HISTORY OF
Yugoslavia

HISTORY OF
Yugoslavia

Vladimir Dedijer
*Serbian Academy of Sciences
and Humanities*

Ivan Božić
University of Belgrade

Sima Ćirković
University of Belgrade

Milorad Ekmečić
University of Sarajevo

McGraw-Hill Book Company
New York   St. Louis   San Francisco   Düsseldorf   Johannesburg
Kuala Lumpur   London   Mexico   Montreal   New Delhi   Panama
Paris   São Paulo   Singapore   Sydney   Tokyo   Toronto

Editor: *Marie Longyear*
Translator: *Kordija Kveder*
Copy editor: *Viola Sperka*
Production supervisor: *Milton Heiberg*
Design: *Pencils Portfolio, Inc.*

The book was set in Patina type by University Graphics, Inc.

It was printed and bound by the Maple Press Company.

Photographs
Figures 1-5, 7, 9, 19, 21, 24, 26, 27, 31, 35, 38, 44: courtesy of the
Yugoslav Information Center, New York
Figures 6, 8, 10-18, 22, 23, 25, 28-30, 32-34, 36, 37, 39, 42, 43: *Yugoslav
Review*, Belgrade
Figures 46-49: Photo Researchers, Inc./John Phillips

History of Yugoslavia

Originally published in Serbo-Croatian by Prosveta, Belgrade, 1972.

1234567890MAMM7987654

Library of Congress Cataloging in Publication Data
Main entry under title:

History of Yugoslavia.

Translation of Istorija Jugoslavije.
1. Yugoslavia—History. I. Dedijer, Vladimir.
DR317.I8613   949.7   74–6164

Contents

Editor's Note on Pronunciation

The vowels in Serbo-Croatian are pronounced approximately as follows:

a as in *car*

e as in *set*

i as in *ravine*

o as in *sought*

u as in *rude*

Most consonants are pronounced approximately as in English, with the following exceptions:

c is always pronounced as *ts*, not as *k* or *s*.

g is always pronounced as in *get*, not as in *gelatin*.

j is always pronounced like the *y* in *yet*.

s is always pronounced as in *set*, not as in *has* or *leisure*.

There are several consonants in Serbo-Croatian that do not occur in the English alphabet:

č has the sound of *ch* in *chop*.

ć has a sound between *t* and *ch*, similar to the *ty* sound in *t(y)une*.

dž has the sound of *j* in *jar*.

š has the sound of *sh* in *ship*.

ž has the sound of *s* in *pleasure*.

lj has the sound of *lli* in *million*.

nj has the sound of *ni* in *minion*.

đ (or *dj*) is similar to the *dy* sound in *d(y)une*.

Preface to the English Edition

The four authors of this book have tried to write a history of Yugoslavia that is scholarly and yet popular, complete though limited in length—one that provides insight into the many economic, social, political, and cultural processes in which the peoples of Yugoslavia have been involved.

The project was begun in 1966 when, working closely together, we decided on the scope and character of the book and determined the subject matter, methodology, and periodization. Then the work was divided among us according to our areas of specialization. We were well aware that our texts would suffer from certain shortcomings, partly because some problems had never been dealt with adequately in previous research and partly because of individual opinions about what is central to various periods in the history of Yugoslavia. We agreed, therefore, to stress, within the context of general European development, those events and phenomena which in our opinion best characterized the era in question or which left an imprint on later development. The work was first published in 1972, in Serbo-Croatian.

We regard this book as an effort to present the past of Yugoslavia as we see it. Perhaps other historians would have approached the task from another point of view. But if our efforts will lead to critical discussion and to fresh attempts to synthesize the complex elements of Yugoslavia's past, we shall have achieved what we set out to do in this pioneering work.

We wish to express our gratitude to the translator, Kordija Kveder, and to the copy editor, Viola Sperka, for their thoughtful and invaluable contributions to the English edition of this book.

Stara Fužina, u Bohinju—May 15, 1973

Vladimir Dedijer
Ivan Božić
Sima Ćirković
Milorad Ekmečić

Part One

THE RISE AND FALL OF THE MEDIEVAL STATES

At the end of their long migration, the ancestors of the South Slavs, alone among the Slavic tribes, settled permanently inside the *limes*, the borders of the Roman Empire. There they came into contact with many aspects of the culture of late antiquity. They found themselves on lands that bore material remains of Roman civilization; they met and had conflicts with the remnants of the old inhabitants of the Balkan provinces; and they were confronted also with the Byzantine Empire, the successor of the eastern half of the Roman Empire. But the Slavs in the Balkans did not succeed in retaining the entire expanse of territory on which they had settled in the seventh century, owing to the arrival later of the Magyars and the Bulgars and to the partial Greek recovery. The Slavic language and traditions were best kept in the parts of the Balkan Peninsula where the Slavs had early formed a sufficiently widespread and strong political organization.

The circumstances of the settlement in the Balkan Peninsula of the different Slavic tribes were not uniform; there were no unified movements by great multitudes, even though their languages were close and their ways of life, economy, and social organization were similar. Spread out over a great area, without good communication and at the same time subjected to different influences from the neighboring world, the Slavs in the Balkans were scattered in many small communities insufficiently strong to resist conquerors. Although in some ways the early medieval states of the South Slavs preserved the differences between the South Slav peoples, they also played a significant role in integrating the Slavic inhabitants over a wide area, creating conditions for cultural and linguistic unity.

The medieval states of the South Slavs nevertheless were not sufficiently strong to resist permanently the expansion of neighboring states, which threatened them from many sides. The south and east were bordered by Byzantium, which at the end of the Middle Ages was replaced by the steadily expanding Ottoman state. At the west the expanding Holy Roman Empire appeared very early, and Hungary advanced from the north.

The most important long-term consequence for the late history of the South Slavs was the acceptance of Christianity in the early Middle Ages. With the new faith the South Slavs entered into the sphere of Christian civilization, and a certain portion acquired writing and a literary language. Christianity provided an element for unity among the different peoples, but at the same time it permitted the formation of deep and permanent gulfs. Roman and Byzantine ecclesiastical jurisdictions, Eastern and Western rites, and different types of church regulations clashed on South Slav soil and for centuries affected the cultural and spiritual life of the people.

CHAPTER I

The Legacy of Antiquity in Yugoslavia

Natural Conditions

The differences between the various regions of Yugoslavia, obvious even to the casual traveler, and the wealth of forms and courses of development, sometimes discouraging to the reader of Yugoslav history, are due to the natural environment and the variety of the area. A glance at the map shows that the territory of Yugoslavia is not, geographically speaking, a simple undiversified region. The not very large area (255,804 square kilometers) is divided by geographers into three distinctive belts: the narrow Adriatic coast, the broad mountainous belt extending from northwest to southeast throughout the entire country, and the northern plains representing the edge of the great Pannonian basin.

The mountainous belt, fanning out eastward, comprises a series of parallel chains of lofty mountains, separating the continental part of Yugoslavia from the coast. Like a towering fence, it prevents the climatic influences of the sea from spreading inland. Also throughout history it has substantially obstructed the movement of people and goods, thus giving rise to appreciable economic and cultural differences between the coast and interior. Within the mountainous region itself are many basins and river valleys, isolated and closeted off, predestined to go their own way until they were included in larger communities by force.

The Yugoslav coast is linked by sea routes, highly favorable for navigation, with the other countries around the Adriatic Sea, especially the coast of Italy and other Mediterranean lands. Also, the northern plains are crisscrossed by lines of communication and rivers connecting them with the Central European countries. On that side, Yugoslavia is open and accessible. The eastern approaches (the present-day constituent republics of Serbia and Macedonia) are bounded by a mountain massif running north-south. Here and there, the cliffs of these mountains provide a rare case of boundaries endowed by nature. Through the eastern reaches of Yugoslav territory run the Morava and Vardar Rivers, the former south-north, and the latter north-south, their broad valleys forming a link between this part of Yugoslav territory and Asia Minor on one side and the Pannonian basin on the other.

These, then, are the links between Yugoslav territory and the outside world. Lying on the shores of the Adriatic Sea, which is really only a great bay of the Mediterranean, it is part of the Mediterranean world; embracing a large part of the Pannonian basin, it belongs to the outskirts of Central Europe; and, in possession of the main land route linking Europe and Asia, it has been caught up in the great movements between continents.

Thus natural conditions favored a separate life in the various regions, hampering communications and frustrating the desire to create greater territorial units. It should not be overlooked, however, that all three large geographic regions comprised in present Yugoslavia cover a fairly extensive area and that their character facilitated the establishment of links and contacts within their own frameworks. This is particularly applicable to the period when ethnic groups were already stable and political organizations were formed. Throughout its entire history the coastal belt, for instance, was relatively consistent, while the mountainous and prairie zones, each unto itself, had their own specific features regardless of the political and other boundaries bisecting them.

In the Yugoslav territories, as elsewhere, natural conditions had a bearing on the possibilities for, and forms of, economic activity and way of life. Along the coast, large tracts of arable land were few and far between, but the narrow strip between the sea and the craggy mountains lent itself admirably to the growing of olives, vines, and southern fruit. There the population supplemented agricultural activity with fishing and navigation. With its harsh climate and scarcity of fertile soil, the mountainous belt, rich in pasturelands and forests, offered ample opportunities for livestock raising. For centuries, until the modern industrial epoch, seminomadic livestock raising was practiced, with the herds alternating between the heights and the valleys. With its typical livestock products and occupations, the world of the highlanders integrated into the trade and division of labor of broader economic and social entities. To the north, the Pannonian prairies, like the river valleys in the central districts, favored farming.

Throughout the various regions there was a constant need for one region to supplement another's economic activity, stimulating closer connections between them and encouraging the population to surmount obstacles and cope with difficulties of transportation. The coast had to maintain ties with the mountainous districts for basic food supplies, especially after the towns became more populous. The inhabitants of the mountain areas had to trade to obtain salt and other articles of food. The central and western mountain districts were rich in ores, exploited in three major waves: in antiquity, in the Middle Ages, and in the modern industrial period.

Traces of the Earliest Cultures

On the whole, the area that is now Yugoslavia provided man with what he needed to sustain life. Thanks to this circumstance, the traces of human habitation date back far into time. Certain parts of Yugoslavia were inhabited in the Paleolithic period. More than forty places in the western districts (Slovenia, Croatia) have yielded, in caves and shallow shelters, the remains of roughhewn stone implements belonging to the late part of the early Stone Age.

During the late Stone Age (Neolithic), the Yugoslav areas were much more densely settled, as attested by numerous findings of the traces of human existence. Archaeological excavations have brought to light many remains of pottery, implements and weapons of bone and stone, traces of settlements, and so on. The archaeological material permits some insight, albeit very general, into the way of life of people at that level of historical development and also throws light on some of the common features of the remains of various cultures, making it possible to pinpoint them in time and space.

The oldest findings were discovered after World War II at Lepenski Vir on the Danube River. The picture of life in those times is rounded out not only by the remains of settlements made up of well-planned houses on pentagonal foundations and a rich assortment of ceramics, but also by unique stone sculptures. One of the first Neolithic cultures in the Yugoslav territories was scattered along the Adriatic coast, on the islands, and along the valleys of rivers flowing into the Adriatic Sea. The turning point in the life of this culture was reached when the people took up agriculture. The "impresso" ornament, impressed into ceramics, is typical of that culture linked with the Mediterranean. Inland, virtually throughout the entire eastern half of the country, spread the Starčevo culture of mud huts and highly specialized ceramics. This culture left its legacy, over an even larger area, to the Vinča culture, named after the Vinča excavations near Belgrade.

In middle and late Neolithic times, with settlements denser and the way of life more complex, differentiation heightened, and it is consequently possible to sift out a larger number of Neolithic cultures, including the most important ones: the Butmir (in Bosnia), famous for its ornamentation; and the Danilo (in Dalmatia and Montenegro), a later extension of which was the Hvar-Lisičiċi. The population of the later Stone Age had spread out to cover a fairly extensive area in Yugoslav territory. Particularly densely populated were the banks of rivers where terrain that was high enough above water level not be subject to inundation provided the people with refuge as well as opportunities for supplementing their crude form of agriculture with fishing. The people knew animal husbandry, raising goats, sheep, pigs, and cattle. Apart from bone and stone implements and tools, and ceramic ware of various forms and ornamentation, Neolithic men also produced a simple kind of textile. Frequently, they dug their abodes into the ground or raised them on stilts.

The use of metal spread to Yugoslav areas in the early second millennium B.C. The large number of excavations and wealth of findings indicate a culture which was more highly differentiated than the preceding ones. There is such a multitude of cultural groups that only archaeologists can identify them and distinguish one from another. Generally speaking, the Bronze Age in Yugoslav territory was divided into three great cultural regions: the Pannonian, the Illyrian, and the region of the tumulus culture.

The cultures of the Pannonian region drew upon earlier Neolithic ones and were marked by a strong linkage with the other cultures of the broad expanses of the Pannonian plains. These people were tillers of the soil who added bronze weapons and implements to earlier achievements. Idols and cult objects reveal that the people of this period were rather well developed in their beliefs. The culture of the tumulus was widespread in Macedonia, and it stands in close connection with the cultural material of Thrace and Thessaly. This culture, too, emerged from that of the late Neolithic, deriving its name from the mounds, or tumuli, rising above the graves. In the western districts of Yugoslav territory, throughout virtually the entire mountainous belt and along the coast, spread the Stone Fort culture (Castellieri) associated with the earliest history of the Illyrian tribes. An essential feature of the culture of this vast area was the stone fortifications for protection.

In the regions of Yugoslavia, iron came to be employed in the early part of the first millennium, when it was gradually put to many different uses. The population of the Iron Age was descended from earlier inhabitants and is ethnically determinable. Apart from the Indo-European tribes known as Illyrians, Thracian tribes lived in the eastern sections of Yugoslav territory; they, too, belonged to the Indo-European community. In the fourth century B.C., they were joined in the Balkan Peninsula by the Celts, who brought with them their characteristic material culture. A section of the Celtic tribes remained forever in what is now Yugoslavia, mingling here and there with adjacent tribes.

Greek Colonies

Whereas the population in the Yugoslav areas lived at the Iron Age level of culture, with productive forces and material culture incomparably more developed than in preceding periods, but yet without writing, in neighboring regions—Greece, Asia Minor, and the Apennine peninsula—the great civilizations of antiquity put in their appearance, and with them the inhabitants of the Balkan Peninsula were bound to come into contact.

The first to arrive on Adriatic shores were the Greeks, who, as seafarers, were eager to explore the islands and coast. After they appeared in the sixth century B.C., they founded a number of colonies, such as Issa (on the island of Vis), Pharos (on the island of Hvar), Korkyra (on the island of Korčula), Herakleia (the location of which is unknown), and others. The Greeks living along the Adriatic also set up their own colonies: Tragurion (Trogir), and Epetion (in the vicinity of Split). The Greeks came into contact with the natives mostly in the guise of traders, for the difference in type of economic activity proved a stimulant to lively trading. Greek influence left its traces on the world of the Illyrian tribes (in crafts, money, literacy), but the latter nevertheless did not change their mode of life, that of highland herdsmen and warriors. Greek influence also penetrated by land, via the Vardar Valley in what is now Macedonia, but it failed to alter the native population's way of living, just as the conquests of Alexander the Great had failed to change political relations in this part of the Balkan Peninsula.

Roman Conquests and Provincial Organization

The world of the Balkan tribes underwent transformation only under the impact of the Romans, who penetrated to the lands lying behind the eastern shores of the Adriatic in stages, by force of arms, relying for support on the strongholds they created gradually. The first stage of Roman expansion to the eastern side of the Adriatic dates back to the third century B.C., when Roman arms were drawn into the conflicts between the Illyrians and the Greek colonists. It was then that the Romans smashed the Illyrian tribal community in which the leading role was played by the Ardideians, whose area extended along the southern part of the Adriatic coast. The Romans then acquired certain strongholds along the Adriatic in their endeavor to secure freedom of navigation and to stop Illyrian piracy, but their gains proved to be temporary. In the second century B.C., the center of Illyrian political power was located in the south, in the southernmost part of what is today Yugoslavia. Gencius, the "king of the Illyrians," reigned in Scodra (now Shkodèr, or Scutari, in Albania) and interfered in Roman attempts to conquer Macedonia. In the war which broke out between 170 and 168 B.C., the Illyrians were not able to stand up to superior Roman power, and consequently this Illyrian state was subordinated to the authority of Rome. At this time, too, the former Greek colonies were incorporated into the Roman state. In 148 B.C. Macedonia became a Roman province, and Yugoslav territories were left vulnerable to Roman penetration from the south.

In the period that followed, pressure built up from the north as the Roman state overflowed the boundaries of the Apennine peninsula. Over the north Italian plains and Alps, the Roman legions thrust into Pannonia as Illyrian centers of resistance moved northward and inland, unreconciled to the presence of the invaders. The Romans won final victory only at the beginning of the Christian epoch when, after fierce fighting, they quelled the great Illyrian insurrection, the *bellum Batonianum*, named after the two Batons, Illyrian chieftains (A.D. 6–9).

The Achievements of Roman Civilization on Yugoslav Soil

All of present-day Yugoslavia, with the exception of the regions north and east of the Danube (now Vojvodina), then found itself administered by Rome. For the first time the area was united, and it was exposed to Roman influence for over five centuries. Under Roman rule, it was shaped and organized, lifted by culture, and urbanized. The later development of communities in the area received many of its impulses from the achievements of Roman civilization.

After their conquests, the Romans established provinces, as they did in other areas brought under their control. The land whose history we are pursuing became part of a number of Roman provinces which in time changed scope and sometimes name as well. What is now Slovenia belonged partly to Italy and partly to the province of Noricum, while Pannonia, later subdivided into two parts, encompassed a large area between the Danube and Sava Rivers and a narrow belt south of the Sava. The province of Dalmatia extended along the Adriatic coast, including the Dinaric mountain belt and the plains in the broad Sava River valley. In the eastern districts were Upper Moesia (in Serbia), Dardania (Serbia and

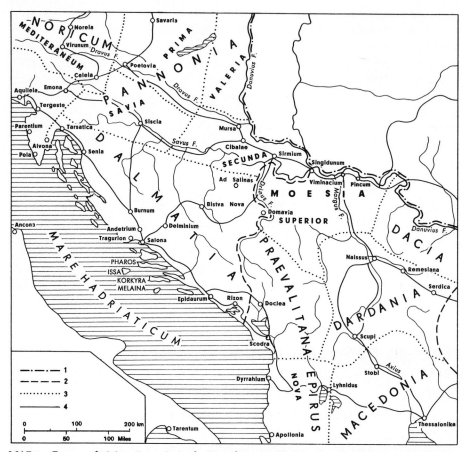

MAP 1. Roman administrative units in the Yugoslav area. Division based on Emperor Diocletian's reforms (284–304). (1) Boundaries of the Roman Empire; (2) boundaries of dioceses; (3) boundaries of provinces; (4) Roman roads.

Macedonia), and Macedonia, which was only the southern part of the present republic of the same name, as its center was far to the south along the shores of the Aegean Sea.

The military encampments and fortifications, with their garrisons, were the true foci of Roman influence in the newly won lands, which had to be defended from attacks originating outside and rebellions welling up inside. From the military camps and the settlements of retired soldiers grew many provincial urban settlements. Also subordinated to the needs of the army was the construction of a well-planned and ramified network of roads linking the provinces with Italy and with each other. The Roman roads, excellent in the execution, long outlived the Roman Empire and later served the incoming Slavs, in substantial measure determining the directions in which people and goods moved.

FIGURE 1. Sculpture from Lepenski Vir.

FIGURE 2. Votive chariot from Dupljaja, Serbia (Bronze Age, ca. 1500 B.C.).

FIGURE 3. Statue of Athena found in
the ruins of Herakleia near
Bitola.

FIGURE 4. Gold mask (Greek, fourth century), found in Macedonia.

Under Roman rule, the economic exploitation of the Balkan regions was intensified and the Roman slave system was introduced. Productive forces surged forward and boundaries became discernible between the economically productive areas and the passive mountainous and forest regions, which were not brought under human control or cultivation. The western and central sections of the Balkan Peninsula, Dalmatia and Moesia, were famed for their mineral wealth and the production of gold, silver, iron, and lead. Agricultural production grew and won for the Danubian provinces the reputation of a breadbasket. In the mountains, livestock raising, traditional among the Balkan tribes, retained its importance and was integrated into the economic life of the empire. Thanks to the sea, the rivers, and the developed road network, vigorous trade was conducted with Italy, the center of the empire, and with more remote provinces.

The urbanization of the Balkan provinces kept pace with the economic upsurge. Besides the military camps and mining centers, the trading towns and tribal townships provided crystallization points for the growth of lively urbanized settlements which in time acquired forums, temples, water mains, large public baths, and other amenities of Roman civilization. Roman towns, like Roman roads, survived the downfall of Rome and were inherited as their Roman legacy by the new Slav settlers. Some of those towns became nuclei around which town life later developed under new conditions.

As time went by, the original antagonism between native population and conquerors gave way to coexistence. In various ways, the local population was drawn into the Roman linguistic and cultural sphere. Inhabitants of the provinces were recruited for the Roman army, in the service of which they spent almost their entire lives, fighting in other parts of the empire and becoming defenders not only of its boundaries but also of the Roman way of life. The more intensive economic life also made the indigenous population emerge from its isolation, subjecting it, particularly in the towns, to the influence of the Latin language and Roman material and spiritual culture. This rapprochement between the Romans and the domestic population and their eventual assimilation enabled the conquerors to assume a more tolerant attitude toward the alien local religion and the merger and fusion of various cults. Not all the Balkan provinces, however, were Romanized to the same degree. The more remote mountain districts were far less susceptible to Roman influence. The provincial system made allowance for the tribes to live their own lives, to retain their rights and to practice their customs (*decuriae* and *conventi*). Although the languages of the pre-Roman Balkan population disappeared, leaving traces only in personal and place names, not even five hundred years of Roman rule sufficed to bring about total cultural and linguistic assimilation. After the Slavs migrated to the Balkan Peninsula, it was therefore possible for various ethnic groups to develop from the remnants of the Roman provincial population.

Greek culture succeeded in maintaining itself in the ancient Greek areas within the fold of the Roman Empire. The Greek language spread to cover an extensive area. The boundary line between the Greek and Latin language areas, which may be established thanks to the numerous Roman inscriptions in stone, bisected Yugoslav territory, running roughly along the line joining Boka Kotorska with Niš. South and east of that line, the Greek language and alphabet held sway. The Greek element was destined to become increasingly important, and finally it took over and continued the entire tradition of the Roman Empire.

The Decline of the Roman Empire and the Incursions of Barbarian Tribes

The widespread economic crisis which shook the Roman Empire in the third century hit the western districts harder than the eastern. There, too, the manpower shortage was in evidence, but such important works as the laying of roads and the construction of settlements continued to be undertaken. Although trade and crafts retrogressed while the latifundia grew, economic life did not come to a standstill, nor did the population decrease dramatically. The eastern part of the empire and the Balkan provinces thus came into the ascendancy. As the empire was transformed from a principate into a dominate, meaning that the emperor enjoyed unlimited and divine power, the focus of empire moved eastward. The founding of Constantinople by Emperor Constantine in 330 was symbolic in its significance. From the name of Byzantium on the Bosporus, next to which Constantine the Great erected the city which came to be called simply Constantinople—in Slavic languages Carigrad, the Emperor's City—by the medieval Slavs, the entire Roman Empire in the East, and its Hellenized extension, by historical tradition came to be called the Byzantine Empire, a name used from the humanistic era onwards.

The Byzantine Empire was invested with its salient features by the Christian religion, which, formerly a persecuted sect, became the state religion under Emperor Constantine. In the Balkan provinces during this period, the church organization was perfected, its beginnings dating back to the time of the apostles and their first disciples. In the sweeping persecutions of the third century, the Illyrian provinces had more than their share of martyrs, and in the succeeding century they produced famous theologians and writers.

The internal weakening of the Empire, resulting from the recession of economic life and the slow decay of state organization, was attended by persistent and growing attacks by the barbarian peoples along the borders. Despite the system of boundary fortifications (limes) extending into Yugoslav territory along the Danube River, the empire found it increasingly difficult to ward off these assaults. The Roman provinces in the Yugoslav region were spared during the great onslaughts of the Goths, who destroyed the boundary system along the

FIGURE 5. Tabula of the Roman Emperor Trajan on the Danube.

FIGURE 6. The amphitheater in Pula.

15

FIGURE 7. Emperor Constantine (fourth century), found in the vicinity of Niš.

FIGURE 8. The Diocletian Palace, Split.

16

lower Danube, but the Hun incursions (448) brought widespread devastation to these areas. Particularly hard hit were the towns in the northern regions, like Sirmium (near the present-day Sremska Mitrovica), Singidunum (at Belgrade), Naissus (Niš), Poetovio (Ptuj), Emona (at Ljubljana), and many others.

After the collapse of the Western Roman Empire in 476, and the establishment of the kingdom of the Ostrogoths in Italy, the provinces which had by the division of the late fourth century been annexed to the western part of the empire were wrested from the Byzantine emperors. Dalmatia, Pannonia, and Noricum joined the Ostrogothic kingdom of King Theodoric. The Ostrogoths did not settle the Yugoslav provinces in any great numbers, and they respected the Roman system they found there. Their rule ensured peace and made it possible to repair the devastations of the Huns. Ostrogoth rule in the western part of the Balkan Peninsula was interrupted by the energetic policy of restoration pursued by the Emperor Justinian (527–565). By reviving the power of the Eastern Empire, Justinian strove to resurrect a state encompassing the entire civilized world. His achievements were noteworthy in Africa, Spain, and Italy. In 535 the emperor's fleet conquered Salona, the center of the province of Dalmatia, and in short order all the Balkan provinces were subordinated to the empire. Great energy was invested in reconstructing the boundary fortifications, as new conquerors were gathering at the gates of the empire.

CHAPTER 2

The Slavs in the Balkan Peninsula

The Puzzle of the Ancient Slav Homeland

The history of the South Slavs begins with their migration to the Balkan Peninsula. Their entire later development is overshadowed by this major turning point, which can barely be reconstructed, even in the roughest outline. The earlier history of the Slavs remains totally obscure, and there is no knowledge whatever of the impulses that led one section of the Slavs to settle the Danube shore along the very boundary of the Byzantine Empire. The ancestors of the South Slavs lived together with other Slavs at one time, but no amount of effort on the part of research workers in a number of scientific disciplines has yielded a reliable picture of that ancient Slav community and the area inhabited by the then undivided and united nation.

Hypothetically, the "ancient homeland" of the Slavs simply represented a long stage of relative stability, a pause, so to speak, in the virtually ceaseless movement of tribes belonging to the Indo-European linguistic family. Actually it is the linguists who have the most to say about this stage, on the grounds of the earliest lexical fund and the oldest loanwords, from which they draw conclusions permitting some insight into the natural environment in which the ancient Slavs lived, and offering a basis for the recognition of their neighbors. Place-names, especially of rivers, make it possible to theorize about the extent of the ancient homeland of the Slavs. However, differences in assessing the significance and value of such data are so great that none of the results achieved meet with general approval or acceptance.

Discussions of the ancient homeland of the Slavs were in progress even toward the end of the Middle Ages and frequently reflected the national and political aspirations and preoccupations of each period. In the first half of the last century, a broad and expansive ancient homeland was reconstructed, winning supporters in the middle of this century. It encompassed the huge area between the Baltic and Black Seas, from the Carpathians in the west to the Don, upper Volga, and Novgorod in the east, covering, apart from all present-day Poland and the Baltic States, also a large segment of the European part of the Soviet Union. More dependable arguments, with a larger number of supporters, can be put forward for the hypothesis that the area was far smaller, embracing the land east of the Carpathians between the Pripyat Marshes, the Dnieper, and the upper courses of the rivers flowing into the Black Sea (Prut, Dniester, Bug), that is, what is now Byelorussia and the Ukraine.

The Slavs on the Lower Danube

Parts of the Slavic population broke off from the nucleus and moved to remote areas, pressed by or engulfed in the migrations of other tribes and nations. The great migrations scattered the Slavs over large areas between the Main and the Volga, between the Baltic and the Mediterranean Seas. As they moved, a section of the Slavs arrived, in the course of the fifth century, in the plains north of the lower Danube (now Romania), stopping before the Byzantine defense system. Even during the sixth century, these Slavs, frequently in combination with tribes and groups of Turk peoples descending from the nearby Black Sea steppes, occasionally broke through the fortified frontier of the empire, penetrating deeply into the interior, even as far as the gates of Constantinople and Salonika. These incursions, although frequent and powerful at times, did not result in any massive or lasting settlement. The Slavs and their allies made sallies across the Danube only to return loaded with booty after their missions had been accomplished.

In the Balkan Peninsula, the presence of the Slavs was first registered by Byzantine writers who took note not only of their harsh methods of warfare and penchant for devastation but also of their way of life and organizational forms. A Byzantine military manual intended for officers making war on the Slavs, which because of its practical intent does not repeat commonplaces about the barbarians, mentions in passing that the Slavs lived along rivers and in forests, in villages that were interconnected and at the same time well protected by natural obstacles, that they were agriculturists who stored food in their houses and also raised livestock, that they were persevering and cunning warriors, lightly equipped and armed, and practicing peculiar tactics. The entire area on that side of the Danube, crisscrossed by rivers, was divided up into belts of small-scale political organizations headed by local princes (archons), whose favor was bought by the Byzantine authorities in their fear that a "monarchy" would be created—a powerful and integral authority—over a large area. Probably such unification was a rare occurrence, as the Slav chieftains were unstable and given to falling out.

Attacks on Byzantine Provinces

The Slavs spent over a century in the vicinity of Byzantium. Numerous but scattered, bound to the land but poorly organized, devoid of an authority capable of combining forces on any large scale, the Slavs were easily subordinated on a temporary basis, or were drawn off by the movement of tribes thrusting from the Black Sea steppes. One such tribe, which wielded considerable influence over the Slavs as they were on the point of settling the Balkan Peninsula, were the Avars. From the area around the mouth of the Danube, they moved westward, interfering in the fighting between the Lombards living in Pannonia, and their neighbors the Gepidae. With their help, the state of the Gepidae was destroyed in 567, and as the Lombards withdrew to Italy the following year, the Avars were left to rule a vast but sparsely populated area in the Pannonian lowlands. Byzantine diplomacy tried to take advantage of the warlike and well-organized Avars to bring pressure to bear on the Slavs, but the Avars were then swift to turn against the boundary towns. The plan of Byzantine diplomacy failed. The Slav groups were forced to pay tribute and to recruit warriors for the wars waged by the Avars. Thus the latter improved their striking power while the Slavs acquired leadership and organization. It is not known, however, how large a section of the Slavs was sucked into this forcible alliance with the Avars which was totally concentrated on warring against the Byzantine Empire. Toward the end of the sixth century, Byzantium succeeded in gathering its forces for an offensive in reply to the Avar-Slav attacks. In the ensuing fighting, the frontier towns were restored and the scene of battle was transferred sporadically to the other side of the Danube.

While fighting was in progress along the middle and lower Danube areas, groups of Slavs were gradually, and without dramatic battles, taking possession of districts in the foothills of the eastern Alps. From the mid-sixth century onwards, they migrated from the north and by the end of that century had penetrated to the north Italian plains, coming face to face with the neighboring Bavarians and Lombards.

The Collapse of the Byzantine Defense System and the Permanent Settlement of the Balkan Peninsula by the Slavs

In the central Balkan Peninsula, the turning point came at the very beginning of the seventh century, when disaffected soldiers forced to spend the winter on hostile Slav territory murdered their vigorous and capable emperor Maurice (602). Phocas, an officer who was proclaimed emperor by acclamation, took picked troops to Constantinople to protect the throne, while the frontier stood unguarded. As there was no practical obstacle thereafter to keep back the flood tide of Slavs, they overflowed the entire Balkan Peninsula. Within a few years, the Slavs had thrust not only to the shores of the Adriatic Sea, where they devastated a number of towns including the provincial capital of Salona (614), but also to the Aegean Sea, where they charged the sturdy walls of Salonika. Around 625, arriving at the extreme south of the Peloponnesus, they boarded ships and attacked the islands, including Crete. The parts of the Balkan Peninsula that were spared were few, most of them well-fortified towns on the Aegean, Ionian, and Adriatic shores.

The Avars also participated in the conquest of the Balkan Peninsula but they directed their forces, and those of the Slavs they led, against the big towns which held out the promise of rich loot. In attacking Constantinople and Salonika, the Avars and Slavs fought side by side, representing the basic mass of the assaulting force. But while the large Slav groups spread about the vast expanses of the Balkan Peninsula, the small but tightly knit Avars returned to their headquarters between the Danube and Tisa Rivers until they set out on new expeditions and raids. In the process of settling the Peninsula, large numbers of Slavs broke away from Avar control.

Despite their large numbers, the Slavs were not able to settle, evenly and densely, the extensive expanses of the Balkan Peninsula. Moving along the ancient Roman roads, they stopped and often tarried forever in areas that promised attractive living conditions, having been cultivated even during Roman times. The inhabited areas were scattered about and separated, like lakes, by mountain chains and inaccessible terrain.

The Roman provincial population fled from the places along the line of

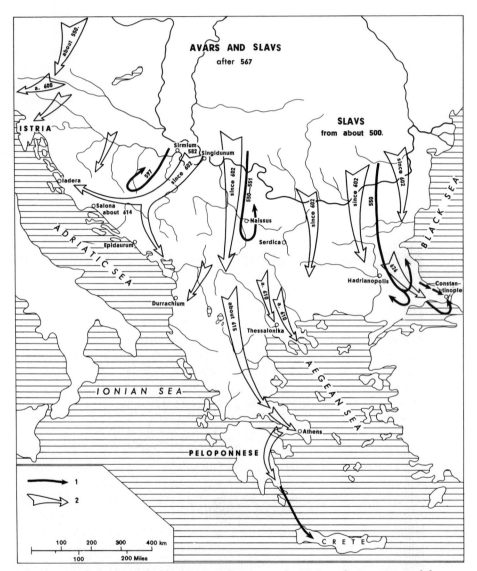

MAP 2. The migrations of the Slavs to the Balkan Peninsula. (1) Sporadic incursions and devastations; (2) permanent settlement.

attack. Thus the inhabitants of Sirmium, near the frontier, withdrew to the better-protected Salona. Inhabitants of the northern provincial towns, who had had an opportunity to become acquainted with the enemy and his methods, withdrew to Salonika, where they were again witness to Avar-Slav assaults. As the entire population from the provinces could not move to the biggest and best-protected towns of the empire, the masses of poor people were forced to flee for their lives to the mountainous and less accessible regions which the Slavs bypassed in their thrust. It thus happened that in the remote mountain regions of the Balkan Peninsula there remained intact islands, of various sizes, of the indigenous population; they lost all traces of ties with the civilization of late antiquity, still alive in the capital and protected parts of the Byzantine Empire. Reduced to the simplest kind of existence and to animal husbandry, these Romanized indigenous groups lived long centuries in utter obscurity, with no memory whatsoever of their historical origins, only to appear later in the guise of Vlachs (Wallachians), Mavro-Vlachs (Black Wallachians), Romans, and Albanians. Gradually they came into closer contact with the agricultural Slav population, finally to merge with it almost completely. But even previous to that, there must have been some contact between the Slavs and the world of the indigenous Balkan peoples. Many place-names, and especially the names of large rivers, were taken from them by the Slavs. The Slav word *car*, meaning emperor, is derived from the Latin *caesar*. Also the Slavs learned the name of the Hellenes in its Latinized form of *Graecus* (from which the Slav version *Grk*).

"Sclavinias"

Little is known about Slav society and organization after the migration to the Balkan Peninsula. The mass of the settlers was certainly made up of parts and segments of various Slav groups, related by linguistic affinity and having reached approximately the same level of socioeconomic development and culture. Old tribal names are found in the place-names for remote areas. Fanning out to the many lowlands and valleys of the Balkan region, the Slavs broke up into many sections which, framed afresh by space, formed new groups. In the first few centuries after settlement, many names of groups and tribes were derived from the place-names of the new area, like Strumljani (from the river Struma—Strymon), Rinhini (from the river Rihios), Timočani (from the river Timok—Timacus), Neretljani (from the river Neretva—Naron), Konavljani (from Canale—the remains of the Roman aqueduct of Epidaurus), Karantani (from civitas Carantana), and so on. The point of departure for the entire further political and ethnical development of the Slavs in the Balkan Peninsula was their division into a large number of groups formed in the new land and bound to it.

The contemporary Byzantines were well aware of the divisions among the Slavs, which were clearly in evidence behind the scenes of their linguistic and cultural unity. "The whole country has become Slav and gone barbarian," says one of the rare Byzantine texts referring to these times, in speaking of Greece. In the eyes of the Byzantines, the European part of the empire had fallen into the possession of the Slavs, but it was not an integral region; rather, it seemed like a conglomeration of separate and independent districts, called by the characteristic plural noun *Sclavinias*.

Knowledge, though scant, is had of only one small belt of Sclavinias, in the vicinity of Salonika. In their attacks on the city, its Slav neighbors left traces of their presence in writings celebrating the miracles of the patron saint of Salonika, Saint Demetrois. There are found the names of the Strumljani, Rinhini, Sagudati, Vajuniti, and Velegeziti, tribes in the near and far vicinity of Salonika who kept the mainland under their control, forcing the city to maintain ties with the capital by sea, which route the Slavs were also wont to cut off during hostilities. These Slavs were still fired by the ambition of conquering Salonika, although when they found conditions unfavorable, or when they were not being pressed into such undertakings by the Avars, whose long arm occasionally extended to these parts, they lived at peace with the city. Under normal conditions, the inhabitants of Salonika bought their food from the Slav agriculturists. Slavs living in remote areas continued to supply the city even when those in the vicinity attacked it.

In the seventh century, the leaders of these Sclavinias had adjusted to the pursuit of policy with Byzantium, negotiating with the authorities in Salonika and even with the emperor himself. In case of need, they were able to pull themselves together, to coordinate actions and to seek Avar help. The life of the Sclavinias inhabiting areas remote from the Byzantine centers was less exposed to Byzantine influence; consequently they turned their attention inward to their own mutual relations but left no trace of this in historical sources. Their remains are sometimes discernible in later and broader political formations.

The Tribal Alliance of Samo

At the opposite end of the spacious territory of which the South Slavs took possession, in the region of the Julian Alps and Karawanken mountains, now the frontier between Yugoslavia and Austria, there existed a Slav principality in the first half of the seventh century upon which historical sources can throw some light. During the time when the Slavs from what is now Czechoslovakia united temporarily under Samo (623–658) to defend themselves from the Avars and Franks, who were trying to push their boundaries eastward, the alliance of Slav tribes also included Prince Valuk (ca. 630). The center of his region, which remained intact even after the collapse of Samo's alliance, was Krnski Grad (civitas Carantana). Its name was transferred to the inhabitants: Carantani, Horutane, Karantanci (Caranthanians), who formed the nucleus of a larger state formation. During Samo's short-lived alliance, a grave blow was struck at supreme Avar authority over sections of the Slavs, rendered even more serious by the failure of the great Avar-Slav assault on Constantinople in 626. For a time, Avar power was on the wane, but they did not disappear from the historical scene nor did all the Slavs then succeed in shaking them off.

Fighting the Avars

The middle of the seventh century still shows no stable picture of the habitation of the Balkan Peninsula, as new waves of settlers were arriving to take possession of empty or abandoned areas. These later waves brought to the central Yugoslav area compact sections of the ancient Slav tribes, the Croats and Serbs. The history of their migration has been pieced together from legends, which were noted down only in the middle of the tenth century by the learned Byzantine emperor Constantine Porphyrogenitus (913–959). According to that version, the Croats arrived in what was once Roman Dalmatia during the reign of Emperor Heraclius (610–641), marking the beginning of the gradual restoration of Byzantine power. Fighting the Avars, they won territory which they were later to settle. This was the hinterland of the central Dalmatian towns, between the Cetina River and the Velebit massif, representing only a small part of the territory which was to be associated with the name of the Croats in the course of the succeeding two centuries. Croats also lived outside of this original nucleus during the migrations; a segment set off on its own for Pannonia and Illyricum, and toponymic data testify to the presence of a considerable number of Croats in the present Slovene lands, with traces found also in other Slav areas all the way to the Peloponnesus. Most probably, these are traces of those sections of the tribes that moved with other waves of migration.

According to the same writings, the Serbs also arrived during the reign of Emperor Heraclius, and with his permission, under the leadership of the son of the chieftain who had been their ruler in their ancient abode. First they moved into the Salonika area, to a district which took its name from them—Servia (Srbica); but finding it not to their liking, they decided to return. Crossing the Danube, they had second thoughts about the matter and asked the Byzantine emperor to allot them another area for settlement. This time they settled in the central regions, somewhere between the Lim River in the east and the Piva River in the west, an area which coincided with the later "Baptized Serbia."

Tribal Distribution

In the plains, highly suitable for cultivation, lying between the sea and the lofty, rockbound mountains, they soon set up small tribal districts, similar to those of the Sclavinias in the Salonika region. One of the Byzantine texts even calls them Sclavinias. In the area between the Cetina River and the Neretva River lay the region of the Neretljani, also extending to the islands of Brač, Hvar, and Korčula, which were, in time, settled by Slavs. To the south, between the Neretva River and Dubrovnik, centering around the plains of the lower Neretva, were the Zahumljani (men from beyond the Hum, that is, beyond the mountain); in the limestone Karst fields, in the hinterland of Dubrovnik and Boka Kotorska, were two groups: the Travunjani, the origin of whose name remains a mystery, and the Konavljani in the plains which still bear the name of Konavli from the Roman aqueduct (canale), the remains of which were long in existence. One "Sclavinia" extended to the plains around Skadar Lake (Lake Scutari), taking its name from a town of antiquity, Dioclea (Duklja in Slav, near present-day Titograd).

In the early days of Slav settlement in the Balkans, there were many more Sclavinias than the few extant sources indicate. Some of them are recognizable in the territorial frameworks and tribal names of later days. Probably the Timo-čani, mentioned at the beginning of the ninth century, had already settled earlier in what is now eastern Serbia around the Timok River (the Timacus of antiquity). In the valley of the Morava River lived a major Slav group which had its own bishopric as early as the ninth century. Also established early was certainly the Slavic principality in the Sisak area, formerly Siscia, later to become part of Croatia. An Armenian manuscript from the second half of the seventh century explicitly states that there were twenty-five "nations" going by the name of "Slavs" in the European provinces of the Byzantine Empire.

After the Slavs settled the Balkan Peninsula, there was as yet no inkling of how the later South Slav peoples would take shape or of the extensive territories of their medieval states. The reality then was the small framework of political organizations in which the tribal communities were formed. Although names are found which were later to be applied to entire nations (Croats, Serbs), those who bore them hardly played any more important role, in the beginning, than the population of the other Sclavinias did. The tribal variety of the Balkan Slavs disappeared gradually, so that some of the Sclavinias were subjugated by the states which started spreading their power over the Balkan Peninsula, while others were dissolved in the extensive organizations of the South Slavs themselves.

CHAPTER 3

The South Slavs between the Byzantine and Frankish Empires

The Transformation of Byzantium and the Beginning of Conquest of Slavic Regions

In the enormous area of the Balkan Peninsula which they had settled, the South Slavs lived in the shadow of two centers of power: the Byzantine Empire and the Avar khaganate. Although they experienced grave crises, and conditions did not favor their subduing and organizing the vast Slavic region, these powers, thanks to their mobility, strength, and superior organization, held the upper hand over the more numerous but dispersed and unenterprising Slavs.

27

Their influence is hardly comparable: the primitive social and military organization of the Avars, tottering from external blows, disappeared without a trace, whereas Byzantium was active among the Balkan Slavs for centuries, imposing upon them more or less permanently the elements of its civilization.

Reaching its lowest point precisely at the beginning of the seventh century, when it was wedged in between the Persians attacking from the east and the allied Avars and Slavs conquering its European provinces, and torn asunder internally by tyranny and faulty administration, the Byzantine Empire slowly began to revive, consolidate, and undertake the offensive, relying on the forces it still had at its disposal. The upsurge is associated with the epoch of Emperor Heraclius (610–641), with his reforms of the military system and administration and the transformation of the late Roman Empire into a Hellenized medieval state. The foundation of military power was laid by the dispensation of property to the warrior-peasants *(stratiotai)*, who were recruited for military service. The remaining, free part of the state was organized along military lines and divided up into "themes"—administrative units run by a military commander (strategos). The expansion of state territory was attended by the setting up of new themes, a reliable sign of the establishment of real Byzantine power.

Not even when it was at its lowest ebb did Byzantium abandon pretensions to gaining mastery over all the territories that had belonged to the Roman Empire. The achievement of these pretensions was the basic objective of Byzantine state policy in relation to the Slavs of the Balkan Peninsula. Emperor Heraclius himself did not succeed in using the awakened forces of the empire against the Slavs, as his principal adversaries were the Persians and Arabians, but his descendants were already in a position to do so when their hands were not tied by fighting the Arabians. Slowly they moved into the offensive and gradually subordinated the Slavs within their reach. Thus began the Byzantine reconquest destined to last for centuries, through which the empire succeeded in bringing a large part of the Slavs under its control and imposing upon them the Greek language and Byzantine culture.

It was said of Emperor Constancse II (641–668) that he warred "on the Sclavinias" and that he "captured many and subjected many." Expeditions against the Slavs terminated in mass resettlement in Asia Minor. The Slavs were thus welded into a force for making war on the Arabians. It was also considered one of the emperor's achievements that the Slavs sent messages suing for peace and friendship. But the periods of peace were nonetheless violated by one side or the other. The Byzantine cavalry was shifted from Asia Minor in 687/88 to deal with the Slavs. The next year, Emperor Justinian II succeeded in making his way by land from Constantinople to Salonika by force of arms. His celebrating this feat as a major victory indicates how weak Byzantium's position had become on European soil. Persevering struggle and a consistently offensive policy slowly brought lasting results. It was during this period that the theme of Thrace was founded in the plains around Constantinople, and at the end of the seventh century, also the theme of Hellas (in central Greece, Attica, and Boeotia). Despite these achievements, Byzantine influence did not reach the inner regions of the Peninsula, which remained under Avar influence.

The Clash of the Alpine Slavs with the Avars and Bavarians

Avar power lay heaviest upon those sections of the South Slavs living in the plains and river valleys through which passed the old Roman roads used by the Avars for their encroachments on Italy and central Europe. The Slavs in the Alpine regions also clashed with the tribes in possession of adjoining territories. In the plains of Friuli they ran into the Germanic Lombards. After protracted fighting the frontier was stabilized along the Lombard system of fortifications *(limes Langobardorum)*, which stopped the Slavs from progressing farther in that direction.

The Alpine Slavs also had disputes with their Bavarian neighbors, and clashes along the borders were frequent. Rapprochement between the Slavs and Bavarians provoked Frankish pressure on the Bavarians and Avar pressure on the Slavs in the eighth century. When the Avars mounted an attack in 745, the Caranthanians applied to the Bavarians for help. The latter did assist them in warding off the Avars but then went on to impose the supreme authority of the Frankish kings, whom the Bavarians themselves had had to recognize two years earlier. The demands on them were not excessive (hostages, tribute) and left considerable margin for independent internal development by the Caranthanians. The greatest change was reflected in the dissemination of Christianity. The Caranthanian prince Borut agreed that his son and nephew, who were among the hostages, were to be reared in the Christian faith. Missionary activities were undertaken from Salzburg, the nearest center of the church, and the construction of church buildings intensified particularly during the reigns of Borut's converted heirs: Gorazd (749–751/52) and Hotimir (751/52–769). There was, however, no lack of resistance to conversion by those sections of society who were dissatisfied with the changes and the strengthening of princely power. Two major insurrections, during the lifetime of Prince Hotimir and after his death, shook the principality but did not alter appreciably the country's already firm Christian orientation.

The Establishment of Supreme Frankish Power

Frankish rule was frustrated for a time (763–788) by Bavarian defection and the separation of Caranthania from the Frankish state. Encompassing almost all western Europe in the mid-eighth century, the Frankish state launched its eastward expansion under the new dynasty, especially following the coronation of Charlemagne (768–814). After dealing with the Saxons, Lombards, and Bavarians, the Frankish state came into direct contact with the Slavs along a broad front. The lands of the Alpine and Pannonian Slavs were subjected to growing pressure and interference by the authorities who would no longer brook token subordination but insisted on organizing the areas they had captured and establishing their own system of administration.

The Collapse of the Avars

Figuring significantly in the development of the South Slavs is the war waged by Charlemagne between 796 and 803 against the Avars. The khaganate crumbled and the Balkan Slavs were rid of Avar domination forever. The Avars soon disappeared as a people from the historic scene. During the war, extensive territories settled by Slavs fell to Frankish rule and were divided up into *marchiae* (marches). The Caranthanian principality was surrounded by Frankish border units although local princes remained in power. The Frankish thrust into Pannonia put pressure on the Croats and the towns of Istria, then ruled by the distant Byzantine emperors.

The Croats and the Frankish State

No cohesive picture can be pieced together for the development of the Croats up to that time. After settling the area and waging war with the Avars, from whose supreme authority they wrested themselves, they were preoccupied with their relations with the Byzantine towns in Dalmatia. Here too, as in Salonika, periods of attacks and attempts to capture the towns alternated with intervals of peace and normal relations. Under certain circumstances, the Croat warriors came to the assistance of the Byzantine Empire, as in 678, when they fought the Arabians on Italian soil. The Croats, whose center was situated in the vicinity of the town of Nin, came into contact with the Franks during the Avar war and recognized the supremacy of Charlemagne even before 803. The war between the Frankish state, which had become an empire in 800, and Byzantium provided the Croats with an opportunity to defect, but the peace concluded between the Eastern and the Western Empires (812) left Croatian territory in the Frankish sphere while the coastal towns, like Venice, fell to Byzantium. Croatian territory was not divided up into boundary marches but remained under the rule of local princes. The oldest dynasty was possibly that of Prince Višeslav, whose name is inscribed in stone on the christening font in Nin.

In Croatia, too, Frankish power paved the way for intensified conversion to Christianity. The focus of such activity was the patriarchate of Aquileia under Frankish rule, as nearby church centers in the coastal towns belonged to Byzantium. This wave of conversion to Christianity created conditions conducive to the founding of a separate Christian bishopric or diocese, centered in Nin.

After the death of Charlemagne (814) relations with the Frankish supreme authority changed. Regents in the frontier areas became overbearing in their attitude, interfering directly in the vassal principalities. Particularly obnoxious in this respect was the margrave of Friuli, who provoked bitterness among the local princes, surrounded by the warrior aristocracy of the clans, and among the population at large. Resistance ran highest in the Sava and Kupa River districts, where a Slav principality had been established earlier; from its later ties with Croatia, it acquired the name of the Sava, or Pannonian, Croatia. Its prince, Ljudevit, chafing from the behavior of the margrave of Friuli applied to Emperor Louis the Pious, son of Charlemagne and, getting no satisfaction in those quarters, raised an insurrection. He found allies among the Caranthanians and neighboring Slavs from Pannonia, to whom were added also the distant Timočani. Borna, the prince of the Croats in Dalmatia, remained loyal to the Franks and warred with them against the insurgents. For three years (819–822) Ljudevit put up a successful resistance. The Franks succeeded in quelling the uprising only after ten expeditions. Ljudevit took refuge among the neighboring Serbs, and later he lost his life in Croatia.

The collapse of this uprising was dire in its consequences for Caranthania, transforming it from a semivassal principality into a county of the Frankish state. The prince, who had been elected by the people and simply confirmed by the Frankish ruler, was replaced by Frankish feudal lords. Feudal institutions and feudal law were gradually introduced, thus interrupting social development on old Slavic foundations. From the very beginning, the Frankish element penetrated powerfully into the internal life of the Caranthanian Slavs, as reflected in the fact that in successive decades, as the Frankish state grew feeble and finally collapsed, no forces appeared to rid the land of the Carolingian system.

Like Byzantium, the Frankish Empire brought a segment of the South Slavs under its control, drawing them into the sphere of Latin Western Christianity and culture. The two medieval empires, so divergent in structure and civilization, dragged the South Slavs in opposite directions, generating and deepening the differences between them. The first wave of Germanic penetration soon reached its furthest limits, however; Byzantine penetration continued for centuries.

The Emergence of the Bulgarian State and Its Expansion

In its policy of "reconquest"—the renewed conquest of former Roman territories in the Balkan Peninsula—Byzantium was soon faced with a rival in the Bulgars, a warlike and well-organized Turkic tribal community which had

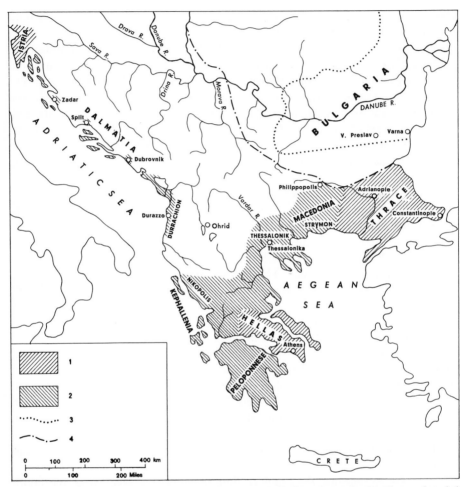

MAP 3. The beginnings of Byzantine reoccupation of the Balkan Peninsula. (1) Themes founded
during the seventh and eighth centuries; (2) themes founded in the ninth century; (3) the
boundaries of the Bulgarian state after the migration of the Bulgars (ca. 680); (4) the boundaries of the Bulgarian state in the early ninth century.

already taken possession of the land between the lower Danube and the Balkan
Mountains (Haemus) by 680. Lording it over the Slavs settled in those territories,
these proto-Bulgars set up a state in which the two racial and ethnical elements
lived separate lives for some time until the language of the Slavs gained the upper
hand. With relative swiftness, the Bulgars, straddling the bordering Balkan Mountains, launched a long and stubborn struggle against Byzantium. The area
settled by Slavs became the theater of war, and the various Sclaviniae fell as the
victims of one or the other rival. The small Slavic principalities either merged

with the extensive but simply organized Bulgar state or were incorporated into the network of Byzantine themes. Byzantium's progress was attended by the founding of new themes which, in the first half of the ninth century, extended from the Ionian Islands, Dyrrachium (Durres, Durazzo), and Epirus (Epeiros) via the Struma district, part of Macedonia, to Thrace and the Black Sea shores.

Early in the ninth century, the Bulgars triumphed over Byzantium, breaking ground for a great westward expansion. The southern flank of their penetration reached through Macedonia to the shores of the Ionian Sea, cutting off the Slavs in the central part of the Peninsula from Byzantium. The northern flank advanced deep into Pannonia only to clash with the Frankish frontier forces at the Drava River.

The free Slavs, inhabiting the western half of the Peninsula, were surrounded on all sides and exposed to pressure from their neighbors. The Serbs stood in the way of Bulgar expansion and a clash was imminent. The earliest available data about the Serbian state and its first dynasty are therefore linked with the war against the Bulgars around 850. Resistance to the Bulgars' westward swing continued through the reign of Prince Mutimir, when a Bulgar army was defeated in the field and the son of the Bulgar khan and a group of boyars were taken captive. For some time afterward, the Bulgar rulers desisted from their attempts to capture the Serbian principality, but they continued interfering in its internal affairs by supporting various members of the ruling family in their attempts to win power.

Byzantium was able to maintain ties with these regions only via the Adriatic Sea and coastal towns. Still, it refused to renounce its pretensions, particularly after Emperor Basil I (867–886) had built up the army and restored the authority shaken by the feeble rulers of the first half of the ninth century. The Bulgar threat caused the Slavic princes to rally to the empire and made them more amenable to accepting the supremacy of Constantinople. Even those members of the Serbian dynasty who had come to power with Bulgar support soon turned to Byzantium to legalize their positions. Byzantium also gained influence through conversion to Christianity. Christian names among the Serbian ruling clan appear among nobles born in the seventies of the ninth century. Because missionary centers could have been only the towns on the Adriatic coast, the earliest Christian influence among the Serbs is traceable to Roman ritual and papal jurisdiction.

The Theme of Dalmatia

One of the important measures in Byzantine offensive policy was the creation of the theme of Dalmatia from the towns and islands remaining under Byzantine rule. Dalmatia acquired a strategos with headquarters in Zadar (Zara); he had to use the sea in order to maintain ties with various parts of his theme and with the central authorities in Constantinople. In founding the theme of Dalmatia, Emperor Basil I had to regulate its relations with the Slavic hinterland. He allowed the Slavic princes in the hinterland to exact a tribute of 10 pounds of gold owed him by the towns.

The Croatian Princes and Byzantium

The nearest and most important neighbor of the theme of Dalmatia was the Croat principality extending from Istria to the Cetina River in the early ninth century. Frankish power was on the wane there, especially since Croatia had forged links with the Carolingian kings of Italy, frequently involved in internal Frankish strife. Together with the Franks, the Croats of the time of Prince Trpimir (ca. 845–ca. 864) warred on the Bulgars, but their attention was really focused seaward. Apart from the Byzantine coastal towns, there were also the merchantmen of Venice, plying the eastern coast of the Adriatic to Constantinople, and the Arabian fleet, which winged its way from the Mediterranean to attack the Adriatic shores. The Croat assaults on Byzantine towns and Venetian ships provoked even greater conflicts with the Byzantine Empire, whereas the Arabian danger cautioned them to peace and cooperation. During the reign of Prince Domagoj (ca. 864–876), the Croats, together with the Serbs, Zahumljani, Travunjani, and Konavljani, who bowed to the supremacy of Byzantium, laid siege to the town of Bari under the joint leadership of the Byzantine and the Holy Roman emperors. Formally, the supreme power of the Western Empire had protected the Croat principality from the impositions of Byzantine power until 875, when Emperor Louis II died. After that, Emperor Basil, exploiting strife among members of the dynasty, supported Prince Zdeslav, son of Trpimir, and achieved his goal through him. When the Croats, too, fell under the supreme authority of the empire, Emperor Basil ceded to their prince and also, but in smaller part to the princes of the Zahumljani and Travunjani, the imperial tribute of 10 pounds of gold due him from the towns of the theme of Dalmatia. Later changes at the Croatian court caused rejection of Byzantine supremacy, but the towns retained the organization of the theme. For long, they were the starting point for the spreading of Byzantine influence. Romanic in the origins of their population, Latin in the language of church services and ecclesiastical culture, and within the papal fold of the still undivided but crumbling Christian world, these towns wielded a uniform influence on the tribes in the Slav hinterland. Linguistic differences and political divisions between the coastal towns and the Slavs raised barriers to the spread of Christianity and church life in this early period. It was precisely at this time, in the second half of the ninth century, that a powerful medium for the dissemination of the faith and Christian culture among the South Slavs came into being in another part of the great Slav area.

The Mission of Saints Cyril and Methodius and Its Results

Rastislav, prince of Great Moravia, intent upon suppressing the influence of the Frankish clergy and accentuating his own independence, applied to the Byzantine emperor for missionaries. Byzantium, then pursuing an active policy toward the Slavic world, selected two learned men of Thessalonika: Constantine, already put to the test in diplomatic and church missions, and his brother Methodius, thoroughly acquainted with the Slavs and their language. The brothers devised a new alphabet (Glagolitic) and translated some of the most important books for the service. Thus the foundations of Slavic literature were laid, and new vistas were opened for the further cultural development of the Slavs.

The Principality in Lower Pannonia

In their mission Constantine (later known by his monastic name Cyril) and Methodius also covered the Slavic principality in Lower Pannonia, established about the middle of the ninth century in the Lake Balaton area among settlers from the Alpine districts, who were enabled by the collapse of the Avar state to settle in the fertile plain. The nucleus of this principality, with headquarters on the southern shores of Lake Balaton Masapurc (Zalavár, Blatenski Kostel) was founded by Pribina, a refugee from Great Moravia and a vassal of the Frankish emperor. His son Kocelj (861–874) received Methodius, who upon returning from Rome, where the pope had blessed his mission, became archbishop of the restored Sirmian-Pannonian diocese. As the growing independence of the church and the introduction of Slavic service were paralleled by the mounting political independence of the Frankish Empire, a new wave of Frankish pressure, both political and ecclesiastical, was not long in coming. Victims of this new offensive were the Lower Pannonian principality, which disappeared in 874 and also Methodius himself, who was first cast into prison and then banished and prevented from continuing his work until his death (885). In consequence of the unfavorable political conditions, the work of the brothers from Thessalonika did not endure in the areas where it was meant to. But thanks to the disciples of Methodius, who after the death of their teacher sought refuge in the south, in the newly converted state of the Bulgar king Boris, Slav literacy spread in the Balkans, where it remained. During the lifetime of the disciples of Methodius, the first alphabet, Glagolitic, which reached as far as Croatia and the Adriatic islands, slowly began to be suppressed by Cyrillic, a more practical alphabet founded on the basis of Greek characters. Glagolitic maintained itself in Croatia and in successive centuries came to be known as the "Croatian alphabet" and later even as one of the essential features of Croathood. Toward the end of the ninth

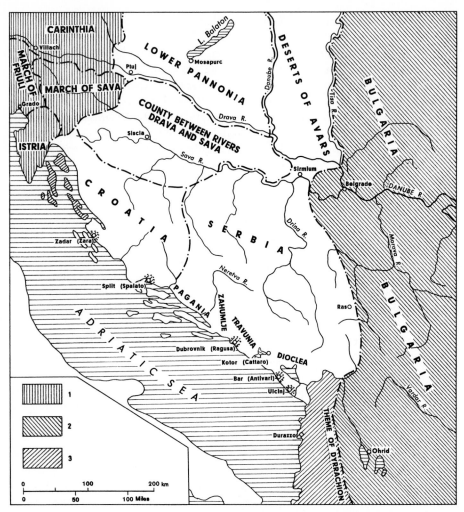

MAP 4.   The South Slavs between the Franks and the Bulgars after the uprising of Ljudevit Posavski.
(1) Under Frankish rule; (2) under Bulgar rule; (3) under Byzantine rule.

century, Ohrid asserted itself as an important Slavic cultural center under
Bulgar rule. Clement (d. 916), a disciple of Methodius, vigorously tackled the
job of training a Slavic clergy, educating the people, translating, and writing
literary works.

The Slav alphabet and the language of church services and texts, understood in various parts of the sprawling Slavic world, were elements cementing
together the Slavic groups that lived and worked under increasingly divergent
conditions. Places of worship and articles for use in ritual were required in the

religious life of Christians, a circumstance which lent impulse to the development of various branches of the arts. Ideas of the forms and shapes of these articles needed for practicing the cult of Christianity arrived from older Christian centers. Little remains of this earliest phase of Christian art among the South Slavs. But in the Dalmatian towns and in the Dalmatian part of Croatia, there have been found important architectural remnants and fragments of stone decoration with the intertwining ornament as the most frequent motif.

CHAPTER 4

The Upsurge and Decline of the Slavic States in the Balkan Peninsula

The Arrival of the Magyars

The position of the Slavs in the Balkan Peninsula was destined to undergo yet another significant change toward the end of the ninth century. Two factors were decisive: the arrival of the Magyars in Pannonia and the sudden upsurge of Bulgaria and its emergence as a powerful empire—rival of Byzantium. Driven from their recent abode on the lower Danube, the Magyars appeared in Pannonia in 895 and swiftly gained mastery not only of the deserted plains, formerly under Avar rule, and the sparsely settled Slav regions, loosely controlled by the Bulgars, but also over Germanic territories up to the Alpine foothills. For the South Slavs, Magyar presence was significant and far-reaching in its consequences. The nearby Slav areas were the first to feel the results of Magyar encroachment and devastation. The Magyars then drove a wedge in the Slavic region, cutting the southern Slavs off from those in the west. Also interrupted was the colonization of Pannonia by the Caranthanians and of Caranthania by the Germans. Finally, the new neighbors of the South Slavs established, in the area of which they had taken possession, a Magyar state, powerful and eminently capable of expanding, and including within its fold a considerable section of the South Slavs.

Byzantine-Bulgar Rivalry for Control of Serbia

Conditions had already been created earlier that permitted the fresh and sudden upsurge of Bulgaria in the early tenth century. All the acquisitions of previous expansion had been retained and the state had undergone important internal transformation. The Bulgars were evangelized in 864, while the then ruler, Boris-Michael, attempted to draw aloof from Byzantium in church matters by exploiting the conflict between the Roman pope and the patriarch in Constantinople. The ties established with the pope and the arrival of Frankish missionaries were fleeting episodes for, in 870, Bulgaria came under the control of the church in Constantinople, and from 885 onwards the disciples of Methodius stepped up their activities in spreading the service in Slavonic, which came to prevail completely in religious life. Attempts to revert to paganism by the Bulgar boyars, whose power was on the wane, were decisively quelled as the Slav element gained ascendancy in the Christianized state. Boris's successor, Simeon (893–927), shifted his ambition to the Byzantine Empire in his dream of acquiring the imperial crown. His intention was not to set up a new empire, but rather, through his own state, to reconstruct a universal empire encompassing the entire Christian world. It was almost as if the Slavicized European provinces, gradually won from Constantinople from the seventh century onwards, were trying to gain mastery over Constantinople, through Simeon's Bulgaria. Superior in the battlefield, Simeon arrived at the very walls of the capital and even at one point succeeded in obtaining an imperial coronation. But forces were always found in Constantinople capable of frustrating his plans after his withdrawal. Nonetheless, Simeon's wars and his imperial coronation echoed widely throughout the Slavic world in the Balkan Peninsula. The reconstruction of Simeon's empire was the goal and ambition of a number of later Balkan Slav movements.

The Byzantine-Bulgar wars influenced the position and development of the remaining South Slavs, especially the Serbs, who were the nearest neighbors of Simeon's Bulgaria. After much internal wrestling for power, Prince Petar Gojniković (893–917) managed to remain on the princely throne for some time,

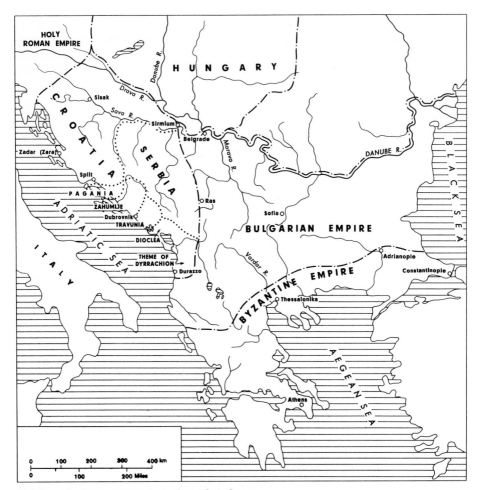

MAP 5. The Balkan Peninsula in the mid-tenth century.

but he had to fight his own relatives to do so, for one of them in particular was bent on gaining control over Serbia with the help of Bulgaria. He recognized the supreme authority of the Byzantine emperor but succeeded, nevertheless, in maintaining friendly relations with Simeon for a time. These relations were spoiled when Byzantium attempted to include the Serbian prince in a broad anti-Bulgarian coalition. Informed by Mihailo, prince of Zahumlje, of Petar's negotiations with Byzantium, Simeon sent an army with another member of the ruling Serbian clan, captured the prince by ruse, and cast him into prison, enthroning his cousin Pavle Branović in his place. Successive events were in substantial measure characteristic of Serbia's position at that time. The Byzantine emperor dispatched another member of the ruling clan, Zaharije Pribislavljević, who failed in his mission. Prince Pavle captured him and surrendered him to the Bulgars. After a brief interval, he shifted to the Byzantine side, while Emperor Simeon sent the previous Byzantine ward, Zaharije, to Serbia and helped him to power. Having established himself on the throne, Zaharije also turned his back on Bulgaria and recognized Byzantium. Emperor Simeon replied in kind: as he had done once before, he dispatched an army with a pretender, but did not enthrone him; rather he captured the district heads (župani) and brought the country under his own personal jurisdiction (924–927). Thus, after a few decades of resistance, Serbia fell victim to Bulgarian expansion then at its zenith.

Remaining beyond the reach of Bulgaria, the coastal principalities (kneževinas) had established closer contacts with Serbia in the intervening period or even recognized its authority for varying intervals. The Travunjani and Konavljani had already combined and forged links with the Serbian dynasty, it being believed in the mid-tenth century that they were descendants of the Serbs who had settled there during the reign of Emperor Heraclius. The principality of Zahumlje, whose inhabitants were also counted as Serbs in the tenth century, pursued an independent policy, dictated apparently by the special interests of the dynasty. The Neretljani were the farthest removed from Bulgar attacks, but because of their incessant buccaneering they were subject to pressure from Byzantium and Venice.

The Ascendant Croatian State

During the first few decades of the tenth century, Croatia also experienced a sudden development. The state had considerable military forces on land and on sea. It was thought in Constantinople in the mid-tenth century that the Croatian ruler had available to him in the thirties an infantry numbering 100,000 men, calvary with 60,000 men, and a navy of over 5,000 seamen. Certainly the numbers are exaggerated, but they do affirm the impression that Croatian military power left on its allies. Croatia was not exposed to the direct threat of Bulgarian conquest but found it necessary to ward off the assaults of Bulgarian detachments which occasionally penetrated deep into its territory. After one such abortive attack, the Bulgar ruler Boris-Michael concluded peace with the Croats. Later, Croatian rulers were to offer sustenance and refuge to the opponents of Bulgaria from Serbia. Consequently, after the subjection of Serbia, the Bulgars mounted a new attack on Croatia which ended in Bulgarian defeat.

During the reign of Tomislav (910—ca. 928), who bore the title of king, Croatia broke the bounds of its mountainous hinterland and spread to the Pannonian plains, previously under Frankish and later Bulgarian rule, and since the late ninth century under attack by the Magyars. This vast territory, extending all the way to the Danube and well within reach of the warlike Magyars, was controlled by Croatian rulers for over a century and a half. Croatia grew with the addition of the new districts, but it was also brought closer to the Magyars, whose attention was consequently directed toward expansion seaward.

During fierce fighting with Bulgaria, the Byzantine emperors could but pursue a moderate and indulgent policy toward Croatia, making their influence felt in more devious ways. The Croatian rulers, including Tomislav, did not encroach upon the Byzantine towns of the theme of Dalmatia, thus facilitating the maintenance of good relations. But difficulties were generated by problems of church jurisdiction in Croatia and Dalmatia, which acquired extremely complicated form. Like other rulers of the early Middle Ages, the Croatian princes and kings strove to place their states under the integral jurisdiction of a single church whose seat and prelate would be in the ruler's vicinity and under his supervision. The territory of Croatia, however, was governed ecclesiastically from Split, as heir of the later provincial metropolis of Salona. Recollections of earlier rights were well preserved in the Romance town, conscious of its continuity with the period of late antiquity. In this it was no doubt supported by the Roman Curia and the Byzantine municipal authorities, among whom church dignitaries figured significantly. By dint of circumstance, therefore, the interests of the Croatian rulers clashed with the traditions of the church order.

The position was exacerbated by the wide use of the Slavonic tongue in the Dalmation church service, which the people of the tenth century, in contrast to their predecessors, energetically condemned. Pope John X, for instance, demanded that King Tomislav and Prince Mihailo of Zahumlje abolish church services in Slavonic. These church problems of Dalmatia and neighboring Slavic states were the subject of consideration at two church synods in Split, in 925 and 927/28. With respect to services in Slavonic, the first synod did not adhere strictly to the pope's wishes, for it merely forbade in future the ordaining of priests who spoke only Slavonic, thus tolerating those who were already active. The second synod did away with the special Croatian bishopric in Nin and set up others under the authority of the archbishop of Split. The synods of Split did not definitely solve the problem of church jurisdiction and the language of the service. They were to crop up again later, engendering fresh conflicts.

Knowledge is scant about the development of Croatia after King Tomislav. Two heirs succeeded him, Krešimir I and Trpimir II, but nothing is known of their reigns except that Croatia's military power remained intact. During the reign of the next prince, Miroslav (945–949), Croatia was rent by internal strife, a frequent manifestation in those times, provoked more often than not by the fact that the ambitions of members of the ruling clan happened to coincide with the interests of foreign powers. As far as is known, however, the consequences for Croatia were not very grave at this time, as no great danger arose to jeopardize its position.

MAP 6.   The restoration of Byzantine rule in the Balkans at the beginning of the eleventh century. (1) Boundary areas under direct Byzantine rule after 1018; (2) boundary areas under the supreme authority of the Byzantine emperor.

The Downfall of the First Bulgar Empire

Major changes occurred in the political situation of the Balkan Peninsula after the death of Emperor Simeon (927). His successor, Petar (927–969), peace-minded and loyal to Byzantium, which recognized his imperial title, was content to preserve what his father had achieved. Simeon's death was exploited by Prince Časlav, who had grown up in Bulgaria with his father, Klonimir, once a ward of Simeon's, to return to Serbia and to reconstruct the state of his forebears. The short period of Bulgarian rule left chaos in its wake. Prince Časlav (927–950), according to contemporary Byzantine sources, was constrained to collect and bring back the people who had fled to neighboring states. In this he enjoyed the support of the Byzantine emperor, whose supreme authority he recognized, as predecessors had. During Časlav's time, Travunija with the district of Konavle also fell under Serbian control. About the mid-tenth century, Magyar incursions far to the south encroached upon Serbia, as well as upon Byzantine territories. One of these attacks was repulsed by Časlav, but according to later sources he lost his life in warring against the Magyars.

The second half of the tenth century saw the dawn of a new epoch of conquests in the history of Byzantium, which again undertook to pursue the policy of "reconquest" of lands settled by Slavs. This policy had had to be abandoned by force of circumstance in the late ninth century. After a string of notable successes in the east, the warlike emperor Nicephorus Phocas refused to pay tribute to the Bulgars and caused the Russian prince Svyatoslav to attack them. The latter emerged victorious but turned the victory to his own account rather than Byzantium's. The upshot was an onslaught against Svyatoslav, his expulsion, and the short-lived reinstatement of the Bulgarian dynasty, and finally the complete subjection of Bulgaria in 971. In substantial degree, this major achievement of Byzantine arms brought the empire closer to its goal. The once superior adversary had suffered total defeat. Bulgaria's fate was probably shared by Serbia, but no information about it is available after the death of Časlav.

The Empire of Samuel

The Byzantine triumph turned out to be of brief duration. After the death of Emperor John I Tzimisces (969–976), who had triumphed over Svyatoslav and the Bulgarian Empire, a major uprising broke out among the Slavs in Macedonia who had been governed by Bulgaria under Simeon and his successors. It flared rapidly over a huge area and literally wiped out the gains of the Byzantine conquest. The insurrection, centered in the region of Ohrid and Prespa (in the southern part of Yugoslav Macedonia), was led by the sons of the local ruler Nicholas: Moses, David, Aron, and Samuel. The Byzantine authorities, paralyzed by struggle over the throne, paid no heed to the uprising for some time. In the fighting, and in private quarrels, three of the brothers were killed, leaving only Samuel, who proclaimed himself emperor, thus letting it be known that his objective was to reconstruct the empire of Simeon and Petar. Contemporaries called Samuel and his subjects Bulgars, as in the intervening period the name of Bulgaria had spread to include the Slavic inhabitants whose language and culture prevailed in the state. Samuel showed no interest in the old Bulgarian centers but directed his expansionist zeal toward the Slavic areas in Macedonia and Greece, where Byzantine rule had been restored in preceding centuries. He attacked the vicinity of Thessalonika, then Thessaly, central Greece, and even the Peloponnesus. The first endeavors of the Byzantine emperor Basil II to stop Samuel, who finally entrenched himself firmly on the throne, ended in total failure. Samuel took advantage of this situation for expansion, bringing under his control the old Bulgar lands in the eastern part of the Peninsula, and also Epeiros (Epirus) and the town of Dyrrachium. After he assailed the Slavic principality of Dioclea near Lake Scutari, transforming it into a vassal district, his detachments devastated the vicinity of the Dalmatian towns. By the year 1000 Samuel had enlarged his state to cover the larger part of the Balkan Peninsula, from Srem in the north to Attica in the south, and from the Ionian Sea in the west to the Black Sea in the east. Early in the eleventh century, Emperor Basil II trained all his forces on Samuel, winning a number of important victories. Successive waves of attack in the course of a few years wrested almost half the territory from under Samuel's control. In 1014 a decisive battle saw Samuel's army beaten and cruelly massacred. Samuel died soon after the defeat, and his son, Gavrilo Radomir, was murdered the next year by Jovan Vladislav, a nephew of Samuel's, who continued fighting Byzantium until his death in 1018. Before long, resistance ceased and the entire empire of Samuel was again under Byzantine control.

The result of this victory was the Byzantine Empire's greatest affirmation in the Balkan Peninsula since the Slavic migrations. The territory was divided up into themes which ran the length and breadth of the entire eastern half of the Peninsula. Once again, Byzantine garrisons established themselves on the shores of the Sava and Danube Rivers, from ancient Sirmium to the mouth of the Black Sea. Realizing the difficulty of organizing and controlling such an enormous area, Emperor Basil II made certain concessions: he gave the entire subject area a separate church organization, the autocephalous archbishopric with a see in Ohrid. He also permitted tribute to be exacted in kind as had been customary in the preceding period. Nevertheless, although the emperor's measures did consolidate Byzantine influence, they did not win over the mass of the population to Byzantine authority; in the course of the eleventh century, a number of major uprisings erupted, whose leaders were inspired by the example of Samuel. Through secular and sacred power, through the towns which were reconstructed and the population that streamed in, the Byzantines made their imprint on the regions subjugated after 1018. In the development of the church, for instance, a clear-cut boundary line is noticeable between the church organizations founded among the Serbs, also under Byzantine influence in the ninth century, and those under the jurisdiction of the archbishopric of Ohrid. It was the latter who were the genuine representatives of Byzantine religious life, and it was they who set the stamp of the eastern Orthodox religion on one section of the South Slavs.

Incessant interference in the order and way of life of the Slavic population inevitably created a mood of rebellion which was expressed among the Slavs under Byzantine rule in the form of revolts and mass uprisings and, among those who were in the position of vassals, in the form of an urge to rid themselves of that influence and to associate themselves with opponents of the Empire. The antagonism characterizing relations between the Byzantine Empire and the South Slav states in the eleventh and twelfth centuries traces its roots back to the situation that arose after 1018.

The Dalmatian Towns under Croatian Control

West of the region where the theme organization had been set up (covering approximately what is now Serbia and Macedonia), the small principalities of Dioclea, Travunija, Zahumlje, and Pagania remained vassals and along with them also Croatia, which came face to face with the resurgence of Byzantine power in a peculiar manner. Whereas previously these regions extending the length of the Adriatic coast had been most susceptible to the Byzantine influence emanating from the towns in the theme of Dalmatia, they now found themselves on the periphery, for the Empire acted as a land power because of the vast inland areas it had conquered. The greatest degree of independence and the highest expenditure of energy in the struggle for more independence in the eleventh century is therefore associated with these coastal areas.

At the turn of the eleventh century, Croatia experienced a crisis generated by the struggle for power which flared up again after the relatively long but little-known reign of King Stjepan Držislav (969–995). The two brothers Krešimir and Gojslav, seeking support in the Byzantine towns, revolted against his son Svetoslav, who was destined to succeed to the Croatian throne. Venice exploited the trouble in Croatia by refusing to pay the tribute exacted from it for centuries for the right to navigate freely along the Adriatic Sea. This launched hostilities between Venice and Croatia, followed by an appeal by the Byzantine towns for help against Svetoslav's attacks. With the permission of the emperor, who was not in a position to send forces to Dalmatia, Venice took control of the towns of the theme of Dalmatia in 1000. This was the first step in Venetian penetration of the eastern shores of the Adriatic. Croatia, where King Krešimir III had sat firmly on the throne since 997, reacted to the attacks on the towns and succeeded in gaining mastery over at least some of them (probably Split and Trogir) for a brief interval. This was followed by an attack by Byzantium in 1024 and reversal to the previous state of affairs.

Before long, the Byzantine Empire started its slow decline. The towns of the theme of Dalmatia grew more independent, and the southern towns formed a separate theme. The principality of Dioclea rid itself of Byzantine control and, under Prince Stefan Vojislav (ca. 1035–1050), successfully withstood the assaults of imperial regents from adjacent areas. Annexing the principalities of Travunija and Zahumlje, Prince Stefan Vojislav created an extensive state organization which replaced in terms of leadership the onetime "baptized" or "evangelized" Serbia, destroyed in the second half of the tenth century. In the southern Adriatic, a situation emerged similar to the one that had long existed in the north. In the immediate hinterland of the Byzantine towns, a large state appeared with the manifest intention of expanding inland, and also of gaining control over the coastal towns. Like Croatia, Dioclea for a time during the reign of Vojislav's successor, Mihailo (1050–1082), won supremacy over the region around the town of Ras deep inland.

The decline of the Byzantine Empire in the eleventh century made the South Slavs more accessible to the influence of neighboring powers whose strength had grown in the meantime. The great uprisings under Petar Odeljan (1040–1042), who claimed to be a grandson of Samuel, and under Djordje Vojteh, who endeavored to rely for support on the principality of Dioclea, did not, it is true, liberate the lands in the Peninsula interior from Byzantium's grip, but the emperors found it increasingly difficult to maintain their positions in the towns of the theme of Dalmatia and to prevent the expansion of Dioclea at the expense of their own territories. During this period, the empire reconciled itself to the existence of independent states and was satisfied to demonstrate its supremacy by assigning Byzantine titles to the Yugoslav rulers. Thus the prince of Dioclea, Mihailo, acquired the title of Prostospatharius, by which he was initiated into the Byzantine official hierarchy. At the same time, this denoted his subordination to the emperor.

In the Byzantine theme of Dalmatia, the ties between the towns grew lax, as did their links with the central power in Constantinople. Until the final quarter of the eleventh century, the emperors appointed administrators of the themes with the title of strategos, later *katepanos* and prior of Zadar, but these regents did not wield real power in all sections of the theme, which consisted of islands and poorly connected towns. Even when the Venetians took control of the theme in 1000, the northern islands of Rab, Krk, and Osor held a different position in relation to the new authority. Early in the eleventh century, the southern part of the theme, the center of which was Dubrovnik, was made a separate theme. In the middle of the century, the emperor ceded Zadar to Venice although the town's inhabitants resisted the change with arms in hand. Croatian pressure on the towns and islands also was not without its effects. Intermittent rule over various towns provided the Croatian kings with an excuse to add Dalmatia to their titles, as the Venetian doges did (after 1000). A document from Rab mentions the Croatian king Petar Krešimir (ca. 1059–1074) as ruler in addition to the Byzantine emperor. Later this king ruled a part of the onetime theme, in which a symbolic concession was made to the supreme power of the Byzantine emperors by reference to it in documents and prayers.

Greater Caranthania

Precisely at the time when the Eastern Empire was being pressed back from the northern part of the Adriatic coast, the Holy Roman Empire tried to strike roots there. After victory over the Magyars in 955, the Caranthanians and Germans from the Alpine regions expanded the frontiers of the revived Western Empire. In the frontier areas bordering on Magyar and adjacent South Slav territory, new frontier units were organized—the marks or marches (of Caranthia, Drava, Sava, Carniola)—which helped to consolidate and maintain the southeast frontiers of the empire. Together with the territory of onetime free Caranthania, these marches were divorced from Bavaria in 976 to form the separate duchy of Greater Caranthania, including Istria and part of Italy (the march of Verona). Greater Caranthania did not last long as an integral political unit; the real political power lay with the marches and feudal lords heading them. These lords frequently pursued an independent policy not only in their mutual relations but also vis-à-vis the central authorities and adjoining states. In alliance with the neighboring Croats and Magyars, Adalberon, herzog of Caranthania, rose in revolt against the Holy Roman Empire in 1035. Three decades later, Ulrich of Weimar, who ruled over a number of marches in the neighborhood of Istria, succeeded in expanding his authority to include the nearby Croatian Littoral and northern islands belonging to Byzantine Dalmatia. From these territories was formed the Dalmatian or Croatian-Dalmatian march (mark); it lasted only a few years, as one of Krešimir's bans (from *banus*), Zvonimir by name, later to become king, was successful in his attempt to annex the Littoral and islands to Croatia after Ulrich's death (1070), with the assistance of the Hungarian Árpáds.

Croatia and the Papacy

While the Holy Roman Empire, with this insignificant exception, remained on South Slav soil within the frameworks of its earlier gains, the papacy, against which the Holy Roman emperors had recently launched a struggle for power over the Western European Christian world, expanded its power and influence. The mounting aloofness between Rome and the Byzantine Empire, marked by periods of polemics and acrimonious exchanges, finally led to the definitive rift in 1054. At that time, the boundary line between the Roman and Constantinopolitan spheres on South Slav soil had not yet been stabilized, but the contours of the great division could already be discerned: under papal jurisdiction were the regions belonging to the Holy Roman Empire, the Adriatic coastal towns, and territories over which the bishops had spiritual jurisdiction. The area was not clearly defined, as church authority was not sufficiently strong in control and organization. In any case, it was an extensive area in the north where it reached the northern frontiers of the Croatian state, whereas in the south, in the Lake Scutari region, it was confined to the surrounding plains. The entire eastern section of the Balkan Peninsula was administered by Byzantium, approximately from the line running through Sirmium, Ras, and Prizren, which were the sees of the westernmost bishoprics of the archbishopric of Ohrid.

In the latter half of the eleventh century, the popes strove to reform the Catholic church and to rid it of secular influence; in this they encountered serious problems on the other side of the Adriatic. Disputes over jurisdiction were no longer waged between the bishops of the towns and the Croatian king— although certain difficulties did crop up in the early eleventh century—but between the towns themselves. Various towns fought for and won the archbishop's see at the expense of Split (Spalato): first Dubrovnik (1022), then also Bar (1089), the former as the center of southern Dalmatia and the latter as the ecclesiastical center of the kingdom of Dioclea, invoking ancient rights and traditions. At papal incentive, a church synod was held (1060) in Split during the movement to reform the church. It adopted decisions to ban marriage, beards, and long hair for priests, and the ordaining of Slav priests unless they learned Latin, and to proscribe marriage among relatives. The reform attempt ran into resistance not only from supporters of service in Slavonic but also from some Dalmatian bishops. Opponents of the reform were bolstered in their endeavors by the antipope, and service in Slavonic was not subject to obstruction in the Croatian-Dalmatian march, where it endured for long.

It is quite possible that order was restored in church relations by the powerful pope Gregory VII (1073–1085), through political pressure. A Norman expedition laid siege to the Dalmatian towns in the spring of 1075, taking the Croatian king captive. The incentive for the attack is ascribed to Pope Gregory and certain of the Dalmatian towns. In the following year, the Normans were expelled from these towns by the Venetians, and Zvonimir, formerly ban, was crowned king. He recognized the supreme authority of the pope and received in return the royal signs and the papal banner. Croatia thereby became part of the systems of vassal papal states developed by Gregory VII throughtout Europe. A similar relation was established with the ruler of Dioclea, Mihailo, whom the pope called "king," promising him the signs of a ruler.

Apparently, it was through Pope Gregory's intercession the Byzantium ceded the towns of its Dalmatian theme to Zvonimir. In the meantime, the German feudal lords had been pushed back from the Croatian-Dalmatian march all the way to Istria, making Zvonimir the first Croatian king to rule the entire region of the Byzantine theme of Dalmatia. Recognition of papal authority provided Croatia with protection from other papal followers, like the Istrian feudal Vezelin, who had been gathering his forces to attack Zvonimir, or the Normans from southern Italy, but at the same time it drew the Croatian ruler into the struggles in which the papacy was involved. Zvonimir therefore found himself on the Normans' side when they made their bid to conquer the entire empire, after winning the Byzantine regions in southern Italy. When the Normans landed to take Dyrrachium, the "Dalmatians" were there to help their fleet, while Bodin, king of Dioclea, although on good terms with the Normans, fought on the side of the Byzantine emperor. At the decisive moment, however, he defected and later exploited Byzantium's misfortunes to conquer Bosnia and Rascia (Raška), expanding his state far inland.

The State in Dioclea

But the consequences of this war proved to be negative for both Dioclea and Croatia. The Byzantine emperor Alexius I Comnenus (1081–1118), whose reign marked the beginning of a new upsurge of the empire, had a free hand for dealing with Dioclea after expelling the Normans. King Bodin was defeated and taken captive, but he regained power and ruled until the early twelfth century.

It was an unfavorable circumstance for Croatia that Emperor Alexius, in his war against the Normans, formed an alliance with Venice, which was eager to win freedom of navigation along the eastern Adriatic shores. Apart from many other privileges granted them by the empire, the Venetians, for services rendered, were also ceded the right to Dalmatia and Croatia. During the lifetime of Zvonimir, they were not able to exercise that right, but in the troubled times following his death they realized their pretensions and actually held mastery over the towns for a brief period.

The Árpáds Expand toward the Adriatic

It was later recounted, although it is probably a legend, that Zvonimir was murdered by his subjects for wishing to lead them into the Crusades. As he left no heir, the crown fell to Stjepan II, the last member of the ancient dynasty of Tripimirović, who had been living quietly in a monastery in Split. He had ruled only a little over a year, from 1089 to 1091, when a faction of the Croatian magnates, headed by the widow of the late King Zvonimir, incited the Hungarian Árpáds to claim the Croatian throne as their inherited right. The Hungarian king Ladislas I, ruling an extensive and consolidated kingdom, was sufficiently strong to capture the continental parts of the Croatian state and a section of the coast early in 1091. For the Croatian throne, he chose his nephew Almos, but the Cuman attack on Hungary forced him to withdraw before the new ruler could receive papal sanction and be crowned. The territory between the Drava River and Petrova Gora (Gvozd) nevertheless remained under the Hungarian rule and a diocese was established in Zagreb in 1094. The Dalmatian towns were withdrawn from Croatia, and the entire theme reverted to Byzantium, the

Byzantine emperor being assisted in his attempt to recover it by one of his Norman vassals.

But in Croatia itself, forces were found who put forth their own ruler, a certain Petar, of whom nothing is known except that he had headquarters at Knin. King Ladislas I was no longer able to give his attention to Croatia, but his nephew Koloman undertook to capture it (1097). Petar resisted him at Gvozd, but with insufficient forces, and was defeated and killed. King Koloman thrust to the coast, of which the Venetian doge had taken possession in the meantime. This time, too, Hungarian power failed to last, as Koloman was pressed back from Croatia after a serious defeat in Galicia in 1099. In a renewed attempt, he succeeded in being crowned king at Biograd na moru in 1102. Croatia thus became part of Hungary, where it remained. Once again, Dalmatia was destined to change hands, from Venice to Byzantium (1103), only to fall to King Koloman two years later. As had happened several times in the course of the eleventh century, the towns were joined to Croatia, but it was at this precise time that they began to withdraw behind their walls. The theme of Dalmatia lived on only in the pretensions of the Byzantine Empire, which was loath to surrender lands that had once been in its possession, and even more unwilling to forget them.

RULERS OF CROATIA

Dynasty Trpimirović

Višeslav (ca. 800)
Borna (ca. 810–821)
Mislav (ca. 835–845)
Trpimir (ca. 845–ca. 864)
Domagoj (ca. 864–876)
Zdeslav (878–879)
Branimir (879–892)
Muncimir (ca. 892–910)
Tomislav (910–ca. 928)
Trpimir II (ca. 928–ca. 935)
Krešimir I (935–945)

Miroslav (945–949)
Mihailo Krešimir II (ca. 949–969)
Stjepan Držislav (969–995)
Svetoslav (995–ca. 997)
Krešimir III (997–ca. 1030)
Stjepan I (ca. 1038–1058)
Petar Krešimir IV (ca. 1059–1074)
Dmitar Zvonimir (1075–1089)
Stjepan II (1089–1091)
Petar (ca. 1093–1097)

RULERS OF SERBIA

Vlastimir (ca. 850–ca. 860)
Mutimir (ca. 860–891, first years with brothers Strojimir and Gojnik)
Pribislav (891–893)
Petar Gojniković (893–917)

Pavle Branović (917–920)
Zaharije Pribislavljević (920–924)
Under Bulgarian rule 924–927
Časlav Klonimirović (927–ca. 950)

RULERS OF DIOCLEA

Jovan Vladimir (ca. 990–1016)   Mihailo (1050–1082)
Stefan Vojislav (1035–1050)   Konstantin Bodin (1081–1116)

CHAPTER 5

Stabilization of Boundaries

THE EMERGENCE OF HISTORICAL PROVINCES IN SLOVENIA / ETH-
NICAL BOUNDARIES / CROATIA UNDER THE ÁRPÁDS / THE FATE OF
THE DALMATIAN TOWNS / THE WITHDRAWAL OF BOSNIA / RASCIA
IN THE STRUGGLE AGAINST BYZANTIUM / THE ACHIEVEMENTS OF
NEMANJA / THE FOUNDING OF THE SERBIAN AUTOCEPHALOUS
ARCHBISHOPRIC / BOSNIA'S RESISTANCE TO CATHOLICISM AND
HUNGARIAN POWER

The Emergence of Historical Provinces in Slovenia

The beginning of the twelfth century marked the close of an important phase in the development of political organizations among the Slavs in the Balkan Peninsula. In terms of leading an independent existence, the South Slav states were in crisis. With the exception of the minor state of Dioclea, and perhaps a few other territories skirting the edges of the Byzantine region, the entire area belonged to various neighboring states. In spite of this, the achievements of the South Slav states were not entirely nullified, nor was it made impossible for them to pursue an independent political life in the future. Later development even demonstrated that frameworks which were to endure for centuries emerged from the living remnants and traces of earlier independent political existence. The fact that these peoples went their own separate ways in the course of historical development and that increasing differences between the various South Slav communities led to the formation of separate Yugoslav nations within the frameworks of territories inhabited by them, can be traced to the stabilization of boundaries and frameworks in the period between the eleventh and thirteenth centuries.

The frontiers of the Holy Roman Empire, which attained stability between the second half of the tenth and the end of the twelfth century, continued for some time to wield a powerful influence on the development of the Slovene and Croat nations. Respected for over four centuries as the boundary between two separate states—Hungary and the Holy Roman Empire—they were not forgotten even during the period when these states found themselves together under Hapsburg rule. This predominantly political boundary was at the same time the ethnical boundary between the Slovenes and the Croats.

Ethnical Boundaries

Within the frontiers of the Holy Roman Empire, the South Slavs, unintegrated, lived in a number of frontier regions—marches or marks. The original boundaries were not fixed but rather shifted, merging and splitting, either by command of the central authorities or as the result of action by local feudal lords who strove to establish ruling houses or dynasties in the regions entrusted to them. In this long process, new territorial entities came into being, with stable boundaries. The marks of Carniola and Savinja were merged into Greater Carniola in the eleventh century, and from this developed the province of Carniola, enduring for centuries and figuring significantly in the development of the Slovene nation. The areas along the eastern frontier (the marks of Caranthania and Drava) and the region of the upper Mura (Mur) merged into one province named Štajerska (Styria, Steiermark) after the feudal family of Traungau, barons of Styria. The once independent principality of Caranthania formed the nucleus of the province which retained its name (Koruška, Carinthia, Kärnten). Unity within the province and stable boundaries were fully established only in the fifteenth century, when provincial assemblies of the estates and other institutions (parliaments) were introduced. After that time, the Slovene provinces provided the framework for development among the Slovenes of their consciousness of national self. Apart from this diffusive feeling of belonging to the Slavs, and the general name Slavs, Slovenes, there developed also a sense of affinity with the

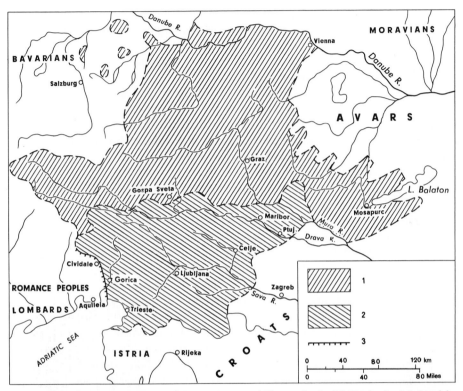

MAP 7.   Results of colonization and Germanization of Slovene lands. (1) Territories inhabited by
Slovenes in the ninth century; (2) Slovene ethnical territory in the mid-twentieth century;
(3) the Lombard *limes*.

province, and hence the name for them: Kranjci, or people of Kranj, Krain, or
Carniola.

From the time of their incorporation into the Frankish state, the Slovenes were subject to intermingling with the Germanic inhabitants and exposed to
German influences. In the first place, the foreigners were members of the feudal
class which in time became more numerous in various ways, among others
through the inclusion of the Slav element, which rose slowly up the social ladder.
Further, the Germans participated in the long and vigorous process of colonizing
the Slovene areas. Clearing the land for cultivation and establishing new settlements among the Slovenes, many German peasants came to make their homes
there, especially in the northern districts. Here and there the Slavs, left in the
minority or cut off from each other and isolated, shed their Slav features as time
went by. Naturally, colonization also worked the other way around, and the

German settlers were sometimes engulfed in the compact Slav area, but the general tendency in development was for the German to prevail and the Slav area to contract. The Slovene-German ethnical boundary became stable in the fifteenth century, when the process of colonization was practically completed, along a line bisecting ancient Caranthania.

The boundary with the Romanic world had stabilized far earlier, during the Slav-Lombard conflicts at the end of the sixth century. The line separating the plains from the mountains was also, on that side, the line denoting the Slovene-Italian ethnical boundary. The later course of colonization led to the establishment of several dozen Slovene villages in the lowlands of Friuli, but they later merged with their Romanic environment.

Very little trace of onetime independent state development was left in the Slavic world, dismembered in this fashion. What did remain was the ritual of investiture of the Caranthanian princes, which the new masters adopted; in somewhat altered form and invested with feudal elements, it was practiced during the ceremonies in which Caranthanian dukes took their oath of office. Although a duke was appointed by the German ruler, still, in the eleventh century, it was the "council of the men-at-arms," descendants of the prince's trusties who had enjoyed special rights and jurisdiction even under German rule, that passed the decision to accept him, reminding him at the same time that he belonged to them through the ritual of his donning peasant dress. Later, when this section of the population died out by developing into nobility, the ritual of investiture became a sheer formality with many picturesque details (the duke, dressed in peasant clothes, replied to questions in the vernacular, purchased the right to be enthroned on the "prince's stone," etc.; in this, the peasant masses played an utterly passive role. In the fifteenth century, the feudal masters came to consider even this ritual as degrading and avoided it, although it lingered on until the seventeenth century.

Croatia under the Árpáds

In contrast to the Slovene lands which fell under foreign rule relatively early, in Croatia independent state development continued in the form of the state order, the legal system, and historical tradition. As part of Hungary, Croatia was a clearly defined area with its own independent state life, imbued with memories of the early medieval *regna* of Croatia and Dalmatia, later joined by the kingdom of Slavonia *(regnum Slavoniae)*. This gave the estate-organized nobility at the end of the Middle Ages an ideological basis for retaining its individuality.

Three boundaries were decisive in defining the area in which the integration of the Croatian nation was to unfold through a long and complex process: the political boundary of Hungary and the Holy Roman Empire, which cut the Croats off from the neighboring Slovenes; the linguistic and legal boundary which separated them from the Hungarians; and the religious boundary setting them apart from their eastern South Slav neighbors (Serbs and Bosnians). Virtually the entire area had been united under Hungarian Árpád rule since the beginning of the twelfth century, but it did not develop along these lines. Three separate entities, the outlines of which were already clear during the period of Croatia's independent development under rulers from the national dynasties, continued their existence under different conditions: early Croatia in the narrow sense, extending from the sea to Petrova Gora; the sparsely settled and poorly organized plains area between the Dinaric mountain chain and the Drava River; and the coastal towns with islands.

Having become the rulers of the Croats, the Árpáds did not, in the spirit of medieval legal conceptions, strive to change the order they found. Even if they had wished to do so, their strength did not suffice for colonization or maintenance of large military garrisons in view of the great expansion of their territory in the second half of the eleventh century, which they had not had the time to develop properly or settle densely. Hungarian warriors came to Croatia only during raids provoked by Venice's taking possession of the coastal towns. The regime of the Árpáds had perforce to rely on the local aristocracy and rulers, leaving thus a considerable margin for independent social evolution and differentiation. The Croatian nobility rose in power, prestige, and organization parallel with the Hungarian nobility. In Croatia the ruler was represented by the ban, a dignitary whose office traced its roots back to an earlier period, and at times by the duke, or *rex iunior* (young king), in cases where representation was entrusted to close relatives of the king.

In the area between Petrova Gora and the Drava River, which had come to be called Slavonia or Slovinia, the Hungarian rulers took stronger and more direct measures in their intervention, as the new regime could not rely for support on the old order and old institutions. In comparison with the coastal belt, the inland districts were poorly organized, probably because less densely populated. There the Árpáds introduced the system of geographic and political units called županijas (comitatus), founding the Zagreb, Varaždin, and Križevac županijas. The royal županijas were more extensive than the earlier Slav counterparts, known to almost the entire Balkan Peninsula. The župan (military and political chief), appointed by the king, usually had his headquarters in a fortified town from which he discharged all the essential functions of state power: raising armies, collecting levies, and dispensing justice. With the creation of large feudal estates and the increase in the number of nobles who were not subject to the authority of the župan but rather responsible directly to the king, the royal županijas lost ground in the system of administration by the central authority, and the vacuum left by them was given new substance through the autonomy of the landowning nobility. Differences in system, and later the existence of separate estate bodies, accentuated a certain detachment between Croatia proper and Slavonia, retarding the integration of the population throughout the entire area.

The Fate of the Dalmatian Towns

Under Hungarian rule, the framework for the old Byzantine Dalmatia collapsed entirely and was relegated to oblivion. Each separate town received confirmation of its ancient rights and autonomy, and each had its own special financial obligations to the ruler (two-thirds of the duties levied on foreigners). Royal privileges gave each town the opportunity to develop into an autonomous commune and to dissociate itself from the hinterland, in terms of rights and system. Consciousness of belonging to a community deepened within the confines of these towns. Thus a boundary line became stabilized along the walls of these towns that for centuries obstructed unification with the hinterland. This boundary was all the more tangible because the patricians of the coastal towns emphasized their superiority over the hinterland, on the basis of their Romanic language and cultural orientation. The original Romanic nucleus dating from the time of the Slav migrations had undergone great changes when the Slavs poured down from the hinterland. The names of citizens and municipal officials during the Byzantine and Croatian periods reveal the important role of Slavs in the life of the towns. During the fresh influx of population, associated with the economic upsurge and the new role of the towns in economic life, and with the social differentiation from which the patrician class emerged, the wealthy older citizens drew aloof from the newcomers, invoking their town traditions which were truly Romanic in origin. The Romanic character of the coastal towns in the late Middle Ages (fourteenth and fifteenth centuries) was the result of the secondary Romanization overlaying and assimilating the Slavic element which had moved into the towns between the seventh and eleventh centuries.

Even after 1105, Venice continued to influence life in the coastal towns and islands. Its ultimate aim was to gain mastery of the area, and a pretext for interference was provided by the ancient rights of the Byzantine Empire to its onetime theme. During the twelfth century, when fierce struggles were in progress for mastery of the Peninsula between Byzantine emperors and Hungarian kings, the towns and islands changed hands a number of times. In 1115 the ten-year Hungarian-Venetian war was launched, during which the Hungarian crown lost towns and islands for longer or shorter periods. In a war of 1133, all towns except Zadar and the island towns reverted to Hungary. The victory of Emperor Manuel I Comnenus in 1167 over Hungary produced the last brief revival of Byzantine Dalmatia, which was organized as the *ducatus* of Dalmatia and Croatia until the emperor's death (1180). This short-lived Byzantine rule left no trace whatever in Croatia. When Byzantium finally lost its grip on Dalmatia, a new Hungarian-Venetian conflict flared up in which Hungary succeeded in retaining Zadar and other towns, while Venice took possession of the northern islands. The latter took advantage of the presence of the Crusaders, on their way to the Fourth Crusade, to conquer Zadar (1202). This state of affairs lasted over a century, with a short interruption in 1242, when the Hungarian king seized Zadar.

The Withdrawal of Bosnia

In the eastern part of Yugoslav territory, boundary stabilization proceeded more slowly, as the decline and contraction of the Byzantine Empire offered possibilities for major changes and ushered in a new period during which
independent state life flourished. The framework created by the expansion of the
oldest Serbian state, "Baptized Serbia," to the Adriatic shore was disrupted in
the second half of the tenth century by a Byzantine conquest, consolidated in
1018. At least one section of that original Serbia, far removed from later centers
of the Serbian people, came under direct Byzantine rule after the appearance of a
strategos of Serbia, a sure sign that a theme of Serbia also existed. Toward the
close of the eleventh century, parts of Serbia were included in the expansion of
the kingdom of Dalmatia and Dioclea, the center of which was located near Lake
Scutari. By that time the western region had broken off to form a separate entity,
Bosnia, with its center in the valley of the same name. Soon after Croatia, in any
case before 1138, Bosnia came to be ruled by the Hungarian king. There, too,
the king was represented by the ban, and sufficient margin was left by Hungarian
rule for independent internal development. Owing to specific circumstances,
first the protracted Hungarian wars against Byzantium and later the situation in
church affairs, Bosnia achieved a high degree of independence.

Rascia in the Struggle against Byzantium

The eastern part of what was once "Baptized Serbia" had as its center
the town of Ras, seat of the bishopric, from which the entire region derived its
name—Ras, or the Raška land, Rascia. Under Byzantine rule from the beginning
of the eleventh century, Rascia was intermittently conquered by the rulers of
Dioclea, and in the twelfth century it figured actively in the struggle against Byzantium, during which its great župans overshadowed the weak kings of Dioclea.
Circumstances did not favor a movement against Byzantium, for the empire
under the Comnenus dynasty was in the ascendancy. It had to devote its attention
to Hungary, a serious rival and pretender to power in the Balkan Peninsula. The
Hungarian-Byzantine wars, waged in several waves (1128–1129, 1150–1151,
1161–1164, 1166–1167), provided the rulers of Rascia with an opportunity to
turn their backs on the Byzantine emperors and attack nearby territories ruled by
Byzantium. The dynasty of the great župans of Rascia formed close ties at this
time with the Hungarian Árpáds, and also contracted marriages with them. The
raids of the Byzantine emperors in the Rascia area and their victories in the war
against Hungary prevented this country from being placed in the same position
as Croatia and Bosnia. The emperors made the great župans recognize their
supreme authority, surrender hostages, and contribute troops, and at times even
removed undesirable members of the dynasty. In 1166, Emperor Manuel I Com-

nenus, during his triumphant offensive, replaced the great župan of Rascia, Desu, by another dynasty member named Tihomir, who in turn was soon overthrown by his youngest brother Stefan Nemanja (1168–1196), the founder of the new dynasty. With the help of the Byzantine army, Tihomir attempted to regain power (1170). Nemanja continued his hostile policy toward Byzantium, placing his reliance on Hungary and Venice, but unfavorable circumstances left him to his own resources, and like his predecessors, he was forced to recognize the emperor's supreme authority and to provide him with auxiliary troops. He was brought to Constantinople and subjected to humiliating treatment in which the triumph of Emperor Manuel I was glorified, but he returned, to continue his rule in the shadow of Byzantine power.

During this initial period of rule, Nemanja in no way differs from his less-known predecessors. There is no information about the relation at that time between Rascia on the one hand and the kingdom of Dalmatia and Dioclea, and the principalities of Travunija and Zahumlje on the other, as the latter lived an independent existence. But the death of Emperor Manuel I Comnenus in 1180 marked a turning point in the development of Rascia and neighboring lands. Nemanja took advantage of the enfeeblement of the empire from internal disorders and external attacks to conquer with relative swiftness the territories lying along the line of Rascia's expansion. He took the plains of Kosovo, against which earlier great župans had also made occasional forays, neighboring Hvosno (today Metohija), and the territory between the Western and the Great Morava up to the town of Ravno (the present-day Ćuprija), where the Hungarian-Serbian boundary ran after Byzantium had been expelled. During fighting on the side of Hungary (1183) and penetration following the passage of the Crusaders during the Third Crusade (1189), Nemanja temporarily took possession of part of eastern Serbia and Macedonia (Polog, the region of today's Tetovo). His activities in the coastal area were meaningful for further development. After Zahumlje and Travunija, which had perhaps been annexed to Rascia even earlier, Dioclea was taken (before 1186).

The Achievements of Nemanja

By his wars, Stefan Nemanja created a state covering two categories of areas: one on which independent political life had prospered earlier, and another which had been ruled directly by Byzantium for almost two centuries. The old principalities lived by their own singular traditions, particularly Dioclea, "a great kingdom from the very first," so that Nemanja's state was an insufficiently cohesive contrivance threatening to fall apart. The assignment of parts of state territory to brothers and nephews for administration only served to augment this danger. Moreover, Stefan Nemanja's state was not safe from outside interference. The Byzantine emperors who succeeded each other always managed to gather enough strength to deal him hard blows and defeats (as in 1190), but they were not able to confine him to the earlier frameworks. Rather they had to be satisfied with the recognition of supreme authority while endeavoring to bind the Rascian dynasty by marriage between the emperor's niece and Stefan Nemanja's son Stefan.

When Stefan Nemanja withdrew in 1196, he was succeeded by his son Stefan (later Stefan Prvovenčani, the First-Crowned), the Byzantine Sevastocrator, whose father-in-law Alexius III Angelus had in the meantime become the Byzantine emperor. Stefan's elder brother Vukan had previously acquired from his father the territory of the onetime kingdom of Dioclea to adminster; his younger brother Sava took vows as a monk and later accompanied his father, in his declining years, to Mount Athos, to the monastery of Chilendarion, constructed by Serbian monks. The new state stood threatened when a struggle for power broke out among the brothers. In 1202 Vukan, assisted by Hungarian troops, expelled his brother and gained mastery over the entire country. The deposed Stefan found support in resurgent Bulgaria and was reinstated the following year, after which he continued fighting his brother for a time.

The political situation in the Balkan Peninsula then underwent a dramatic change. The Crusaders of the Fourth Crusade, led by Venice and incited by internal struggles for power, conquered Constantinople and brought down the Byzantine Empire in 1204. The result was an extremely complicated map of the Balkan Peninsula. Latin Crusade states were formed on the ruins of Byzantium: the empire of Constantinople, the kingdom of Salonika, and others; unconquered parts of Byzantium in Epirus and Asia Minor continued an independent existence under local dynasties and strove persistently to restore the empire. Bulgaria had already won independence (1185), and Hungarian influence was no longer offset by that of Byzantium. The Serbian state confronted not the Byzantine Empire but rather a whole series of states, each of which was potentially hostile. Under the circumstances, Serbia's new-won independence could easily be jeopardized. Consequently, Nemanja's heir was forced to pursue a dynamic policy, warding off the attacks of the Bulgarian tsar Boril, the Latin emperor of Constantinople, Henry of Flanders, and the master of Epirus, Michael Angelus, and to dissuade the Hungarian king Andrew II from attacking Serbia, which he at one time intended to do.

The Founding of the Serbian Autocephalous Archbishopric

Some time before the Latin triumph, Stefan the First-Crowned had substituted reliance on Rome and Venice for the earlier Byzantine orientation, but even after 1204 he did not neglect relations with the Greek states, guardians of

Byzantine traditions. Ties with the papacy led to Stefan's being crowned king by the papal legate in 1217. The coronation signified Serbia's affirmation among the states of that day and the strengthening of the ruler's position and authority in the country. According to contemporary conceptions, political independence was also reflected in separate church organization, but after all the political changes, the Serbian state remained under the ecclesiastical authority of the archbishopric of Ohrid. The king's brother Sava, who had lived in Serbia for a number of years, helping his brother in political matters, went to Nicaea, the seat of the emperor and patriarch, where he applied for and won an imperial decision establishing an autocephalous archbishopric for the state under the Serbian king. In Nicaea, Sava was invested as the first archbishop. This significant change was fiercely but vainly opposed by the archbishop of Ohrid, who thereby lost ecclesiastical power over Rascia. Sava set up a number of new bishoprics and trained a domestic clergy and church hierarchy, drawing support from the already well-established monastic communities of Serbia. The network of sacred institutions covered territories where the Christian church had been superficial in its proselytizing. The creation of the autocephalous Serbian archbishopric altered considerably the boundary between the Eastern and the Western Churches. Although the Serbian king and the archbishopric assumed an extremely moderate attitude in the great Greco-Roman church controversy, which had been exacerbated by the Crusades, and although they maintained ties with the popes, their activity for the development of the autocephalous church worked to the detriment of papal jurisdiction. The area of Orthodox bishoprics was extended to the Neretva River and Adriatic coast, almost up to the very walls of the towns where the sees of the Roman bishops were situated. The hardest hit was the archdiocese of Dubrovnik, to which belonged the entire hinterland, including Bosnia. The new boundary between the Catholic and Orthodox regions did not remain permanent; rather, it changed under the influence of political events, as will be seen later, but it never went back to the boundary line of 1020.

The creation of a separate church organization was instrumental in consolidating the several parts of the Nemanid state and, in time, merging them into a whole. In Serbia, as in other lands of Eastern Christianity, the sacred and secular spheres were not separate, the state being conceived of as both a religious and a political community. Church activity was therefore important for its integrating function, which was all the more explicit here for the very early emergence of the cult of the founders of the independent state and church, Saint Simeon (Stefan Nemanja) and Saint Sava (his son), with a number of other rulers being added to the cult later. Through them the political history of the Serbian state was interwoven with church tradition, enabling the church to maintain continuity of historical consciousness, so important in helping the Serbian nation remain intact under periods of alien rule.

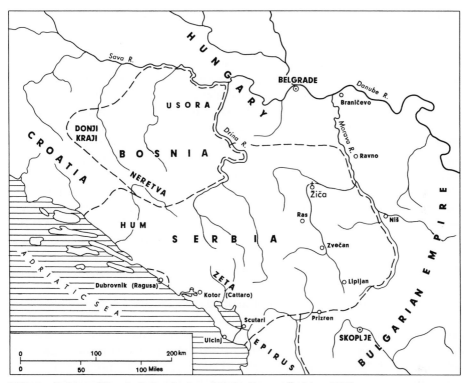

MAP 8.   Serbia and Bosnia during the time of Stefan Prvovenčani (ca. 1214).

In the first half of the thirteenth century, the Serbian state was in the morning of its independent development and its area changed with the tides of expansion and withdrawal. The lasting boundary remained the one which, in the human consciousness, separated the surrounding world from those who belonged to the Serbian state and church. This religious and political boundary was very clear-cut in relation to Bosnia, which embarked upon a more independent political development toward the end of the twelfth century.

Bosnia's Resistance to Catholicism and Hungarian Power

The retreat of Byzantium and the growing independence of Nemanja's state set Bosnia apart from the empire, which ruled it for the last time between 1167 and 1180. After this, Hungarian power had no countervailing force, and the Bosnian ruler, Ban Kulin (1180–1204), found himself under the authority of the Hungarian king. Conditions in the church began to aggravate the position of the state. In the diocese where service was held in Slavonic, under the ecclesiastical jurisdiction of Dubrovnik, dualistic heretics appeared at the close of the twelfth century, contemporary with those in neighboring Dalmatia and in the state of Serbia, and also with those in Macedonia, who had a longer tradition behind them. Their activities alarmed the Roman Curia, which had just launched an offensive against them in France and Italy. In dealing with the heretics in Bosnia, the pope drew support from the Hungarian kings. During the reign of Ban Kulin, the legate of Pope Innocent III, active in Bosnia, succeeded in persuading the Bosnian monks under heretic influence to atone for their sins and to undertake an obligation to respect the teachings and norms of the Roman church. But this did not stop the penetration and dissemination of dualistic beliefs in Bosnia. Again the heretics were condemned in 1221, this time provoking external intervention. The consolidation of Catholic positions and the endeavor to reform the Bosnian diocese on the model of other Catholic dioceses of that time caused a massive revolt and several waves of bitter wars between the Hungarian army, with whom the Dominicans sided, and the domestic forces led by Ban Matej Ninoslav (1233–1250). The fortunes of war favored first one side and then the other, but the Catholic church failed to attain its goal: the heretics remained to obtain control over the old Bosnian diocese, which was transformed into the dualistic "Bosnian church." Catholicism was expelled from the country and regained its foothold only after long and patient work by the Franciscan order. It thus happened that in Bosnia, the political framework of the Bosnian state was supplemented by an integral and altogether unique church organization. This state and church boundary distinguished Bosnia from adjacent South Slav regions, simultaneously preventing it from being transformed into a part of the Hungarian state or from uniting with Serbia, from which it had once withdrawn.

RULERS OF CROATIA AND HUNGARY

Dynasty Árpád

Koloman (1095–1116)	Ladislas III (1204–1205)
Stephen II (1116–1131)	Andrew II (1205–1235)
Béla II (1131–1141)	Béla IV (1235–1270)
Géza II (1141–1162)	Stephen V (1270–1272)
Stephen III (1162–1172)	Ladislas IV the Cumanian (1272–1290)
Béla III (1172–1196)	Andrew III (1290–1301)
Emeric (1196–1204)	

CHAPTER 6

Economic Development

Agrarian Economy

Little is known about economic life during the first few centuries after the Slav migrations. Some light has been shed on the subject only for places where the Slavic agrarian world came into contact with the towns in which the flame of late classical culture still burned. A very early source states that the Dalmatian townships maintained themselves in spite of Avar-Slav pressure "because the sea gave them a means of livelihood." This must be taken to mean that the towns were economically independent of their agricultural hinterland, which had fallen into the hands of unfamiliar and hostile conquerors, and that the sea remained as a link with the islands and other parts of the world to which fate had been kinder, above all Constantinople; the statement also implies that fishing was an important occupation. This state of affairs could not endure long. Necessity had brought together the citizens of Thessalonika and the people of the Slav hinterland in a rudimentary form of economic cooperation. As early as the seventh century, the town population had purchased food from neighboring Slavs, or even from more distant Slavic tribes when its closer neighbors laid siege to the city. So, too, was the population of the Adriatic coastal towns forced to trade with neighbors. Periods of hostility no doubt alternated with periods of normal relations. In the eighth century the Slavs settled the area where the Istrian Romanic towns were located, and in the ninth century, when the towns paid tribute to adjacent Slavic princes, their interdependence reached a high level.

During the initial contacts between the rural Slavic world and the remnants of the classical urbanized groups, the two approximated each other in degree of social and economic development. But shifting political fortunes, poverty, and isolation during the decline and decay of the empire engendered a general depression in the towns, where the population nevertheless did not revert to a far more primitive economy, as has been the case with the population of late antiquity in the Peninsula interior. On Yugoslav soil, the coastal towns were the harbingers of urban development and the standard-bearers of urbanized economy.

Throughout the Middle Ages, the urban and agrarian economies developed and progressed side by side, changing and complementing each other but going their own separate ways. Urban economy, associated initially with a few privileged points, spread throughout the entire territory with the growth, in waves, of urban settlements which relieved the otherwise uniformly agrarian landscape.

As in other parts of the world, agrarian economy here was conservative, changing only gradually over a long period of time. The South Slav regions were also affected by the slow but steady advancement of agrarian techniques. The heavy asymmetrical plow came into use but failed to displace the far more primitive wooden plowshare. In all South Slav lands, the three-field system of cultivation was introduced, the plots of land being sown alternately to winter and summer crops, with some left to lie fallow, but there is no information as to whether the system was applied generally or only on the large estates and in areas where land for tilling was abundant. Some sources refer to irrigation and the use of fertilizers here and there. On the whole, yields were small and farming that was dependent on the whims of nature was uncertain as a livelihood. When climatic conditions were unfavorable, the result was a veritable catastrophe; knowledge about the extent of such disasters is available from periods for which historical sources exist.

Underdeveloped agrarian techniques and low yields forced the farmers to increase the area under cultivation in order to raise food output for the growing population, of whom many had no means of subsistence. The land acquired upon settlement had to be expanded by clearing forests and undergrowth and taking possession of unsettled mountain terrain. This internal colonization in all Yugoslav regions gave shape to the cultural landscape and extended the settled zone considerably, but this subject has been studied adequately only for the Slovene districts, where the course and the stages of the process are discernible.

The System of Exploitation

As time passed, the system of exploitation changed. Even in the first few centuries after the migrations, two types of production were in evidence: first, land cultivation by the free peasants, working their plots independently, but utilizing water, forests, and pastures in common with other members of their village community; and second, the work of the serfs or captives who tilled the land for their masters, the latter reaping all the fruits of their labor and giving them only sustenance in return. In the beginning the holdings cultivated by serfs, belonging usually to the ruler or to prominent clan and tribal aristocrats, were a rare phenomenon. In time, however, the large feudal estate tilled by persons dependent in varying degrees upon the owner came to prevail and suppress free peasant production. Freemen came to be connected with the feudal estates under various conditions: if the ruler granted land to church or temporal lords for whom the freemen then tilled the land; if freeman submitted to bondage of their own free will in order to obtain "protection"; if a powerful feudatory forced them into such a relation.

The Organization of the Feudal Estates

The principle of exploitation was basically the same everywhere, irrespective of regional and local features, in regard to the type and magnitude of the obligation of the men working on the estate. One part of the estate was divided up among the peasants, who had their homes on the tenures, and another part was cultivated for the landlord by peasants subject to corvée. Apart from the corvée, the peasant on the estate was obliged to turn in a part of his basic crops (one-fourth, one-third) as well as a part of his other products (usually a tenth or ninth of wine, honey, livestock), certain token payments in kind, and frequently levies in money. Under the influence of the Frankish feudal system, in the Slovene areas the *huba* (from the German *Hufe*, homestead) was introduced as the unit of the peasant holding; this gave the families of the dependent peasants a source of livelihood and was also used to determine the amount of their obligation. This region was characterized by a reduction and even abandonment of the seigneurial land, attended by a diminishment of the peasant's corvée, as there was nowhere to apply it. Even on the estates where corvée was retained, it did not amount to much, and more often than not labor dues were commuted to money payments. In the thirteenth century and fourteenth centuries the leasing of land to peasants on a fixed contract basis became widespread in this part of Yugoslav territory, and characteristic also of the coastal districts and the area of the Dalmatian communes. By the close of the Middle Ages, payment in money had come to prevail.

In the organization of landed estates in Croatia, there was a noticeable difference between the older regions, where the stronger families and village communes were successful in maintaining their independence of the landlords, and Slavonia, where the feudal possessions began to expand suddenly during the period of the Árpáds. Everywhere, however, the serfs and the less dependent categories formed an integral, subject part of the population which retained a significant degree of freedom of movement and rendered relatively small corvée. Payment of taxes also spread in Croatia. In Serbia only the church estates are known, where the same basic elements are found: the seigneurial land under different names and the tenures of the tenants in varying degrees of dependency. The position of the *otroci* (slaves) resembled that of the serfs in Western regions; the *meropsi* (serfs) were a counterpart of the Byzantine *paroikoi*; and the *sokalnici* (cooks, helpers, servants) and artisans had their own special obligations. The labor dues were fairly high and were determined by the amount of soil that a peasant household was obliged to till. After the fourteenth century, two days of corvée weekly were introduced, meaning that the landlord took one-third of the peasant's labor. In Serbia, too, the tenants owned dues in kind and labor, but there was no noticeable tendency toward replacing prestations and corvées by money payments.

The Byzantine system of agrarian exploitation, in which money dues were of first-rate importance, did not take root in the Yugoslav territories. When direct Byzantine power was established in the early eleventh century, the general level of the economy in the Balkan Peninsula was such that the Byzantine authorities had to adjust themselves to payment of dues in kind. The estates were totally undeveloped, judging from the state of the bishoprics of the Ohrid archbishopric. In Macedonia, which remained under Byzantine rule until the end of the thirteenth century, money payments played a more important role, but as in Serbia, the economy of the estates rested on corvées and prestations (one-fourth of the crops for the right to tenure).

In the mountainous areas of the entire Yugoslav region, from Istria to Macedonia, livestock raising was the basic of the economy. It was seminomadic;

the Vlach community regularly moved with its herds from summer pastures in the mountains to winter abodes in warm and protected valleys. With their traditional commodities—livestock, cured meat, cheese, and hides—they traded with the surrounding agriculturists, thus supplementing their one-sided means of existence. The herdsmen were much slower than the tillers of the soil to be subordinated to the bonds of the feudal estates, and when they were as in Serbia, their dues were commensurate with their way of life and their economy. Apart from payments in kind (livestock, hides), the herdsmen's corvées consisted of tending the lord's herds and supplying transport services. The transport of goods in the Balkan Peninsula depended largely on the labor of the Vlach herdsmen.

The exploitation of the land created the means of existence for all sections of society and for the functioning of the entire state mechanism. The labor of the peasants supported the feudal warrior class and the church organization. Thus the land, settled by people who were bound to till it, represented the greatest wealth and, up to the thirteenth century, actually the only real wealth. Rulers awarded their warriors and officials grants of land—fiefs—thus enabling them to discharge their functions and at the same time binding them to service and fealty. The conditions under which fiefs were granted and enjoyed differed considerably from one part of Yugoslav territory to another although their economic function was everywhere the same. In the Slovene regions, which were the only Yugoslav areas where the classic, Western European type of feudalism was known, the fief was not only a source of income but also an essential requisite for belonging to the ruling class. In the other lands, from Croatia through Bosnia to Serbia, it was the type of unconditional grant from the ruler that was prevalent, the land remaining in the family of the warrior who had received the fief as long as the ruler enjoyed his service and fealty. After territories in Macedonia had been conquered from Byzantium, the *pronoia* became widespread in Serbia. This was a Byzantine form of fief, granted by the ruler for life on condition of military service. The *pronoia* was a small holding as a rule, and the spread of this system created a large number of small estates.

Trade and Mining; The Emergence of Towns

This essentially peasant, and in large part closed, type of economy with underdeveloped division of labor, little trade, even less money, began to be invigorated, at first slowly and then with increasing rapidity, by trade, which substantially changed the entire economy and way of life. Unfortunately, reliable data on the substance and techniques of that trade are available only from the time when it had already established itself firmly (from the thirteenth century onwards). Certainly products were exchanged much earlier, on a small scale and locally, between coastal towns and the adjoining hinterland, between the highland herdsmen and the cultivators, but this did not have any appreciable influence on the economy. Apparently, it was the coastal towns which first drew Yugoslav territories into trade with the Mediterranean on a larger scale. Together with the Byzantine towns in Italy, they are the harbingers of the upsurge that was to set its imprint on an entire era in European history. From the middle of the tenth century, we have the information that Dubrovnik (Ragusa), called Ragusion under Byzantium, grew so quickly that it had to enlarge its walls three times. It is possible that this town enjoyed a privileged position as reflected in its later role in the development of trade. Nevertheless, its sudden prosperity is a sure sign that other towns, too, had passed the crisis of isolation and the period when they eked their living from the sea; further, that they exploited their ties with the capital of the empire, still economically active, for trade with the hinterland. The influence of these towns is justifiably ascribed to the relatively advanced social differentiation and higher level of organization of regions in the immediate hinterland as compared with districts far inland.

The more densely populated regions in the Slovene lands led the way in development of trade and formation of nonagrarian economic centers. The intermittent marketplaces, which satisfied the growing requirements of the population, gave rise to settlements of traders and artisans. The marketplace of Breže (Frisach) was in existence as early as the eleventh century; later it developed into a town and center for minting silver coins known as "frisatics," used over a wide area. Several other merchant colonies grew up in the twelfth century, followed by towns which were to play an important role in economic life for centuries: Maribor, Ptuj, Celje, Ljubljana, Kranj. In time, the Roman roads came back into use, determining the directions in which the traders moved unless forced to make detours to points where fees were charged by the feudal lords.

The Byzantine "reconquest" figured significantly in the development of town life in the eastern regions. By penetrating to the Danube and Sava Rivers in 1018, Byzantium acquired an ancient network of roads, including the old military road which ran the length of the entire Peninsula from Belgrade to Constantinople. The Byzantine authorities reurbanized the regions under their control for political reasons. The old towns, more or less devastated, in some cases deserted, were resettled and revived for the purpose of gaining the upper hand over the agrarian Slav surroundings. Singidunum (Belgrade), Viminacium (Braničevo), Naissus (Niš), Scupi (Skoplje), and a number of other towns figured as political and economic centers from the eleventh century onward. In the twelfth century Byzantine traders along the Danube dealt with the Magyars. Apparently this trade was conducted between distant markets and did not have a direct effect on these Byzantine towns.

The countries in the interior (Slavonia, Bosnia, Serbia) were to acquire their nonagrarian economic centers somewhat later. Mainly foreigners were instrumental in forming them. The nucleus of the marketplaces that began to appear in Slavonia in the early thirteenth century consisted of "guests," immigrant traders from Germany or Italy. In Serbia and Bosnia, German Saxon miners stimulated the beginning nonagrarian economic activities and the emergence of urban settlements, first in Serbia in the mid-thirteenth century, and then in Bosnia in the early fourteenth century. Following the traces of Roman mines, they launched the extraction and melting of ores. The metals produced were silver, frequently mixed with gold, lead, and copper—goods very much in demand, which attracted traders. The mining centers thus grew into merchant colonies and gradually into important economic centers.

The mainstream of trade linked the towns along the coast with the marketplaces in the interior, from the Slovene lands in the west to Serbia in the east. Goods in transit between Austrian and Hungarian territories and the economic centers of the Mediterranean, above all Venice, moved along the roads negotiating the mountains of the Dinaric system, parallel with the sea at several relatively passable places. The South Slav countries traded on a broader, international scale their agrarian and livestock products (meat, livestock, cheese, hides, furs, honey, wax) and the output of their mines: silver, copper, lead from Bosnia and Serbia and iron from Slovenia. The countries in the interior purchased from the coast large quantities of salt, textiles (mostly of Italian origin), spices and luxury articles (perfumes, jewelry) from the Middle East, and also wine, oil, and subtropical fruit, usually produced domestically. In the course of the thirteenth century, the foundations were laid for the entire future economic development of the South Slav countries.

The upsurge of trade and crafts and mining production also affected the centers of political power and the functioning of state machinery. Rulers and lords of territories took upon themselves the prerogatives of exacting tolls, payable by traders either en route or in the marketplaces. These taxes proved to be such an important source of income that the rulers of various areas favored the roads and places under their control to the detriment of adjoining marketplaces and merchants. Stimulating trade, from which they reaped direct benefit, the political authorities found themselves saddled with new tasks: maintaining security along the roads, settling disputes, establishing monetary systems. Mining also brought rulers considerable revenue from the purchase of rights to the "treasure" in the bowels of the earth. Apart from a high percentage of the ore and melted metal (about 10 percent), the mineowners also had their own mints, which later netted them additional income. Silver money was minted in all Yugoslav regions in the Middle Ages. Slavonia had its well-known *banovci*, the Serbian rulers minted their dinars and grosus for over two centuries, and Bosnia had its own money beginning with the first half of the fourteenth century.

The rulers also had need of officials to conduct the increasing bulk of financial affairs. Initially, they made use on a large scale of customs collectors, experienced merchants who set up systems for exacting tolls and for supervision; later, traders became court functionaries. Income from trade, mining, and crafts became a more important source of rulers' revenues than the taxes collected from cultivators. The resulting growth in resources enabled the rulers to maintain armies, hire mercenaries, and undertake ambitious construction plans.

CHAPTER 7

Society
in Formation

The Partitioned Population

Political development up to the thirteenth century had led to the establishment of extensive and stable political frameworks, while economic advancement, generated by revival of trade and regular communications, facilitated connections between territories which were already far more densely populated and cultivated than they had been in the first few centuries after the arrival of the Slavs. Thus conditions were created for the establishment of large stabilized social groups, cohesive, organized, and united by a common consciousness, at a time when societies were still highly parcelized and closeted off from each other by numerous horizontal and vertical boundaries. Progress in this respect tended to be extremely slow and uneven as forces of integration and disintegration were at work simultaneously; while some boundaries became indistinct and disappeared, others appeared or were strengthened.

The Dependent Peasantry

In various parts of the South Slav region, society was being organized and was taking shape under the impact of a number of factors. More or less similar traditions merged with outside influences, differing from one region to another, the consequence being the emergence of specific forms and appreciable divergencies. Nevertheless, certain general processes paralleled each other, leading irrespective of the wealth of concrete forms to essentially the same results. One such common result was the great division of society into the ruling and the subordinate classes. Its origins go back to an earlier phase when the local aristocracy of the župans, together with the ruler, his family, and warriors, was pitted against the large mass of freemen and the relatively small number of serfs and villeins, frequently alien captives. The requirements of the economy, the formation of feudal estates and their expansion had placed even the freemen in the position of tenants on the estates. The variety of circumstances by which men came to be bound to the feudal estates and undertook the unequal obligations with which they were encumbered led to the formation and tenacious maintenance of various categories and degrees of dependence. However, as conditions of labor tended to become similar under pressure of changes in agrarian techniques and also equalization of obligations everywhere, the differences were erased and a massive class of subordinates was created whose position was far better, in terms of their relation with the feudatory and the degree of their freedom, than it had been at the beginning of this trend in development.

The Nobility

A like result had been produced in the upper classes of society. The old clan aristocracy had been suppressed or interrupted in its development, as in the Slovene lands, and replaced by a ruling class of foreigners which, while absorbing domestic elements or expanding through the addition of newcomers, was transformed into an extensive class of landowners and warriors, that is, the feudal nobility.

In the Slovene lands, court functionaries and warriors played an important role in the formation of this new feudal nobility. These *ministeriales* and knights, who were authorized to bear arms and receive feuds, were counted among the nobility although some of them barely differed from the peasants in property status or way of life. In Croatia, the king's warriors and soldiers of the royal cities (*servientes regis* and *iobagiones castri*), recipients of royal charters, were obdurate in their resistance to the big magnates who threatened to degrade them to the status of tenants. They succeeded in winning legal protection (the Golden Bull of 1222, confirmed a number of times), maintained their rank, and finally in the middle of the fourteenth century obtained formal equality of rights with the old and high nobility. In Bosnia a mass of nobles was created of persons who had resisted subordination to the feudatories and were successful in refusing to do service or labor that was considered socially degrading. The nobility were supported by the broad community of blood relations—the clan—frequently numerous and firmly rooted in the "noble lands." In Serbia the "soldiers" who appeared on the scene as early as the beginning of the thirteenth century came to be counted among the nobles or minor nobility unless for some reason they slid down the social scale.

The Estates Rights of the Nobility

In virtually all South Slav lands, the nobility strove to secure positions and acquire certain special prerogatives for the entire estate. They fought for and won special lawcourts or guarantees for the inviolability of their persons and freedom in disposing of their holdings. In the Slovene lands, for instance, the entire nobility came under the jurisdiction of the provincial prince's court. In Croatia lawsuits involving the nobility, "the twelve tribes of the Croatian kingdom," were held in special courts under special law. In Slavonia, the županija courts were basically nobles' courts, the only higher one being the royal court. In Bosnia nobles were not subject to capital punishment, imprisonment, or confiscation of property unless tried by a court of their peers and representatives of the Bosnian church. A growing role in safeguarding the privileges of the nobility was played by the assemblies, which were gradually transformed into representatives of the estate, meeting regularly and participating formally in the conduct of state affairs. Only in Serbia, owing to the lasting influence of Byzantine law and the strong position of the ruler, the nobles had no special courts for their estate but enjoyed privileged treatment under the general penal system. There the assembly did not become a body of the estate of nobles, but rather remained a formal gathering at which the ruler's decisions were announced.

The emergence of the estate of nobles and the largely equalized and massive stratum of sebars (commoners), as they were called in the central and eastern regions, generated the formation of vast social groups and destroyed the barriers between various categories of society. Large segments were integrated into already stable political frameworks (provinces, the boundaries of earlier states, the boundaries of existing states), but new barriers sprang into being as the estate of nobles withdrew into exclusivity. These barriers became so rigid and difficult to surmount that they obstructed further integration all the way up until the onset of modern democracy and the national movements of the nineteenth century.

Organized in its own estate, pursuing its own interests and imbued with a singular consciousness, the nobility was an important factor in ethnical processes. Bearing tribal or land names (Croatians, Bosnians, Carniolans) and acting as guardians of the rights and specific features of their territories, the nobles' estate fostered its own peculiar brand of patriotism.

Influence of State Organization

State power proved to be extremely imperfect as a factor promoting integration. It had not yet developed efficient techniques of administration for knitting territory into an organized whole. This was also to be the problem facing absolutist states several centuries later. Only rather small areas could be effectively controlled; consequently state territory could be kept cohesive only with the aid of a large number of strongholds and local centers of power. Previously local leaders had taken evident part in important political events; in Macedonia they came to the forefront with their fortifications during the collapse of Samuel's empire, incorporating themselves into the Byzantine system; in Serbia the župans were called upon to recognize the ruler in 924, their subjugation signifying the final subduing of the entire country; in Croatia even their names are found in the ruler's documents. This system of rule endured for a very long time, during which the ruler's relatives or members of branches of the dynasty appeared as the heads of smaller or larger regions. This not only tended to maintain the special traditions of various regions, noticeable in the example of the Serbian state in the thirteenth century, but also gave rise to centrifugal tendencies. The system in which the ruler could, at will, appoint and recall local leaders was applied at least for some time in the županijas (established in Slavonia) and in the Serbian state before the mid-fourteenth century.

Immunity and Autonomy

In all the South Slav lands, the functions of state power were slowly ceded to the feudatories through the assignment of immunity. By the thirteenth century, the feudal estates were units so comprehensive and cohesive that the peasants had no contact with provincial organs in Slovene areas. The landlord held court for his serfs except in cases warranting the death penalty. Court fees were collected by the landlord, and the župan was transformed into a functionary of the feudal estate. Apart from the superior forms of immunity enjoyed by church estates in Croatia, assigned during the reigns of rulers belonging to national dynasties, at the close of the twelfth century the kings donated entire župas to feudal lords, complete with all royal prerogatives, and the right to rule over the entire population. The most familiar immunities in the Serbian state were those of the great monastic estates. Not only did the feudatories collect dues owed to the state and sit in judgment over tenants in their courts, except in a few cases reserved for the royal court, but the ruler's functionaries were forbidden even to set foot on the grounds of estates enjoying immunity. The transformation of the estates, originally economic units, into administrative entities disrupted the public authority. The growing jurisdiction of the estates intensified the already salient diversity of regimes, multiplying customs and administrative practices so much that the people inhabiting these extensive areas came to live under very different conditions.

Like the estates, the townships represented separate entities in the feudal social fabric. In time, the townships withdrew from the jurisdiction of local authorities or shed their feudal masters. The towns along the Adriatic coast from Istria to Lake Scutari experienced a singular development. Even while they had been under Byzantine rule, autonomous forces of considerable power had established themselves under the leadership of the bishops or wealthier citizens who, as consuls, wielded juridical and administrative authority. In the Istrian towns this autonomy withered as the municipalities were subjected to pressure from the patriarch of Aquileia on one hand and Venice on the other. Under Venetian rule the Istrian towns retained their statutes intact, but the "chiefs" appointed by Venice had the last word in the administration and courts of law.

Towns which had fallen to Árpád power in the early twelfth century preserved a high degree of autonomy that permitted the unhampered differentiation of society and reserved for each town the right, codified in its statute, to retain administrative and juridical functions. Towns south of Dubrovnik ruled by the state of the Nemani dynasty at the close of the twelfth century were administered by municipal courts delegated by the ruler. In time, however, the courts had to surrender their competence to the municipal magistrates as autonomous organs.

The Patriciate in the Dalmatian Towns

During the period of economic development, the older, wealthy families in the coastal towns congealed into a separate group holding municipal administrative and juridical power in their hands. As early as the fourteenth century, they formed the patriciate, the town nobility which dissociated itself from the flood of new inhabitants. The great social partition referred to above was thus repeated within the walls surrounding the autonomous towns. The patriciate persistently nurtured and stressed Romance cultural traditions, bent upon divorcing itself from the purely Slavic newcomers and accentuating its independence of the hinterland. On the same basis, the patriciate fostered the consciousness of belonging to the special world living inside the town bulwarks and promoted municipal patriotism to the point of resisting inclusion in broader communities. Parcelized into a large number of communes, the citizens were not in a position to feel themselves a social force apart. It was only during the late Renaissance that some of the intelligentsia from the Dalmatian towns were persuaded to accept the "Slovenian" tongue and Slavic historic traditions.

Inland the towns did not resemble each other to the same degree. They differed in origin, population, and system, but they too kept aloof from their agricultural surroundings. In the Slovene lands towns gradually won the right to elect all court and administrative authorities, but owing to increasing social stratification, this autonomy came to be exploited by a small group of citizens who tended to suppress the wider "commune" to the benefit of the "council." Nevertheless, all citizens enjoyed personal freedom, which was acquired also by peasants after they had spent a year and a day in town. In some cases, municipal jurisdiction transcended town walls but did not extend to the clergy and nobility residing in the towns. In Croatia and Slavonia, the exceptional position of town residents rested on the privileges granted by kings of the Árpád dynasty to "guests," the foreign settlers—merchants and artisans. The "guests" were exempted from the authority of the royal župans and were responsible directly to the ban or king. Apart from autonomous administration and courts, personified in the elected magistrate, "free towns" owned property managed by the commune in the capacity of a lord. The privileges of the free communes were not uniform, but all of them were exempted from levies on trade within the kingdom. The most privileged, like Gradec, forerunner of the present-day Zagreb, enjoyed the right to pass administrative regulations and hold weekly fairs and the great annual fair. In time, foreigners became a minority in these communes.

Within the Serbian state, the old towns, reconstructed during the period of Byzantine rule, retained their Byzantine order in which the town bishop and clergy had the last word, together with the king's functionary. The town did not withdraw from its environs, but rather lorded it over the surrounding area. As time went on, this type of town did not spread; it remained confined to the territories that had long been under Byzantine rule. From the mid-thirteenth century, however, there came to develop in the old territories of the Serbian state types of towns that closely resembled those in the western districts of Yugoslavia. These were the privileged communes of the German Saxon miners who had enjoyed autonomy ever since their arrival in the country. Personal liberty and freedom of religion, a free hand in mining activities, special courts, and a town council consisting of twelve burghers, flanking the mayor who had most probably been appointed by the ruler, spread through the Saxons to all residents of market towns and even those which had no connection with mining. Thus in a large part of Serbia the world of the townspeople and the world of the peasants took different paths. In Bosnia, too, the same type of township and townspeople was found. The communes in the eastern half of the country are too unfamiliar to us to permit any conjecture about social differentiation or possible barriers between various groups and sections of the population.

The Vlach Herdsmen

The communities of Vlach herdsmen, roaming about Serbia, Bosnia, and Croatia, were also not part of larger territorial or social entities. Their basic organizational cell was the *katun*, a group bound together by real or fictive blood ties, under the leadership of chieftains (the *katunari* or *primićuri*). The Vlachs were judged and tried by their elders and lived out their lives without feeling the influence of any other authority. Owing to their specific occupation and way of life, their obligations differed considerably from those of the cultivators once they were incorporated into the feudal estates. Raising livestock and producing meat, cheese, and skins, the Vlachs also discharged the obligation of providing transport services for their masters, or for merchants on a free-lance basis. Stratification in Vlach communities was based on property ownership and rights and obligations. Although they acquired the language of their Slav surroundings and came under the jurisdiction of the same church, though only superficially so, the Vlachs were not accepted by those among whom they lived as members of the same social and ethnical community. Throughout the Middle Ages, the name of the Vlachs is used in writings as an ethnical designation, like that for the Greeks, Albanians, and Bulgarians.

Within the larger communities, prerogatives were enjoyed by certain groups to whom the principle of special rights was applied. These were the German miners whose special rights were instrumental in giving form to the free communes in the townships and market towns. Merchants from the coastal towns also belonged to such groups in Serbia and in Bosnia. Although they were numerous in the towns and marketplaces, living there for years and even decades, they were not subject to the local authorities or courts, but rather to the courts of their city, that is, to its "consuls," in disputes among themselves, and to mixed courts in suits with the native population. More or less the same applied to real foreigners, merchants from Italian towns, who were far fewer. As far as the local population and authorities were concerned, these were all "Latins" although most of them were of Slavic descent and spoke Slavonic.

The Role of Church Organizations in the Process of Social Integration

South Slav countries had been situated in evangelized surroundings, so that allegiance to the Christian church offered no foundation for a feeling of belonging or solidarity in relation to the world of the infidels and pagans, until the Turks appeared in their conquest of these territories. Certain churches, how-

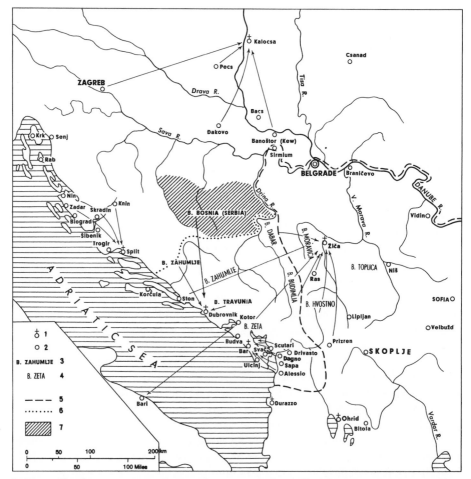

MAP 9.   Church organization in the Yugoslav area in the first half of the thirteenth century. (1) See of the archbishopric; (2) see of the bishopric; (3) Catholic bishopric; (4) Orthodox bishopric; (5) boundaries of the Constantinople and Roman spheres in the late twelfth century; (6) boundary shifts during the founding of the Serbian autocephalous archbishopric; (7) the area of the dualistic Bosnian church.

ever, were an important factor of integration. We have already seen that the territory of Yugoslavia had been divided up between, first, the Catholic church, covering areas within the Holy Roman Empire, the Hungarian state, and all the towns along the Adriatic coast with immediate surroundings, and, second, the Eastern or Orthodox church, which held sway in the Serbian state and the Byzantine Empire. The dualistic Bosnian church prevailed within the limits of the Bosnian state. Each one of these churches knit its faithful together into an ideal entity bound by the same beliefs, rituals, and symbols. In the Catholic sphere these elements were virtually universal and common to a large part of Europe, but in Bosnia and Serbia the churches were limited to a smaller area and a particular political framework.

Church influence was not equally powerful, however, in all regions and throughout all sections of society. Whereas the Catholic and the Eastern Orthodox churches, in addition to their hierarchy and monastic orders, maintained a pervasive influence over the lives of their flocks, bringing them together for religious services and initiating them into the holy sacraments, the Bosnian church was confined to a small circle of "the perfect," of "true Christians who had no love of sin," strictly ascetic groups, introverted and uninterested in the large mass of the faithful who had no place to worship or receive the sacraments. Consequently the majority of the population in Bosnia remained virtually at the level of heathens until near the end of the Middle Ages, when the two other and more powerful churches gained the upper hand there. The itinerant Vlach communities hardly felt the presence of the church at all, and clergymen visited them only rarely. Even less frequently were places of worship found among them.

The power of the church was far stronger in the townships. In the Catholic areas the influence of Franciscans and Dominicans spread quickly after the thirteenth century. As in other countries, they built their monasteries in towns where they could hold sway over larger sections of the population more easily. Through merchant colonies in the fourteenth century, the Franciscans gained ground also in Bosnia, suppressing the Bosnian church in ever-growing degree. The Franciscans penetrated to Orthodox Serbia, again through the market towns, where the Saxons and merchants from the coastal townships had their places of worship. Throughout the Catholic territory the religious fraternities in the towns wielded power over smaller or larger groups of the population. In parts, as in Croatia, their organizations were the forerunners of the later guilds. Thus the religious organizations welded the people into large church communities and at the same time divided them into smaller social groups based on property status or profession.

CHAPTER 8

State Expansion and Consolidation of the Ruler's Power

Consolidation of the Serbian State in the Thirteenth Century

As early as the second half of the thirteenth century, internal development and foreign relations had progressed to a point that enabled Serbia to
expand its territory and entrench central authority more firmly. The same
process took place in Bosnia in the course of the fourteenth century. The old
boundaries underwent alteration, and former political frameworks were temporarily disrupted. In the western areas the region under Hungarian control
experienced internal changes engendered by the crisis of royal power under the

last of the Árpáds, only to revive the Angevins. In the second half of the thirteenth century, a process of political integration was launched in the Slovene provinces belonging to the Holy Roman Empire.

By proclaiming itself a kingdom and founding the autocephalous archbishopric, Serbia was established as an independent state after Constantinople had been conquered and Westerners started their encroachment on the Byzantine world. Later, when the various parts of the Balkan Peninsula were locked in struggle for power and predominance, the first to gain temporary ascendancy was Epirus under the Greek despots, followed by resurgent Bulgaria, but in the face of these developments the grandsons of Nemanja stood firm. The youngest of them, Uroš I (1243–1276), who succeeded to the throne at a period when the Tatar invasions were leaving devastation in their wake, launched his preparations for transforming the country internally. Mines were opened, silver money was minted in considerable quantities, and trade ties with the outside world were multiplied. The mining settlements and marketplaces became veritable townships, changing the rural landscape of Serbian areas. Uros's descendants reaped income not only from their holdings, but also from regalia—royal rights and prerogatives, such as customs, mines, and minting. The modesty of their predecessors gave way to splendor and pomp in court appointments and manner of dress. For their military requirements, they were in a position to maintain mercenary units, so that their victories in war depended not so much on a fortunate choice of allies as on their own forces.

By the end of the thirteenth century, the links of Zahumlje, Travunija, and Zeta with the mother Serbian lands had consolidated. Uroš's son Dragutin (1276–1282), after abdicating in favor of his brother Milutin (1282–1321), received the banovina of Mačva (Machow), including Belgrade, from the Hungarian king to administer. Later, together with his brother, he gained mastery over Braničevo, formerly a bone of contention between Hungarians and Bulgarians. The frontier of lands under Serbian rule therefore moved to the Sava and Danube Rivers, either temporarily or permanently. By that time Serbian colonization had definitely penetrated northward.

Laws had not yet been codified, but many legal norms had been established in royal charters. Regulations defined the organization of monastic estates and the legal position and privileges of foreign merchants. The Saxon miners brought their own laws with them, and it was in accordance with these that they lived in their settlements and elected their administrative bodies. Church life was regulated by the *Krmčija* of Saint Sava—the Nomocanon in translation. The rulers relied on the church for support, and state interests were identified with those of the church. In this close relation, the cult of Nemanid saints developed very early, with the result that the dynasty acquired a charismatic character. Spiritual life drew inspiration from the great Byzantine tradition, although in their foreign policy the Serbian rulers frequently sought the support of Western powers and directed their expansionist aims toward Byzantine dominions. There were some attempts at rapprochement between Uroš I and Michael VIII Palaeologus, who had reconstructed the empire (1261), but the hostility between the two was rekindled when the Byzantine emperor, negotiating with the pope for a union of the churches, displayed readiness to sacrifice to his purposes the autocephalous rights of the Serbian church.

Expansion Southward

Uroš's thrust southward did not result in territorial expansion for Serbia. Upon ascending the throne, however, Milutin succeeded in gaining mastery over northern Macedonia and retaining it for Serbian power. The Byzantine emperor's endeavors to restore lost lands degenerated into futile warfare, and finally peace was concluded, opening wide the doors to Byzantine influence. In organization and splendor, and the adoption of Byzantine titles for dignitaries, the Serbian court began to emulate Constantinople. The Byzantine institution of the *pronoia*, a military fief or feud spread throughout the Serbian lands: land was granted, complete with peasants, during the life-span of the beneficiary in return for military service.

The first few decades of the fourteenth century brought a temporary stagnation in territorial expansion. First, the country was shaken by Milutin's clash with his brother Dragutin, the "king of Srem," over the right of succession to the Serbian throne. After Dragutin's death (1316) Milutin attempted to obtain control over his entire patrimony, including even the Hungarian areas that had been ceded on a temporary basis. The Hungarian king and the pope responded by forming a broad coalition of neighboring Catholic countries against the "schismatic king." Even greater upheavals were avoided when the Hungarian king satisfied himself with restoration of the banovina of Mačva. When Milutin presented the church of Saint Nicholas in Bari with a silver altar, he was able to style himself, in the inscription, as the master of the entire country "from the Adriatic Gulf, from the sea, to the great river of the Danube." But the danger of internal resistance ran high.

Conflict between the Nobility and the Increasingly Powerful Ruler

The nobles, discontented with the growth in kingly power, stood poised to exploit dynastic conflicts and to turn them to their own ends. In Milutin's clash with his brother Dragutin, the feudal lords extended more support to the latter in the hope of winning greater indulgence. Temporarily obstructed in their

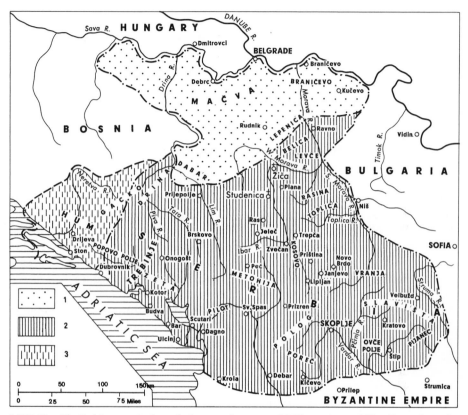

MAP 10.   The Serbian state in the early fourteenth century. (1) The territory of King Dragutin established from areas received from Hungary and conquered from Bulgarian magnates; (2) the territory of King Milutin established from inherited lands and conquests from Byzantium; (3) territory lost in 1326.

plans, they eagerly took advantage of dynastic differences after Milutin's death to provoke chaos. After victory was won by Milutin's unwarlike son Stefan (1321–1331), called Stefan Dečanski after the great church and monastery that he founded, they began to support the *rex iunior* (the king's son Stefan Dušan) in the hope that he would lead them into war and victory, from which they expected land and position. The civil war that had shaken Byzantium was drawing to a close with the young emperor Andronicus III emerging triumphant after rallying the most prominent landowners against the old emperor, his grandfather. Serbia was threatened with the loss of eastern Macedonia, as Andronicus III had won Bulgaria over as an ally for an assault on Stefan Dečanski. The Serbian army defeated the Bulgarian at Velbužd (1330) and succeeded in preserving Macedonia intact, largely through the merit of Stefan Dušan and the great magnates who supported him. The same nobles helped overthrow the old king and enthrone their favorite, Stefan Dušan (1331–1355).

The Conquests of Stefan Dušan

Changes had occurred also at the court of Bulgaria, and the way was paved for establishment of good relations between the two courts. Responding to the wishes of the restless Serbian, Albanian, and Greek lords, Stefan Dušan undertook several successive attacks on Byzantine dominions (1334, 1341–1345, 1347–1348). The Serbian victories helped fan a new civil war in Byzantium. In the conflict between the minor emperor John V and his regent, John Cantacuzenus, the old rivals of Venice and Genoa interfered as allies on either side. Supporting Cantacuzenus, the Osmanli Turks plundered Byzantine territory. Moreover, the country was torn by religious differences and social unrest provoked by extreme poverty. Stefan Dušan took the remaining Macedonian towns, acquired all of Albania with the exception of Durazzo, and then conquered Serres. Finally he also obtained extensive parts of Greece as far as the Gulf of Corinth. The conquests assuaged the appetites of the Serbian and Albanian lords and warriors, and Stefan Dušan began thinking along the lines of restoring the defunct empire under his rule.

Proclamation of the Patriarchate and the Empire

As soon as he had taken possession of Serres, the Serbian king styled himself the "master of Romania" (Byzantium) and by the end of 1345 had proclaimed himself emperor of the Serbs and Greeks. With the approval of the patriarch of Trnovo and the archbishop of Ohrid, he elevated the archbishop of Peć to the rank of patriarch and, with them performing the ceremony of investiture, had himself crowned emperor at a synod held in Skoplje April 16, 1346. Although the imperial title no longer reflected the desire for universal power, it did reveal the plans of the Serbian ruler to impose his mastery on the empire. After fresh victories and territorial expansion, Stefan Dušan applied to the Venetians for help by sea to conquer Constantinople. Although addressed to allies, his appeals went unanswered. The Western powers were in no mood to sustain his program, and they continued to call him king rather than emperor. Stefan Dušan's plan to form a coalition against the Turks and his negotiations with the pope at Avignon to get himself appointed a "captain" of the Crusaders bore no fruit although he held out the promise of a union of churches. The Hungarian king was the first to offer resistance. And when Dušan's achievements were interrupted by his untimely death (1355), there still remained the anathema pronounced by the patriarch of Constantinople against the new emperor and patriarch and the new church functionaries, meaning the very persons who were the standard-bearers of Serbian state ideology.

Under Stefan Dušan, the Serbian state attained its greatest expansion, reaching the Adriatic, Ionian, and Aegean Seas. He himself, carried away by victories and visions, behaved like an emperor of Byzantium. State synods, attended by eminent Serbs and Albanians, no longer discussed sacred and secular affairs as they previously had, but simply acclaimed the emperor's proposals and laws. But the new state was not cohesive internally, nor was its emperor all-powerful.

The Empire's Internal Weaknesses

The new state was centered in the Greek lands, ruled by the emperor himself, who usually resided in the Macedonian towns of Skoplje and Serres. The Serbian lands were administered by his son Uroš, bearing the title of king. The counts and chiefs (ćefalije) who replaced the former župans were not a very powerful force in the structure of state authority. The new monasteries had been granted vast lands and virtually total immunity, wrenching themselves from under the direct influence of the ruler's functionaries. The feudal landlords with ancient patrimonies, and the warriors with their pronoia, enjoyed broad rights. Moreover, the most outstanding Serbian lords and relatives of the emperor, who stood at the head of entire provinces, displayed a tendency to become independent rulers on a minor scale. Stefan Dušan's power depended on the devotion of the landlords. Once the wars stopped, that devotion could easily give way to defection.

Furthermore, among the landlords themselves, both ecclesiastical and temporal, antagonism rooted in different ethnical origins grew. Although many Greeks retained holdings, positions, and functions, they felt only scorn for the Serbian nobles; those who had been forced to abdicate their former posts were bitter in the extreme. The Byzantine writer Nicephorus Gregoras said of his compatriots: "Happy is he who was born a Hellene, and not a barbarian." The suppressed Albanian lords were hostile to the new authority, whereas the minor Albanian feudatories, uplifted to high positions in Epirus and Thessaly, provoked the fury of the deposed Greek archons. The high-ranking Greek clergy, replaced by Serbian prelates, incited conflict between the patriarchates of Peć and Constantinople. An inimical attitude was also assumed by the Greek population of the Macedonian towns. The Slav population in Macedonia, consisting largely of peasants, and forever oppressed, saw no difference between their Greek and Serbian masters.

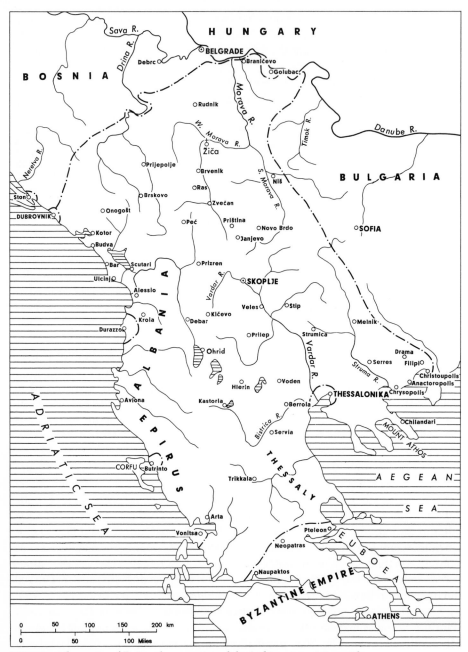

MAP 11. The empire of Dušan: the expansion of the Serbian state at its zenith.

The Code of Laws of Stefan Dušan

This new society, a patchwork of divergent elements, had to be welded together and subjected to the common norms of an integral legal order. At the state synod in Skoplje, the Code of Laws of Stefan Dušan was published in 1349 and supplemented by new provisions later (1354). His aim was to unify legal practice and to buttress the positions acquired by the Serbian church and lords. The decree demonstrates that the lords and imperial functionaries frequently abused their rights to the detriment of imperial authority and a stable feudal order. New provisions were needed to prevent the uncontrolled movement of dependent persons on the one hand, and on the other to put an end to the lawlessness of the arrogant lords and the abuses of unconscientious judges and imperial functionaries. Actually they reveal the internal crisis that was building up within the empire and corroding it. After Dušan the edifice began to crack, finally to collapse altogether.

The Rise and Fall of Šubić and Baboneg

At the same time that Nemanja's descendants were paving the way for the upsurge of the Serbian states, the power of the last Árpáds in Hungary was on the wane, with the result that the division of land into županijus no longer had any meaning. Prominent feudal families gained mastery over entire provinces and shared out the land between them. Three families in Croatia rose to a new zenith of power: the Babonegs in Slavonia, the Frankapans in the Croatian Littoral, and the Šubićs in the hinterland of the Dalmatian towns. The administrative unity of the Croatian lands was disrupted, as two bans ruled where there had previously been one: one controlled Croatian Dalmatia, and the other Slavonia. The position of the ban was a bone of contention among the prominent families who fought to make it an inherited right.

Pavle Šubić (1272–1312), ban of Croatia and Dalmatia, brought surrounding areas into his fold and set about creating a veritable state. Dalmatian towns formerly held by Venice, as well as the *Neretljanska krajina* (Neretva March) and the larger part of Bosnia, all found themselves under Šubić rule. Ban Pavle Šubić apportioned lands and towns to his brothers to administer and handed the power of the ban down to his son Mladen II (1301–ca.1341) as an inheritance. He drew support from the Angevins of Naples in return for siding with them in their struggle for the Hungarian crown.

The "kingdom of Serbia," encompassing regions south of the Sava and Danube Rivers, ruled by the "king of Srem, Dragutin," was also considered a Hungarian area that had acquired independence, as its nucleus consisted of the banovina of Mačva.

Consolidation of Central Power in Hungary under the Angevins

When Charles I (Charles Robert of Anjou, 1301–1342) entrenched himself on the throne of Hungary after introducing economic and financial reforms, he joined battle with the independent magnates, breaking them one by one. After foiling an attempt by the Serbian king Milutin to retain the banovina of Mačva, he bore down on the Šubićs. The growth in royal power provoked all local adversaries to revolt. The Dalmatian towns complained of the plundering policies of Mladen II, turning to Venice for help. The Croatian nobility sought to restore its ancient rights and, by joining forces, deposed Mladen II in 1322. Rather than helping him, the king sent him into exile. Mladen's heirs, stripped of their holdings, waited a quarter of a century before being assigned Zrinj in Slavonia and from this area they styled themselves Zrinski. Soon after dealing with Šubić, Charles I turned on the Babonegs in Slavonia as the most powerful of the big families in the country. Their demise did not bring the country peace, however, as the Croatian nobles launched a fierce battle among themselves. But the second Anjou to sit on the throne of Hungary, Louis I (1342–1382), the son of Charles, consolidated royal power throughout the area ruled by the Hungarian crown and put an end to anarchy in Croatian lands.

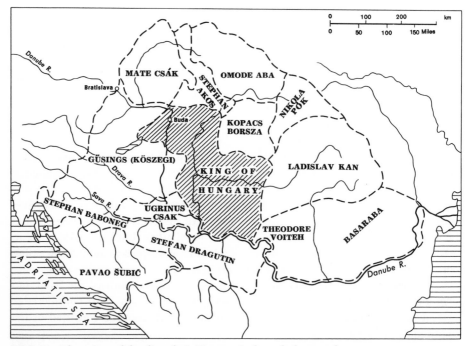

MAP 12.   The regions of the oligarchs in Hungary in the early fourteenth century.

The Revival of Hungarian Power in Dalmatia

Louis I dreamed of bringing the entire Balkan Peninsula to heel. To achieve this, he intensified his influence over Bosnia and on several occasions struck at Serbian lands from the north. The great conqueror of Byzantine lands, Stefan Dušan, was more than happy to conclude peace with the Hungarian king in 1346. The latter also became involved in an endeavor to expel the Venetians from Dalmatian cities for having struck an alliance with Dušan, his aim being to attain undisputed mastery over the Adriatic coast and execute his grandiose dynastic plan of merging the kingdoms of Hungary and Naples. Louis I did not succeed in bringing the Hungarian and Neapolitan holdings of the Angevins under his own power, and evicted the Venetians from Dalmatia only after Dušan's death. When Louis's powerful army set out for Dalmatia, the Hungarian envoy explained to the pope in Avignon that the Republic of Saint Mark deserved no better fate, owing to its ties with the "schismatic Serbs." By 1358 Louis I had taken possession of the Dalmatian towns and subdued the restive Croatian magnates. In a peace treaty he forced the Venetians to renounce all rights to the Adriatic coast from the Gulf of Kvarner (Quarnero) to Durazzo. From that time on, the entire region of Croatia and Slavonia bent to the king's will.

As it turned out, the consolidation of royal power in Hungary was transitory. After Louis's death in 1382, internal strife again began to disrupt the country. Resistance to the central power was strongest along the state's periphery, particularly in the Croatian lands.

The Growing Vigor and Territorial Expansion of Bosnia

The collapse of Šubić, the disruption of the Serbian Empire, and, finally, the Hungarian crises offered Bosnia an opportunity to surge forward politically and expand its state boundaries. The ban of Bosnia, Stjepan II Kotromanić (1314–1353), had lived until 1322 in the shadow of the powerful Šubićs; it was no wonder that he allied himself with the forceful Angevins against the former, and maintained good relations with the Hungarian court after their downfall. Louis I even married his daughter. Taking advantage of the strife among the Croatian nobility, the Bosnian ban extended his boundaries westward by annexing the Donji Kraji (Lower Regions) and the Neretva March. At approximately the same time, he gained control over the larger part of Zahumlje, where a native feudal family had acquired independent power during the dynastic struggles. All subsequent attempts by Stefan Dušan to regain the lost regions ended in failure. And when Stjepan II rounded out his possessions by restoring Soli and Usore, he proudly claimed that his authority extended "from the Sava River to the sea and from the Cetina to the Drina River."

At the same time, Bosnia grew in strength internally. The Saxons opened mines; foreign merchants, chiefly from the coast, arrived in increasing numbers and trade reached unprecedented heights. The domestic population engaged in trade found their incomes growing with the expanding economy, and the ban himself, imitating the Hungarian Angevins, resorted to fiscal measures which augmented his revenues appreciably. He also proved himself capable of undertaking major political moves. The effect of these, however, was undermined by old and new causes of internal weakness. The state structure was not in keeping with the powerful central authority, still dependent on the personal fealty of the magnates to the ruler. To a great extent the power of the Bosnian ban depended upon their "faithful service." The diet of nobles *(stanak)* had to approve all important decisions taken by the ruler and could oppose him at every step. Furthermore, in expanding its boundaries, Bosnia had lost its earlier religious unity. The Catholic inhabitants in the west and the Orthodox in the east were both hostile to the Bosnian church. Through the Franciscans, the pope stepped up his struggle against the Patarenes. True, the inquisition did not succeed, not did papal accusations break the Bosnian ban. Nonetheless, internal antagonisms and the ruler's dependence on the Hungarian crown created a potentially explosive situation. Latently or actively, Bosnia was in crisis during the first twenty years of the rule of Tvrtko I, the nephew and successor of Stjepan II Kotromanić.

Tvrtko I and Proclamation of the Kingdom

The support extended by the lords to Stjepan II was transformed into hostility toward the new ban, Tvrtko I (1353–1391), and even into open rebellion. The previous benevolence of the Hungarian king gave way to political pressure, including the dispatch of armies under the banner of struggle against the Patarenes. Tvrtko I was forced also to reconcile himself to territorial losses. Ultimately he made peace with the Hungarian king in order to obtain help in dealing with the lords' revolt. At one time, under the weight of internal opposition, he lost control over almost the entire country. It was only in the seventies that he succeeded in restoring power over Bosnia, as a direct result of his first foreign policy success.

In alliance with the Serbian prince Lazar, Tvrtko brought about the downfall of the lord of Podrinje, Nikola Altomanović, who had provoked fierce conflicts with his neighbors. Sharing out his lands, the Bosnian ban annexed to Bosnia the western districts of Serbian territory. As master of a part of the regions that had once belonged to the Nemanid dynasty, he was quick to hit upon the idea of continuing their state traditions. He was himself a distant Nemanid relative and made the most of his position. After regaining control over the entire territory of the Bosnian state, he achieved greater power than any previous re-

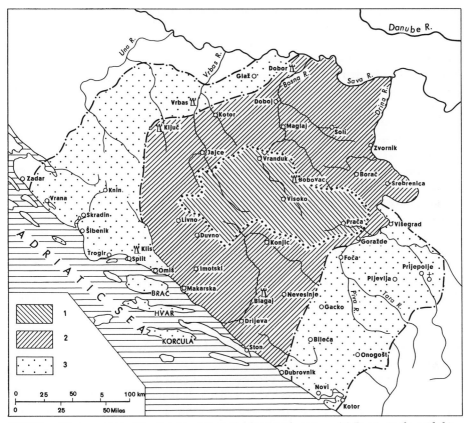

MAP 13.   The expansion of the Bosnian state in the fourteenth century. (1) Bosnia in the mid-thirteenth century; (2) expansion during the time of Ban Stjepan II Kotromanic (1322–1353);
(3) expansion during the time of King Tvrtko (1354–1391).

gional lord in Serbia. Tvrtko I was therefore extremely susceptible to the suggestion of his logothete Vlatko, a refugee from Serbia, that the "double wreath"
was rightfully his (referring to the royal crown of Bosnia and the Serbian lands).
Tvrtko I had himself crowned king in 1377 on newly acquired Serbian territory,
in the monastery of Milesevo, and added to his national name one that was
symbolically borne by all Serbian rulers—Stefan. After Tvrtko, every Bosnian
ruler included it in his name, even when his name was already Stipan, a popular variant of Stefan. Tvrtko's coronation was recognized by the most prominent
Serbian lords, as well as by Dubrovnik and Venice. Joining the ranks of rulers,
he adopted the signs and ceremonies of the Serbian court, thereby consolidating
his authority in Bosnia. He did not, however, restore the old Serbian state,
nor did he continue its traditions. As master of heretic Bosnia and annexed

Catholic territories, his religious beliefs, and concepts generally, were far-removed from those of the charismatic Serbian kings. Continuing to gain power until the end of his life, he did not seek to buttress it with support from the East but rather from the zone of Western influence, toward which all new territorial claims were directed.

After Louis, Tvrtko restored the lands once ceded to the Hungarians; erected a town, Novi, at the entrance to the fjord of Boka Kotorska; took control of Kotor, and then of the central Dalmatian towns with a wide band of hinterland. The west Bosnian boundary bisected the Una, Sana, and Vrbas Rivers, and Tvrtko I was styled "by the mercy of God, the glorious King of Rascia, Bosnia, Dalmatia, Croatia, Primorje [the Littoral]," and so on. Politically, eyes were trained westward. Refusing to recognize the new Hungarian king, Sigismund of Luxembourg, he even considered contracting marital ties with the Hapsburgs of Austria.

Tvrtko's death (1391) marked the end of a brilliant period in Bosnian history. Regional lords, whose internecine struggle had led more than once to internal upheaval, began to prevail again, to the detriment of royal power. The absence of a strong state organization hastened the dissolution of what had once been firm royal rule.

The Slovene Lands under the Rule of the Hapsburgs

In the Slovene lands a process of political integration such as feudal families had not been able to achieve earlier was inaugurated in the second half of the thirteenth century. The first attempt was made by the Czech king Otakar II Premysl, who, taking advantage of the interregnum in Germany, obtained control of Austria and then Styria, Carinthia, and Carniola, thus bringing the majority of the Slovene provinces under a single authority. When Rudolf of Hapsburg came to the throne of Germany, however, he defeated the Czech king in the field (1278) and by that very fact disrupted the unity of the Slovene provinces. The victor was forced to parcel them out and share them with his allies. His successors, pursuing a patient and consistent policy, annexed to the Hapsburg patrimony the lands of other lords, thrust to the sea, and in somewhat over a hundred years brought all Slovene dominions under their control.

Consolidating the power of their house, the Hapsburgs found support among the nobles of the Slovene provinces (the nobility also being of Germanic origin) and in return granted them certain privileges: juridical power over subjects and the right to be tried for their own crimes by "provincial courts." Certain affairs in the provincial administration were left to the estates (the clergy, the nobility, and the few representatives of the towns) in the anticipation of approval for special levies. In the fourteenth century they won the right to sit first in a provincial and then in a general land assembly. It was only at the turn of the

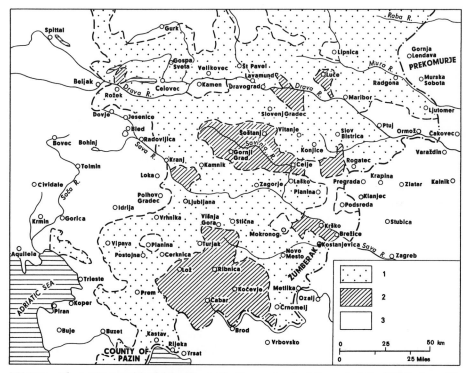

MAP 14.   The territories of feudal families in the Slovene lands at the end of the Middle Ages. (1) Hapsburg possessions; (2) possessions of the barons of Cilli (Celje); (3) possessions of other sacred and profane feudatories and towns.

seventeenth century, with the introduction of centralized policies, that the power and jurisdiction of the estates began to be curtailed.

In contrast to the slow, steady rise of the Hapsburgs, the achievements of the Nemanid dynasty, the Hungarian Angevins, and the Bosnian Kotro-manićs were destined to be short-lived. Created at a time when the Balkan and Central European countries were being incorporated into the economy of the Western countries, they developed on a solid economic base. However, Serbia did not succeed in replacing the foundered Byzantine Empire, nor was Bosnia able to become a significant political factor by taking advantage of sporadic Hungarian crises. Both countries became the prey of Turkish conquest. Hungary exhausted all its strength in a protracted struggle to establish a great political power in the area of the extremely parceled Holy Roman Empire and around it. Losing the dynastic struggle for dominance in Central Europe, it also finally fell victim to Turkish expansion. On the other hand, the Hapsburgs were successful in establishing a powerful Danubian monarchy and in stopping the Turkish onslaught.

RULERS OF SERBIA

Dynasty Nemanjić

Stefan Nemanja, Great Župan
(1168–1196)
Stefan Prvovenčani, Great Župan
(1196–1217), King (1217–1227)
Radoslav, King (1227–1234)
Vladislav, King (1234–1243)
Stefan Uroš I, King (1243–1276)

Stefan Dragutin, King (1276–1282),
after abdication King of Srem
(1282–1316)
Stefan Uroš II Milutin, King
(1282–1321)
Stefan Uroš III Dečanski, King
(1321–1331)
Stefan Dušan, King (1331–1346),
Emperor (1346–1355)
Stefan Uroš, Emperor (1355–1371)

RULERS OF BOSNIA

Dynasty Kotromanić

Prijezda, ban (ca. 1250–1278)
Stjepan I Kotromanić, ban
(1290–1310)
Pavao, Mladen I and Mladen II of
Bribir, who styled themselves
"banus Bosne" (1299–1322)
Stjepan II Kotromanić, ban
(1314–1353)
Tvrtko I, ban (1353–1377), King
Stefan (1377–1391)
Dabiša, King (1391–1395)

Jelena Gruba, Queen (1395–1398)
Stefan Ostoja, King (1398–1404,
1409–1418)
Stefan Tvrtko II, King (1404–1409,
1421–1443)
Stefan Ostojić, King (1418–1421)
Stefan Tomaš, King (1443–1461)
Stefan Tomašević, King (1461–1463)

CHAPTER 9

The Eastern
and Western
Cultural Zones

The Influence of Byzantium and Western Europe

The line segregating the eastern (Hellenic) from the western (Roman) zone of political and cultural influence had run since antiquity down the center of the Balkan Peninsula. It also divided the South Slavs into two parts. During the early centuries of their habitation of the Balkan Peninsula, when the Western world was still culturally and economically backward, the Byzantine Empire, heir and guardian of classical culture and the mainstay of palpably modified artistic traditions, sent its impulses far to the west, setting its imprint on the still primitive occidental culture. The tenth and eleventh centuries saw the beginnings of economic development in the western lands, the awakening of thought and explicit tendencies toward creating a singular artistic style. Demographic expansion propelled Western European society into the Crusades, posing a threat to the political and economic position of the Byzantine Empire. The schism of 1054 and the strengthening of the papacy exposed all South Slavs along the coast and in western regions to the direct influence of Western European culture. This development was furthered by the fact that Croatia and Dalmatia had long been ruled by the Hungarian crown, which had always looked to Rome, and that the Slavs in the Alpine areas were politically associated with the Germans.

In the eastern regions (Serbia and Macedonia) Byzantine influence prevailed. Although the Nemanid state was born in the struggle against the Byzantine Empire, which itself remained in a state of dismemberment for half a century (1204–1261), owing to the founding of the Latin Empire of Constantinople and a plethora of small Crusade states, culture in the eastern part of the Balkan Peninsula was fostered on Byzantine models. Macedonia was long part of Byzantium. The autocephalous Serbian church had been organized along Byzantine lines, translating from Greek the liturgy, canon law, and other religious texts. The Serbian state itself grew as it conquered Byzantine districts. Byzantine influence was dominant in spite of endeavors to uproot the "Greek word" in order to consolidate the new power.

Their affiliation with two different worlds, the Western European and the Byzantine, deepened the cultural differences between the South Slavs, creating cultural zones of diverse bent, particularly in the world of the spirit and in the circles which ruled over others from their position at the apex of society. In spite of divergent cultural orientations, remains of the fructifying influence of Byzantium from earlier times lingered on here and there in the western zone and disappeared gradually, whereas the eastern regions, linked economically with the coast, adopted the products of Western European craftsmen and artisans from the littoral, especially experienced masons. Western and Eastern elements intermingled in everyday life. Men in the eastern regions, in contrast to those in the West, wore beards and moustaches; but in their hunts, heroic games, gambling in the inns, and plays performed by itinerant actors, Western influence was present. Wage laborers in Serbia counted among their number vagabonds and adventurers from the West; "Latin" quarters existed in the Serbian marketplaces, and mining, at least in the initial phase, was in the hands of the Saxons of Transylvania. In the daily life of both feudal lords and ordinary citizens, numerous Western habits and customs had taken hold and endured.

Between the eastern and western zones lay Bosnia, sunk in its mountains and pursuing its own religious beliefs, equally distant from East and West. Consequently its culture, bearing strong traces of the patriarchal legacy, reflected both cultural trends, neither of which gained precedence.

The tone in cultural activity was set by the church centers, the courts, the regional lords and nobles, and finally the town communes. This is where the schools and offices were located, the archives and libraries. The literate and the schooled, the artisans and the artists, provided for the needs of the spiritual and temporal lords, the town patriciate, and the rich citizens, to whose tastes they had to cater.

The written languages were Slavonic, Greek, Latin, and even German, for the ruling class in Macedonia long remained Greek, the patriciate in the Dalmatian towns was of Romance origin, and the feudal lords in the Slovene Provinces were German. The official language of the Catholic church, and the only one permitted, was Latin.

Greek and Latin Literature

In the eastern zone, the people had to know Greek because it was from this language that most of the theological and legal writings were translated. Especially after the conquest of Byzantine areas, the Serbian rulers were compelled to employ Greek scribes to maintain ties with their closest neighbors. In Macedonia, ecclesiastical texts in Greek were copied and used. Distinguished heads of the church, like the archbishop of Ohrid, Theophilactos (1084–1107), and Demetrios Chomatenos (1216–1234), wrote in Greek. A Greek from Euboea, Theophilactos, whose Slav flock "stank of sheepskin," left, apart from numerous letters, also an interpretation of the Gospels, the lives of Christian martyrs from Tiberiopolis, a polemical manuscript on the "errors of the Latins," and a lengthy life of Clement of Ohrid. Demetrios Chomatenos, an uncompromising adversary of the Serbian autocephalous church, bequeathed to posterity a short biography of Clement *(Legend of Ohrid)* as part of his canonic and theological legacy.

In the western zone, Latin was not only the official language of the Roman church, but also the common medium of expression for Western European culture. Except in areas where services were held in Slavonic, all ritual, liturgical, and canonic writings were in Latin. This also applied to administrative documents, official correspondence, and legal monuments. The statutes of the coastal towns, imbued with the principles of Roman law and frequently imitating the statutes of Italian communes, were also in Latin (Split 1241, Korčula 1265, Dubrovnik 1272, Zadar and Brač 1305, Lastovo and Mljet 1310, Trogir 1322, Rab 1330, and Hvar 1330, Poreč 1363, Senj 1388, and so on). Every town school was called *grammatica*, indicating that its primary purpose was teaching Latin. Many local writers also used it as their medium of expression. The chronicles of "Pop Dukljanin" (the presbyter of Diocles), assumed to have been written in the second half of the twelfth century and containing an imaginary history of the state of Dioclea, were in Latin. Along with the theologian Paulus Dalmata, who wrote

FIGURE 9.   The church of St. Donat, Zadar.

FIGURE 10.   St. John Kaneo, Ohrid.

FIGURE 11.   The necropolis at Radimlje near Stolac.

FIGURE 12.   Interior of St. Naum monastery, Ohrid.

De poenitentia, and the poet and historian Syfridus Swevus, the archdeacon of Split, Toma (Thomas, 1200–1268), was preeminent in Latin literature; his *Historia Salonitana* abounds in information not only about the past of Split and its church, but also about the other Dalmatian towns. In the course of the fourteenth century there were written, in addition to theological tracts, a number of historical works—the anonymous *Obsidio Iadrensis* and the *Chronica Iadrensis*, the *Memoriale* of Paul of Zadar, works by Marinus a Cutheis, Miha Madii de Barbazanis, and Janez, the abbot of the monastery of Vetrinje near Celovec. Verses were still a rarity, although knightly poems from which rhymed chronicles in German later derived were produced in the provincial courts in Slovenia, as well as at the court of Spanheim in Carinthia. A wealth of Latin literature was contained in the numerous monastery and chapter libraries, where precious old manuscripts, bound, copied, and illustrated by domestic scribes and illuminators, are still preserved.

The Glagolitic and Cyrillic Alphabets

Texts in Slavonic are extant in two alphabets—Glagolitic and Cyrillic. Only after the fourteenth century did the Roman alphabet come into its own in the western cultural zone.

In the region encompassed by Catholic church organizations, the Roman Curia was adamant in its opposition to services in Slavonic and the use of the Glagolitic; consequently this earliest Slavonic alphabet maintained itself only on the island of Krk and in the diocese of Senj. Only after Pope Innocent IV permitted that tiny area to retain its traditions (1248, 1252) did the Glagolitic alphabet begin its slow diffusion, almost illegally as it were, penetrating to Istria and along the Adriatic coast as far as Dubrovnik and Kotor, and making its way to Lika, from which it passed on to Slavonia, and southern Solvene lands (Bela Krajina, Istria, Venetian Slovenes). It was also occasionally in use in certain Benedictine monasteries, where Latin was otherwise the exclusive language. Monasteries using Glagolitic characters were even founded by the Czech king Karl IV, in Emaus near Prague (1347), as well as by the Polish king Wladislaus Jagiello, in Cracow (1390).

Cyrillic prevailed throughout the zone of Byzantine influence. It also spread to Bosnia, where it was retained until the nineteenth century, and to the entire coastal region south of Split. It was employed not only in Poljica (between Split and the Cetina) but also at Sinj, Klis (above Split), and on the island of Brac. In these Western-oriented areas, Cyrillic was not replaced by Glagolitic but rather suppressed slowly by the Roman alphabet in the period of humanism and the Renaissance.

Versions of Old Slavonic and the Use of the Vernacular in Written Texts

In the Slovene lands, ruled by German feudal lords, development of literature in Slavonic was blocked. As of the fourteenth and fifteenth centuries, a growing number of Slavonic writings appeared using the Latin alphabet. Two linguistic tendencies were noticeable in the remaining areas where Slavonic literature was fostered: (1) the retention of the Old Slavonic, or Church Slavonic, in the spirit of the traditions established by Cyril and Methodius, with minor adjustments to the local features of the vernacular (Bulgarian, Serbian, and Croatian variants), and (2) the establishment of the vernacular as the principal mode of expression in writing as well as speaking.

Books for the service in the Western ritual demonstrate the slow evolution of the pure Old Slavonic tongue, as found in the Vatican Missal, toward the considerably modified church language influenced by popular speech (the Missal of Hrvoje), especially in the čakavian dialect,[1] which then extended along the coast from Istria to the Cetina and from there far inland up to the Kupa, Una, and Sana Rivers. The vernacular established itself in legal documents with even greater ease (the Code of Vinodol, 1288). When the influx of Slavs tangibly altered the ethnical structure of the coastal towns which had been predominantly Romance, Slav literacy and literature began to fan out only in the popular spoken tongue as the towns had no tradition of Glagolitic, used only for literature and worship. In any case, the tendency was for lay literature and church texts devised for the faithful (evangelistaries, lectionaries) to be read in the language understood by the people. In the western cultural zone, the stage was being set for the vernacular with its dialectical features to become the language of literature.

In the Nemanid state, literature, both original and in translation, was firmly rooted in the only slightly modified Old Slavonic tongue. Like art, it achieved an enviable level but was marked by an unfortunate tendency to petrify values, as was the case with Byzantine culture in its entirety. The literature that developed in the Nemanid state persisted in repeating the old models and preserving the already dead Church Slavonic language all the way up to the

---

[1] The Serbo-Croatian language is divided into three basic dialects according to the form of the interrogative pronoun *what:* kajkavian (what = *kaj*), čakavian (what = *ča*), and štokavian (what = *što*). Kajkavian is spoken today in northwestern parts of Croatia, čakavian in the northern coast area and on the Adriatic islands, štokavian in all other regions. Štokavian is the basis of modern standard Serbo-Croatian. Štokavian has three subdialects according to the pronunciation of the original Slavic vowel represented by the letter *jat.* In the ikavian subdialect *jat* developed into *i*, in the *jekavian* (or *ijekavian*) into *je (ije)*, and in the *ekavian* into *e*. For example, the word for *milk* in ikavian is *mliko*, in jekavian *mlijeko*, and in ekavian *mleko*. In modern standard Serbo-Croatian, only ekavian (eastern regions) and jekavian (western regions) are used.

eighteenth century. During its golden age, from the thirteenth to the fifteenth century, it eclipsed all the works written by learned men in other parts of what is now Yugoslavia, but as the brilliant reflection of a great culture on the wane, it provided no fertilizing incentive for new and substantively different achievements. The vernacular was able to establish itself only in legal monuments (rulers' charters, the Code of Laws of Dušan) and in correspondence. The diplomatic documents of Bosnia, Hum, Zeta, and Dubrovnik mirrored this inflexible process even more.

Sacred and Secular Literature

Literary activity in Slavonic, among both Serbs and Croats, was directed mainly toward meeting the requirements of the church and religious teaching. Apart from copying the old Glagolitic texts, the Catholic church issued instructive and moralistic works for the common man, translated from Italian or Czech, such as, for instance, the *Lucidar*, a small encyclopedia in the form of a dialogue on religion and nature. In addition to translations of Gospels, accounts of apostles, psalters, menologies, proluges (collections of short lives of the saints, divided up into months and days) and collections of ritual poems, Serbian medieval literature included compositions celebrating native saints. Saint Sava was the first to compose a service to Saint Simeon (Nemanja), his father. Similar services with short lives were later written for other canonized rulers, as well as for all Serbian archbishops and patriarchs, and finally brought together in a special edition called *Srbljak* (from the sixteenth century onwards). As the monastic orders spread, rules governing life in the monasteries were drawn up and came to be known as *typica*. Also associated with Sava's name is a translation of the Nomocanon (a collection of secular and sacred rules associated with church life), a work which later came to be known among all Orthodox Slavs by the name *Krmčija* (from the verb *krmiti* or *krmaniti*, meaning to steer, administer, rule). These same rules were systematized by Matthias Blastares of Salonika in 1335, and his *Syntagma* was translated into Church Slavonic only twelve years later by order of Emperor Stefan Dušan. As exemplary models of church teaching, selected pages from the eloquent addresses of John Chrysostom, Basil the Great, Andrew of Crete, and others were also translated.

In both cultural zones the people eagerly read apocrypha, in which biblical themes intermingled with fascinating legends and visions rejected by the official church (*The Proto-Gospels of Jacob*, *The Gospels of Nikodemos*, *The Vision of the Madonna*, *The Second Coming of Christ*, and so on). These beloved tales also made their way into folk songs. The same or similar motives were found in Greek and Latin apocryphal literature, and thus reached the Yugoslav regions from both sides. Also popular was the hagiographic literature, which no church rejected. Among the Serbs, some of the most widely known were the lives of Saint George, Saint Demetrios, Alexius "the Man of God," Mary of Egypt, and among the Croats the life of Saint Jerome (considered a Croat because of his Dalmatian origin), the Miracles of the Virgin, and similar compositions. In the attempt to bring religious themes home to the people, a new step was taken in the form of performances, under Italian and German influence, illustrating parts of the Bible (*The Lamentation of the Blessed Virgin Mary*, *The Passion of Christ*, and so on); they were later (in the fifteenth century) taken up by the monasteries and religious orders along the entire Adriatic coast and thus became the beginning of the domestic theater.

Hagiographic literature in the Nemanid state was supplemented by the lives of Serbian rulers and archbishops. These were original works containing, apart from quotations from the Bible and biblical reminiscences, valuable historical data on the political and ecclesiastical activities of distinguished persons in Serbian society, permeated by an emphatically panegyric tone. Two of Nemanja's sons, Saint Sava and Stefan Prvovenčani (the First-Crowned), wrote—the first briefly and the latter at length—biographies of their father, Saint Simeon, who had assumed that name as a monk. Domentiyan produced a life of Saint Sava (1253), and Theodosius rewrote it at the close of the thirteenth century, replacing Domentiyan's turgid style with lively and picturesque narration. In the fourteenth century, Archbishop Danilo II wrote the lives of all the Nemanid rulers, from Stefan Prvovenčani to Dušan, and of all Serbian archbishops. As the work was left unfinished, Danilo's disciple added the lives of Danilo II and Dušan's father, Stefan Dečanski, with a great deal more literary finish than his teacher. The enfeeblement and decline of the empire signified the end of this literary activity, which had surpassed in quality and significance everything else produced in Yugoslav medieval literature.

Secular literature was generally far rarer than sacred, as though it were a fugitive in "the atmosphere of incense and prayer." Most of the engrossing, instructive tales, laced with Indian and Arabic motifs, were derived from Byzantine literature. Some of them *(Of the All-Wise Akira, Barlaam and Joasaph)* also reached the Catholic littoral. Meanwhile the Western European chivalric romance also made its way to the Serbian dominions, probably via the coast. *Rumanac trojski* (*rumanac* from the Italian *romanzo*, i.e., *Romance of Troy*), in which Homer's heroes are depicted as medieval knights, was translated in 1300 in the Croatian Littoral, from which it reached Bulgaria and Russia, through Serbia. The romance of Alexander the Great, popular among both Serbs and Croats, was imported into Russia as *The Serbian Alexandris*. The same was undoubtedly true of the celebrated romance *Trištan and Ižota (Tristan and Isolde)*, preserved in a Byelorussian manuscript.

Although many of the sacred and secular works were translated from originals that were in verse form, in Yugoslav literature they appeared as prose, with only occasional consideration shown for the number of syllables and rhyme. True verse appeared sporadically, like that from a Brač inscription in the Byzantine twelve-beat line. It made headway in the eastern regions in the fifteenth century, when its spread along the coast was parallel with the diffusion of Renaissance literature.

Oral poetry, both lyric and epic, was a beloved form with the people. When the Byzantine chronicler Nicephorus Gregoras visited Serbia as imperial envoy, the men dispatched to escort him sang of their heroes, although the words, echoing in the gorges and ravines, were incomprehensible to him. According to Saint Sava, the folk poetry was "impure and harmful." Feudal society, with its learned literature, in any case found folk poetry revolting not only for its freedom of expression, but also for its patent disapproval of the social system. In order to establish closer contact with the folk, the Catholic church paved the way for establishment of the folk rhyme in octameter in plebeian performances of the lives of saints.

Scientific knowledge was scant. The *Physiologus*, a Greek text of the second or third century, was translated by the Serbs, but it was merely a collection of fantastic descriptions of animals with a Christian moral attached to the end of each. Books of medicine were imported from Byzantium, teaching the use of nature cures, reinforced by prayers and magical incantations. The rulers and their closest associates had more confidence in the physicians imported by the coastal towns from Italy whose knowledge was limited, however, by their insufficient acquaintance with the human body and the nature of illness.

Romanesque and Gothic

The art of the western cultural zone developed within the scope of two major styles—Romanesque and Gothic. Spreading outward from their provenance, Romanesque from the tenth century and Gothic from the twelfth, these two styles reached the Yugoslav dominions in their original form and there they acquired regional and local features. Two great regions are distinguishable—the coastal and the continental, to which influences came from countries of differing artistic development.

The coastal belt, from Istria to the Montenegrin coast, adopted the artistic models of adjacent Italy. There the Romanesque style struck deep roots and held its own in some places until the sixteenth century. Built in this style were the earliest loggias, communal palaces, and many churches, mostly triple-aisled:

Saint Anastasia and Saint Chrysogonus (Krševan) in Zadar, the cathedral of Trogir, the ancient cathedral of Dubrovnik (destroyed in the earthquake of 1667), with here and there a single-aisle church (Saint Mary's on Mljet Island) or one with octagonal base (the Holy Trinity in Rovinj). Bell towers were freestanding or attached. When Franciscan and Dominican monasteries began to be founded in the thirteenth century, their monks usually commissioned single-aisle churches, to which Gothic elements were added. Native masters also constructed for them cloisters in the late Romanesque style. Unfinished monumental cathedrals were invested by builders with elements of the Gothic (Šibenik, Trogir, Korčula), leaving room for the addition of some of the most salient features of the Renaissance. Gothic came in on the tide of Venetian rule, building into highly simplified wall surfaces the triforia, quadriforia, and portals for which Venetian architecture was celebrated. In the face of the Renaissance, the taste for Gothic slowly disappeared from the coastal towns.

In the interior, segregated from the coast by mountain chains, and open toward the Danubian region, the foreign (German) feudal lords erected their "burgs" with the resulting establishment of the Central European variants of the foregoing styles. Although this zone is a broad one, it lagged behind the coast, owing to the belated development of the towns. The Romanesque penetrated but poorly, and few Romanesque buildings, or traces of them, remain in the area. The earliest cathedral of Zagreb was demolished during the Tatar invasions, but others have been preserved: the church of Saint Mary in Topusko, the monastery of Stična in Slovenia, and the remains of secular buildings repaired or reconstructed later. Most of them were commissioned by the monastic orders arriving from the Germanic lands as part of the great wave of German colonizers, although there was already some Italian and French influence. Once Gothic appeared, it tended to suppress Romanesque forms. The new style was quick to establish itself and showed considerable staying power, lasting until the seventeenth century. The cathedral of Zagreb was already being reconstructed in the thirteenth century on the model of the church of Saint Urban in the French town of Troyes. Gothic stylistic features are in evidence also in the remains of fifteenth-century palaces and feudal architecture in Bosnia.

The power of Romanesque architecture along the coast was so overwhelming that it penetrated from Zeta towns to the Nemanid state. Tying in and intermingling with elements of the Byzantine buildings, it was instrumental in producing the singular Rascia School. From Studenica, through Žiča, Mileševo, Sopoćani, and other churches, the traditions of the Rascia School flourished in architecture until the fourteenth century, when Banjska, Dečani, and the Holy Archangel near Prizren were erected. These usually single-aisle churches with domes underwent reconstruction in the thirteenth century, when large-narthexes with side chapels and belfries were built at the entrance.

The Byzantine Art Style

In the twelfth and thirteenth centuries, churches in Macedonia were constructed under the direct influence of the Byzantine style. The floor plan was the cross-in-square with a cupola rising above each section of the cross (Nerezi near Skoplje). Built of bricks, these churches were notable for the ceramic meanders on their facades, the interrupted friezes, and above the doors and windows blind niches with volutes (Our Lady Peribleptos, now called the church of Saint Clement in Ohrid). After the arrival of the Serbs in Macedonian lands, the Byzantine style began to be reflected in Serbian architecture (Our Lady Ljeviška in Prizren, Gračancia in Kosovo), from which it gradually suppressed elements of the Rascia School. Ultimately, the Byzantine style of the Palaeologue era gained sway over Serbian building techniques.

During the Romanesque and Gothic periods, sculpture developed as a component part of architecture. The floral, animal, and geometric motifs on the capitals and portals were supplemented by the figures of saints, biblical scenes in bas-relief, and illustrations from everyday life. In the continental region, sculptural details were scarce — perhaps a relief of the Lamb of God added to the architectural ornamentation in Slovenia. It was only after the Gothic had entrenched itself that a larger number of statues were produced: the Crucified Christ, the Madonna with Child, Pietà — mostly from the fifteenth century. In medieval Slavonia the most impressive monument is the southern portal of the church of Saint Mark in Zagreb, with Gothic figures of saints. Romanesque sculpture underwent a turbulent development along the coast, where the appearance of Gothic only served to enrich it. Byzantine traditions, still lingering in the carving of the capitals, the great wooden crosses, and the marble relief of Christ Enthroned (the cathedral of Rab, fifteenth century), retreated as Romanesque set its imprint on the most important works. At the beginning of the thirteenth century, Andrija Buvina and his associates fashioned a carved wooden portal for the cathedral of Split with twenty-eight New Testament scenes in polychrome relief. About 1240 Master Radovan carved the monumental portal of the cathedral of Trogir, his fine sense of realism evident in the statues of Adam and Eve, and the reliefs of the Labors of the Months, portraying the appropriate tasks of each season. Two of his disciples had already adopted the artistic concepts of Gothic. These elements asserted themselves first in crosses, altars, altar statues, and church furniture. They were also applied by local goldsmiths in fashioning crosses, reliquaries, vessels, and ornaments for book covers. The most distinctive monument in goldwork is the sepulcher of Saint Simon in Zadar, dating from the second half of the fourteenth century.

Sculpture suffered from neglect in the zone of Byzantine influence. The wooden statue of Saint Clement in Ohrid (fourteenth century) may therefore be considered a rarity. Western influence was apparent in churches of the Rascia

School, like Studenica and Dečani, in the portals and windows with their sumptuous floral decoration into which are interwoven the figures of real and fantastic animals, reliefs of the figure of Christ, the apostles, saints, and archangels.

The Bosnian Tombstones

Thousands of tombstones of varying form, called *stećci*, have been preserved in Bosnia, some of them recalling Roman sarcophagi, and others simplified human forms. Extensive necropolises are found at Zgošća near Visoko, in Olovo, and in Radimlje, near Stolac. A few of these *stećci* bear inscriptions and carvings of geometric and floral ornaments, scenes of hunting and games, and processions of horsemen. The rustic craftsmen took their inspiration from the monuments of antiquity, from Gothic carving, and from painted textiles. The *stećci* themselves cannot be associated with the Patarenes or the Bosnian church alone, as they were erected also by Catholics and Orthodox.

Painters worked on wet plaster along the inner walls of churches (frescoes), on wood panels (icons), and on the parchment pages of codices (miniatures).

Although the names of many coastal painters are known to us today, remains of frescoes are extremely rare in Dalmatia; they are found much more frequently in Istria. This style of painting, developed by the Benedictines in Italy, was invested still with emphatic Byzantine elements. In the interior, only the cathedral of Zagreb contains the remains of frescoes, executed by an artist of Rome. During the Gothic period the reconstructed cathedral was again painted by a foreign artist of Rimini. In the Slovene regions, under Italian influence on the one hand, and Czech and Tirolean on the other, the inside and sometimes the outside walls and a large number of churches were painted. The iconographic system that had been adopted dictated the distribution of the basic themes — God in Majesty, the apostles, the Annunciation, the Adoration of the Magi, and the Last Judgment.

But the real wealth of wall painting is to be found preserved in the eastern, Orthodox zone, where there is not a single church whose inner walls are not covered with frescoes. Foundations from the early period of the Nemanid dynasty were painted by Greek masters on the model of Byzantine art of the Comnenus period. Here are grandiose compositions from the life of Christ, illustrations of church holidays, processions of saints and historical personalities. These were paralleled by the development of monastic painting, an austere offshoot with its rows of monks and hermits. In the thirteenth century, while Constantinople was under Latin rule, Serbian painting gained independence to achieve supreme aesthetic values. Motifs were enriched with portraits of native rulers and historical compositions, depictions of ecumenical synods and the Last

FIGURE 13.   Fresco from Mileševo monastery.

FIGURE 14.   Fresco from Nerezi.

110

FIGURE 15. Dubrovnik.

FIGURE 16. Studenica.

Judgment. All these themes are portrayed at the Sopoćani monastery (built ca. 1265), which by virtue of its monumentality, symmetrical distribution of figures, broad painted surfaces, and sensitivity of artistic expression is without peer in the European art of that period. A similar process may be traced through the frescoes of the Macedonian churches, where the figures of saints, previously stereotyped, begin to give the impression of genuine portraits.

From the end of the thirteenth century, when Macedonia was part of the Nemanid state, the entire region reflected the overpowering influence of renascent Byzantine painting from the Palaeologue period, characterized by the models of antiquity which inspired it. In a large number of the new cycles (there are nineteen in Dečani), a sense of drama and symbolism permeates the narration, and scenes from everyday life have been inserted into the sacred compositions. The overly sumptuous painting of the new period (fourteenth century) lost something of the earlier cohesion for, apart from the use of models from Constantinople and Mount Athos, "Greek painters" from the coast, who had modified their artistic conceptions in Italy, added their special touch. The result was a coarser and more naïve expression.

A considerable number of icons are extant, a few Byzantine ones from Dalmatia, and those produced in Macedonia and Serbia, worked in the same spirit that pervaded the frescoes. Scriptoria were kept busy in all regions, not only copying books but also illuminating them with miniatures in the dominant style of the time.

The gradual defining of the two zones of differing influences demonstrates how the South Slav peoples began to drift apart. Within these same zones, however, certain elements of rapprochement were also evident. The dissemination of the Glagolitic alphabet in Slavonia, and even in the southern Slovene areas, and the religious books into which the Ča dialect began to infiltrate, are the timid expressions of kinship in the cultural climate of the Croats and Slovenes. The intimacy was even greater between the Serbian, Macedonian, and Bulgarian cultures. Approximately the same literary language, based on Old Slavonic, and the same Byzantine influence in ecclesiastical and state organization, in law, and in artistic creativity, made it easy for writers and artists who wished to travel from one country to another to continue their activities without undue difficulty. Future development was destined to stop this process of cultural rapprochement, here earlier, there later, and to set the various peoples moving along new roads of creativity.

CHAPTER 10

The Balkan World during the Turkish Conquests

The Spread of the Osmanlis

From the time of their migration from Asia as a nomadic tribe, when they joined the service of the sultan of Iconium (Konya) in return for the right to enjoy the territory near the Byzantine boundary on the Sea of Marmara, until the middle of the fourteenth century, the Turks underwent a metamorphosis that transformed them from mere fear-inspiring plunderers into a dangerous conquering force. Called Osmanlis, from the name of their chieftain Osman, they interfered in internal Byzantine conflicts, expanded their territory, and in 1354 set

113

foot on Balkan soil. The weakness of the Balkan rulers facilitated their swift penetration, and eventually they moved the capital of their sultan to Edirne (Adrianople) and brought in their own people to replace the uprooted population. From their new strongholds they were able to make incursions into Bulgarian, Greek, and Serbian lands.

The concessions made to the Genoese by John V Palaeologus, an emperor without an army, a fleet, or money; his promise to the pope of a union of churches accompanied by a request for help from the West; his travels to Hungary; his entreaties for money in Venice—none of these yielded the desired results. The remnants of the once mighty Byzantine Empire (Constantinople with its environs, Morea, and Salonika) were now ranked among the tiny Balkan states of which there were twenty-four, with the exception of Hungarian, Genoese, and Venetian possessions.

Bulgaria was dismembered and impotent. The court at Trnovo placed its reliance on Turkey, helping it in its assaults on Hungary while the emperor in Vidin accepted the protection of the Hungarian king.

The Collapse of Dušan's Empire

Dušan's heir, Emperor Uroš, pressed by the powerful landlords, found it impossible to keep his father's empire intact. Whole areas fell away. Dušan's half brother Simeon (Siniša) rallied to himself the regents in Greece and Albania to oppose the emperor. Unable to gain mastery over the entire country, he withdrew to lead an independent life in Greek lands. The Serbian lords remaining faithful to the emperor considered themselves the masters of their territories and styled themselves his "allies and friends." Ruthlessly they joined battle over possessions and power. In an atmosphere of insecurity and disintegration, the country's power to resist declined. Regional lords behaved like rulers on a small scale, minted money, and exacted tolls, depriving the emperor of his rights and revenues. Many monastic estates were abandoned, and merchants setting out for Serbia frequently turned back. Stagnation set in where economy had flourished.

The first to gain predominance among the feudal magnates were two brothers of the Mrnjavčević family. Formerly the master of Prilep, Vukašin had won control of the region west of the Vardar River in 1369, taken the title of king, and become a coruler with Emperor Uroš I. His brother, Despot Uglješa, established a separate state in eastern Macedonia, around the towns of Serres and Drama. In Zeta the Balšićs held sway, striking an alliance with the Mrnjavčevićs to facilitate dealing with their neighbors. As the Mrnjavčević lands were the first to reel from Turkish blows, Despot Uglješa called upon the surrounding lords to unite for resistance, condemning Dušan's coronation as emperor and the establishment of the patriarchate, in order to win the favor of Constantinople. However, in the battle against the Turks near Černomen on the Maritsa River in 1371, only his brother Vukašin stood by him. Both brothers were slain in the field, and the Turks smashed their armies. Many of the feudal lords in the vicinity became vassals and tributaries of the sultan, among them Vukašin's successor, King Marko (the legendary hero of many folk songs that become popular among all the South Slavs), the lord of Bulgaria, and the Byzantine emperor himself. The Turks set up around their borders the first band of small dependent states.

The Morava River Region under Prince Lazar as a New Political Center

The Maritsa defeat was soon followed by the death of Emperor Uroš I, who had provided at least a formal link among the independent Serbian magnates; his place was assumed among them by the lord of the Morava region, Prince Lazar, bound to the Nemanid family tree by tenuous ties, through his wife Milica. Also, greater influence was gained by his son-in-law Vuk Branković, the lord of Kosovo, who expanded his territory by eliminating the weaker lords and taking a part of Vukašin's inheritance, among others the town of Skoplje. Prince Lazar also formed an alliance with the Balsićs of Zeta. The obstinate zupan Nikola Altomanović was broken with the assistance of King Tvrtko I, and Lazar took over the eastern districts of his region. Although remaining but a prince to the end of his life, he followed in the footsteps of the Nemanid rulers. Supported by the Serbian church, he also succeeded in achieving reconciliation with the patriarchate of Constantinople in 1375. Embarking on a program of construction, he commissioned monasteries in the Morava River region where none had existed before and where the population was not so closely bound to its church; continuing his activities across the Danube, he sent missionaries to the Vlachs and raised foundations there as well. Monks fleeing from the Turks found refuge at his court. Once-neglected areas began to revive culturally and economically and to provide the reconstructed state with a number of new centers. Lazar then took up residence in the newly built fortress of Kruševac. Tvrtko's coronation and adoption of the name borne by Serbian rulers, and the assumption of a royal title by the Turkish vassal Marko, did nothing to alter Lazar's position. In popular legend, the prince was fondly remembered as an emperor.

The Defeat at Kosovo (1389)

It was natural, too, for Lazar to organize defenses against Turkish encroachments. He was successful in beating back the forces of Sultan Murad (1381, 1386), just as Tvrtko brought defeat upon them when they attempted to invade

Bosnia (1386, 1388). The sultan's failures caused him to make sounder preparations for his next sally. On June 28, 1389, at the Battle of Kosovo, between Priština and Lab, Lazar's forces were joined in the field by those of Vuk Branković and the Bosnian king Tvrtko I. The Serbian army won some initial battles, as one of Lazar's nobles, Miloš (called Obilić in folk poetry), killed Murad I in his tent. But the Turks were swift to recover from the ensuing confusion. Murad's son Bajazet took over command and won the day. Prince Lazar was captured and put to death, and his widow, acting on behalf of her minor son Stefan, was subjected to the payment of annual tribute and to raising reinforcements. Vuk Branković salvaged his army by withdrawing it from the battlefield but continued to offer resistance until, under pressure, he had to surrender Skoplje to the Turks in 1392 and also to undertake an obligation to pay tribute. The grave consequences of the defeat at Kosovo were assuaged in legend only: "Tsar" Lazar achieved the kingdom of heaven whereas Vuk Branković was damned as a traitor responsible for the collapse on the battlefield. The glorification of dead heroes, fostered by the church, which made haste to proclaim Prince Lazar a saint, inspired later fighters against Turkish rule with the desire to "avenge Kosovo." Actually, after Kosovo, the Turks set up a new belt of vassal states, soon acquired eastern Bulgaria (1393), and carried their assaults to the Danubian area, to the very gateway of Hungary.

Hungary then faced the task of mustering its forces for war against Turkey. After Louis I, clashes between prominent feudal families had provoked a civil war. Sigismund of Luxembourg was crowned king in 1387, but the entire south of the country was in the hands of his adversaries. The Croatian regions south of the Drava River were firmly held by the Horvat brothers, who kept the country in a state of revolt against the court at Budapest, never abandoning the idea of placing Ladislas of Naples on the throne there. They were supported in their efforts by King Tvrtko I and also the Serbian Prince Lazar, until he made his peace with Sigismund before the Battle of Kosovo so as to forestall trouble on his northern boundaries. It was only after Tvrtko's death that the new Hungarian king won influence in Bosnia, crushing the resistance of the Horvats and their followers. Then he rallied his former adversaries in preparation for the war against the Turks.

Temporary Crises in Turkey

Leading the Christian forces, he undertook two expeditions. Defending the prince of Wallachia as his vassal, he defeated the sultan's forces in 1395 at Rovine. But the next year (1396), with the knights he had gathered in the western lands, he suffered a resounding defeat at Nicopolis which cost him his hard-won prestige in his own kingdom. But regardless of their success or failure in individual battles, the Turks faced a divided Europe. And they had on their side the

MAP 15.   Regions of the Serbian feudal lords before the Battle of Kosovo.

sultan's vassals of the Balkan Peninsula, including Stefan Lazarević "if not will-
ingly, then of necessity," as his biographer declares. These continued to lay down
their lives, as King Marko had at Rovine. Their vassal lands were thereupon
transformed by the sultan into sanjaks and annexed to the empire. It seemed as if
a great offensive was about to be launched against the Hungarian lands, but then
came a fresh Mongol invasion to thwart the Turks in their designs.

Triumphant Bajazet I suffered defeat in Asia Minor, where many of the
Seljuk emirs, disgruntled with the centralistic policies of the Osmanlis, offered
their support to the lord of Samarkand, Tamerlane, who in creating a great state
in central Asia penetrated Anadolia. Clashing with Osmanli forces at Angora
in 1402, Tamerlane emerged victorious, taking Bajazet I captive. After this defeat,

the sultan's sons squabbled over their father's inheritance while the emirs of Asia Minor strove for independence. Dynastic strife and feudal reaction temporarily arrested Osmanli expansion. The surrounding Christian countries won a breathing spell and could turn their attention to their own differences.

King Sigismund no longer had the faintest intention of starting a new war against the Turks. Rather he was carried away by the idea of gaining mastery over Bohemia and Germany to form a community of countries under one dynasty. After he had achieved this and was duly crowned Holy Roman emperor, the Hussite wars and problems with the Council occupied his attention. For a full forty years, with rare interruptions, he avoided any major conflicts with the sultan. But he was forced to reconcile himself to losses in the Balkan region.

Internal Croatian and Bosnian Conflicts

The Dalmatian towns and islands were also lost for the crown. The Croatian landlords, in their opposition, did not succeed in posing a serious threat to Sigismund in Hungary with their plans for enthroning Ladislas of Naples, although they were instrumental in bringing the latter to Zadar (Zara), where he was crowned king in 1403. But Ladislas was plunged by them into a long war with the Venetians, who bought from him his rights to Dalmatia in 1409. Sigismund crushed the opposition in Croatia and Slavonia with the assistance of the powerful family of the counts of Cilli (Celje), who proved reliable allies in the pursuit of his European policies.

That family, once bound to the Hapsburgs, had accumulated power in the Slovene provinces through the acquisition of extensive possessions between the twelfth and fourteenth centuries. It derived its name from the castle and town of Cilli. Herman II of Cilli tied his fortunes to Sigismund, receiving in return large tracts of land in Slavonia, Medjumurje, and the dignity of ban in Croatia, Dalmatia, and Slavonia. Herman was largely responsible for easing tensions in the Croatian lands and helping Sigismund consolidate power in Hungary. Raising Herman's heirs to new dignities, the Luxembourgian secured for them the position of princes of the empire with the right to mint money, exact tolls, and receive revenues from the mines. The natural result was an open clash between the barons of Cilli and their former masters, the Hapsburgs, with whom Sigismund also inevitably came into conflict in his European policies. The war between the barons of Cilli and the Hapsburgs waned only after the death of Sigismund, leaving devastation in its wake throughout the Slovene provinces.

In Bosnia the Hungarian king was not able to secure lasting influence. The decisive role there was played by the landlords rallied around three powerful families who had divided most of the state territory among themselves, leaving the king a minor part. The possessions of the Hrvatinići in the northwest were expanded in the direction of Croatia and Dalmatia. The Kosača-Hranićs held territory running from Onogost (Nikšić, in present-day Montenegro) to the Cetina River in Dalmatia. The Pavlovići owned the eastern districts but extended their possessions to include part of the littoral. As regional lords, the representatives of these houses acted with total independence, replacing the king at will and even striking alliances with his adversaries. Falling out among themselves, they began to draw the Hungarians and Turks alternately into their quarrels. Sigismund could never depend on more than one of the belligerents at a time and even that not for long. Endeavoring to consolidate his influence over Bosnia and to retain a reliable ally on the throne there, he was forced to undertake a number of expeditions, but they brought more suffering to the people than consolidation of Hungarian positions.

The Brief Upsurge of the Serbian Despotate

In Serbia Sigismund found a dependable ally in Stefan Lazarević. The son and heir of Lazar, he had fought in the Battle of Angora in Bajazet's army. Upon his return to Constantinople, he had been elevated to the rank of despot, the highest title after that of emperor. His rise was swift from the position of an obedient vassal of the sultan to the powerful ruler of renascent Serbia. Locked in internal conflict with his own brother and the sons of Vuk Branković, he turned to Sigismund for aid, became his vassal in 1403, and received in return Mačva and Belgrade, and later, in 1411, the biggest Bosnian mine of Srebrenica with environs, an area Sigismund had taken after doing battle with the Bosnian king, and finally extensive lands in Hungary. Despot Stefan selected Belgrade for his capital, investing every effort to reconstruct it and assure its economic advancement. His new possessions netted him considerable revenues.

While dynastic quarrels were in progress in Turkey, the despot could not rally the Serbian lands or strengthen his position and authority. He was opposed by his brother and nephews, who took up first with one and then another Turkish pretender, persisting in their demands to share power with Stefan. Only after they had been killed in the Turkish conflicts was the despot reconciled with Djuradj Branković, the only nephew to survive. The two of them, with the most prominent sanjakbegs, King Sigismund and the Bosnian lord voivode Sandalj Hranić, took sides in the final squaring of accounts between the two remaining sons of Bajazet and helped Mehmed I gain the throne in 1413. It was then that Despot Stefan renewed his old obligations to the sultan, winning for the country a twenty-year period of peace. His association with the rulers of both "East" and "West" (the sultan and the Hungarian king) caused him no difficulty as long as the two respected the peace on the borders.

Djuradj Branković retained his father's region, but after reconciliation

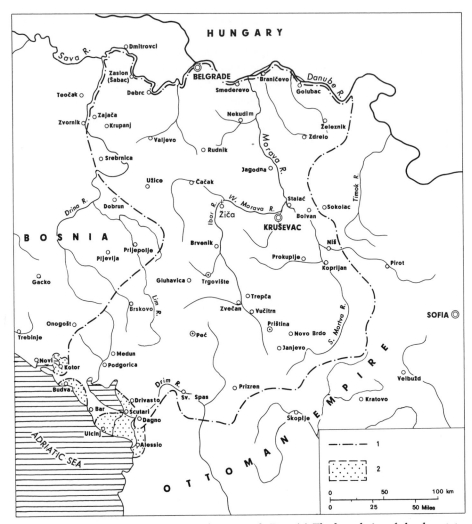

MAP 16. The Serbian despotate after unification with Zeta. (1) The boundaries of the despotate around 1422; (2) towns and territories under the rule of Venice.

he recognized his uncle as the supreme lord of the land. When the last Balšić died in 1421, Despot Stefan took control of Zeta, leaving it to his nephew Djuradj to rule. Merging three great Serbian regions, he continued his father's policy of reconstructing the Nemanid state, with a new center in the Morava River area. This was a district with no foreign strongholds, whereas the land held by the Brankovićs had had Turkish garrisons and towns since the late fourteenth century where Turkish authorities functioned parallel with the Serbian. In Zeta a number of coastal towns were under Venetian administration.

While still playing tribute to Bajazet, Stefan Lazarević, with the sultan's support, had quelled the arrogant nobles and developed a strong central authority. For purposes of local administration, he replaced the earlier župas by new divisions, headed by commanders appointed by himself with headquarters in the most important towns. He relied for support on his standing army and so was not dependent on the goodwill of the landlords. These reforms could not be implemented in the Branković region, laced by Turkish garrisons, leaving the state unity incomplete in parts. But in contrast to the disunity typical of Serbian lands during the second half of the fourteenth century, the despot's firm hand could be felt throughout the extensive territory. As his biographer Constantine the Philosopher put it, "Neither did the powerful take the districts of their neighbors, nor did the mighty draw their swords, nor was the blood of the just spilled."

Judging from incomplete sources, it may be assumed that the revenues of the Serbian despot from mining multiplied more than fivefold. The amount grew, thanks not only to intensive exploitation of old mines but also to the opening of new ones, particularly in the Rudnik and Kopaonik areas. Metallurgy advanced with mining, as the number of metalworking craftsmen in the towns increased. It is no wonder then that Despot Stefan Lazarević caused legal norms and regulations pertaining to mining in Novo Brdo to be compiled for his mine law (1412). A similar development was noticeable in Bosnia, although that country was frequently torn by strife. Foreign merchants invested their resources in expanding the mines of both countries, thus giving impulse to the revival of the economy. Apart from hides, wax, and smoked meat, they exported silver, lead, iron, and copper in growing quantities. Via Split, Drijevo on the Neretva, Dubrovnik, Kotor, Scutari, and Durazzo these commodities were also shipped overseas. In exchange, Serbia imported textiles, salt, wine, and luxury articles. The mining settlements flourished, and along with them market towns like Belgrade, Paraćin, Kruševac, Zaslom (Šabac), Valjevo, Čačak, and many others. In Bosnia towns developed in the shadow of fortified castles—Podvisoko, Podborač, Podzvonik, Podolovo, and so on.

The growth of foreign trade provided incentive, especially in Dubrovnik, to those crafts that could not count on a steady supply of raw materials from the Balkan hinterland—leatherworking, waxmaking, gold working, and also the manufacture of textiles. Weavers in Dubrovnik and somewhat later in Novi produced fabrics from Castilian wool, satisfying most of the demand for this article along the coast and in the hinterland. The owners of textile manufacturing workshops in Dubrovnik also engaged in trade and credit business, apart from employing master craftsmen and unskilled workers, thereby turning a neat profit. Growing production and expanding trade brought Serbia and Bosnia all forms of monetary transactions, gradually changing the barter economy and the earlier social relation.

In the mining settlements and marketplaces of Serbia and Bosnia lived a large number of "Latins," mostly from Dubrovnik. Their importance in the econ-

FIGURE 17.   Remains of the medieval fortress in Smederevo.

FIGURE 18.   Island of Rab.

FIGURE 19. Manasija monastery.

FIGURE 20. Patriarchate of Peć.

omy far surpassed their numbers, as they had financial means, goods, and ramified business connections. The majority of the populace in the Serbian and Bosnian towns were local people, craftsmen, and merchants who traded with foreigners. The Serbian despot, frequently in conflict with the Dubrovnik merchants, endeavored to strip them of their privileges and place them on a par with the local population. But recurrent conflicts with the Turks prevented him from implementing a more independent economic policy.

Stefan Lazarević had command of the resources needed to assure the continuation of the cultural advancement initiated by his father. Well-educated himself, he brought learned monks to Serbia, and built, in his fortified monastery of Manasija, a literary center called the Resava School, named after the Resava River. Old manuscripts were copied and corrected, and work was continued on the reform of grammar, which had begun in Trnovo before defeat by the Turks. Among the cultivated foreigners was a Bulgarian, Constantine the Philosopher, who later became the despot's biographer. Interest in historical writings was revived at the close of the fourteenth and beginning of the fifteenth century. Apart from the works written in praise of Prince Lazar and the histories in which the past of Serbia predominated over general and Byzantine history penned by the Greek chroniclers, a special literary category came into being—the genealogies—which endeavored to show that the Nemanid Dynasty traced its origins to the Roman emperors. Works by Byzantine historians were also translated. Biographies of local rulers shed the hagiographic features of earlier life stories, concentrating rather on secular achievements and activities.

In the arts there was a patent tendency for architecture to break away from the slavish imitation of early Byzantine models. The monasteries of ·Prince Lazar, Despot Stefan, and their lords were constructed with more originality, whereas the wall paintings, although concentrating on old themes, reflected a richer palette, more lyricism, and sensitivity. Before the state collapsed, a new Morava School had established itself, its finest monuments, the monasteries of Manasija and Kalenić, being the last two great buildings constructed in Serbia before the Turkish conquest.

Despot Stefan did not live out his days in peace with the Turks. Obligations toward Sigismund, and Hungarian movements along the boundaries, brought the Turks back to take Niš 'and Kruševac and to build a Turkish fleet on the Morava River. Stefan, who died in 1427, was succeeded by Djuradj Branković. The succession took place under the most difficult of circumstances. According to an earlier agreement, he restored Mačva and Belgrade to Sigismund, and found himself in a situation marked by general disorder and disruption of trade ties with the outside world. A truce was declared only after the Hungarians had concluded peace with the Turks and the new despot had agreed to increase his obligations to the sultan. Mustering all his resources, Branković commissioned

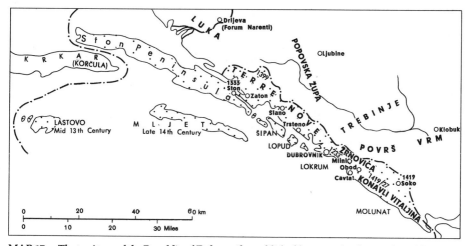

MAP 17.   The territory of the Republic of Dubrovnik established between the thirteenth and fifteenth centuries. Dates indicate when various parts of the territory were acquired.

the construction of a new capital, Smederevo, a fortified town on the Danube completed by 1430, thus consolidating his position and temporarily prolonging the life of his despotate.

Venetian Consolidation in Zeta and Dalmatia

In the meantime, the Venetians, using money and mercenaries, strove to acquire a belt along the eastern Adriatic coast, a singularly important undertaking for them after their retreat before Turkish pressure from the Levant. Two earlier peace treaties with the Hungarian king had hampered them along the entire coast from Quarnero to Durazzo. Therefore they first gained control of Corfu (1386) and then Durazzo in Albania. From the Balšićs, they acquired Scutari and its surroundings (1396). The promised protection from the Turkish threat failed to materialize, while economic pressure generated such bitterness that the last Balšić, Balša III, waged two wars against the Republic of Venice with support from the Turks. After conflicts were terminated through negotiations with the Serbian despot, the Venetians retained their expanded possessions along the Zeta coast. In the intervening period, they took Kotor (1420) and finally secured control over the Dalmatian towns and islands, for which they paid Ladislas of Naples 100,000 ducats. With the western shores of Istria also under their control, they now ruled most of the Adriatic Sea. All that was left to the Hungarian king was Senj in the north and Dubrovnik in the south. The latter, territorially removed from the other Hungarian lands, lived an independent existence, considering and calling itself a republic.

Venetian rule in Dalmatia endured several centuries, bringing economic retrogression in the towns, largely due to their separation from the hinterland, which was soon to fall to the Turks, and to the system of economic restrictions introduced by the Venetians to protect the interests of their metropolis. They had succeeded in establishing control over the Adriatic coast, in which they had a direct interest, before the onset of major changes that were to take place in the Balkan Peninsula.

KINGS OF HUNGARY AND CROATIA

Charles I Robert of Anjou (1301–1342)
Louis I of Anjou (1342–1382)
Maria, daughter of Louis (1382–1385)

Charles of Durazzo, Angevin line of Naples (1385–1386)
Ladislas of Naples (1386–1409)
Sigismund of Luxembourg (1387–1437)

Albrecht of Hapsburg (1437–1439)

Wladislas I Jagiellon (1440–1444)
Ladislas V the Posthumous, son of Albrecht (1444–1457)
Matthias Hunyady Corvinus (1458–1490)
Wladislas II Jagiellon (1490–1516)
Louis II Jagiellon (1516–1526)

RULERS IN DIVIDED SERBIA

1. Zeta
Stracimir Balšić (1360–?)
Djuradj I Balšic (?–1378)

Balša II Balšić (1378–1385)
Djuradj II Stracimirović Balšić (1385–1403)
Balša III Balšić (1403–1421)

2. Kosovo
Vuk Branković (ca. 1371–1397)
Widow Mara with sons (1397–1412)

3. Pomoravlje
Lazar Hrebeljanović, Prince (ca. 1370–1389)
Stefan Lazarević, Prince (1389–1402)

DESPOTS OF SERBIA

Stefan Lazarević, Despot (1402–1427)
Djuradj Branković, Despot (1427–1456)
Lazar Branković, Despot (1456–1458)
Regency: Stefan Branković and Jelena Palaeolog (1458–1459)
Stefan Tomašević, heir to the throne of Bosnia (1459)

CHAPTER II

The Establishment of Turkish Power

Hungary's Preoccupation with Central European Politics

During the fifteenth century and the first few decades of the sixteenth, most of the Yugoslav lands finally fell to Turkish power. The states which had maintained themselves by maneuvering between Hungary and Turkey were erased from the-face of the earth. Up to the middle of the fifteenth century, a tenuous balance had existed between the Christian and Osmanli forces. But when internal Hungarian conflicts were intensified, and when the crisis generated in the Osmanli empire by its defeat at Angora had been settled, the outcome of the great confrontation became clear.

127

After King Sigismund's death, in 1437 the star of the Austrian Hapsburgs began to rise. Having secured power for their house in Germany, they
claimed the Hungarian throne and on two occasions succeeded in making that
claim good. Hungary not only was no longer in a position to resist their grandiose
plans, but even objectively helped them to power by indulging in internal conflicts. The native lords defended the throne from Hapsburg pretensions, stressing
the principle that royal power in Hungary was elective and bringing kings from
the Polish Jagiello dynasty to rule their land. Internal strife centered on the
attempt to crush the mighty families of the magnates, in which a nobleman of
Transylvania, John Hunyadi (remembered in Serbian folk poetry under the name
of Sibinjanin Janko), played a prominent role. Influential in the army and
political life, for a time Hungarian regent, and enjoying the support of nobles of
intermediary rank, he had been instrumental in bringing about the downfall of
the all-powerful barons of Cilli. But the collapse of the latter simply served to
augment the strength of the Hapsburg house, which made haste to grab their
lands. When his son Matthias Corvinus assumed the throne (1458–1490), Hungary experienced an internal renaissance. The king continued the policy of breaking the power of the great magnates, including the family of the Frankapan
princes of Croatia, from Krk. He temporarily ameliorated the lot of the peasants
and opened the doors to cultural influences from Italy but was unsuccessful in
implementing a single plan of Hungarian foreign policy. Engagement in European
politics brought him no results. Failing to establish a great monarchy in Central
Europe, he also neglected the Turkish threat of which his father had been so
acutely aware.

Turkish Ascendancy

At this time Turkey established itself as a mighty power, thanks primarily to military reforms. The ranks of the Janissaries, the celebrated standing
army which the sultans originally reinforced with captives, now began to be
strengthened with the children of Christians. Taken from their parents in the
subjugated lands as "levy in blood," the children were educated in special schools
set up for that purpose, reared in the spirit of Islam and of utter devotion to the
sultan. The Turkish cavalry, the spahis, had previously been composed of the
minor Osmanli nobility. It, too, was reinforced with converted Christians, and
even prominent Christians who kept their faith. Among the military commanders
descended from Osmanli bey families and from the circles of the Seljuk emirs,
opposition to the unlimited power of the sultan smoldered. To offset this, the
sultan appointed distinguished converts to high military posts. In their total
dependency on him, these men became his blindly obedient servants. Everything was geared to enhancing the sultan's omnipotence, including the laws

regulating administration and economic activity. The European states of the time knew no such concentration of political power and economic resources.

The thought of launching a crusade had long been considered in the Western countries. The rulers of these countries, however, agreed to participate in an anti-Turkish alliance only on condition that they could thereby resolve certain internal conflicts. The Roman Curia allocated funds, hoping to bring the Eastern world into its sphere of influence through the union of churches, solemnly proclaimed in Florence in 1439. The Venetians preferred trading with the Turks to making war on them and were willing to engage in open fighting with them only when it became obvious that Osmanli expansion would destroy their remaining positions in the Levant. The Aragonese of Naples, like their predecessors the Angevins, still believed in the possibility of consolidation in the Balkan Peninsula and the eastern Mediterranean. For the dukes of Milan and Burgundy, these eastern regions were a distant world. They had no real grasp of what was happening there, believed in the facile achievement of a crusade, and assigned insignificant forces and resources for various undertakings. The burden of the war devolved in substantial part on Hungary, where responsible persons were frequently given to underestimating the danger and overestimating their own forces. Distracted by internal conflicts and deceived by passing success in fighting the Turks, they rushed headlong and heedlessly into disaster.

Even before the great sultan Mehmed II, known as El Fatih (the Conqueror), took power in Turkey, the Serbian despotate had become the booty of the invaders. The efforts of Djuradj Branković to improve ties with the Porte achieved nothing, as the Turks considered his despotate a temporary contrivance, destined to last only until the first big clash with the Hungarians. When, immediately after the death of King Sigismund, Murad II mounted an expedition against the Danubian region, he was resolved first to subjugate Serbia and secure a dependable rear for his fighting men before launching new operations. After two years of fighting, by 1439 the Turks had brought all the Serbian lands and towns to heel except Novo Brdo, which surrendered in 1441.

The Double Vassalage of the Serbian Despotate

Despot Djuradj Branković took refuge in Hungary. He seems to have believed in the possibility of profiting from dynastic conflicts there to secure the Hungarian throne for his son. Later, he went to Zeta and from there endeavored to raise an insurrection in Serbia with the help of two of his sons, to whom the sultan had ceded power in the old Branković lands in order to win them over. The Turks discovered the plot and demanded that the despot surrender himself. Uneasy even among his closest associates, the despot had to return to Hungary. To prevent the Bosnian lord Stefan Vukčić-Kosača, long under the sultan's patronage, from taking possession of all Zeta, the despot naïvely and gullibly entrusted its remnants, largely the coastal towns, to the Venetians to look after and protect.

In Hungary he joined in the preparations to attack Turkish territory. The effort proved to be justified, for the "great war" waged in 1443 by numerous Hungarian, Serbian, Polish, and German fighting men enabled Djuradj to restore his despotate. With no particular difficulty, moving via Belgrade and Niš, the Christian army penetrated deep into Bulgaria, from which it withdrew as victor, in fear of hunger and winter. The resulting enthusiasm gave impulse to many anti-Turkish actions. For example, Djuradj Castrioti, the son of a minor Albanian landowner and a convert to Islam, had served in the Turkish army, where he was known as Scanderbeg; at this time he abandoned the sultan, made his way to the fortress of Kruya in Albania, rid the country of Turkish garrisons, and launched a struggle against his former master in which he persisted, under the most grueling circumstances, until his death. The Turks realized the time was not yet ripe for their great offensive.

The sultan offered the Hungarian king Vladislas I a ten-year truce, and the Serbian despot the restoration of power in his lost lands. Djuradj Branković then received from the Turks a number of townships previously held by Turkish garrisons, renewed his former obligations to the sultan, and left the anti-Turkish coalition.

But both he and the entire country found themselves in straitened circumstances, as the Hungarian king first accepted the proffered truce and ratified the treaty (the Peace of Szeged, 1444) only to violate it almost immediately and take an army to the Black Sea coast, where he was to be met by the Christian fleet. The same year, the Turks had no difficulty in routing his small force at Varna. The Hungarian king and the papal legate lost their lives on the battlefield. The Turkish-Hungarian clashes continued, frequently on Serbian soil, working great suffering upon the population although its lord was not at war with either side. His own forces were being spent in war with the Venetians over the Zeta towns, and with the Bosnian king over Srebrenica.

The balance between Turkish and Hungarian forces was upset when Mehmed II assumed the throne in 1451. The new sultan was quick to undertake fresh offensives. In 1453 alarm in Europe grew at the news that he had stormed and captured Constantinople. The small Italian states agreed to drop hostilities, and two German states councils gave consideration to the Turkish threat. But no action was taken, for each of the Italian rulers sought means of concluding individual agreements with the sultan, while the German princes simply chafed under the demands of the emperor and pope for financial assistance. All of them were lulled by the unrealistic hope that Turkish power would be stopped by the lords of Karamania, the Crimean Tatars, or the grand prince of Moscow. No one even dreamed of helping the Balkan states.

Temporary and Final Collapse of the Serbian Despotate

Disregarding the fact that the Serbian despot had helped him to conquer Constantinople, the sultan waited only a year to send an army against Serbia. The Turks captured the central regions of the despotate, ravaged the country, and took about 50,000 captives. Again Djuradj Branković had to apply to the Hungarians. But the victory of John Hunyadi over the Turks at Kruševac (1454) came too late, and two small Serbian armies vainly offered resistance at Sitnica and Dubočica. By 1455 the Turks had subjugated most of the country and after protracted bombardment forced Novo Brdo to surrender. True, the succeeding year the defenders of Smederevo inflicted heavy losses on them and Hungarian Belgrade stood up to a siege of many months, but these events, regardless of their repercussions in Europe, held out little promise of a turning point, especially after both John Hunyadi and Djuradj Branković died in 1456. The new Hungarian king, Matthias Corvinus (1458–1490), intervened southward only sporadically, and belatedly, leaving the Turks to pursue their plans unmolested.

In what remained of Serbia, the descendants of Djuradj Branković and the great magnates fell to quarreling. Some believed that they could preserve the remnants of their power in the devastated land only if they relied on Hungary, whereas others demanded the unconditional acceptance of Turkish authority. The latter were joined by Mara, the daughter of Djuradj, who had spent her youth in the harem of Mehmed's father and enjoyed the respect of the ruthless conquerors. At the height of contention, the pro-Turkish side threw open the gates of Smederevo to a Turkish contingent, which was promptly massacred by the other side. In the ensuing confusion the invaders found it easy to take possession of the country's remnants. Only Smederevo held out. There the friends of Hungary endeavored to unite Serbia and Bosnia by marrying Djuradj's granddaughter to the Bosnian crown prince Stefan Tomašević, in the hope that they would thereby be able to continue resistance. They flung the gates open to Hungarian troops, which did nothing to help, as the Turks, meeting no resistance, entered the city in 1459, and the subjugation of Serbia was complete. Four years later they gained control of Bosnia.

Western and Turkish Influences in Bosnia

Bosnia had long been victimized by internal conflicts and external intervention. Its southeastern districts, where Stefan Vukčić had expanded the Kosača inheritance, gradually withdrew from the state to become an independent region, called Hercegovina, the name derived from the title of the "Herceg (duke) of Saint Sava," which had been assumed by its lord in 1448. As the sultan's vassal and ally, Stefan Vukčić was the enemy of the Bosnian king, particularly when the latter drew closer to Hungary and Christian Europe in the anticipation that under their wing he would be able to withstand Turkish pressure. King Stefan Tomaš (1443–1461) became a Hungarian vassal, was converted to Catholicism, and permitted the Franciscans to construct monasteries in Bosnia and to suppress the Bosnian church. Although many feudal lords followed in his footsteps and although he, too, gave up his skillful maneuvering and turned to persecuting the Patarines, they nevertheless retained strong positions in the country. When necessary, the herceg gave them refuge. The Turks exhausted the country by exacting exorbitant tribute. They also acquired important strongholds, one of which was situated near present-day Sarajevo. From there they plundered and looted, keeping the population in a constant state of insecurity.

The Fall of Bosnia, Hercegovina, and Montenegro

When Stefan Tomaš was succeeded by his son Stefan Tomašević (1461–1463), with the approval of the great magnates, Bosnia finally joined the West. The new king also had the support of the old herceg, Stefan Vukčić, who, disillusioned, had dissociated himself from the Turks and sought sustenance among their Western adversaries. When the king refused to pay tribute to the sultan, the latter sent an expedition to Bosnia in 1463. The anticipated help from the West failed to materialize, and the resistance of local forces was not strong enough to stop Mehmed II. Vainly the king sought to flee. Captured at Ključ on the Sana River, he ordered the towns to surrender, expecting to save his own life by this gesture. But the Turks put him to death along with the most prominent nobles who surrendered to them during their inexorable progress. Herceg Stefan Vukčić alone withstood their attacks in his own region. After he had lost most of it in a new Turkish onslaught, he withdrew to the town of Novi. There his son held out until the end of 1481, when he had to abandon Novi under siege by the local Turkish army.

Only in Zeta did the local lords of Montenegro continue to hang on. These were the Crnojevićs, the original masters of the mountainous area rising above Boka Kotorska, where they alternated between cooperation with or opposition to the Balšićs and the Serbian despots. While Djuradj Branković was at war with the Venetians, Stefan Crnojević joined the Republic of Venice, quelled in blood the revolt of the peasants allied with Djuradj in the vicinity of Kotor (1452), and then defeated the despot's army that arrived in Zeta to do battle with the Venetians. The Turks were putting pressure on the despotate; one of their commanders gained control over the Medun Fortress in Zeta. From that time onward, Stefan Crnojević as a Venetian "captain" beat off Turkish attacks. His son and heir Ivan, dissatisfied with Venetian policy, drew aloof from the Republic and started paying tribute to the sultan, only to return to the fold of

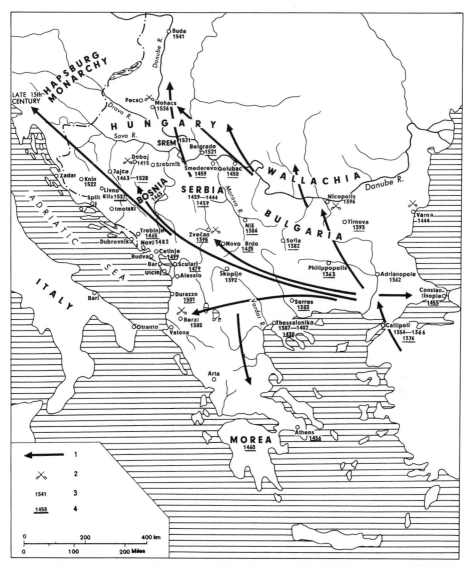

MAP 18.   Turkish advances and conquests. (1) The directions of Turkish advancement; (2) localities
of important battles; (3) year of temporary conquest; (4) year of permanent conquest.

Venice and give it valuable assistance during the two sieges of Scutari. When the
Venetians concluded peace with the Porte and surrendered Scutari to the Turks
(1479), Ivan had to take refuge in Italy.

The Balkans began to seethe after the death of Mehmed II in 1481.
Hungarian troops raided Bosnia, the Albanian chieftains returned to continue

the battle, and Ivan Crnojević came back to his native land. There he remained, as the sultan was satisfied with the restoration of the vassal relationship between them. Headquarters were transferred to Cetinje, a tiny village high up in the mountains, where he commissioned a monastery consecrated to the Birth of the Virgin, the new see of the metropolitans of Zeta. Ivan's son Djuradj distinguished himself during his brief reign by establishing the first Cyrillic alphabet printing press in the South Slav lands. Owing to his political connections with the sultan's opponents, he was forced to leave Montenegro in 1496. With his departure, the last ray of a free life and of the power of local feudal lords was extinguished in the Montenegrin mountains.

Turkish Assaults on Croatian and Slovene Lands

The Hungarian boundary had long been subject to attack by the Turks. In spite of this situation, the court in Budapest still failed to pay sufficient attention to the danger threatening from the south. It was only after the collapse of Bosnia that King Matthias conquered its northern districts and set up two boundary banovinas with headquarters in Jajce and Srebrnik. The Danubian fleet and the frontier army in southern Hungary had been reinforced by Serbs who had taken refuge in those areas. Desirous of winning even greater loyalty from these new settlers and of persuading them to defend the boundary with their very lives, King Matthias bestowed the title of despot and extensive lands on one of the descendants of Djuradj Branković. He and his successors participated in Hungarian assaults on Turkish territory, and when their line died out, their functions and title were acquired by a Croatian landowning family. Since the days of King Sigismund, there had been two "camps" of local militia in the Croatian regions. They were supplemented by a special "captainship" established in Senj (1469) but this defense system was too weak to withstand Turkish raids.

Plundering detachments of Turks started their attacks in 1468. These were repeated year in and year out, and stopped only during periods of truce. The directions of attack were across the Sava and Danube Rivers toward Slavonia and southern Hungary on the one hand, and on the other from Bosnia toward Croatia and Dalmatia. Roughly forty-five Turkish assaults against Slovene provinces were recorded between 1469 and 1526, sometimes as many as four in the course of a single year. During the Turkish-Venetian wars (1463–1479, 1499–1503), Turkish forces made incursions into Dalmatia, Istria, and Friuli, returning with rich loot and large numbers of captives. Leaving devastation in their wake, they were described by a chronicler, not without reason, as "destroying the Croats."

From time to time, the Croatian army succeeded in making short shrift of Turkish detachments returning from their raids and bearing booty, but in

1493 it suffered total defeat. It was then that the pasha of Bosnia, returning from Styria with his troops raised in Serbia, Bosnia, and Eastern Rumelia, plundered Croatian lands as well. The newly appointed ban, Emerik Derenčin, met the Turks at Udbina, with his warriors from Slavonia and Croatia and a multitude of poorly equipped peasants. Despite fierce resistance, the Turks won the day at Krbava Field. The ban was captured, and the flower of the old Croatian nobility was shattered. This battle, remembered in history as the "Croatian defeat," brought the Turks no territorial conquest but left a large area defenseless. The onslaught undertaken by the Hungarians against Serbia and Bulgaria did not alter the situation. Clashes continued, only to demonstrate that not a single foot of land could be taken from the sultan, although no large-scale Turkish armies appeared on European soil after the siege of Scutari (1479) and the great offensives undertaken by Suleiman II the Lawmaker against Central Europe.

The Background of Turkish Successes

During this period, the Turks were winding up their conquests in the East while Hungary catapulted toward total disaster. Furthermore, the country was rent asunder by strife between domestic landlords and foreigners, between church and citizenry. Resources for defense fell off noticeably. The French sovereign persuaded the Porte to launch an attack on Central Europe, not in order to break the already weak state of Hungary but to strike a blow at his most dangerous rivals, the Hapsburgs. The Polish king had no thought of rescuing the country governed by his kin, but on the contrary was happy to conclude peace with the sultan. In the interval of a few months, Suleiman's forces smashed the Hungarian defense system by taking Belgrade, Šabac, and Zemun (1521), followed by the Croatian towns of Skradin, Knin (1522), Ostrovica (1523), and Sinj (1524). Then the sultan moved a large army against the Danubian region (1526), charging and capturing Petrovaradin on the Danube and Osijek on the Drava and bringing total defeat upon the Hungarian army, reinforced by Serbian and Croatian detachments, at Mohács. Following this, he laid Buda waste, but he did not subjugate Hungary, well aware that it would finish itself off through internal strife. From experience, he knew this would be the best way to bring the country to its knees.

Some time before Turkish expansion reached its zenith, the majority of Yugoslavs found themselves under the sultan's power. But conflict between the two irreconcilable worlds, the Islamic and the Christian, was not the sole feature of the century and a half under consideration. Conquests were also accompanied by inevitable cooperation and mutual influences. The sultan's tributaries furthered Turkish victories with money and influence and by supplying the Turks

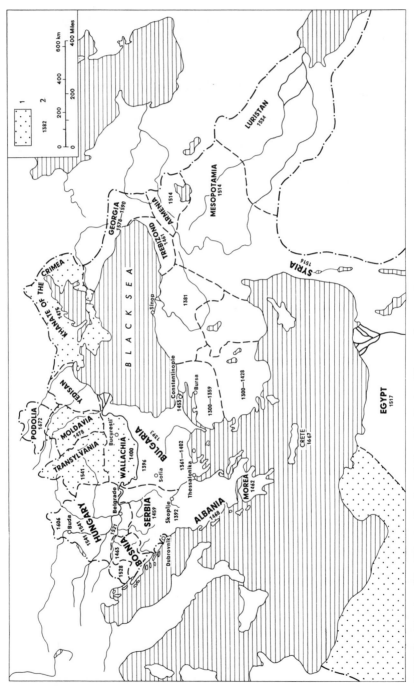

MAP 19.   The rise of the Ottoman Empire. (1) Vassal territories; (2) year of conquest.

with reinforcements; through their fiscal and paramilitary obligations, the subject peoples were also instrumental in helping the Turks. The Balkan rank and file, primarily the peasants, suffered horribly from the creation of a no-man's-land around the Turkish borders and from the conflicts between the lords. They therefore frequently welcomed Turkish administration as an emancipation from their poverty and misfortunes. The last Bosnian sovereign told the pope that by treating the peasants well, the Turks had succeeded in winning them away from their own rulers and nobles with promises of a better life. And indeed, the areas of which the Turks had taken possession did enjoy a period of temporary relaxation, for people no longer had to worry about keeping body and soul together or to trouble themselves about the uncertainties of the future. And all those who were converted to Islam and thereby accepted the new authority found the doors to the highest posts open to them, regardless of their previous position in society. On the other hand, the plundering, the raids, and the conquests had left economic chaos in their wake, breaking the established frameworks of the Balkan states, destroying the social and political order, and provoking major demographic changes. In a word, they changed the historical course of the Yugoslav peoples and introduced new elements of cultural and spiritual orientation.

Part Two

LIFE AND STRUGGLE
WITHIN
THE GREAT EMPIRES

The South Slav peoples found themselves from the sixteenth to the eighteenth century under the authority of two great empires, the Ottomans and the Hapsburgs. The Adriatic coast was held for most of the period from the first half of the fifteenth century by the Venetian Republic. After the uninterrupted expansion of the Ottoman power, the western states launched themselves into a counteroffensive. The wars in the course of the seventeenth and eighteenth centuries reduced the Turkish territory. The Ottoman Empire faced an internal crisis, which seriously threatened its very survival in the Balkan Peninsula and ushered in the Eastern Question.

The expansion and later the contraction of the Ottoman Empire on the soil of present-day Yugoslavia brought about significant demographic dislocations. The Serbian people settled a great area in southern Hungary, Slavonia, western Bosnia, Croatia, and Dalmatia; the Croatian people, retreating before the Ottoman advance, drew back to the west and north, and then after Christian victories they returned into the regions wrenched away from the sultan. This movement broke up ethnic concentrations, brought about crisscrossed ethnic boundaries, and caused considerable changes in the territorial extent of different dialects.

In the wars between the great powers the local inhabitants found themselves included in the Turkish, Hapsburg, or Venetian defense systems. In the military border marches which were organized by the Hapsburgs on the soil of Croatia and Slavonia, the soldiers were chiefly Serbs, commanded by Germans, but financed by the estates of the Slovenian crownlands. The crisis of the Ottoman system brought about great pressure on the Christian populace under the authority of the sultan and provoked, besides flight and migration, internal movements of resistance, the ever-present haiduks, and the turning for aid toward the Western powers. These negotiations were now and then participated in by the patriarchate at Peć, which had been reestablished with the agreement of the Porte in the fifteenth century, and which had gathered under its authority the Serbian people throughout great stretches of the Balkan Peninsula and Central Europe. In the anti-Turkish struggle the independent Montenegrins also participated under the authority of their own local vladika (bishop). Under the Hapsburgs, meanwhile, popular dissatisfaction brought about peasant uprisings, while the centralizing policy of the Vienna court provoked the resistance of the Croatian nobility, which through its own institutions strove to maintain its own state sovereignty.

The political and social changes influenced the cultural and religious course of development. Accompanying the Turkish conquest was the process of Islamization of the local inhabitants, chiefly in Bosnia. The towns in the Turkish regions acquired Eastern appearance with great emphasis on different ethnic groupings, each living in its own separate mahala (quarter). The development of Islamic culture also made its influence felt among Christians in speech, attitudes, and daily customs. The raya (subjected peasants) retained their patriarchal culture and firmly stuck to their own customs, church holidays, and oral folklore, which transmitted their deeply rooted view of life and moral values. The Serbian church continued to preserve art and literature in the spirit of the petrified medieval tradition. In regions under the authority of the Christian states, reverberations of the religious and cultural movements of Western Europe were felt. In Dalmatia, especially in Dubrovnik, whose inhabitants lived freely as Turkish tribute payers, there blossomed a renaissance of literature and art. The Slovenian lands, and also to some extent the Croatian lands, were gripped by the wave of Protestantism; this was quickly beaten back by the strict measures of the Hapsburgs, who were closely connected with the Catholic Counter-Reformation. Then in all these regions the style and tastes of the baroque flourished. At the same time the works of writers, whether in foreign or in native languages, began to excite thoughts about the broader Slavic world and their unfortunate fate under foreign rulers.

CHAPTER 12

The Yugoslav Peoples under the Hapsburg Monarchy and the Republic of Venice

The Emergence of the Hapsburg Monarchy

While the Turks were occupied raiding Hungary, conditions had already ripened for the establishment of an extensive Danubian monarchy as a counterpoise to the Ottoman Empire. What Matthias Corvinus failed to accomplish in the fifteenth century was achieved by his rivals, the Hapsburgs, in the German, Slovene, and Hungarian lands.

Formerly petty princes, who occasionally acceded to the throne of the Holy Roman Empire, they had gained control of vast regions in Europe and parts of America by the beginning of the sixteenth century. Through their marital

142

ties, their house acquired the larger part of the lands of the Burgundian inheritance, and took the Spanish throne and with it control of southern Italy and Sicily, as well as the Spanish colonies in America. It was truly an empire upon which "the sun never set." Charles V, ruler of Spain from 1516 and Holy Roman emperor from 1519, conceded the Austrian lands to his brother Ferdinand I, who became the founder of the Austrian branch of the powerful house of Hapsburg and of the mighty Danubian monarchy.

The Crises and Collapse of Hungary (1526)

Ferdinand's star began to rise after the Battle of Mohács. Invoking ties of marriage and an earlier treaty, he claimed the right to rule all lands under the Hungarian crown. Only a section of the Hungarian nobles consented to his demands, although he offered them extensive holdings in return for their support. The majority, consisting mostly of lesser nobles, chose the duke of Transylvania, John Zápolya, a wealthy landowner, for their king in November 1526. Slavonia also bowed to his rule. After protracted negotiations, the Croatian nobles, few in number, elected Ferdinand I king at an assembly in Cetingrad, on January 1, 1527, won over by his promise to defend the country from the Turks. The Serbs living in southern Hungary also upheld Ferdinand.

After the Turkish incursions, Bačka was so thoroughly devastated that the big Hungarian landowners abandoned their possessions there. Among them was Jovan Nenada, a man of uncertain origin, styled the "Emperor" and the "Black One," who rallied the Serbian peasants to his banner. Nenada held out the promise of liberating Serbia and gained popularity by apportioning land and livestock to the peasants. He joined Zápolya until Ferdinand lured him over with gifts and guile. Both pretenders fought for his allegiance, for the peasant controlled an army of some 15,000 strong at a time when even Ferdinand could not muster more than 10,000 fighting men and Zápolya hardly 3,000. The Black One triumphed over the forces of the Hungarian magnates sent into the field against him by Zápolya, only to be slain in an ambush. The peasant army disintegrated, and Ferdinand found a new ally in Pavle Bakić. Arriving from Serbia in 1525 with a large number of his compatriots, Bakić had fought with them at Mohács, initially throwing his support to Zápolya. Then joining Ferdinand, he and his men did battle along all the fronts where the Hapsburgs clashed with the Turks.

The Turkish Offensive against Central Europe

The sultan backed Zápolya in the conviction that the Hapsburgs were the more dangerous rivals. As his ally, he laid siege to Vienna in 1529. But the town walls, defended by about 18,000 men, withstood the attack. In a fresh attempt three years later, the Turks were stopped by a small garrison in the Hungarian town of Kiszeg commanded by Nikola Jurišić of Senj. Later, instead of undertaking massive attacks, the Turks slowly captured one town after another in Slavonia, moving their boundary with Croatia and Dalmatia all the way to Karlobag, at the foot of the Velebit massif, finally to celebrate the year 1537 with a double victory. The Austrian army, which included Bakić's detachments, was smashed at Gorjane, and Turkish authority was firmly established over most of Slavonia. In Dalmatia they captured the fortress of Klis, towering over Split, where refugees (known as Uskoks) from the subjugated areas had gathered and warded off attacks for decades. The Uskoks then took off for Senj, where they organized a new center of resistance. Boundary skirmishes and small-scale attacks did nothing to alter the established frontier with Croatia, reduced to the "remnants of the remnants" *(reliquiae reliquiarum)*, as it was then called. By a new thrust into the heart of Hungary, the Turks captured Budapest (1541), extending control into Slavonia and taking possession of the Banat. After these changes, Hungary was divided into three parts: the Hapsburg possessions in the west, the Turkish in the middle, and Transylvania in the east. Most of the Yugoslav lands swore allegiance to the sultan. Even the Republic of Dubrovnik, which had preserved its independence, paid tribute to the Porte as agreed upon in the fifteenth century. In the mid-sixteenth century, the Ottoman Empire was at the zenith of its power. Then began the descent.

The Turkish attack on Malta brought no reward, and the thirteenth assault on the Danubian region ended in a truce. True, in 1566 the Turks did take Szigetvar in the Hapsburg part of Hungary, a town defended by a small garrison led by Nikola Zrinski, former Croatian-Slavonian-Dalmatian ban. During the final charge, the garrison was wiped out but not before it had left 20,000 Janissaries dead in the field. Gravely ill, Suleiman died in his tent. His heir was satisfied with an annual tribute of 30,000 ducats as compensation for the cessation of hostilities. In the Cyprus War (1570–1573) the Venetians lost their large island in the eastern Mediterranean to the Turks. Nonetheless, the victory of the Christian fleet at Lepanto, in Greece (1571), demonstrated that the powerful adversary was not invincible. Even then, the Ottoman Empire displayed signs of internal crisis. In the meantime, the Hapsburg monarchy waxed strong and continued constructing a powerful defense system.

The Defense System of the Slovene Provinces

In accordance with an obligation to the Croatian nobles given before the decisions taken at Cetingrad, Ferdinand I was to provide for the upkeep of 200 infantrymen and 1,000 cavalrymen, 800 of whom were to be commanded by local men, for purposes of defending the Croatian region. Ferdinand took over direct command of only two captainships, with headquarters at Senj and Bihać. The Croatian nobles reaped very little income from the territory of Croatia and Slavonia, which had been diminished and ravaged, and so they were more than content to allow the king to assume command over the remaining frontier captainships. However, even his revenues from war levies in the mid-sixteenth century covered hardly 1 percent of expenditures for defense, and court coffers were more often empty than full. Consequently, in the second half of the six-teenth century, the boundary defense system was made to depend on the financial resources and manpower of the Slovene provinces of Carniola, Carinthia, and Styria.

In places, these provinces were a bare 15 kilometers from the Turkish frontier and had been forced, as early as the first half of the sixteenth century, to organize their own defenses accordingly. All feudal landowners were under the

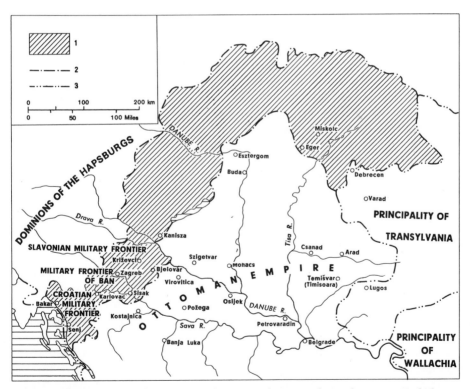

MAP 20.   The "remnants of the remnants" of Croatia and Hungary during the greatest Turkish conquests (second half of the sixteenth century). (1) Free territories of Croatia and Hungary;
(2) the boundaries of Croatia and Hungary; (3) the boundaries of Turkish vassal lands and
Venetian possessions.

obligation to provide the provincial armies with a stipulated number of men and to participate personally in defense. The towns supplied infantrymen and looked after their own security. In case of emergency, the system of "insurrection" was resorted to, that is, the mobilization of the free peasants. This involved every thirtieth, twentieth, and sometimes even tenth or fifth peasant. The peasants set up fortified camps on hills, from which they were able, by a special system of signals, to keep the countryside informed of impending danger.

The Uskoks

Apart from the free peasants, the local defense system also included mercenaries and Uskoks, men who had fled to Hapsburg territory from Turkish frontier areas. These Uskoks, or refugees, are referred to in various terms: Turks, Vlachs, Serbs, Rasciani, Ćići. In occupation, they were usually herdsmen or soldiers, of the Orthodox faith, with a few Catholics, and ethnically speaking descended from the ancient Balkan Romans, Slavicized, and from all those Slavs (Serbs and Croats) who had joined their communities, so that in doing military service they could derive some benefit from the privileged position enjoyed by the Vlachs in Turkey. Still few in number, the Uskoks gathered around Žumberak and Metlika in Carniola, under the leadership of their own captains and army commanders. They were paid salaries, had the right to retain two-thirds of the booty they captured, and enjoyed other prerogatives. The entire system of defense in the Slovene provinces rested under the control of the feudal lords, who also collected revenues for its maintenance. Military expenditures grew apace, from 10,000 forints in 1520 to 550,000 forints in 1578, at a time when taxes for purposes of defense in Croatia and Slavonia netted only 5,000 forints.

The Croatian Military Frontier

When the boundary defenses were linked up in 1553 with the military system of the Slovene provinces, all the frontier military forces were placed under the command of a supreme captain. Later Rudolf II entrusted the supreme command in the Croatian districts and the defense of the frontier to his uncle, Archduke Charles, who was also the provincial prince of Styria, Carinthia, and Carniola. In 1579 Archduke Charles initiated the construction of a town at the confluence of the Korana and Mrežnica Rivers, as the headquarters for the generals of the Croatian Military Frontier. From him it derived its name, Karlovac. The town of Varaždin later became the headquarters of the general of the Slavonian Military Frontier. Along the entire boundary, towns of stone and many wooden fortifications were erected. It was from these that smaller forces struck out to raid Turkish territory, and that scouts gathered information about conditions in Turkish areas, mainly from the Uskoks, who had relatives on the other side. Thus organized, the Military Frontier first delayed and finally stopped Turkish progress altogether.

The Economy of the Croatian and Slovene Lands under the Hapsburgs

The creation of the Hapsburg monarchy, which assumed the task of preventing Turkey's expansion and suppressing Protestantism, was attended by gradual centralization and growing bureaucracy in internal administration. The Hapsburgs entrusted finances to paid officials, set up central administrations to assure the sovereign a decisive role in administering the country and to smash the power of the feudal forces whose strongholds were the provincial assemblies of their estate.

These changes were applicable only to the Hapsburg crownlands. The Croatian lands were in a different position. The Croatian and Slavonian nobility, as masters of territories incorporated into Hungary, accepted rule by the Hapsburgs. They maintained only formal ties with the Hapsburg part of Hungary, while accentuating the significance and role of the institutions they had preserved as the keepers of their own independence. These were the assemblies, both Croatian and Slavonian, which merged into a single body at the close of the sixteenth century, and the two bans, whose functions were also fused and discharged by one person. The influence of the ban, who maintained ties with the king through the court offices of Hungary which moved to Vienna in 1531, began to wane the moment that military matters were transferred to the Royal Military Council in Vienna. His revenues were insignificant, his military forces small (only the Zrinski family was capable of raising more than 400 fighting men), and he could not retain that part of the boundary that was under his command, known as the "Ban's Frontier," from Ivanić to Karlovac. Once the Military Frontier was established, he lost control over a considerable part of the already-decimated Croatian territory. The upshot was the eruption of a conflict between the Viennese court and Croatian nobility which was exacerbated in the course of the seventeenth century.

Social Changes

Two factors acted to influence economic life and social relations in the countries under Hapsburg rule: the Turkish menace and the beginning of the development of capitalism in Central Europe. The threat of Turkey made it necessary to allocate large sums for defense, which bore down increasingly hard on those sections of society that created wealth but enjoyed no privileges in a state ruled by the nobility. The penetration of early capitalist relations, particularly in the lands of Slovenia, opened the doors to foreign, and especially German, commercial societies which subordinated domestic production to their own business interests. Their role was most prominent in mining, metallurgy, and foreign trade.

In the Croatian lands, hardest hit by Turkish expansion, mineral wealth was exploited but little. The Zrinski family owned iron and lead mines in Gvozdansko, but knowledge of them is scanty. In the Slovene provinces mining had been developing steadily since the fourteenth century. The improvement of metallurgy ran parallel with the exploitation of the mines. In number of smelters and in terms of techniques (the utilization of running water for power) mining reached its peak at the turn of the sixteenth century, particularly in Carniola. Iron, lead, mercury, and, from the sixteenth century, copper were produced for domestic needs and for export. Citizens, who also traded in metal, owned the mines and smelters. The peasants were employed in the mines and thus escaped dependence on the feudal lords. The mine in Idrija, which yielded about 50 tons of mercury and cinnabar, eventually grew into the largest enterprise. Traders turned a large profit, as did the provincial prince from his regalia, or royal rights and prerogatives. However, domestic traders, lacking resources, could not withstand the competition of foreign trading companies on the European market. Receding before them, in the end they had to turn their own mine shares over to them. In 1575 Archduke Charles became the sole mineowner in Idrija. A small number of manufacturing plants were also set up, where the hired laborers produced cannon balls, paper, beer, and glassware. Here, too, foreign capital was quick to appear. The house of Fugger constructed a copper refinery at Podklošter and thereby won for itself a place of paramount importance in foreign trade.

Situated between Central Europe and Italy, the lands of Croatia and Slovenia were important only as transit points in European trade. Apart from this, they exported agricultural produce (grains, livestock), and the Slovene provinces exported considerable quantities of metals. Imports consisted largely of textiles, foodstuffs, and luxury articles. As Turkey expanded, the Croatian lands lost their main arteries of communication and the volume of foreign trade diminished. The first to be abandoned was the road running along the Una Valley, and then the one to Senj, via Gorski Kotar. Ties with the outside world could be maintained only through the Slovene provinces, whose role in international trade was growing. But the local merchants failed to profit from the house of Fugger the trade in copper and lead, and the peasants retained control over trading in agricultural products. After the expulsion of Jews, foreigners also acquired the credit business. In Croatia foreigners had long been omnipotent, supplying the army and raising prices at will.

This state of affairs forced the guilds to take more stringent measures to defend themselves from the competition of the villages, the manufacturers, and foreign traders. The citizens thus found themselves in the same position as the feudal landlords, whose support they won in the fight for municipal self-government. Together they resisted the provincial prince, who posed a threat to both. He not only tried to make guild representatives his obedient servants, but encroached upon municipal rights while throwing his weight behind the foreign merchants. The role of the town population in Croatia was negligible. It was virtually pauperized in the remnants of Slavonia, a stone's throw from the Turkish frontier. In the royal towns all power resided in the hands of the few patricians, and in those towns that depended on the feudal landlords, the formerly free citizens (burghers) became serfs. In the interior they looked largely to livestock raising for a livelihood, and along the coast to fishing and salt production.

Even more profound changes took place in the social structure of Croatian lands. Districts fallen to the Turks were stripped of their nobility, who fled to the "relics of relics" of the kingdom. Owning no land there, they were quickly impoverished unless the king took them into service. Only the most powerful were able to keep their heads above water. The greatest among these few was the Zrinski family, which acquired large possessions between the Adriatic Sea and the Mura River, at the expense of landowning families that had died out or succumbed to poverty. True, the Hapsburgs created the nucleus of a new nobility by assigning coats of arms to freemen (townspeople and foreigners), but their rights as nobles were recognized only if and when they acquired the land of other noblemen. Formerly, particularly in the watershed of the Una River, "communes of nobles" had once existed with their own judiciary, self-government, and fortresses that were part of the royal defense system. These lesser nobles could not withstand the onslaught of the Turks. In unsubjugated areas they had to subordinate themselves to the magnates and undertake obligations of corvée (various forms of personal labor), so that, in fact, they lost their privileges and freedom.

Peasant Movements

But it was the Croatian and Slovene peasantry who suffered the most. Under the impact of capitalist economy, a great differentiation in terms of landownership took place among the peasants of the Slovene provinces, beginning in the mid-fifteenth century, and many were no longer able to eke a livelihood from their land. Those who were better off waxed prosperous by trading and endeavored to throw off the yoke of feudal dependence. Their masters, the landowners with their insignificant incomes from land rent paid in money which steadily lost value, forced them out of the trading business, raised and multiplied their levies, and demanded agricultural produce and personal labor in place of rent. The state increased taxes and in 1475 also levied a special tax for defense from the Turks. Under pressure from landlords, church, and state, the peasants threatened to move elsewhere. First they formed alliances to protect themselves from the provincial prince and then, from 1478 onwards, raised insurrections, demanding the "old rights," which meant restoration of the obligations that had been in force up to the middle of the fifteenth century. A revolt of large dimensions flared up in 1515 in all Slovene provinces. About 80,000 rebels attacked and took possession of castles in the hope that Emperor Maximilian I would keep his promise to uphold their demands. Although numerous, the insurgents had many shortcomings in their organization. They tended to act individually, lacked cavalry, and were not prepared for attack but only for defense from the Turks. Consequently, as soon as they had gathered their forces, the provincial nobles were able to defeat them over a broad area, and to quell their insurrection by the cruelest of measures. But the uprising was of paramount significance, for, after six centuries spent under alien rule, the Slovenes had begun to take independent political action. Their fight for social justice paved the way for the formation of the Slovene nation. The revolt itself did not, however, repair the position of the peasants. Fiscal levies burgeoned, and peasants were forced to pay high prices for their own patrimony. The result was revolt. It was with good reason that they joined the great peasant uprisings in Croatia in the second half of the sixteenth century.

The lot of the Croatian peasants worsened after the death of Matthias Corvinus, whose memory was revered by them for his suppression of the arrogant landlords. Toward the end of the fifteenth and in the first few decades of the sixteenth century, no one questioned the right of the landlords to demand greater corvee from their subjects and to restrict their right to dispose of their own patrimony as they saw fit. But there were still no peasant movements even after the consequences began to be felt of the Dozsa Uprising in southern Hungary (1514), in which many Serbs were involved, besides Hungarians. After the revolt had been put down, the Hungarian Diet adopted the laws *(tripartitum)* proposed by Istvan Werböczy, acting to the detriment of the dependent peasantry and including a ban on the serfs that forbade them to change masters of their own free will. The Hungarian and Croatian nobles managed to retain the Werböczy laws, as the principal pillar of their class privileges, until 1848. The position of the Croatian peasant failed to improve even after the lifting of the ban on changing masters (1538), for everywhere he met increased corvée, new levies, taxes payable in money, fines, imprisonment, and sentences involving flogging handed down by the landlords' courts. For in the lands of Croatia, as in those of Slovenia, the burden on the peasants increased, owing partially to Turkish penetration. Huge resources were needed to organize defense. Discontent was bred among the more prosperous peasants by the fact that the citizens and landlords were squeezing them out of commercial affairs. Many therefore solved their problems by joining the emperor's frontier forces.

The "tyranny of the lords" and the exceptionally grueling conditions on the lands belonging to Franjo Tahi, in the vicinity of Zagreb, provoked a major uprising. In April 1572 the peasants took Donja Stubica, one of the two towns over possession of which Tahi contested the claims of the local landowners. At year's end, the peasants rose also on his lands south of Ptuj, in Slovenia. As the Croatian landlords were not able to pacify the peasants, the emperor had to promise to investigate the situation. Believing in "imperial justice," all those who were dissatisfied with the feudal order joined the insurgents. From these local revolts grew a broad movement with an organized army and courts. A Croatian peasant, Matija Gubec,[1] headed the rebellion. Armed actions were initiated at the end of January 1573, but they were short-lived. One detachment advanced in the direction of Styria. When danger ran high, the nobles gathered their forces, and by February 9 they smashed the insurgents, who were poorly armed and lacked cavalry. Their revenge was savage: the peasants were massacred, their homes leveled with the ground, and the leaders, including Matija Gubec, put to death. These sacrifices did nothing to improve the peasants' lot. The Hapsburgs continued to curtail the power of the landlords, separatist in their leanings, so as to consolidate the central authority and weld the disunited feudal forces together. Under the circumstances, the peasants could not become the allies of the ruler, except as fighting men in the field.

Venetian Dalmatia

Internal development differed in the coastal region, ruled by the Republic of Venice. Territorially, its fortunes fluctuated, depending on the outcome of the various Turco-Venetian wars. In the towns Venice retained the patrician order, developed in the Middle Ages, and the ancient communal system. Each town and surrounding district remained an entity. Life was regulated by the provisions of statutes that had changed but insignificantly; economic opportunities were few and minor everyday problems many. The commune was administered by the *conte*, or podesta; the fortress was guarded by mercenaries, all of them under the control of the Venetian Senate and its auxiliary organs. The towns in Zeta, Dalmatia, and Istria fell upon hard days, languishing in poverty and burdened by the obligation to build fortresses and complete public buildings initiated earlier. Educated individuals persisted in their literary endeavors to enrich their microcosmic environment and to dispel their own boredom. The population made its living from fishing, cultivating land not very fit for agriculture, and petty trading along the Adriatic coast, subject to the Venetian system of restrictions.

The peasant, completely subordinated to the control of the communal

---

[1] The name Matija is not found in historical sources from the time of the uprising. Presumably it derives from popular legends about the peasant leader. However, mention is made of the name Ambroz.

authorities, found himself in the position of a *colonus* (tenant-laborer), the relatively free tiller of land belonging to others. In the towns, weakly bound together since the late sixteenth century by a special regent in Zadar, ancient strife smoldered and sometimes flared up between the landlords and townspeople over participation in the administration of the municipality. Bloody clashes erupted on the island of Hvar, their repercussions affecting other towns. In 1510, plebeians led by Matija Ivanić entered the town of Hvar, killed a number of landlords, and gained control of the entire island. The Venetians maintained power with small forces, in their reliance on the antagonism between nobles and plebeians. Meeting certain plebeian demands, they curtailed municipal autonomy, meaning the influence of the patricians, who were in power in name alone, alongside the Venetian "rector." In the Hvar uprising, the Venetians acted as mediators and intermediaries, but when mediation failed to produce results, the Venetian military commander restored order by banishing 65 plebeians. A fresh insurrection compelled him to abandon the island, and in 1514 the plebeians massacred the landlords. It was only then that the Venetian fleet intervened to smash the revolt by force.

Although the Republic, in encroaching upon the autonomous rights of the nobles, drew support from the plebeians, it did not permit any deep-rooted change in the old order for fear of undesirable upheavals. Only by safeguarding the peace and creating confidence in the "justice" dispensed by its functionaries and organs in the metropolis could it maintain itself in an area of overwhelming strategic and commercial significance in its maritime system.

SERBIAN DESPOTS IN HUNGARY

Vuk Branković, Despot (1465–1485)

Djuradj Branković, Despot (1486–1493), as monk Maxim from 1497

Jovan Branković, Despot (1493–1502)

Ivaniš Berislavić, of Trogir descent, Despot (1502–1514)

Stjepan Berislavić, Despot (1514–1535)

Pavle Bakić, immigrant from Serbia, Despot (1537)

KINGS OF HUNGARY AND CROATIA

Dynasty Hapsburg

Ferdinand I (1527–1564)
Maximilian II (1564–1576)
Rudolf II (1576–1608)
Matthias (1608–1619)
Ferdinand II (1619–1637)

Ferdinand III (1637–1657)
Leopold I (1657–1705)
Joseph I (1705–1711)
Karl VI (1711–1740)
Maria Theresa (1740–1780)

Dynasty Hapsburg-Lothringen

Joseph II (1780–1790)   Ferdinand I (1835–1848)
Leopold II (1790–1792)   Franz Joseph (1848–1916)
Franz II (1792–1835)   Karl I (1916–1918)

CHAPTER 13

Cultural and Religious Movements

Humanism in the Coastal Areas

The period of Turkish conquests magnified the differentiation in the cultural orientation of the eastern and western parts of Yugoslavia. In the lands under Ottoman rule, the culture of the Orthodox East lived on, preserving the medieval traditions. In the inaccessible mountain areas, isolated from the rest of the world, the patriarchal culture of the folk went its own way. Where large segments of the population had been converted to Islam, the culture associated with that religion struck root. The western areas and the entire Adriatic coast remained responsive to Western European culture and its ideological and religious movements. True, owing to their marginal position and retarded economic development, obstructed by the proximity of the Turkish boundary, they could not keep pace with the sudden cultural and scientific development of the West, but they drew sustenance from it and in a sense merged with it. Several centuries were to pass before the other areas caught up and, in a development parallel with emancipation from Turkish rule, became Europeanized to the extent that they could incorporate their way of life and customs into the Continent's mainstream.

During the fifteenth and sixteenth centuries, the culture and spiritual life of the western districts reflected the profound influence of Italian humanism and the Renaissance, the impact of scientific advancement, the Reformation, and finally the Counter-Reformation through which the Catholic world opposed Protestantism. Humanism and the Renaissance gained ground most rapidly in the towns along the eastern Adriatic coast, whereas the Reformation achieved passing success in the areas gravitating toward Central Europe. Also, the Catholic reaction set in throughout the entire area. All influences were mingled, succeeding each other in literature and science, with humanistic views found among both champions of the Reformation and ardent Catholics. No one could withstand the pressure of the new scientific outlook.

The towns of Dalmatia and Istria were ripe for the acceptance of Renaissance culture and humanistic enlightenment, thanks to their educated citizenry and unbroken ties with Italy. There were no such centers in Croatia and Slavonia, where only individuals stood out from the mass, prelates and secular leaders, educated at universities abroad, most of whom flocked to the court of Matthias Corvinus. Humanistic ideas were spread by nationals and foreigners—teachers, notary publics, chancellors, doctors and pharmacists, traders and diplomats, elders of the church, and Venetian functionaries. Thus the clergy was divested of its role as the sole standard-bearer of culture and the master of spiritual affairs. Libraries were no longer to be found only in monasteries but in the homes of individual citizens who collected both sacred texts and the works of national writers and distinguished humanists. In the fifteenth century, humanist Enlightenment spread throughout the Istrian towns, thence to Zadar, Šibenik, Trogir, Split, Hvar, Dubrovnik, and Kotor. An environment was created in which men of letters could discuss logic, compose verse in Latin, and foster interest in the heritage of antiquity. Wherever there was money for it, teachers were brought in, and municipal schools were established in which Latin was taught to an extent far surpassing the requirements of composing stereotyped commercial documents. Reorganizing education in Dubrovnik, Filip de Diversis made provision during his sojourn in that city (1434–1441) for the teaching of logic, rhetoric, and other humanistic subjects. Tideo Acciarini, a prominent Italian humanist, lectured in Zadar, Split, and Dubrovnik. His compatriot Palladio Fosco dedicated his efforts to developing the school in Zadar at the turn of the sixteenth century. Only in the poorer towns did education remain in the hands of the local clergy.

The advancement of secular schooling engendered new concepts of education. They were formulated by an eminent representative of early humanism from Koper (Capodistria), Peter Paul Vergerius the Elder (1370–1444) in his work *De ingenuis moribus et liberalibus studiis adulescentiae.* His ideas were quick to win acceptance. A merchant of Dubrovnik, Benko Kotruljević, long in the service of the king of Naples, stated in his work *On Trade and the Perfect Trader* (1458) the modern view that knowledge about the world could be gained only through the study of natural sciences, that religion should not provoke conflicts and intolerance nor should it blind people, and that a harmonious human personality could be formed only through education and schooling. "Many of my Dubrovnik friends," he wrote, "upbraid me for teaching my daughters grammar and for requiring them to learn Vergil's verses by rote. I do not do this to make grammarians and orators out of them, but to educate them as intelligent and worthy women."

The mode of life also underwent change. Whereas Chancellor Giovanni da Ravenna de Conversino, having come from Italy, found Dubrovnik boring at the end of the fourteenth century, young men in the succeeding century sang gay and salacious songs in the streets, acted out farces while masked for carnival, danced the tripud (three-step) and reel. Women wore sumptuous apparel, reading was a popular pastime, and voyages were undertaken not only for gain but in the search for new knowledge.

The Development of Literature in the Vernacular

Numerous foreigners and a steadily increasing number of nationals wrote verse and prose, epic, historical, and scientific works in Latin, and also translated classical masterpieces. Later, lyrics, epics, and dramatic literature began to be written in the vernacular, which men of letters called not only Croatian or Slavonic but also Illyrian in the endeavor to revive the ancient roots of their culture. And just as Latin literature, in form and spirit, drew inspiration from classical models (all literary forms were pursued—epics, satires, epigrams, idylls, odes, elegies, and so on) so did literature in the vernacular look to contemporary Italian works, frequently imitating them but also investing them with the atmosphere of the environment from which they emerged, and with motives derived from the life, customs, and traditions of the Slavic inhabitants. In contrast to earlier times, literature in both languages was permeated largely by a secular spirit. Works on religious themes were adapted to the new movements and currents.

Outstanding among the numerous writers in Latin were Ivan Česmički of Slavonia (1434–1472) and Ilija Crijević of Dubrovnik (1463–1520). The former acquired an excellent education in Italy, and climbing the ladder of the church

FIGURE 21.   Sultan Murad I (right) and Sultan Bajazit I (left).

FIGURE 22.   Mosque, Sarajevo.

FIGURE 23.   Mostar.

FIGURE 24.   The bridge on the Drina at Višegrad.

158

hierarchy, he quickly became a Hungarian primate and the most distinguished of the learned group around Matthias Corvinus. His poems were celebrated for their profound feeling and inventiveness, reflecting his fine classical education. He was known to friends and admirers under the Latin name Ianus Pannonius. Ilija Crijević, disciple and admirer of Pomponio Leto, a humanist of Rome, was crowned with the laurel wreath, at the Campidoglio in 1484, for the beauty of his love poems, penned with enviable facility and true poetic fervor. Upon his return to Dubrovnik, he was the center of a group of modern literati and humanist enthusiasts.

Also deserving of mention are Juraj Šišgorić of Šibenik (ca. 1420–1509), whose poems were published in Venice in 1477 (the first Yugoslav incunabulum); Karlo Pučić of Dubrovnik (1461–1552); Damljan Beněsić also of Dubrovnik (1477–1539); and Ludovik Paskvalić of Kotor (1500–1551). In the mid-sixteenth century, the learned formed a circle around Didacus Pyrrhus, actually a Jew, Isaiah Cohen, whose sensitive lyrical verses they found inspiring; banished from his native Portugal, he wandered around Europe, finally to settle in Dubrovnik. All these and other poets in Latin, browsing over classical mythology, writing poems in praise of friends and patrons, giving themselves over to love affairs, were very much involved in life, its contentments, conflicts, and woes. Frequently the perfection of their verses and their excellent Latin betrayed their imitation of classical sources. As in the case of most humanists, this rendered their output artificial and somewhat stale. Writers of epic works, modeled on Vergil's poems, sang chiefly in praise of Christian themes. Prominent among these was Marko Marulić (1450–1524), a citizen of Split who, though thoroughly acquainted with the classics, wrote works of moralizing instruction and Christian didactics. His epic *Davidias* elaborates upon the biblical legend of David. His approach was the same to the story of Judith, "composed in Croatian verse" (1501), a work whose realistic passages are interspersed with prayers and morals.

However, just as Marulić's considerably older contemporary, Juraj Šišgorić, collected popular sayings with great élan, in addition to writing Latin verse, so did Marulić demonstrate his affection for his native land and its people, whose language he poured into metrical molds unknown to folk poetry.

Ilija Crijević of Dubrovnik was carried away by the idea of the spiritual revival of the Roman Empire, and at times he believed that Dubrovnik would become a true colony of Romulus. Although Romance language had once been spoken there, as in other coastal towns, in Crijević's youth only a few elderly persons could have used it. Because of their business ties, the traders knew Italian, but most of the town population spoke Slavonic. Also, the spirit and culture of the new era could be expressed only in the vernacular, as was the case in Italy, where the popular tongue came to prevail over Latin, revived by the humanists, in the belles lettres. The poems written by the young bloods of Dubrovnik and other coastal towns rang with the Slavonic word, present also in the war cries of the Slovene insurgents in 1515.

Poetry and Drama

In the first half of the fifteenth century, an anonymous employee of the Dubrovnik Customs House entered in his ledger a few verses in the Cyrillic alphabet, and in the vernacular, describing his delight at some poems written by young noblemen. At the close of the same century, Crijević's contemporaries Sisko Menčetić and Džore Držić were already composing love songs in the vernacular, in the style of the Italian Petrarchists. In Držić's work the freshness of folk songs shone through the Italian models. A Benedictine monk, Mavro Vetranović (after 1482–1576), residing on a deserted island, composed many verses about the political events of his day and his life of solitude (*Remeta*, or *The Hermit*) with little genuine lyricism and a great deal of moralizing, similar to that found in Marulić's work. He also remained faithful to church tradition in writing on biblical themes, which were no longer to the public taste.

Presumably he realized this and so produced a number of poems for carnival processions. Toward the end of the first half of the sixteenth century, during carnival time and for wedding ceremonies, theatrical pieces of varying content began to be presented in Dubrovnik. The happy-go-lucky theatrical ensembles produced dramas written for them by two national writers; the first, the astronomer Nikola Nalješković (1500–1587), and the second, the greatest representative of Renaissance literature, a poor clergyman, clerk, servant of adventurous voyagers, and finally conspirator, Marin Držić (1508–1567). Besides lyrical poems, the two men composed pastorals. This highly appreciated product of Renaissance literature, with its dreams of an idyllic Arcady, brought to life a world of fairies and shepherds, to the accompaniment of verse, music, and dance. Držić also introduced the element of peasant farce, thus increasing the success of his plays *Tyrrhenia* and *Venus and Adonis*. But it was genuine comedy that lovers of comic situations found most gratifying. A writer of modest talents, Nalješković failed to achieve any notable popularity with his audiences, leaving Marin Držić the undisputed master of the theater. Clashing with the conservative attitudes of ruling circles and the narrow-mindedness of the nobility, Držić strove to depict life as it was. His comedies (*Dundo Maroje*, *The Miser*, *Mande*, and others) occasionally drew their motives from Plautus or Boccaccio, but his greatest value lies in his bringing to life the environment in which he lived, poking fun at the failings of his contemporaries and portraying for audiences such familiar types as the rich merchant, the conceited teacher, the avaricious servant, the sly peasant, and the always clumsy characters unfortunate enough to reside outside the limits of Dubrovnik. Tragedy fared poorly and actually stopped with Držić's retelling of the Italian version of *Hecuba*.

Works for the theater were also produced in the literary circle of Hvar. Nikša Benetović (ca. 1500–1562) composed a carnival play *The Gypsy*, outstanding for its wit and reflectiveness. Hanibal Lucić (1485–1553), who also composed love poems and epistles, wrote a naïvely emotional drama entitled *The Slave Girl*. An organist, Martin Benetović, younger than the other two (d. 1607), left two comedies. In *Hvarkinja (The Woman of Hvar)* the usual love plot is brought to a climax by characters whose behavior and speech abound in local color.

Other coastal writers of the sixteenth century introduced domestic themes into their works, demonstrating their inclination for folk songs and popular legends while abandoning the mythological motifs of antiquity. In an idyllic poem about a three-day fishing venture off the island of Hvar, *Fishing and Fishermen's Conversation* (1556), Petar Hektorović of Hvar (1487–1572) produced three folk songs (known as bugarštice) which his fishermen sang in "the Serbian manner." A nobleman of Zadar, Petar Zoranić, wrote the first national novel in verse and prose, *Planine (The Mountains,* 1536), which reflected a profound malaise at Turkish devastations and Venetian rule along the coast, as well as love for the people and the language spoken by them. Another citizen of Zadar, Brne Karnarutić (1515/20–1572/73) told the epic story of Nikola Zrinski of 1566 in his *Conquest of Szigetvár* (1584). His compatriot, Juraj Baraković (1548–1628), a priest who wrote in Glagolitic, brought to life the past of the environs of Zadar in the poems *Vila Slovinka (The Slav Fairy)* and *Jerula*, deeply national in consciousness. It should be remembered that they had all had more or less humanistic educations and were well acquainted with the humanistic literature of their day. Crijević's ambiguous fantasies were imbued with the lively awareness of belonging to the great Slavic nation, in whose traditions, language, and lore the humanistically reared authors sought creative inspiration.

Scientific and Theological Works

Scientific and theological works were written in Latin. Men of learning had not yet begun to specialize and frequently, besides verse, they also wrote about various spheres of human endeavor. Along with moralistic-philosophical and rather vacuous rhetorical compositions there are found genuinely scientific writings, the result of observation and investigation of natural phenomena. Mathematicians, physicists, astronomers, and physicians, torn between scholastic concepts and natural laws, strained to find formulas enabling them to maintain an ideological balance. Among them, certainly the most distinguished was a mathematician of Dubrovnik, Marin Getaldić (1568–1626)—*angelus in moribus, diabolus in mathematicis;* he wrote on the application of algebra to the solution of geometrical problems. The versatile writer and inventor Faust Vrančić (1551–1617) set out his various inventive ideas (the parachute, turbine, tide-driven mills) in his work *Machinae novae* (1595). After comprehensive knowledge had been gained about the works of antiquity, the old school textbooks were no longer satisfactory; new lexicons in a number of languages and Latin grammar books were produced. Bernhard Perger of Styria (where humanism was slow to penetrate because of the general backwardness of the secular sections of society in the Slovene provinces) wrote a Latin textbook in the humanistic spirit. The aforementioned Faust Vrančić composed a *Dictionary of the Five Most Distinguished European Languages*—Latin, Italian, German, Croatian, and Hungarian.

The history and historical monuments of various towns or entire regions also became a subject of investigation. Outstanding among chroniclers for his sobriety in portraying and assessing contemporary events was Ludovik Tuberon Crijević of Dubrovnik (1459–1527), who had completed his studies in Paris. He had adopted from his teachers a critical attitude toward the dissolute life of high-ranking members of the Roman church. In his *Commentaries*, he described events in southeastern Europe between 1490 and 1522, devoting ample space to his native town and the theme of Ottoman expansion and searching for the causes of events in geographic and economic conditions, the ratio of military and political forces, the collective mentality of the people, and the character of individuals. He knew that the South Slavs were not descendants of the Illyrians but rather members of the Slavic nation, which had originated in Russia and settled the area in the seventh century. His contemporaries, however, favored the concept that the Slavs were the indigenous inhabitants of the Balkan Peninsula. Vinko Pribojević of Hvar (*De origine successibusque Slavorum*, 1525) considered Illyria the original homeland of all the Slavs and erroneously counted among their forebears many of the great men of the classical age, including Alexander the Great and Aristotle.

The Spread of Protestantism and Its Influence on the Development of Slovene Literature

Whereas humanism was strongest in its repercussions in the coastal towns, the Reformation left deep traces in the Slovene provinces, penetrating to Croatia and Slavonia in lesser degree. Despite the resistance of the Hapsburgs, literary and cultural activities by Protestant preachers made their mark among the people and engendered the growth of consciousness. The new faith was brought to the Military Frontier by German soldiers, and to the lands of Slovenia by soldiers, miners, and merchants from Germany, or by nationals returning after having received their education at German universities. Conditions were ripe for the acceptance of Martin Luther's teachings as the wealth and power of the church were looked upon with disfavor. The nobility wanted the church lands secularized, the citizens hoped to oust the clergy from affairs of commerce, and the peasants were anxious to free themselves of its pressures and abuses. Protestant circles were in existence in the Slovene provinces as early as 1528, and by the second half of the sixteenth century Protestantism had spread widely, especially among the aristocracy and citizenry. Enjoying the wholehearted support of the estates' assemblies, its followers won temporary concessions from the Hapsburgs, particularly when the latter needed support in their plans for collecting financial resources earmarked for defense of the empire from the Turks. Archduke Charles promised freedom of worship to the Styrian nobles in 1572, and in 1578 he recognized the same rights for the nobility of Carinthia and Carniola, as well as for the citizenry of four cities (Grac, Ljubljana, Judenburg, and Celovac). The temporary victory satisfied both nobility and citizenry. The peasants saw nothing particularly attractive about the Lutheran religion, as it also demanded subordination to the landlords. Consequently, from the very beginning they were drawn to Anabaptism, the most radical, plebeian section of the Reformation, opposed by both the Lutheran nobles and the Catholic church.

During its upsurge, the Lutheran church developed its own organization, with superintendents and preachers in the Slovene provinces; it opened churches and schools and offered the faithful worship in the vernacular, which in Styria and Carinthia meant principally in German. In Carniola a "Slovene church" was formed, where services were held in Slovenian. The credit for this achievement belongs to Primož Trubar (1508–1586), the chief exponent of Protestantism among the Slovenes, who styled himself an "Illyrian patriot." Trubar developed his activities along these lines as canon of Ljubljana during the incumbency of Bishop Fran Kocijaner, who was partial to Luther. When Kocijaner was succeeded in 1543 by a staunch champion of the Catholic church, Trubar found it wise to leave Austrian territory. He moved to Germany, where other propagators of the Reformation, from Slovene and Croatian areas, also took refuge later. In Tübingen he published the *ABC's* and *Catechism* in Slovenian, and then wrote other books, brief and modest, for the requirements of the service and education. His associates also published their own works; between 1550 and 1595, fifty works were printed in Slovenian, of which Trubar himself was the author of twenty-five. Trubar concentrated much of his effort on getting published a translation of the Holy Bible; he finally succeeded in 1584.

The idea itself originated in 1554 with a banished citizen of Koper, Petar Paul Vergerius the Younger (1495–1565), who felt that the Holy Bible, as the basic medium for spreading the Reformation, should be translated into a language understood by all South Slavs. Many difficulties naturally cropped up, as champions of the Reformation knew only their own local dialects. An attempt was therefore made, with which Trubar initially agreed, to bring together translators from various regions. It was imagined that reformed Christianity would attract not only all Christians but even Muslims, including the sultan himself. Trubar, Vergerius, and Ivan Ungnad, former head of Styria, gathered to their fold two Istrians who wrote in the Glagolitic alphabet, Stjepan Konzul and Ivan

FIGURE 25.   Primož Trubar.

FIGURE 26.   Sveti Janez at Bohinj.

FIGURE 27. Cetinje.

Dalmatin, as well as two Orthodox monks from Hercegovina, presumably Uskoks, valuable for their knowledge of Cyrillic. The duke of Württemberg provided some funds for setting up a printing press in Urach (near Tübingen), where books were printed in the Glagolitic, Latin, and Cyrillic alphabets. In contrast to the expectations of these enthusiasts, Cyrillic books from the Protestant press, which had to be smuggled across the Turkish frontier, made little headway among the Serbs. Furthermore, the effort to translate the Holy Bible into some sort of general Slavonic language was unsuccessful, particularly after the originator of the idea, Vergerius, lost interest in it and Trubar also drew aloof from the group, divested himself of grandiose plans, and set about completing the work of organizing a Protestant church in Carniola. He also presented his compatriots with a complete translation of the Holy Bible. Trubar himself published only parts of it up to 1555; the complete text was translated, in consultation with him, by a younger associate and also by the most distinguished Slovene writer of the sixteenth century, Jurij Dalmatin (1547–1589). This translation, published in 1584, was to become the basis of the Slovene literary language. The same year, Dalmatin's teacher and close associate, Adam Bohorič (ca. 1520–ca. 1600), made public the first grammar of the Slovene language, *Arcticae horulae*, in which he developed the basic rules for Slovene orthography; known as *Bohorčica*, it remained in use until the nineteenth century.

Although most of the books for the South Slav region were printed in Germany (in Urach) during the height of the Reformation, a printing press was also in operation in Ljubljana (1575–1580), and another, established by Juraj Zrinski, functioned first in Nedelište (1570–1584) and later Varaždin. Trubar demanded that schools be opened in all towns, but no noteworthy results were achieved along these lines. For Slovenes, the most important school, where Latin and German were taught, was located in Ljubljana. In the first grade all teaching was done in Slovenian; in the second grade only catechism was taught in the native language.

The Reformation had considerable significance for the Slovene provinces for, in the process of pursuing its religious objectives, it laid the groundwork for the Slovene literary language. Slovene literature, previously nonexistent, became the foundation for the Slovenes' unity and the gradual development of their consciousness of belonging to one community, of their national self. The work of the Slovene reformers, built into the foundations of the Slovene national renaissance, remained even after the Counter-Reformation had effaced all the achievements of Protestantism itself.

There had been no notable progress along these lines in Croatia, where the Catholic church consequently found it easy to suppress Protestantism. The literary efforts of its propagators, however, did offer impetus to the development of literature in the vernacular, for the most part religious poetry in the Kaj dialect, published anonymously in small anthologies. The most important contribution of the Croats to the general movement of the Reformation may be considered the work of several distinguished theoreticians, headed by Matthias Flacius Illyricus (1520–1575), who wrote one of the fundamental Protestant books, *Centuriae Magdeburgenses*, presenting the history of Christianity; it was imbued with anti-Roman church attitudes in the spirit of his firm Protestant persuasion. In the coastal towns the Reformation echoed here and there, as reflected in the work of the learned archbishop of Split, Marco Antoniode Dominus (1560–1624), from whose pen flowed more than a little gall against the Roman pope and his policies. He even fled to England in 1616, only to return disillusioned and desperate to Rome, where he finished his days interned in the Castel Sant' Angelo.

The Success of the Counter-Reformation

After the Council of Trent (1545–1563), where proposals for reconcilia-tion were rejected, the Catholic church launched resolute action and, with the help of the Jesuit order, found it fairly easy to inhibit Protestantism in the Haps-burg territories. Giving it their full support, the Hapsburgs welcomed the Jesuits to Graz as early as 1573, and later, in 1586, endowed their school with the rank of a university. They had persecuted the Protestants even before this, unless the general situation was such that they found it wiser to take conciliatory attitude. Bishop Juraj Drašković (1525–1587), later cardinal and ban, established a semi-nary in Zagreb in 1565 for the training of a militant clergy while he himself re-jected the freethinking humanism in whose traditions he had been educated, and renounced the attitude of reconciliation he had assumed in Trent. From 1582 onwards, Archduke Charles brought pressure to bear on the Protestants to return to the Catholic church, punished the recalcitrant, and restored to the church the lands of which it had been dispossessed. His son, later the Holy Roman Emperor Ferdinand II (1619–1637), used force to uproot Protestantism. After the decision to banish Protestant preachers (1598) and the issuance of a decree ordering commoners to return to the Catholic church (1599), "religious commissions" went into action with the help of the military. Protestant churches were destroyed, cemeteries were violated, and books were burned. Resistance was negligible. In Styria, Carinthia, and Carniola, however, the nobility maintained their religious freedom until 1628, although they were not free to perform church rituals.

The Jesuits took over schools and generally supervised the life of the faithful. By 1596 they had entrenched themselves in Ljubljana and later in places where Protestantism presented little or no threat: in Dubrovnik (1604), Zagreb (1606), Trieste (1619), Rijeka (1628), Varaždin (1632), and so on. The Croatian Assembly recognized only the Catholic church in Croatia and Slavonia by a decision of 1608. The Jesuits reared the young people in a militant Catholic spirit and held sway over intellectual life. Members of other orders and clergymen saw to it that the unlettered mass of the people were duly assiduous in their re-ligious duties, developing among them a feeling of intolerance toward other con-fessions. Notions of the church's omnipotence were heightened by solemn pro-cessions, elaborate church rituals, and pilgrimages by the penitent. As the church drew closer to the people, it resorted to the same methods that had been employed by the Protestants. In literature the churchmen accepted the vernacular, wrote popular books of a religious nature, and encouraged lay church poetry. In the atmosphere of religious bigotry, intolerance, and readiness to exterminate those of a different mind, the gay and sometimes unbridled way of life, introduced by the Renaissance into the coastal towns, withered; free humanist thought receded and critical intelligence was blunted in its observation of life and the behavior of representatives of the Roman church. The discipline required by the Counter-Reformation changed those who implemented it. Catholic reaction celebrated its victory in the Yugoslav lands and set its seal upon the public and cultural life of the region.

Renaissance Art

In the arts the style of the Italian Renaissance made inroads during the second half of the fifteenth and the first half of the sixteenth century, superimposing itself on the already-developed Gothic forms. The style did not assert itself fully in architecture, as the Dalmatian towns under Venetian rule simply set about completing monumental edifices begun earlier. Then stagnation set in as a reflection of general conditions, except in Dubrovnik, where the prince's palace was reconstructed and new secular buildings were erected, such as the Sponza (Customs House) and the nobles' summer residences in the vicinity, where Renaissance and late Gothic elements intermingle. In the other towns ornamental and decorative Renaissance elements were introduced when old buildings were repaired.

The Renaissance was most in evidence in decorative carving and sculpture. The realistic portraits by Juraj Dalmatinac, with their explicitly individualistic features, reflect the influence of Florentine sculpture. Niccolò Fiorentino, unknown in Italy, revealed his talents as a disciple of Donatello in his reliefs and statues. Andrea Alessi, a native of Durazzo, remained a Gothic artist in his statues and reliefs; he adopted Renaissance forms and motifs which were easily imitated even by ordinary stonemasons only in his later ornamental work. In the sixteenth century, sculpture was patently in its decline. Portraits and tombs in the Slovene lands reflect the influence of the Renaissance style as it appeared in Central Europe.

Also in decline were the quantity and quality of paintings. Only in Dubrovnik did a local school develop, its many representatives advancing from Byzantine models to Renaissance conceptions. The most talented painters had been trained in Italy; Nikola Božidarević in Venice, Mihailo Hamzić in Padua. In the sixteenth century, when the Dubrovnik school too was in full decline, the coastal towns commissioned their paintings from Italy. There the finest painters of Yugoslav descent remained, never returning to their native land but rather leaving their work to posterity in their adopted country; among them were Franjo and Lucijan Vranjani, the former a sculptor and the latter an architect; the sculptor Ivan Duknović Dalmata; and the painters Juraj Čulinović Schiavone and Andrija Medulić Schiavone.

FIGURE 28. Cathedral in Korčula.

FIGURE 29.   Ivan Gundulič.

FIGURE 30.   Franciscan monastery in Dubrovnik.

Ideas of Slavdom

Scientists, writers, and artists in areas which looked to Western European culture contributed to their progress and paved the way for later development. The establishment of the vernacular in the literature of Slovene provinces, the strong assertion of the Što dialect in artistic and instructive literature, and the awakening consciousness of affinity with the Slavic or "Illyrian" community of all South Slavs are elements which were destined to figure importantly in the later national renaissance. In various ways they were to influence the formation of the national consciousness on a scale much broader than the local and regional consciousness within which life at that time still revolved.

CHAPTER 14

The Yugoslav Peoples under Turkish Rule

The Organization of Turkish Administrative, Military, and Judicial Authority

Beyond a narrow belt of deserted no-man's-land, and bordering on Hapsburg and Venetian possessions, began a world differing considerably from them in its political and social order, its economic development, its culture, and its mentality. Within the boundaries of the mighty Ottoman Empire lived about 20 million inhabitants of diverse nationalities, subject to the despotic power of the sultan. This empire had at its disposal a powerful military organization, and it showed scant respect for hereditary titles or the class prerogatives of any kind of established nobility. And yet it was not a homogeneous empire, for Ottoman institutions had adapted themselves to the inherited traditions of various regions in which the majority of the population, particularly in the Balkan Peninsula, lived according to its ancient customs, remaining outside the orbit represented by the state structure, the religion, and the culture of their masters.

The sultan's will was done through the grand vizier, as his deputy, and the divan, consisting of from three to five Kube-visiers with advisory powers. Two kazaskers (chief justices) concerned themselves with judicial affairs and two defterdars (finance ministers) with finances. The laws were interpreted and the legality of the divan's decisions was confirmed by the sheikh ul Islam (the grand mufti). Also among the high-ranking dignitaries was the nishanji (keeper of the great seal) in whose office the ornamental signature of the sultan was painted on official documents: firmans (decrees), berats (appointments), ahdams (treaties), and correspondence. All these bodies and the building in which they were housed were known in the West as the Sublime Porte.

The state was divided into large military-administrative regions, eyalets (later vilayets), each headed by a beglerbeg; later they were also called pashalics if the head bore the title of pasha or vizier. After the fall of Budapest, all Balkan lands were incorporated into the Rumelian eyalet with headquarters in Sofia, but they were later divided into a number of pashalics, the most important of which, from the standpoint of the Yugoslav peoples' history, was the Bosnian pashalic (dating from 1580). The eyalets were in turn subdivided into sanjaks (banners) headed by sanjakbegs, and later by pashas. When Turkish expansion reached its culmination, the Yugoslav lands included twenty-five sanjaks, more than a third of which had their capitals and the larger part of their territory outside the borders of present-day Yugoslavia. As conquests proceeded, greater importance was attached to the frontier sanjaks with their system of fortresses and strong garrisons. This was the position of the Smederevo sanjak for roughly a hundred years (1459–1552). Then the Turkish frontier with the Croatian lands was stabilized in the second half of the sixteenth century, and the Turks organized kapudanlics (captainships) along similar lines in Bosnia and Slavonia. The sanjaks were subdivided into smaller administrative districts—nahiyas—headed by muselemins. And that was the bottom of the ladder of Turkish power. Considerably larger than the nahiyas were the judicial districts, the khadilics. The Islamic judges, khadis, dispensing justice according to the holy books and the sultan's kanun-names (collections of laws) were independent of regional authorities and subordinate only to central judicial organs.

The Spahis and the Raya

In addition to its navy and river fleet, the empire was equipped with a powerful land army, divided into the imperial guard and the eyalet army. Outstanding in the guard were the "sons of the emperor"—the Janissaries, who, deprived of the right to raise a family or to acquire private property, were maintained by salaries from the imperial coffers. The ranking citizens of the eyalets were the spahis (feudal cavalry), who lived off the rent from their holdings. Apart from various branches of infantry and fortress garrisons, there were also ancillary detachments of cavalry, transport, and frontier guardsmen, frequently reinforced by Vlach Voinuks and Armatoles.

Owing to its paramount role in the empire, the army gave the ruling class its name—the asker (soldiers). Irrespective of name, to this class belonged all administrative, judicial, and financial officials, religious elders, and professors, all those whose role in the state contributed to the glory of the padishah (sultan). The masses, whose duty it was to work and produce everything needed by the ruling class, were called raya (flock, subjects, common folk). Members of the ruling class enjoyed rights and income in accordance with their role and rank. Social equality did not exist among the raya either, for many of them acquired a variety of privileges in return for minor services. It thus happened that the social position of many people ranged between the raya and the asker. The Muslim raya were in a better position than the Christian, and from the middle of the seventeenth century onwards the term *raya* was applied exclusively to the latter. Prominent individuals and groups among the Christians who accepted the new authority without complaint and offered it support became members of the privileged class.

The rights and privileges of the ruling class and the obligations of the raya are best explained by the system of land tenure and resource utilization. In principle these belonged to Allah but were disposed of by the sultan as his regent. The richest sources of income were the khasses—mines, lakes, hunting grounds, great expanses of arable land, and entire villages, particularly those along the frontiers and around mines. The khasses were exploited by the sultan himself or granted to viziers, beglerbegs, and sanjakbegs as long as they discharged their functions. The spahis and distinguished individuals were granted holdings, the smallest of which were called timars (with an income of up to 20,000 aspers a year), and the larger ziamets (with incomes ranging from 20,000 to 100,000 aspers a year). The masters of the timars and ziamets were actually Ottoman feudatories whose rights were established by law and who could never gain enough power to pose a threat to the central authority. Their holdings (spahilics) were enjoyed conditionally; to be more precise, the holder of a spahilic was the beneficiary of a specifically determined income from a specific holding, provided that he could muster a stipulated number of soldiers for war, the number depending on the size of the land grant. The right of inheritance was restricted, and the right to convey or sell land was precluded. From the very outset Christians were numbered among those who held timars; these were members of the onetime lesser nobility or the elders of Vlach groups of herdsmen who had joined the service of the emperor. Only occasionally do we find more Christian than Muslim spahis (for example, in Braničevo, Serbia); in most cases Christians were in the minority and their incomes were small. During the sixteenth century their number declined considerably, despite the increase in the number of spahis and the consolidation of the timar system. Tolerant of other religions, the Turks left untouched the estates belonging to monasteries and church institutions. At the same time, there emerged in the Balkan lands a system of endowed estates of Islamic religious and philanthropic institutions—mosques, schools, hammams (public baths), khans (caravansaries)—known as wakfs, largely from land that was privately owned by prominent individuals. As total ownership with unlimited rights to bequeath, convey, or sell land was at odds with the general property principles of the Ottoman Empire, by bequeathing land to the wakfs these individuals secured for their families the inherited rights to manage them.

The tillers of the soil, who composed the larger part of the raya, had heritable property in the form of family farms (čiftliks) and were subject to feudal obligations to the sultan and feudatories—the masters of the khasses, ziamets, timars, or wakfs. By paying an inheritance tax to the spahi, they were able to hand their land down to their heirs, and also, with their master's consent, to convey or sell it. Apart from the taxes and levies compulsory for all, the non-Muslim raya owed the sultan a head tax (jizya) payable by every able-bodied male; a blood levy; a tenth of all products for the spahi (actually, from one-seventh to one-tenth of the harvest); a money fee—the ispendje per head tax payee; and some lesser obligations of corvée and products. The tribute levied on the Muslim raya was considerably less severe. As the entire system was adapted to local conditions, in certain regions formerly under Hungarian rule (Srem, Slavonia), the sultan was owed, instead of the head tax per working male and other tributes, a filuriya (ducat) and vojnica (military tax) per household. The filuriya was also payable by the Vlach herdsmen, who met other obligations with livestock. The form of relief was granted them in return for their discharging military and paramilitary obligations. Also partially released from levies were those persons who maintained khans, passes, or roads; worked on ferries or bridges; repaired fortresses or ships; or produced arrows. The Sokolari, Vlach Voinuks, and Armatoles (armed Christians in the imperial frontier service) possessed free heritable property which carried no obligations. Fiscal relief or exemption was actually a form of reward for the discharge of certain functions. Also in a better position were the raya in the towns, for they paid only state and personal levies. As they owned no land, or only negligible plots in the vicinity of the town, no agrarian taxes were levied.

In the second half of the sixteenth century, the social and economic differentiation of the raya began to be carried to the opposite extreme. Prominent individuals received deserted land as čiftlik to which they brought peasants and established villages. They paid the agrarian levies for the newly settled peasants but extracted much larger sums from them in return. As they were able to dis-

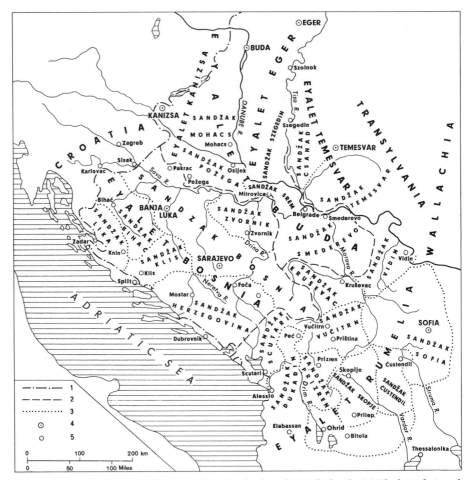

MAP 21.   The administrative division of Yugoslav lands under Turkish rule. (1) The boundaries of
the Ottoman Empire at the beginning of the seventeenth century; (2) the boundaries of
eyalets; (3) the boundaries of sanjaks (sandžaks); (4) the seat of eyalet; (5) the seat of
sanjak.

possess the peasants at will, the latter found themselves in an extremely difficult
position. They were truly serfs of their masters, the čiftlik-sahibis. But the process of čiftlik creation was only in its inception, and it may therefore be considered that during the initial period of Turkish rule the peasantry was in a better
position than previously, under its domestic masters, and that the landlords
oppressed them less than was the case in neighboring European states. Consequently, at that time there was no appreciable resistance to the new authority.

The Migrations

The process of destroying the Balkan states and the former society, launched by the Turkish conquests, was also attended by great migrations and demographic changes. While the course of conquest was still in progress, the indigenous population withdrew northward. During the fifteenth and sixteenth centuries, the Serbs settled in southern Hungary and remained in Srem, Bačka, and the Banat even after the Turks had subjugated those areas. Turkish raids on Croatian lands, especially after the defeat at Krbava Field, caused much of the population to retreat from areas that had once represented the nucleus of the Croatian state. They crossed the Kupa River into Istria and advanced farther to the islands. People also left the coastal areas, individually and in groups, to move to Italy. With these migrations, the name of Croatia established itself more firmly in Slavonia (Slovinia). When the Turks took possession of abandoned areas in Croatia and Slavonia, they brought to them the Christian population from their territories to reconstruct the ravaged economy, as well as a large number of Muslims to organize the defense of the frontier. The highly mobile Vlach herdsmen figured importantly in these internal migrations. At the turn of the sixteenth century, they settled northern and western Serbia, afterwards crossing the Danube and Drina Rivers. During this process they finally merged with the Serbian agricultural population, helping to form a broad ethnical, religious, and cultural community of the Serbian people scattered over a vast area from which the indigenous population had withdrawn. Fleeing over the borders, many joined the Hapsburg defense system and lived side by side with the Croats in the same area. The mountain people of the Dinaric region later settled areas that had been depopulated by epidemics, starvation, and war devastations. In any case, for economic reasons the mountain dwellers were not loath to leave their homes and to settle less forbidding areas.

In consequence of these migrations, certain traditions were transmitted and disseminated, and a change took place in the former distribution of the various dialects of the Serbo-Croatian language (see footnote, page 103). The Ča dialect had previously been spoken along the coast between Istria and the Cetina River all the way to Gvozd and the Sava; the Kaj dialect extended to the north; and of the Što dialect, the *i* version was used in areas all the way to the Drina River, the *e* version in Kosovo, Metohija, and along the Morava River, and the *ije* version in Hum and Zeta. After the migrations, the *ije* version spread across the Drina River, penetrated to the Sava River, and suppressed the Kaj dialect as far back as the Croatian Zagorje, and the Ča dialect to the narrow coastal belt. Conditions were thereby created for the Što dialect to become the common spoken language of the larger part of the Croats and all Serbs. In areas where Serbs and Croats lived side by side, they followed the same customs and together created a common tradition. Consequently the earlier process of rapprochement among the Serbs, Macedonians, and Bulgarians, through the medium of a common literary tongue and similar cultural heritage, lost its previous significance.

New ethical elements also appeared with the Turks. The Yuruks, Asia Minor herdsmen of Turco-Tatar origin, settled in Macedonia while the Gypsies, descended from India, moved with the Turkish armies and found a new homeland in the Balkan countries, whence they spread throughout Europe. After the pogroms in Spain, Jews came to reside in the towns, plying their trades and crafts. During a period when they were being banished from the Slovene provinces and Croatia, and when they likewise found a hostile environment in the Dalmatian towns resulting from the anti-Jewish decrees of the Venetian Republic, they were able to settle in Bitola, Skoplje, Belgrade, and Sarajevo under the wing of Ottoman power. From there they scattered to other towns from the seventeenth century onwards. Members of their community maintained business ties with the Jewish community in Dubrovnik, where repressive measures were taken in the course of the sixteenth century, despite protests from the Porte.

Features of Ottoman Economy

The military-administrative apparatus, the timar system, the legislative and colonizing measures all had the same objective—harnessing the entire economic potential of the country to serve the empire and its new martial undertakings. But it was able to act as a foundation for Ottoman power only temporarily. The new power severed the established course of the economy and interrupted the active incorporation of the Balkan countries into European economic development. Implanting a primitive feudal system and bureaucratic exploitation of natural resources and manpower, and effecting a return to barter economy, it stunted the growth of a "money economy" and capitalist development, to which the feudal monarchies in Europe had accommodated. This type of economy inevitably drove the empire into a grave crisis, causing it to lag permanently behind neighboring European states.

Although the Turks introduced some new crops into the Balkans (cotton, rice, sesame, poppies), and although the Vlachs, having settled in the valleys, took up the plow and the hoe, livestock raising played an increasingly important role in agriculture. Vlach expansion and the requirements of the Turkish army for their transport services and for large quantities of meat, gave animal husbandry an advantage over other branches of agriculture.

Mining was condemned to failure. Mine exploitation in the medieval Balkan states had opened up new vistas for the consolidation and expansion of a money economy. During the Turkish wars, professional miners had left their jobs to move elsewhere. Businessmen who leased the mines on a long-term basis—and they included a large number of the citizens of Dubrovnik—either withdrew or switched their attention to other undertakings. Mehmed II promulgated laws designed to revive mining, but the resulting reconstruction was short-lived. Tools and techniques remained medieval. The local population, Serbs and Albanians, accustomed to unskilled labor, went to work in the mines. The mines were regulated by customary law based on the old Saxon legislation. As part of the imperial khasses, the mines were leased on a short-term basis, which offered no incentive for investment. The metal was used above all for the needs of the army and mints. Merchants, money changers, and businessmen generally abandoned this otherwise extremely profitable line of endeavor, and state workshops were set up to discharge the functions no longer found lucrative by others. Toward the end of the fifteenth and in the course of the sixteenth century, mining advanced to some extent, especially in Macedonia, although many pits were deserted even during the prosperous period, whereas the biggest mines, like those of Novo Brdo and Srebrenica, did not produce anything approaching their onetime output under domestic masters. The Muslim population was not at all attracted to the mines, and this branch of economy was left mostly to the Christians. By the end of the sixteenth century, the mines were in crisis again, and thereafter they were extinguished one by one.

Not even the manifest development of towns could change the overall picture of economic life. Turkish towns grew up at the sites of former urban settlements; improvised military fortifications sprang up along the roads and around military and administrative centers. Some of them remained small towns (kasabas), whereas others flowered into important centers of crafts and trade with a large population and many public institutions (mosques, schools, khans, hammams, and so on). The largest towns in Macedonia were Bitola, Skoplje, Kratovo, Štip, and Prilep; in Serbia—Smederevo, Belgrade, Novo Brdo, and later Niš and Užice; in Bosnia—Sarajevo, Banja Luka, Jajce, Travnik, and Visoko; in what is now Vojvodina—Sremska Mitrovica, Bač, Sombor, Bečkerek; in Srem—Ilok, and in Slavonia—Osijek. These towns showed oriental features as in the course of time the Muslim population, largely domestic in origin, came to predominate. Foreign settlers (Jews, Armenians, Greeks, Italians, men from Dubrovnik, etc.) added to the generally motley impression, particularly evident when the peasants brought their wares to market. In the trading center of the towns (čaršija) were concentrated the shops of the craftsmen, usually Muslims, who fashioned a great variety of products. Many more crafts were practiced then than in the Middle Ages, the Turks having brought new ones with them. Nonetheless, the majority of craftsmen worked for the needs of the army, producing such articles as sabers, rifles, and daggers. Plying their trade in the medieval manner, the craftsmen, members of guilds, worked by hand in their tiny shops. Manufacturing of the type developing in the Western countries was nonexistent.

Towns and Villages

Trading was vigorous in the towns. Extraordinary development was registered by towns located at important junctions of routes connecting productive areas or centers for the sale and purchase of agricultural and livestock products (grains, wax, wool, hides, furs, livestock on the hoof, and cheese). In trading with Europe, the Ottoman Empire exported raw materials and imported Western manufactures. Economically, therefore, it was in a subordinate position. Merchants were both nationals (largely Muslims) and foreigners, among whom the men of Dubrovnik were outstanding for their ability. As early as the fifteenth century, the Republic of Dubrovnik had acquired for its merchants an exceptionally advantageous position throughout the empire as reflected in the payment of a uniform customs levy of 2 percent of the value of goods. On the whole, there were always about 300 to 400 Dubrovnik traders in the Turkish towns; the value of the goods they exported ran to an average of 150,000 ducats, although in wartime years that figure was quadrupled or even septupled. In the sixteenth century Dubrovnik was in possession of a maritime fleet of from 170 to 200 ships, which not only transported goods from the Balkan Peninsula to all Mediterranean countries, but also provided transport services for others. Dubrovnik's economic upsurge in the sixteenth century may be ascribed to its favored position on the Turkish market and the crisis that struck the big Italian centers.

Conversion to Islam

Prosperity in the towns did not suffice, however, to repair the empire's economic situation. Incomes were high, money circulated in large quantities, and property was privately owned, but even at the empire's zenith a deep gap divided the town from the rural districts. Later, when certain forms of commodity-money economy began to wield an influence over the villages as well, they simply acted to destroy the Ottoman feudal system and bring it to the brink of the abyss. Whoever wished to advance in the military and administrative apparatus of the empire, to get rich quick by engaging in economic activities in the towns, or simply to show that he accepted the new social order, converted to Islam. Conversions were far more common in the towns than in the countryside. Outside the towns, the new faith was accepted by the lesser nobility, by Christian spahis bent on retaining their timars, and occasionally by peasants. Conversion was the most widespread in Bosnia; this may partially be explained by the fact that there the mass of the population had no support from a strong church organization when the Turks came. Furthermore, after the Battle of Mohács (1526), large groups of privileged Vlachs in Hercegovina were transformed into raya, whereupon they converted to make life easier for themselves. But the Islamization of the peasantry and lesser nobility in Bosnia was nevertheless a gradual process.

In consequence of the Islamic religious premise that all Muslims are Muhammad's people, it was made possible for those belonging to diverse ethnical communities to achieve the highest positions. Even converted Slavs, thanks to their personal abilities and the sultan's favor, attained to the position of Janissary agas, beglerbegs, viziers, and grand viziers. They owed their rise to the sultan, who was therefore able to rely on them completely. At one time, in the mid-sixteenth century, the grand vizier and two of the three viziers were Yugoslavs from Bosnia. Other converts who succeeded in attaining to brilliant careers were Mehmed Pasha Sokolović (Sokollu), a Serb from the Višegrad area. He achieved great success, becoming one of the most prominent associates of Suleiman II, as well as his son-in-law, and finally grand vizier. He commanded many raids, victoriously fought the Hapsburgs in Europe, paved the way for Hungary's collapse, and subdued Arabia. The influence of Yugoslav converts at the Porte was so strong that Serbo-Croatian was used in offices and in diplomatic negotiations as the second language. It was also spoken by the beglerbegs and sanjakbegs in their correspondence with Croatian commanders along the frontier and in conversation with the latter's Slovene and Croat envoys.

Islamic Culture

The section of the population that converted to Islam was also profoundly affected by Islamic culture, the centers of which were the educational-religious institutions. All Muslim towns had their mektebs (elementary schools), where Arabic letters were taught and the Koran was read; there were seventy in Sarajevo. In the larger towns, medresas (intermediate schools) were established; there religious teaching was supplemented by the eastern languages, Islamic law, philosophy, and mathematics. The most famous medresas were in Sarajevo, Belgrade, and Skoplje. Talented individuals obtained a higher education in Istanbul (Constantinople), Cairo, Damascus, and other centers of oriental culture, later achieving prominent positions in education, the courts, and the administration. Other educational institutions were the mosques, as places of worship, and the tekyas, headquarters of the order of dervishes, characterized by mysticism and fanaticism. Macedonia, Kosovo, and Metohija had the largest number of tekyas. These institutions were in possession of rich libraries, even in smaller towns. In many of these, Arabic, Persian, and Turkish manuscripts have been preserved to this day.

Numerous members of the native population also gained prominence in literature, both prose and poetry. Prose works, usually written in Arabic, were concerned mainly with religious and legal matters. There were a number of well-known historians (Rustem Pasha in the sixteenth century, Ibrahim Alajbegović in the seventeenth, and Omar Effendi in the eighteenth), writers of political dissertations (Lufti Pasha, Hasan Khadi), and mathematicians of note (Ahmed Hatem and Husam the Bosnian). Poets, of whom about a hundred are known to us today, composed poems in Persian and Turkish about war and the homeland, frequently setting out ideas that deviated from official concepts and consequently ending their days in banishment. The poets destined to gain the greatest distinction were Suzi Čelebiya of Prizren (fifteenth–sixteenth century), Dervish Pasha Bajazidović of Mostar, and Vahdeti of Dobrun near Višegrad (sixteenth century), Nerkesi of Sarajevo, Sabit of Užice (seventeenth century), and Fevzi of Mostar (eighteenth century).

The influence of Islamic poetry and particularly oriental music was most evident in South Slav folk songs and dances; in the addition of about 3,000 Slavicized words of Turkish provenance to the Serbo-Croat and Macedonian languages; and in the influx of words of Arabic, Turkish, and Persian origin. The intermingling was inevitable, and it comes as no surprise that many Serbo-Croat verses were penned in Arabic characters or that Muslims in Bosnia retained the Cyrillic alphabet for private and official use until the most recent period.

Islamic-oriental arts, primarily architecture, and material culture, superimposed themselves not only on the towns but also on the villages wherever Muslims lived. Towns far from the frontier and therefore not exposed to the threat of invasion were not within walls but spread out over broad expanses in order to give each house a garden, a souce of water, and a fine view. The central part of the towns consisted of the čaršija, where public buildings, shops, and offices clustered. The residential quarters were divided up into mahalas, where various religious and ethnical groups lived separately. In layout and appearance, these mahalas differed noticeably from the čaršija.

The most distinguished public buildings, religious and commercial, had been erected by the end of the sixteenth century. Mosques were cube-shaped and topped by domes, their freestanding slender minarets piercing the sky. The loveliest ones to have been preserved are found in Sarajevo, Foča, Banja Luka, Skoplje, and Prizren. The burial places of prominent individuals were marked by turbehs (mausoleums) in the mosque courtyards and cemeteries. One of the finest bridges was constructed at Mostar, a graceful arch spanning the Neretva, and another at Višegrad on the Drina River, a monument to Mehmed Pasha Sokolović. Bezistans (commercial houses) in the business part of town were constructed of stone and covered with domes. Caravansaries and khans were rectangular in shape, with a courtyard in the center; warehouses and stalls were situated on the ground floor and bedrooms on the story above. Public buildings had water mains, šedrvans (fountains), drinking fountains, and hammams. Residences, usually of brick, were distinctive for their divanhanes (rooms for conversation and smoking), terminating in an overhanging balcony pleasant for sunning during the day and making the rooms cooler by night. The balcony was usually screened from the eyes of passersby with grillwork. Household articles of wood, metal, and leather showed the high achievement of these handicrafts.

Prerogatives and Self-government

Islamic culture, as reflected in articles of everyday use, way of life, and mentality, left a deep imprint on the Christian population as well. Nonetheless, the majority of Christians made up a separate world, bound to the past by many traditions and profoundly patriarchal in outlook. The Turks did not attempt to interfere in that world as long as their authority was accepted without resistance. Representing local pockets and cut off from the large centers with which they had no political, cultural, or religious ties, the Christians posed no threat as yet to the conquerors. Ottoman administration permitted them to run local affairs, especially in the villages, and conceded certain auxiliary functions to them in the administrative apparatus.

The Vlach herdsmen who had settled in northern Serbia while it was still a frontier zone had their own peculiar organization. They were grouped into katuns; during the first wave of settlement there were twenty families to a katun and in the second there were fifty. Their leadership was provided by chiefs— *knezovi* and *primićuri*. In 1536, when they were shorn of their privileged position and many of them moved to the northwest, to newly conquered Turkish regions, those who remained in Serbia as tillers of the soil mingled with the rest of the raya but retained their old organization. Their knezes were no longer the elders of the Vlach herdsmen but rather local functionaries in a small area called the Knežina. Villages in the knežina were administered by primićurs. Both functions were inherited. The knezes and primićurs helped the authorities collect tithes, bring back the fleeing raya for use on public works, etc. In return, they enjoyed the right to free heritable property or even timar. Thus they were incorporated into the asker class and linked with the state apparatus while the people administered by them enjoyed a certain degree of autonomy. This type of local administration was established also in other Yugoslav lands.

In Montenegro, the Turks abolished the timar land tenure system introduced earlier, considering the land too rocky and unproductive, and proclaimed its inhabitants free peasants bound by the obligation to pay a ducat per household. They did not establish their own authorities but left the nahiyas and knežinas to local persons who governed their areas in accordance with common law. In civil suits Christians were not obliged to submit their cases to the khadis but rather to juries of their own people, who settled them in line with the old traditions, in large part relying on the legal codes of the state to which they had once belonged. This was one of the reasons why the Code of Laws of Stefan Dušan retained its significance even after the collapse of the medieval Serbian state. Frequently rewritten and brought up to date in details, it continued to be used by the Serbian people in their dealings under law. Many rewritten and edited copies have been preserved, thanks to this practice. In the knežinas of Montenegro, assemblies were held on a nationwide scale and thus helped pave the way toward autonomy. Mention is made in the early seventeenth century of a native, Vujo Rajčev, styled the "Prince of Montenegro," representing the country vis-à-vis the Turkish authorities. Turkish functionaries were not allowed in Montenegro with the exception of an envoy of the sultan, who collected the head tax after the ducat payments were abolished. The Montenegrins were under the obligation to go to war for the sultan, although actually they used their weapons to ward off any attempts by the Turkish army to enter their land. The development of autonomy was paralleled by the process of tribal formation not only in Montenegro and in Brda but also in the neighboring countries of Hercegovina and Albania. In the Middle Ages the katuns, powerful groups of herdsmen, also served as military groups. Furthermore, family ties were extremely strong, with large communities of kinsmen, the clans, passing down lore from father to son about their distant ancestors and the development of the clan. Some of the katuns acted as a rallying point for the population in their area, and the nucleus of the clan thus formed frequently provided the name for entire nahiyas. As time went by, tribes comprising a number of clans developed in these areas as organized territorial communities with economic, administrative, and military functions. The tribe was headed by an elected elder who had to abide by decisions passed at assemblies of all adult warriors. In the tribe, and outside, individuals were protected through the medium of the blood feud which, once started, could stop only with the pacification of the involved families through the contraction of marriages and the establishment of ties such as those of the *kum* (godfather). The tribes owned such common property as forests, pastures, and waterways, and these were used by all members. The private holdings of individual families were small, for arable land was scarce. Territorial communities that varied in size and enjoyed autonomous rights thus came into being within the empire.

The Revival of the Patriarchate of Peć

The Christians were also bound together by their religious organizations. The Catholics were in a particularly difficult position, for the Turks, waging war against Catholic countries in Europe, were extremely suspicious of their Catholic subjects. Priests and papal envoys arriving from the west were looked upon as spies. The authorities displayed an extraordinary tolerance toward the Bosnian Franciscans, who had been active since 1517 in a special province, Bosna

Argentinea. This area was later extended to include other territories taken by the Turks in Dalmatia and Slavonia, where the Franciscans made efforts to establish and organize the Catholic church.

Until a powerful Russia appeared on the international scene, the Orthodox church presented no threat to the empire because the most important centers of the Eastern church were situated in its territory. The archbishopric of Ohrid remained, and it expanded the area of its jurisdiction. From 1455 onwards, it encompassed even the southern eparchy of the patriarchate of Peć and its center in Peć. The Serbian church preserved its autonomy up to the 1530s; then it was subordinated to the jurisdiction of the archbishop of Ohrid. However, the important role played by the Serbs in Turkish conquests, and the personal influence of Mehmed Sokolović, were instrumental in persuading Suleiman II to consent to the reconstruction of the patriarchate of Peć in 1557. The first patriarch to be appointed was Makarije, the brother of Mehmed Sokolović; after Makarije's death, his nephew Antonije and cousin Gerasim became patriarchs. The patriarchate of Peć expanded its jurisdiction over Serbia, Montenegro, part of Bulgaria, the northern districts of Macedonia, and all settlements of the Serbs in Dalmatia, Croatia, Slavonia, and Hungary through the medium of over forty metropolitans and bishops. The patriarchate and its eparchies were granted estates and the right to collect fees of twelve aspers per household and one ducat for each priest. The Serbian church was autonomous (electing its own patriarch and bishops) and empowered to settle marital disputes between its faithful. At the top it was a feudal organization, but with its multitude of clergymen, its reconstructed or newly built churches and monasteries, it was a gathering place for the Serbian people, scattered over the wide expanses of the Ottoman Empire, welding them into a whole, acting as their representatives, and promoting the idea of their unity. In comparison with the church organization, the autonomous local units of the Serbian people were second-rate in significance.

Patriarchal Culture

Fostering the traditions of the Nemanid dynasty and state, the Serbian church continued to pursue its cultural activities both before and after the reconstruction of the patriarchate. During the sixteenth century, a number of presses were established for printing ecclesiastical texts (at Mileševo, Belgrade, Rujna, Scutari), and books were also copied by scribes in the monasteries. Patriarch Pajsije (sixteenth–seventeenth century) composed a biography of Emperor Uroš, and others wrote or rewrote chronicles in the Serbian version of Old Slavonic. In reconstructing old or erecting new churches, painters were commissioned to decorate the walls with frescoes, which began to include subjects from old biographies; icons were also painted, magnificent iconostases were

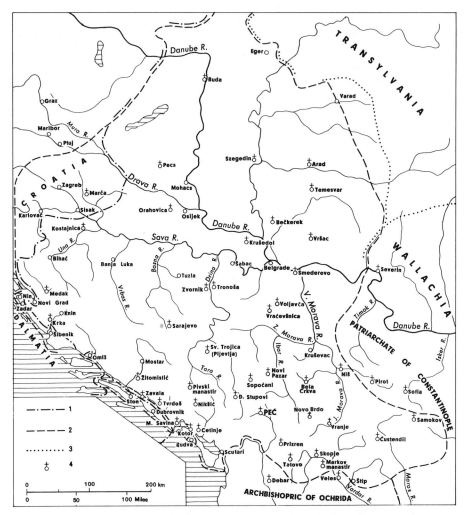

MAP 22.   The area under the jurisdiction of the patriarchate of Peć in the mid-seventeenth century. (1) The boundaries of the Ottoman Empire; (2) the boundaries of the area under the jurisdiction of the patriarchate of Peć; (3) the boundaries of vassal principalities; (4) the see of bishoprics.

erected, and many ritual and ornamental objects were fashioned. There being no powerful donors, church buildings and works of art were far more modest than they had been in the Middle Ages. Rather, they reflected the possibilities of the church itself, or of wealthier citizens and the small peasant holders, with the result that the final outcropping of this art found expression in wooden churches. The area of this artistic and cultural activity extended to all districts where the revived patriarchate exercised jurisdiction over the Orthodox part of the population. Similar activity was in progress in the area of the archbishopric of Ohrid; linguistically, its role differed from that of the patriarchate of Peć. The archbishops were Greeks, and from the end of the sixteenth century onwards most of the bishops also were Greeks; under their influence the use of Slavonic books in worship and in schools was slowly suppressed. It thus happened that the archbishopric of Ohrid dissociated itself completely from the Slav people among whom it functioned.

The nurturing of the remnants of the old feudal culture in traditional forms was paralleled by the flowering of folk culture bearing the imprint of profound patriarchalism. Rising from the narrow coastal belt that was exposed to the fructifying impulses of the Mediterranean and largely subordinated to Venetian power, the lofty mountains of the Dinaric system stretched to the fertile plains of the Sava Valley. With little arable land to speak of, the highlanders jealously guarded the remnants of ancient social relations. To them, patriarchal concepts were very much a part of life. This was a singularly archaic world of ancient Balkan culture which, under Turkish rule, left to its own resources, and free of the pressure that had been brought to bear on it by the feudal institutions of the medieval states, grew even more set in its ways. Its isolation deprived it of the possibility of promoting production and changing the way of life. Most needs were satisfied by the products of cottage industries, sometimes brought to perfection. Scant attention was paid to the home, and furniture consisted of only the most essential articles required for rest and the preparation of food (mats, woven covers, low tables and chairs, clay and wooden vessels and utensils). Much greater importance was attached to wearing apparel for festive occasions, and on this the industrious weavers and embroiderers spent all their inventiveness, decorating both men's and women's clothing with richly wrought motifs in silver, woolen, and silk thread in glowing natural colors. The numerous ornamental designs worked into belts, vests, headkerchiefs, and aprons occasionally containing elements typical of classical decoration, gave village and family holidays a picturesque air.

Festivities connected with religious holidays (Christmas, Easter) or important family occasions (birthdays, weddings, burials) or work in the fields, unfolded according to a rigidly established ritual based on ancient customs in which pagan symbols outnumbered Christian. Man's life ran its course from birth to death through fixed and inviolable forms, into which new elements could be introduced only with the greatest of difficulty and in the teeth of stubborn resistance. The people possessed a highly developed sense of solidarity and were governed in their behavior by strict moral principles, within the framework of small communities like the joint family, the village, and the clan, which sometimes embraced distant relatives and tribes. Everything was sacred: honor, property, and human life. These principles were far less prevalent in other communities nearby or far away. As the communities rested on blood ties, there developed a very rich terminology covering all degrees of kinship. Foreigners, travelers, and all peaceable passersby enjoyed the protection of the community in which they found themselves. Hospitality was a lasting and respected feature of patriarchal society. Virtue was demanded of young women, and of married women devotion to their husbands and the family; men were required to show a stout heart and courage, severity, and justice. Greater prestige accrued to those who, besides possessing their own admirable personal qualities, could name their ancestors and faithfully recount their deeds. Traditions were consequently preserved. But the farther removed tradition was from the event in question, the more it lost the freshness of accuracy, tending to confuse personalities and chronology and to mingle legend with history.

In this social setup, a rich folk literature developed, fostered in the vernacular and handed down by word of mouth from one generation to the next. Its authors are anonymous, for it expressed the broad and generally adopted attitudes of the community, its tastes, mentality, and requirements. To make them more memorable, experiences and wisdom were given the form of pithy folk sayings, used in everyday speech whenever an occasion arose to confirm their authenticity. Folktales and prose fables, frequently laced with ancient motifs transmitted through written literature, revealed to listeners an unreal world full of infinite possibilities (omnipotent and supernatural beings, acts independent of the operation of natural laws) and released them for a fleeting moment from the ordinarily grueling grind of everyday life. The lyrical song was the handmaiden of toil, ritual, entertainment, and love situations. But pride of place belonged to the epic poem in a ten-beat line. These poems, recited by elderly and frequently blind men who accompanied themselves on the gusle, excited the hearers with their descriptions of actual or imagined events from the past and present. Such songs had also existed in the Middle Ages, but it is characteristic that few have come down to us with motifs from mythology or the life of the times of the Nemanid dynasty. Most of the songs are linked with happenings from the period of the Turkish invasions (the cycle of the Battle of Kosovo, Kraljević Marko, the despots) or with heroes celebrated for their feats during the period of Turkish rule (cycles about the haiduks and Uskoks), especially when the empire started to decline. Similar songs were known to the Muslims, who, however, sang of their own heroes fighting against the resistance of the Christian multitude. All these songs underwent change as time went by and they were sung in larger areas. The ones that have been written down are those which were preserved up to the nineteenth century, when collection and study of them was begun. It was then that the language of the folk songs, the language of the ordinary cattle raisers, was taken to serve as the basis for the new Serbo-Croat literature and the modern literary Serbo-Croat language.

CHAPTER 15

The Crisis
of the Ottoman System
and the Beginning
of Resistance

THE DECLINE OF THE OTTOMAN EMPIRE / SOCIAL CHANGES (CREA-
TION OF ČIFTLIKS) / THE TURKISH REIGN OF TERROR AND RESIS-
TANCE BY THE HAIDUKS / THE CURTAILMENT OF TURKISH EXPAN-
SION / INSURGENTS AGAINST TURKISH POWER / THE CANDIAN
WAR / WESTERN PROPAGANDA AMONG THE CHRISTIANS IN THE
TURKISH EMPIRE / THE TEMPORARY RECOVERY OF THE ECONOMY
IN DALMATIA

The Decline of the Ottoman Empire

It was impossible for the Ottoman Empire to maintain for long its superiority over the European countries. Although it enjoyed the support of France,
ancient rival of the Hapsburg monarchy, its "capitulations" with the French king
in 1535 ("capitulations" was the name for agreements signed by Western countries
with the Porte) gave European traders a privileged position in the empire, allot-

ting Turkey the status of a semicolonial country in the European economic system. Exports accounted for the flourishing cities. By 1632 Belgrade had grown to 40,000 inhabitants; at roughly the same time Sarajevo had 8,000 and Banja Luka 3,000 houses. The towns offered abundant opportunities for prosperous business, and all sections of the population flocked there in droves. For the luxury articles that were on sale, huge quantities of grains had to be traded, the result being that entire areas were threatened with starvation. The fact that these expensive wares could be purchased only for large sums of money launched a veritable stampede to get rich quick. As early as the second half of the sixteenth century, processes began which were to lead to the military and financial crisis of the empire.

The Hapsburg monarchy succeeded in putting a stop to Turkish expansion. The conquerors failed in their attempts to acquire booty and new timars, and so, in order to secure the needed income, they appropriated a greater share of the goods produced on the same, unchanged holdings. The state increased the estates of individual spahis, but by the second half of the sixteenth century their number had been reduced by 50 percent. No replacements were sought for those who had lost their lives in the wars, as there was nothing to offer them. The remaining spahis in Bosnia, Macedonia, and other lands fought to retain their timars within their own families and to win the right to dispose of them as they saw fit. The central authorities permitted the creation of what were known as *ojakluk* timars (family timars), and even gave their owners money to help them prepare for war. Still it happened in the early seventeenth century that barely half of those from whom service was expected answered the call to arms. Army discipline deteriorated, and the prestige of the central government declined rapidly. The Janissaries, once the pillar of the sultan's power, raised revolts, blackmailed, overthrew, and even murdered the sultans. Their ranks were no longer reinforced by the "levy of boys," which was abolished in the first half of the seventeenth century. Instead they accepted into their fold the sons of influential Muslims and scattered over the empire, waxing rich from crafts or trade. They also took to raising families, despite the sultan's prohibition.

In the face of dissolution of the old military-feudal system, the central authorities had to rely in growing degree on mercenaries. For their maintenance and the improvement of military equipment, which was developing apace in the West, enormous sums were needed, but much of the revenue was being swallowed by wasteful courtly spending on luxury living and expensive administration. The Porte raised taxes, debased money, and leased state property on a long-term basis. The situation improved only temporarily, for even worse days set in after the brief spell of relief. As the sixteenth century drew to a close, expenditures were three times the amount of revenues. Furthermore, gold and silver flowed out of the country for the purchase of luxury articles. Work ground to a halt in the mines, and agriculture showed no betterment, for new methods of land cultivation were not being applied in spite of constantly fluctuating manpower. The scramble for land and property rights was on.

Social Changes (Creation of Čiftliks)

Under the old system very little land was left at the free disposal of individuals. If the peasant sold his heritable property with the permission of the spahi, a buyer of the same social position would take over his obligations along with the land, thereby freezing the entire social structure. The number of feudatories with čiftliks was small. Toward the end of the sixteenth and in the course of the seventeenth century, transformation of lands into private property became a regular occurrence. Land abandoned by peasants fleeing from hunger, pestilence, and the savagery of tax collectors was conceded by one spahi to another as čiftlik. The peasants themselves turned it over to town merchants and moneylenders against unpaid debts. These then traded with the land and the people they found on it. Onetime Vlach warriors and Armatoles lost their heritable property, which the new masters acquired as čiftlik. In Serbia military commanders took the land from district chiefs (knezovi) and chieftains (primićuri) and even divested churches and monasteries of their holdings for the purpose of creating čiftliks. This form of land possession and disposal became increasingly widespread also in Macedonia, Serbia, and Bosnia. The peasants who stayed on the čiftliks to work or those who were brought in by the new master became serfs without any rights. Their lord, a Janissary, aga, bey, spahi, or merchant, collected all levies, both imperial and spahi, thus appropriating for himself the lion's share of income.

On the whole, the peasant's lot deteriorated. Taxes and levies weighed heavily upon him, as they continued their upward spiraling. By the end of the sixteenth century, they were five and even eight times as high as before. Furthermore, the peasants were made to do forced labor repairing fortresses, towers, and roads. In Srem, Bačka, and Banat they also had to put up with taxes levied by the Hungarian landlords, who lived outside Turkish borders but acted through the haiduks. The peasants fled from these areas or, in order to conceal themselves, built their homes underground, the roofs and chimneys barely visible through the trees. In Serbia, along the Istanbul road over which all Turkish armies passed, not a settlement could be seen, for the armies plundered and murdered the population along the way. Tax collectors, seeking protection from aroused peasants, arrived with armed escorts who shrank from no form of violence and terror. The flight of peasants to the hills, towns, or other areas threatened to leave the landowners without manpower. The laws bound the peasants to the land, and here and there the spahis had the right to return peasants by force wherever they found them within a period of fifteen years.

The Turkish Reign of Terror and Resistance by the Haiduks

Security and law were a thing of the past. No one could count on a fair trial, as the khadis were greedy for bribes. The entire military-administrative apparatus also reeked of corruption from top to bottom, relying on graft for the major part of its income. Titles and honors were purchased. Data were entered in tax ledgers according to the amount the payee was able to deposit in bribes. The wealthy concealed their riches to protect them from the avarice of the Turkish authorities. The shattered prestige of the central authorities made for anarchy in the eyalets and sandjaks. In the first few decades of the seventeenth century, beglerbegs and sandjakbegs followed upon one another in rapid succession, undertaking raids on their own along the Croatian and Dalmatian boundaries, clashing and crossing swords with the Janissaries, feudatories, and merchants, and fostering lawlessness from which it was the rank and file of the people who suffered most. Discontent mounted, driving people to resist. A permanent form of this resistance was the *hajdučija* (resistance by haiduks). Revolts, which broke out when conditions for their achieving success were ripe, were due to multiplying Turkish difficulties and outside impetus.

The haiduks were an extremely complex phenomenon of social and political resistance. Even before the arrival of the Turks, men had become individual outlaws, gathering together in the forests and hills and plundering the merchants that carried rich wares along the roads. Under the Turks, large numbers of men joined the haiduks. Looting by haiduks along the roads was a regular occurrence. To combat it, the authorities set up *palanke* (minor settlements) as the centers of small garrisons. These also served for refuge in case of attacks. Furthermore, for a minimum of protection, they imposed upon entire villages the obligation to guard the lines of communication and at the same time forced them to shoulder collective responsibility for any damage done. Ordinary cases of highway robbery were abundant, but apart from these the mountain clans and tribes, like those of the heroic Greek period, considered raids and looting beyond the boundaries of their own territory as feats of courage and an acceptable form of economic activity. When terror and violence began to prevail in the empire, and people were forced to flee their homes where they were in arm's reach of the authorities, the mountains hummed with activity. Detachments of from ten to thirty haiduks were led by their commanders, called *harambaša* and *barjaktar* (standard-bearer), into attacks on Turkish caravans, merchants, and wealthy individuals. The haiduks accumulated booty from spring to autumn (from Saint George's Day to Saint Demetrius' Day) and then hid out with yataks, their secret allies in the villages, who concealed and helped them and among whom representatives of the authorities themselves were sometimes numbered. Haiduks also operated in the plains of southern Hungary, enjoying the support of the boundary authorities of the Hapsburg monarchy and often taking cover in the vassal Turkish principalities of Transylvania, Wallachia, and Moldavia. Their activities acquired some of the features of political struggle. Occasionally, as in Macedonia, Muslim outlaws joined the haiduks, but the majority of the latter were Christians. The Turks pursued them, offered rewards for their capture, persecuted their contacts, and made short shrift of those whom they caught by torture, impalement, and hanging. In spite of these stringent measures, they failed to suppress the haiduks. During wars against Christian countries, the phenomenon assumed even broader proportions, and haiduks frequently became the standard-bearers of struggle. In popular uprisings their detachments were the backbone of striking power. In war and in insurrection, without changing their way of life or the activities in which they engaged, the haiduks became fighters for the emancipation of the people from social and national oppression.

In role and function the haiduks were not different from the Uskoks (refugees), who were wont to raid Turkish territory and to plunder under the leadership of their commanders. The Uskoks of Senj had their own seafaring vessels, which they sailed up rivers to attack Turkish territory. The Venetians supported the Uskok operations while they were at war with the sultan, for instance, during the Cyprus War (1570–1573). When peace reigned between the Turks and the Venetian Republic, the Uskoks again became bothersome as they menaced trade along the Adriatic coast and plundered Venetian ships.

The haiduks and Uskoks were not the only forces of resistance. When the empire fell into crisis and lawlessness threatened, many local citizens were left without their former privileges and the church was deprived of its possessions. The antagonism between the asker and the raya increasingly came to be identified with the earlier but less emphatic antagonism between Muslims and Christians. The Turks then became virtually the sole mainstay of social and political suppression, while the Christian people, the Serbs, Macedonians, and Croats were the oppressed raya. When revolts flared up toward the end of the sixteenth century, they were supported by the highest representatives of the Serbian church. Heading them, apart from the haiduk commanders, were persons who had previously enjoyed a privileged position in the feudal system of the Ottoman Empire. The earliest organized movements of this type appeared during the Turco-Austrian War of 1593–1606.

The Curtailment of Turkish Expansion

The pasha of Bosnia attacked the Croatian border as early as 1574 although the Porte and the Viennese court were at peace. Slowly he dislodged the border, moving it westward and thus prompting the Hapsburgs to organize the Military Frontier with thoroughness. The raids of 1591 were continued by the Bosnian convert to Islam, Hasan Pasha Predojević, when he came to rule

Bosnia. By the following year he had captured Bihać and the area surrounding it. Many Croatian fortified towns fell, and Turkish troops took large numbers captive for use as slaves. However, successive attacks on Sisak brought no result and even terminated in a Turkish defeat in 1593, in which Hasan Pasha himself and four sanjakbegs lost their lives. The Porte responded to the defeat, the gravest it had experienced on its boundaries in the past hundred years, by declaring war on Austria. This Turco-Austrian War was waged chiefly in Hungary. It demonstrated the impotence of the Ottoman Empire and its inability to undertake the kind of offensive that had once been successfully prosecuted by Suleiman II. The forces warring along the Croatian boundary won back part of the lost territory and retained it until peace was concluded in 1606.

As soon as the Turks launched raids along the Croatian boundary, the old idea of forming a league against them was revived. But the pope, finding it impossible to persuade even a single Western European power to take action, undertook steps to attract Poland, Russia, Wallachia, and Moldavia to the league. It was believed that Russia would show some concern for its coreligionaries in the Balkan Peninsula, particularly if Russia itself decided to move against the empire. Most of the countries still stood aloof. Only Wallachia and Moldavia joined the war on Austria's side. The propaganda designed to persuade the Serbs to answer the call to revolt was effective. Unknown to the Turks and Venetians, inhabitants of the coastal area established contact with leaders of the people in Hercegovina. The Serbs in the Banat particularly took courage when the prince of Transylvania, whose support they had enjoyed even earlier, started talks with the court in Vienna for a common front against the Turks. Revolts flared up one after another in several quarters only to end in defeat for lack of proper preparation and adequate coordination.

Insurgents against Turkish Power

First came the uprising in the Banat (1594), which achieved enviable success while Turkish troops were otherwise occupied in Hungary. The rebels captured a number of towns. A few months later the Turks, no longer pressed along the main front, annihilated two detachments of rebels one after the other. Assistance from Austria and Transylvania failed to materialize, and the surviving fighting men had no recourse but to join the troops of those countries in order to pursue the struggle against the Turks. In a vengeful mood the grand vizier and the commander in chief of the Turkish forces, Sinan Pasha, ordered the remains of Saint Sava to be disinterred from the monastery of Mileševo and removed to Belgrade, where they were burned in retaliation for the revolts, and as a warning. The act had exactly the opposite effect.

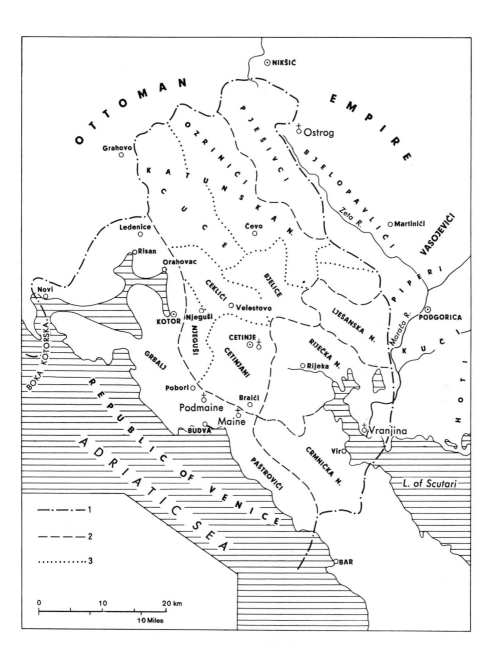

MAP 23.   Montenegro in the early eighteenth century. (1) Boundary of Montenegro and Venetian possessions; (2) boundaries of nahiyas; (3) boundaries of tribes.

Envoys of the pope and of the Austrian and Spanish Hapsburgs won over for their plans the archbishop of Hercegovina and the vladika of Montenegro. They also persuaded the archbishop of Ohrid to generate activity among the Albanians. Monks informed them that the people were ready to fight on condition that they would receive assistance from abroad. Although the Western powers did not form an alliance, and there were no joint operations, prominent haiduk leaders set out against Turkish detachments, destroying them and capturing Turkish strongholds. Hapsburg followers in Split, in spite of official Venetian policy, gained temporary control of the Klis fortress. The insurgent movement spread like wildfire among the Hercegovinians and the highland tribes in present-day Montenegro. Stranded without the promised help, the leader of the Hercegovinian tribes, Grdan, was forced to capitulate to the superior enemy in 1597, the year in which he had raised the insurrection. But he continued to maintain ties with the Austrian Hapsburgs, particularly after Jovan, the patriarch of Peć, had also established contact with them. After the conclusion of peace between the Austrians and Turks, he made an effort to find support in Spain, Tuscany, and Savoy. In the presence of Patriarch Jovan, a gathering of people was held in Morača toward the end of 1608. Those present expressed their readiness to accept the duke of Savoy as their king in exchange for assistance and a promise to respect the Orthodox religion. The duke of Savoy had no forces to speak of, whereas mutual conflicts held the attention of other European powers. The insurgents could pin their hopes only on the unrealistic plans of isolated adventurers. Finally, Voivode Grdan and Patriarch Jovan broke off ties with the Western powers and terminated the activities that had been initiated with such enthusiasm.

The situation created along the western borders of the Ottoman Empire held out the promise of a relatively peaceful period. In 1615 the court of Vienna renewed the peace that had been concluded earlier. Soon the Thirty Years' War (1618–1648) was to engage all its forces. Before that war engulfed Western Europe, the Hapsburgs had to regulate their relations with the Republic of Venice, which had not participated in the last war against the Turks. The Venetians had even profited from that war to expand their trading privileges in Turkey. They obstructed papal and Hapsburg propaganda at every turn while keeping a watchful eye on the insurgent movement lest it spread to their territory along the coast. They were thorough in suppressing Uskok activities, claiming that it was precisely these that had prevented their achieving agreement with the Viennese court. When the Hapsburgs, concluding peace with the Porte, forbade Uskok activities along their frontiers, the Uskoks, left without plunder, turned their attention to Venetian ships and possessions. Their ruthless courage finally led to the Venetian-Austrian War, commonly called the Uskok War (1615–1617). Although Uskok corsairs posed a threat to Venice itself, the Hapsburgs, in warring along the land border with Venice, failed to bring the Venetians to heel and finally agreed to peace, after which they resettled the Uskoks of Senj in the Military Frontier. Finding previous obstacles had melted away, the Venetians revived trade with Turkey via Dalmatia. Plundering continued along the Turkish-Hapsburg frontier, but war operations were not undertaken and trade, especially smuggling, began to develop more freely.

The Candian War

During the first half of the seventeenth century, revolts and disorders shook the capital of the Ottoman Empire as well as its Asian and African provinces. Algeria, Tunisia, and Tripoli won their independence. The central government frittered away its strength in crushing disorders. Wars against Poland and Persia ended abortively. But just when the recapture of Baghdad (1638) held out hope that the old glory of Turkish arms could be revived, the luxury-loving Sultan Ibrahim I, desirous of wresting Crete from the Venetians, succeeded only in involving himself in the protracted Candian War (1645–1669). The Turks prosecuted the war without success until 1656, when Sultan Mehmed IV entrusted imperial policy and the title of grand vizier to the elderly Mehmed Köprülü of Albanian descent. Finally the Turks managed to capture Crete, leaving the Venetians only three ports. Although the Republic of Venice was disinclined to fight, once war was forced upon it, it pursued it in the Mediterranean and in Dalmatia with all the forces at its command, including those against whom it had fought during the Turco-Austrian War.

From 1646 onwards, the Turks undertook raids from Bosnia into Dalmatia in the endeavor to capture Šibenik, Zadar, Split, and Kotor. The Venetians' mercenaries warded off the attacks only to indulge in an occasional raid themselves during which they took possession of boundary fortifications. The Venetians' greatest achievement was the capture of Klis Fortress, Poljica (the area between Split and the Cetina River), and the Makarska Frontier. Although only minor boundary changes were the upshot, the war area suffered horribly from starvation and pestilence, having been left without even the scant income it eked from agriculture. Whereas the Venetians had previously taken savage action against the Uskoks, now they invited Turkish subjects, mostly Vlach herdsmen called Morlaci, to settle on their territory with their families and livestock and to take upon themselves the burden of patrolling the boundary. The Morlaci (actually Orthodox herdsmen who considered themselves Serbs) formed haiduk detachments and made their way along river valleys and over the mountains to Turkish territory, plundering along the way and giving impetus to action by the haiduks in Bosnia and Hercegovina. The most famous Uskok commander in the Venetian fold was Stojan Janković, who could muster 1,200 fighting men. Refugees from Hercegovina, led by Bajo Nikolić Pivljanin and

Limo Barjaktar, attacked Turkish territory from Boka Kotorska while guarding Venetian possessions at the same time. Many of the natives who had accepted Islam also won fame for their feats of daring and were celebrated in folk songs together with their Christian brothers.

The Hercegovinian tribes of the Nikšići, Ridjani, and Drobnjaci raised two insurrections during the war (1649, 1657). In the course of the second, certain highland tribes (from the Albanian border) also rose in revolt. In 1648 the Montenegrins offered to become subjects of Venice if the same rights recognized by the Turks were accorded them. The following year, detachments made up of Venetian subjects from the coast arrived in Cetinje. The Turks, however, defeated them at the Morača River, forced them to retire, and pacified Montenegro. Finally collaboration between them was reduced to the Montenegrins' promising the Venetians at a Montenegrin assembly held in 1660 that they would not permit any armed forces intending to strike against Venice to cross Montenegrin territory.

Western Propaganda among the Christians in the Turkish Empire

During the Candian War the Roman Catholic church continued its propaganda among the higher Orthodox clergy. Although Jovan's successor, Patriarch Pajsije (1614–1647), devoted his energies largely to the life of the church, its reconstruction, and cultural activity, he did not entirely disrupt talks with the papal plenipotentiaries. But he exercised great caution, for in Rome's view an anti-Turkish alliance could be realized only if attended by agreement on the union of the churches. Like his predecessors, he put pressure on the Catholic inhabitants of the empire and tried to make them pay church levies. Closer ties were established by Mardarije, the Montenegrin metropolitan, through whom the pope wished to influence Patriarch Pajsije. The new patriarch, elected at the synod held in Morača in 1648, agreed to talks on the matter of the union. The notion of union, however, was distasteful to the lower clergy. When the Turks removed the bishop who had been designated to go to Rome for talks, Patriarch Gavrilo took refuge in Russia. Intensified reprisals and the death sentence meted out to Patriarch Gavrilo upon his return from Russia (he was hanged in Brusa in 1659), coupled with the loss of faith in the Western powers, caused a growth in opposition to any negotiation whatsoever for a union of churches. The new patriarch, Maxim, elected in 1656 in Gavrilo's absence, devoted himself to church affairs in the endeavor to avoid arousing the ire of the Turkish authorities. But by the end of the seventeenth century, such a policy was no longer tenable.

Regardless of all the shifts in position of the patriarchs and church elders of Montenegro and Hercegovina, during the Candian War the Christian raya took a definite stand favoring war against the Turks. After 1669 the Venetians retained Klis, Poljica, and the Makarska Frontier in Dalmatia.

The Temporary Recovery of the Economy in Dalmatia

The Candian War brought dislocation to established relations in the economic life of Dalmatia on one hand and Bosnia on the other. After the war these relations were reestablished. Between the seventies of the sixteenth century and the Candian War, the Venetians made an effort to revive trade in the Adriatic Sea. Through the Dalmatian cities, and particularly Split, they maintained commercial ties not only with the Balkan lands but also with other regions of the empire. Dalmatia experienced a period of economic advancement. Dubrovnik gradually lost its trade monopoly in Turkish territory and, owing to Venetian pressure at sea and the strong competition of Western countries in the Levant, decreased its fleet perceptibly. Dubrovnik traders moved away from many towns in Turkey, withdrawing before the hordes of local Muslims, Armenians, Jews, and others, to found colonies in the larger towns. During the Candian War, Dubrovnik trading again became important in the empire, as Dubrovnik remained the sole port along the Adriatic Sea where goods could pass in transit to Turkish territories. When the war ended, the Venetians again took over their previous role, trying to press the traders of Dubrovnik out of business wherever they could. The latter no longer had the strength to fight for their earlier positions, for, to top everything off, a terrible earthquake destroyed the city in 1667, bringing death to three to four thousand of its inhabitants and devastating property. And while Dubrovnik fought for its very existence, standing up to Turkish and Venetian pressure, the Venetians opened their ports in Dalmatia to trade with the continent.

The restoration of trade ties through Dalmatia led to the temporary recovery of Bosnian towns and trade, which was abruptly cut off by the new Turco-Austrian War. But this upsurge, too, carried the hallmarks of the crisis that lurked beneath the surface, corroding society and the economy of the Ottoman Empire. The rural districts could not produce the quantity of goods required by the tumultuous development of urban economy. Production, oriented largely to livestock raising, was exhausted for the purchase of luxury goods in the West. Individuals grew prosperous while the mass of peasants and town dwellers could not keep body and soul together. Class differentiation in the towns provoked disputes between craftsmen and guilds, or between craftsmen and rich traders, who paid extremely low prices for the craftsmen's products. Finally, in 1682, rebellion broke out in Sarajevo. The peasants from the surrounding area and the poor town dwellers stormed and destroyed the sumptuous buildings housing public institutions and the stately homes of the rich.

In comparison with the state of affairs during the first half of the seventeenth century, the Ottoman Empire succeeded, on the whole, in advancing after 1656 and again joining the ranks of powers that had to be taken seriously into consideration by both East and West. But all the signs of its profound internal crisis smoldered on. Retreat in fresh wars undermined the empire anew, transforming it into the sick old man of the Bosporus.

OTTOMAN SULTANS

Othman (1281–1324)
Orkhan (1324–1360)
Murad I (1360–1389)
Bajazed I Jildrim (1389–1402)
Suleiman I Çelebi (1402–1410)
Musa (1410–1413)
Mehmed I (1413–1421)
Murad II (1421–1451)
Mehmed I el Fatih (1451–1481)
Bajazed II (1481–1512)
Selim I (1512–1520)
Suleiman II Kanuni (1520–1566)
Selim II (1566–1574)
Murad III (1574–1595)
Mehmed III (1595–1603)
Ahmed I (1603–1617)
Mustafa I (1617–1618)
Othman II (1618–1622)

Murad IV (1623–1640)
Ibrahim I (1640–1648)
Mehmed IV (1648–1687)
Suleiman III (1687–1691)
Ahmed II (1691–1695)
Mustafa II (1695–1703)
Ahmed III (1703–1730)
Mahmud I (1730–1754)
Othman III (1754–1757)
Mustafa III (1757–1774)
Abd ul-Hamid I (1774–1789)
Selim III (1789–1808)
Mahmud II (1808–1839)
Abd ul-Medjid (1839–1861)
Abd ul-Azis (1861–1876)
Murad V (1876, only three months)
Abd ul-Hamid II (1876–1909)
Mehmed V (1909–1918)
Mehmed VI (1918–1922)

CHAPTER 16

The Hapsburg Lands and the Anti-Turkish Offensive in the Seventeenth Century

The Centralist and Absolutist Policies of the Viennese Court

In the final decades of the seventeenth century, the Hapsburg monarchy was in a position to replace its previous defensive position with offensive action against the Turks. The growth of its forces was preceded by a period in which internal resistance to the absolutist policies of the Viennese court was crushed, although the Hapsburgs did not succeed in imposing their will on the entire empire despite the power emanating from the imperial crown they had worn. The German princes opposed the measures of the Counter-Reformation, which could celebrate victory only in the Hapsburg crownlands. In Hungary opposition was stiff.

The grandson of Ferdinand I, Rudolf II (emperor from 1576 to 1612), failed to preserve to the end of his life the title of Croatian-Hungarian and Czech king and the title of Austrian archduke. His struggle against the Protestants was defied by the Hungarian nobility under the leadership of István Bocskay (prince of Transylvania from 1605 onwards). In 1606 the emperor's brother Matthias had to concede the right to religious freedom and internal self-government in the Hapsburg part of Hungary. And when Matthias took the lead among the nobility, which was partly Protestant, in Austria, Hungary, and Moravia, Rudolf ceded power to Austria, Hungary, and Moravia in 1608 and to Bohemia in 1611. Matthias's successor, his cousin Ferdinand II, gathered up all the ruler's dignities— imperial, royal, and archducal—resolved to crush the Protestants by force. After the rebellion of the Czech Protestants he became involved in the Thirty Years' War (1618–1648), which engulfed a large part of Europe, bringing terrible devastation to German lands. When peace was restored, the German princes were free to impose their religion on their subjects, but the Hapsburgs retrieved imperial power in form alone.

The horrors of the Thirty Years' War did not directly affect the lands of Croatia and Slovenia. The Croat estates and the ban sided with the Catholic ruler Ferdinand II, as Protestantism had been uprooted in Croatia long ago. In the Slovene provinces, the nobility fawned on the ruler in order to win lucrative positions in the frontier service and obtain military assistance to quell the peasant uprisings; the citizens followed suit, anxious to acquire privileges in trade and crafts in which the peasants competed with them with increasing success, threatening to undermine their positions. A large number of Slovenes, Croats, and Serbs from Hungary and the Military Frontier in Croatia fought on the emperor's side with the light cavalry in the great battles of the Thirty Years' War, their courage and ruthlessness striking terror in the heart of enemy ranks.

The Collapse of the Reformation Movement; The Resistance to Centralism in Croatia and Hungary

During the Thirty Years' War and afterwards, the court in Vienna resorted to various measures to consolidate the absolutist power of the monarch, drawing support from the Catholic church, the higher nobility dependent on the court, the powerful standing army, and the highly developed bureaucratic apparatus. Austria was gradually withdrawing from the Holy Roman Empire into a separate political unit. The process of consolidating central power directly affected the Slovene regions as Hapsburg crownlands. In Hungary and Croatia, where the Hapsburgs were kings by election, the old institutions of the autonomous structure resisted this pressure longer and with more notable success.

In 1628 Ferdinand II ordered the Protestant nobility in Austrian lands either to convert to Catholicism or to emigrate. Over 750 noblemen left Inner Austria for other parts. Until the final decades of the eighteenth century, Catholicism remained as the sole confession permitted in Slovene lands. The only exceptions were Prekomurje, which was part of Hungary, and Trieste and Gorizia, where Jews persecuted in other areas had come to settle. Church institutions increased their landholdings while simultaneously falling under the influence of the central authorities, who maintained full supervision over the people through them. The clergy attained a better education, became highly disciplined, and kept orderly parochial ledgers with data about parishioners.

The reforms failed to abolish the old political institutions, but they did reduce their competence and significance, whereby the provincial governor and the estates were divested of their earlier role in the country's political life. Although Inner Austria remained a separate administrative unit, the Court Office moved from Graz to Vienna, where it existed another one-hundred-odd years. The provincial estates, gradually transformed into representative bodies of the nobility, approved the collection of certain taxes and discharged specific military, administrative, and judicial functions. But the domestic army and fortified feudal castles lost importance, for no direct danger from outside enemies threatened. Warriors left for Austria and Italy to serve as mercenaries. Even the right to collect certain taxes expired when the ruler himself began to levy some of them without approval of the estates (1682). In view of its new status, the nobility was no longer inclined to offer resistance. In crushing provincial separatism, the ruler made no inroads on either their interests or their incomes. The victims were the serfs.

Irrespective of how taxes were levied, they grew appreciably, as considerable resources were required to maintain the mercenary army and the expensive administrative apparatus, and to pursue the sweeping policies. The serfs on the large estates bore the brunt of the financial burden of the monarchy, paying new and old levies on homes, on lands, and even on themselves. Their dissatisfaction erupted into the great uprising of 1635, which spread through most of the Slovene lands. The peasants' position was in any case deteriorating. The landlords raised levies, and the peasants brought suit, which they always lost, not knowing where to turn or to whom to appeal. The state did not interfere to any serious extent in the relation between the landlords and their serfs except in the gravest cases.

In Croatia, however, the old structure seemed there to stay. It was considered a component part of the lands under the Hungarian crown, now ruled by the Hapsburgs, who, as kings, provided the sole tie with other lands under the monarchy. Actually, Croatia's reduced territory was not a single entity, nor was it entirely subordinate to the ban and the estates, as the Military Frontier was directly responsible to the ruler through the military administration. Croatia's political life unfolded through a series of conflicts over jurisdiction in the Military Frontier and power over its population. In these conflicts the Military Frontier slowly took shape as a separate area, set apart from the Croatian kingdom.

Until the Turco-Austrian War of 1593–1606, the Military Frontier comprised a system of fortified strongholds with two centers—Karlovac and Varaždin. In Slavonia the area around the generalate of Varaždin was deserted, the villages burned and empty. In Croatia, in the area of the Karlovac generalate, the population was sparse; the land the people used was subject to the payment of certain fees to the lords, largely the most prominent representatives of the big Croatian families—Zrinski and Frankapan. As the population supplied the military command with fighting men, called Frontiersmen, they enjoyed personal liberty. During the war the Frontier commanders invited Serbs, still called Vlachs, from the surrounding territories and settled them in large numbers on the abandoned lands first in Slavonia and later in Croatia. The settlers were happy to leave Turkish territory, for the Austrian archduke Ferdinand II, later emperor, had promised them the same privileges they had enjoyed under Turkish rule or, as in Croatia proper, the exercise of "Uskok freedoms." The revival of the deserted villages stimulated the landholders, Croatian ecclesiastical and temporal lords, to demand the same feudal obligations of the new settlers, while the Croatian Assembly posed the question of its jurisdiction over the newly formed settlements. The new Frontiersmen put up a staunch opposition, requesting self-government and religious freedom. They were supported by their commanders, largely Germans from Styria, who were eager to maintain power over all Frontiersmen. Unwilling to dispute the rights of the Croatian landlords, the ruler set up commissions charged with the task of proposing solutions. These commissions were of the opinion that the Catholic population, comprising one-third of Slavonia, and over one-half of Croatia, could be made subject to the competence of the Croatian Assembly and ban. All the Frontiersmen, however, were unanimous in demanding their rights and stiffly opposed the suggested solutions. In Slavonia the Vlachs succeeded in having their rights formulated in writing in 1630. According to the Vlach Statutes (*statuta Valachorum*), the villages were granted self-government and elected chiefs who drew up military lists. In each captainship the Vlachs elected a grand judge with eight assessors. For criminal acts they were answerable to the military commands and had the right of appeal from lower courts to the general at Varaždin. For the rights granted them, they were expected to undertake the obligation of fighting and building fortifications.

In the territory of Croatia, where there were fewer new settlers, and where the Zrinski and Frankapan counts, and occasionally also the high-ranking commanders in the Military Frontier, succeeded in realizing their land rights, the Frontiersmen remained disunited. The new settlers clashed with the indigenous population and landowners, their quarrels terminating either by their purchasing land themselves or leaving for Slavonia or Venetian territory.

In any case, the Frontier military authorities were successful in their endeavor to keep the control over the population of the Military Frontier out of the hands of the Croatian Assembly. In time, they violated the privileges of the Frontiersmen and finally acquired all administrative and judicial power over them. Most of the Vlachs were Orthodox Serbs with their own church organization and a bishop in the newly erected monastery of Marči, under the jurisdiction of the patriarch of Peć. This was an intolerable situation from the Hapsburg point of view, and the bishop of Marči was asked to express his support for the idea of a union of churches. The declaration was formally given. But when a union was actually effected in the monastery of Marči, in 1672, the people revolted. Their rebellion, however, was easily crushed.

The Carnolian, Carinthian, and Styrian estates, whose revenues maintained the Frontier, lost interest in its destiny as the Turkish threat was no longer imminent. In the early seventeenth century, when they still hoped to forestall the absolutist aspirations of the Hapsburgs, they supported the Croatian estates and their demands in order to win them over as allies in the contest with Vienna. When their resistance was broken, they reversed their overtures of solidarity and in 1625 agreed to the upkeep of the generalate in Karlovac, winning in return the right to dispense posts there. The Croatian estates retaliated by trying to suppress them but failed, as the Carniolan, Carinthian, and Styrian estates demanded compensation for all the resources they had invested in return for conceding such profitable positions in the Frontier area. The extremely modest income of Croatia made it impossible for the Croats to meet their demand.

The gradual erosion of Vlach self-government, the inroads on the autonomy of all towns acting as the headquarters of military commanders (Senj, Koprivnica, Križevci), and the suppression of the old ruling families from those towns assured the Hapsburgs supreme authority in the Frontier territory. Finally the king proclaimed all Frontier land his feud, making empty promises to the onetime feudal lords that he would grant them other lands in exchange. It thus happened that the Military Frontier became a separate territory within Croatia, where the Hapsburgs kept a permanent body of troops and created a foothold for absolutist policies. The Croatian kingdom became a weak protector of the class interests of its nobility which, itself stripped of power and disunited, was no match in its aspirations for statehood for the mounting pressure of the Viennese court.

Many of the church and temporal lords in Croatia were shorn of their onetime holdings and income. The serfs also fled from these possessions to the Frontier so as to attain to the status of free men by becoming soldiers. Those who remained raised rebellions, thus exhausting further the already-debilitated Croatian nobles. A profound gap had long existed between a few of the biggest landowning families and their vassals with considerably smaller possessions. The lesser nobility, suppressed altogether, endeavored to curry favor with court circles and obtain posts of some kind or other. The big families differed in the political positions they assumed, clashing constantly over the pursuit of their own private interests. The ancient Frankapan family was dying out and had already lost most of its possessions in the sixteenth century. Between the Sava and Kupa Rivers, the most powerful were the Erdödis, members of whom had achieved high posts in the Frontier and enjoyed the king's favor. The most prominent was the Zrinski family, whose purchases of land and kinship with the Frankapan family created an estate extending from Medjumurje to Bakar on the coast. Members of this family were regularly appointed to the post of ban. In view of their exceptional power, the Zrinskis became standard-bearers of resistance to Viennese absolutist policies and fighters for the preservation of Croatian statehood.

Dissatisfaction with Viennese policies was far more widespread among the Hungarian nobility, which began to fear, a few years after the termination of the Thirty Years' War, for the special position of the Hungarian lands and to chafe at the neglect of struggle against the Turks and the consequent erosion of Hungarian lands to Turkish power. In the conspiracy involving the highest representatives of the Hungarian nobles (the palatine, the supreme judge, the archbishop of Gran) the most conspicuous role was played by the Croatian ban Nikola Zrinski, who had distinguished himself in boundary clashes with the Turks. The short-lived Turco-Austrian war of 1663–1664 and its abortive end gave the plotters the incentive to take action. Although worn by protracted warfare against the Venetians (the Candian War, 1645–1669), the Porte sent armies to the Hungarian lands, embittered at Austrian meddling in the choice of the prince of Transylvania and furious over the erection of a fortress on Turkish territory (at the confluence of the Mura and Drava Rivers) by Nikola Zrinski in 1661. The army, led by Mehmed Köprili, penetrated to a point 130 kilometers from Vienna, again posing a threat to Europe. Assistance to thwart the attack came from all sides, even from opponents of the Hapsburgs. Finally Austrian forces won the day at Saint Gotthard, but Emperor Leopold I (1658–1705) hastened to Warsaw to conclude peace with the sultan under extremely unfavorable terms, recognizing the right of the Turks to captured lands and agreeing to pay them war indemnity. Nikola Zrinski, who had gained distinction for this thrust to Osijek, withdrew from battle before the conclusion of peace, accusing the Austrian command of refusing to help him defend his fortress. The Hungarian nobility for its part was galled at the court's violation of its rights in concluding a peace without the approval of the Hungarian Diet. The conspirators, relying on Vienna's perennial rival France, decided to move against the Hapsburgs.

Three months after the conclusion of the Vásvár Peace Pact (1664), Nikola Zrinski lost his life during a hunt. After his death, the anti-Hapsburg movement lost its cohesion. Nikola's brother Petar Zrinski, chosen ban the next year, continued negotiations with the French. The negotiations were exploited by the French only to achieve a tactical advantage over the Viennese court for exacting an agreement on the question of the Spanish inheritance. When this agreement was concluded in 1668, negotiations were disrupted. In the meantime the conspirators had established contact with the Turks and with the Poles, meeting only rejection wherever they turned. In 1668 the court of Vienna confirmed the appointment of Petar Zrinski as ban, leaving him with the impression that faithful service might gain him the favor of Leopold I. In this way the final blow to the plans of the conspirators was struck, for Petar's hopes turned out to be unfounded. Vienna did not make him the general of Karlovac, a post he coveted.

The Zrinski-Frankapan Conspiracy and Its Failure

Disillusioned by this failure, Petar Zrinski determined to instigate an uprising, with the support of his brother-in-law Franja Krsta Frankapan and his son-in-law Ferenz Rákóczy, a Hungarian magnate. As the plotters were few in number, Petar called upon the sultan for help, dreaming of becoming, under his wing, the ruler of all lands to be wrenched from the monarchy. The Porte was in no mood to prosecute another war with Austria and replied ambiguously. Through its intelligence, the Viennese court learned of the negotiations and kept track of developments. The conspirators could not muster any great force, as they were opposed to Erdödi, the bishop of Zagreb, and the lesser nobility in service in the Frontier area, and they could not count on the people or Frontiersmen in Slavonia. In 1670 they led into battle only the soldiers of the ban's Frontier and his serfs, but they scattered quickly after the commander of Karlovac defeated the detachment of the ban's Frontiersmen without great difficulty. Petar Zrinski continued to maintain ties with the Turks while at the same time, through intermediaries, he threw himself upon the mercy of Leopold I. False promises were given him on both sides. In April Petar Zrinski and Franja Krsta Frankapan left for Vienna with high hopes of reconciliation and the acceptance of their immodest demands. Ignoring the fact that only the Hungarian Diet had the right to pass judgment on them, Leopold I appointed a court made up of adherents of Viennese absolutism. In accordance with a prior decision, the court sentenced both men to death and confiscation of property. As this denouement was designed to consolidate absolutist policies in Croatia, there was no question of amnesty. Petar Zrinski and Franja Krsta Frankapan were put to death in April 1671 in Wiener Neustadt, and their possessions, covering half of that part of Croatia that was ruled by the ban, fell into the emperor's hands. Having dealt summarily with the strongest Croatian magnate, the Hapsburgs could pursue without obstruction, at least for a brief period, the objectives of their absolutist policy.

Leopold I entrusted the functions of the ban to two ban regents, one of whom, a faithful adherent, Nikola Erdödi, was charged with military affairs. He did not abolish the Croatian Assembly, in the conviction that in the atmosphere of fear and confusion following the crushing of the conspiracy it could easily be transformed into the kind of estate representative body that existed in all Austrian crownlands. The centralistic policies of the Viennese court were implemented by General Herberstein of Karlovac, who elaborated a plan calling for the separation of Croatia from Hungary and the annexation of the ban's Frontier to the generalates of Karlovac and Varaždin, in the endeavor to place the entire Military Frontier under one command and in the same political position. This plan, adopted in 1672 by the War Council in Graz, was opposed by Nikola Erdödi. No longer fearing pressure from the powerful Zrinski family, he stood up in defense of the state rights of Croatia. He was able to assume this posture because the centralistic policy was fiercely resisted by the Magyars, who acted to frustrate its complete affirmation in Croatia as well. When Leopold I abolished the estates order in Hungary and transferred the functions of the palatine to the regency in Pozsony (Bratislava), the incursions of the Protestant *kurucz* (Crusaders), who had taken refuge from persecution in Transylvania, provoked a veritable civil war. In 1677 the *kurucz* received assistance from France and from the prominent leader, Imre Thölköly, sworn enemy of the Hapsburgs, thus forcing the court to relent. In 1680 Leopold restored the ban's rights in Croatia, and at the Assembly in Sopron he reinstated the estates order in Hungary. Thököly, in danger of being left without broad support, concluded an alliance with the Turks and married the daughter of Petar Zrinski, Jelena, widow of Ferenz Rákóczy, who burned with the desire to avenge her family's downfall. Thököly then set about inciting the Porte to prepare for a major war against Vienna. The weakness of Hungary and the enmity of France filled the sultan with hope of fresh victories.

Hapsburg Successes in the Great War of the Holy League against Turkey

The grand vizier Kara Mustafa Pasha led a large host against Vienna in 1683, launching a protracted war against the Hapsburgs (1683–1699), the consequences of which were unforeseeable. After a two-month siege of Vienna, the Turks sustained a telling defeat chiefly because the Polish king Jan Sobieski hastened to aid the Austrian capital. The great Christian victory, echoing joyously throughout Europe, was a turning point in the conflict between the Ottoman Empire and the Hapsburg monarchy, between the Christian West and the Islamic East, for after a period during which power had been more or less bal-

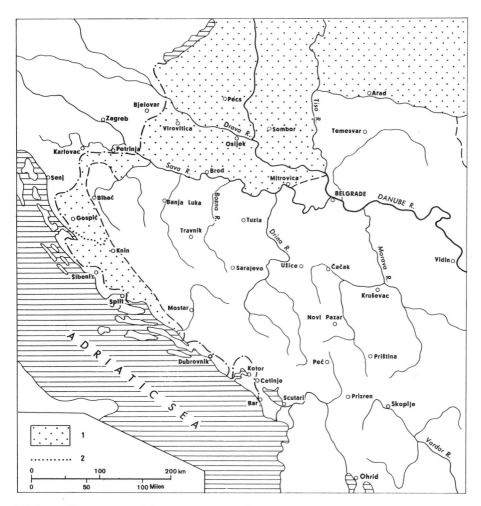

MAP 24. The expansion of the Hapsburg monarchy and the decline of the Ottoman Empire. (1) Territories liberated during the Treaty of Karlowitz (Karlovci), 1699; (2) boundary of Venetian and Hapsburg territories.

anced, the Turks were compelled to withdraw. Beyond all expectations, the Austrian forces penetrated deep into the Balkan Peninsula. The Hapsburg monarchy was not left alone in the war. In February 1684, at the incentive of the pope, Austria, Poland, and the Venetian Republic formed the Holy League, forcing the Turks to offer resistance on several fronts. The Venetians threw their troops against Turkish possessions in Morea (for them it was the "Morean War") and simultaneously joined battle along the borders in Dalmatia and the Montenegrin coast. The war was prosecuted by the Holy League in two phases, before and after 1689, when the fortunes of the Austrian army were reversed. After several attacks on German lands in the Rhine area, France declared war on the Hapsburg monarchy, constraining it to withdraw most of its troops from the Balkan theater.

In addition to the Austrian army, which pressed the Turks from Hungary, Croats, Frontier Serbs, Uskoks from Dalmatia, and haiduk detachments from Slavonia, Bosnia, and Hercegovina also took part in the battles. The people rose on all sides, ready to support the regular troops. By 1687 the Austrian army had taken all of Hungary, Bačka, and a large slice of Slavonia. The Muslim inhabitants fled from the Turkish cities while the Turkish army beat a disorderly retreat. The Janissaries in Belgrade rose in revolt and advanced on Istanbul to depose the sultan, enabling the Austrian army to take possession of Srem and enter Belgrade in 1688, and then to consolidate its positions in northern Serbia and Bosnia along the Sava and Danube Rivers.

Activities of Venice

Simultaneously the Venetian forces, made up largely of Uskoks and local inhabitants, cleaned the Turks out of northern Dalmatia, took Sinj (1686) and Herceg Novi in Boka Kotorska (1687). Austrian victories created confusion among Venetian ranks and cautioned them to be wary of their allies. They therefore undertook to sever all Dubrovnik's ties with its hinterland, where the imperial envoy was busy gaining adherents among the Hercegovinian tribes, and to bring the town under their control. The Republic itself then developed vigorous propaganda activities in Hercegovina, Montenegro, and Albania, for, when the Austrian army began thrusting southward from Belgrade in 1689, the Venetians feared encroachment on their sphere of interest, particularly the Adriatic seacoast. Concluding an alliance, the two powers had agreed that each one should take the regions that had belonged to it earlier. Now, with the Austrians recording unexpected victories and penetrating areas they had never occupied before, suspicion was aroused and friction broke out over spheres of interest. In the autumn of 1688, the Venetians sent a detachment to Cetinje.

Austrian Conquests and the Abandonment of Serbia and Macedonia

Before advancing southward, the Austrian command headed by Ludwig of Baden attempted to fill in the vacuum created by the departure of its units to the western front and called upon the people of Serbia to rebel. There were already many Serbs in the Austrian army who had joined during its triumphant passage through Hungarian lands. The people of Serbia rose against the Turks, formed detachments, and liberated entire areas. By the autumn of 1689, the

"Serbian Militia" had grown to the strength of a regiment, divided into ten companies. At about this time, the Austrian forces defeated the Turks at Niš, captured the town, and continued penetrating in two directions. Ludwig of Baden advanced on Vidin, which he took, while his general, Piccolomini, thrust toward Macedonia, where he entered Skoplje.

Austrian successes had already provoked movements in Macedonia even before he arrived. The people made common cause with the haiduks, and in the summer of 1689 an uprising led by Karpoš encompassed the northeastern part of the country. The Austrian presence only served to broaden the insurrection, but disillusionment was quick to set in. Piccolomini ordered Skoplje, Štip, and Veles razed to protect his army from the pestilence raging there; afterwards he withdrew it to Priština. In the meantime, Turkish forces mustered and went into the offensive. First they quelled the uprising, impaled Karpoš on the stake, and then defeated the Austrian army at Kačanik, heralding the defeat of Austrian arms in Serbia.

The Austrians were engaged in a persistent endeavor to win the allegiance of prominent personalities through whom they hoped to wield influence over the people. They found two such men among the Serbs, one of whom they immediately discarded, taking the other with them. The first was Djordje Branković, who had spent a goodly part of his life in the diplomatic service of the prince of Transylvania. On the basis of his surname, he claimed to be a descendant of the last Serbian despots and tried to persuade the court in Vienna of his power over the people. The emperor bestowed the title of baron on him on the grounds of a forged certificate issued by the patriarch of Peć in return for a payment. He needed the title to pursue his objective of rallying the Serbs around himself. With the emperor's charter in his hands, in 1689, as the "hereditary heir to all Illyria," he began to gather Serbian rebels. Ludwig of Baden, intimidated by his pretensions and ties with the Vlachs and with Russia, ordered him taken captive. Djordje Branković remained in captivity until the end of his days, shorn of all influence over the course of events. Another prominent personality for whose favor the Venetians and Austrians fought was the patriarch of Peć, Arsenije III Čarnojević. Wealthy in his own right, he incited the people to rebel, provoking simultaneous sentiments of hatred and avarice among the Turks. During the Austrian army's southward thrust, he stood in danger of falling into Turkish hands. Leaving Peć to take refuge first in Nikšić and then in Cetinje, he entreated the Venetians to move their armies as soon as possible. Piccolomini, already infected by the plague, moved to Prizren, threatening the patriarch with replacement if he continued his collaboration with the Venetians. Arsenije III returned to welcome him. Together with leaders of the Serbs and Albanians, they reached agreement on the recognition of imperial power and future assistance. Early in November, Piccolomini succumbed to his illness and the Austrian army started to withdraw.

The Great Migration of Serbs to Hungary

Fleeing from Turkish revenge, Arsenije III Čarnojević led the rebellious people toward Belgrade, collecting along the way all those who had cause to fear the arrival of the Turks, especially traders and craftsmen from the Turkish towns. The Austrians supported the migration, seeing in the refugees a fresh source of troops, while the Turks tried unsuccessfully to dissuade them, promising them mercy and even temporary relief from paying the head tax. At the end of March 1690, the fleeing Serbs and Macedonians found themselves at the gateway to Belgrade. In response to a call from Leopold I, many returned to battle, but their participation actually failed to change the course of events in any way. The Turks captured Niš, and the Austrian army arrived at Belgrade reinforced by refugees from the Morava River area. In Belgrade the Serbs held an assembly, from which they sent the emperor an envoy in the person of Vladika Isaija Djaković with an appeal for recognition of freedom of confession and church self-administration, and the message that they recognized him as their hereditary ruler. Leopold accepted their proposals, although with trepidation, and conceded the patriarch's jurisdiction over Orthodox inhabitants of the monarchy. Before the emperor's reply arrived, however, Arsenije III led the people across the Sava and Danube Rivers, in the face of powerful Turkish pressure. In late October 1690 the Turks entered Belgrade, successfully prosecuting the war in the Banat. Consequently the "Great Serb Migration" did not dare stop in Bačka. Under Arsenije III, the people arrived in Komarom and Szent Endre, settling in Hungary. In March 1691 they held a new assembly in Budapest, for the emperor was demanding troop reinforcements. Aware of the fate of Djordje Branković and convinced of his royal origins, they asked the emperor to appoint him their voivode (commander). Leopold I, reluctant to permit revival of notions about the restoration of the Serbian state, rejected the request and appointed a "subcommander" while at the same time transferring to the patriarch, as a less dangerous personality, all jurisdiction over secular and sacred affairs. As the Hungarian estates agreed with the emperor's measures, the Serbs had no need to feel unwanted in their new environment.

Having abandoned Serbia, Austria was no longer in a position to undertake offensives south of the Sava and Danube Rivers. The war dragged on in Bačka, Srem, and Slavonia with intermittent success. During Austrian operations in Serbia in 1689, the Frontier Command finally took Lika and Krbava. The ban's army two years later thrust along the right bank of the Sava River all the way to Brod, and after withdrawing retained the area between the Kupa and Una Rivers. Although satisfied at the withdrawal of the Austrians from the Balkan Peninsula, the Venetians did no more than endeavor to keep their spheres in Dalmatia, Hercegovina, and Montenegro. In this they failed, and were forced to withdraw from Cetinje by Turkish pressure. In 1692 the Turks set fire to the monastery and razed the town, returning then to Scutari. The Hapsburgs and Venetians were prostrated by the seemingly endless war. The Turkish forces, too, had been dealt a telling blow when the Austrian army, commanded by Prince Eugene of Savoy, defeated them in 1697 at Senta and then made a lightning thrust to Sarajevo, which the celebrated commander subdued in three days. Consequently everyone accepted with relief the mediation of Hapsburg allies, England and the Netherlands. Late in January 1699 a peace treaty was signed in Sremski Karlovci (Treaty of Karlowitz). Each side kept what it possessed at that moment. Morea and minor territories in the Dalmatian hinterland were retained by Venice. To escape the encroachments of Venice, the Republic of Dubrovnik permitted the Turks passage to the sea on both sides of Dubrovnik territory. The Hapsburg monarchy, although occupied on two fronts, expanded its area considerably at Turkish expense, demonstrating its might as a power fully capable of pressing the Ottomans back from Central Europe and the Balkan Peninsula.

Success in warfare offered Leopold I opportunities for new ways to entrench his absolutist power. In the flush of gratitude for the liberation of the country, in 1687 the Hungarian Diet in Bratislava recognized the Hapsburgs as hereditary successors to the throne of Saint Stephen. Two years later the Court Office worked out a plan for restructuring Hungary, elements of which were a mixed Hungarian-German standing army, the curtailment of religious freedom in the newly liberated regions, and colonization by Germans. Land was partitioned out among the Austrian generals, who established a new nobility. These measures provoked revolts from 1697 onwards, preventing Vienna from implementing its plans. In Croatia a tug of war ensued between the aspirants to power over the lands taken from the Turks—the Croatian Diet and the central organs of the empire. The Croatian representative in the Hungarian Diet stressed that the Croats had defended the country with their own forces, while the court in Vienna naturally laid emphasis on the merits of the Military Frontier. In controversy with the Croatian Diet, the emperor formally backed down, appointing župans in Slavonia in accordance with the request of the Croatian Diet, but in actual fact he left all power in the hands of the military commanders. In 1693 he agreed that Lika and Krbava should join Croatia, but he did not restore the županija system. The only area recognized in 1695 as coming within the jurisdiction of the Croatian Diet was that between the Kupa and Una Rivers. The central organs ignored demands put forward by the Croatian nobles, skillfully exploiting class and religious differences in the country itself. Looting, killing, and rebelling, the Croatian peasants gave vent to their dissatisfaction with their masters, with no thought whatever of supporting their struggle to maintain the estates. The Frontier Serbs were inimical to the nobles for trying to reduce them to serfs. Added to this were the attempts by the Catholic clergy to draw them into a union. It was therefore natural for them to support the imperial army and its positions. Court policies were also promoted by disputes between the Croatian and Hungarian estates, particularly over the Hungarian notion of the subordination of the Croatian Diet to the Hungarian Diet, as representative of all lands under the Crown of Saint Stephen. Vienna was slowly paving the way toward a centralized monarchy under the absolutist power of the Hapsburgs.

The Development of Capitalist Relations in the Yugoslav Lands under Hapsburg Rule

In the course of the seventeenth century, capitalism started developing slowly in Hapsburg lands. The flight of wealthy Protestants during the height of the Counter-Reformation had initiated a growing dissociation of these lands from Germany, both culturally and economically, and attention was shifted to neighboring Italy. Furthermore, German capital was withdrawing owing to the failure of the biggest business houses when the focus of economic life, particularly trade, moved to Atlantic coastal countries. The Italians invested commercial capital in businesses as permitted by the development of the domestic economy. Capacities had remained unchanged in agriculture, but nonagrarian activities showed signs of recession. In Slovene lands earlier manufacturing plants had closed down, and new ones did not take their place until the eighteenth century. The mine in Idrija raised its production of mercury, much in demand on the world market, but after 1658 the production of cinnabar was stopped as insufficiently competitive. In mining and metallurgy, techniques had improved, it is true, with the utilization of water power, but in smelters many of the furnaces stood idle. Iron production kept its earlier level, while lead declined after the fall of the house of Fugger. Town crafts, enriched by only a few new branches (casting of bells and cannon), produced largely for the local market. But they could not satisfy the demand even of this market and had to be supplemented by cottage industries in the rural districts, with silk raising and embroidery making rather widespread in certain areas. The town craftsmen, jealously guarding the exclusiveness of their guilds, were vigilant to see that their number did not increase. After the foreign traders and entrepreneurs left, they were highly instrumental in bringing on the decline of the towns. Ljubljana had 7,000 inhabitants, Gorizia about 4,000 to 5,000, and Maribor only 2,000. The towns in Croatia lagged far behind them. In some, guilds were just being founded, setting the imprint of the Middle Ages on the modest volume of crafts production.

In times of peace, trade in the Croatian lands revived, interlaced in the boundary areas with smuggling and looting. In the Slovene provinces, which were spared many of the Hapsburg wars, thanks to their geographic position, trade affairs maintained a certain rhythm despite the poor state of the roads, which began to be repaired only about 1660. Apart from petty town trading, against which the peasants continued putting up stiff competition, the domestic merchants also sometimes engaged in business on a large scale, buying up all the products of a certain branch of economy. In foreign trade aliens purchased from the court monopolies for the export of livestock on the hoof, grains, or honey, arousing discontent and resistance on the part of domestic traders. The largest quantities were exported to Italy (livestock, wood, metals). Mercury came from Amsterdam (especially after Dutch capitalists appeared on the scene), Regensburg, and other important trade centers. Grains were imported from Croatia and Hungary, and luxury articles from the Western countries.

The state paid scant attention to economic policies, seeking only to assure itself adequate income. For this purpose, it leased everything it could lay hands on, bestowing titles of nobility on foreign traders who had waxed prosperous. Economic theorists in Austria proposed measures to revitalize the economy and increase revenues. In the spirit of mercantilist policies, they suggested decreasing exports of raw materials, setting up domestic manufacturing for processing those materials, and exporting finished products. The East Company, established in 1667, failed as a result of the Turco-Austrian War. Vienna strove to assure its merchants an outlet to the Mediterranean area through Rijeka and Senj, where it ran up against Venetian restrictions and the competition of Bakar, part of the Zrinski possessions. After their downfall, the court hit upon the idea of opening those ports to Dutch traders. All these, however, were modest attempts to incorporate the Hapsburg lands into the capitalist development of Europe. The Commercial Collegium, established in Vienna for the purpose of promoting trade, setting up manufacturing plants, and controlling prices and circulation of money, had only a negligible influence over the economic affairs of the Austrian lands. The capitalist economy was destined to develop only in the eighteenth century, along with the triumph of imperial absolutism.

CHAPTER 17

The Decline
of the Ottoman Empire
and the Inception of
the Eastern Question

THE TREATY OF PASSAROWITZ AND ITS CONSEQUENCES / AUS-
TRIAN ADMINISTRATION IN NORTHERN SERBIA / THE PEACE OF
BELGRADE / INTERNAL DIFFICULTIES OF THE OTTOMAN EMPIRE /
THE ABOLITION OF THE PATRIARCHATE OF PEĆ AND THE ARCH-
BISHOPRIC OF OHRID / THE POSITION OF MONTENEGRO AND ITS
STRUGGLE AGAINST THE TURKS

The Treaty of Passarowitz and Its Consequences

The Treaty of Karlowitz in 1699 terminated only one long phase in the
war between the Turkish Empire and the Christian powers. Greater stability and
more lasting peace could not be achieved for a number of reasons, one of them
that restive European policy reflected on the relations between individual states
and Turkey. Hardly a decade had passed since the Treaty of Karlowitz, when
Russia entered the war against Turkey for its own specific reasons (1710). The war

came to a quick end as Russia under Peter the Great was compelled to conclude peace (1711) after defeat on the Prut River. Its brief engagement in the war did, however, have repercussions in the Balkan Peninsula. Strongly influenced by the Russians, and responding to a call from the emperor, the Montenegrins took arms against the Turks, but unfavorable developments resulted in their isolation. Nothing stood in the way of the Porte's sending a large invasion army against Montenegro, which even heroic resistance was unable to stop. The fact that refugees were offered shelter in the territory of the Venetian Republic provoked first tension and then war between Venice and Turkey (1714). While the Venetian army battled the Turks in Dalmatia and in the Peloponnesus, its diplomats were busy seeking allies. In 1716 the chain of belligerents grew to include Austria.

Following this development, a larger part of Yugoslav territory became a theater of war. Hapsburg troops entered Bosnia while the main force of the Turkish army crossed the Sava River, sustaining a ringing defeat at Petrovaradin. The path was clear for the war to be transferred entirely to Turkish territory and for the siege of Belgrade. Yet another Turkish army sent to relieve Belgrade was repelled. No decisive battles took place in the Dalmatian or Montenegrin theaters. After a number of defeats, Turkey indicated it was ready to sue for peace. After lengthy negotiations, the rival states concluded the Treaty of Passarowitz (Požarevac) in the year 1718. Because of its reverses, Turkey was forced to agree to major concessions. It ceded to Austria the Banat and Little Wallachia, northern Serbia, the remaining part of Srem, and a belt of territory south of the Sava River, while also agreeing to changes in the boundary along the Una River. The changes were far less significant on the Venetian side. Expansion near Imotski and in Boka Kotorska could not compensate for the Republic's losses in the Peloponnesus. This treaty also secured favorable trading concessions for Austria in Turkey.

Austrian Administration in Northern Serbia

The peace remained in force a bare two decades, during which the belligerents from the past war were drawn into various European conflicts. When that situation subsided, political activity again came to focus on Turkey. This time it was Russia that embarked upon war in 1735, with Austria joining in 1737. Exaggerated optimism attended the launching of these operations, as the Christian population, to which a call to arms had been directed, was expected to support them. Through the patriarchate of Peć and church elders, the Austrian military commanders secured promises of intensified assistance from the insurgents as soon as the emperor's army entered Turkish territory. In the summer of 1737, operations began with uneven success. The Austrians were repulsed in minor boundary clashes while the main body of troops advanced southward, taking Niš,

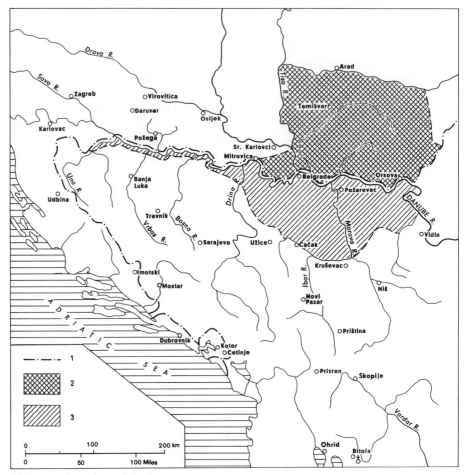

MAP 25. The curbing of the Ottoman Empire in the eighteenth century. (1) Boundaries according to the Peace of Belgrade, 1739; (2) territories permanently liberated by the Treaty of Passarowitz (Požarevac), 1718; (3) territories temporarily liberated by the Treaty of Passarowitz (Požarevac), 1718.

and the rebels captured Novi Pazar. As in the great war of 1690, the patriarch and Serbian elders, as well as tribal representatives from Montenegro and Albania, joined the emperor's army and asked that action be coordinated. But the situation took a turn for the worse as the Turkish army registered one victory after another in Bosnia, from which it thoroughly routed the Austrians. An offensive followed in Serbia, where the imperial army lost everything it had gained in the past war with the exception of Belgrade. War with the Turks was transferred to the other side of the Danube.

The Peace of Belgrade

The Christian population was victimized by Turkish reprisals. A section of the Serbs and Albanians, headed by Patriarch Arsenije IV, entered Austrian territory. Those who stayed behind suffered not only the devastations of war but the ravages of a raging plague. A peace concluded in Belgrade in 1739 moved the Turco-Austrian boundary to the lower reaches of the Sava and to the Danube, leaving all of Serbia under Turkish domination. As this boundary line was destined to remain in force for some time, first as the Austrian-Turkish and later as the Austrian-Serbian border, the Serbs were split in two. Those in Hungary were on the threshold of a brighter future, but even greater trials and tribulations awaited those in Turkey.

The Peace of Belgrade terminated twenty years of Austrian administration (1718–1739) in the northern part of Serbia, from which no significant achievements ensued. The new administration made an effort to compensate for the enormous losses in manpower caused by war and migration by resettling the Serbs from the depopulated areas and bringing colonists from distant parts, largely Germans, to live in the towns, especially Belgrade. The endeavor was designed to replace the Islamic craftsmen and to revive town crafts, leaving trade in the hands of the Balkan Christians. Some attempt was also made to revitalize mining, once an important economic activity in this region. The old mines were worked with the help of foreign experts, but the achievement was negligible. Small quantities of silver, lead, copper, and iron were produced (Rudnik, Avala, Majdanpek), but the entire undertaking was too short-lived for major development and mining came to a halt again along with Austrian rule.

Austrian rule in Serbia had introduced a completely new administrative system in which military and civil power were combined. The entire territory was directly subordinated to central state organs (the Court Chamber Council); lower administrative headquarters were located in Belgrade and Timişoara. The boundary line with Turkey bristled with fortifications, lookout towers, and militia composed of refugees from Austrian territory. The country's interior was divided into about fifteen districts, the highest units under Austrian administration. Beneath them were the *obor-knezovi*, district chiefs of local origin, as the elders of smaller districts, where they collected taxes, maintained law and order, and discharged judicial functions. These *obor-knezovi* belonged to the higher echelons of society which maintained themselves even after the restoration of Turkish power. Likewise their districts were not extinguished entirely. They were perhaps the most important remnant of Austrian rule, calling up among the people unhappy memories of exorbitant fiscal levies, a corrupt body of civil servants, and a ruthless attitude toward the religious sentiments of the population.

The restoration of Turkish power in 1739 was total: the spahis' lands were returned to them, the former Turkish administrative units were reconstructed, troops came to garrison the fortifications, part of the Turkish town population moved back. But the general level of economic and social development declined because resettlement activities were discontinued and part of the working population withdrew with the Austrian army.

Internal Difficulties of the Ottoman Empire

The general difficulties and weaknesses undermining the Ottoman Empire, whose internal decline was manifest in a number of ways, were also evident in these areas. Economically it lagged behind even further as a result of its insufficiently advanced money-economy trade and the paucity of manufacturing during a period when the European countries were experiencing an economic transformation that brought them to the threshold of the industrial revolution. Mining, once a major economic activity, virtually died out altogether in the territories under Turkish rule. In Macedonia the lead mines near Kratovo were utilized still, but the ore was mined by forced labor *(angaria)* of peasants in the vicinity. Mining products were not traded through regular channels but sent directly to state organs which used them for military purposes. The Turkish authorities had no success in their efforts to revive mining in Trepča, a former mining center. In Bosnia, also an ancient mining area, only iron ore was extracted to enable toolmakers to ply their crafts.

Trading showed some progress, especially during the relatively long peaceful period after 1739. Impetus to commercial activity was frequently given by the interest of European countries in a broad market such as the Ottoman Empire. Thanks to Western merchants and local Jews, Salonika in the eighteenth century emerged as the biggest Balkan trading center. Macedonia was well connected by road with Salonika, where it could sell its agricultural and livestock products and purchase what it needed in return. Bosnia's links ran to the Adriatic ports of Dubrovnik and Split and through them to Italy and the Mediterranean basin. Wares traded in for centuries (hides, leather goods, footwear, harnesses, blankets, etc.) were exported still, while staple foodstuffs, salt, textiles, and southern fruits were imported. But new articles also appeared for broad consumption, like coffee and tobacco, and others like steel, tin, and copper met the needs of craftsmen. During this period, trade was monopolized by domestic merchants, notably those from Sarajevo and Mostar, closely connected with their counterparts in coastal towns. After 1739 considerable trade passed in transit between Austria and Turkey over Serbian territory, as the most important road to Istanbul began at Belgrade. In time Serbia also won part of that trade by exporting livestock to Austria. Intensified commerce was useful not only for those engaged in it and for the producers of goods in high demand, but also for the state coffers filled with revenues from levies on trade.

The Ottoman Empire was in need of huge resources, however, to maintain its army and state apparatus and to satisfy the requirements of the sultan and other dignitaries. The result was fiscal pressure that aggravated the position of all those engaged in business. The self-seeking tax collectors brought on deterioration, by their abuses, in the already difficult situation of taxpayers.

The empire's military power waned perceptibly. The timar system of land tenure was in crisis, as the spahis refused to discharge their military obligations devotedly and unreservedly as they once had. On the one hand the timars were not sufficient for the maintenance of the spahis, and on the other a process of their alienation set in. More čiftliks were created, leading in Macedonia to the formation of large estates. The new masters of the čiftliks, the čiftlik-sahibis, stepped up exploitation of the peasantry while dissociating themselves increasingly from the spahis and state authorities. Consequently the creation of landed estates by the Janissaries and military commanders provided with a material base the centrifugal tendencies of increasingly powerful local rulers in various parts of the empire.

Discipline was no longer maintained, and insubordination to the central authorities became regular practice in many areas. Powerful groups of *haramis*, defectors consisting at times of 400 to 500 men who enslaved and bled village and town, were very active in Macedonia. The Armatoles, keepers of the roads and passes whose function it was to protect lines of communication from robbers, frequently resorted to extortion and violence themselves, and in some cases even became outlaws and criminals. In Bosnia the captains and local feudatories waxed powerful and independent. The large Muslim population, its numbers swelled by the southward march of Turkish rule, was mindful of its role in defending the empire, consisting of a well-linked system of fortifications with garrisons and commanders who put up stiff and effective resistance to Hapsburg advancement. Apart from bearing its part of the burden of defense, Bosnia provided the sultan with fighting men for distant theaters of war. Bosnian viziers, whose headquarters had been situated in Travnik from the beginning of the eighteenth century, tried to increase levies, but their attempts met with opposition from local Muslims, who sought relief through legal organs (councils of *ayans*, notables) and also in the form of revolts. In the middle of the eighteenth century the authority of the vizier, as representative of the sultan, had so dwindled that the country suffered from total anarchy for a number of years. In the second half of the century, strife subsided, making it possible for the defense system in the war with Austria to function properly again. In Serbia the town garrisons with their commanders were an important political force which gained mastery over the Christian population through the mass introduction of čiftlik relations, while trying at the same time to resist the influence of the central authority to the utmost. Consequently the moderate regime which the Turkish authorities wished to institute after 1739 to keep the frontier lands as secure as possible, was undermined by the Janissaries and their leaders who controlled the fortifications.

The Abolition of the Patriarchate of Peć and the Archbishopric of Ohrid

A significant change in the position of the Christian population of the Ottoman Empire resulted from the abolition of the patriarchate of Peć (1766) and the archbishopric of Ohrid (1767). Under Turkish power the church hierarchy had been in crisis for some time. The patriarch's support of the Austrian army and his withdrawal with it in 1690 caused the Porte to appoint a Greek to the post of patriarch, provoking a rift in the church when the Serbian bishops refused to accept him. Under successive patriarchs, of Serbian origin, unity was restored and the patriarch was even considered the ranking personage among the Serbs under Hapsburg rule, organized in the see of Sremski Karlovci. Actually, the church in Hapsburg lands lived a life of its own within the framework of imperial privileges. As it was in an incomparably better material position, the see of Karlovci rendered assistance to the patriarchate of Peć, heavily taxed and pressed by the Porte. In the meantime, Greek church dignitaries closely linked with influential traders and financiers (Phanariots, monied Greeks from Constantinople) were gaining ground. Arsenije IV, who had left Turkish territory and joined the Austrian army, was succeeded by a number of Serb and Greek patriarchs, some of whom resigned their posts because of overindebtedness. It was only exceptionally during this entire period that some Serbian patriarchs maintained ties between the patriarchate of Peć and the see of Karlovci. The entire life of the patriarchate, which had only thirteen eparchies after 1739, was quite paralyzed and in rapid decline. The patriarchate of Istanbul bided its time, waiting for the propitious moment to insist on the abolition of Balkan church organizations and to subordinate their territories to its own rule. The last Serbian patriarch was deposed by denunciation, and his Greek successor tendered his resignation himself. A formal act by the sultan abolishing the patriarchate was undertaken in September 1766 at the request of the patriarch of Istanbul, who undertook to pay the debts of the Serbian patriarchate. This was followed by the removal of Serbian bishops and their replacement by Greeks.

During the same period, the autocephalous archbishopric of Ohrid encountered similar difficulties. Frequent replacements at the see of Ohrid were not the consequence of Turkish meddling alone, but of strife among the members of the hierarchy who spared no means to seize high posts which cost a great deal (tribute to the Turkish state, gifts to the sultan, bribes) but were lucrative nonetheless. Like their counterparts in Istanbul and Peć, the church leaders of Ohrid tried to extract as much money as possible from their flocks. The archbishops of Ohrid were also under suspicion at the Porte for their ties with Austria and Rome. Early in the eighteenth century, efforts were made to propagate the idea of a union of churches in Macedonia, whereas the archbishop of Ohrid himself took active part in the war of 1737–1739 on the side of the Austrians. These doubts made it easier for the patriarchs of Istanbul to attain their goal. After the resignation of Archbishop Arsenije early in 1767, the area of the Ohrid archbishopric was annexed to the patriarchate of Istanbul.

The abolition of autocephalous church organizations also provided a tangible sign of the change that had taken place in the attitude toward the Christian population in the Ottoman Empire. Privileged elements had disappeared long before and the domestic church hierarchy had been uprooted, causing social equalization among all the Christian inhabitants. The term *raya*, once used to designate all dependent toilers, was now applied to the entire Christian population. This trend was paralleled by increasing tension between the Muslims, who out of a sense of duty and also in defense of their own interests supported Turkish authority, and the raya who strove to get rid of it. In the eighteenth century strict provisions were adopted forbidding Christians to wear luxurious clothing and even certain colors. They were also required to behave humbly in their relations with Muslims. Thus segregation and social subordination acquired outward symbols.

The Position of Montenegro and Its Struggle against the Turks

Two separate societies were living within the fold of the Ottoman Empire, with few ties or points of contact. In Serbia, for instance, there were no Turks in the rural districts at all and few Serbs could be found in the larger villages and small towns. In Montenegro the Christians and Turks lived in separate territories. Communities were closeted off from each other, and their political organizations differed. As had previously been the case, the Turks were influential only in the plains in the vicinity of fortified towns like Podgorica, Žabljak, Spuž, and Bar. In the mountainous area of the Katunska nahija (district), the center of which was Cetinje (the see of the metropolitan), the Turks penetrated only if they broke their way through with a well-organized army. Although Turkey considered this rockbound land its own, and its claim was recognized by adjacent states, the population refused to pay the head tax, thereby in fact rejecting the sultan's authority.

The true masters of that unproductive and sparsely settled area (it has been estimated that all Montenegro had only 14,000 to 15,000 people in the eighteenth century) were the Montenegrin tribes, whose formation was completed in the eighteenth century. In their demarcated territory, with their chieftains and warriors, and their tribal organization, they lived the lives of herdsmen and fighting men, their time devoted to raiding, cattle rustling, and sundry feats of heroism. Their sworn enemies, apart from the Turks, were their own nationals who had been converted to Islam. The extermination of these converts at the beginning of the eighteenth century was celebrated in later historical tradition. The tribes also fell out among themselves, but customary law provided means for reconciliation and the ironing out of disputes. But vis-à-vis the surrounding world, primarily the Turks, the tribes put up a common front of solidarity.

The metropolitans of Cetinje were a significant factor of cohesion in Montenegrin tribal life. Their ecclesiastical authority extended beyond Montenegro to neighboring Venetian territory and the territory of Brda, which had its own tribal organization. The vladika was elected by an all-Montenegrin assembly and confirmed, before 1766, by the patriarch of Peć. In the eighteenth century, the choice was restricted to members of one family, so that the dignity of vladika actually became hereditary in the Petrović family, from which the Montenegrin ruling dynasty later emerged. The vladikas of Montenegro, as pastors of their flocks, were also duty-bound to participate vigorously in the political affairs of Montenegro. In the eighteenth century certain vladikas also trained their attention on the international scene, developing activities at Christian courts, above all in St. Petersburg. Gaining for Montenegro an international reputation, they also paved the way for influence by the big powers over its position.

In their struggle against the Turks, the Montenegrins had relied for help on Venice since the end of the Middle Ages. The Venetian Republic had an interest in enlisting courageous warriors for its fight to preserve its possessions, and therefore extended them assistance, helped them obtain supplies for military requirements, paid tribal chieftains, and offered them protection in time of need. Warfare against the Turks toward the end of the seventeenth century revealed that Austria and Russia were the two great powers which could be expected to bring about the downfall of the Turkish Empire, whereas Venice, weakened, played a role of secondary importance. Events in the early eighteenth century simply confirmed this development in the ratio of forces and led the Montenegrins to seek patrons elsewhere, while not disrupting their ties with Venice. Venice, itself desirous of preserving peace, tried to persuade the Montenegrins to pursue a conciliatory policy designed to maintain the status quo.

On the basis of old religious ties, the Montenegrins drew closer to Russia, a land of Orthodox confession and Slav brothers, who they hopefully expected would emancipate Christians from the Turkish yoke. In response to an appeal from Russian imperial emissaries who visited Montenegro, the Montenegrins joined the Russo-Turkish War in 1711, but severe casualties were the only result. The Turkish onslaught, which advanced as far as Cetinje in 1712, and another punitive expedition in 1714 were attended by terror and devastation. In the teeth of setbacks and suffering, the Montenegrins continued to participate in the war.

However, despite financial assistance brought back from Russia by Vladika Danilo, they reverted to collaboration with Venice. In 1717, after negotiations with the tribal chieftains, the Venetian Republic became the patron of Montenegro, undertaking to respect its internal independence, extend assistance, and pay the Montenegrin chieftains. The peace concluded the following year frustrated the implementation of this treaty and left Montenegro entirely within the framework of the Turkish Empire. The Montenegrins continued their practice of raiding even after this development, and they managed to strike serious blows at the Turks in Hercegovina during the war of 1737.

In the mid-eighteenth century, Montenegro's policy of linking its fate with that of Russia was given fresh impetus by the activities of Vladika Vasilije Petrović, who was, formally speaking, simply an aide of his cousin, Vladika Sava, but in actual fact ruled the see of Cetinje and Montenegro itself. Vasilije endeavored to expand the limits of Russo-Montenegrin relations, which had been reduced to the extension of regular annual assistance. He applied to the Russian court to accept the role of protector of Montenegro (the same offer had been made earlier to Empress Maria Theresa) and to add the name of Montenegro to the imperial title. He also attempted to form a regiment of Montenegrins for the imperial army, paying scant attention to the realistic possibilities. In his desire to acquaint the Russian public with Montenegro's struggle, Vasilije published his *History of Montenegro* in Moscow in 1754, actually a political tract in praise of the centuries of struggle of the Montenegrin people and the role of the vladika and his family. His actual achievement was negligible, although he paid three long visits to Russia. Nonetheless, he undoubtedly increased interest in and understanding of his land and procured greater assistance from the Russians.

His pretensions in European politics were paralleled by attempts to pursue an unrelenting policy toward the Turks. Montenegrin raids and the refusal to pay head tax called forth more determined action by the Turkish authorities. The Bosnian vizier was ordered to bring Montenegro to its knees. When the vizier approached Montenegro's boundaries, Metropolitan Sava, the guvernadur installed by the Venetians in 1717, and the chieftains promised to pay head tax and to desist from attacking the sultan's subjects, in an attempt to avoid devastation. Vladika Vasilije, who had returned from Russia in the meantime, frustrated that agreement and simultaneously initiated agitation against Venice among its subjects in the vicinity of Montenegro. The Turkish attack was unavoidable, and help was not forthcoming from any quarter. The Venetians cut off the country's supplies and called for Vasilije's head, while the Turks, with a large army meeting tenacious resistance, thrust to the center of Montenegro. They did not reach Cetinje, for the Montenegrins managed to stop them en route. Although tradition celebrates this war as a Montenegrin victory, head tax began to be paid in 1757 and an obligation was undertaken not to attack the sultan's subjects or receive foreign emissaries.

Vladika Vasilije, who had left the country on the eve of the Turkish invasion, adopted a more conciliatory attitude after his return from his second trip to Russia. In this atmosphere of veneration for Russia and its dynasty, developed during several decades of regular ties, it was possible for an adventurer to appear on the scene who rose almost to the position of ruler in Montenegro in a few short years, although he had no roots in the country and no legal basis for his authority. He was first heard of in the middle of 1766, when he began representing himself as the Russian tsar Peter III. This impostor, Šćepan Mali (Stephen the Little), won over followers among some of the chieftains and monks who helped him spread the conviction that he was truly the Russian tsar. When Vladika Sava tried to unmask him, calling him an "ordinary deceiver and impostor," Šćepan Mali had him sentenced to a short term in prison and later brushed him aside.

In short order, Šćepan Mali gained influence over all the Montenegrin tribes, who frequently quarreled among themselves during this period, and attained great prestige among the neighboring tribes in Brda, Hercegovina, etc. He spoke and wrote like a religious fanatic, promising to emancipate the Serbs from Turkish and Venetian power. But his real successes were registered in internal policy. He managed to introduce peace and order among the tribes by bearing down hard on blood feuds and cattle rustling. The measures to which he resorted were severe and unusual in a tribal society (execution, imprisonment, flogging), justice being dispensed with the help of a detachment of several dozen men. This military detachment of the self-styled tsar, reorganized in 1772 on instructions from Petrograd and placed under the command of a Montenegrin, was the forerunner of organs of central power that after a few decades became regular and stabilized central government bodies.

Šćepan Mali's activities alarmed the powers interested in Montenegro. Venice secretly sentenced him to death for the influence he wielded over the population under its control; the sultan dispatched an invasion army against Montenegro, in the face of which Šćepan Mali disappeared temporarily until the Turks were made to withdraw by resistance and inclement weather. The Russian court was also anxious to remove Šćepan from the scene in Montenegro. Later, however, when Prince Jurij Dolgorukov (1740–1830) had him imprisoned, it reconciled itself to leaving him in power in order to win the Montenegrins over to the battle against Turkey, with which Russia went to war in 1768. Šćepan was murdered by a servant in 1773, probably at the instigation of the Turks.

The period of history during which Šćepan Mali held sway lasted only a few years and wrought no profound changes in the life of Montenegro. It simply heralded further developments in the building of state power and revealed that secular leaders could play a significant role in this process. Conditions were thus created for the "guvernadur of Montenegro," the leader of the entire country, to come out from behind the vladika's shadow and assume the principal role in political life.

CHAPTER 18

The South Slavs in the Hapsburg Monarchy during the Period of Absolutist Reforms

The Viennese Court's Program of Centralization and Resistance by the Estates

Although it retained its possessions on the Atlantic coast (in what is now Belgium), and although the Hapsburgs continued to rule as Holy Roman emperors, the Hapsburg monarchy was oriented largely toward Turkey after its extensive conquests of land from the Ottomans. The focus moved to the Danubian lands, while the Austro-Hungarian nucleus grew in importance as the symbol of the entire monarchy—*Austriaca Monarchia*. In spite of all the results achieved by the absolutist policies pursued by the emperors throughout the seventeenth century, the monarchy was still a loose assemblage of poorly linked and even territorially segregated lands, inhabited by people speaking various languages and belonging to diverse nationalities, developing in different ways under a variety of systems through the medium of social forces that acted with vigor in defending their special rights and traditional order. This incohesive state found difficulty in defending its influential place among the European powers and functioning successfully under the increasingly complex conditions of European politics. Consequently, at the beginning of the eighteenth century, the idea was born —tersely expressed in the recommendation of the Secret Conference of Emperor Charles VI—to "form a whole" out of the great and splendid monarchy. From this idea emerged a program which the Hapsburgs strove to implement during the entire eighteenth century in spite of divergent pressures and resistance.

The Yugoslav lands under Hapsburg rule did not represent an entity; they were not bound together more effectively by Hapsburg policies, nor was any attempt made to create balance in their development. Owing to the uneven success of absolutist reforms, certain differences even intensified and new boundaries came into being. Above all, differences grew in the crownland area, meaning present-day Slovenia, and the part within Hungarian borders—present-day Croatia and Vojvodina. The Slovene provinces of Carinthia, Carniola, and Styria, encompassed by Viennese centralization measures, were the object of a number of administrative and other reforms, generating more favorable conditions for economic resurgence.

In the other section, a notable difference existed between the Croatian and Hungarian lands, and also within those regions that were ruled by civil administration and estates organs and those run by military administration (the Military Frontier), responsible directly to Austrian central organs. The Hungarian and Croatian nobility aspired, after expelling the Turks, to restore the power of their estates order and, equally important, to revive the landed estates and exploit the lands from which they had been displaced in times long past. The Viennese court and its military organs were in pursuit of entirely different objectives, seeing the newly acquired territories both as a source of the revenues the state so sorely required and also as an opportune means to maintain a gigantic military camp from which reinforcements could be drawn for war against the Turks as well as for other European battlefields. The problem of the destiny of the new lands, after success in the war against the Turks, was the wellspring of fresh tension between the court with its absolutist tendencies and the nobles of Hungary and Croatia, assembled in their estates. During the eighteenth century the population of those areas took a more active part in forging its destiny, rendering the political struggle even more complex.

The first few decades of the eighteenth century were a period of open strife between the rulers and a large section of their Hungarian subjects. The peasant revolt of the *kurucz* (the ancient Hungarian term for the Crusaders), directed against high taxes and feudal magnates, was blunted in terms of its social substances as it came to be led by Hapsburg opponents headed by Ferenz Rákóczy, transforming it into a struggle for the estates rights of the nobility, or rather for the revival of the estates system. This rebellion, occasionally massive and radical (for instance, the rebels called for the overthrow of the Hapsburgs at the Diet of 1708), terminated in 1711 in a compromise providing for the rebels' accepting the Hapsburg dynasty while the king promised to restore the estates system, a serious blow to Viennese absolutism.

The Hungarian nobles, energetic in the defense of their estates rights, were unwilling to respect the independence of the Croatian estates and their rights. During Rákóczy's rebellion an assembly of the nobility faithful to the Hapsburgs appealed to the king to sanction only those "legal articles," that is, the legal decisions of the Croatian Diet, which were not at odds with Hungarian laws. Restrictions on Croatian legislation were not imposed at this time, but a tendency was clearly in evidence to deny the Croatian Diet equality. Somewhat later (1711) the Hungarian Diet endeavored to deprive Croatia of its ancient privilege of paying only half of the war tax *(dika)*.

The Pragmatic Sanction in Croatia

The Croatian Diet was offered an opportunity to react to the policies of the Hungarian nobility, and to emphasize its equality with the Hungarian estates Diet, when it was enabled to assume an autonomous position, independently of the Hungarian Diet, on the rights of inheritance and the order of succession in the Hapsburg dynasty. A resolution which gained currency under the name of the Croatian Pragmatic Sanction was passed by the Croatian Diet, recognizing the female line of the Hapsburg dynasty which ruled Austria and Styria, Carinthia, and Carniola. In return Charles VI undertook the obligation for himself and his successors to respect the "rights, privileges, and freedoms" of the Croatian kingdom. Following this, the Hungarian Diet demonstrated its flexibility by recognizing the validity of earlier Diet decisions and leaving the sanctioning of Croatian Diet decisions to the will of the ruler.

As Charles VI later asked all Hapsburg lands, and even foreign powers, to confirm the Pragmatic Sanction, he had to make concessions to win their recognition of the female Hapsburg line. He therefore promised the Hungarian Diet that he and his heirs would respect the indivisibility of lands under the Crown of Saint Stephen, thereby denying Croatia the right to withdraw from Hungary.

The Reforms Instituted by Maria Theresa

In spite of the Pragmatic Sanction's recognition by the interested powers, changes on the throne were attended by wars in which Maria Theresa (1740–

1780) succeeded in preserving all lands intact with the exception of Silesia. When she had stabilized her position on the throne, this ruler embarked upon a series of meaningful reforms in many spheres. Her general objective was to increase the state's military power, for which greater financial resources were of course required. The measures undertaken to achieve this purpose suppressed, or destroyed altogether, traditional forms of the order as well as many provincial and local rights. The reforms permitted the state to interfere in numerous aspects of life that had previously been beyond its reach and to embark on a policy of modernization.

Theresa's reforms were implemented most thoroughly in the Austrian part of the country, although even there they were met with resistance. Carniola and Carinthia were among the first provinces to receive provincial governments (1747) as bodies of civil servants which in substantial measure replaced the role of the estates. Extended to other territories as well, these governments, under the name of gubernium, or "provincial executives," remained the basis for the entire administrative system; they were further subdivided into districts, lower units important for their control of the landed estates and the regime governing them.

Eager to acquire the revenues it needed, the state interfered in the landed estates to assure that the serf remained capable of paying state taxes. As no appreciable increase could be squeezed from the peasants, the state resorted to taxing the domanial parts of the estates cultivated for the landlords by their serfs. Changes were introduced also in the manner of tax collection, the basis being the income, which was carefully scrutinized and recorded (the Theresian cadastre). The reform of the tax system soon showed important financial results (over a million forints) while placing the estates in the position of formally approving the taxes for several years at a time.

The serfs were protected from unfair demands on the part of their masters by the possibility of appealing to special courts handling such cases, but this did not close the door on abuses, especially in the exploitation of corvée. Disputes were frequent, and in Styria peasant revolts broke out. Finally corvée was strictly limited and standardized, for Styria and Carinthia in 1778 and for Carniola in 1782. The peasants also staggered under the burden of the charges levied by the masters when peasant landholdings changed hands; consequently a demand was raised for the introduction of the right of purchase of heritable serfs' rights. Here, too, the state interfered by prohibiting the temporary conveyance of land, that is, by demanding that the peasants be permitted to purchase heritable rights. In this way numerous peasant families repaired their positions, despite tenacious opposition from the estates.

In stimulating trade and nonagricultural economic activities, the offices in charge of economic questions, and the central organs as well, continued the policies whose foundations had been laid by Charles VI. The process of Trieste's emerging as a large commercial port and trading center of the southern sections of Hapsburg lands was stopped after the abolition of the Oriental Company in 1732. But freedom of navigation remained, as did the roads constructed in the hinterland. This network of roads was completed and improved while goods flowed into Trieste and Rijeka in increasing quantities. These two cities accommodated most of the exports from Slovene lands. Under the circumstances, Trieste was able to develop rapidly after the mid-eighteenth century. The mercantilist economic policies of the state as a whole collided inevitably with internal tariffs in the provinces and the latters' local economic policies. As had been the case in other spheres, here too the central organs had their way and internal tariffs were abolished. The sole ones remaining were those between the Hungarian and the Austrian parts of the state. The monetary reform (1750) and the coordination of provincial measures with those of Vienna served the same purpose of promoting trade.

Exports could be increased only if production for the market also rose. The authorities therefore supported incentives for manufacturing. Textile plants producing cotton and silk were established in the larger towns. Glass production, which underwent considerable expansion in the eighteenth century, was also earmarked for export. A number of crafts products were intended for distant markets. Mining figured importantly in the economy of the Slovene lands at this time. Iron and steel production was rising slowly, but it came to a standstill toward the end of the eighteenth century, although blast furnaces continued to be constructed, creating conditions conducive to the later revival of this branch. Idrija continued to hold pride of place in mercury mining, thanks to the discovery of new deposits and improvements in technology. Its products were much in demand as far afield as the Atlantic coast.

During the initial period the reform made no encroachments on the foundations of the feudal order but rather buttressed them by removing the gravest abuses. Nevertheless, it did pave the way for a profound transformation of the Slovene lands. Improvement in the peasant's position, cultivation of new land, sowing of new crops (maize, potatoes), and betterment of agrarian techniques broke the ground for modernization of the rural districts. Reversal of restrictions on production and trade in commodities opened the door to greater penetration of capitalist economy, permitting new social forces and political aspirations to surface.

In the Hungarian part of the state, absolutist reforms failed to show the same results, not only because of resilient opposition from the nobles and estates, but also because of the essentially different situation of certain regions and the different tasks with which the state authority had to cope. Only Civil Croatia, the small part under the authority of ban and Diet, was uninterrupted in its development in the same sense as the Slovene lands from the end of the Middle Ages. All other territories either belonged to the frontier defense system, exposed to the ravages of war, or had recently been liberated from the Turks. Some territories were virtually vacant or totally depopulated, the most urgent task there being to bring the soil back under cultivation and revive life in the villages. For this purpose, the spontaneous settlement of the population did not suffice, not even when people arrived in large waves, like those following the unsuccessful war of 1737–1739 and the abandonment of Serbia. The Hapsburg authorities had to undertake planned colonization measures to repopulate the plains of southern Hungary, above all the Banat, which had been liberated in 1718 and maintained under the control of central military organs until 1779. Large numbers of people were brought as settlers from the southern parts of Germany; smaller groups of Frenchmen, Spaniards, and Italians joined them and either disappeared gradually or were engulfed by their more massively German environment. The example set by the central authorities was followed by the feudal lords, who moved the population from their estates in other parts of Hungary to the newly conquered areas. Hungarians, Slovaks, and Ruthenians were brought in. Romanians descended from mountainous areas to the plains of Banat, frequently against the will of the Hapsburg authorities. The Serbian population grew, boosted by fresh arrivals from Turkish territory or by shifts within Hungary itself. This complex and long-lasting colonization produced an extremely motley ethnical map of southern Hungary (now Vojvodina). Vast marshes and wastelands were put to the plow, resulting in the transformation of this territory into the breadbasket of Hungary.

The Position of the Areas Won from the Turks

One of the most urgent tasks facing the central state authorities was the introduction of a stable administrative system into the lands liberated from Turkey. In both Croatia and Hungary the estates pursued the idea of restoration in the form of expansion of the competence of estates assemblies, revival of the županija system and the feudal estates. The Hapsburg military organs, who had first taken possession of and organized these territories, were unwilling to surrender them to anyone else. Furthermore, they were under constant pressure from the population of these territories, Serbs in the large majority, who feared the županija type of administration and the landlords in the conviction that these would reduce them to serfdom and curtail freedom of conscience. These fears proved to be founded, as the restored županija authorities in Bačka set about disarming the Serbian militia (peasant soldiers) with a total disregard for Serbian privileges. The upshot was resistance, revolts, and clashes with the authorities. As the Hungarian estates refused to accept solutions allowing military authorities jurisdiction over Serbian soldiers living in županija frameworks, in 1702 the Hapsburg court established the Sava-Danube and the Tisa-Maroš Military Frontier, the territories of which were withdrawn from županija and Diet control.

The same problem arose in Croatia, but in milder form. The territory between the Kupa and Una Rivers was controlled by the Diet, whereas Lika and Krbava, despite the ruler's formal consent to reinstate županijas authority, were annexed to the Military Frontier. The restoration of three županijas in Slavonia and Srem (Virovitica, Požega, and Srem) was attended by the usual difficulties. The population vigorously fought being transformed into dependents and insisted on treatment as Frontiersmen, inhabitants of the Military Frontier, although the Royal Court Administration in Vienna had also established landed estates there and tolerated exorbitant levies on the peasants. The županija system was introduced, but parts of Slavonian and Srem territory along the Sava River from Gradiška to Zemun and along the Danube River from Zemun to Petrovaradin were incorporated into the Military Frontier, which acquired its final contours in this area.

Conflict over the Military Frontier

The Hungarian estates and Serbian Frontiersmen were locked in struggle over the abolition of the Tisa-Maroš Frontier, promised by the empress to the Hungarian Diet in 1741 after the eruption of a new war with Prussia. For a full ten years the "incorporation" was postponed because of resistance, protests, and the need for fighting men from the Military Frontier. One form of resistance manifested itself in the emigration of a considerable segment of Serbs to Russia between 1751 and 1753. The creation of new military territories along the Sava and Danube Rivers, and of privileged districts, made it possible to preserve the basic liberties of the Serbs who refused to live under županija control.

When the territory of the Military Frontier along the Sava and Danube Rivers stabilized in the second half of the eighteenth century with the creation of the Šajkaš battalion and the Banat regiments, the resulting belt of land under military organization extended from the Adriatic Sea to the Carpathians. The Military Frontier encompassed over a third of what is now Yugoslavia, in the Hungarian part of the Hapsburg monarchy. As it was administered by military commands and central military organs, the Military Frontier was subjected to centralistic reforms and unification attempts to a far greater extent than the lands administered by the Croatian or the Hungarian assemblies. Defiance here involved the broadest masses of Frontiersmen, perennially dissatisfied with their position but also in no mood for drastic change. For decades parts of the frontier were in constant upheaval, at times on account of abuses perpetrated by officers and authorities, at others because of measures

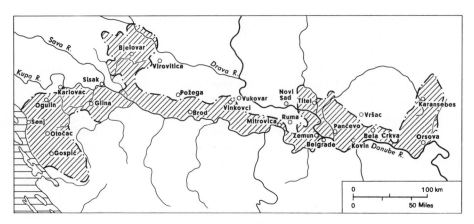

MAP 26.   Territory of the Military Frontier in the eighteenth century.

designed to repair the situation. The perceptible differences between various parts of the boundary area, or frontiers as they were then called, were nevertheless slowly eradicated and frontier regimes were gradually equalized. Major undertakings to reform the Frontier were paralleled by the reform of the administrative system in other parts of the empire. An important step along these lines was the introduction of regiments transforming the Frontiersmen into a regular army. Their use on battlefields everywhere had been initiated long ago. Subdivided into companies, the regiments were stationed in large fortresses. Among the Frontiersmen a difference was drawn between those on active service and those whose labor sustained the soldiery. One-third of the Frontiersmen were always on the battlefield. They made their livelihood from the lands allocated to them as heritable property and were released from the obligation to pay taxes. But they had to supply their own uniforms and to help build military objects and officers' quarters, for which, it is true, they received some monetary compensation. The junior officers sometimes also received half a salary in addition to the land allotted them, whereas the senior officers, mainly Germans, were paid their salaries in full. Rebellion was directed against the compulsory purchase of uniforms and the threat to freedom of confession. In mid-century, those in the forefront of revolt were Serbian officers who could not accommodate themselves to modernization of the army. One of the most widespread revolts was that in the generalate of Varaždin in 1755. In the second half of the eighteenth century, conditions finally stabilized in the Military Frontier. The old Frontier self-administration disappeared, but the Frontiersmen preserved their personal and religious liberties, and the material conditions enabling them to discharge their duties were bettered. The Hapsburg monarchy thereby gained several tens of thousands of soldiers eminently fit for warfare and imbued with a spirit of the utmost devotion.

Economic Development in Croatia

The Croat lands outside the Military Frontier experienced a significant advance in productive forces in the course of the eighteenth century. The first manufacturing shops were set up and production grew. The copper mine near Samobor prospered, although iron production continued to be limited to small foundries with several dozen workers each. Forests were exploited to a greater degree, and the timber was processed in sawmills; trees were also burned for potash. In Gorski Kotar and Slavonia, Czech specialists helped promote glass production, whereas in Rijeka and Senj, two large shipyards were in operation, with ropemakers, sailmakers, and so on nearby.

The sugar refinery founded in Rijeka in the middle of the eighteenth century employed 1,000 workers by the end of the same century and was the biggest manufacturing plant in Croatia.

Agriculture continued to be the backbone of economic activity. A significant innovation was the large-scale planting of maize, particularly on the serfs' holdings, while the domanial lands persevered in growing traditional crops. Whereas Croatia proper was densely populated, Slavonia was not and land was brought but gradually under cultivation. Slavonia was further characterized by the underdevelopment of the small noble's holding, for the Viennese authorities had sold large tracts of land to import foreign feudatories.

Although the peasants' load of tithes and corvée was already unevenly distributed, as time went by, conditions worsened as a result of abuses of corvée by the landlords. It is evident from peasants' appeals that their burden was increased in a number of different ways. Discontent sometimes took the form of peasants' demands to be annexed to the Military Frontier, and sometimes of support for frontier rebellions, but in 1755, when the Tax Reform was implemented in Croatia, a massive revolt broke out and the peasants burned the manor houses of their masters, calling for "the old rights." The crushing of this revolt, which caused considerable loss of life, and parallel movements in Slavonia provided a motive for state interference in the regime of exploitation of the peasants on the estates (the urbarial regulations). Beginning with 1737, the urbariums (the Slavonia and Srem urbariums) precisely assessed a peasant's obligations in produce and corvée, depending on the size of his holding. Although the urbariums were not always implemented everywhere, they did improve the peasants' position and prevented further exacerbation of their lot. Feudal relations were thereby preserved by the state and given a staying power that helped them endure until the middle of the nineteenth century.

Absolutist Administrative Reforms

The reforms also covered the administrative system in Croatia as, after 1764, the court consistently implemented its absolutist system in the Hungarian part of the state as well. Civil government was introduced in Croatia in 1767, in the form of a Royal Council headed by the ban *(banus)*. Here too the Diet was suppressed and deprived even of influence over tax collecting and the spending of financial resources. Apart from carrying through the tax reforms, the Royal Council did significant work in organizing school-ing, which became the concern of the state for the first time in the history of the area. The network of elementary schools was expanded considerably and a Royal Academy was established, later to develop into the University of Zagreb.

The Royal Council was the butt of dissatisfaction on the part of the Croatian nobility and Hungarian estates. Consequently, it was abolished in 1779 and all Civil Croatia was assigned to the Hungarian Regency Council. Two other legal acts in the second half of the eighteenth century were un-favorable in their effects on the later development of Croatia. Rijeka with its environs was restored to Croatia in 1776, but its autonomy was so broadly interpreted that it was considered a "special body, associated with the sacred crown of the Hungarian kingdom." This served as the basis for later demands that this economically important center enjoy a special position vis-à-vis Hungary. On the other hand, Slavonia's ties with Croatia slackened. With the Military Frontier wedged in between itself and Croatia, Slavonia was under the jurisdiction of the Hungarian Regency Council up to 1769 and after 1779, although it remained under the juridical authority of the ban and also had representatives in the Croatian Diet.

Controversy over the "Privileges" of the Serbs in Hungary

The position of the Serbs in Hungary was to have been regulated by the dispensation of "privileges" which the Hapsburg rulers assigned at the end of the seventeenth century, when the Serbs raised an insurrection against the Turks and were settled on Hungarian territory during the Turkish counteroffensive that followed. Owing to opposition from the Hungarian estates and authorities in areas where the Serbs had settled, and also by reason of its own special interests, the Viennese court failed to heed two essential

Serbian demands: it did not allot them a special territory where they might settle and it did not permit the development of secular government headed by a "despot." The court recognized members of the Eastern Orthodox church hierarchy, headed by the patriarch and later by the metropolitan of Karlovci, as the elders of the Serbs. Confirmed but also curtailed in the interpretation, the "privileges" gave protection above all to freedom of confession for the Serbs and the rights of the hierarchy and clergy in relation to their faithful. This represented belated application of the principle of personal rights, for the Serbs enjoyed their "privileges" as Serbs and as members of the Serbian Orthodox church, irrespective of the area they inhabited and the laws in force in that territory.

The "privileges" enabled representatives of the Serbs from all parts of Hapsburg territory to hold assemblies, naturally with the permission of the court and in the presence of one of its envoys. The assemblies had no specific terms of reference, their principal task being to elect a metropolitan, especially as "discussional" assemblies had been suppressed in the middle of the eighteenth century. After 1749, the assembly's composition was regulated: bishops, twenty-five clergymen, twenty-five representatives of the Military Frontier, and twenty-five representatives of other territories and towns.

The assemblies concerned themselves with the exercise of privileges and registered protests in cases of violation, but they also discussed relations within the Serbian community, and heard complaints by all sections of the population about oppressive behavior by the landlords, civil servants, proprietors, etc. Matters of current importance included relations between the people and the clergy, who had a free hand in collecting church tithes and were inclined to abuse these rights beyond the limits established by custom. Having put up a hard fight to defend themselves from the demands of the Catholic hierarchy that they pay tithes to them, too, and from attempts at church union, the Orthodox faithful clashed also with their own hierarchy and clergymen on account of exorbitant obligations.

Among a large section of Serbs, problems of personal liberty, public obligations, tax burdens, and the question of jurisdiction were settled independently of privileges. Apart from the peasant-soldiers in the Military Frontier and their officers, who were subject to a special regime as discussed above, Serbian traders and craftsmen living in the small towns, then in the process of being reconstructed and on the threshold of a long resurgence, took advantage of the autonomy of free royal towns. Serbian traders and craftsmen figured importantly in the revival of economic activities in ravaged Hungary, finding it easy to adjust to a legal system offering them freedom of action. The Serbs in Taban, a suburb of Budapest, were granted self-government in their community at the end of the seventeenth century. In areas under the županija system, citizens purchased the rights of the free royal city, at high cost as a rule, and thus achieved personal liberty, strictly regulated obligations, and the enjoyment of self-administration. Novi Sad and Sombor, where the Serbs made up the great majority, purchased these rights as early as 1747 and 1749. In the latter half of the century, Serbs were granted these liberties in the towns of the Banat, where the population had become ethnically mixed as a result of colonization measures undertaken in the meantime. Inhabitants were awarded considerable freedom by the "free military communities," nonagrarian settlements within the Military Frontier, such as Zemun, Karlovci, Mitrovica, Bela Crkva, and Pančevo. By paying obligations in money, the inhabitants of these communities rid themselves of military service and were thus able to pursue their trading or crafts activities unhampered.

Conditions favoring trade in the developing regions traversed by roads connecting Turkey with Central Europe promoted the prosperity of Serbian and Cincar[1] traders. In the course of the eighteenth century, they developed into a numerous and economically powerful section of the population, destined to play an important role in the advancement of culture and in the national-political struggle. The craftsmen, the other essential element among the citizenry, were economically weaker but also numerous, and they organized in guilds to defend their interests.

Despite all the expansions of the Military Frontier, the emigrations, and resistance, a section of the immigrant Serbs declined into peonage, as dependent peasants on landed estates. But differences in position were considerable among them. The best off were those living in privileged districts (Tisa from 1751 and Velika Kikinda from 1774) ruled by the Court Chamber. They could not be turned over to private landowners for exploitation, and they paid strictly fixed taxes collected by the magistrates of the district itself. On other possessions of the Court Chamber the position of the serfs was aggravated by the abuses of tax collectors and civil servants. The peasants on the spahilics, the estates of the big magnates, felt only the belated and incomplete benefits of urbarial regulation, limited in the best of cases. The Slavonian urbarium was in effect in Srem from 1737 onwards, whereas in Bačka an urbarium on the same general principles as obtained in Hungary was applied after 1772. Urbariums in this part of the state did not provide for the possibility of serfs purchasing land.

As applied to the Serbs, Vienna's absolutist policies were under double

---

[1] The Cincars (pronounced Tzintzars) were descendants of the pre-Slavic Romanized inhabitants of the Balkan Peninsula. Displaced by the Turkish authorities from their centers in southern Albania at the end of the eighteenth century, the Cincars became dispersed over broad areas in the Balkans and Hungary. Confessionally they belonged to the Eastern Orthodox church; culturally they were close to the Greeks. The Cincars were an important component in the creation of the Balkan population. Wherever they settled, the Cincars adapted themselves to their environment, forgot their Romance dialect, and eventually disappeared as an ethnic entity.

fire: by the Hungarian estates, who opposed all forms of privileges by or for the Serbs, and by the Serbs, who clung tenaciously to these rights and offered fierce resistance to any concessions to Hungarian demands violating their privileges. Depending on its needs and requirements, the court bent one way and then the other, agreeing first to the revival of the županija system but immediately afterwards sifting out the area settled by Serbs and giving them military organization so as to appease the other side. The court had set up a special body to deal with Serbian affairs, the Illyrian Court Commission (Illyrische Hofcommission, 1745), transformed in 1747 into the Illyrian Court Deputation (Illyrische Hofdeputation). A stronger absolutist undertaking was initiated in the seventies by restrictions on the rights of the Serbian clergy, against whom the faithful themselves had lodged protests. The metropolitan was divested of competence in secular matters, and by the school statute of 1776 religious schools had to adapt to the requirements of state schools. Finally, the abolition of the Illyrian Court Deputation in 1777 ushered in a new wave of absolutist measures during the period of Joseph II.

CHAPTER 19

The Assertion
of the Baroque

JESUIT SCHOOLING / BAROQUE INFLUENCES ON ART / BAROQUE
LITERATURE / ACADEMIES AND THEATERS / PRINTING PRESSES AND
NEWSPAPERS / THE IMAGE OF THE SLAV PAST / BAROQUE CULTURE
IN THE ORTHODOX SETTING

Jesuit Schooling

The victory of the Counter-Reformation, which practically uprooted
Protestantism from Yugoslav lands, paved the way for baroque penetration into
the South Slav world not only in art and the development of taste, of the general
atmosphere, but also in the entire spiritual climate. This applies above all to
those parts of the South Slav area whose bulwarks protected them from the
Turks, as in the Dalmatian towns, or where the same purpose was served by the
defensive belt of the Military Frontier, as in portions of Croatia proper and the

Slovene lands. There alone conditions were conducive to normal cultural development, to the nurturing of earlier traditions and the fostering of historical ties. The baroque set its imprint also on areas liberated only at the end of the seventeenth century, where it arrived, however, intermingled with elements of a civilization that had to be planted on neglected soil.

The work of education was taken over by the Jesuits, the most militant champions of the Counter-Reformation. Scattered in large numbers about the Catholic parts of the South Slav lands, the Jesuits organized a broad network of intermediary education through their own high schools and colleges. Until the abolition of the order in the latter half of the eighteenth century, and before the state began to interfere in education, the Jesuit schools, with all the virtues and failings of Jesuit educational practices, spread not only education but devotion to Catholicism and respect for the order that had functioned for two centuries as an intellectual force of paramount significance. Although intended primarily for the aristocratic section of the population, the Jesuit schools enrolled pupils from other strata and undoubtedly contributed to the dissemination of learning and to terminating the monopoly of the highest echelons in society. They were certainly instrumental in elevating the level of the parochial clergy and monastic orders, which experienced a belated development on the threshold of the epoch of the Enlightenment. While adhering firmly to the use of Latin as the medium of instruction, the Jesuit schools nonetheless helped make Italian and German favored languages in schools.

Baroque Influences on Art

The triumph of traditionalist Catholicism over austere Protestantism, of adherents of a sumptuous church and pomp in worship over the opponents of paintings and ceremony, ushered in an era during which art was advanced for the purposes of the church. Economic growth, which came sooner or later to all Catholic regions, provided the material possibilities for artistic activity on a grand scale. As early as the first half of the seventeenth century, fresh currents were circulating in the Yugoslav areas. Stepped-up building activity in the Dalmatian towns looked first to Roman and later to Venetian baroque models. In the Slovene regions direct influences from Italy intermingled with impulses from Austrian church centers. Jesuit churches, along with the churches of certain other monastic orders, led the way in disseminating early baroque forms until all building and decorative arts came to be imbued with the baroque aesthetic. Baroque set its seal on new buildings and it insinuated itself into old ones during repair and reconstruction work. Many monuments were invested with baroque features long after they were constructed, during the "baroquization" of the seventeenth and eighteenth centuries. But it was the interior of churches where the baroque spirit was most eloquently expressed. Ornate altars with much gilt, richly fashioned carved-wood church furniture, numerous sculptures, wall decorations, icons, and frescoes merged to create an impression of magnificence which the faithful found it hard to resist.

Many crafts flourished during this period of works commissioned to refurbish the interiors of churches, when material resources set the sole limits on the magnitude of such undertakings. Some master craftsmen had to be imported because domestic artists did not suffice for the work at hand. Dalmatia, for instance, had no major artists of note during this period with the exception of Tripo Kokolja, whose masterpieces have been preserved in an island church in Boka Kotorska and on the island of Brač. In Croatia proper, painters and sculptors from Slovenia, where domestic artists had formed groups, plied their art alongside foreigners. Apart from graphic artists belonging to the circle of the nobleman J. V. Valvasor (1641–1693), who depicted the monuments and celebrated places of Carniola and Carinthia in their paintings, Ljubljana could boast of several painters working in the generally accepted style. Among them were Valentin Mecinger (1699–1759), Franc Jelovšek (1700–1764), Fortunat Bergant (1720–1769), and Anton Cebej (1722–1744). Outstanding among the sculptors' studios was that headed by Frano Roba (1727–1757), a distinguished artist whose works adorn Ljubljana, Celovec (Klagenfurt), and Zagreb.

Baroque art was not limited to church buildings. Also built or reconstructed in the baroque style were mansions and palaces, their interiors informed with all the features of the new ornate art style. Landscaping also developed under the influence of baroque parks abroad, as attested by paintings of the time. Finally, baroque left its imprint on the appearance of towns. Apart from the churches and baroque palaces, the facades of other edifices were subjected to decoration with characteristic baroque features, and architectural complexes, like squares with monuments and fountains, also took shape. The towns of Slovenia and Croatia are therefore distinctive not only for fine individual buildings but also for excellent baroque complexes.

Baroque Literature

In literature the baroque period was less fruitful. The overwhelming pressure of stagnant forms and means of expression in all literary disciplines, compounded by the rigid frameworks of Counter-Reformationist ideology, left little margin for fresh thinking or originality. Literary production increased with the number of educated persons, so that its bulk was greater than ever before, but it never broke the bonds of monotony. The dominant overtones were religious and didactic, extremely learned to be sure, and writings were couched in various poetic and prose forms. The type of literature is reflected to some extent in the titles of works which may be considered above average: *The Sin of Our First Father, Adam* by Juraj Habdelić; *Mandaljena Pokornica (The Penitent Magdalene)* by Dživo Bunić of Dubrovnik; *The Life of Saint John, Bishop of Trogir* by Petar Kanavelović of Korčula; *Bogatsvo i Uboštvo (Wealth and Poverty)* by Jeronim Kavanjin of Split. The writers found it difficult to shed stereotypes even when they dealt with historical subject matter. Outstanding in eighteenth-century Croatia in this field were Petar Zrinski and Franja Frankapan, champions of the struggle against Viennese absolutism and victims of it themselves. The former was the author of the poem *The Siren of the Adriatic Sea*, actually a translation of his brother Nikola's work in Hungarian. Frankapan composed a collection of lyrics under the influence of contemporary Italian poetry.

Academies and Theaters

In general cultural terms, the baroque period was characterized by the creation of a cultivated environment, the expansion of the number of people who knew and enjoyed works of art and literature. An interesting development was the foundation of academies on the Italian model, providing a gathering place for poetry lovers and intellectuals with a linguistic bent. Private academies of this type were in existence in a number of cultural centers. Toward the end of the seventeenth century, an academy of devotees of the arts was founded in Dubrovnik to which those with time to spare flocked. Another society in Dubrovnik was dedicated solely to literary work in Slavonic. This purpose was served also by the Illyrian Academy in Split, of the same period. In Ljubljana the Academia Operosorum fostered artistic activity with an eye on the Italian baroque as the supreme ideal. In the second half of the eighteenth century, these societies bent their energies to practical objectives: the dissemination of useful knowledge, the promotion of agriculture, and so on. In furthering theatrical and musical performances, the palaces of the nobles or homes of patricians in the coastal towns led the way. In time this role was taken over by the towns and larger communities. Temporal entertainment for the public appeared in Zagreb at the close of the eighteenth century with performances by a German acting ensemble. In their schools the Jesuits had been encouraging school performances for quite some time. In Ljubljana local music lovers saw to it that operas were presented as early as the seventeenth century. Theatrical life may be said to have begun in the first half of the eighteenth century, and by 1865 Ljubljana had its first theater housed in a special building constructed for that purpose. In 1701 a society was founded under the name of Academia Philharmonicorum, which deserves a great deal of the credit for the enviable development of musical life in that town.

Printing Presses and Newspapers

Along with all these other manifestations, printing presses and newspapers were signs of the new cultural atmosphere. They were not so dependent on church activity, after the impetus provided by the Counter-Reformation, as they were on the growing number of educated persons and the creation of a cultivated environment. Important towns in eighteenth-century Slovenia established printers' shops (Celje, Ptuj, Maribor, Gorica); Ljubljana had had newspapers since 1782. This was a period marked by the founding of large libraries and the preoccupation of local personages with scientific research. The Slovene lands, like the Republic of Dubrovnik, produced a number of scientists, although they achieved their prominence abroad. Among them are the astronomer and philosopher Rudjer Bošković (Ruggiero Boscovich, 1711–1787) and the numismatics expert Anselmo Banduri (1671–1743).

The Image of the Slav Past

In Yugoslavia as elsewhere, the baroque world was fascinated by history: not only biblical and ecclesiastical history, fostered in didactic literature, and the history of classical antiquity, popularized by "classical" education, but also national and local history, foundations for the study of which had been laid during the period of humanism. The example of the Italians, to whom humanism revealed glorious ancestors in the classical Romans, and of the Germans, who, after the discovery of Tacitus's *Germania*, placed their virtuous and warlike forebears on the same pedestal as the Romans, was followed by the Slav humanists. Even in the sixteenth century, realizing the linguistic affinity of the Slavic peoples, they regarded the splendid past of the Slavs as stretching back in time through the inhabitants of the Balkan Peninsula in antiquity all the way to the period of Alexander the Great. The history of the Slavs was not so well known as it deserved to be for the simple reason that the Slavs, largely a warlike people, had had no writers of note to celebrate their deeds. After the short work *De origine successibusque Sclavorum* by Vinko Pribojević of Hvar, the total vision of the Slav past was popularized in a voluminous book by a Benedictine monk of Dubrovnik, Mauro Orbini. In *Il regno degli Slavi* (1601) he added to early Slavic history, in which he included many classical peoples and Germanic tribes, a survey of the medieval history of the South Slavs. This rather uncritical work nevertheless provided basic and concrete knowledge about the history of the South Slavs while it consolidated a comprehensive view of the Slav past which was invested with an ideological function.

Their eyes trained on the Romans and Germans, the South Slavs failed to differentiate among themselves. Consequently, Slav history as it appears in writings of the seventeenth and eighteenth centuries embraces elements of the history of various peoples, lands, dynasties, towns, and individuals, with evidently no effort being made, as it was in the romantic and later periods, to determine which elements were associated with individual South Slav nations. This generalized Slavic background persisted even when writers turned their glance to one part of the South Slav world; such a writer was the canon of Zagreb, Juraj Ratkaj (1612–1666), who wrote a history of Croatia *(Memoria regum et banorum regnorum Dalmatiae, Croatiae et Slavoniae)*. For Juraj Križanić (1618–1683) South Slav unity was the point of departure for an unrealistic political plan to unite all Slavs under the Russian tsar, who would then supposedly convert his country to Catholicism. Križanić was also carried away by the notion that the Russian tsar should invest efforts in "correcting" the Slavonic tongue so as to arrive at a common language for all Slavs. He thus went one step further than the Roman Catholic propagators of the Counter-Reformation, who endeavored to use the Bosnian Što dialect as a basis for literary works intended for all South Slavs generally.

Križanić's elder contemporary Dživo Gundulić (1589–1638), the great baroque poet of Dubrovnik, reflected the hope that Turkish crises and Christian victories, still rare at that time (like the victory of the Polish king at Hotin in 1621), would eventually liberate Balkan Christians from Turkish power and, opening up vistas for the future, persuade men to turn to the past in order to find strength and solutions for the morrow. Apart from numerous reminiscences from the history of Poland, Turkey, Serbia, and Dubrovnik, Gundulić also expressed the wish, in his poem *Osman*, for the victor over the Ottoman Turks to take charge of Dušan's empire.

The political topicality of the "Slavic" vision of the past became quite explicit in the work of the Croat writer Pavle Riter-Vitezović, active after the great victories of the Christians and the retreat of the Turks at the end of the seventeenth century. The author of a number of extremely popular historical works, such as *Kronika aliti spomen svega svieta vikov*, *Croatia rediviva regnate Leopoldo Magno Caesare*, *Serbia illustrata*, *Stemmatographia*, Vitezović found a formula in early South Slav history for future unification. Working on the basis of the geography contained in a twelfth-century work, the *Chronicles of the Presbyter of Dioclea*, where "Red" Croatia along the southern shores of the Adriatic is found along with "White" Croatia, Vitezović applied the name of Croatia to all the South Slavs of his period (Serbia, Macedonia, and Bulgaria being included in "Red" Croatia). This initial attempt to replace the actual division of the South Slavs by unity, destined to become a political objective and program, was only a utopian notion at the beginning of the eighteenth century, although in time it came to have a strong influence. In the eighteenth century the picture of the South Slav past as created by Mavro Orbin was popularized by Andrija Kačić Miošić, a Franciscan monk, in many poems written in the national style [*Korabljica (Schooner); Razgovor ugodni naroda slovinskog (Pleasant Talk of the Slavonic People)*].

No reference to history can overlook the work of Ivan Lučić (Johannes Lucius) of Trogir, whose highly developed critical sense and erudite efforts kept step with the forerunners of European historiography in the seventeenth century, heralding a much later critical approach. His voluminous history *De regno Dalmatiae et Croatiae libri VI* is a storehouse of valuable information.

Views of history were not imbued with this "Slavism" in the Slovene lands. There, provincial consciousness and local patriotism provided the frameworks for delving into the past. Although the Slovene language came to play a greater role as education advanced, and although the absolutist administration took it into account, it did not serve the purpose of setting the Slovenes apart from their provincial environment and persuading them to associate themselves with other Slavs. Distinguished intellectuals looked upon both Slovene and German as their own languages. Martin Baučer (1595–1668), a Slovene Jesuit of Gorizia, took Noricum and Friuli as the subject of his historical interest *(Historia rerum Noricarum et Forojuliensium)*; Ivan Ludvig Schönleben (1618–1681) wrote the earliest history of Carniola *(Carniola antiqua et nova)*. The culmination was achieved by J. V. Valvasor, who, continuing the work of Schönleben, wrote not only a history but also a comprehensive description of contemporary Carniola *(Die Ehre des Herzogthums Crain)*.

Baroque Culture in the Orthodox Setting

The course of baroque culture among the Serbs was quite specific in its manifestations. During the period of Turkish rule, medieval literary and artistic traditions were fostered by the Serbian church. Patriarch Pajsije produced a biography of Emperor Uroš in the early seventeenth century, totally in the spirit and style of his distant predecessors. Although church building did not take place in circumstances that favored any great achievement, the period of Patriarch Pajsije is outstanding for the reconstruction and erection of churches. Painting is well represented by Djordje Mitrofanović, whose works still remain in a number of Serbian churches and on Mount Athos. Cut off from cultural developments in Europe, in an environment marked by growing impoverishment, medieval traditions gradually dried up and petrified. Beyond the sphere of the church, the people pursued the patriarchal life typical at that time of all Balkan regions under Turkish control.

When the Turks were pressed back from Hungary and town life was revitalized, these two processes being attended by the economic and social advancement of the Serbian population there, conditions were created for the influx of European culture and its acceptance. In the course of one century, between approximately 1690 and 1790, the Serbs in Hungary traveled the long road from the introduction of elementary schooling to the adoption of rationalistic philosophy.

At the end of the seventeenth century Orthodox believers residing in Budapest and Szent Endre erected a church with baroque stylistic features. Even after the arrival of fresh waves of Serbian emigrants and a new church hierarchy, this development in church building was not interrupted. In a brief period, and in confined frameworks, the same transformations known to Catholic countries took place among the Serbs. New churches were built in the baroque manner, and earlier monastic buildings were reconstructed along baroque lines. Church interiors, although hostile to works of sculpture, were endowed with a baroque brilliance. A number of painters gained distinction by catering to the requirements of the church (Teodor Dimitrijević Kračun, Teodor Ilić Češljar, and others). Despite the suspicion of Western influence engendered by attempts at unification of the churches, the Serbian Orthodox church in Hungary accepted baroque as its official art.

Temporal circles among the nobility and citizenry found it even easier to adjust to the new art. The result was large number of baroque summer residences, town mansions, and magistrates' buildings in Vojvodina.

Western influences were far slower in making headway in literature. The Serbian church hierarchy clung tenaciously to Orthodox Russia as a model for literature and education. Books were imported from Russia, and from there, too, came teachers who established the first "Slavonic-Latin school" in Sremski Karlovci, the see of the metropolitan (Maksim Suvorov, Emanuil Kozačinski). This Russophile orientation brought strong Russian influence to bear on the Serbian literary language, setting its stamp on an entire epoch in the development of the language (Slaviano-Serbian). During the reign of Maria Theresa, the environment of the towns gave impetus to the cultural reorientation of the Serbs and the strengthening of European influences, with special emphasis on German.

Serbian historical studies in the eighteenth century merged the medieval traditions of the lives of saints and martyrs and chronicles with the traditions of the Dalmatian writers. In the unpublished chronicles of Count Djordje Branković, information gleaned from learned writers and autobiographical data about the author are mingled with the medieval type of reporting. This merger was to reach its culmination in the later monumental opus of Jovan Rajić. History was also popularized through the graphic arts. For instance, the copper engraver Hristofer Žefarović translated, reworked, and richly illustrated the *Stemmatographia* of Pavle Riter-Vitezović.

As the baroque thus imposed its forms on the ways of life and artistic expression of a significant section of the South Slavs, it linked them simultaneously with the principal trends in Europe.

Part Three

THE STRUGGLE
FOR NATION STATES
AND MODERN SOCIETY

At the end of the eighteenth century the process of creating the Yugoslav nations and modern societies began. The development of towns and of the bourgeoisie, the breakup of feudal relations, and agrarian revolutions all unfolded in the shadow of the great European wars and the interests of the great powers in the Balkan territory. The national revivals, which were to appear at different times among the different Yugoslav peoples, introduced the concept of states and societies based on the principle of a common language. Religious differences, however, made it difficult for the Yugoslav intelligentsia to create an integrated society on the basis of common language; throughout the nineteenth century religion provided the framework of distinct communities.

The Serbian national revolution of 1804 brought the peasants onto the Balkan scene as a decisive historical force; after the revolution, and throughout the nineteenth century, the agricultural free peasantry was the basis for social progress in the Balkans. The South Slav lands of the Hapsburg empire after 1848, under conditions that preserved the old class and state institutions, contrasted sharply with the Eastern South Slav lands, where feudal relations were destroyed by popular revolution in which the old class and state institutions passed from the historical scene. In the western parts of Yugoslavia the unfavorable solution to the agrarian question was characterized by greater concentrations of capital among the upper classes and a lack of stable financial institutions; these were to be the basic cause for both social and economic backwardness. The northern regions developed most quickly, for they lay on the European transport routes from the west to the Near East (along the rivers Sava and Danube) and the north-south route from Vienna and Budapest to Trieste and Rijeka. (It was in the north, along the former borders of Turkey and Europe, that the Yugoslav bourgeoisie originated.) Not until the end of the nineteenth century would national capital grow, although it still was weak compared with foreign capital. All the great industrial and transport enterprises depended on foreign investment. The Slavicization of the South Slav towns took great strides only after 1848, although it progressed more slowly in the southern regions, under the Turkish Empire.

Throughout this period the Balkans were a stage on which the interests of the great powers (Russia, France, and Austria) clashed. Not one significant event or social process could occur without their supervision and intervention, particularly after the failure of the revolution in the Hapsburg empire in 1848–

1849. In connection with all this was the question of political institutions and political freedom. In the Hapsburg empire an unfavorable electoral system, established in 1861, favored the political interests of the upper classes, administrative functionaries, the church, and foreign ethnic elements of the towns. In Serbia, because the free peasantry was the social foundation of the state, the degree of freedom was greater and the development of political institutions more rapid and more directly traceable to Western European, especially French, patterns.

In the course of all this, from the end of the eighteenth to the beginning of the twentieth century, the foundations of modern society were laid in all the Yugoslav lands except Macedonia, where, because of greater engagement of foreign powers and because of the mosaic-like ethnic character of its territory, the process of creating a national society lagged behind. Despite all their differences, the trend of the national movements of the Yugoslav people was toward unification. Up to 1903 the programs for Yugoslav state unification were ideologically based, and the societies of the various Yugoslav lands were preparing themselves more and more for the task.

CHAPTER 20

The Reign of Joseph II and the Awakening of the Yugoslav Peoples

---

The Reforms of Joseph II and Opposition from the Aristocracy

During the reign of Joseph II (1780–1790), the entire structure of the Hapsburg monarchy underwent change through a series of successive reforms touching upon every single sphere of society's life. The Yugoslav peoples also felt the repercussions of these modifications. The state, assumed to be serving the public good, endeavored through concentration of power and decision making in the hands of one man to achieve equality with the powerful European states of that time. The centralistic policy was pursued in opposition to tendencies on the part of various provinces to establish the new order on a local basis, independently of the common interest of the empire as a whole. At the same time, the landed aristocracy, which together with the church and army had been one of the principal pillars of the state throughout history, bent its efforts to perpetuating the status quo. In spite of its heterogeneity, the new state set about the business of restructuring as though only one nation were involved. By a decree of 1784, German was raised to the level of the official language also in the Hungarian part of the empire, attempts having failed to work out a common orthography for all branches of the South Slavs.

In the effort to gain the upper hand over the nobility, solidly imbued with the feudal spirit, the emperor's absolutism did not find the strong support it sought in the towns. Of the 9.5 million inhabitants of Hungary (together with Croatia and Slavonia), 5 percent were the nobility and clergy and about 5 percent the population of towns and mining settlements. The peasants spoke various Slavonic, Romanian, and Hungarian tongues, but German was slowly coming to prevail in the towns. Only one-third of the population spoke Hungarian. In order to improve the position of the towns, guilds were abolished and the serf system was modified and restricted in 1785. The ideas and needs of state centralization were furthered in terms of its peasant emancipation policy by a sanguinary agrarian rebellion in Transylvania that took the lives of 4,000 people, as well as by the effort to introduce effective control over tax collection by extending tax levies to include the nobility. The emperor nevertheless did not allow the peasants to become owners of the land they cultivated; they remained tenants who owed their feudatories specific obligations in money and kind.

Apart from the social aspects of the situation, subjects of the realm had to be made to feel they belonged to the state. To this end, from 1777 onwards, measures were undertaken to bring the reform home to the church, tenacious and conservative guardian of the old order. Links between the Catholic bishops and the pope were obstructed. The organization of convents was changed, and an order was issued to monasteries forbidding anyone to take monastic vows for a period of twenty years.

Administrative innovations were even more damaging to the nobility. The Slovene lands were grouped into two guberniyas at the same time that twelve earlier provincial governments in the crownlands were concentrated in six guberniyas. Nothing was left to the old estates' colleges except two estate representatives in the guberniya organs. The nobility was thus shorn of its earlier political role in state affairs. Under the new administrative system, Hungary retained certain specific features. It was promised greater independence in financial, judicial, and certain political matters. The counties (županijas) were abolished, and the country was divided into ten districts, with no consideration displayed for earlier historical boundaries or the specific features to which the backward society was so sensitive. Royal commissioners were appointed to head them, destroying in

Croatia and Slavonia the županija assemblies of nobles which had elected delegates to the assembly; with them also disappeared the old freedom of the nobles. Croatia was transformed into a separate district, and Slavonia and Baranja were linked with the district of Pečuj. Certain administrative and political changes were also carried out in the Military Frontier (the "cantonal system").

These thoroughgoing reforms generated major consequences in the empire at large. A substantial part of the nobility, its position as the pillar of society threatened, formed an opposition. Among the South Slav lands, this was most noticeable in Croatia, the only one of the Yugoslav areas in the empire with a powerful national nobility. In 1785 in Civil Croatia and Slavonia, there were 25,000 nobles (9,260 noble families) to 589,620 inhabitants. The heterogeneous bourgeoisie in the small towns (28,490) was not capable of opposing the nobility, nor could it serve the reform-bent court as a support replacing the nobility. The biggest towns of that time (Varaždin, Rijeka, Bakar, Zagreb, Osijek) had no more than 8,000 inhabitants each; in some of them, more people were employed in and around the church than in trade. In large part the Croatian nobility was conservative in its loyalty to the old constitutional system of Hungary. It shared with the Hungarian nobility a common tongue (Latin) and political creed.

In Hungary a Hungarian national movement came into being, defiant of the Germanization efforts of Joseph II and determined to introduce the Hungarian national language in place of Latin. Repercussions were felt in Croatia, where German had not taken root.

Reaction after Joseph and the Association of Croatia with Hungary

Shortly before his death in 1790, Joseph II, disillusioned and ailing, desisted from his reforming notions, and his successors at court were to be more permissive. The nobility then attempted to turn back the clock of history, although desirous itself of implementing certain changes in society. Originally the Croatian nobility made common cause with the Hungarian nobles, raising the slogan of "constitutional fraternalism" with them. In May 1790 the Croatian Diet passed a decision to establish stronger ties with Hungary, ceding to the Hungarian Regency Council the administration of Croatia. In Croatia the old power of the nobles was revived, predicated on the autonomous županijas. At the same Assembly, the nobility agreed to the introduction of the Hungarian language in Croatian schools, but not as a compulsory subject.

Although the serf reverted to his previous position, the Diet of 1790 nevertheless established the possibility for him to leave the feudal estate if he wished, after settling accounts with the nobleman and any obligations he may have owed to others. Thus began the corrosion of the ancient system marked by the serf's personal dependence on the landlord; also, social relations in their entirety were somewhat liberalized. By 1802 the Diet had completed its system of laws designed to counter any innovations, thus confirming the earlier decision to establish as the basis of the state order the rule that nobles paid no taxes and did not serve in the army.

In its fear of fresh centralizing measures by the court, the Croatian nobility hitched the Croatian wagon to Hungary after the death of Joseph II. In acting thus, it sacrificed far more traditional Croatian autonomy than could have been expected. Military taxes were left up to the joint Hungarian Diet, while Croatian administration was subordinated to the Hungarian government with the provision that the rights of the Croatian županijas to issue decrees were transferred to the Hungarian Regency Council. A real union was thereby forged between Croatia and Hungary, leaving the former in substantial measure at the mercy of the Hungarian nobility, which found a lasting cure for centralization in the Magyarization of its state institutions and of the entire culture. The Magyarization drive thus came to be transmitted to Croatia as well.

The Serbs' Struggle for Autonomy

At this time the Serbs in Hungary were in somewhat the same position except that their mood was more sympathetic to Joseph's reforms. They could not, however, justify their resistance to Hungarian domination by invoking special historical rights and the traditions of a separate statehood, as Croatia could. The Serbs were thrown into confusion after the death of Joseph II, who, through his "toleration patent" and alleviations for the serfs, had opened up for Serbia the prospect of a better national future. In heated discussions in 1790, the Serbs demanded that, as a recognized nation, they enjoy the right of access to all sections of society, that they have a hand in administration and "now and in future participate in the general prosperity and improvement of their own situation." Demands for a special territory and autonomy were submitted most insistently in the Timişoara Assembly of 1790, at which all Serbian estates with the exception of peasants were represented (bourgeoisie, soldiers, clergymen, nobles). After this the court in Vienna instituted an office for Serbian affairs (the Illyrian Court Office) which concerned itself with their problems in 1791 and 1792. In the latter year the Hungarians agreed to concede the rights of citizenship to the Serbs in Hungary, and to permit their metropolitan and bishops to have a say in the Diet. The Serbs therefore succeeded in winning recognition for their church leaders and national political leaders, despite the fact that they had no genuine authority.

The Jacobin Conspiracy

Defeated by the nobility, the reform spirit found expression in various secret societies; the most significant was initiated by the abbot Ignazius Martinovics and some of his companions in Hungary. His Serbian parents had migrated to the other side of the Sava River under the leadership of Arsenije III Čarnojević, had been converted to Catholicism, and had enrolled their son in the Franciscan order. In time he became a professor at the University of Lvov. His followers were called the Hungarian Jacobins. Martinovics left behind him important projects for the political restructuring of the state. In November 1792 he secretly published the *Status regni Hungariae*, in which he referred to a bicameral parliament on the British model. In his project of September 1793 for a federal "Republic of Hungary" he provided for the establishment of a federated state divided up into provinces and nationalities (Hungary, Illyria, Slovakia, and Wallachia). The common tongue would be Hungarian although "every province would have the right to introduce its provincial language in schools and public institutions."

The court in Vienna was aware of these movements in Hungary and for a time, until they acquired the proportions of dangerous plots against the dynasty, clandestinely supported them as a means of blackmailing the Hungarian magnates who opposed the court. Initially, Martinovics, believing in the reforms of the new emperor Leopold II, joined the service of the emperor as a paid agent. Finally, in May 1794, he started forming a revolutionary organization, uncovered after only three months, during which brief interval he had presumably enlisted about 200 members, most of them young intellectuals, nobles, and bourgeoisie. For his conspiracy Martinovics and his comrades were arrested in the middle of 1794. He was later executed at the "Bloody Field," a square in Budapest.

Although by nature a Magyar movement, Martinovics's conspiracy figured significantly in South Slav history, where it undoubtedly belongs, for it was supported by a considerable number of people in Croatia (Zagreb and Varaždin) and in Vojvodina. That they were organized in cells is known, although it is difficult to reconstruct their network in Yugoslav lands, as the principal personality in the organization was Josip Kralj, a prefect on the crown-owned estate of Kutjevo, who committed suicide as he faced arrest in 1795. He left a defiant message to the effect that he had "lived freely and would rather die free than to be chained even for an hour." Another Serb member of the movement was Jakov Sečanac, a lawyer, arrested as an accomplice of Martinovics but later released.

The supporters of the ideas of French Revolution and Jacobinism organized a bloody insurrection in Dalmatia and Istria in 1797. Traditionally, educated aristocrats there were divided into two groups, liberal and conservative, under the names of the universities they were educated in ("Sorbonnes" and "Salamancaes"). After the collapse of the Venetian Republic in 1797 mutiny broke out in Dalmatian towns (Šibenik, Split, Zadar, and others). The objective of the rebels was the prevention of occupation of the Adriatic coast by the Austrian army. The insurrection was unsuccessful.

Similar defiance is discernible in the ideas of the Greek revolutionary Riga of Fera (Konstantinos Rhigas Velestinlis, 1755–1798). His works, the most significant being the *Declaration on the Rights of Man* and the *Draft of the Constitution*, preached the ideas of the French Revolution. In 1797 he foresaw the raising of a general insurrection against the Turks and the creation of a new Hellenic republic predicated on the sovereignty of the people. Equally dangerous to Turks and Austrians, he was apprehended by the latter and extradited to the Turks, who executed him in Belgrade.

Quest for a New Culture and National Awakening

Profound consequences emanated not only from these political changes and events but also from new achievements along cultural lines. In Slovenia the fight for use of the national language had been launched in 1768 by the publication of Pohlin's *Carniolan Grammar*. Thenceforward the recession of Latin was paralleled by the entrenchment of German. The Slovene national awakening was initiated then, slowly at first but gaining momentum, although some time had yet to pass before its full flowering. An essential characteristic of the first phase, which lasted until 1848, was the belated maturing of political methods of struggle and the reliance on culture in which provincial motives were the first to prevail, surrendering later to all-national Slovene motives. Anton Linhart (1756–1795) wrote *An Attempt at a History of Carniolan and Other South Slavs in Austria*. Baron Žiga Zois (1747–1819) collected national poetry and offered encouragement to national poets and the few practicing scientists. Belonging to the same circle was the poet Valentin Vodnik (1758–1819), whose poem *Zadovoljni Kranjac (The Satisfied Carniolan)* opened the way to national literature in the nineteenth century.

But this national renaissance, slow to manifest itself in culture, had no very deep foundations. Furthermore, it was politically devoted to Vienna, with which it shared a certain fear of Russia. Catholicism was to remain one of the lasting bases upon which the awakening was grounded, just as national awakening in the Balkan Peninsula generally can hardly be divorced from the national churches.

The leading classes in Slovenia were the Germans, who represented the thin layer of public opinion and the pillar of official policy. They included virtually the entire nobility, the higher echelons of citizens, and a part of the intelligentsia. In Hungary and Croatia the Germans had no national policy of their own in the towns, but they did have one in Slovenia. Within the framework of that policy, they endeavored to assimilate all those who were rising in the social hierarchy.

The Serbian bourgeoisie in Hungary during this period was preoccupied with the development of a national culture under the dual influence of Western Europe and Russia. At first the orientation to Orthodox Russia prevailed, for the Serbs always turned to Russia partly out of fear of Austrian attempts to unify the churches, and partly as a result of the underdevelopment of their own society, which still drew no great difference between communities belonging to the same religion. The situation was not changed by the fact that a section of the educated Serbs, like all educated sections of the population in the Balkan Peninsula outside of Turkey, shuddered at the thought of the oppressive Russian political regime.

The new times struck blows at Serbian national customs, at the still-living forms of the earlier society and the old mentality. In the conviction that these customs were heathenish, the churches of both Serbs and Croats tried to stamp them out. Some of them were common to Christians of both churches and also to the Muslims in the Yugoslav lands, but the Catholic church made the most headway in uprooting them. The consequence of these actions was to cause even greater differentiation along religious lines among the people of various denominations.

Beginning with 1776, the Serbs celebrated the New Year on January 1, rather than September 1, the former date. Six years earlier they had begun to decrease the number of Orthodox religious holidays in their calendar. Previously, including Sundays, there had been 170 holidays, meaning that for Serbs almost every second day was a holiday. Embarked upon the new age of businesslike attitudes and reason, patriarchal agrarian society staggered under the burden of medieval customs. The Serbian town population in Hungary took upon itself the major historic task of ridding it of that burden. At a number of successive church synods up to 1787, the excessive number of holidays was reduced to eighty-one a year. Here too could be sensed the meddling hand of the Austrian authorities, who were hopeful that through these changes Serbian political traditions would suffer and the Serbian church would draw closer to the Catholic. They achieved some temporary success along these lines, as the changes concerned the peculiar customs surrounding the canonization of Serbian saints, in which national magnates and political personalities from the history of the Serbian state had suppressed other names in the calendar. This had been a powerful means to arouse the people's consciousness that they belonged to the same religious, church, and political framework.

Furthermore, the Serbian bourgeoisie in Hungary had already begun the struggle against the existing literary language, an artificial contrivance of recent date, incomprehensible to the ordinary people. A number of valuable literary works had been written in this Slaviano-Serbian language. The rank and file profited little from this literacy, however, for as Dositej Obradović (1742-1811) stated, "it was understood properly by one in ten thousand." Obradović was responsible for giving the most powerful impetus to the new trend. The principal messages contained in his works were that a more simple alphabet should be created (Latinized Cyrillic), the vernacular should be used in literature, and culture should be separated from the church. He offered no lasting solutions to any one of these problems, but his thinking on the subject created profound misgivings among his contemporaries, which were to lead to reforms several decades later. Similarly, his ideas about the nation as a community based on language, and not religious or church affiliation, made a deep impression and were to inspire later generations. Obradović himself, in working out his ideas, was influenced by rational philosophy.

Toward the end of the eighteenth century a general and strong tendency was noticeable among all South Slavs to emancipate national culture from its slavish dependence on religion and to redirect it toward national sources. Andrija Kačić Miošić's poem *Pleasant Talk of the Slavonic People*, published in 1759, had a strong influence on later literature and politics. Among the Bulgarians, Pajsije of Chilendarion published *The History of Slaviano-Bulgaria* in 1762. The *Slaveno-Serbian News*, printed in Vienna in 1792, made its way even to readers under Turkish rule. Archimandrite Jovan Rajić published in Vienna in 1794 *The History of Various Slav Peoples, Particularly Bulgarians, Croats, and Serbs*, which was powerful and direct in deepening the perception of later champions of national renaissance.

Wars with Turkey

These cultural and social changes among the South Slavs were given impetus by the fact that the Balkan area was being increasingly transformed into one of the most important centers of the European diplomatic scene. Russia and Austria considered the Balkan Peninsula a region where they could expand and augment their territories. In spite of the Kuchuk Kainarji peace treaty of 1774, a series of wars was pursued by Russia against Turkey, between 1787 and 1856, in the search for an outlet to the southern seas. At the end of the eighteenth century, it was fighting for the right to trusteeship over the Balkan peoples of Orthodox faith, just as Austria sought to do for the Balkan Catholics. But when territorial gains at the expense of crumbling Turkey were involved, this principle went by the board.

First Russia and Austria (1781) and then Russia and France (1807) endeavored to reach agreement over partition of the Balkan Peninsula. Gnawing though petty mistrust and boundless rivalry prevented them from fulfilling their intention, but the division of the Balkan Peninsula into various spheres of interest did actually begin then. In 1782 Joseph II and Catherine tried to agree on the establishment of the independent state of Dacia and revival of the Greek Empire with its capital in Constantinople. The line of division in the South Slav lands ran from Belgrade to the Bay of the Drim, whereas Austria was nursing a secret longing for Venetian Dalmatia, whose isolation from its Balkan hinterland was felt increasingly.

The most incisive minds among the South Slavs made an effort to turn this situation to advantage, laying stress on their national unity, as Dositej Obradović did, or prodding the big powers into action against the Turks. David Nerandžić, the brother of a favorite of Catherine II, was advised by the Montenegrin bishop Petar I, the head of both state and church, to write a memorandum in 1785 on the liberation of the Balkan nations. These peoples, he said, "had once had their own celebrated lords, who were masters of Illyria and other lands up to the Black Sea. . . . The minute Russia takes action, these peoples, desirous of liberty, will rise against the Turks." But without any really strong national movements on which to rely, such appeals for unity and liberation remained isolated testimony to the historical maturity of leading minds but not to the capabilities of entire societies.

In the war that Austria and Russia fought in 1787 against Turkey, the people in Serbia were clamorous in their rebellion. While Austrian agents rallied monks and petty traders to their cause, the Turks executed sixty-five prominent Serbs in 1788. As Austria's frontier with Turkey ran from Dalmatia to Hotin, Austria was concerned to cover part of the vast front with native volunteers. In December 1787 a detachment of volunteers was formed (Freikorps), led by Mihailo Mihailović and operating between the Morava and Drina Rivers. East of the Morava the Banat Freikorps conducted its operations, and a Bosnian volunteer detachment was formed for Bosnia. This, however, was of minor significance. In eastern Serbia a detachment raised by Koča Andjelković, a wealthy merchant, gained prominence. Detachments of rebellious Serbs in this war ranged up to 3,000 men, their tasks being to obstruct communications and the transport of Turkish troops along the roads from Istanbul to Belgrade, to burn crops as a menace to the Turkish armies' supply lines, and to fell trees along rivers to hamper navigation. In Serbia the people fled in masses to forest hideouts, where they often remained an entire year. In 1788 there were 50,000 refugees on the northern (Austrian) side of the Sava River.

The war was called Koča's War in Serbia, after Koča Andjelković, who of all the leaders of the day impressed himself most indelibly on the peasant consciousness. Their guerrilla activities in this war were a great lesson in history for the Serbian people. They lost their former confidence in the Austrian emperor, who betrayed them in the war; on the Turkish side, these mass peasant movements disrupted the old Turkish society, which was never again to achieve its former glory. All signs indicated that it would be easier to win liberation from the Turks than to try to restore the old harmony under them.

Movements came into being also in Montenegro, which, through its guvernadur, Jovan Radonić, received assistance in arms. Its bishop, Petar, intended to win international recognition of Montenegro's independence. A detachment of Montenegrins under Filip Vukasović was transported to Croatia, where it fought but was sent home after the Army Mutiny of 1789. Austria's objectives in this war were limited. It had captured Belgrade, while its soldiers in Bosnia laid a long siege to Dubica, from which the entire campaign derived its name, the Dubica War. With great effort, Dubica, Novi, and Gradiška were taken.

The war ended abortively with the Treaty of Sistova in 1791, concluded on the basis of the status quo. Austria left Serbia and in Bosnia won a rectified boundary on the Una River. The people who had risen against the Turks were amnestied, and the majority of refugees from Austria returned to Turkey, embittered by the ill-treatment to which they had been subjected. In future conflicts the experience of their failure to get help was to mean more to them than if they had obtained it.

CHAPTER 21

The Serbian Revolution and the Yugoslav Lands during the Napoleonic Wars

---

THE DECLINE OF TURKEY / THE DAHIYAS AND THE BEHEADING OF THE KNEZES / THE FIRST SERBIAN UPRISING / THE STATE OF RELATIONS BETWEEN FRANCE AND RUSSIA / THE FAILURE OF THE FIRST SERBIAN UPRISING / THE PEACE OF BUCHAREST / THE SECOND UPRISING AND THE GENERAL SIGNIFICANCE OF THE SERBIAN REVOLUTION / THE POLICIES OF AUSTRIA

The Decline of Turkey

Despite occasional and unexpected spurts of resurgence, Turkey declined slowly but steadily throughout the eighteenth century. In an effort to reverse the process, the sultan-reformer Selim III (1789–1807) instituted reforms the consequences of which only aggravated the situation. New levies were imposed upon the peasants. In most cases, in the process of restructuring feudal holdings (*čitlučenje*) already well under way, another intermediary (the čiftlik-sahibi) intervened between the old spahi and his serfs, debasing the earlier form of social relations and doubling the burden on the peasants. During these troubled and generally insecure times, the peasant world adopted the new owner as protector. The general result of these social changes was protracted social instability against the background of political anarchy throughout the empire.

Turkey's steady retrogression may also be attributed to another factor, its inability to revitalize its cities at a time when towns in the rest of Europe were experiencing one of the most important evolutions known to history in all spheres, social, political, and economic. In the Turkey of that time, the Balkan town was predominantly Muslim. In the pashalic of Belgrade in 1785 the Serbian population in the towns amounted to only 35 percent of the inhabitants, in addition to Cincars and some Greeks who far outnumbered the Serbs in places. The Muslim population in the towns was even larger in Bosnia, Macedonia, and northern Albania, although in Bosnia the Muslims were ethnically Slavs. In consequence of customs regulations, all trade along the boundaries was transit in character; the traders' mentality became geared to their acting as intermediaries between the Islamic East and Europe. The merchants set the tone in the towns.

The empire was being dismembered into provincial and to some extent ethnical entities. All those who were not real Turks turned against the sultan, including the Muslims of Bosnia and Albania. The Muslims' resistance to Turkish authority, however, had different social roots and a different political tradition from those of their Christian brothers. In Vidin, Pazvan-Oglu set up his own separate authority in 1794. In northern Albania, Mahmud Pasha Bushatliya, after securing his position, tried to establish contact with Joseph II in 1786. In Bosnia a growth in power was registered by the magnates' families, which discharged, by inheritance, the function of "captains," of whom there were twenty-four in Bosnia and twelve in Hercegovina. They imposed taxes and levies at will, did the work of the police authorities, and went to war at the head of military units.

Partly in discharge of peace obligations arising from the Treaty of Sistova, and partly out of the urgent need to improve the situation, the Turks tried to establish peace in the Belgrade pashalic, but no headway could be made in reestablishing the old order under the altered conditions and amid the shambles of earlier social institutions. Soon after 1791 the Turks were hardly able to enforce the old decrees about the wearing apparel of the raya, which set the Christians apart as a second-class section of society. Realizing the danger threatening from Serbia, Sultan Selim III personally participated in drafting the reforms of 1791–1801 for that "Frontier," as he called the Belgrade pashalic. The first step that had to be taken was eviction of the Janissaries, about whom the people complained bitterly, followed by attempts to persuade those who had taken refuge on the other side of the Sava River to return to Serbia. This pashalic was in any case sparsely settled, the estimate being that before the uprising of 1804 it counted only about 368,000 persons.

The menace of the Janissaries' returning was always present. Actually

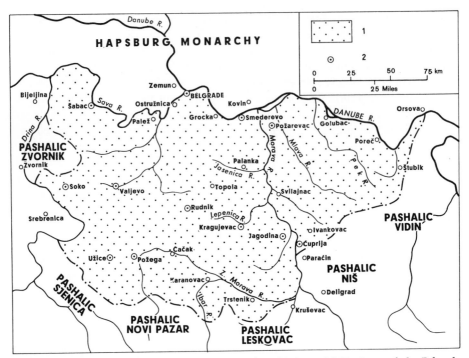

MAP 27.   The Belgrade pashalic before the First Serbian Uprising. (1) Territory of the Belgrade
pashalic; (2) seat of nahiya.

they did succeed in capturing Belgrade in an invasion of 1792 which the town was
unable to resist. The authorities endeavored to forbid Turks to carry arms and
to prevent the old spahis, who regained their possessions, from settling anywhere
near the raya in the villages. The most significant of the new measures recognized
the right of the Serbs to local government. They won the right to self-government
and not only showed great staying power in their autonomous local territory
(knežina) but developed a social mechanism fostering the consciousness that
they were not raya. The Turks fixed the exact amount of taxes payable by the
entire pashalic, and spahis were permitted to live only in Belgrade. The raya
were allowed to erect churches wherever they wished. Serbian military units
were engaged to help pursue the Janissaries. For the first time in the recent history
of the empire, Serbian military organizations acquired legality and were commanded by natives. The Turkish authorities were even thinking of entrusting
them with the obligation of defending the pashalic from outside opponents.
The process of restructuring feudal holdings stopped with the disappearance of
the Janissaries, and the people thenceforward paid only two taxes—to the empire
and to the spahis. The taxes were collected by local chiefs (knezes) and their
superiors (ober-knezes), reducing the movements of Turks among the people

to a minimum. The people elected their chiefs on an annual basis, their choice being confirmed by the pasha.

The Dahiyas and the Beheading of the Knezes

The Janissaries in neighboring regions continued to regard the Belgrade pashalic as the "sweetest morsel." In 1797/98 they attacked but failed to capture it. The defense brought to the fore the excellent qualities of the Serbian people's army, for whom this was the first important school for the future. Nevertheless, with the approval of the Turkish government, the Janissaries lawfully returned to the pashalic and in 1801 introduced a reign of terror in Serbia. Under the new setup the pashalic was divided into four parts headed by dahiyas (provincial dignitaries), and čiftliks were restored. The new division into "čiftliks and dahilics" canceled the privileges previously won by the Serbs, placing Serbia once again on an equal footing with the other provinces, but it nevertheless caused dissatisfaction among the old spahis in Belgrade, who had been accustomed to collecting their own dues from the peasants. The Janissary authority thus found itself between two fires: between the old Muslim spahis and the new Serbian leadership that had emerged in the villages and knežinas. The Janissaries divested the former of their land, and the latter of local power, wealth, and security. The period of relative peace and gradual progress between 1791 and 1801 had been conducive to the growth of prosperity among that section of the population. An increase was recorded in the number of merchants in the villages who tried to have a hand in all affairs. Historians call them the "village bourgeoisie," and there is no doubt that they represented the inception of a new social leadership of the people. Their wealth derived largely from export trade, as evidenced in the statistic that 200,000 pigs were annually exported from Serbia during the end of the eighteenth century.

In defending themselves from the Janissaries, the Serbs struck a temporary alliance with the spahis, whom they considered decent Turks loyal to the empire, and whose presence in their midst lent their rebellion the appearance of legality and held out the hope of success. There was also a widespread belief that Austria and Russia would not leave them in the lurch. From an intercepted letter from Austria, the dahiyas got wind of the approaching storms, and in order to nip the plans in the bud, they began the "execution of the knezes" toward the end of January 1804, killing prominent persons throughout the pashalic, wherever they found them. This gave the people sufficient cause to revolt. A powerful personality immediately established himself among the Serbs in the person of Karadjordje ("Black" or "Handsome" George) Petrović (1768–1817), whom the dahiyas failed to apprehend. He was a small trader and one of the seniors in the Serbian volunteer army from the last war between Austria and Turkey. At an assembly in Orašac early in February 1804, the rebels, deciding to rouse the people to a general rebellion, elected him their leader. It was the custom to persuade the hesitant to join the rebellion by having more resolute neighbors set fire to their houses or for Karadjordje to hang a Turk on their threshold.

The First Serbian Uprising

The focus of the movement was Šumadija, in the nahiyas (districts) of Rudnik, Kragujevac, and Belgrade. The uprising spread rapidly, and in the process the original, immature objectives also changed. The movement for the "old rights" metamorphosed into a liberation war for political autonomy. Most of the mass of peasants participating in the uprising were those who lived in family cooperatives, but they were joined, in time, by small detachments of volunteers (usually homeless persons) who provided the nucleus of the standing army. Most of these came from Hercegovina, Bosnia, the Austrian Yugoslav provinces, Bulgaria, and Macedonia. Volunteers from Macedonia formed their own detachments bearing banners with the Macedonian emblem and name. A Greek folk song of that period refers to the Serbian army, in which comrades-in-arms do not recognize each other because of the ethnical admixture, including Serbs, Bulgarians, Romanians, and Greeks.

Appeals to Austria and Russia for help (a deputation was sent to the latter at the end of 1804) lent the uprising the character of a grass-roots rebellion with far-reaching objectives.

Up to 1807, the uprising was conciliatory in its attitude toward Turkey. The aim was autonomy with international guarantees. During this period, the rebels had to regulate two matters: (1) to draft clear-cut demands to be laid before the sultan; (2) to develop an internal state mechanism. In the first case they elaborated the Serbian objectives step by step. Originally a peasant uprising, led by local knezes and merchants, its participants were carried away by the idea of expanding and guaranteeing the rights enjoyed by Serbia before 1801. In line with this approach, Janissaries were run down in the captured towns (Rudnik, Valjevo, Šabac, Požarevac, Smederevo), but the Muslim craftsmen and merchants, considered friends and allies, were left in peace. This later changed, and in time the Muslim population disappeared from Serbia.

At an assembly in Pećane on May 13, 1805, no mention is made of the spahis and feudal order, as though it were self-evident that the old social system could not be reinstated. The chain of victories over the imperial army stimulated political ambitions and speeded the achievement of general objectives, with the result that a deputation, which found it rough going to reach Istanbul, placed certain demands before the sultan: a separate prince for Serbia, independent collection of taxes, and defense of the pashalic by the Serbs.

By early 1806, with alternating successes, the insurgents captured Karanovac, Užice (without the stronghold of Soko), Paraćin, Ražanj, and Aleksinac. Trenches were fortified at Deligrad, and in August 1805 Commanders Milojko Stojković and Petar Dobrnjac foiled the plans of the newly appointed vizier, who had set out from Niš with an army to take Belgrade. He was thoroughly routed at Ivankovac. The shift from local raids in the nahiyas to the offensive tactics of lengthy and unprecedented winter marches to join battle with the Turkish army resulted in two more celebrated triumphs: in August 1806 at Mišar against the Bosnian army and at Aleksinac and Deligrad against the Rumelian army. This chain of rebel victories was slated to terminate with the definitive capture of Belgrade (the town in December 1806 and the fortress the next month). Finally the triumphant army entered Šabac, to the roll of drums and the sound of music, in January 1807. The successful outcome of these battles filled the Serbs with confidence and removed many of the obstacles to the formation of the natural objectives of the revolution. From time immemorial a myth had prevailed about a lasting desire for an independent state, and eyes turned to the expanses of surrounding territories reaching to the Adriatic Sea and the boundaries of Bosnia. In 1805 the tribal community of the Drobnjaci rebelled, and in 1807 the peasants around Pirot, Niš, and Leskovac and in the Bosnian part of the Drina River valley. Bulgarians in the boundary areas began to flee to Serbia. Early in April 1807 peasants in Srem rose (at Voganj near Ruma) under the leadership of Teodor Avramović and Andrija Popović in a revolt named Tican's Revolt after one of the commanders. After crushing this revolt, the Austrian authorities set about interfering with the circulation of Serbian patriotic books in Vojvodina, but another rebellion erupted in the Banat in 1808. Also, Janić's Revolt broke out in the Bosnian March but was thoroughly quelled in 1809. Peasants on Austrian territory across the Danube River, in the Banat, also rose in rebellion.

The other matter concerned the regulation of internal affairs and the creation of state machinery in Serbia. This was far more difficult. Not only had there been a tradition of self-government in the knežinas, which the central government had persisted in violating, but the people had no clear idea of their national self. It was still not evident exactly what Serbia was. In the popular image created by history and tradition, it encompassed something far larger than the pashalic. In Šumadija itself, provincial and local names were associated with local patriotism in sentiment and in final objectives. Lasting strife among the local leaders over political prestige and the agrarian self-sufficiency of the peasants favored this segmentation. In the knežinas there emerged new arrogant commanders (vojvodas) whom the central authorities could not bend to their will. Great families arose to manage the affairs of the people in their areas, like minor kings ruling their own territory.

A joint executive organ was established—the Administrative Council under the presidency of the distinguished leader Matija Nenadović (1777–1854) who was respected for his wisdom both in politics and in the church, where he served as a priest. However, the Council was actually directed by its secretary Boža Grujović (1778-1807), an educated Serb from Hungary who had been a university professor in Russia. He had his own ideas about the organization of the new Serbian state and Serbian government, worked out under the influence of French rationalism. He declared that "lords, chieftains, and the Administrative Council, and the clergy, the army, and the whole people must be ruled by one and the same law." The Serbs were assisted in the work of developing a new statehood by some learned Russians who wished to make of Serbia something that like-minded individuals had not succeeded in doing at home: partially to limit the autocratic power of the ruler by the constitution, and to establish a representative body, albeit imperfect. The first draft of the Serbian constitutional law (August 8, 1807) comprising twelve articles was worked out by a commission of three Russians and five Serbs. The assembly rejected it, and it failed to win the approval of the Russian tsar. Karadjordje himself attempted to promulgate a constitutional law quite at odds with it. The constitution of 1807 attempted to curtail Karadjordje's power by provisionally creating a federation of nahiya states out of Serbia. But the nahiyas wanted to make their own laws for their regions. Karadjordje was to oppose this federalism later, too, and in the Constitution of 1811 he broke up the big vojvodstvos (areas under a vojvoda, or commander) to create smaller ones, in the conviction that this was the cure for centralism.

The Administrative Council passed through a number of phases up to 1813, adapting itself to the conflict between local commanders and joint leaders, external circumstances, and various political currents. Before 1811 the Council was representative in character, seventeen councilmen representing seventeen districts.

The local leaders had learned the art of ruling the people from their former Turkish masters. The itch for wealth among some of them developed into the ambition to create a new Serbian feudalism on the ruins of the Turkish; on the holdings of some of these vojvodas, the peasants toiled as they had under the spahis. In a number of ways, Karadjordje was an exceptional leader. He was elected by the people and accepted by them as their leader, an essential feature of all peasant uprisings before and after. The peasants singled out for their leader a strong personality who gradually emerged as a monarch. Karadjordje was tough, but in his toughness he exercised reasonable caution. His character reflected the record of suffering of the Balkan peasants over the past few centuries. Barely literate, he was a rare historical case of a peasant merchant who founded a dynasty. Physically and mentally, he corresponded to a child's image of a king—the tallest, strongest, and most intelligent of them all. Songs about him were sung by all peasant peoples in the Balkan Peninsula, and even the Turks felt a healthy respect for him. A person as powerful as he, whose achievements were interwoven with the myths produced by the ordinary folk, was considered capable of performing miracles. But the one thing he could not do was bridle the arrogant commanders who followed his example. The question of internal statehood and power was to remain unsolved until the end of the revolution.

The State of Relations between France and Russia

During the entire course of the uprising, external factors and the influence of European powers were to have a bearing on its development. In Europe the star of France under Napoleon was rising. On December 2, 1805, when Napoleon defeated the Russians and Austrians at Austerlitz, France loomed as a factor of major importance for the Balkans. But there was no need to go far back into history to find a tradition for this. During the collapse of the Venetian Republic in 1797, France had conceded to Austria what had formerly been Venetian Istria with the Quarnero Islands, Dalmatia, and Boka Kotorska. This placed within the confines of the Hapsburg empire yet another half million South Slavs and large territories with strategic significance for the entire Balkan area. Under Venice, Dalmatia with its quarter of a million inhabitants had been the largest and the poorest province of the Republic, with the most backward population. The new Austrian government (the First Austrian Occupation of Dalmatia) did nothing to change the old Venetian institutions. But this state of affairs did not last long, for at the end of 1805, in a number of sweeping strategic moves, Napoleon annexed these Dalmatian and littoral regions to the newly formed kingdom of Italy, of which he himself was king. Italian remained the official language in the area, ruled by a *provveditore general* whose function was discharged by the Venetian Vicenzo Dandolo (1758–1819).

In 1805 the Russians, in control of the nearby strategically important Ionian Islands, tried to persuade Montenegro to commit itself to the struggle against France. The Russian fleet sailed into Boka Kotorska (1804), where a Russian consulate had been opened. The Montenegrin demand that this region be annexed to Montenegro was brusquely rejected by its traditional protector. The Russian counselor Stefan Sankovski visited Montenegro to deal with the matter. By 1806 the wartime alliance began to show results, and 2,500 Russians with twice as many Montenegrins, joined by rebellious peasants from the Konavle area, set off for Dubrovnik, which had unwillingly opened its gates to the French general Jacques-Alexandre Lauriston.

The march on Dubrovnik of 1806 failed, but better fortune awaited the attackers along the road to Pelješac and Korčula. True, in these coastal engagements, the major question was whether Russia would acquire a secure stronghold in this part of the Mediterranean. As a world power, it was eager to play the role of arbiter in its political affairs. Thus it drew the Serbs and South Slavs generally onto the world diplomatic scene, primarily through its relations with France.

In the face of events so important to its possessions, Turkey made haste to set matters right in its own house. Late in August 1806 it accepted an offer of peace from the Serbs, brought by a representative of the uprising, Petar Ička, delegate of Belgrade's merchants. The Turks agreed to some measure of Serbian autonomy and more precise stipulation of taxes. But the Serbian leadership, intoxicated with the victories of its army, did not consider the bargain struck as a realistic basis for their power or as offering firm international guarantees, so cautiously avoided by the Turks. The Serbs themselves did not observe "Ička's Peace" and hitched their destiny to Russia, which had taken Moldavia and Wallachia. Consequently the sultan declared war on them in December 1806. This gave the Serbs cause to disbelieve the Turkish promises made in Ička's Peace. At an assembly in Belgrade, they opted for military and political cooperation with the Russians. It was to bring them initial successes and take them to the zenith of their revolution, after which the revolution collapsed when Russia withdrew in 1812.

In the spring of 1807 they attacked on all fronts, capturing Užice, Jadar, and Radjevina (from the Bosnian pashalic) in the west. The Serbs' Achilles' heel was the length of the borders they had to defend. From the east came attacks by the Rumelian army, sometimes led by the grand vizier himself; in the south they were menaced by the pasha of Scutari, who did not, however, have the audacity to make any major advances, and from the west by the Bosnian vizier, who usually marched along the Šabac-Belgrade route. In each of these directions the Turks were able to put more men in the field than the Serbs on all three fronts together.

The Russians endeavored to establish a stable relation with the Serbs, and on July 10, 1807, Colonel Filipp Osipovič Paulucci signed a convention with them at Negotin ("Paulucci's Convention," which some historians term the Serbian-Russian Alliance) in which the Serbs, exhausted by the ceaseless strife among their leaders for primacy and power, asked for a Russian regent to rule Serbia, Russian garrisons for fortified towns in the interior, and defense of the eastern and southern borders by the Russians (in the direction of Montenegro and Dalmatia).

Pressed and defeated by the French in Prussia, the Russians concluded peace with them in Tilsit (July 7, 1807); in a subsequent alliance with France, Russia was compelled to remain at peace with the Turks, although in a later oral interpretation Napoleon left it the possibility of not withdrawing its armies from the Turkish theater. Soon afterward, when Russia concluded a truce in Slobozia (August 24, 1807), not a word was said about the Serbs. True, Alexander I did appoint Prince A. A. Prozorovski to head the army in Wallachia, thus repairing the situation somewhat, as this move forced the Turks to desist from their plan of sending troops to subdue Serbia. For two years an uncertain truce reigned, revealing the internal weaknesses of the uprising. The fight for power intensified, and the failure to find the expected support in Russia strengthened the position of those who favored obtaining assistance from Austria. After fresh defeats, the leadership called for a high-ranking Russian functionary to consolidate the situation in the pashalic. A diplomat was dispatched to the Serbs, R. R. Rodofinikin, of Greek descent, who toyed with the idea of creating a Greek legion of 2,500 men with the intention of arousing Greece, which had been considered Russian diplomacy's principal base in the Balkans since 1803. The Russians thereby established a permanent diplomatic mission in Serbia, and later endeavored to have Karadjordje's son sent to Russia for schooling "so that devotion to Russia might be instilled in his blood through education."

By the Treaty of Tilsit and the Alliance with France of 1807, the Russians ceded the Ionian Islands and Boka Kotorska to Napoleon, but in this great allocation of spheres of interest they acquired the opportunity to increase their influence in Turkey, including Serbia. Boka Kotorska and Dubrovnik were crushed economically. Further, in the clashes with Napoleon, Boka lost four-fifths of its once-celebrated navy (then roughly 700 ships).

Appeased by the Tilsit Alliance, Napoleon was able to turn his attention to these coastal possessions. And actually, he did establish a new administrative entity, including the Slovene lands and part of the Croatian, all of which were annexed to the French Empire. In instructions issued to Rade Vučinić (January 1810), whom he dispatched to Paris, Karadjordje hinted, between the lines, that Serbia might find a place in the new French possessions in the Balkans. By the Treaty of Schönbrunn, October 14, 1809, Napoleon stripped Austria of its entire Istrian possession with Trieste and Gorizia, western Carinthia, Carniola, and the part of Croatia lying south of the Sava River to Jasenovac. In the process of dismemberment, little concern was shown for ethnical and linguistic boundaries. Strategic and geographic considerations were paramount. Napoleon seemed not to realize that in these regions beat a national heart that could cause him trouble later. On the very day of the Treaty of Schönbrunn, talk circulated about the "Illyrian Provinces," which the French emperor apparently considered a fine gain as "they would yield excellent soldiers." Before the "Illyrian Provinces" were created, Dubrovnik had also been formally annexed on January 31, 1808.

The Illyrian Provinces were formed to check commercial contact between Central Europe and the Danube region on the one hand and England on the other; to secure the French commercial route over which cotton was transported from Salonika through Bosnia, to the Yugoslav West through Turkish possessions in the central Balkans, and thence to European spinning mills; and to maintain control over the strategic foundations for future plans to restructure Eastern Europe, while keeping a watchful eye on Austria, for in Napoleon's opinion, "Illyria was an outpost at the very gates of Vienna." The center of these provinces was Ljubljana, headquarters of the governor-general. They were divided into six civil provinces: Carniola, Carinthia, Istria, Civil Croatia, Dalmatia, and Dubrovnik.

MAP 28.   Illyrian Provinces under Napoleon's rule. (1) Territory of the Illyrian Provinces: (2) Montenegro.

Special attention was paid to the Military Frontier south of the Sava River, where the military organization of the Austrian frontier was kept intact as, in the assessment of Marshal Marmont, it had been "deeply and brilliantly conceived."

The attempt to introduce a common South Slav literary language based on the Dubrovnik dialect was destined to fail in Slovenia, whose people found the name of Illyria artificial. However, no other name could be distilled from the historical past. The foundations were laid for modern education through twenty-five high schools and nine lycées; in Ljubljana and Zadar, education at the university level began to take shape. For the first time in the history of this country, human rights as conceived of in modern times were formulated and religions were granted equality before the law, meaning that under the French one-fifth of Dalmatia's population belonging to the Orthodox faith won equality in terms of church organization. Newspapers were published in the vernacular, printing presses were founded, and roads were driven through the mountain fastnesses (the Rijeka-Karlovac road and the roads through Dalmatia).

Napoleon's rule no doubt influenced the development of the idea of a single Yugoslavia, although it had existed even before that in the isolated world of intellectuals. In instructions issued by Alexander I to Admiral Chichagov early in 1812, Russia too promised "the peoples of Serbia, Bosnia, Dalmatia, Montenegro, Croatia, and Illyria independence and the establishment of a Slavic kingdom." A learned nobleman, Sava Tekelija (1761–1842), on two occasions made proposals for a joint state of the South Slavs; the same ideas were propagated by Cobenzl, a Slovene. The Montenegrin Bishop Petar I (1747–1830) drew up a limited proposal for a Slavo-Serbian state under the sponsorship of the Russian tsar (Montenegro, Hercegovina, Bosnia, and Dalmatia), with its center in Dubrovnik. But this project was more a reflection of the weakness than the strength of this agrarian world, bisected by the old and the new boundaries of far-flung empires.

The Failure of the First Serbian Uprising

The final fate of this process of negotiation among the big powers to restructure parts of the Balkans depended also on the destiny of Turkey and of the Serbian Revolution within its borders. The truce in Serbia lasted until March 1809, when war broke out again. Now the Serbs lunged in all directions: toward Bosnia, Vidin, Niš, and the Sanjak of Novi Bazar, the strip of territory between Serbia and Montenegro. Karadjordje himself intended advancing southward via Sjenica to establish contact with Montenegro and the Adriatic Sea, from which points it would be easier for him to arouse the Greeks to rebellion. The Montenegrins had set out for fortified Nikšić, but their move failed. Along other directions, too, the insurgents ran into trouble. Under the command of the grand vizier Yusuf Pasha, who attacked with a mass of 40,000 men, the Turks struck at the Serbian formation on its way to Niš and on May 31, owing to a falling out among the Serbian leaders and the delay of the Russians in crossing the Danube, defeated it at Kamenica. The Serbs fled toward Deligrad, although a company commanded by Stevan Sindjelić offered fierce resistance at Čegar. Desperate and overwhelmed by the odds against him, Sindjelić set fire to the stores of gunpowder on which he himself sat, leaving to posterity the memory of a courageous deed of a caliber rare even in this heroic period. The defeat marked the onset of the Serbian collapse, but a new Russian advance set the Turks reeling back to their former positions. Victories at Jasika, Varvarin, and Loznica postponed the inevitable while the appearance of Russian garrisons (1811) in Belgrade and Šabac raised hopes temporarily.

Karadjordje set about trying to solve in two ways the profound crisis into which rebellious Serbia had fallen: to seek help from Austria (to which he had once offered Belgrade in a gesture of despair) and also from Napoleon, to whom he sent Rade Vučinić with an offer of permission to establish French garrisons in Serbia, assuring him of the loyalty not only of Serbs, but of their fellow Slavs from Bosnia and Hercegovina, and even from Bulgaria. Vučinić stayed in France four years (1810–1814), by the end of which time he had achieved nothing.

Another measure to which Karadjordje resorted was establishment of a firm authority in Serbia capable of transforming it into a modern state. Finally, he made attempts to break the burgeoning power of the provincial chiefs, some of whom had amassed considerable wealth by looting and trade monopoly. The process of creating a state mechanism was furthered by three successive reforms — 1807, 1808 (the Constitutional Act of December 26), and early 1811. The Administrative Council was transformed into a government with six ministers. A Supreme Court was set up and Karadjordje, the "Supreme Leader" ("Vrhovni vožd"), was recognized as monarch. The nahiyas became magistratures ruled no longer by the willful vojvodas but by salaried officials educated in Austria. This change was paralleled by the establishment of a regular army (the "regulars"). From 1809 onwards, the army was divided into the people's army and the regular army, the latter being the main force.

Thus there was created a regular state with a monarch at the head, at the cost of abolishing the traditional self-government of the knežinas, in which the people had exercised local autonomy for centuries. The assemblies of the knežinas and other assemblies had been institutions not of the Serbian state but of the people. The degeneration of the peasant people's uprising into the social process of creation of a centralized monarchy, inherent in the historical nature of all agrarian rebellions in the Balkans, was thereby complete. The theoretical underpinnings for this transformation were put foward by Ivan Jugović (1775–1813) in an address in the Soviet (Council) on February 24, 1810, his main point being that God had not created people equal and that society would not exist "if everyone in the world were on the same footing," although "no one can make himself great but supreme power will make each one great and respect the extent of his greatness." This was a singular attempt to define the severely centralized state as the lasting fate of the people.

But the suppression of local self-government and autonomy in the knežinas was not a coincidence; rather it indicated how powerless that self-government was to maintain itself in a sweeping revolution. Even if it had prevailed, it would not have obstructed the centralized state (just as it had not presented an obstacle in Turkey) and might even have become once again the foundation for a new despotism.

In the meantime the seething society was building a strong emotional basis for nationhood. The cult of the Nemanid dynasty was fostered, no longer through the myth of Kosovo and the traditional sentiments associated with immeasurable suffering throughout history but now through rational knowledge gained from historiography. Jovan Rajić's history of the medieval state[1] was read for indications of what the objectives of the movement of 1804 should be. The relics of Stefan the First-Crowned were transferred to Serbia, and the cult of Tsar Dušan, whose portrait looked down on the Administrative Council of 1808 in Smederevo ("the town of our despots and tsars"), was strong and pervasive in its influence on the spiritual environment. The leaders of the uprising even referred to the boundaries of the medieval Serbian state, having convinced themselves that their insurrection was a step in the sequence of state continuity. This emotional nexus, developing with the uprising, was powerful enough to prevent a reversion to the former state of affairs, irrespective of the extent of the defeat suffered by the people in the uprising.

The Peace of Bucharest

The First Serbian Uprising came to an end in 1812 with the Peace of Bucharest concluded between Russia and Turkey, which (in Article 8) guaranteed the Serbs amnesty and internal self-government. Turkish garrisons were to be stationed in the towns, and agreement was to be reached with the Porte for the payment of moderate levies. Both sides tried to prolong the negotiations, providing the Turks with a motive to launch a general attack. In the middle of 1813 the Turks mounted an assault from all sides. On October 3, 1813, disillusioned by the rampant strife and decline in morale, Karadjordje left Serbia. The Turks captured Belgrade. Over 100,000 people fled to Srem and the Banat, but they did not tarry long there and returned gradually to Serbia.

The Second Uprising and the General Significance of the Serbian Revolution

After the defeat of the uprising, Turkish authority could not be stabilized in the pashalic. Almost a decade of warfare had left deep scars on the people, who refused to accommodate to the situation. Turkish terror provoked the Second Serbian Uprising after the resourceful Miloš Obrenović (1780–1860), a rival vojvoda of Karadjordje, had been elected leader at a gathering in Takovo on

[1] *The History of Various Slav Peoples, Particularly Bulgarians, Croats, and Serbs*, 4 vols., Vienna, 1794.

April 23, 1815. In a few months the insurgents liberated most Serbian towns. Fearing Russian intervention, the Turkish government left it to the Rumelian governor Marashli Pasha, the vizier of Belgrade, to come to terms with Miloš Obrenović about the new position of Serbs in the empire. The resulting agreement brought the Turkish army back to the towns.

Two aspects of the agreement struck on that occasion are distinctive: only Serbs were to collect levies for the sultan, and a National Office of twelve Serbian knezes was to be established in Belgrade. The spahis, and the muslims as judges, were allowed to remain, but their authority was curtailed. It was on this tenuous achievement won after twenty years of grueling fighting that Miloš Obrenović was to develop Serbian state independence, avoiding rash action and slowly corrupting the Turkish masters of Serbia. Karadjordje's approach had been determined by his taste of victory, whereas that of Miloš was predicated on the bitterness of defeat. In 1817, Karadjordje attempted to return to Serbia, inspired by the ideal of the Greek Philike Hetairia—a grandiose Balkan liberation. Miloš replied by having him beheaded (1817).

The historical significance of the Serbian Revolution of 1804–1815 is manifold: (1) A new Serbian society was created, engendered by the emancipated peasants and the developing mentality of a cohesive nation in Serbia proper and among the townspeople of Vojvodina. (2) The revolution, as a social movement of the peasantry bent on liberation through protracted guerrilla and frontal war, determined the methods to be used in all later peasant and national movements in the Balkan Peninsula. This struggle against feudalism and for free peasant holdings provided the basic motive for social progress throughout the Balkan Peninsula. As such, it injected the Eastern Question into history and posed the problem of small nations and liberation movements. (3) The peasantry and landholdings assumed a new role on the stage of history. (4) It opened, in the Balkans, the process of conflict between the big powers and the liberation movements of small peoples.

The Policies of Austria

France's withdrawal in 1814 cleared the ground for Austria's return among the South Slavs. This time it was forced to take into account the existence of the new factor of national uprisings in the Balkans. In 1814 the Austrian army recaptured the area along the Adriatic coast (the Second Austrian Occupation of Dalmatia), and although ostensibly the people breathed a sigh of relief when it came, it was patently clear at the outset that they expected an improved version of Austrian government. In Carniola they refused to pay urbarial levies to the old landowners under the pretext that the Napoleonic Code, which remained in force for some time, had abolished them. Ljubljana launched a movement which the police called the Illyrian uprising.

The spirit of the Croatian nobility, strengthened during the post-Joseph reaction, remained unshaken within the confines of Hungarian constitutionality, based on the estates. After the Napoleonic storm had passed, the nobility strove to reconstruct and consolidate the constitutional system of Hungary and the position of the estates. Metternich, the Austrian chancellor and one of the standard-bearers of European reaction, was highly cognizant of the dangers threatening the Hapsburg empire from Hungarian separatism and national movements among the South Slavs. Motivated by the idea that "events which cannot be prevented should be managed," he made a provisional attempt to take advantage of Napoleon's Illyrian legacy in the Balkans for future use. In the comfortable drawing rooms of Vienna, at the time of the successful termination of the Serbian Revolution in 1815, more fear was generated by the possibility of a Yugoslav national movement than was warranted by the actual situation. This was the reason why Metternich in 1815 staunchly opposed the Serbian uprising, extending the Turks material and political assistance in their endeavor to crush it even at the cost of the possible physical extermination of the "Serbian nation," as he himself declared. The system of the Holy Alliance was being developed in an effort to advance an ideology, based on Christian morality, dedicated to quelling any revolution in Europe directed against legal rulers. The Serbian Revolution was the first test of that principle and the first effective demonstration of its futility, manifested later in full force. As Russia took a different view of the Serbian movement and of a possible movement by the Greeks, Metternich feared that its stance might influence the South Slavs in the Hapsburg empire. For a while he championed the creation of a great Illyrian kingdom to provide "an effective antithesis to Russian influence and machinations among the people in those parts." In May 1816 he explained to the Austrian emperor that such a kingdom "could only bring advantages, especially where this nationalism coincided with the Catholic religion."

By the Emperor's Patent of August 3, 1816, the "kingdom of Illyria" was created, including Slovene lands in somewhat more expanded form than in Napoleon's time, as well as southern Croatia without Dalmatia. This was conceived not only as an excellent point of departure for solving Balkan problems in the future but as a means for foiling the intentions of the Hungarians, who sought an outlet to the sea, the road to which had always passed through Croatia. This official Illyrism was opposed by the Croatian nobility, and the Slovene as well, in the fear that the nobles' freedoms and provincial identity would be lost in the sea of such an extensive land invested with a national character. Official Illyrian policy was formally maintained in Croatia until 1822 and in Slovenia until 1849.

The departure of the French army from Boka paved the way for attempts to bring about a unification of this area with Montenegro into a single state. An assembly was held in Dobrota to proclaim the union of Montenegro and Boka Kotorska under a joint government (the "Central Commission") the president of which was Bishop Petar I. By occupying Boka, Austria frustrated these plans.

CHAPTER 22

Social Transformation in the First Half of the Nineteenth Century

A salient feature of social development in the South Slav countries during
the first half of the nineteenth century was the striving by the peasants to emancipate themselves from feudal dependence or its remnants. In Serbia a state of free
peasants was in formation; in Montenegro it had in one form or another existed
even earlier. In Croatia and Slovenia towns consolidated. In Vojvodina the towns
were preponderantly Slav, although with large German and Hungarian oases
(Bečkerek, Pančevo, Vršac). In Serbia, Macedonia, and Bosnia, towns retained
their heterogeneous ethnical structure ("Balkan çarşi"), except that Muslims were
melting away as an ethnical component of the Serbian towns. In Bosnia the towns

278

were Slavic (Muslim Slavs and fewer Christian Slavs). The Macedonian towns showed the strongest admixture of Turks, Greeks, Macedonians, and others.

In most Yugoslav lands the peasantry had one institution in common—the family cooperative, or family community (zadruga). These communities, linked by family ties, worked together, cooked together, and bore the same name. Property was held in common by all members. The elders were customarily elected, although their function was frequently heritable.

The Building of the Serbian State and a Society of Free Peasants in Serbia

Until 1842 the autonomous Serbian state developed under the full sovereignty of the Turkish sultan. Pressure brought to bear on the Turks to recognize the Peace of Bucharest of 1812 was designed to treat Serbia as an international rather than an internal Turkish problem. The response to that pressure brought recognition by Turkey. In the Akkerman Convention of 1826, Russia compelled Turkey to apply the provisions of the Bucharest treaty to Serbia. The development of an internal state administration had as its purpose the transformation of Serbia into a heritable monarchy, to which end the entire early political process was subordinated.

Pressed by the people's unrelenting insistence that Serbia emancipate itself from Turkish authority. Miloš Obrenović proved to be the most skillful of all Serbia's leaders. Having amassed considerable wealth through a monopoly on trade and the lease of Turkish imperial lands, the right to collect customs and operate ferry boats on the bordering rivers, he was eminently capable of exploiting the disadvantages of all his rivals.

The growth of Serbian statehood in the first half of the nineteenth century may be divided into two periods—before and after 1830. During the earlier period Serbia fought for recognition of autonomy and liquidation of Turkey's role in the country's internal affairs. Miloš used all his resourcefulness to force the Turks to withdraw the khadiyas and muselims from the nahiya centers and to evacuate the Muslim population from the Serbian interior. Between 1812 and 1826 the Turkish agrarian system was abolished and the rights of the spahis were curtailed radically. The Turkish army, stationed in certain frontier towns, was allowed at first to move along the main roads. In 1818 Miloš took upon himself the right to pass the death sentence, which he exercised just as energetically as the Turkish authorities before him. Popular revolt after 1825 provided him with an opportunity to build up a regular army. Having sustained defeat in the widespread national revolution between 1804 and 1815, the Turks could be expelled from Serbia with greater facility, the expulsion bearing all the hallmarks of historic inevitability.

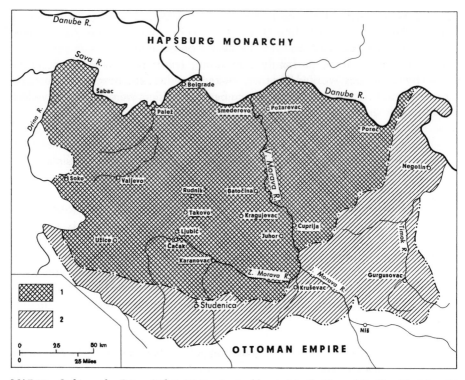

MAP 29. Serbia under Prince Miloš. (1) Territories liberated in the Second Serbian Uprising; (2) expansion between 1831 and 1833.

In building up the new Serbian state, Miloš wrested power from both the Turks and his own people. A number of assembly elders between 1817 and 1830 proclaimed Miloš the supreme hereditary prince of Serbia. As such, he assumed the right to appoint local chiefs in the knežinas, which were called captainships after 1830. From 1839 onwards, the nahiyas were termed okrugs. Threatened by popular revolts, Miloš passed a law in 1836 assigning to military commanders military and civil authority over the entire local administration. As the "principal policemen" they were also entrusted with keeping a watchful eye on public opinion.

In the beginning, Miloš had shared power with the "National Office" and the representatives in it, but as they endeavored to exploit this institution in order to restrict the prince's prerogatives, he got rid of his rivals one by one. Some were publicly condemned at meetings, others disappeared in the middle of the night (on some such flimsy pretext as "rifles having gone off by mistake"). Among those who disappeared were Petar Moler, at one time the prince's chief rival in the National Office, and Metropolitan Melentije Nikšić, Pavle Čukić, Sima Marković, and others. The revolt of chiefs Stevan Todorović Abdula and Resavac in the nahiyas of Požarevac, the Diak's Revolt of 1825, the Čarapić Conspiracy of 1826, Mileta's Revolt in 1835, and the Katana Revolt (or "Cavalry Revolt") in 1844 were the outward manifestations of the process by which the new state was being created. The most significant of these was the massive Diak's Revolt, so called because of the nickname (Diak) of its young leader, triggered by an assembly of the people in Topola on January 20, 1825. The people demanded abolition of forced labor, reduced taxes, monopoly-free trade, and free circulation of money. Most of all, they called for personal security, protection from courts-martial, and curtailment of the prince's self-will, which frequently caused the summary execution of those under suspicion.

This resistance to despotism began to serve as a basis for democratic orientation after it shed some of its anarchical qualities and acquired philosophical and ideological overtones, as evidenced in a letter written to the prince by the linguistic reformer Vuk Karadžić (1787–1864) on April 12, 1832. In his epistle Karadžić presented the prince with a new conception of the Serbian people as living in a legal state.

By an article of the Treaty of Adrianople, concluded after the Russo-Turkish War of 1828–1829, Russia had become the international protector of Serbia. Its consul in Belgrade endeavored to solve some of the country's crucial problems, in accordance with instructions from his government, and even sat in on government sessions occasionally. In 1830 the sultan recognized the right of the Serbs to internal self-government and the creation of an independent state administration. All levies, as well as the tribute paid by Serbia to Turkey, were precisely defined. It was ordained that Serbia would be administered by a prince with the help of a "council." The hatti-sherif of 1830 founded the bases for Serbian independence, but it was not until later that all Serbian claims could be fulfilled. The hatti-sherif of 1833 restored six nahiyas to Serbia. It also acquired its own flag and shared the right to maintain a consul in certain centers. In 1852 its church was separated from the patriarchate of Constantinople.

A legislative commission entrusted with drafting laws proposed the Napoleonic Code as the basis for Serbian legislation, an approach regarded with suspicion by Russia and Austria. Popular leaders, officials, and wealthy merchants bent their efforts toward promulgating a constitution. The people's dissatisfaction at the belated adoption of more liberal laws erupted into Mileta's Revolt in January 1835. That year the National Assembly presented the country with a constitution on the holy day celebrating the Presentation in the Temple (the Presentation Day Constitution), acting on the demands raised by this movement. The constitution was a modern one, taking as its point of departure the up-to-date principle of separation of powers into legislative, judicial, and executive. In its conception of freedom, the constitution was far too liberal for the Europe of that time and was for that reason dubbed by some as a "French transplant to the Turkish forest." The diplomats of the big powers, assessing it as deadly and contagious, persisted in their attempts to have it abolished. This was true particularly of Russia, whose envoys to Serbia stated that Serbia needed no constitution other than the good, old hatti-sherif. Serbia was subjected to tremendous pressure by the big powers, some favoring its having no constitution at all, others opposing this solution, depending on how much influence they hoped to gain over Serbia. Consequently the Constitution was suspended in 1835, destroying any chance for the building of more democratic conceptions of freedom into the foundations of the state.

In 1838 Serbia was given a new constitution (the "Turkish Constitution") in the form of the sultan's hatti-sherif "for the people of my province of Serbia in recognition of their loyalty and devotion." This constitution was imposed on Serbia by the big powers, supported by the Serbian magnates (Defenders of the Constitution). A council of seventeen members was set up to assist the prince. Their posts were heritable, and they were responsible to the sultan. The institution of the people's assembly was abolished, but the memory of it lingered on and was to influence the development of modern Serbian democracy.

Disillusioned by this train of events, Prince Miloš abdicated in favor of his son Michael. Vučić's Revolt in Serbia in 1842 complicated the situation to such an extent that Michael himself had to flee from the Serbian army; afterwards the Defenders of the Constitution elected Aleksandar Karadjordjević, member of the rival dynasty and a son of Karadjordje, to the position of prince of Serbia. The new government of the Defenders of the Constitution consolidated the administration of Serbia by 1858. Serbia became a stable state administered by a well-educated civil service, with the help of the police. Once Jovan Hadžić (1799–1869), acting on instructions from the Serbian government, had drafted the first civil code of laws in 1844, laws began to be passed one after another. The lawyers, graduates of schools in Vojvodina and Hungary, were inclined to model their statutes on Austrian laws, partly out of fear of more radical legislation, and partly in response to Metternich's pressure. The Serbian administration, which was to endure throughout the nineteenth century on the same basis, was modernized with the sum of money collected by Miloš Obrenović—he had 13 million groschen of his own when he embarked upon his ambitious venture in 1839.

And so the new Serbian society acquired political organization. The foundation was the emancipated Serbian peasant. In Europe, it was the only society of small peasants protected by the state. The spahis disappeared after 1830, having been indemnified by the Serbian state. On January 1, 1833, Prince Miloš announced in the Assembly that the spahilics "had been destroyed forever in Serbia and would never be restored in any form whatsoever." However, until the law of 1839 was promulgated, there were no legal norms for protection of the communal and peasant lands from the propensity of the rich to snatch them away. Consequently the peasants were not yet altogether secure.

In agricultural production a transformation was in progress. Slowly the land came to be cultivated more intensively. The population, predominantly occupied with animal husbandry, turned its attention to crops. Potatoes and maize were raised. In 1827 regulation of the villages was undertaken but had to be abandoned for a decade and a half owing to resistance by the people. The peasants were still unskilled as farmers and had no suitable implements. Even forty years later, Svetozar Marković (1848–1875), the socialist writer, was provoked into complaining that Serbian craftsmen in the towns were not producing scythes, shovels, and rakes for the peasant, who had therefore to import his implements from Austria.

Radical agrarian policies began to be pursued by the state in an attempt to solve the agrarian question. Prince Miloš set norms for the size of peasant holdings, determined the minimal amount of property that could not be sold for debts, made decisions on the dispensation of areas that were not under cultivation, and shifted peasants from one part of the country to another. The mainstream of Balkan migration flowed into Šumadija. The estimate is that over 200,000 people moved into Serbia at that time; the dynamic growth of the population was stabilized only after 1840. In 1815 there had been 12.5 inhabitants per square kilometer; by 1844 the figure reached 22.6. The concomitant growth in number of villages has been assessed as 1,400 in 1815 and 2,018 in 1844. These measures laid the foundations of modern Serbian society, which, with its 680,000 people (1834), was 94 percent agricultural. Most of them were free peasants living outside the joint families, although in Miloš's time one-fourth of the peasants still maintained these family cooperatives. But the institution as such was far from the tenacious one it had once been.

Only 6 percent of the population lived in towns, surrounded by a veritable sea of peasants. These towns numbered only thirty-five, and they, too, were semiagrarian in character. The monotonous agricultural landscape was punctuated here and there by the holdings of rich individuals who had acquired wealth in trade and speculation. It was they who provided the social basis for the official policy and, struggling against the prince, ruled the state. They wielded political influence by grouping themselves around the two rival dynasties and seeking support in either Russia or Austria. As constitutional freedoms were lacking, political parties in the democratic sense of the word were replaced by political conspiracies as the accepted mode of political activity.

The free peasant was the pillar not only of the state but of the modern Serbian nation. All peasant rebellions in the surrounding areas—both in Bosnia and in western Bulgaria—had Serbia before their eyes as a model of liberation. For several decades, their political programs called for unification with Serbia into a single state.

The Structure of Society in Croatia and the Position of the Towns

These developments were paralleled by fundamental changes in Croatian society, although there was as yet no question of unity throughout the Croatian ethnical area. Struggling to preserve its old privileges, the numerous Croatian nobility, through its estate, gave the changes taking place a special political direction. Royal absolutism was to endure until 1825, and Metternich's Reaction (to the democratic movements and ideas introduced by the French Revolution and the Napoleonic wars) until 1848. Absolutism undermined the nobility, but Metternich's Reaction struck largely at the intellectual sections of society.

The twenties saw a mounting danger of rebellions in Italy and of Serbian movements linked with the Greek uprising. The economic crisis also aroused the Hungarian nobility to action. Under these circumstances, the ruler in fear of popular uprising decided to meet the feudal opposition halfway. In 1825 permission was given for convocation of the Hungarian Diet, which continued its opposition to the court where it had left off earlier. The nobility strove to replace Latin and German with Hungarian in all state and cultural institutions. Moreover, the general reforms demanded by the nobility were designed to encompass all aspects of life, to emancipate the serfs and create a free society, and to introduce religious tolerance for Jews and Protestants. But politically, the old estates Assembly and županijas were jealously guarded, and guarantees were sought that changes would be effected by the nobility alone, through the projected reforms.

As long as their struggle focused on Viennese centralism, the Hungarians were regarded with sympathy in Croatia. But when it was sensed that the reform movement also had as its objective the incorporation of Croatia into the new Hungarian national state, a segment of Croatian society put up resistance, although it saw no clear way out of the situation. Inferior to Hungary, Croatia was easy prey for the latter. In the middle of the nineteenth century Croatia together with Slavonia had somewhat over 850,000 inhabitants (the Military Frontier over 673,000, Dalmatia 415,000, and Istria 234,000). Of this number, 85 percent were peasants on feudal holdings, with three-quarters of the land in the hands of feudatories. The nobility accounted for 4 percent of the entire nation, concentrated largely in Civil Croatia and much less densely in Slavonia. The higher nobility were aliens. In Slavonia the large landed estate predominated, and in Croatia the small and medium-sized. As it was not capable of withstanding competition from modernized landed estates in the Pannonian plain, the Croatian nobility was feudal both in spirit and in its hope to conserve the old institutions. Croatian towns did not play nearly the same important role as other towns in the empire. In 1857 Zagreb could boast only 16,653 inhabitants, Osijek 13,883, Rijeka 15,319, Krapina 12,888. By the end of the eighteenth century, the towns had been Germanized extensively, and it was the Germans who were responsible for the creation of the first cultural institutions, newspapers, and theaters, all in German. These towns grew along the waterways and continental roads leading to the coast. In the second half of the eighteenth century three fine roads ran from Karlovac to the sea. As far as Karlovac, export trade was carried along the Danube, Sava, and Kupa Rivers. Slowly the focus of activity shifted from Varaž-din to Zagreb. During the period of the Metternich Reaction, these towns, although undoubtedly developing, were still cut off from the world and dozed on in provincial slumber.

The railway line was late in arriving in Croatia (by 1846 it had been laid only as far as Zidani Most in Slovenia). In the towns the craftsmen, merchants, landed gentry, and civil servants constituted the small bourgeoisie. The focus of rising industry (Rijeka, Osijek) was situated in territory under Hungarian control. The Hungarian Trading Society transformed Rijeka into the principal Hungarian port, where the first steamship put in an appearance in 1840. The Croatian nobility lived in constant fear that the reform-bent Hungarian Diet would abolish feudalism and free the peasants, or introduce religious tolerance. Moreover, the town youth and a segment of the lesser nobility were showing signs of restiveness in their desire to transform Croatian society. They were joined by the lower Catholic clergy, which strove from the beginning of the century to separate the church from Hungary and create an independent archdiocese in Zagreb.

Croatian policy deviated from Hungarian on four major issues: (1) the state-legal relation between Croatia and Hungary *(iura municipalia);* (2) the official language; (3) the peasant's feudal status and religious tolerance; (4) Rijeka's affiliation. In 1827 the Hungarian Diet referred to Croatia as a subject Hungarian land. This was to provoke a reaction in Croatia, where a struggle was pursued until 1848 for recognition of Croatian federal status in Hungary. The view prevailed that Croatia's relation with Hungary was a voluntary one and that therefore the joint Hungarian-Croatian Diet in Pozsony (Bratislava) could not take action to change that status. During the attempts at Magyarization through introduction of the Hungarian language, the nobility capitulated, and in 1827 and 1830 the Croatian Assembly agreed that Hungarian should be introduced as a compulsory subject in schools. In 1844 the Hungarians also succeeded in passing a ruling which stipulated that Croatian deputies to the joint Diet should speak Hungarian there from 1853 onwards.

This trend caused a wave of profound remorse at the incautious decisions adopted during the post-Joseph reaction when the Croatian nobility surrendered

Croatian power to the Hungarians to a much greater extent than was wise or warranted. The Assembly endeavored to bolster its power by restoring the right to decision making on tax matters (1832), thus abrogating the decisions of 1790. Other demands concerned the strengthening of the ban's functions and annexation of the Military Frontier and Dalmatia to Croatia. The Croatian nobles systematically fought the abolition of serfdom under the pretext that they would be too impoverished to pay for hired labor on such small holdings.

All this, combined with social changes in the towns and the nobility's efforts to rectify its mistake of 1790, created the background for the emergence of the Croatian national movement.

Dalmatia after 1815

After Napoleon left Dalmatia, Austria allowed the use of Italian to continue in the administration although, in 1820, the "Dalmatian literary language" was also introduced as an admixture of various Dalmatian dialects, with the exception of that spoken in Dubrovnik. With the establishment of the new authority, a large segment of the old Dalmatian town nobility, the pillar of local policies, disappeared. The town merchants, moneylenders, and village priests were a poor replacement. The Austrian government had no wish to see Dalmatia united with Croatia, supported in this view by the fact that no strong internal impetus to unification seemed to exist. The Italianized town's only alternative was the backward village.

Dalmatia was still largely an agrarian land in 1870, 90 percent of its people living in a patchwork of various forms of feudal dependence, from the type of serfdom prevalent in Dubrovnik to the status of the *colonatus* (tenant-farmer). Trade ties with Croatia were virtually nonexistent, whereas with Bosnia and Hercegovina caravans provided the only form of transportation. Dalmatia was oriented to the sea, from which it made its living. With Napoleon's departure, at least 1,000 of the 1,599 pre-1815 seagoing ships disappeared from Dalmatia's ports. When the Austrian Lloyd of Trieste, supported by the state and exempted from harbor taxes, gained the upper hand in Dalmatian ports in 1836, Dalmatia surrendered its previous importance to Rijeka and Trieste.

Society in Slovenia: Industrialization and Germanization

In contrast to societies in other Yugoslav lands in the Austrian Empire, Slovene society showed all the signs of dramatic economic advancement, despite the fact that in the Austrian part of the monarchy the Slovenes were one of the most backward and most exploited of groups. Slovenia was framed by the great

Illyrian area to which Croatia also belonged until 1822, but this was a sheer political formality. Until 1849 this formality was to remain for the Slovene lands only an external framework within which very little change took place. After the collapse of Napoleon's power, the estates bodies were not reinstated in the coastal areas. In Carniola, this body was organized anew in 1818, whereas in Styria and Carinthia they retained their earlier form. The Carniolan body was made up of four estates, current affairs being looked after by a council of four members headed by the governor. The basis of society was the nobility, the powerful civil servants, the military, and the church, whose role was even intensified through the medium of the Jesuits in Austria in 1816.

Joseph's reforms, meaning the personal emancipation of the peasants, remained in force in the villages. This was to the great advantage of fledgling Slovene industries which were thus supplied with cheap manpower. The peasant rebellion of 1845 resulted in the Imperial Patent of 1846, according to which landowners and serfs could come to mutual agreement for the payment of all the peasants' obligations in money rather than in kind.

That town life continued to intensify in Slovene lands is evidenced by the growth of Ljubljana by mid-century to 20,000 inhabitants and Trieste to 80,000. The Slovenes took ample advantage of the fact that their lands were situated along the principal Austrian road to the sea and beyond. A chain of industries came into being, creating an industrial base far more complete than anything in the other South Slav lands. Basic industry comprised a network of iron-manufacturing plants of various sizes. The construction of railways (the first in Austria in 1838 and the first in Slovenia—the Celje-Graz line—in 1846), as well as improved utilization of the Sava River for navigation, injected even greater vigor into the market. In the first half of the century, the industrial revolution bore early fruit. The basic industries and industrial classes were formed and established. The bourgeoisie, and all capital in the banks, were of alien provenance, largely German and Italian. The first steamship sailed in the port of Trieste in 1818. By 1847 Slovenia boasted twenty-five steamships. Croatia was the only other South Slav area where steamships were in use at that time. Between 1825 and 1847, iron production doubled and iron ore was smelted in twenty-one places. Large business firms grew up on the basis of iron production (Ruard, Zois, and others). Also significant was the textile industry in the first half of the century. Of the forty-one steam-driven plants in the whole empire, three were situated in Slovenia. Other important products were paper, sugar, soap, silver, and mercury. Increasing iron production stimulated the search for fresh coal and iron ore deposits. Before 1848 the foundations had been laid for all later coal mines and ironworks in Slovenia.

Still, the Slovenes were in substantial measure a peasant people without a bourgeoisie or towns of their own. When the national bourgeoisie started to grow, it was mostly in the area between the Sava River and the sea. National sentiments were not developed among the then 1 million Slovenes (1846), and strange demographic changes were in progress. The natural population increase was canceled out by rapid Germanization. The towns in the hands of foreigners were another source of alienation of Slovenes from their own people. Later the course of this process was such that the growth of the Slovene ethnical mass was only two-thirds as much as the German. The Slovenes seemed to be receding particularly in the northern regions (Carinthia, Styria).

As there was no national bourgeoisie, the leading national section of the population consisted of the lower clergy, craftsmen, and merchants in the towns, who were conservative by virtue of their occupations. The want of a national state made it necessary for national culture to act as a poor substitute for a national policy. This was especially true as the national bourgeoisie, lacking strong positions in industry, established itself through the medium of the schools and the intelligentsia.

Social and Political Changes in Bosnia

Yugoslav societies under Turkish rule presented an entirely different picture. They clung tenaciously to their patriarchal patterns even more than would otherwise have been the case if the state machine had been not so under-developed and capital not so scarce. Through trade, capital fled westward, leaving the feeble trading bourgeoisie in the towns and the rebellious peasants in the villages to fend for themselves in creating new social relations.

Bosnian society in the first half of the nineteenth century embarked upon a period of stabilization after the profound dislocations and anarchy that had lasted until 1815. Vizier Ali Jellaludin Pasha was successful in suppressing the resistance of certain mutinous captains, abolishing the Janissaries in 1826 and quelling in blood their last convulsive attempts at opposition in the towns (particularly Sarajevo). After that, sporadic internal anarchy was replaced by the collective defection of the entire province. After an attempted uprising in 1828, this collective withdrawal succeeded and the Bosnian beys, condemning the sultan as an infidel, elected a native vizier, Husein Aga, a captain from Gradačac (the "dragon of Bosnia," 1802–1834). The latter tried to link his destiny with that of another defector, the pasha of Scutari. After defeating a Turkish army at Kosovo (Banjska), he was given deceptive promises by the Turks. Lulled, he returned to Bosnia, but the sultan sent an army after him. He was beaten in the field and was forced to flee to Austria.

The reforms in Turkey provided for the abolition of captains in Bosnia; the Hatti-sherif of Gilhana in 1839 endeavored to introduce a new administration. Proclaiming the reform of the empire, that Hatti-sherif was designed primarily to create a new army on the basis of shorter military service. The consequence was the disappearance of earlier local autonomy which had existed within empire confines (Bosnia, Albania) and under which local chieftains, as vassals of the sultan, undertook to provide soldiers for the state when it was at war but were otherwise independent in internal affairs. After the new reforms, the state was to be centralized, but attempts along these lines provoked resistance among the Muslim population whose positions they undermined.

The Christian population also was seething, notably the peasants upon whom tax policies bore down hard. Of the three peasant rebellions in Bosnia in the first half of the nineteenth century (1834, 1842, 1848), the greatest significance attaches to the first, led by Presbyter Jovica Ilić (Presbyter Jovica's Rebellion). After it was crushed, Ilić fled to Serbia but was extradited to the Turkish authorities by the Serbian prince. The rebellious peasants (Orthodox and Catholic) were severely punished although they claimed they had revolted not against the sultan but against the unbearable social order and native aristocracy. Although these peasant rebellions were disorganized and spontaneous revolts against the social order and injustice, exorbitant taxes, and starvation, they were the only genuine strivings for social progress. Basically, even when unaware of it themselves, these peasants were undermining the Turkish state and aspiring toward the creation of a national state which would protect the small free landholding.

Peasant uprisings, alternating with rebellions by the Muslim aristocracy, each group pulling in a different direction but equally opposed to the sultan, provided the background for the crisis of the empire's social order, which could not be resolved in the way the government wanted.

One of the important movements in Bosnia was that of the Catholic clergy. The chapters and orders enjoyed privileges bestowed upon them by both pope and sultan. But disagreement set in after Bishop Barišić (1796–1863) was appointed apostolic vicar in 1832. As he was devoted to Austria, the Austrian government hoped to use him for tightening its grip on the Bosnian people, especially because after the denouement of the Eastern Question in 1841, it claimed the right of protectorate over all Catholics in the Turkish Empire. Barišić was moved by the desire to modernize the Catholic church in Bosnia by introducing parochial clergy in addition to the chapters, and setting up a seminary in Travnik. He also suspected the orders of collusion with the Serbs in planning an uprising against the Turks. The old privileges of the friars were in jeopardy and they resisted. The "Barišić affair" was to last a full fourteen years, until the presumptuous bishop lost the battle and was removed elsewhere.

Macedonia in the First Half of the Nineteenth Century

The crisis of the Turkish feudal system also involved Macedonia as attendant social changes began to be felt in that area. The defection of local pashas (particularly Ali Pasha of Janjina) was one of the external manifestations of these changes, which were in progress throughout the entire Turkish Empire of that time. The creation of čiftliks had progressed to the point of altering the entire picture of the Macedonian and Albanian villages. The population, divided into two basic religions and several ethnical groups of different sizes, was far from integrated. The Macedonians themselves were sentimentally attached to their various provinces, and people tended to identify themselves with their tribes more than anything else (Brsjaci, Mijaci, Koponovci, Pijanci, Bandevci, Pulina-kovci, Brzilevci, Mrvaci). In mid-century, animal husbandry with 8 million head of livestock provided the dominant feature of the rural districts in Macedonia.

The reform policies of the Turkish state and the requirements of the new Turkish army began gradually to change the Macedonian towns. The towns grew, and by the middle of the century a number of them could boast over 5,000 inhabitants: Salonika, Bitolj, Skoplje, Ohrid, Prilep, and Veles. The population was an ethnical mélange of peoples, with Greeks and Cincars predominating, and Macedonians, Jews, and Armenians also present in considerable numbers. The guilds were ethnically mixed although the Slavic guild members stood aloof in several Macedonian towns—Skoplje, Veles, Prilep, and even Salonika.

Caravans bearing goods moved from Salonika along the Vardar and Morava Valleys to the Danube, whence the wares were carried along European routes. Thus the Macedonian towns became foci for the devious formation of the Macedonian bourgeoisie. In continual rivalry with other ethnical groups and the Muslim state machine, it was long on the defensive. Like the Greek and Bulgarian, the Macedonian bourgeoisie aspired to its own church communes and schools, and to the use of Slavonic in church ritual. The brunt of this struggle was borne by the Macedonian traders and craftsmen. But their path was crossed by the vir-tually insurmountable resistance of Greek nationalism, which conceived of the northern borders of Greece as running all the way to Scutari, Skoplje, and the Balkan range in Hungary. The struggle to emancipate the church from Greek in-fluence provides the sum total of the political history of the Macedonian bour-geoisie of that time. The communes competed with each other in the construction of new churches. Slavic schools were opened, and in 1847 a report appeared in the *Serbian News* to the effect that there were seven national schools in Mace-donia. The first educated teachers were Serbs from Vojvodina, and books were by and large obtained from Serbia and Russia. A Slavonic printing press was set up in Salonika in 1834 by Theodosie Sinaitski, destined, however, to exist but briefly.

Efforts to Create the State of Montenegro

The internal transformation of Montenegrin society made possible the process of building an independent state. This process was furthered with great effort by two bishops, Petar I (1782–1830) and Petar Petrović Njegoš (1830–1851), but it was brought to completion by Prince Danilo (1851–1860) on the basis of endeavors that had preceded him. The pursuit of this aim was obstructed largely by the Radonjić family of guvernadurs, which strove to frustrate the rise of the Petrović family, metropolitans by heritage. Achievement of this objective was also hampered by the total lack of any concept of private property in the modern sense.

The state began to be formed around the bishop see of Cetinje. Although the rank and file saw it as a representative of continuity and as the pillar of Orthodoxy and Serbian political traditions, it was still a church rather than a state institution. In order to discharge its role in the creation of a state, it first had to transform itself, just as it had to reeducate the Petrović family to effect a painless transition from the flowing gowns of the bishop to the apparel of a temporal dynasty. Ten years after the defeat of the Turks at Kruse (1796), Montenegro, by annexing the tribes of the Pipers and Bjelopavlićs, rounded out a territory on which it could develop its statehood. Thenceforward the Montenegrins no longer considered themselves part of the Turkish state, and because of the tenuous fragility of earlier ties, the younger generation scarcely knew that they had ever existed. The first Code of Montenegro and Brda was promulgated on October 18, 1798, paralleled by the establishment of a Court of Justice of Montenegro and Brda called the *kuluk*. The Assembly of Cetinje amended the Code in 1803.

A fierce struggle had raged between the see and the guvernadur since 1781. Petar I originally tried to diminish the competence of the guvernadur's office and the Radonjić family by reducing it to the local frameworks of the Njegoš tribe and in 1818 tried to abolish the institution altogether. As the attempt failed, the guvernadur returned, but the Radonjić family's policy of looking to Austria in the conflict between that country and Russia had no future among the Orthodox population. Working in their favor, however, was the inclination of the small community inertly to retain its old institutions despite their obsolescence, a feature of all underdeveloped and patriarchal societies motivated by the conservative desire to preserve their ways.

The state took shape against the background of the country's low level of material development. The average family could subsist from its own labor for only six to eight months out of the year, and some members had to migrate even to find food. Frequent droughts resulted in many unproductive years, and the general scarcity in the country frustrated normal social development. In the first half of the century, the people were divided into thirty-six tribes. The number of inhabitants cannot be ascertained accurately, but it has been estimated at 120,000 people living in 240 villages. The fighting men numbered 20,000. Among these peasant people, sustained more by animal husbandry than agriculture, there were no towns. Even in the middle of the nineteenth century, Cetinje, the capital of the country, had only nine houses constructed of durable materials. Until the forties, no roads were cut into the mountain fastnesses.

In the struggle for statehood, the efforts of Petar I initiated many processes but hardly completed them. His attempt to introduce taxes failed, and it was later recounted that no one paid them except the bishop who had thought them up. Even the courts, instituted to bridle the blood feuds, could make no headway until such time as the state was able to curtail the tribal autonomy on which society was based. Among the border tribes, many considered the state run from Cetinje as suspect, and even turned to the Turks, offering their services as volunteers or accepting bribes from the surrounding pashas. The philosophy by which this small rockbound state was steered is staggering in its simplicity: "Pray to God and hang on to Russia"—the testament handed down to Njegoš by his predecessor as he lay on his deathbed.

Among the powerful rulers who created and headed the state for a whole century, Petar II Petrović Njegoš towers above the rest for the tremendous force of his statesmanlike spirit, recognized throughout the Balkans. A talented writer and poet, he bequeathed to the Serbian and all South Slav renaissance movements an unending source of inspiration. An inveterate traveler, he raised the prestige of his homeland throughout the Europe of his day. As soon as he took over the helm of state, Njegoš endeavored, with Russia's help, to restructure the state institutions which, through the reforms of his predecessor, still shared power with various tribes. In 1831 an Administrative Senate of Montenegro and Brda was formed to replace the previous central organization established in 1798. Its sixteen members were nahiyas and tribal chieftains, but no attempt was made to assure all tribes equal representation. They had to bow down to the new state, but were not destined to disappear soon. The members of the Senate were paid for discharging their duties, but despite the existence of this body, Njegoš's rule was absolute. When the last guvernadur was finally banished in 1832, the final obstacle had been removed to consolidation of the state. A small army was also formed (Guardia), numbering fewer than 400 men and designed to extend support to the court rather than for external defense, which was the affair of the entire nation. In 1837 the bishop appointed a captain for each tribe to discharge the functions of state authority. Regular collection of taxes from 1833 onwards was attended by endeavors to introduce a state budget. After 1838 augmented Russian assistance, which exceeded domestic income, assured the basic resources for the maintenance of the tiny state apparatus. When the first schools and printing presses were opened in 1834, the foundations had been laid by the new state for national education. Politically, Njegoš drew Montenegro closer to Serbia and even took part in certain secret plans of the Serbian government in the Balkan Peninsula.

RULERS OF SERBIA

Dynasty Obrenović

Miloš, Prince (1815–1839 and 1858–1860)

Milan, Prince (1839)

Mihailo, Prince (1839–1842 and 1860–1868)

Milan, Prince (1868–1882), King (1882–1889)

Alexander, King (1889–1903)

CHAPTER 23

National Renaissances

The Institutionalized Struggle for National Consciousness

National renaissances have the nature of democratic movements dedicated to a new concept of the state. The striving for a new state has always been
concealed behind national ideas. Consciously or unconsciously, the aspiration
has ever been toward a state resting on the principle of national sovereignty.
Simultaneously the struggle for nationhood is the struggle for a new pattern of
society in which the old ruling class will step down from the stage, the peasant

will achieve emancipation and the towns will assume political and social leader-ship.

The historical frameworks within which foundations were laid for specific nations during times of renaissance were determined by religion, lan-guage, and mentality, the latter predicated on the consciousness of a particular origin. Among all these factors, religion and the church were decisive in the Serbo-Croatian linguistic area, and it was they that divided the nation on a permanent basis. For the Slovenes and Macedonians, it was their languages that determined their frameworks as separate nations.

The method of developing national consciousness within these confines was institutionalized, that is, fostered through specific institutions: the church, state administration, schools, literature, historical science, newspapers, reading rooms, national cultural societies under the name of "matice," as theaters, museums, celebration of important events and historical personalities, national savings banks, and the army. Later these institutions were supplemented by others: universities, academies of science, sports organizations, and political parties. Through the medium of these institutions, it was first culture that was nationalized, followed by the welding of the leading class in society into a co-hesive entity on the basis of sentiment. The basic means in this struggle was language. The quest for a literary language was directed toward pursuit not only of the most effective means of social communication but also of a covert means of struggle for social prestige. The national class whose language pre-vailed was the one that held sway over others. Its breadth was determined by the area in which the language was spoken.

Language as the Basis of Nationhood

Yugoslav national renaissance inherited from rationalist philosophies the idea that language is the basis of the nation, although domestic sources were also present in the works of the historian Mavro Orbini. The romanticism of the first half of the nineteenth century upheld this idea completely. Its concepts were made available to the South Slavs especially through the works of J. G. Herder. Carried away by his ideas of Slavdom's future, people everywhere read, translated, and interpreted Herder's works. Other rationalists also influenced the South Slav awakeners. The conceptions of Sava Mrkalj (1783–1835), a little-known Serbian philologist, about language are similar to those expounded by John Locke and indeed took shape under his influence. In some degree they influenced the work of the founding father of Serbian literary language, Vuk Karadžić. Basically, the democratic conception of the nation separated the nation from religion and treated it as a temporal factor. Implementing this idea, the

South Slav awakeners succeeded only partly in literature and culture, whereas politically they were frustrated by the backward agrarian reality of the Balkan Peninsula.

Reforming the Serbian Literary Language

The cultural achievements of the Vojvodina town dwellers at the end of the eighteenth century and the emancipation of the peasants of Šumadija in the early nineteenth century figured significantly in the development of the modern Serbian nation. But the process of laying foundations for the new Serbian nationhood was to terminate only after culture had thoroughly nationalized ideology through the medium of national institutions. It was marked by two essential circumstances: (1) the struggle for purity of the national language determined its character; (2) the struggle for national consciousness did not unfold of itself but was encouraged through well-organized national institutions. In 1826 there were sixteen small-town schools and a few village schools functioning in Serbia. They were taught partly by teachers from Vojvodina and partly by native sons. Education was regulated by a decree of the State Council dating from 1835. A high school for civil servants was opened in Belgrade in 1831, and in 1838 a lycée, as the first steps toward the establishment of a university. These were followed by a seminary (1836) and a military academy. All of them were national schools where instruction, given in the national language, was imbued with the national spirit. A state printing press was opened in Belgrade in 1831 but soon moved to Kragujevac, where, in 1833, the works of the first great national writer of these times, Dositej Obradović, were published at government expense. During the period of the Defenders of the Constitution, the Serbian Literary Society was formed (1842) to promote national science, with the emphasis on historiography. The opening of the National Library, the National Museum (1848), the Serbian Reading Room, and a number of newspapers completed this network of institutions. The Matica Srpska publishing house, founded in Budapest in 1826, together with its publication, the *Letopis (Yearbook)*, discharged an important function in the nationalization of culture. The same may be said of the *Srpske novine (Serbian News)* published by Frušić-Davidović (1813–1822) and Pavlović (1836–1848) in Vienna and Budapest, respectively, and the *Novine srpske (Serbian News)* published in Belgrade.

The highest attainment of the Serbian national renaissance was the creation of the new literary language, the quest for which was transferred from the eighteenth to the nineteenth century. It was through language that the struggle was pursued for future Serbian nationhood. This historic mission is intimately associated with the name of Vuk Stefanović Karadžić (1787–1864). After the collapse of Karadjordje's uprising Karadžić left for Vienna where he made the acquaintance of the Slovene Jernej Kopitar (1780–1844), whose disciple he became. In 1814 Karadžić published a collection of Serbian poems and the significant *Grammar of the Serbian Language According to the Speech of the Ordinary People*. When he also published the *Serbian Dictionary* in 1818 he had laid the foundation for the modern Serbian literary language while at the same time pacifying the "revolt of the Slav alphabets." His conception of the literary language was based on the principle of "write as you speak and read as it is written." The basis for this literary language was the popular speech of eastern Hercegovina (the *ije* version of the Što dialect). Karadžić simplified the Serbian Cyrillic alphabet by deleting superfluous characters and creating new ones in line with the idea that each sound should have an alphabetical symbol. It was in this language that he published Serbian ballads and tales (which he collected with remarkable industry by visiting with common folk, etc.) and historical and other works. He also made a translation of the Holy Bible which he undertook when Jernej Kopitar in reply to a query from the British and Foreign Biblical Society in 1815, stated that he considered Karadžić would be the best man for the job.

The consequences of Karadžić's philological reforms were reflected in the general democratization of Serbian culture, which, having its roots in Russian and Old Slavonic sources, was definitely turning to the European West. Supporters of the old order were adamant in their resistance. From Budapest to Belgrade, Karadžić's followers and his opponents indulged in heated polemics. At the same time Vuk Karadžić, in the tradition of eighteenth-century rationalists, secularized Serbian national ideology, separating the concept of the Serbian nation from religion and reducing the basis of the nation to its common denominator—a common tongue. Those who spoke one language were one people according to him, but not everyone was persuaded that this was so. The conception undermined the idea of a general Slavic nation and regarded the Serbs as a separate people within the South Slav community. This idea of the linguistic foundations of the Serbian people gave their ideology a powerful push in the direction of the European West, transcending the traditional boundaries of Orthodoxy.

In his conviction that the limits of the Serbian nation were represented by the boundaries within which the Što dialect was spoken, irrespective of the religion of the population, Karadžić was supported and inspired by many European scientists of that time. In this respect he was not at all original, for the idea preceded him by far. In 1809 Kopitar, responding to a request by the French that he define the limits of the Slavonic languages, recognized only Slovene and Serbian among the South Slavs. The same ideas were preached by Pavle Šafarik, who published his *History of Slavonic Language and Literature* in Budapest in 1826. In it, he divided the Serbs according to religion, one section belonging to the Orthodox faith and another, living in Dubrovnik, Dalmatia, Bosnia, and Slavonia, to the Catholic. In another work, dating from 1842, Šafarik identified the Serbs with the Illyrians, counting among them all those who spoke the Što

FIGURE 31.   Karadjordje.

FIGURE 32.   Vuk Karadžić.

FIGURE 33. France Prešern.

FIGURE 34. Petar Petrović Njegoš.

dialect regardless of whether they belonged to the Orthodox, Catholic, or Muhammadan faith, as well as the population of northern Albania. Consequently Karadžić indirectly inherited this conception of nationality based on a single language from European rationalist philosophy. It was able to sway him because the ordinary peasant folk in the backward agrarian areas in Turkey and parts of Dalmatia had not, in his time, yet experienced a national awakening and gave little thought to the name of their nationality. National names were to be inscribed on banners only when the people began their quest for a new state.

In these linguistic and cultural endeavors the standard-bearers of Serbian national renaissance were soon to meet on common ground with similar Croatian forces. That meeting of minds was to define one of the most important stages in the history of the Yugoslav peoples.

Illyrism

The national awakening in Croatia was political and cultural in character. Its basis was the conviction that the Croats were simply a segment of the integral Yugoslav nation, although the name "Yugoslav," apart from the general use of the synonym "Illyrian," was not yet employed for that concept. Linguistically, the renaissance succeeded in equalizing the literary language of the Croats and Serbs, but politically it did not prevail, and the modern Croatian nation was united within the context of general Yugoslav ideas. Among the Croats of that time, it is not possible to draw a difference between linguistic and purely political movements. The struggle for the new Croatian literary language was widely supported throughout society. At the beginning of the nineteenth century, the Croatian people were using seven different orthographies: in Civil Croatia the Kaj dialect in the "Hungarian orthography" and in Slavonia the Što dialect in the "Slavonian orthography," while the Croatian Littoral, Dalmatia, Istria, Dubrovnik, and the Bosnian Croats had their own specific orthographies. Earlier concepts of the Croatian language soon surrendered to the struggle for a language based on the Što dialect in the Hercegovinian version. But the transition from ideas to practice was not an easy one, as part of the Croatian nobility, steeped in the spirit of the old Hungarian Constitution, waxed enthusiastic about the Hungarian national awakening. The section that opposed the Hungarian language in Croatia grabbed at the straw of preserving Latin in public life. In 1832, the Croatian Assembly sought the right to use Latin as the official language. Attempts along these lines were continued until 1847.

It was soon perceived by the Croats that they could not long maintain these positions against the Hungarians. In the first programmatic article written in the national language, in 1832, known as the *Dissertation*, Count Janko Drašković (1770–1856) fought for the use of the Što dialect, which he himself spoke at home. The struggle for the literary language had, of course, been in progress much earlier, but this was the first time it was given practical political application and invested with the powerful political arguments of the national awakening. This *Dissertation* revealed the historical significance of the movement in which all Croatia was caught up; within the narrow confines of Civil Croatia it was to remain subordinate to Hungary, and Croatia was able to tip the political scales in its own favor only if it opposed the Hungarians with the broader Slav idea of a "Great Illyria" from the Adriatic Sea to the Drina River which should, in time, also include Slovenia. Later, in the article *Words to Illyrian Daughters* Drašković was to extend the limits of Great Illyria to encompass all South Slav lands, including parts of Albania, and Bulgaria, in a political complex comprising 8 million persons. Although these radical ideas shared with Drašković by the Croatian public, were still, formally speaking, not beyond the bounds of the legitimate policies and traditions of the Hapsburg empire, they reveal the true intentions of the Croatian national renaissance as it slowly shifted from the domain of literature to that of politics.

The Croatian national awakening was promoted by the middle nobility, the citizens, and the lesser clergy. It also embraced most of the Croatian youth in the towns, although the masses of the people were not included in the political struggle. Its fundamental tone was set by the Croatian youth headed by Ljudevit Gaj (1809–1872). The son of German settlers in Krapina, he had already joined the fight for the literary language in the twenties and in his youth collaborated occasionally with a students' association in Graz (called Serbian Government). After he met the Slovak Jan Kolar in Budapest and became acquainted with the ideas of Šafarik, he had a closer notion as to just what he wished to achieve in Croatia. His *Short Basis for Croatian-Slavonian Orthography*, published in 1830, reformed Croatian orthography.

Gaj counted among his associates a number of writers, most of them commoners. Pavao Štos (1806–1862; *The Statue of the Homeland*, 1830), Ivan Derkos (1808–1834; *Genius Patriae super dormientibus suis filiis*, 1832), and others joined the linguistic fray. The turning point came in 1835, when Gaj began publishing the *Croatian News* with a literary supplement called the *Morning Star of Croatia, Slavonia, and Dalmatia*, for which he had great difficulty obtaining approval during an audience with the emperor in 1833. The first few issues were printed in the Kaj dialect, but in 1836 the Što dialect was used; the name of Croatia was also replaced by that of Illyria. Thus a new and far-reaching national strategy of the Croats was determined; from the hundred years of Danubian orientation and community with their coreligionaries the Hungarians, the Croats turned to the Balkan Peninsula and community with the Serbs.

The name of Illyria was taken for the same reasons that the Germans had taken the classical name of Germany: to unify heterogeneous provinces which lacked the consciousness of community. Thus the South Slavs acquired the classical name of Illyria as a common denominator embracing different provincial and genetic names. Some of them labored with dedication to prove that the South Slavs really could trace their origins to the classical Illyrians. Like Gaj, Illyrists were inspired by the idea of the existence of a South Slav language with a number of variants (Illyrian in the center, and Slovenian and Bulgarian as dialects) and a general Slavonic tongue, thereby running the risk of being dubbed Pan-Slavists by their opponents. The struggle for this Illyrian tongue was conceived by contemporaries as a struggle for the new Yugoslav or, at the very least, for Serbo-Croatian nationhood.

Consequently they strove for a common alphabet with the Serbs. Gaj reformed the Roman alphabet (Gajica) by introducing Czech diacritical symbols, with a special sign for the letter *e* that allowed for its being written in one way and read differently in each dialect.

Apart from striving for the literary language and newspapers, Illyrism had as its goal the founding of a joint cultural society to concentrate on this objective. This need was elaborated upon by Gaj in 1836 in an article entitled *The Society of Friends of Illyrian National Education*. The same year, when the assembly adopted the idea of organizing in Zagreb a center to foster language and culture, the Viennese court made no haste to give its consent. Impatient, the Illyrists decided not to wait for approval and began opening reading rooms in the towns for which the approval of local authorities sufficed. In 1838 reading rooms sprang up in Varaždin, Karlovac, and Zagreb. From the Illyrian Reading Room in Zagreb later developed, with the assistance of Count Drašković, the *Matica ilirska* (Illyrian Matica) in 1842 [later the *Matica hrvatska* (Croatian Matica)]. Guiding the national culture of the Croatian people, the organization was to try repeatedly to fashion the nation's entire historical strategy.

Moreover, the Illyrists were the first to give impetus to the establishment of a learned Croatian society in response to the earlier creation of the Hungarian Academy of Science. After prolonged effort, they finally succeeded in laying the foundations for the first national theater, in addition to the German one, which had existed in Zagreb since 1780. In 1840, with the help of actors from Novi Sad, a drama was performed. It was through these institutions that Croatian culture was to be nationalized. A key role was played by the Illyrian Matica with its magazine the *Reel* in 1847 and *Marigold* in 1852, but the entire effort to open reading rooms, newspapers, national schools, and museums was for some time determined among the Croats by the institutionalized method of struggle for building up a national consciousness although their actual functioning was always provoked by an immediate political need.

By the end of 1841 the Illyrists had strengthened to the extent that in Croatia they could shift activities from the literary to the political scene. The Illyrian League, as the group was called, was in fact the embryo of the later National party, opposed by the pro-Hungarian Croatian-Hungarian party. It was an unnatural social admixture of the lesser higher and rural nobility devoted to the tradition of the Hungarian estates system and the Kaj dialect as a framework for Croatia. North of the Sava River the lesser nobility was solidly in support of the Illyrists. This rural, Hungarian-oriented nobility was concentrated in Turopolje, Draganić, and Cvetković and numbered about 25,000 persons at the beginning of the century. The rural noble differed from the ordinary peasant in being exempt from taxes, bearing a title, and enjoying the right to vote in local assemblies and in the principal assembly. In 1845 the emperor forbade them to participate personally in the Croatian Diet, thus heightening their resistance. Representatives of the pro-Hungarian faction, Graf Josipović (1806–1874) and the vice župan of Slavonia, Ivan Salopek, wrote in Latin the *Letters of a Croat*, supporting the right of Protestants to settle in Croatia and the administrative annexation of Slavonia to Hungary.

At all meetings where discussions were held and voting took place, the Illyrists and pro-Hungarians sat in separate chambers. On one side were the Illyrists in their national tunics and on the other the coarse rural feudals in their shirts and moccasins. Some of their conflicts resembled those between Vienna and Budapest, only on a minor scale. Among their clashes, the most important one, over the reelection of members of the Zagreb županija, occurred on July 29, 1845, in Saint Mark's Square in Zagreb, when several people lost their lives (the July Victims). From then on, the prestige of the Illyrists, although they were defeated that day, was to draw sustenance from martyrdom and legend.

The Illyrian movement had followers beyond the limits of Croatia proper, in Slavonia, Dalmatia, and Bosnia. In Slovenia Illyrism appeared during the height of struggle for Slovene national consciousness, which was still embattled over regional and provincial names. There the Što dialect had been rejected even in Napoleon's time. Later no one thought seriously of restoring it until such time as the spreading of national renaissances in the south posed the idea again in Slovenia as well. During the period of Croatian Illyrism the Illyrian camp in Slovenia was a meeting ground for isolated representatives of the middle classes and a few prominent personalities like the poet Stanko Vraz. Slovene Illyrism helped to terminate the "ABC war," which had been waged for thirty years, and to introduce Gaj's alphabet, through which the Slovenes arrived at characters most suitable to their needs. This was the greatest achievement of Slovene Illyrism.

It was in Dalmatia that Illyrism performed the most important function in historical terms. The citizens in the towns used Italian; as a matter of fact, 11 percent of the Dalmatian people spoke it. It was the language of administration, trade, art, and Mediterranean rhetoric. Dalmatia was said to be a land where Italian was thought and spoken, German was used for commands, and Slavonic was heard. The difference between town and countryside was enormous. The linguistic reforms of Vuk Karadžić and the Illyrian movement in Croatia echoed widely in Dalmatia. A merchant of Šibenik, Božidar Petranović (1809–1874), began to publish in 1835 the *Lover of Enlightenment: A Serbian-Dalmatian Almanac*, which was renamed the *Serbian-Dalmatian Magazine* in 1838. Illyrian ideas and teachings about language began to spread in Dalmatia through the medium of this publication. Groups of Illyrists formed in the towns, extending support to Gaj's Illyrism. In 1844 the *Dalmatian Dawn* began to come out, with the ambitious notion of building the Dalmatian *i* version of the Što dialect into the foundations of the Croatian literary language. This Dalmatian literary separatism was to endure until the revolution of 1848 with sporadic attempts even afterwards to make a comeback.

In Bosnia the Illyrists were supported by the Catholic chapters, largely those who revolted against Bishop Barišić (Ivan Franjo Jukić, 1818–1857; Grgo Martić, 1822–1885; and Martin Nedić, 1810–1885). The most prominent member of the group, Ivan Franjo Jukić, was the author of a number of works about his travels through Bosnia and is considered the first modern writer of Bosnian history and geography, as well as the first collector of popular ballads. Later in life, he published the magazine *Bosnian Friend*. Politically his ideal was the creation of a Yugoslav state centering around Serbia, which Bosnia would join as an independent unit, as the Bosnians according to him were neither Serbs nor Croats but a separate people.

On the whole, Illyrism's historical mission was the creation, under its standard, of modern Croatian national ideology. It became the ideological foundation of the new Croatian society that was emerging, and the root of all future changes and movements among the Croatian people. Above all, in the shipwreck of the old society before the revolution of 1848, Illyrism was the sole pathfinder to the future. The striving for a single language brought down the spiritual barriers between the Croats in the north and those in the south. and brought about a cohesion that was formerly lacking. By championing the language of the lower classes, Illyrism, regardless of who its standard-bearers were, became a democratic movement with a different conception of society and the state, although it was to remain incomplete in many aspects for some time to come. The Croatian national renaissance worked for close cooperation with the other South Slav peoples, all of whom it regarded as forming one national entity. Under that banner, Croatia won temporary political leadership among the South Slavs.

Basically Illyrism was not successful anywhere except in Croatia proper and among the Što-speaking Catholics who in time were integrated in the Croatian nation. Most important of all, it did not succeed in turning the Serbian national renaissance in the direction of Yugoslav nationhood on the historical foundations determined by Illyrism, although the majority of the Serb nationalists of the time, and later, preached the need for formation of a Yugoslav community. A section of the Serbian intellectuals and merchants in Croatia and Slavonia upheld Illyrism (Mojsije Georgijević, Justin Mihajlović), especially in its early phase.

From the political standpoint, Illyrists did not always have a clear picture of the kind of Yugoslav community they wished to create. In 1841 Gaj exclaimed, "God save the constitution of Hungary, the kingdom of Croatia, and Illyrian nationhood." There was nothing radical about their attitude toward the Hapsburg state. Ivan Kukuljević (1816–1889), speaking in the name of one faction of Illyrism, stated that "we will not, we do not wish to proclaim any kind of Slavic independence in the south now, for which we truly are not ready." After the name of Illyria was banned in 1843, the National party shifted to the right; also, Vienna wielded a certain degree of influence over it. Moreover, the Illyrists gave little thought to the agrarian problem. A section of the Serbian government and Serbian public opinion was distrustful of the activities of Illyrists fighting for the national language while speaking German at home. In 1845 a member of the Serbian government, Avram Petronijević by name (1791–1852), explained this lack of confidence by saying that the Illyrists "were under the strong influence of Austria, particularly Catholicsm." It was true that one section of the Croats rejected Karadžić's *ije* version of the Što dialect because, in their interpretation, it was the language of people of the Orthodox faith.

Political differences between the Serbian and Illyrian movements were manifested in 1844, when the Serbs made plans for the creation of a big, independent state in the desire to avoid the dangers threatening the Serbian nation from Austria and Russia. With the help of Polish exiles headed by Prince Adam Czartoryski in Paris and his representative in Belgrade, Franz Zach (1807–1892), the Serbian minister of internal affairs Ilija Garašanin (1812–1874) produced in 1874 a long-term program for Serbia entitled *Načertanije (Memoir)*, hoping to establish the Serbian question as one of interest to all Europe. His attempt failed, as the document was not made known to the public for fifty years. The idea was to create a large state around Serbia (including Bosnia, Hercegovina, northern Albania) which would have some sort of connection with a liberated Bulgaria. After the *Memoir*, young political activists in Belgrade (most of them from Croatia, Dalmatia, Bosnia, and Serbia, and in larger part Catholic) began to disseminate these ideas among the people. They were carried away by the notion of creating a common Yugoslav language and Yugoslav nation on the foundations of the Serbian state. Some called them the "Secret Pan-Slavist Circle in Belgrade" although the name was utterly inadequate and bore no relation to the nature of their activities. They maintained contacts with the Croatian and Bosnian Illyrists, and with some champions of the Bulgarian renaissance. The Illyrian newspaper *Branislav* was published underground in Belgrade and briefly circulated in Croatia, the first uncensored newspaper in Croatia.

If not in practical action to be undertaken, then at least in the final objective of creating an integral Yugoslav community, the Serbian nationalists were in agreement with the Croatian Illyrists. In their fear of Austria and Catholicism, the Serbs were less unitarian in their leanings. On March 28, 1850, a number of representatives of Serbian and Croatian culture (including Vuk Karadžić) signed, in Vienna. a "Literary Agreement" relevant to a literary language, their point of departure being that "one people should have one literature."

But between the two sides there remained a great deal of margin for misunderstanding and disagreement. The backbone of the common nation in the Illyrian conception encompassed the area of the Sava River valley from Slovenia and Zagreb in the east, through Belgrade to Bulgaria, centering on the northern towns, largely denationalized. In the conception of Karadžić and Garašanin, the axis ran from Belgrade to the southern sea. For the Illyrists, culture was classical in its sources; for Karadžić its wellspring was the ordinary peasant and his sense of history. This difference was in itself sufficient to engender conflicts involving prestige among people who were actually one nation. One conception focused on Zagreb, the other on Belgrade. Furthermore, the two sides were supported by two social classes of diverse origins; in Serbia it was the "Balkan carsi" headed by the Cincars and in Croatia the fragile bourgeoisie headed by the Germans. The question was which center would prevail and how Yugoslavia'a future would be defined. Disagreements over language were actually disagreements over its social background. "When our language prevails, then we too shall prevail," stated *Dalmatian Dawn* in 1848.

Religion as the Watershed and Dividing Line between Nations in the Serbo-Croatian Area

Even if the renaissance standard-bearers had agreed on a common name and composition for the future community, they could not have succeeded in their endeavors. The nation, proclaimed as a linguistic community in the Balkan world which still used religion as a yardstick, could not eradicate the boundaries established by churches over a period of centuries. Religion remained the dividing line of nations in the Serbo-Croatian area, and the learned linguists and the entire culture were too weak to transcend the old boundary lines. Religion was not the reason for the creation of nations but simply the external framework within which social ferment in the last century generated the national consciousness. Among the Serbs this ferment was promoted by the struggle for the free peasant holding; among the Croats it was the battle for reform of society in a manner maintaining continuity with the old glories and the old rights. In that profoundly conservative agrarian society, language was not a unifying factor. Ljubomir Martić, a fervent Illyrist, noted that in Hercegovina Christians of both churches refused even to eat together out of religious hatred. Virtually the entire spiritual life of this peasant world was determined by the quarreling religions to which they were deeply attached.

One of the reasons for this was also the religious historical background of the modern Yugoslav intelligentsia. Historically the intelligentsia began to emerge in the eighteenth century within the fold of the church. Intellectuals were educated in church schools, and a substantial number of them prepared for the priesthood; the first language they spoke was the language of their church. This is particularly characteristic of the Catholic part of Yugoslavia and the sections of the Hapsburg empire inhabited by South Slavs, who had no considerable upper classes of their own. There are some areas (like those inhabited by the Bosnian Catholics) where the intelligentsia during the period of national awakening was totally composed of members of the priesthood. Its origin reflected not only on its culture but even more on the particular concept of the nation for which it fought. The religious origins of the intelligentsia were to be manifest for a whole century, although this continuity was interrupted among the Serbs with the appearance of Vuk Karadžić, and among the Croats Ljudevit Gaj. After the papal "Letter to the Orthodox" ("Literae ad Orientales") of January 6, 1848, an endeavor was made to equalize and unify the churches. In Croatia there were those who called for the introduction of Slavonic services and Slavonic vestments. When this failed, the rift widened. Applied in this patriarchal and agrarian Christian world of religious intolerance, the linguistic formula for unity, borrowed from intellectual circles in Europe, was not sufficiently realistic. In later decades this prejudice of the learned was to become the source of many evils, for entire regions on both sides were forced to accommodate to names which the people living in them did not accept as their own. The failure of this agrarian society to build into the foundations of the nation the secularized idea of language (the only possible one for a democratic conception of the state) was to have many repercussions for South Slav history, at times wielding a decisive influence.

The Slovene National Renaissance

The national renaissance in Slovenia kept step with the development of Slovene society. The fact that the Slovene towns were dominated by Germans and Italians was repressive to their awakening, for the Slovenes found it extremely difficult to establish their own national institutions. As in Croatia, schooling was in Latin and partly also in German. The Slovene language was used only in the elementary schools, but not in all of them; usually it was simply employed as a stepping-stone to the study of German. Although the first history book in the Slovene language appeared as early as 1845 (Anton Kremple's *History of Styria with Special Reference to Slovenes*), most national institutions in Slovenia were established by Germans. The conservative domestic intelligentsia, largely clerical, cared little for development of the national spirit and language. France Prešern (1800–1849) wrote in one of his poems that German was the language of ladies and gentlemen and Slovene of those who served them. The state system saw to it that education and political obedience went hand in hand. "I do not need intellectuals," the emperor told the professors of Ljubljana, "but good, honest citizens." Any pursuit of new avenues of thought carried with it great personal risk.

From the time Kopitar's grammar appeared in 1808 as the first thorough and scientific attempt to fashion a literary language from local and largely Germanized dialects, and a Slovene alphabet came to replace the old Bohorčica, persevering effort was made to codify the literary language. In a grammar published in 1825, a clergyman, Fran Serafin Metelko (1789–1860), narrowed the basis for the literary language to the dialect of Dolenjska. In the conviction that he was providing western and southern Slavs with a new alphabet, he created a successful combination of the Roman and Cyrillic alphabets, called Metelčica. At the same time, a clergyman of Styria, Petar Dajnko (1787–1873), presented his version of the alphabet, Dajnčica, basing the Slovene literary language on the speech of Styria.

The struggle to raise one or the other dialect to the level of a literary language demonstrated that the Slovenes were not yet sufficiently integrated as a nation. The provinces were still locked in battle for prestige. Before 1848 there was no national consciousness at all among the Slovenes, an indication of the absence of a national class interested in defining its social boundaries through the medium of language. The national movement was divided into two basic camps: conservative and democratic, dominated by the former, which satisfied itself with concessions from the Viennese court in the guise of the strong development of schooling and industry. The political tone was inherited from Jernej Kopitar, who opposed any solution outside Austrian boundaries. The democratic camp, in the minority, concealed its ideology in poetry and unbinding declarations of sympathy for the peasant world. The tone of this camp was set by distinguished writers like France Prešern, Andrej Smole (1800–1840), and Matija Čop (1798–1835).

The maximum achievement in this process, with the exception of the arts, was reflected in the publication of the peasants' and craftsmen's *News* in 1843, written in an unpolished but integrated literary language and edited by the secretary of the Peasant Society, Dr. Janez Blajvajz (1808–1881), who was himself more at home in German than in Slovene.

The Beginnings of the Macedonian National Renaissance

This period also saw the appearance of the first premature forerunner of the Macedonian national awakening. The Turkish social system clamped down on all activities along the lines of renaissance, the frameworks for which were still provided by an utterly different civilization. The national renaissance movements already in existence (Bosnia, Greece) in the Turkish area looked to regions outside that system. But church activities and church books reflected tendencies that were to be expressed more powerfully at a later date. Kiril Pejčinović (1717–1845), iguman (head) of the monastery of Leška near Tetovo, published a book in the Macedonian language entitled *The Mirror* in Budapest in 1818, and *Consolation for Sinners* in Salonika in 1840. But these early flickerings of Macedonian awakening were still only signs of the striving for the general emancipation of the Slavic peoples in Turkey.

CHAPTER 24

The Revolution
of 1848-1849

The long-smoldering dissatisfaction with the social system of feudal subjugation, combined with the general social underdevelopment of the South Slavs,
determined their special place in the European revolutions of 1848–1849. In the
Hapsburg empire it was mainly the South Slav peoples who rebelled. There were
as many revolutionary objectives and ways in which they manifested themselves
as there were different societies and diverse provincial identities, diffused and not
integrated into nations.

Ideas of a "United Slovenia"

In Slovenia the political problem was presented by the need to unify the provinces into a national homeland and to create a national consciousness among the Slovenes under conditions in which the national bourgeoisie was distinguished only by its stagnation. In Croatia the chief problem was agrarian, compounded by the political need to unite into an independent unit vis-à-vis Hungary. In Vojvodina the revolution, by democratizing society, was to give the people and the area a Serbian political identity. In Dalmatia the towns had to be diverted from their still-living Venetian traditions in the north and guided inward, toward the national nucleus, through unification with Croatia. The little movement there was in the Turkish area, which never developed into a real revolution, had as its goal the posing of the Serbian and Bulgarian questions in Turkey. It was the task of the revolution, and in this it failed, to solve problems that in the sluggish development of the times had been postponed for decades. By the spring of 1848 peasant unrest was at its height everywhere.

Movements in towns and rural districts were set in motion by the revolution in Slovenia. On March 16 demonstrations were held in Ljubljana. Toll stations were burned, and the town fathers fled for their lives against the background of sporadic revolts by the peasants. But all this simply provoked a conservative reaction on the part of the majority of the townspeople and clergy. When the new constitution was promulgated in Vienna, three camps could be distinguished in Slovene society: conservatives, liberals, and democrats. The last was represented by some individuals only. Continued social ferment was toned down by the Decree of September 7 abolishing serfdom, with the result that a salient feature of this revolution in Slovenia was the estrangement of the lower from the middle class, the latter fighting for the political expression of the national idea. A section of the middle class strove for a restructuring of the Hapsburg empire on federal lines in which Slovenia would figure as a separate unit. In this respect it made common cause with the official policies of the South Slav movements of the time. But the restiveness of many was alleviated when the benign emperor announced new reforms in the old provincial structure, leaving the Slovenes still divided into a number of parts. The writer Matia Majar (1809–1872), active among the Slovenian students, or someone else in his group, demanded in Celovec (Klagenfurt) that "the Slovenes should be treated as one people with an assembly of their own" and that firmer political ties should be established with the other South Slav peoples in the empire.

When the majority of Slovene lands, together with Austria, entered the German Union, they were called upon, on April 15, 1848, to elect deputies to the All-German Parliament in Frankfurt. Some Slovenes were persuaded that only the German Union could assure them independence, but another current sought unification of the Slovenes in Austria outside the commonwealth of the German state.

The principal achievement of the revolution in Slovenia was the hammering out of a program for unification of the Slovenes. This solution was demanded by a group of Viennese Slovenes on March 29, 1848, who also mapped out the image of a united Slovenia: protection of Slovene nationality, unity of the Slovene literary language and orthography and its introduction in schools and offices, and the overall regeneration of Austria. This "United Slovenia" was to remain the Slovene national program for many decades.

When, in the autumn of 1848, the Austrian Parliament in Kroměříž (Kremsier) presented the bill of a constitution reorganizing the empire, provision was made for restructuring Slovene lands. But the outcome depended on the fate of the revolution throughout the empire as a whole. Promulgation of the new constitution in March 1849 terminated this turbulent activity. Lethargy set in, ending in absolutism by 1851.

Hungary's Revolutionary Policies

In the Hungarian part of the empire, including Croatia and Vojvodina, the nobility sensed its precarious position and met the demands of the peasantry with such alacrity that the latter could hardly get their bearings. The agrarian revolution that had been on the threshold therefore suffered a setback. Fearing that the Viennese government might solve the peasant problem on Hungarian holdings in its own way, the Hungarian nobility hastened to anticipate it. Intoxicated with messianic notions of bringing its own national renaissance to fruition, that nobility was unable to take a sufficiently realistic view of the situation. The nobles regarded their nation in its historic frameworks extending from the Carpathians to the Adriatic Sea. The session of the Hungarian Diet in 1847, where some of the foregoing issues were discussed, incited the Croats to defiance; even if there had been no impulses coming from Europe, radical dislocation would have taken place in Hungarian-Croatian relations. The same year, the Croatian Assembly resolved to establish the national language in public life, despite the fact that the Hungarian Diet had adopted a decision to introduce the Hungarian language throughout Hungary on money and seals and in elementary schools. Latin was to be used locally in Croatia and Italian in Rijeka.

The Hungarians were bent on winning a number of concessions from Vienna. Demands for an annual parliament in Budapest, with a responsible government, national army, and constitutional liberties, were simply the prelude to more troubled times. The court complied with the demands, and by a decision of March 17, 1848, the first Hungarian ministry, headed by Lajos Batthyány (1806–1849), abolished the feudal dependency of the peasants, lifting the lid off the Pandora's box of revolution throughout the empire. Formally, this made the empire a state to be ruled by two peoples—Germans and Hungarians. And when the dual state was constituted, it was actually a personal union between Austria and Hungary. Neither side was able to consolidate smoothly on that basis. In April a constitution was promulgated by the court in Vienna providing for a bicameral system and franchise restricted by property census. The emperor retained the right of absolute veto. In Slovene lands, Istria, and Dalmatia, under obligation to send deputies to Parliament, the constitution was upheld by the upper classes; in Hungary linguistic and peasant problems complicated the revolution from its very inception. Through the medium of the compulsory common tongue, Magyarization jeopardized the very national existence of Croats and Serbs. Basically this was the reason why sympathy for the Hungarian revolution began to wane rapidly.

The Movement in Vojvodina

In Vojvodina and Budapest the Serbs in assemblies formed national committees which, in places, sat in public session. The growing Serbian bourgeoisie in the Vojvodina towns took the banner of struggle from the hands of the old church leadership. After the revolution broke out, the Serbs in Hungary initially put forward moderate demands which did nothing to estrange their movement from the Hungarian. At a number of gatherings (Budapest, Novi Sad, Zemun, Sremski Karlovci) in March 1848, they called for recognition of the right to use their mother tongue, protection of their religion, the right to hold government posts, regular annual convocation of the national assembly, abolition of feudalism in certain areas, tax relief, free election of officers in the Military Frontier, municipal self-government, civil courts, and freedom of trade. But nowhere were these demands submitted in integral form. The movement soon dropped its moderate tone, however, and as early as April 1848 the "requests" made by some of the village communes in the Petrovaradin area also mentioned the right to the "election of a Serbian vojvoda (military commander) for the Serbian army," recognition of the Serbian flag and emblem, the Serbo-Croatian tongue and the Cyrillic alphabet in public affairs, a national assembly, national schools, and employment of Serbs in the županija and town administrations. Thus local demands evolved into the demand for national state autonomy, with Vojvodina as a separate unit seen as part of the state framework of the Croats. Metropolitan Josif Rajačić (1785–1861), under pressure from the masses, sallied forth into the crowded streets and with crucifix in hand convened a national assembly. On May 1, 1848, that assembly, meeting in Karlovci, elected a patriarch and vojvoda, thus fulfilling the age-old dream of autonomy and separate territory. In the month of May, the movement for state autonomy intensified. De-

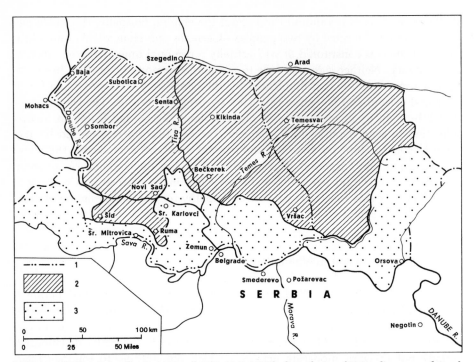

MAP 30.   Serbian Vojvodina in 1848 and 1849–1860. (1) The boundaries of Vojvodina as proclaimed
in May 1848; (2) territory of Vojvodina and the Banat, 1849–1860; (3) territory of the
Military Frontier.

mands were raised for equality in a democratic Hungary, an annual Serbian assembly, Serbian schools, and protection of the Serbian church from attempts at
union. The latter issue was raised by the papal "Letter to the Orthodox" of January 6, 1848, condemned by the Orthodox church in the East as a call for unification. Another demand asked for exemption from the obligation to pay taxes to
the Catholic church. Although the Assembly of Serbs in Budapest on March 6,
1848, in its manifesto entitled "Demands of the Serbian People," still acknowledged the political superiority of the Hungarians, doubts in that superiority were
soon to be aroused.

In the Military Frontier (Zemun, Pančevo) uprisings erupted, and the
citizenry destroyed the old military administration, set up civil guards, and introduced freedom of the press. The peasants began to portion out the land of monasteries and other estates, the uncontrolled wave showing up all of a sudden the
archaic nature of earlier political demands by the citizens who had been satisfied
with legitimist solutions.

At the National Assembly in Sremski Karlovci on May 1–3, 1848, the
Serbian Main Committee was formed to conduct public affairs. In demanding

autonomy, it had an eye on the formation of a "Serbian Vojvodina" (the civil and frontier sections of Srem, the Banat, Bačka, and Baranja). During the revolution the entire region which was controlled by the Serbian movement was soon covered by a network of "people's committees" whose territorial frameworks were fluid. These people's committees constituted the new system of authority. Consequently it was in Vojvodina that the revolution was implemented most consistently and thoroughly, for nowhere else in the empire were the former authorities routed as decisively as they were in that province. Despite this, however, the Serbian bourgeoisie of Vojvodina was powerless and immature, too much so to carry through the social revolution which, having begun as a peasant movement, continued later to destroy the old županija system, as it had no nobility of its own to try to transform the system from within. Funds were raised to equip the new army under the command of Colonel Stefan Šupljikac (1786–1848).

The Main Committee was headed by the dynamic Djordje Stratimirović (1822–1908), who forged a military organization out of local volunteers and newcomers from other parts. The conservative wing led by Patriarch Rajačić grew in strength with the passage of time.

Considering the May Assembly illegal, the Hungarians refused to recognize its decisions, thus provoking military skirmishes. In June 1848 an imperial army under the command of the Hungarian government mounted an attack on Karlovac. There could no longer be any question of returning to the initial fraternization. Legal oversights amounting to nonrecognition of nationhood presented problems that had to be solved by cannon. The new emperor, Franz Joseph, who thought to turn the rebellion against the Hungarians to his own advantage, approved the Serbian patriarch and commander by a patent of December 15, 1848, although in the spring and summer the emperor had refused to recognize the decisions of the May Assembly and prevented Šupljikac from leaving Italy for Vojvodina. He appointed General Meyerhofer the first provisional head (after Šupljikac died suddenly), but warily avoided committing himself on the extent of Vojvodina's territory. The proclaimed unity with Croatia was difficult to materialize, as the old administrative system had been retained in Croatia (the feudal županijas, the power of the ban, the Assembly), and even though modified, its restoration in Vojvodina would have been tantamount to counterrevolution. Srem was ruled by the dual authority of the old županijas and the new people's committees, constituting a Serbo-Croatian condominium over Srem. It was destined to become an obstruction rather than a bridge of cooperation between Serbs and Croats in that area.

The strength of the Hungarians lay in their cavalry, that of the Serbs in their infantry and in defensive tactics generally. By the end of 1848 the result of the hard fighting was still not clear, but soon after, the entire territory of Bačka and Banat was liberated. However, the new organs of government were no longer imbued with the original revolutionary spirit. Everywhere conservatives surged forward, bowing to Vienna and hitching the Serbian movement to the wagon of counterrevolution. Because of the pitched battle that took place there, Saint Thomas was renamed Srbobran (Serbian defense).

Revolution in Croatia

The very first rumblings of resistance in Hungary resounded powerfully in Croatia; as soon as news arrived that revolution had broken out in Vienna, turmoil was triggered off in Zagreb. It was insisted that the emperor recognize for Croatia a number of the same kind of independent institutions that the Hungarians sought. The movement was led by the National party, with an Illyrian nucleus. Ljudevit Gaj hastened to Graz to consider with Archduke Johann the position in which Croatia found itself; he also met with spirited young revolutionaries from Slovenia. Vienna had decided to appoint a capable Frontier colonel, Josip Jelačić (1801–1859), to the post of ban of Croatia in the belief that he could divert the rebellion in Croatia in the desired direction, that is, against Hungary. At Gaj's proposal, the national assembly on March 25 appointed Jelačić ban of Croatia and submitted to the king a long list of "Demands of the People." They included the demand for unification of Croatian lands (Croatia, Slavonia, the Military Frontier, Dalmatia, and Rijeka); abolition of the assembly of the estates and election of a new assembly in accordance with a new electoral law, as well as the establishment of responsible government. A new assembly was duly instituted. It abrogated the union with Hungary introduced by the nobility in 1790. With this exception, the revolution made no particular headway in destroying the old institutions. The "Demands of the People" had called for the abolition of serfdom in Croatia. When this demand was transformed into an official act by proclamation of Jelačić on April 25, Croatian policy won broader support from the masses, although in 1848 and 1849 the peasants of northern Croatia were inclined to favor the Hungarians. In summer and autumn of 1848 there were some peasant resistance to the Ban's Council, and local revolts were cruelly suppressed.

The Hungarians were still strong in Slavonia; they retained Osijek for a time, while in Vukovar, too, their adherents held out until mid-August 1848. Rijeka stood somewhat aloof from these trends in Croatia. Jelačić's proclamation of martial law temporarily pacified the excited villagers and put an end to Hungarian intrigues in the rural districts. The Assembly, elected in accordance with the new provisions (with a certain number of permanent "virilist"[1] members nominated by Jelačić) appointed a new ban on June 5. By April 19 he had severed all official ties between the local authorities in Croatia and the Hungarian govern-

---

[1] Virilists were feudal and church dignitaries who were not elected to the Assembly but appointed by virtue of their position; their vote was called the *votum virile,* from which they took their name.

ment. The Assembly adopted the principle of universal taxation and submitted a far-reaching program for the reorganization of the empire on a federal basis. The demand for merger of the Military Frontier and Dalmatia with Croatia and alliance with Serbian Vojvodina was approved, and Baron Franjo Kulmer, a conservative intimately connected with the court camarilla, was selected to maintain contact with the court.

In the hope of achieving agreement with Hungary, on May 7, 1848, the court agreed that all military forces in Croatia and the Military Frontier should be under the command of the Hungarian Defense Ministry. Baron Hrabovski was delegated as the imperial commissioner to take charge of these military forces. The court even removed Jelačić temporarily. It wished to play the trump card of Croatia in its bargaining with the Hungarians. There seemed to be a possibility of negotiations between the Croats and Hungarians when the ban left for Innsbruck on June 12 for an audience with the emperor, who had withdrawn from Vienna as revolution loomed. The negotiations broke off when the Croats demanded that the Hungarians submit to the government in Vienna and recognize Serbian Vojvodina.

Vienna's intentions were quite clear and were complicated even further by misunderstanding over the deployment of the army in both parts of the empire, and the expenses for its upkeep. Vienna sought ways of raising funds to equip Jelačić's frontier troops. The Hungarians assessed the situation in Croatia as representing rebellion which it was the duty of the emperor himself to crush. They feared that a court decision favoring neutrality in the conflict between Hungarians and Croats would simply serve to aggravate those relations.

Jelačić's March on Hungary

In the meantime, the revolutionary movement had burst like a bubble. Count Radetzky had taken the offensive in Italy, and Prince Alfred Windisch-Grätz had quelled the revolt in Prague. Encouraged by this turn of events, the Military party in Vienna calculated that it was capable of squaring accounts with the Hungarians, trusting to Jelačić to crush their revolution. He had called his Frontiersmen to Italy to fight for the emperor, while fearing that the Hungarians might do just the opposite.

The first spark flew when Jelačić occupied Rijeka on August 31. The court, cheered, decided to introduce central authority in finances and the army. On September 11, 1848, Jelačić and his army crossed the Drava River, annexing Medjumurje to Croatia. The march of the Croatian army on Hungary was complicated by military setbacks and the development of the revolution in Vienna. Failing to take Budapest, Jelačić turned on rebellious Vienna, which he subdued on November 1, 1848, with the aid of Windisch-Grätz, to the rejoicing of the military and feudal reactionaries and the dismay of democratic forces throughout the empire. In South Slav lands the defeat was even welcomed by these forces, as victory would have jeopardized the Slavs and helped the Germans and Hungarians.

After the government under Prince Felix Schwarzenberg was formed, reaction consolidated and Hungary was assaulted again. Serbs from Vojvodina participated in the battles against the Hungarians, as they had done before. They were assisted by an army of volunteers from Serbia and looked upon with favor by the Serbian government headed by Senator Stevan Knićanin (1807–1855).

There were few forces in this South Slav movement capable of switching it from the path of salvaging the empire to revolutionary struggle for a Yugoslav state. Democratic forces in Croatia were associated with the opposition to Ban Jelačić, whom the most sober minds of the Croatian national movement began to suspect as a reactionary. The Croatian democratic left wing rallied around the most radical newspaper in the whole empire, the *Slavic South*, edited by the "Red Baron" Dragojlo Kušlan (1817–1867). This group waxed enthusiastic about transforming the empire and even considered collaborating with Hungary. Another important organization was the Slavic Linden Society of Slavic Linden in the Slavic South, which submitted an explicitly progressive program in Croatia on November 29, 1848. It drew political support from the Czech movement of the same name and also to some extent from the Serbs of the *Progress* (newspaper) group in Sremski Karlovci, as well as from the like-minded who subscribed to the newspaper *Slovenia* in Slovenia. In the autumn of 1848, radical democrats among Croats and Serbs who favored the idea of a federal Austrian state came to prevail in the Slavic Linden. This was in any case a period of flourishing Slavic ideas, associated particularly with the convening of the Slav Congress in Prague in the spring of 1848, at which a very strong South Slav delegation was present. The ideology harbored by the South Slavs of common ties among the Slavs was still totally unrealistic. The situation was aptly defined by a British diplomat in Belgrade who described it as "calling little things by big names." Ljudevit Gaj, although convinced that the empire would survive the revolution and that no great changes could be expected from this—the greatest crisis of the century—had in mind as the future goal the creation of a Yugoslavia with Belgrade as its capital. "It is destined for that role," he told the French envoy Bistranovski, "by national sentiments, by virtue of its position and the fact that it is the junction of Yugoslavia's waterways."

The arrival of the former Serbian prince Miloš Obrenović in Zagreb toward the end of May 1848 was also associated with this idea of reorganizing the empire. Rumor had it that he was making preparations for the creation of a state to be headed by himself. Arriving in Zagreb with huge amounts of money, he was forced to leave by both Vienna and the Serbian government. Miloš Obrenović's money was the cause of a scandal that involved Ljudevit Gaj and cost him his good name.

The Situation in Dalmatia

Also associated with South Slav policies was the mission of Matija Ban (1818–1903), writer and representative of the Serbian government, to Vojvodina, Croatia, and Dalmatia in April 1848. Through him the Serbian government attempted to pave the way for Serbo-Croatian cooperation and to explore the possibility of obtaining assistance for the launching of an uprising in Turkey.

The conception of a federal Austria, in which Dalmatia would be a separate unit using Italian as the official language, was most suitable to the majority of the politically conscious world of Dalmatia, in which the towns led the way. Hence they opposed sending delegates to the joint Croatian Assembly in Zagreb. The only exceptions were Dubrovnik, where the pro-Yugoslav orientation ran strong and where a national guard had been formed at the beginning of the revolution, and Boka Kotorska, in which this ideal was translated into a political program by decision of the assembly of Boka communes held in Prčanj on June 13, 1848. Their aim was a South Slav state (a "Slavic empire" of "Slavic-Serbian nationality") within the framework of the Hapsburg empire. In Dalmatia itself, consciousness of nationhood had to cope with the social leadership of the Italianized towns and the prejudice that alliance with Croatia would bring the misfortunes of Hungarian nationalism down upon the heads of the Dalmatians. "Only the people in the mountain regions," declared Matija Ban in a report from Dalmatia, "are not infected by alien ideas, but they have no common national consciousness outside of speaking their own language, adhering to their own customs, and resenting townspeople." No serious complications were posed by followers of the Venetian Republic in Dalmatia, who waited in vain for Venetian ships to appear. The Venetian fleet never ventured near Dalmatian shores after a warning of November 20, 1848, issued by Lord Palmerston, speaking on behalf of the British government (after having received information that Venice intended taking the island of Vis). He cautioned the government of the Venetian Republic that its ships must not "take possession of any port on the Dalmatian coast."

Serbia and the Revolution of 1848

In April 1848 the Democratic Pan-Slavic Club in Belgrade put up posters all over town propagating the idea of creating a Yugoslav kingdom (Serbia, Bosnia, Bulgaria, Croatia, Slavonia, Srem, and southern Hungary) headed by Aleksandar Karadjordjević. It was also probably responsible for printing an appeal to boundary units to come back from Italy, to which end Michael Bakunin, Russian revolutionary and later ideologue of anarchism, also bent his energies from Prague. The Serbian government itself was working to expand its state with areas from Turkey.

Through the good offices of French diplomacy, it asked the sultan to permit it to annex neighboring regions over which he would continue to exercise supreme control. Late in December 1848 the Serbian government announced its acceptance of federal union with the Bulgarians in the conviction that "only a federation of Slavs under the suzerainty of His Highness the Sultan can save and consolidate the integrity of the Ottoman Empire." At the beginning of the revolution, the opinion in Paris was that Russia had forfeited the influence it had previously wielded over Central and Eastern Europe and would therefore "seek in the Bosporus the pillar of support it lacked." A French military mission was dispatched to Serbia in the middle of 1848. A letter from the Serbian prince to the president of the French Republic in late February 1849 expressed the hope that France would do something for all the South Slavs. Stating that he was speaking "in the name of my homeland and in the interests of the freedom and political salvation of all South Slavs," he complained of the danger threatening these peoples from Russia. France's endeavor to persuade Turkey to implement reforms in Bosnia and Bulgaria, where according to their plan Turkish viziers would have Serbs for deputies, bore no fruit save that Turkey itself, without outside assistance, hastened to implement reforms, especially in Bosnia.

It thus happened that in the revolutions of 1848, the entire Yugoslav policy never got beyond the limits of ideology, encumbered in practice by the political sterility of leading South Slav classes who pinned their hopes more on changes in the world at large and diplomatic assistance than on the popular movements in their own countries.

In the spring of 1849 the Hungarians undertook the offensive. They defeated the Serbs in Vojvodina, won back Budapest, and on April 14, 1849, issued a "manifesto of independence" in Debrecen proclaiming the Hapsburgs dethroned. Jelačić had left for Srem to attack the Hungarians in Bačka and crush the Serbian movement in Srem with his "southern army" at the request of Windisch-Grätz. In the meantime the new Austrian government under Felix Schwarzenberg promulgated the new, imposed constitution (March 9, 1849) transforming the empire into a centralized state. Various provinces became crownlands, independent of each other. Provision was made for a central parliament in Vienna and assemblies in the provinces. South Slav conservative forces who had helped the court in their effort to promote the federal reorganization of the empire were thereby duped, just as the Hungarian revolutionaries had been. Croatia was not unified, nor were boundaries ever clearly determined for Serbian Vojvodina, which remained without a permanent vojvoda. Belated efforts to reconcile the South Slavs and Hungarians failed even before Hungary capitulated on August 13, 1849, in the face of the Russian imperial army, which had hastened to the assistance of the Austrian emperor. The revolution among the South Slavs was definitely extinguished. The Croats continued to hope in vain for at least formal compliance with national demands for unification. In the Slovene towns persistent illusions of unification paled.

The revolution's defeat brought reversal of all its political achievements. Toward the end of 1851, even the imposed constitution was suspended and political absolutism was restored. But feudalism had been abolished, and despite flagrant relapses the foundations had been laid for new societies which were to become stabilized in the next few decades. After the failure of the revolution, Austria focused more attention on solving South Slav political problems within and beyond its boundaries. In 1849 it began to open a network of consulates in Bosnia and Hercegovina. After 1849 the South Slavs were in a worse position than before.

CHAPTER 25

The Consequences of the Revolution, 1849-1860

After the failure of the revolutions of 1848–1849, the Yugoslav lands were enmeshed in a profound political crisis. Its two essential elements were: (1) a gradual transition from national movements and rebellions to consolidation of bourgeois societies; the estrangement of peasant movements from the legitimist policies of stabilized societies, resulting in the general postponement of national revolutions; (2) abolition of earlier legal institutions in Austria and the establishment of absolutism, the historical mission of which was to create a stable political framework for legal transition to a new social structure.

322

Garašanin's Secret Organizations

At this time Serbia was a state in which the official oligarchy, relying on the traditional constitutional mechanism, successfully resisted the new emerging liberal spirit. Freethinking writers and societies were persecuted, but the seeds of liberalism began to germinate among students and youth associations. In Serbia it was customary that all great ideas originated with the students, the most dangerous section of the population in terms of posing a threat to the police system. Failing to achieve anything essential or lasting from its program of unifying the Serbian nation with the consent of the Turkish sultan or with support from the French government and Polish exiles, the Serbian government set out in another direction in 1849. It organized secret organizations in Turkish areas for the purpose of promoting Serbian national liberation. Such clandestine organizations had existed before, but this was the first time that a widespread system was brought into being. These were to last from 1849 to 1874, with certain interruptions and changes in leadership, program, and political objectives. The government made every effort to retain strict control over such organizations and always considered them conspiratorial. Their goal was to pave the way for a Serbian national revolution and the constituting of a Serbian state that later came to be called by journalists the "Piedmont of the South Slavs."

In May 1849 a "statute for political propaganda to be pursued in Slavic-Turkish lands" was adopted, to prepare for the moment of liberation, which was to be effected by means of guerrilla warfare. While the statute was under preparation, "rules on guerrilla warfare" were printed on the model of similar rules from Poland. This strategic basis for a guerrilla liberation war was elaborated by Ljubomir Ivanović (1836–1879) twenty years later in a study entitled *Guerrilla Activities and Guerrilla Warfare*. Fundamentally this meant that the chain of peasant uprisings around Serbia was to be firmly controlled by Belgrade and that this policy had been adopted as a long-term strategic method for unification of the nation.

After 1849 propaganda activity was directed by Ilija Garašanin and the Serbian Prince Alexander Karadordević. The areas in which propaganda was to be conducted were broken up into "provinces" (pokrajine), the latter into "areas" (predeli), and the "areas" into "nahiyas" (nahija). Salaried functionaries subordinated to Garašanin were called "ringleaders" (kolovođe); below them were the "agents and their men," followed by "district chiefs" and "village chiefs." The territory covered by the propaganda network included Bosnia, Hercegovina, Dalmatia, the Military Frontier (in Croatia, Slavonia, and Vojvodina), Montenegro, northern Albania (Miridit), Macedonia, and at least two-thirds of Bulgaria. The objective of the propaganda was to prepare for the fusion of neighboring areas with Serbia and the formation of a single state. Provision was made for extending assistance to neighboring peoples, especially Bulgarians. The presence of invincible Austria made it practically impossible even to mention the Croatian problem in this propaganda, whereas in decadent Turkey, the situation was ripe for change in the territories of Bosnia, Bulgaria, and Albania. Propaganda activity was controlled from two centers—Belgrade and Dubrovnik. Practical results were forthcoming only from those regions which had previously decided of their own accord that such activity was desirable. The leading functionaries and ideologists were educated men, most of them Catholics from Serbia, Croatia, Dalmatia, and Bosnia. Also involved were a number of people from the onetime Illyrian movement. After learning of the existence of this propaganda network in 1850, the Austrian government was persuaded that its goal was the creation of a "big empire" of South Slav peoples living in Turkey and Austria.

Petar Petrović Njegoš of Montenegro also was actively engaged in the movement. Girding for a possible war against the Turks, he displayed enthusiasm over the existence of this secret organization, stating that "nothing like it has ever been done among our people since the Battle of Kosovo." He extended his preparations for an uprising against the Turks also to Hercegovina and northern Albania, where the Miriditi, as part of the Scutari province, had an old autonomous tribal organization, the head of which bore the title of captain (kepedan). Through the offices of a Catholic clergyman, Don Karlo Krasnik, the Serbian government also won over for cooperation the Miriditi captain Bib Doda in 1846. Doda promised to participate in the uprising against the Turks on condition that the Miriditi would enjoy autonomy and freedom of conscience in the Serbian state. In Kosovo and Metohija four Serbian merchants and monks conducted the propaganda in preparation for the uprising, although their activities among the Muslim Albanians produced no tangible results.

Basically, the work was carried on by minor traders and ordinary clergymen. The writer Ivan Franjo Jukić and priest Blaž Josić were among the Catholic clergymen in Bosnia who operated as regular propaganda agents, while a large number of friars supported the work. The Muslims were given guarantees of the security of their person, property, and religion. Nowhere, however, did the organization succeed in controlling a single peasant uprising, although a number of them broke out at the time. The mercantile bourgeoisie in Turkey were not at all capable of leading a large-scale national movement, the upshot being that conservative political thinking, which officially held sway in Serbia itself, also entrenched itself in these organizations. The movement parted ways with the peasant agrarian movement, which it had never in any case led, while endeavoring at the same time to tone it down in the sense of persuading it to show more political, social, and religious tolerance.

Fear of Austrian intervention led to the gradual extinction of the secret organizations by 1853, although they were revived again in 1858. Between that time and 1862, they systematically worked out a program of cooperation with the Muslim aristocrats, who were offered guarantees that their estates would be preserved after liberation from the Turks. In an 1868 project for the uprising, provision was made for the issuance of a proclamation to the Muslim nobility promising that "their spahilics would never be taken away, but that the relation between them and the Christian peasants would be regulated differently and that it would be legalized firmly and forever by consensus at the general national assembly so that no side would find fault with it."

Reform Attempts in Turkey

Menaced by the peasant uprising and persuaded by a friendly France, Turkey resumed implementation of reforms in 1848. France, uneasy at the thought that the liberation movement of Slavic peoples in the Balkan Peninsula might be exploited by Russia to buttress its position in Europe, endeavored to pry Russia out of the area. From 1849 to 1851 a large-scale peasant uprising, savagely quelled by the Turks, raged around Vidin and Niš and throughout the northwestern part of Bulgaria and eastern Siberia. The peasants' hopes in Serbia were dashed by the Serbian leadership's fear of antagonizing Turkey, which had, just in case, sent an army to the western boundary of Serbia. At the same time there was reason to believe that a peasant uprising was in the offing in Bosnia and Hercegovina which Montenegro would undertake to assist.

For crushing the uprising around Niš and Vidin, Turkey had formed a powerful Rumelian army headed by one of its most capable commanders, Omer Pasha Latas (1806–1871). A Serb from Lika (Mihajlo Latas), he had been converted to Islam after fleeing to Turkey to escape punishment in his native land. His career in the army had been meteoric. After putting down the revolt in Vidin and Niš, he turned to Bosnia to assure the implementation of the reforms France had persuaded Turkey to undertake in its anxiety that a popular uprising there could easily throw the area "into Russia's arms." In a note of January 6, 1849, France asked Turkey to carry out the reforms; Bulgarian demands for the creation of a Bulgarian national church should be met; a Serb from the principality of Serbia should be appointed to each of the Turkish viziers in Bulgaria and Bosnia and "permitted by the Sublime Porte to supervise the affairs and interests of Christians and to protect them from violence by the Muslims." The Turkish government rejected all these suggestions, but admitted to French representatives that the situation of the Christians ruled by Muslim nobles in Bosnia was truly abominable. It was therefore necessary to remedy the situation swiftly by introducing reforms.

On August 4, 1850, Omer Pasha arrived in Bosnia with a firman for the reforms. The reading of the firman was attended by two viziers, ten pashas, and all the principal leaders of the Bosnian Muslim aristocracy whom he had invited, or forced, to come to Sarajevo to pay homage. The reforms consisted of a new administrative division of the country in which local Christians were also to have some part. The judiciary was to be improved, and minor changes were made in the position of the peasantry. The institution of bourgeois society was also introduced in the empire through the reforms although none of the social assumptions for its existence had been created. The emancipation of the peasants dragged on slowly and had not been achieved by the time Turkish rule terminated. Actually Bosnia lost its old autonomy and the Bosnian Muslims were divested of power over their province, while the running of the new administration was entrusted to educated civil servants, mostly foreigners. The Bosnian Muslims rose in revolt.

Pacification of Bosnia, 1851

During several consecutive battles lasting eight winter months in 1850/51 in Hercegovina, the Bosnian Krajina, and the Sava River valley, Omer Pasha succeeded in crushing the Bosnian resistance. The leaders of the revolt were executed or dispatched in chains to Istanbul. These savage methods broke the power of the Bosnian Muslim landowners. In 1851 Omer Pasha sent Istanbul 24 million piasters from taxes and war levies. The province was carved up into districts and counties headed by military personnel. At the summit of power in the province was the governor (vali) and an administrative council (mejlis). The head tax was abolished in 1855 and replaced by a military tax. The old landowners were stripped of certain rights, with some resulting modifications in the feudal system.

The introduction of the new administration in Bosnia brought some benefit to the new landowners, the newly arrived officials who battened on blackmail and fines, and the Christian population. In keeping with the proclaimed tolerance, Christians won the right to conduct their own schools, maintained by a fund set up in 1851 in Sarajevo from voluntary contributions. After his success in Bosnia, Omer Pasha turned his attention to Montenegro, but his attempt to bring it to its knees was foiled by Austrian diplomacy.

To prevent Russia from penetrating the Balkan Peninsula, France and England (later joined by Piedmont) embarked on a war against Russia in 1854. After protracted fighting in the Crimea, Russia was defeated in 1856. The Treaty of Paris concluded in 1856 replaced Russian protection of Balkan Christians by the protection of the "guarantee" powers, of whom France and Austria were foremost. In announcing the reformed constitutional law *(hatti-humayun)* in 1856, Turkey undertook the obligation of implementing reforms; the social ferment among the Balkan peasants was thereafter under international surveillance. No solution could be achieved any longer without the big European powers, and when solutions were found, they were always accompanied by the creation of spheres of interest and territorial divisions.

In the Bosnian Krajina and the Sava River area, a widespread peasant revolt broke out in 1858 under the leadership of the haiduk Petar Petrović-Pecija. Fierce clashes with the Turkish army ensued, the major one being that near the village of Ivanjska. Both Orthodox and Catholic peasants fought in the uprising. Before revolting, the peasants had sent petitions to the sultan and requests for help to European governments. In one such letter, they stressed that their complaint concerned "all of Bosnia—not only the Christians but also the poorest Muslims, who find just as unbearable as we do the terror of their authorities." The crushing defeat of the peasant uprising resulted in 1859 in the issuance of the Safer Decree, through which the Turkish government regulated agrarian relations by law, and thus they remained, without radical changes, until 1918. In 1862 Christians were granted the right to organize their own church and school communities, which Serbs, Macedonians, and Bulgarians exercised. In the towns of European Turkey, the Slav population launched a struggle against the upper echelons of the Greek hierarchy in the Orthodox church. In Macedonia this struggle, more deeply rooted among the people than it was in Bosnia, was soon complicated by the meddling of the big powers and smaller Christian neighbors.

The uprising of Christians in eastern Hercegovina, led by Luka Vukalović (1823-1873), lasted with interruptions from 1852 until 1861, with regular assistance extended by Montenegro. The fighting dragged on with intermittent success, but on May 13, 1858, the Turks were routed at Grahovo by the combined forces of the rebels and Montenegrins. The Turkish government's compliance with the demand of boundary tribes for tax relief restored peace, which lasted a full thirteen years. The peace was disrupted by a Turkish march on Montenegro in 1862, into which the Turks threw 50,000 men moving in three directions.

Prince Danilo and Montenegro

Montenegro figured significantly in all these movements as it enjoyed considerable prestige among the Christian peoples of Turkey. Its prince declared that the rockbound land could not feed two-thirds of the population, numbering 120,000 in the 1850s. War with neighboring pashas was part of the Montenegrins' everyday life and their only dependable source of income. In contrast to Petar II Petrović Njegoš, who wished to rid himself of Russian assistance, the new ruler rejected financial help from Serbia as too negligible and associated himself more closely with Russia. When he took over the leadership of Montenegro, Danilo Petrović was twenty-five years old—a ruler of sudden rages and hasty decisions. As a layman, he broke the chain of holy men and poets who had governed Montenegro. With Russia's agreement and the tacit approval of Austria, Danilo became the temporal ruler of Montenegro. Internal opposition to him ran strong and the quarreling tribes united only to stave off the Turks. It was Danilo's in-

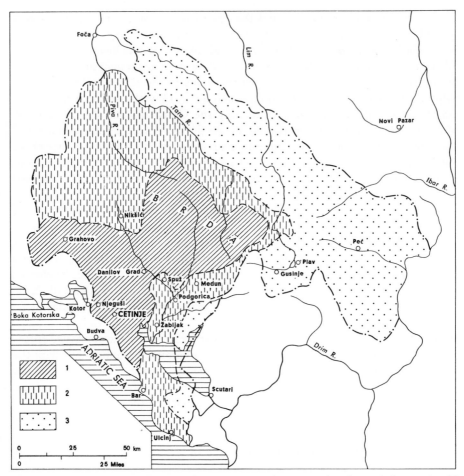

MAP 31.   The territorial development of Montenegro in the nineteenth and twentieth centuries. (1) Territory of Montenegro, 1859; (2) additions by the Treaty of Berlin and subsequent treaties; (3) additions in 1913.

tention to fashion a modern centralized state out of Montenegro. In May 1855 he published the General National Code of Laws, a Montenegrin constitution in a manner of speaking. The national army was formed after a census was taken of all able-bodied males. The prince eliminated the opposition in the reorganized Senate, thereby crushing resistance among the tribes. The system of power consisted of the prince and a general tribal assembly of chieftains. Elated by military victories (1858, 1862) and enjoying enhanced prestige among the surrounding peoples, Montenegro stabilized its position for some time after Turkey agreed to demarcation of the boundaries.

The Situation in the Western Yugoslav Provinces after the Revolution

In the South Slav lands under Austrian rule, reaction had the unenviable task, after the revolutions of 1849, of completing the process initiated by the democratic-minded movements. This refers in the first place to stabilization of the new social structure on the basis of the emancipated peasantry. By an "Open Command" of March 2, 1853, the emperor amply indemnified the nobility for their lost feudal rights. Landed estates, church and temporal, existed side by side with free peasant holdings. The peasant had received little land and was partially relegated to the position of a hired laborer although the Imperial Patent of 1853 offered him some protection. The dissolution of feudalism and its remnants extended, however, into the next century.

After the revolution the peasant in Dalmatia remained dependent on the landowner as a tenant-laborer *(colonatus)*, a position that did not change until 1930. Dissatisfied with his lot, the peasant constantly strove for a free landholding with the simple justification that the land belonged to God and labor was free *(La Terra è di Dio e lavoro è mio)*. Differences in forms of landholdings and in the tempo of their transformation engendered profound consequences, feeding Dalmatian aspirations toward separatism from northern Croatia.

In Slovenia the domestic capitalist economy reaped greater benefit from the agrarian reform. Of the 600 million forints paid to the Austrian nobility, the peasants provided 20 million in the form of compensation. But there, too, the peasants received little land. In Carniola there were only 334 large landowners with over 1,000 hectares of land, and the average peasant holding ran to under 10 hectares.

After the revolution the Austrian part of the South Slav area experienced a relatively dynamic advancement. The political framework and stable foundation for that advancement, as well as the initial basis for the building of the new society, was the political absolutism introduced by the emperor's New Year's Patent of December 31, 1851, also dubbed "Bach's absolutism" after Alexander Bach, the minister of internal affairs. The old institutions sank into oblivion, having been sustained by the nobility since the Middle Ages. The basic feature of this political system was the abolition of obsolete legal institutions and the effort to generate a new integrated Austrian society, through the medium of political centralism, while preventing the creation of separate national societies or one single Yugoslav society. The entire system rested on German civil servants. Official reference was made to the "Austrian people," but no social basis for this assumption had been created.

Political slumber and police-maintained peace were the conditions upon which unobstructed economic dynamism depended. To supplement the police, the state also introduced the gendarmerie—a military formation with a directly political function. Suspicion ran high, and the primitive police found everything suspect, even ambiguous sentences in Latin copybooks which could be interpreted as political allusions. Their suspicions were well-founded, as in the dearth of political liberty, literature became the refuge of politics. A conviction arose that national culture was a substitute for the nonexistent national state. Flogging was legalized.

Underlying the new regime was the idea that bureaucratic administration should be concentrated in the hands of the government. The state was strongly centralized but administratively divided into provinces which had their own local governments. The church became one of the foundation stones of the system. In 1849 concessions were made to the Orthodox church, and in 1855 a concordat was concluded with the pope abolishing state control over bishops. Croatia also won a concession in the form of separation of its church from the Hungarian in 1852, when the bishop of Zagreb was invested with the title of archbishop.

Striving to ward off any future Hungarian opposition and to give some minor satisfaction to the small national oligarchies that were faithful to their religion, the government set up "Serbian Vojvodina and Tamiš (Timis) Banat." With a population of 1,500,000 people (prior to 1860), the area numbered 400,000 Romanians, 350,000 Germans, and roughly 300,000 Serbs. The center of the province, to which a part of Srem was added, was located in Temišvar (Timişoara). The title of vojvoda was borne by the emperor himself. In accordance with earlier privileges, it was left to the patriarch to represent the Serbian people in moral and ecclesiastical matters. Serbian Vojvodina was not purely Serbian from the standpoint of national composition; it had been so skillfully tailored that the Germans ruled while the Serbs and Romanians bickered.

Certain administrative changes were effected in Slovenia, although the promise that assemblies would be established in the provinces remained a dead letter. Emancipation of the peasants put an end to movements in the villages; the bourgeoisie and townspeople in general, busily occupied with new economic activities, were disinclined to bother with politics. In 1853 all newspapers were forced out of business except the *Slovene Church Magazine*, later rechristened *Vzgodnja Danica (Early Dawn)*. The leaders of the Slovene national movement, Bishop Martin Slomšek (1800–1862), Luka Jeran (1818–1896), and Dr. Blajvajz, were legitimists who, while defending the Slovene language, opposed the unification of Slovenia. It was they who laid the foundations for modern Slovene clericalism. Although not ignoring the nation, in the list of general spiritual values they placed it last. In 1860 Bishop Slomšek declared that the Slovenes should remain first conscious "Catholics and Austrians, and then Slovenes."

Within the scope of general administrative changes, Slavonia was joined to Croatia. As in other provinces, German was established as the official language in 1854. Civil servants speaking fluent German ("Bach's Hussars") flowed into Croatia from Slovenia, Bohemia, and Austria while the church attracted German clergymen from the Tirol. In Croatia, Dalmatia, and Vojvodina the regime made certain concessions to the national cultures. The introduction of new literary languages was a lasting achievement, although the old Illyrian spirit and the political ideology associated with it were persecuted. Literature and historiography, adapted to the development of national consciousness, were without a doubt its most significant pillar of support. Their cautious avoidance of political barbs and programs against Austrian state integrity did the regime no harm; furthermore, the gradual development through the magazines of concealed or even open polemics between the Serbs and Croats was more advantageous to the state than all its gendarmerie together.

Austria in the Balkan Peninsula

Stabilized internally by artificial means and political force, the empire was capable of launching a new Balkan policy of far-reaching consequences after 1849. First of all, it succeeded in winning the sympathies of Catholics in the Turkish empire. It was decided to double the annual grants to bishops in Bosnia and Albania, who were asked to influence the Catholics in the spirit of Austrian policies, to teach them to light candles on the emperor's birthday, and to attend church services on that day.

The motive behind this entire policy was the official conviction that Austria must at all costs prevent a new revolution, the inspiration for which would come from Paris, with the Balkan Peninsula as one of the possible foci. The youthful Emperor Francis Joseph, who on December 2, 1848, succeeded the abdicated Ferdinand I, believed that providence had ordained him to uproot revolution. In 1851 he was already engaged in an endeavor in Central Europe to set up "a strong dam against the strivings of the revolutionary spirit." It was feared that a South Slav revolution in the Turkish part of the Balkans could instigate democratic movements in Croatia, Hungary, and Bohemia. The government in Vienna began to keep a close check on political movements in Turkey, and when it got wind of the organizing of secret activities by the Serbs in nearby Turkish provinces, it set its own spies to work and persecuted those engaged in such activity. From time to time, political emissaries were sent out among the people from the Una River to Greece. They advised the Slavs in Turkey to "wait patiently for improvement of their lot by legal means, for in no case would Austria tolerate revolution along its boundaries." These Austrian agents were regarded with benign tolerance by the Turkish authorities; at times their influence was so strong and so systematically pursued that they could immobilize movements throughout an entire province. Considerable sums were spent by Vienna for this work in Turkey; after 1856 they amounted to 20,000 forints annually.

This wary vigilance against South Slav movements and revolutions in continguous Turkish territory was part and parcel of Austria's Balkan policy for many decades to come. Particular concern was shown to prevent unification of Catholics and Orthodox. As late as 1869 the Austrian consular agent in Banja Luka told the Turks, "Such unification would be your end and ours."

Austria's pressure on Montenegro was particularly significant in this respect. After the death of Petar II Petrović Njegoš, the government in Vienna endeavored to subordinate the Montenegrin church to the diocese in Zadar and to take upon itself the education of its priests, just as it had intended doing with Orthodox priests from Bosnia and Hercegovina. The Austrian court began to apply a new policy toward the Orthodox religion in the Balkans, leading it to separate the Romanian church in the Banat from the Serbian patriarch (in 1864), which the Romanian national assembly in Lugos had demanded in vain in 1848.

In this way Austria, fearing a South Slav revolution, came into conflict in Turkish territory with the Belgrade-organized Serbian national movement, which it began to suppress. The government in Vienna, alarmed by the prospect that the European revolutionary movement might exploit South Slav restiveness, sent its overzealous police in all directions searching high and low for any possible adherents of European revolutionary organizations and ideologies. They kept specially close watch on workers and the few workers' associations then in existence, and also on the movements of craftsmen and apprentices leaving for the West from Yugoslav lands. In September 1851 the police sent instructions to local organs to be on the lookout for agitators among the workers on construction sites, and especially along railway lines. Followers of socialist ideas were singled out for attention, and a police warrant in Dalmatia even mentioned Marx and Engels. Austria thus put up barriers, during the emergence of modern democracy and consolidation of the initial foundations of socialism, to the penetration of ideas from their original Western European sources, mainly French and British. When these democratic ideas did come through later, Vienna was the intermediary: thence the difference, in the early stages, between socialism in Serbia and that in the South Slav countries under Austrian rule.

Austria thus gradually became a decisive factor in Balkan history. From 1849 onwards, it frustrated any liberation movement it feared might rally all the South Slavs and did not flag in this effort between 1849 and 1878. By these thoroughgoing changes, pressures, and control of all national institutions, Austria assured the peaceful development of its new society and brought its leading class release from the mentality of defeat. By 1860 it had truly secured political stability in its Balkan possessions and no clamorous or insistent voice of political protest disrupted the peace. The national spirit could not be suppressed altogether however, for it was precisely during this period that firm foundations were laid for the national literary languages, Slovene and Serbo-Croatian.

CHAPTER 26

Political Development, 1860-1875

CONSTITUTIONAL CHANGES IN CROATIA AND THE COMPROMISE
OF 1868 / CONFLICT BETWEEN THE POPULISTS AND THE AUTONO-
MISTS IN DALMATIA / THE SITUATION IN SLOVENIA / THE QUEST
FOR AUTONOMY IN VOJVODINA AND THE ROLE OF SVETOZAR
MILETIĆ / SERBIAN LIBERALISM / THE POLITICAL DEVELOPMENT OF
SERBIA / THE NEW ADMINISTRATIVE STRUCTURE AND TURKIZATION
IN BOSNIA / CHANGES IN MACEDONIA AND THE NEW PHASE OF THE
RENAISSANCE / NEGOTIATIONS BETWEEN THE SERBIAN GOVERN-
MENT AND SURROUNDING STATES AND MOVEMENTS / CLERICAL-
ISM AMONG THE SERBS AND CROATS

Important changes occurred in Yugoslav lands in the sixties of the nineteenth century. The regime of the Defenders of the Constitution in Serbia, entangled in mounting difficulties and pressed by increasingly insistent demands
for greater freedom, began to make concessions. Torture was abolished in 1858,
and discussion of political rights was permitted. Resistance from the Serbian
bourgeoisie then becoming conspicuous, particularly in Belgrade, jeopardized
the regime. In December 1858, during Saint Andrew's Assembly, two-thirds
of whose deputies were peasants, Prince Aleksandar Karadjordjević was deposed
and replaced by Miloš Obrenović, who was erroneously believed to respect the

newly laid foundations of Serbian liberalism. But the new leader lost no time disillusioning the public, for he stated, "No one is going to tell me what to do."

Already feeble, he was soon succeeded by his son Mihajlo Obrenović (1823–1868), who followed the pattern of dynastic behavior to which he owed his position. (This was the second time the Obrenovićs came to power. The first time was 1815–1842.) In the sixties, Serbia found itself torn internally between the old autocratic spirit and the new process of democratization. The dynasty concealed the rift by a lively show of active foreign policy directed toward South Slav and Balkan rapprochement, in the conviction that the new European spirit would have a profound effect on Austria and Turkey.

Constitutional Changes in Croatia and the Compromise of 1868

Having lost the war with France in 1859, and after the proclamation of the kingdom of Italy over which that war had been waged, Austria was gripped by crisis. The old state apparatus tottered, exhausted by domestic strife and warfare with its neighbors. Seeking to repair the situation, the emperor wished first to come to an understanding with the Hungarian national opposition, which posed the greatest danger. The Hungarians insisted that the ruler restore the original borders of the Hungarian kingdom within the frameworks of which Hungarian nationality and language would be acknowledged. They also called for recognition of the old municipal institutions, freedom of conscience for Protestants, and acknowledgment of separate Hungarian statehood, thereby canceling the secession of Croatia and Vojvodina. By 1867 the court had still not made up its mind. After the collapse of absolutism in 1859, an attempt was made to complete the state reform by establishing a federally organized monarchy with its center in Vienna (the October Diploma of 1860). When this failed, a centralized state order was introduced the following year (the February Patent, 1861), remaining in force until 1865. The system provided for a joint parliament in which the lower chamber consisted of deputies from the provincial assemblies.

On February 19, 1861, the "land system for the kingdom of Dalmatia" was proclaimed and an electoral law was adopted for the Dalmatian Assembly. Istria also constituted a separate province with assembly in Poreč. Medjumurje was separated from Croatia; in Rijeka the citizens declared themselves against union. By the Imperial Patent of December 1860, Serbian Vojvodina was abolished, part of Srem was annexed to Croatia, and the rest of it to Hungary.

Problems that had lain dormant since 1849 were resurrected after the revival of constitutional life in Croatia. Ban Šokčević convened the Ban's Conference in Zagreb on November 26, 1860, attended by fifty-six people. The Conference demanded not only that the national language be used in the administration and that a special office for Croatia be opened in Vienna, but also that Dalmatia, the Kvarner (Quarnero) islands, and three Istrian counties be annexed to Croatia. When it convened in 1861, the Croatian Assembly also raised the demand for annexation of Dalmatia, the Military Frontier, the Kvarner islands, and, if the Eastern Question was solved, also part of Bosnia extending to the Vrbas River. The only one of the demands to be satisfied concerned the election of Frontier representatives to the Croatian Assembly. This was the first time in official Croatian policy that Serbs also became a legal political factor.

A rift was provoked over the basic question occupying the attention of the Assembly—the state and legal relation with Vienna for the settlement of which it had been convened. A section of the Croatian National party, imbued with the incandescent spirit of the National party of Illyrian days, favored negotiations with the Hungarians for regulation of relations with Croatia. A smaller section of the party later broke off to form the Independent National party, striving for the annexation of Croatia to Austria. The two independent representatives in the Assembly, Ante Starčević (1823–1896) and Eugen Kvaternik (1825–1871), laid the foundation for the later Croatian Party of Rights. Before it was dissolved by force, the Assembly succeeded at the last minute in passing Assembly Article 42, referring to conditions for the reunification of Croatia with Hungary: Croatia's only tie with Hungary was the joint king, as the earlier tie of union had definitely ceased in 1748; Hungary was to recognize the territorial unity of Croatia, Slavonia, and Dalmatia (with Medjumurje); Croatia was to preserve its separate legislation and supreme administration over political, educational, religious, and judicial affairs. After this dissolution, Croatia had no representative body until 1865, but only a chancellor, the writer Ivan Mažuranić (1814–1890), who looked at Vienna, considering Croatia merely a unit in the future federation of Austria. In 1865 the emperor abolished the centralized system inaugurated by the February Patent. Alarmed at the possibility that Prussia and Italy might defeat him, which they did in 1866, he decided on a new move and negotiations with the transigent Hungarians.

The result of the negotiations was the Austro-Hungarian compromise (*nagodba; Ausgleich*) of 1867, transforming the Hapsburg empire from a single state into a dual monarchy. Mastery by one nation was replaced by the mastery of two, that is, government by two national oligarchies. The state was territorially divided into two parts with the boundary line running along the Leitha River (Cisleithania and Transleithania). It was left up to the Hungarians to come to terms with the Croats on the future position of Croatia in the Hungarian part of the state, which was an independent entity in every way with the exception of the joint ruler, army, diplomacy, and finances. In this great division, the Yugoslav peoples were portioned out between Austria and Hungary, both sides demonstrating a willingness to concede some autonomy to their old administrative and political entities. The Hungarian part included Croatia with Slavonia, as well as Vojvodina, and the Austrian included Dalmatia, Istria, and the Slovene lands, each of them with its own administration.

Between April 16 and June 16, 1866, the Croats negotiated to prevent this outcome, using Article 42 of their Assembly as a basis for their arguments. In this they failed. The Hungarians refused to recognize the territorial unity of Croatia, Slavonia, and Dalmatia, and they would not allow Rijeka and Medjumurje to join Croatia. Croatia proper with Slavonia, later joined by the Military Frontier, was considered a single unit to which the Hungarians granted autonomy in administration and in judicial and educational affairs. Vojvodina, losing all traces of a separate political identity, remained an integral part of Hungary. In actual fact, therefore, the Austro-Hungarian Compromise of 1867 proved to be a great historical setback for all South Slavs, who thenceforward had to reconcile themselves to the realities of a stabilized dual monarchy.

Croatia's agreement with Hungary was achieved under extremely irregular political circumstances. A new electoral system had been imposed on Croatia; the ban's regent, Levin Rauch (1818–1890), favored the party of unification with the Hungarians, which functioned under the name of the Unionist party in line with the old pro-Hungarian legacy. It won a majority vote in "fixed" elections. The small opposition of the National party left the Assembly, and in September 1868 an Assembly delegation signed the Croatian-Hungarian Compromise with a delegation of the Hungarian Assembly, canceling the separation of Croatia from Hungary dating from 1848. According to this compromise, they now constituted one state with one ruler and one joint national representative body. All economic and financial affairs and railways were managed by joint ministries in Budapest, equipped with special sections for Croatia. Financial arrangements were to be renewed every ten years, and as taxation was also conducted jointly, the Hungarian government long succeeded in utilizing for its own purposes most of the revenues originating in Croatia. A Croatian minister also sat in the Hungarian cabinet.

Despite this, however, Croatia acquired some measure of autonomy: a separate assembly which sent forty deputies to the joint Hungarian Assembly; and separate internal affairs, justice, education, and church. In Croatia, Croatian was the official language, although for joint business (especially railways and finances), the Hungarians preferred that Hungarian be spoken. The Croatian ban was appointed by the dual monarch with the approval of the Hungarian prime minister, who always saw to it that someone completely devoted to Budapest was chosen. The emperor ceded Rijeka (Fiume) to Hungary, which interpreted its provisional administration as a permanent solution. Glued to the telegram from Vienna announcing this decision was a scrap of paper dealing with the Rijeka question (the so-called "Rijeka rag"), a subsequent order that Croatia had to accept without protest.

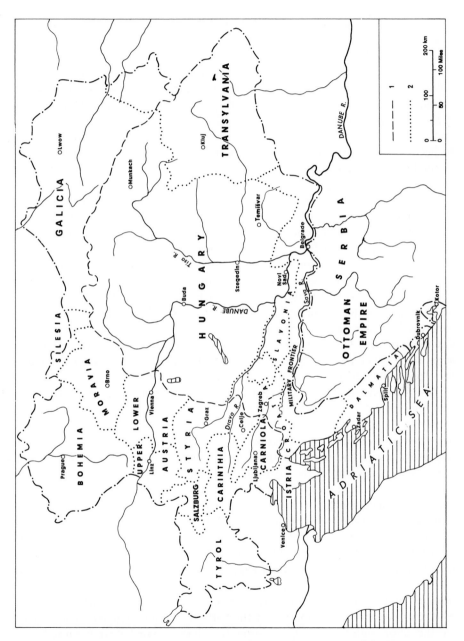

MAP 32. Austria-Hungary after 1867. (1) Boundary between the Austrian and the Hungarian part
of the monarchy; (2) boundaries between lands.

Conflict between the Populists and the Autonomists in Dalmatia

The collapse of absolutism was followed by the slow progress of a new wave of national awakening in Dalmatia, concentrating on language and national culture. As it was at this precise moment that the question of Dalmatia's unification with Croatia was posed anew, the town intelligentsia of Dalmatia was divided in two—one segment favored Dalmatia's autonomy within the empire, and the other aspired toward association with Croatia. *La Voce Dalmatica* was to become the newspaper of the Autonomists; *Il Nazionale* reflected the views of the Populists (Narodnjaks). Zagreb sent out frequent appeals for Dalmatia's unification with Croatia.

The question of unification, raised just as a real national awakening began to spread throughout Dalmatia, touched off a conflict over the future of this province. The Autonomists, although making no claim as to the Italian ethnical character of Dalmatia, took the view that Dalmatia was possessed of certain specific features, and even called its language "Slavo-Dalmatian," while the Populists formed a joint Serbo-Croatian bloc. Their principal spokesman, Natko Nodilo (1834–1912), wrote: "We in Dalmatia are of either Serbian or Croatian origin, and we speak no language other than Serbian or Croatian. Therefore, the language of our dictionaries can be only Croatian-Serbian, or Serbo-Croatian; or only Croatian, or only Serbian, which actually means one and the same thing." The concept of "Serbo-Croatian" was still considered the banner for a policy of integration.

The national renaissance in Dalmatia was given powerful impetus by two important factors: the establishment of a chain of reading rooms and the formation of the National party. The first of these "Slavianic" reading rooms appeared in Dobrota (Boka Kotorska) in April 1862, and subsequently other important towns had them. In time, these reading rooms became focal points of national policy and of the National party itself. The men who came together to form the National party acquired their experience through engaging in polemics over the language in land registers, activity during celebrations of historic dates, and preparations to open the Dalmatian Matica (national cultural society). In 1860 and 1861 they labored with zeal and energy to launch a newspaper; their efforts were crowned with success on March 1, 1862, when *Il Nazionale (Narodni List)* began publication, carrying a supplement in the Serbo-Croatian language.

Up to 1875 the newspaper was published in Italian. It provided a meeting ground for the formation and development of the National party (Populists), as it struggled for the affirmation of the Serbo-Croatian language in society and for the union with Croatia. Quite some time had to pass before it surged to the forefront of Dalmatian political life. In terms of social pattern, the National party was a movement of the town intelligentsia (lawyers, professors, sea captains, merchants, and some clergymen), a social mélange that was to replace the more powerful national bourgeoisie. They asserted themselves in public life during the drive for communal administration in 1865. The Populists gained adherents through their position on language, especially after 1866, when "Illyro-Dalmatian" was introduced as the second compulsory language for civil servants.

In 1870 the Populists won control of the Dalmatian Assembly. But the basic motive of their policy began to pale when unification with Croatia receded as a realistic possibility. Not only did the Croatian-Hungarian Compromise hamper the attainment of this goal, but considerable differences between the societies of the two areas had to be admitted. The two aristocracies differed from each other, as had their role in the development of the social mentality in Dalmatia and Croatia. Also, social relations in the villages varied to such an extent that in 1861 Governor Mamula was moved to state that "in Croatia the land had become free with land reforms and the peasant had become a free landholder. On the contrary in Dalmatia, the system of serfdom is an extremely complicated one." One of the basic reasons why the will for unification was lacking was certainly the exclusion of the peasant from voting.

Until 1870 the National party represented a common front of Serbs and Croats in Dalmatia; after that time it disintegrated into various national parties that differed radically on essential issues. The method by which new parties were created was similar throughout the South Slav area: a group of the politically like-minded would come together around a newspaper serving as a pivotal point. Separation of Serbs from Croats was also characteristic of Croatia, so that in the emergence of purely Croatian national ideas, Serbs adhered to those forces that were most closely allied with official policy. In Dalmatia they favored the policy of Dalmatian autonomy, considering—as the writer Stjepan Mitrov Ljubiša (1824–1878) once expressed it—that Croatia's state rights could not extend throughout all Dalmatia, which included Boka and Dubrovnik. The historic mission of the Dalmatian National party lay in its promoting Croatian and Serbian national consciousness in that region, although it did for a time negate the difference between Serbs and Croats and followed the general Yugoslav line. Its Yugoslav ideas were manifested in a number of variants (Slav, Dalmatian, regional), although inherent in each of them was the concept of a general Yugoslav nation, and of the Dalmatians as part of that nation. From that time onwards, the Autonomists in Dalmatia, at least the section that spoke İtalian, oriented themselves more and more to Italian as the nationality of their choice.

The Situation in Slovenia

Although there were stirrings of national awakening in Istria during the sixties, the process developed under the least favorable of circumstances. As in Dalmatia, the people were grouped according to nationality: Italians in the towns and Slavs in the rural districts. The ruling class, rising steadily after 1848, moved to Istria from western Italian cities or emerged from the old Italian nucleus. That class was almost exclusively composed of Italians, all the way down to the village saloonkeepers and retail traders. In some areas, the peasants complained that eight months of the year they had to go abroad to earn their daily bread. The deputy from Istria in the Parliament of Vienna stated in 1862 that there were districts in Istria where the people ate food without salt and where "most of the population consumed raw grass or wild strawberries when hard times fell upon them." Between 70 and 80 percent of the population in some areas were infected with malaria. The peasants had no schools to go to, the provincial Diet having seen to it that only Italian schools were established. On the other hand, the feeling of belonging to an entity was dissipated even in the Croatian part of Istria by the existence of three dialects in a relatively small linguistic community. The unity of the people was largely manifested through the church and the role of the lesser clergy who lived close to the people. Dominant figures among them were Bishop Dobrila (1812–1882), an Illyrist by upbringing and long the Istrian representative in the Viennese Parliament, and other leading intellectuals, such as Bastijan and Vitezić.

The tie with Croatia was emotional and lacked any economic basis. Here the Croatian national awakeners, like their Slovene counterparts in Trieste, had no possibility of developing national institutions to promote national sentiments. The Italian bourgeoisie was aware that the consequence of its social power over the South Slavs was the latter's denationalization. Their ideologue Carlo de Franceschi wrote in 1848 that the Istrian Slavs "would be Italianized as they became more civilized." From 1861 the Diet in Poreč almost exclusively numbered Italians among its deputies, the Croatian language being heard only if a deputy wished to quote something in Croatian. The dormant society employed the constitutional mechanism favoring only the upper classes, and the province was headed by Italian political leaders. Of the thirty deputies in the Diet, only one was a Croat, in addition to two Croatian bishops and one Slovene. In 1870 the newspaper *Our Concord (Naša Sloga)* was started in Trieste, but the movement to open reading rooms met with a favorable reception only in eastern Istria. The first one was established in Kastva. It was only after 1870 that a genuine national renaissance began in Istria, but even then it was not strong enough to withstand the competition of accelerated Italianization and the burgeoning power of the Italian bourgeoisie, all the less so as, after the Italian unification of 1871, reasons for animosity between Austria and Italy disappeared and all manner of ties with Italy became legal within the monarchy. The Croats drew support from the equally jeopardized Slovenes in western Istria and Trieste. The Croatian-Slovene National party had to put up with political inferiority everywhere, except in the agrarian districts of central Istria, but despite its position it managed to feed the flame of national life.

During this period, the basic program pursued by Slovene politics was that of a "United Slovenia" dating from 1848. The methods used were still essentially legitimistic, in line with the need to educate the people in political consciousness. In the sixties, reading rooms were set up, the most important being those in Ljubljana, from which the Slovene Matica and the Drama Society later emerged. The establishment of a constitutional order made it possible for political activity to take new forms through the medium of legal newspapers. In 1863 the poet Miroslav Vilhar (1818–1871) launched the newspaper *Forward (Naprej)*, whose editor and principal columnist was Fran Levstik (1831–1887). When Vilhar began to maintain that it was necessary to eradicate the old political boundaries which divided people speaking one language, the government placed a ban on the newspaper. But Levstik's activities were not without their effect, and his support of the idea of a "United Slovenia" echoed widely among the people, especially students. Levstik's *Forward* was opposed by Blajvajz's old *News (Novice)*, which supported obsolescent solutions.

Devoted to the Catholic faith, which they elevated above the interests of the nation, the conservatives strove for the right of Slovenes in each province to have a separate representative body in the form of provincial "national curiae." In their view, these could also meet at general provincial gatherings in the land assemblies, which would have separate national chambers. The idea was submitted at a meeting of political leaders on September 25, 1865, in Maribor (the Maribor Program).

The political struggle of conservatives and liberals was waged through the reading rooms, which figured as centers of patriotic literature and oratory, and through newspapers and meetings ("camps"). The liberals (the Young Slovenes) refused to renounce the project of a "United Slovenia" dating from 1848, while the conservatives (the Old Slovenes) remained basically legitimists, even when they became slightly more pliable in their positions and joined the general movement of the camp. Still, their only ideal was to repair the situation somewhat, within the old frameworks.

The first camps made their appearance after 1868 as meetings of the people at some suitable place outside of town; some of them brought together as many as several thousand persons. With their banners and their speakers' stands, it seemed at times as though entire provinces had congregated. Imbued with a democratic spirit, they aspired to the elusive goal of a "United Slovenia," invoked in solemn speeches. A similar camp movement, although of lesser intensity, then existed in Istria, receiving its impulses of political inspiration from Bohemia. The camp movement was a powerful and popular one which influenced all society and at one time even succeeded in the attempt to unify both currents in Slovene politics. When the camps began to fade away after 1871, the old division into conservatives and liberals was restored, and they stood separately for the elections of 1873.

The Quest for Autonomy in Vojvodina and the Role of Svetozar Miletić

The political activities of the Vojvodina Serbs were facilitated by the fact that the collapse of absolutism in 1859 left at their disposal a network of institutions which guaranteed their old privileges. When "Serbian Vojvodina and Tamiš Banat" were abolished in 1860, the Serbs began to suspect that they had lost their last dependable stronghold of national autonomy. The Annunciation Day Assembly in 1861 accepted the emperor's condition that all Serbian demands should be made within Hungarian frameworks; in its sixteen-point program, it called for the creation of "Serbian Vojvodina" (Srem, Lower Bačka with Šajkaška, the Banat with the Military Frontier) of whose 600,000 inhabitants the Serbs would be less than half, although the Serbo-Croatian language was spoken by a majority including the South Slav Catholics living there. The region would be headed by a vojvoda, elected also by Serbs from Croatia and Dalmatia (about a million persons), and a vojvoda's council. The government in Vienna rejected these demands of the Annunciation Day Assembly for fear of provoking the Hungarians, who had insisted on recognition of Hungary's territorial unity as a condition for agreement. This rejection closed the door forever on Serbian hopes of political autonomy although in 1864 the new patriarch was still praying that the merciful emperor would fulfill their wishes so that "we may glorify him, and serve him and fight for him forever and a day, as long as the race, the tribe, and the name of Serbs live."

Having lost their territorial autonomy, the Vojvodina Serbs were left to occupy themselves with their schools and church problems through the traditional church synods, which they persevered in believing to be general representative bodies of the people. Before 1875 nine such synods were convened, although none, with the exception of the synod of 1861, had anything more than a trifling political significance.

In this area, too, the new bourgeois movement formed around a newspaper, the *Serbian Daily (Srpski Dnevnik)*. Outstanding among its contributors was Svetozar Miletić (1826–1901), a distinguished politician, the first of his type among the Serbs of the Hapsburg empire. Miletić concerned himself not only with current political problems but also with the ideology which was to determine the historical strategy of the Serbian people throughout the Balkan Peninsula. A commoner, son of an ordinary Bačka bootmaker, Miletić was a deputy to the Hungarian Diet several times, and twice mayor of Novi Sad. Originally he was of the persuasion that the Parliament in Budapest was a better solution for the Vojvodina Serbs than were the commissioners from Vienna with their political autonomy on paper alone, concealing actual rule by the Germans. The Serbs had greater leeway, in the enfeebled Hapsburg monarchy, to work toward the posing of the Eastern Question by relying on the Hungarians. After the creation of a national state consisting of Serbs in Turkey, the Serbian problem was raised in its entirety. Throughout his politically active career, Miletić considered the Eastern Question the key issue in the Serbian national movement. His newspaper *Banner (Zastava)* was the loudest and clearest voice and the most regular political organ of all Slavs in the Turkish empire.

Miletić's Serbian National Freethinking party was formally constituted at a congress in Bečkerek (January 1, 1869). The program demanded Hungary's transformation into a democratic state with equal rights for all its numerous peoples and their right to speak their own language in parliament and also for that language to be the official one in communes where they had a numerical majority. This rule was also to be applied to higher schools of learning and in military units where non-Hungarian conscripts were in the majority.

This party was opposed by the conservative current of Vojvodina Serbs who took their inspiration from the church and the old Serbian estates, or classes. Among its opponents, it was popularly known as the "party of monks" although it was not a monkish party in the literal sense. In its opposition to Hungary's policies, it relied by tradition on the court in Vienna. Its meeting ground was the newspapers *Progress (Napredak)* and *Serbian Defense (Srbobran)*, and its leader was for a time General Djordje Stratimirović.

Serbian Liberalism

A broad, dynamic movement, the United Serbian Youth, functioned parallel with the National party, to which it rendered considerable assistance. Founded at an assembly in Novi Sad in August 1866, this youth movement represented a liberal front of the Serbian people as a whole. Formally, it devoted its energies to the field of education while making underground preparations for the uprising in Turkey. The objective of these young people, who did not always share exactly the same views, was a democratic republic based on the principle of "everything by the people, for the people." This principle was closely associated with the idea of a Balkan state alliance and Balkan federation. At an assembly in Vršac in August 1871, the youth refused to comply with a Hungarian government demand that they restrict their activities to Hungary. This brought their movement to an end. Attempts to transfer their program of action to secret organizations under another name did not succeed.

Their defeat in the Austro-Hungarian Compromise of 1867, and defeat again over the Eastern Question, revealed the full historical importance of political events among the South Slavs in the sixties, for the Serbs were never again, until 1914, to have an opportunity to discuss their destiny legally. Thenceforward they were jeopardized not only in terms of their position in the empire but also as citizens in their own homeland.

The Political Development of Serbia

In the sixties, with Austrian and Turkish enfeeblement, Serbia found the possibility of guiding its own future, and that of South Slavs generally, in another direction. Losing the chance then, as well as its other opportunity in 1878, it was never to be given another one until the First Balkan War.

In Serbia the new ruler, Miloš Obrenović, who ascended the throne by a decision of the Serbian assembly late in December 1858, adhered to the old formulas, making a mockery of the demands of the liberal youth for freedom, and relied rather on the old conservatives from the previous regime of the Defenders of the Constitution (Garašanin, Hristić). The ruler had the habit of encircling with question marks newspaper articles in which reference was made to the people as a factor of power. No matter how many groups he included in his government, he always tried to run everything himself. His personal philosophy, on which he predicated his behavior as a statesman, was based on the conviction that in every state there are those who rule and those who obey. The more backward a people is, the more centralized must be the state, and the greater the ruler's absolutism. Persuaded that internal restraints only served to strengthen Serbia's foreign position, he persecuted Serbian liberals and looked with disfavor upon the National party of Svetozar Miletić in Vojvodina.

The slogan of Serbian liberals—"Find yourself in yourself"—coined by their ideologue, Vladimir Jovanović (1833–1912), was instrumental in convincing the Serbs to build their new political order on the foundations of their mythical past: the Serb was born free and had become accustomed to the institution of the national assembly, which could only be the best of all parliamentary systems. This liberalism struggled for the ideas of the European revolutions of 1848: constitutionality, government by consensus, national sovereignty. Secretly, the liberals believed that monarchy and oligarchy had been imposed on Serbia by Russia and that as such they were not typical of the Serbs. The concentration of the youth movement on culture and science, although to some extent the consequence of its looking to similar European organizations for models, reflected the historical shift in Serbian national policy from its preoccupation with the village and political oligarchy to the bourgeoisie and urban intelligentsia. The objective of the youth organization was to transfer the work of liberating and unifying the Serbian people to conspiratorial groups and individuals having access to government funds and, as a matter of fact, to include the entire Serbian nation in the underground activity. Garašanin's secret organizations were replaced by a nationwide conspiracy. The medium of struggle was literature and journalism to a far greater extent than political activity, although it too was not lacking.

Generally speaking, Serbian official policy at that time accentuated preparations for war with Turkey. On June 3, 1862, the Turkish and Serbian inhabitants of Belgrade clashed (over the murder of a Serbian boy at Čukur Fountain), and afterwards the Turks in the fortress of Kalemegdan bombarded the town. Representatives of the big powers sitting in conference in Kanlidža brought pressure on Turkey, demanding that the Turkish population withdraw from all Serbian towns. The fortresses of Soko and Užice were to be destroyed and irregulars replaced by regular Turkish troops in the other fortresses (Šabac, Belgrade, Smederevo, and Kladovo).

Serbia failed in its endeavor to call attention to the Eastern Question for, until the termination of strife over Italian and German national unification (1871), sufficient support for this cause was not forthcoming from Europe. Russia's defeat in the Crimean War (1854–1856) spared the Balkans any military interventions by that power until 1877. In 1867 the sultan turned the fortified towns over to Serbia. Bent upon enlarging Serbian territory, Prince Mihajlo revived the secret organizations in Turkey after 1860 and tried to achieve political agreement with all surrounding states and national movements. Serbia was not isolated in the pursuit of its South Slav policy, as all South Slavs and a section of the Albanians were strongly Yugoslav-oriented. The idea of creating a separate Serbian state may truly be said to have reached its zenith in the sixties.

The New Administrative Structure and Turkization in Bosnia

Bosnia was a key area in this Yugoslav policy, and it was precisely in Bosnia that the situation stabilized temporarily in the sixties. The modernization of the system after Omer Pasha Latas's time began to bear the first fruits. Reforms after 1856 increased legal machinery in Turkey. The national Christian bourgeoisie, powerless to do more, satisfied itself with opening more churches and schools, and only rarely with participating in secret Serbian committees. That bourgeoisie definitely grew more prosperous in Bosnia in the sixties. The Safer Decree stabilized agrarian relations for a time, consolidated the system of taxation which presented a growing burden on the people, and, legally speaking, alleviated somewhat the position of the peasant. The general advancement of the Yugoslav peoples during this period, in spite of all their political defeats, forced Istanbul to do something for its Balkan provinces, all the more so as, with all their poverty, they were still the most progressive in the entire empire (with the exception of Istanbul and its environs). This applied particularly to Bosnia, the westernmost part of the empire.

Between 1861 and 1869 the vizier of Bosnia was Topal Sherif Osman Pasha, former commander of the fortress of Belgrade, a sagacious statesman who had enjoyed the benefits of a European education. In 1860 telegraph lines began to be laid in Bosnia, followed by roads toward the Sava River and along the Neretva Valley. The doors were also flung open to the first capitalist enterprises. The Constitutional Law of 1865 was intended to provide a stable framework for all these reforms. The province was called a vilayet, and the vizier in charge was the head of the entire military and civilian administration. The earlier Administrative Council as it had existed in the time of Omer Pasha Latas was reformed and renamed the Administrative Council of the Vilayet, but it was rumored that the Christian members of the Council simply served to hand the Muslims their chibouks.

Although European administrative methods were not instituted, the state system was improved and modernized appreciably. The authorities also made an effort to introduce changes in the sphere of culture to help them consolidate their power further. With the arrival of a printer from Zemun, Ignjat Sopron, in 1866, Sarajevo acquired its first modern printing press, which turned out books in the national and Turkish tongues, largely for the requirements of the administration and the new schools. The first newspapers were also launched [*Bosnia (Bosna)* and *Sarajevo Flowerbed (Sarajevski Cvjetnik)*] using the Cyrillic alphabet and the Karadžić orthography. A number of new commercial schools and the first school for girls (Staka Skenderova) were opened. Some of the schools were maintained by foreign governments through their consulates, and one was run by two English missionary women, the Misses Irby and McKenzie. The Muslims had their own religious schools; state schools, under the new reformed administration, were designed to train junior civil servants. These schools were of the rank of junior high schools and although they had been in existence since 1847, really began to flourish only in the seventies, when their number grew to twenty-five. In 1865 the new vizier opened the Civil Service School and the teachers college, and in 1873 one military academy. In all of them, and in the junior high schools, teaching was conducted exclusively in Turkish.

The administrative apparatus acted steadily and warily to prevent legalization of national renaissance movements; they were systematically suppressed and their exponents were persecuted. Most of them, like Vasa Pelagić (1833–1899) and the Perović brothers, were of Serbian bourgeois origin or intellectuals. The Muslims were favored and held all posts in the administration without exception. Native Muslims, although fluent in Turkish, had to start with the very lowest rating if they wished to make any sort of career for themselves.

Changes in Macedonia and the New Phase of the Renaissance

Divided into a number of vilayets and with strong internal administrative boundaries, Macedonia had a political development that differed considerably from that of other South Slav lands. Politically, unification began with the Macedonian national renaissance, which unfolded through struggle for national schools and a separate church. The demand for Slav bishops aroused the animosity of the Constantinople patriarchate; supporting the Greeks, it refused to budge on the issue of allowing the Slav population to hear service in their own language.

MAP 33.   Macedonia under Turkish rule. (1) Seats of vilayets; (2) seats of sanjaks; (3) important towns.

Macedonia was the last of all the South Slav lands in the Balkans to win its own national institutions (above all schools) through which it could promote national consciousness. The bourgeoisie could not constitute itself into a national entity, a contributing factor to this inability being the four great wars that were to rumble over Macedonia late in the nineteenth and early in the twentieth century, dissecting it successively into a number of different variants. Until 1944 institutions of culture, education, and politics were in the hands of neighboring countries, and as a result the institutionalized development of national consciousness arrived late on the scene.

Some of the outstanding figures in the national awakening were two writers, the Miladinov brothers from Ohrid (Dimitrije, 1810–1862, and Konstantin, 1830–1863) and the educationalist Jovan Džinot. The Miladinov brothers maintained lively contacts with their colleagues throughout Macedonia and the entire Balkan Peninsula, particularly with the Robev brothers of Bitolj and Šapkarov of Ohrid. This phase of the Macedonian national renaissance was characterized by the profundity of the Slavic spirit which moved it. Opposing these strivings were Hellenic aspirations toward a northern boundary extending as far as Skoplje and Scutari. To the north, Serbia manifested its interest in Macedonia, just as the Bulgarian bourgeoisie considered that Macedonia belonged within its fold. Under the circumstances, some of the Macedonian nationalists fell prey to the influence of policies pursued by the Greek, Bulgarian, and Serbian leaders, thereby unwittingly diverting the national renaissance in the wrong direction.

Russia's policy also had substantial bearing on this question. While it was the principal political factor in this part of the Balkans, before its defeat in the Crimean War, its tsars supported the unity of the Orthodox church in the Balkans, their policy acting to buttress the Constantinople Phanariot patriarchate. After Russia lost the Crimean War, forcing it to seek new and more reliable allies in the Balkans, it decided to throw its weight behind the Bulgarian national movement, which was the strongest in Turkey. The Serbian movement was paralyzed by its position between Austria and Turkey, and in consequence the Russian tsars began aiding Bulgaria in its demand for a separate national church. Alarmed at Russia's favoring the Bulgarians, Serbia stirred itself to activity in Macedonia. The conflict of the Serbs and Bulgarians over Macedonia was destined to drag on interminably, although the Serbian government, fearing the loss of urgently needed Russian diplomatic assistance, made every effort to avoid an outright clash over this matter with Russia. It was to the Bulgarians' advantage that the motive for their national renaissance was similar to that for the Macedonian struggle for church autonomy.

From 1868 onwards, Serbian activities in Macedonia became more systematic as greater political weight was attached to them. A committee was formed in Belgrade to promote Serbian education in Macedonia and old Serbia, to which end two men especially bent their energies: Archimandrite Ničifor Dučić (1832-1900) and the historian Stojan Novaković (1842–1915). In 1873 the Belgrade Theological Seminary opened a new section for boys from Turkey. Although the seminary was a combination of teachers college and theological school, more lessons were devoted to military training than to the Serbian language.

The measure of success attained by neighboring states in their activities throughout Macedonia may be ascribed to certain weaknesses of the Macedonian national renaissance. As in Slovenia, Dalmatia, and Bosnia, in Macedonia too the estrangement of the town from the countryside postponed the full flowering of the national spirit. But whereas in neighboring lands, the towns became national-minded and progressed, in Macedonia the traditionally heterogeneous ethnical pattern of the urban areas intensified. The trend toward disunity was encouraged by the wholesale departure of the Macedonian town population to adjacent states. Most of the emigrants moved to Bulgaria and Serbia, where the process of national assimilation was to provide both Bulgarian and Serbian nationalism with powerful arguments for several decades. The town, retrogressing socially and presenting the ethnical patchwork quilt, could not offer the people political leadership, despite the fact that those very same people had aspired to political and cultural autonomy for a full half century.

Here too attempts were made to use affiliation with the church as the decisive factor of demarcation in the national movement. A firman issued by the sultan on February 28, 1870, recognized the autonomy of the Bulgarian church throughout all the Slav districts of Turkey (with the exception of Bosnia, the Sanjak, and Greek areas); this was tantamount to political recognition not only of church but also of artificially determined national Bulgarian boundaries. Representatives from Niš, Pirot, Skoplje, Veles, Bitolj, and Ohrid did take some part in the work of the Exarchate, although it was only by the sultan's berats of 1890 and 1894 that Bulgarian prelates were permitted to do church organizational work in Macedonia. Although both are Orthodox, the Macedonians and Bulgarians differ somewhat in religious matters: like the Serbs, they celebrate the day of their patron saint, and like the Greeks also their name day. Some attempts were made to win permission from the sultan for revival of the autonomous archbishopric in Ohrid, and even to effect a union between it and the Catholic church and pope in Rome. The church, followed by the schools and literature, began to foster national consciousness among the people, endeavoring to stamp out traces of separate culture and literature. According to Stojan Novaković, literature in their own language predated "literature in Serbian and Bulgarian."

One section of the intellectuals fell victim to the influence of neighboring nationalisms which in time led to the paradox that children from a single family, educated in three different national schools, were proclaimed Serbs, Greeks, or Bulgarians (Srbomans, Grekomans, or Bulgaromans). Those who strove for a Macedonian national consciousness were still on the defensive. They complained of the books and influences coming from adjacent countries, which moved the writer S. Čilingirov to declare that the Bulgarian reading room in Istanbul had been opened in 1866 for the purpose, among others, of "implanting Bulgarian ideas among the Macedonians."

Sensing the ferment in Macedonia, the Turks endeavored from time to time to prevent development along these lines by arresting the principal Macedonian nationalists who, despite their awkwardness and shortcomings, were still the only ones capable of showing the people the right way out of their situations. Dimitrije Miladinov was accused of being a Russian agent and was interned. Nevertheless, Turkey considered independent Serbia its principal opponent and tried in every way imaginable to parry its enormous political and cultural influence. When it was found that the smuggling ·of books from Serbia to Macedonian and Bulgarian schools could not be stopped, Turkey resolved to build a living wall around Serbia, cutting it off from its Slav neighbors. The areas

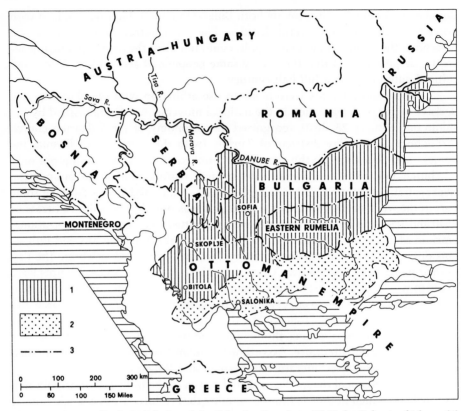

MAP 34. Area under the jurisdiction of the Bulgarian Exarchate. (1) Under Bulgarian bishops; (2) without Bulgarian bishops; (3) the political frontiers are those of the Treaty of Berlin, July 1878.

along the Serbian boundary were settled with a buffer belt of Cherkess families, from Vidin on the Danube to Prizren in Kosovo. Later this belt disintegrated completely.

Negotiations between the Serbian Government and Surrounding States and Movements

But whatever conflicts there may have been, the spirit of South Slav cooperation ran strong in all the South Slav lands, manifesting itself in the attempt to create a Balkan alliance between the Balkan states, and almost all Balkan national movements, centering on Serbia. In September 1866 an alliance was concluded between Serbia and Montenegro, where Prince Danilo had been succeeded in 1860 by his nephew Nikola (1841–1921). Nikola, in the Montenegrin tradition, was both poet and ruler. After he assumed power, Montenegro was to figure importantly in seething Balkan activity. An alliance was concluded in August 1867 with Greece, and in January 1868 with Romania. These were agreements between states, and it now remained to strike similar alliances with national movements fighting for independent statehood or for improvement of their state's position. Negotiations with the Bulgarian national leadership in exile bore fruit as, despite all the rivalry, beneath the surface a deep tradition of cooperation was still alive.

In 1867 Belgrade accepted the proposal put forward by the Bulgarian Revolutionary Committee relevant to the founding of a "Yugoslav Empire" headed by Prince Mihajlo, but those concerned were still wondering whether to name it "Bulgaro-Serbia" or "Serbo-Bulgaria." Later another Bulgarian league, consisting of Bulgarian exiles, was formed in Belgrade. According to plan, parliament, the capital (not designated), the sovereign, legislation, the flag, and money would be common to both, but there would be separate administrations and both literary languages would be retained. Originally, provision was made for a joint patriarch, but it was finally decided that a joint synod would suffice and that the "ruling religion was Orthodox although freedom of religion would prevail." The empire would be organized as a federation, with Bulgaria including Thrace and Macedonia. On neither side was there complete agreement on the projects. Among the Bulgarians, a strong anti-Serbian group inveighed against those who favored Belgrade, whereas in Serbia there was a great deal of suspicion, open or concealed, over Macedonia.

Early in September 1866 a parole agreement was concluded between Ilija Garašanin and Bishop Strossmayer (1815–1905), the leader of the National party of Croatia, on the need for joint action to establish a Yugoslav state independent of Austria and Turkey. The talks were renewed in the course of 1867 for the purpose of creating a federal state based on common nationality after a jointly prepared uprising had been carried out in Bosnia and Hercegovina. Garašanin stated on that occasion: "The Croatian and Serbian nationalities are one and the same thing—Yugoslav (Slav); religion should not interfere at all in national matters; nationality is the sole basis for the state; religion divides us into three parts and separates us, therefore it can never be the principle underlying unification into one state; only nationality can play that role, because we are one."

This idealism was clouded, however, by the troubled political reality. On both sides the classes that had taken shape nursed ambitions generating mutual distrust and posing, overtly or covertly, the question of prestige in the Balkan Peninsula, particularly in Bosnia. In Croatia linguistic strife persisted, and in that disturbed social atmosphere attempts were made to puzzle out the real boundary between the two peoples, Serbian and Croatian, on the basis of language. Religion was a major factor, and the church fathers who took part in official policy making were unwilling to sacrifice it even when, out of consideration, they tended to sidestep the issue in political dialogues. Until the Austro-Hungarian Compromise, many members of the Croatian National party expected Austria to solve the Eastern Question in favor of the South Slavs and refused to see the court in Vienna in the role of rival. Their feeling was that Serbia, under the sway of European diplomacy and poorly developed in the cultural sense, could not serve as the focus of South Slav liberation, a task which in their thinking would be better left to Croatia. Moreover, it was their conviction that an Austria reorganized on the federal principle would make an autonomous and unified Croatia, rid of the Hungarian specter, an attractive proposition for all South Slavs. This naïve trust in a federated Austria was to persevere until disenchantment set in among the members of the National party after the reality of the defeat of 1867 was brought home to them, demonstrating that the only realistic agreement to be expected in Austria was agreement between the German and Hungarian oligarchies.

Cooperation between the Serbian government and the Croatian National party was disturbed by the political crisis in Croatia and the inclination shown by Prince Mihajlo of Serbia to come to terms with the Hungarians in the second half of 1867. When faced with two alternatives, he chose to have a free hand in the Turkish area rather than helping the internal opposition in Croatia and Vojvodina. Consequently, the Serbian liberals condemned the prince for his behind-the scenes activities. On the other hand, Garašanin evaded recognizing the right of Croatia to rally the Hapsburg Yugoslavs to their banner, especially not to attempt the assimilation of the Slovenes. Croatia was regarded as a rival center, and suspicions of the Croatian leaders' intentions in relation to Vienna were never dispelled. From the very beginning, therefore, the idea of a Serbo-Croatian Yugoslavia as a "federal state" staggered under the burden of the struggle for prestige.

Negotiations between the Serbian government and Greece relevant to the formation of an alliance also provided for joint activities designed to propel the Albanians into rebelling, and for regulation of relations with other Balkan peoples. A Serbo-Greek agreement was signed in Weslau near Vienna in 1867, one of its articles stating that the "right of self-determination will be recognized for those peoples who take part in the struggle if they wish to establish separate states which will certainly be organized in a Balkan confederation."

The Serbian government succeeded in persuading a number of Albanian leaders to cooperate, among them Naum Sido (presumably from the Toska tribe), who in 1866 won over to the anti-Turkish cause the reputable Djelal Pasha, member of the powerful feudal family of Zogu from the Mat River area. It was thought that he would attract the broad masses of Muslims in Albania to the struggle against the Turks.

These conspiratorial activities in the Balkans created the conviction among those who participated in them that the time was at hand when a new Yugoslav state would be formed around Serbia. Without doubt, its policies were a factor of integration in the Balkans at that time, despite the fact that it never got beyond the level of inconclusive understandings between official diplomacies and sections of the national oligarchies. The national question in the Balkans and the creation of free societies were not decided by agreements between princes and bishops, but by national movements. Every agreement, no matter how ideally formulated, tended to break down if they were left out of the picture. Finally, the United Serbian Youth, through its program and activities, made every effort to surmount the narrow frameworks of official policy as pursued by the princes and to shift the focus to Serbian society in its entirety, and from there to the other peoples of the Balkan Peninsula.

On June 10, 1868, Prince Mihajlo was assassinated in Košutnjak Park in Belgrade, and work on the establishment of a new Yugoslav state came to a halt. The regency, which ruled Serbia on behalf of the new prince Milan Obrenović, consisted of Jovan Ristić (1831–1899), Milivoj Blaznavac (1824–1873), and Jovan Gavrilović (1796–1877), who continued pursuing that policy in all directions, but unconvincingly and lethargically. In Serbia's internal policies the old political rule of the iron hand, instituted by Prince Mihajlo, was continued.

In Croatia the mood swung increasingly in favor of the National party, which faithfully interpreted the will of the majority for some time. After the successive defeats of 1867 and 1868, it pinned its hopes on the external situation and on public opinion in the Yugoslav provinces of the Austro-Hungarian monarchy, as well as on the possible expansion of Serbia, which could then serve as a free nucleus for the future Yugoslav community. This was looked upon as a possibility that could effect a radical change in the unfavorable course of Croatian history. When nothing came of this, the National party endeavored, at the Yugoslav Congress convened in Ljubljana in 1870 and attended by about a hundred Yugoslav politicians, to lay the foundations for South Slav cooperation in the Hapsburg monarchy. The organizational leader of the National party, Matija Mrazović (1824–1896), was the moving spirit behind the preparations for this important meeting in Ljubljana. Laza Kostić (1841–1910) also attended in the capacity of representative of the board of the United Serbian Youth. Before the meeting Croatian policy makers met in Sisak, although the Dalmatians were kept away by inclement weather along the coast. The Croats were eager to rid themselves of the Hungarian shackles binding them after the 1868 Compromise; they wished to unify Croatia, Dalmatia, and Slovenia into an integral political entity and then, as a federation, to embark on a real union with Hungary. Slovenia would have a special place in such a union. Some of the Serbs in the monarchy, like the leader of the National party from Vojvodina, Svetozar Miletić, opposed such a solution, fearing that, thus strengthened, Austria would have an open door to the Balkans and frustrate Serbia in its intention of creating an independent Yugoslav nucleus around itself. Miletić's lack of confidence in the Hapsburg Slavs was condemned by some Slovene politicians, among them Josip Jurčič (1844–1881), who wrote that "while humble, we Slovenes are nevertheless convinced that we are not a burden of any kind on Yugoslavdom but rather that we bring Yugoslavdom elements that can only be useful to it; we are certain that in the northwest we are the primary guardians of Yugoslavdom."

The Yugoslav Congress was held in Ljubljana in December 1870. Its conclusions were passed under the shadow of the Franco-Prussian War, which was considered as having a most important bearing on the fate of Austria. Consequently one section favored bringing together Serbs, Croats, and Slovenes in Hungary, whereas another would have left the Slovenes to Austria. As hopes in the outcome of the war were dashed, the conclusions of the meeting remained rather ambiguous. It was proclaimed that the South Slavs "wish to strive in every possible legal way for the achievement of their unity." Stress was laid on literary, economic, and political unity inside the monarchy and outside of it. Some (like Bishop Strossmayer and Laza Kostić) considered this as applicable to Serbia as well and thought of the Ljubljana Program of 1870 as some sort of moral foundation for the future Yugoslavia.

When these expectations failed to materialize, it dawned on all those concerned that dualism in the monarchy was becoming a lasting historical achievement. The consequence of this awareness was catastrophic in its effects on the Yugoslavs in Austria-Hungary. In Dalmatia, Serbs and Croats who had pulled together in the National party began to draw apart. In 1870 the Serbs formed a separate movement, but it was slow to mature. In part, they were discouraged by the influx of clerical ideas propounded by Don Mihovil Pavlinović (1831–1887), who invested the Dalmatian National party with a narrow Croatian purpose. In Istria pro-Italians gained ground just as in Slovenia bourgeois conservatives, encouraged by the turn events were taking, threw increasing weight behind the Germans. In Croatia the futility of previous hopes caused the National party to start supporting the 1868 Compromise with the Hungarians in spite of its former opposition to it. Now, it accepted that compromise on condition that certain negligible and more or less formal corrections were introduced in financial and political matters (September 5, 1873). By assuming this posture, the National party lost prestige; in the next decade the disastrous consequences of the compromise were felt throughout Dalmatia.

The dualism established in 1867, although extremely unfavorable for the South Slav lands, created a stable political mechanism. Except for local revolts in Krivošije in 1869 and Rakovica in 1871, and disorders in Croatia in 1883, no major unheavals threatened to upset the system.

Clericalism among the Serbs and Croats

But the victory of dualism and its consolidation, and the defeat of South Slav aspirations, were not the sole reasons for the dissipation of South Slav political solidarity. There were other reasons, less dramatic than pressure from Austria, Hungary, and Russia, and as a matter of fact so subtle that originally the nationalists were not even particularly aware of them. Danger threatened from the erosion of the historical assumptions on which their national renaissances had been built and on the basis of which they had taken shape as separate nations. The Christian religions began to drift apart as the political atmosphere was polluted by the spirit of clericalism insidiously infiltrating the ranks of both Serbs and Croats.

Orthodox clericalism was closely associated with the growing influence of Russian Pan-Slavism in the Balkan Peninsula. Although the Serbian government struggled valiantly to avoid injecting Orthodoxy into its ideological parlance, it could hardly dodge the issue altogether. In Serbia itself an effort was made to clericalize Orthodoxy through Metropolitan Mihajlo, who had studied in Russia and was one of the most capable Serbian theologians. At the Archbishops' Synod of 1871 he tried to commit the church to the struggle against Serbian democracy, claiming that "it is the duty of the church and state to work with the utmost seriousness to stop the flood of atheism and materialism which has begun to invade our country." For this clericalism to succeed, a disciplined and sufficiently numerous clergy would have been needed to mold the spirit of the people to these ideas. Serbia had no such clergy as, by tradition, its clergymen were closer to the realities of life than to dogma. Consequently this Orthodox clericalism was more influential among the political leaders than it was among the people. It made no headway among the Serbian youth, nor did it affect Serbian culture. It was, however, undoubtedly instrumental, particularly after the "Epistle to the Serbs" sent by Russian Pan-Slavists in 1860, in awakening doubts among official circles of the appropriateness of cooperating with the Catholic part of Yugoslavia. It was far worse in its consequences for Serbs living side by side with Catholics than it was for those in Serbia. The upshot was intensified mistrust between the Catholic and Orthodox South Slavs. Furthermore, as the Russian Pan-Slavists in their practical policies favored the Bulgarians more than the Serbs, mistrust between Serbs and Bulgarians was also intensified.

Approximately coinciding with these developments was the growth of Catholic clericalism, which did not wane until the close of the century. In 1864 papal instructions marked the end of the Catholic church's defensive position and its launching of an offensive (the 1864 encyclical "Quanta cura" supplemented in 1870 by the Syllabus, a list of modern sins of which the faithful should cleanse themselves). Through them, the church endeavored to control intellectual trends in the world. By attacking individualism as a sin, the Catholic church brought into question the entire democratic spirit of the modern era. The consequences manifested themselves in various ways. In Slovenia nationality was negated, whereas in Croatia an attempt was made to influence the people to avoid the political ideologies of parties.

Catholic clericalism registered an upsurge particularly in the seventies, and showed exceptional tenacity after the Catholic Congress in Vienna in 1877. It had been working out its position for a full twenty years in reaction to the democratic revolutions of 1848. Against the background of the realities of the South Slav situation of that time, this meant that a section of the clergy, disciplined by celibacy and wielding a tremendous influence over the peasants, who were accustomed to accept rather unquestioningly whatever they were told by the men "in holy apparel," played an extremely important role as they strove for revival of the Papal State and threw all their support to Austria. Unconsciously, these policies could but lead to the greater or lesser isolation of the patriotic clergy which had pursued the policy of cooperation on a Yugoslav-wide basis. The full significance of their sway is reflected in a remark made by Pavlinović: "Son, stick to your priest, and God will stick by you."

During the crucial period of South Slav national awakenings and the formation of the Yugoslav ideology, the question arose as to whether political movements greatly influenced by clergymen were at all capable of solving the problem of rapprochement between peoples divided by their religions. Naturally the principal reason for the failure of rapprochement lay not in clericalism but in the fact that closed agrarian societies, sufficient unto themselves, were forming among the South Slavs. And it would appear, as a rule, that agrarian lands have no need of one another and are ridden by the instinct of division.

CHAPTER 27

Profiles of Societies in the Second Half of the Nineteenth Century

In Serbia society continued developing on the basis of the free peasant holding and urban advancement. After the revolution of 1848–1849, the feudal order collapsed in the lands of the Hapsburg monarchy, and bourgeois society grew rapidly on capitalist economic foundations among all the South Slav peoples of the empire. Remnants of feudalism persisted in Turkish areas of the Balkan Peninsula until the end of the century, when they began to disappear from Bosnia, Hercegovina, Macedonia, the Sanjak, and Kosovo. Furthermore, South Slav societies were still divided into two basic parts: in the north, new ones were in the process of emerging under the political and social dominance of the petty bourgeoisie which drew sustenance from its own and foreign capital. In the south (largely Dalmatia and Montenegro) society lagged behind, incapable of accumulating capital itself and faced with the indifference of foreign capital. This trend tended to promote consolidation of the petty bourgeoisie in the north, living in their small national communities and depending for advancement on the international road running from Vienna to Istanbul. The turbulent capitalist development of Europe and the Hapsburg empire also lent impetus to these Balkan societies, although it was only laboriously and on pain of political concessions that they could even try to keep step.

The Structure of New Croatian Society

Societies that evolved within the Hapsburg empire did so in the shadow of ascendant Hungarian and German society, and this may be considered one of their salient features.

The creation of capitalist landholdings on the ruins of feudalism in the Hapsburg empire left the peasant outside of the political mechanism, the consequence being that the western sections of the Yugoslav people developed a social mentality that differed from the eastern. Through the agrarian reform, the nobleman became a big landholder, or a new type of proprietor in the towns, or simply fell by the roadside if he was too small to stand up to competition. However, in the latter case, he was better off with his meaningless nobleman's title than without it in the hierarchical structure of the monarchy. The mentality of the old aristocratic society, preserved in its entirety, was transmitted to successive generations, especially as the tottering aristocracy and the entire ruling class labored after 1849 under the illusion that it was they who had liberated the people from feudal bonds, and not vice versa. Josip Jelačić , the obedient imperial soldier, was transformed by imagination into a mythical liberator. Society lived in accordance with the old rules of behavior applying to various rungs of the ladder; in the tales of Ksaver Šandor Djalski, *From the Days of the Vármegyaks*, persons who address each other use a scale of twenty different nuances to express varying degrees of respect and social distance. The new ruling class felt only annoyance at the crude undercurrent of egalitarianism redolent of the patriarchal world, issuing not only from the Yugoslav east but also from their own peasants. That feeling was summed up by the Serbian leader of the Defenders of the Constitution group, Toma Vučić Perišić, when he declared, "We are all equal; a prince is the same as a swineherd, and a swineherd differs not from a civil servant."

The new Croatian society was an amalgam of emancipated peasants, nouveau riche landholders, townspeople, workers, and civil servants. The ruling class consisted of the big landowners drawn from the old nobility, the old rich and the new rich bourgeoisie, and the powerful government beaurocracy, composed partly of Germans and partly of native nobility and intelligentsia. The mentality of the ruling class was subjected to the powerful influence of changes in society's ethnical composition. Foreigners came to settle in the cities and rural estates. Of Zagreb's 40,000 inhabitants in 1890, one-fourth were aliens, largely Germans, and German was spoken in the better Zagreb homes even by those who were not of German origin. Osijek was a Germanized town, whereas Rijeka (Fiume) was undergoing a rapid process of Magyarization and Italianization. Simultaneously the number of Serbs fell off rapidly; from one-third of the population they declined to one-fourth by 1880. In 1880 Croatia had a population of 1,841,000; by 1910, another 729,000 people had been added.

By 1873 the empire was covered by a network of railways. Up to 1867 the railways had gravitated toward their center in Vienna; afterwards a second center was added—Budapest. Slovenia lay on the southern railway route (Vienna-Trieste), along which most Austrian exports flowed. For a time Croatia was connected with this principal export route, after the construction of the Zidani Most–Sisak section. In 1873 Rijeka was linked by railway with Budapest. This again brought Croatian economy into dependence on Hungarian lines of transportation and Croatia in its entirety on the southern route of Hungary's outlet to the world's seas. Croatia's domestic bourgeoisie, operating from 1850 onwards through its "chambers of commerce and crafts," continued to prosper from the sale of unprocessed and manufactured wheat and timber. Moreover, steam-driven mills and sugar refineries were established, also drawing their raw materials from agriculture. At the turn of the century, 84 percent of the population in Croatia still lived on the land, the highest percentage of the whole monarchy, in which Croatia followed close upon Istria as the most backward area. Croatia and Slavonia together could count only seventeen settlements. Zagreb grew fastest, and four other large towns absorbed most of the remaining urban population. The Croatian bourgeoisie—a petty bourgeoisie—doubled its number, growing from 8,788 to 16,825 between 1881 and 1890. The percentage of peasants coincided approximately with the percentage of illiteracy. There was a very real danger that foreigners with greater amounts of capital at their command would be more capable of implementing the industrial revolution than the domestic bourgeoisie. In Croatia banks with small savings accounts, deposited by the petty bourgeoisie of town and country, prevailed. Foreigners held key positions in all important financial institutions. Before the great depression of 1873, domestic capital in Croatia, laboriously accumulated from transit trade and the agrarian reform, could still feel itself up to the task of developing an independent society. From then until 1903 it limped behind, especially after cheaper Russian and American wheat systematically forced the Pannonian product from the world market. The situation deteriorated even further after the Compromise of 1868, which assured the Hungarian government the right to dispose of Croatia's revenues.

Under the new conditions the rural districts could hardly make ends meet. The iron plow was to replace the wooden plowshare extensively only after 1895, and even then several decades had to pass before it became predominant. The villages were heavily taxed for the benefit of the Hungarian ruling class, but in the political mechanism of society their voice was heard only indirectly.

Development of Society in Slovenia

In Slovenia this type of development worsened the social conditions necessary for unification of the nation. Even more than in Croatia the new society discriminated in favor of foreigners, who comprised the upper class, the intellectuals, and in places the entire urban population in the divided Slovene provinces. The Slovenes had no nobles of their own to keep at least part of the capital from the agrarian reform within national confines. Half the Slovenes lived in provinces where Germans and Italians made up the ethnical majority and where they, as Slavs, were a suppressed national minority.

In the second half of the nineteenth century, the Slovene people underwent changes that were to weld them into an industrial society before any other South Slav people. They were, however, integrated into Austrian society. The population of what is now Slovenia grew from 1,100,000 in 1857 to 1,320,000 in 1910. The industrial towns advanced rapidly, while the number of peasants declined with equal swiftness. In 1857 peasants accounted for 83 percent of all society, only to fall to 73 percent by century's end and showing a tendency toward even more accelerated decline. The process of Germanization associated with these changes continued apace, notably in the regions north of the Sava River.

A number of important industrial centers came into being in Slovenia, dominated by multinational Trieste. By 1910 Ljubljana had a population of over 41,000. Other centers were Maribor, Celje, Beljak (Villach), Jesenice, Tržič (Treviso). But national spirit was lacking among the Slovenes, and this was one of the manifest weaknesses of their society. Foreigners were the vehicles of economic and social progress. The Slovene bourgeoisie was powerless and still dominated by intellectuals, the church, and the traders. Only after the seventies was it given an opportunity to take a more lively interest in industry, but even then it could make no particular headway. National savings banks on the Czech model were opened in Slovenia. The purpose of these banks was to help the national bourgeoisie resist the domination of foreign capital. At one time, the newspaper *Slovene People* wrote that an attempt was being made through the savings banks to form "companies or cooperatives so as to emancipate ourselves materially from foreign capital." Nonetheless, at the turn of the century the ratio of foreign to domestic capital in the Slovene economy stood roughly at 10:1. With the exception of backward Istria, this was the worst ratio in all the South Slav provinces. It was only at the beginning of the twentieth century that Slovene bank capital appeared in any considerable amount, but the prevalence of the Viennese, Berlin, Czech, and Italian banks, with branches all over Slovenia, continued.

Industrial stock companies, which began to be formed in the sixties, were established largely with German, and also with French, capital. In 1888 Viennese and Berlin capital was to galvanize Jesenice into an up-to-date industrial center. In 1873 a Viennese stock company, beginning with Trbovlje, soon won control of, and integrated, mines in Zagorje, Hrastnik, Liboje, and other places all the way to Raša in Istria. The same was the case of the Hüttenberg Railroad Company in Carinthia. Modern industry in Slovenia was built up on the basis of ironworks and railways, although other industries were also transformed and expanded.

Industrialization and the Protection of Peasant Holdings in Serbia

In the second half of the nineteenth century, Serbian society gradually shed its old oriental forms and habits. Belgrade blossomed into a true capital, acquiring an increasingly European appearance and reaching the figure of 40,000 inhabitants by 1844. But the transformation was long and laborious. In Serbian towns the once-leading stratum of Greeks and Cincars was soon assimilated by the Serbs. The style of living in Serbian, Bosnian, and Macedonian towns was similar, although changes were recorded earlier in Serbia than elsewhere.

The Serbian state was instrumental in promoting the growth of capitalism. For instance, a law of 1873 offered incentives to domestic industries. Another law on public land routes in Serbia, in 1864, also facilitated the development of the national market. In half a century trade in Serbia was multiplied sevenfold. Before 1878, Serbia could boast of no customs of its own. The Austrian economic vise closed every more tightly around Serbia, with Austria accounting in 1875 for over 80 percent of Serbian imports. The danger threatened, as it did in Croatia and Slovenia, that Austria, with its powerful German and European hinterland, rather than Serbia would be the one to create the new capitalist society.

Serbia continued its predominantly agrarian existence, rural overpopulation running a close race with the efforts of the government to create prosperous national cities. In 1866 there were 15,000 craftsmen in a population of 1,215,000, and in 1900 still only 33,467 craftsmen among 2,497,000 people. In other words, the agrarian status quo was maintained. A law passed in 1873 forbade peasants to sell all their land and stipulated that they must retain a minimum holding of 6 jutros[1] as part of the government policy of protecting the small peasant from destitution. But these measures acted to transform Serbia into a realm of small holders. In time the small and medium-sized holdings came to represent 96 percent of all peasant landholdings, with only every fiftieth peasant family owning a cart, and every sixth a plowshare. Population growth was admittedly slow in comparison with the natural possibilities of Serbia; a government report of 1889 noted that "in view of its natural wealth, Serbia's population growth is still small."

One phenomenon was common to Serbia and the western areas of the South Slav lands: the decline of the remaining peasant cooperatives (joint families) and the creation of the individual form of peasant holding. From 1860 onwards, the few joint families that were left went into sudden collapse, and after 1870 virtually the entire peasant population was given over to individual production. The same process of disappearance of joint families was in progress in Croatia (Slavonia, the Military Frontier, Zagorje). New lands (1853, 1870, 1874, 1876, 1880) intensified this process still further, although on two successive occasions (1889, 1902) an attempt was made to reverse the process of decline of the joint families. As these family cooperatives left the scene, the great complexes of land were parceled out and new settlements emerged with tiny houses in which small families resided. Zagorje, and then other areas, soon fell prey to agrarian overpopulation. The surplus population emigrated to other countries in a steady stream.

The sluggish advance of capitalist economy in Serbia was attended by the slow introduction of banking and credit institutions. There were no organized monetary institutions before 1862 in this land where taxes payable in money had been introduced only in 1835, and national money began to be issued in 1868. The First Serbian Bank, which was literally the first, was organized in Belgrade in 1869, with half of its capital Hungarian and its director a German who knew no Serbian. It financed the construction of a railway line to Trieste and the export of Bosnian plums, but the crash of 1873 in Vienna occasioned its collapse. Ten years later the banks pulled out of the depression and the Belgrade Cooperative was formed in Belgrade with branches in other centers.

It was only after 1880 that railways began to be built in Serbia (Belgrade-Niš, 1884; Niš-Vranje, 1886), but even then they were part of the international system of transportation and not an integral part of the national economy, which hardly needed them.

The general tendency in Yugoslav lands in the nineteenth and twentieth centuries was reflected in the creation of societies marked by agrarian overpopulation, with small towns and weak economies resting on a thin crust of

---

[1] A jutro was equal to 0.57 hectare.

capital wrung from the rural districts. Foreign capital figured importantly in these economies, especially in the western areas. Slovenia had already begun to extricate itself away from the agrarian economy in which the other districts were so hopelessly involved.

Differences between Societies in North and South

Differences in development between the Yugoslav north and south were very much in evidence in Dalmatia, Istria, and Montenegro.

Dalmatia was sunk in stagnation during the second part of the century. With 440,000 inhabitants, it had only fourteen towns; Split alone numbered over 10,000. The pillar of society was the peasant, who lived in a variety of mixed social relation. He was a tenant-laborer *(colonatus)* and also held land of his own. But the land was divided up into tiny parcels hardly sufficient to support life. Traditional activities like olive growing and animal husbandry were in decline. The only crop that fared better was the vine, but it too depended on a capricious market which the producers were not skilled in following or winning. In the fifties and seventies wine production experienced upsurges owing to the opening of Italian and French markets, but afterwards slid downhill steadily. A "wine clause" inserted in a trade agreement with Italy concluded in 1891, followed by importation of inexpensive Italian wines, provoked a catastrophe in Yugoslav lands, the hardest hit being Dalmatia and Istria.

The economy displayed somewhat more dynamism along the coast and in the towns, but there, too, it was encumbered by the unfavorable social structure: in the sixties, there were 3,300 craftsmen and traders, 3,000 civil servants, and 2,000 clergymen. Besides three naval academies and two parochial high schools, there were seventy-nine monasteries. Also, the state gave the church 2.5 times as much help as it gave to the schools. In terms of communications, the Dalmatian coast was severed more and more from its mountainous hinterland and oriented to Rijeka and Trieste. The basic means of inland transportation was the donkey, and Dalmatia was still a roadless land. Railways were not being constructed. The Siverić-Split line, with a branch running to Šibenik, was opened in 1877 but had no link with the internal railway network. It was only in 1891 that Metković was connected with the Bosnian hinterland.

Under the circumstances, Dalmatia was relegated even further to the background when clippers were replaced by steamships. In the eighties the mean value of a steamship (per gross registered ton) was almost five times that of a sailing ship. As the construction of steamships required greater capital investment, the rush for capital along the Adriatic coast acquired the proportions of a historic problem. The entire Yugoslav coast could not scrape together enough capital to effect the shift to steam-driven ships, not even on the most modest scale. The authorities favored the Austrian Lloyd of Trieste and skillfully supervised its expansion. The weak national banks, and banking generally (the first small bank was opened in Split in 1868, followed by the Adriatic Bank in Trieste and some smaller ones in other towns), could do nothing to help domestic shipping, which required increasing amounts of money. Attempts by the government in Vienna in 1895 to help Dalmatia advance were virtually fruitless.

The situation was identical in Istria and along the Slovene coast, where three prosperous towns (Trieste, Pula, and Rijeka) diverted the attention of the Peninsula in various directions. Towns were being Italianized. In 1853 Pula became a naval port and in 1876 was linked by rail with the Austrian hinterland, divorcing Istria even further from its Croatian motherland. The strengthening of the Italian ethnical element in Istria was in full swing. In 1846 there were 60,000 Italians among 228,000 inhabitants, but by century's end, of 317,000 inhabitants 136,000 were Italian. Numerically they approached the Croats and Slovenes, although they were always to remain a minority in comparison.

Montenegrin society faced the problem of acquiring a basis for its existence in the second half of the nineteenth century. Most of its 196,238 inhabitants (according to the census of 1863/64) made their living from animal husbandry, banded together in family cooperatives and bound by the old tribal structure which, though weak, still provided the foundation of society. The entire nation was armed and ever ready for external or intertribal warfare. This community, which had to melt down the font of its first printing press for bullets to meet the Turkish challenge of 1853, could give little thought to changing the ways tradition had set for it.

The state was maintained by taxes *(dačija)*, irregular Russian assistance in money and wheat, and Austrian aid in money (from 1866 onwards). Taxes began to be collected from the people in 1853, but they gave so unwillingly that in 1861 a new law prescribed severer penalties for tax evasion. Taxes were paid on land and livestock, and from 1882 on wine. The government's principal worry centered on feeding the population; in all projects, events, and intrigues, it looked to obtain neighboring Turkish districts with fertile land where it could implant strong roots for its independence. This was achieved in the liberation war of 1876–1878. Montenegro's territory doubled and its arable land increased even more. Besides vast forest reserves, it acquired an outlet to the sea. In the towns it came into possession of, it found an urban population (Podgorica, Nikšić, Bar, Ulcinj, Kolašin, Spuž, Žabljak).

The growth of population surpassed the natural possibilities of feeding it; a report of the Serbian government of 1889 stated that "in Montenegro, sources of livelihood do not develop parallel with the growth of population." People left en masse to earn a better living elsewhere, mostly to ethnically the same regions in Serbia. The number of those who sought to improve their status by moving away exceeded 10 percent of the entire population, unusual even for countries with a high rate of economic emigration. The townspeople consisted of petty traders, craftsmen, and intellectuals. There was hardly any question of industry or banking before 1901. And even where there was, capital reserves in some of the banks, considered quite large there, did not exceed the wealth of a Viennese shopkeeper. Skillful speculation by the prince on European stock markets helped maintain state finances. Road construction began in the seventies, chiefly by forced labor paid for in wheat rather than money.

Society in the Turkish Area

In the Yugoslav lands under Turkish rule, reform of the old social structure was stabilized for several decades by Safer Decree of 1859. The agrarian system did not get beyond the beginning of transition from classical feudalism to the new latifundia system of landholding designed to be based on commodity production but with rent paid in kind. Progress could hardly be made on the basis of such a hodgepodge, and even that system was in constant jeopardy from the peasants' rebellions. The want of capitalist industry or the spirit of industrial civilization left that agrarian system to die a lingering death until its forced collapse in 1912 and 1918.

From the end of the Crimean War in 1856, the Muslim town population in Bosnia and Macedonia receded steadily, giving way to Christians. This was particularly true in Macedonia. The travel writer Bianconi calculated the population of that area to be 1,450,000 in 1888, of whom 180,000 were Turks. The majority of the few Muslim peasants were Slavic rather than Turk. In Macedonia the Turks were mostly big landowners, civil servants, craftsmen, and merchants. Except for Salonika, there were no towns over 30,000, and most of them were considerably smaller. Trade caravans made their way along the Vardar River valley to Belgrade, loaded with tobacco, cotton, wool, and hides. Banking and credit institutions rested substantially on foreign capital. After 1856 the Imperial Ottoman Bank opened branches all over Macedonia, and in 1860 the Turkish authorities established village "coffers" *(menafi sanduklari)* to help the agriculturists. Counterparts were set up also in Bosnia.

The state of affairs in Bosnia was similar, although there the Muslim section of the population was Slavic to a greater extent and fully capable of assimilating the incoming Turks. There are no reliable data as to the number of inhabitants in Bosnia and Hercegovina at that time, but in 1865 the official estimate was 1,278,850, of which 593,548 were Orthodox, 257,920 Catholic, and 419,628 Muslim. Numerically, Muslims were decreasing.

Turkey stood threatened in Bosnia by the fact that a large section of the poorer population had for social reasons become emotionally attached to Serbia, and the upper classes had been won over by Austria. After 1849 Austria made increasing economic headway in Bosnia. For purposes of tax relief, wholesale traders along the borders sought Austrian citizenship and asked for consular protection in the interior. Big Muslim landowners produced for Austria's markets and during crises mortgaged their lands to obtain Austrian capital.

Omer Pasha Latas launched modern road building in Bosnia and Hercegovina (the Sarajevo-Travnik road and others), thus cutting the length of the trip from Sarajevo to the Sava River by more than half. In the sixties, and particularly during the administration of Topal Osman Pasha, communications expanded even further, although the old practice remained of using forced labor for this construction work. The first industrial plants (sawmills, breweries, small woodworking and stave making shops, as well as primitive potash works) were owned by merchants and entrepreneurs on the other, Austrian side of the Sava River. Lumber was the principal industrial and export article. Wheat, livestock, and lumber prices in Bosnia depended on Austrian market prices. In 1845 two men of Vienna, Ernest Schönfeldt and Leone Kluky, set up the first industrial enterprise in Hercegovina for timber exploitation. Both Turkish and Austrian money was in circulation in Bosnia, although the latter became prevalent after the introduction of Turkish paper money (*kaima*) in 1876. Banja Luka began to prosper in mid-century. Steamships transported European goods along the Sava River, carried thence by wagons to Banja Luka, making it the closest Bosnian emporium to Europe.

The economic penetration of foreigners and the circulation of alarming amounts of foreign currencies in Bosnia were telling signs that Turkey's boundaries were again shifting eastward. The economic prosperity generated a powerful stratum of Christian merchants who, for the first time after four centuries, tried to take the leadership of society into their own hands. This historical turning point was attended by boundless rivalry, jealousy, and sporadic violence. The Christian bourgeoisie in the Turkish towns was the first to embrace enthusiastically the spirit of European modernization expounded by the state and to adapt itself with the most dedicated thoroughness to European models.

Despite all this, Bosnia's capital, Sarajevo, with 50,000 people on the eve of the uprising of 1878, had no bookshops. Also, all roads from it led to the Sava River and Dalmatia. In the middle of the century, only a good horse could get the traveler from the heart of Bosnia to Zvornik and in the direction of Serbia.

Although this early development of capitalism in the South Slav lands under Turkish control proceeded under politically unfavorable circumstances, the foundations of future society were nevertheless laid in Macedonia and Bosnia. Trading and urban centers, established in the past, waxed richer and were to remain the principal foci of production and city life. The roads built then were later consolidated into an improved network of communications.

Owing to the peasant's predominance in Bosnian society, the agrarian problem set its stamp on the times as its chief characteristic. Even in the twentieth century, 90 percent of the population has made its livelihood from agriculture. Some of the peasants were free, others were serfs; in 1878 the percentage of free peasants and serfs were 47.5 and 52.5 percent respectively. Most of the serfs were Orthodox. The territorial distribution of free and unfree peasants was uneven. This was the principal reason why peasant uprisings occurred in greater numbers in Hercegovina, the Bosnian Krajina, and the Sava and Drina River valleys, whereas the central Bosnian districts were spared. In 1878 there were 85,000 families of serfs and 6,000 to 7,000 families of agas and beys. Among the latter were such as had negligible holdings with only one serf, thus bringing exploitation to its maximum: one man exploiting one other man.

The peasant's position on the land was also aggravated by numerous levies, small and large, including the strange tax on the bey's teeth while he ate the peasants' food (the "chew tax"). The peasant was exhausted by the system of leasing tax collection privileges. In 1886 the "tithe"[1] in Hercegovina amounted to more than all other taxes together. The situation was similar in other provinces of the empire, taxes being collected at four levels: village, district, provincial, and imperial. The violence perpetrated during collection of taxes and debts (the peasants were hanged by the feet, head down in smoke from wet straw) produced a long and ugly epic of suffering for which later generations of peasants took revenge. The position of the Bosnian peasant and the Bosnian social situation in general were of prominent significance for Yugoslav history in its entirety, as the uprising of 1875–1878 in Bosnia was one of the most fateful turning points in that history.

Railroad Construction and the Role of the Great Powers

Foreign capital in the Balkan Peninsula began to perform a decisive role, for major undertakings, like the construction of railways as the sole great technological enterprise of the times, depended on it. In the sixties European imperialist states sought the best route to the Middle East and the Suez Canal (opened in 1869) through the Balkan Peninsula. The political interests of the European and Balkan national states in eastern and southern seas were just as tortuous as the railway lines mapped out by their engineers. Istanbul, Salonika, and a port on the Adriatic coast near Scutari were three strategic areas around which history revolved. Austria, Russia, Germany, England, Serbia, and Bulgaria trained their glances on these three points, where the main railway lines terminated. After its defeat in the Crimean War, Russia was to come back to this area in 1871 as a technologically modernized imperialist state. Russia's encounter with Western imperialism in the Balkan Peninsula, along strategic lines inspired

---

[1] Literally a tenth *(desetina)*, but in practice the tax amounted to far more than the name implies.

perhaps by the ghost of Peter the Great, generated a new phase in the history of spheres of interest in this area.

By a law of 1854, Austria planned the extension of its southern railways toward Istanbul via Zemun. This policy of railroad expansion was to accelerate Austria's defeat in Europe in 1866. From then on, penetration of the Balkan Peninsula and Near East became not only a matter of the utmost urgency but a question of life and death for it. The best route for the planned line ran through Bosnia, Serbia, and Romania to Istanbul, but Hungary and Serbia blocked the way. A signed agreement between the Turkish government and Baron Maurice de Hirsch, a leading European banker, brought to the Balkans one of the most prominent representatives of world imperialism, who figured more importantly in Balkan history than any of its rulers of that day. With Austrian capital to back him, de Hirsch succeeded in corrupting the highest Turkish authorities to such an extent that they provided him with forced labor for the construction of the first embankments.

Serbia's failure over the Eastern Question in 1875–1878 bound its economy even more closely to that of Austria-Hungary. At the Congress of Berlin in July 1878, Serbian and Austrian ministers signed a convention favorable to Austria for the construction of a railway through Serbia.

Planning railway construction itself, the Serbian government had concluded an agreement with the French banking house of l'Union Générale, the president of which was Paul Eugène Bontoux (1820–1904). On favorable terms, it was to construct a single-track railway line from Belgrade to Niš and Vranje, and after completion the banking house was to enjoy the right of utilizing it for twenty-five years. Bontoux calculated that he would earn 30 million francs on this deal in Serbia, for which the government of Prince Milan Obrenović (1854–1901) offered him attractive financial conditions and guarantees. The Austrian banks also were interested in the construction of Serbian railways. A scandal followed the exposure of Bontoux's corruption of Serbian politicians, including the prince himself, and the public's interest in this affair smoldered on for decades. When Bontoux crashed, a consortium with mixed capital replaced him in Serbia. The consequence was a powerful breakthrough of foreign capital into Serbia; in time, the influence of that capital on politics and society became immeasurable though not always discernible. From the corruption of ministers and the enrichment of resourceful individuals to the ways of foreign policy, everywhere the secret finger of foreign capital was present. With somewhat over 500 kilometers of railway lines, most of them transit, Serbia held last place in Europe.

In the meantime, de Hirsch constructed a line from Novi to Banja Luka in 1872, and the Salonika-Skoplje line in Macedonia, which he took as far as Mitrovica in 1874. The intention of extending it later to Bosnia never materialized for, in 1888, it was linked up with the Serbian railways via Vranje. Bosnia was left without a railway line to Istanbul, and it was only later that Austria laid a

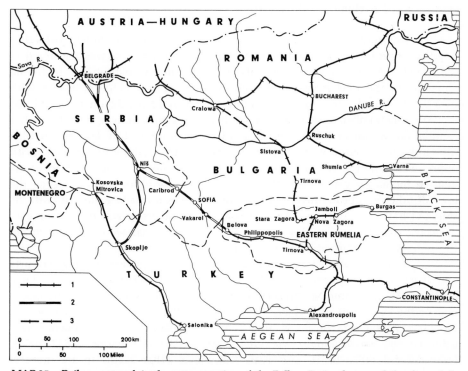

MAP 35.   Railway network in the eastern section of the Balkan Peninsula toward the close of the nineteenth century. (1) Railways which began operation before 1886; (2) railways which began operation before 1897; (3) Bomberg's railway plan.

narrow-gage line from Brod to Sarajevo (after 1879), lengthened in 1891 to Metković, whence lines ran to Gruž and Zelenika.

For strategic considerations Russia was keenly interested in lines along the Danube and Vardar River valley. In 1878 the Russian banking house of Günzburg began to construct a line through Bulgaria, Turkey, and Macedonia, supported not only by Russian capital but by the strategic interest of Russia in the Balkan Peninsula. The upshot was a clash of Russian and Austrian capital in this area. The struggle of European capital for control of Balkan railways was one of the principal reasons for the Serbo-Bulgarian War of 1885.

In 1880, when de Hirsch sold his right to construct Turkish railways, German capital appeared on the scene in guise of the Deutschbank, one of the principal purchasers of de Hirsch's vast interests. German capital intended to lengthen these lines in the Balkan Peninsula to Asia Minor and Baghdad (later known as the Baghdad Line) and, by controlling this main artery, to draw off the commercial and economic cream produced by the Balkan peoples.

The Development of Culture

Yugoslav culture in the second half of the nineteenth century yielded to impulses from the realities of the historical situation. Progress was registered in the growth of the number of educational and cultural institutions. In Serbia alone the number of elementary schools rose from 274 in 1855 to 936 in 1900 with over 100,000 pupils. In Croatia the number increased from 221 in 1851 to 1,337 in 1903. The number of secondary schools rose proportionately, and the earlier foundations of universities in Serbia and Croatia continued to develop. In 1865 the old lycée in Serbia was transformed into a higher school of learning. With improvements in the system of teaching, the expansion of various departments, and the increasing capabilities of professors, this institution soon achieved the level of other European universities, although it was formally endowed with the status of university only in 1905. In Croatia the university was opened on old, neglected foundations in 1874, and although its diplomas were not recognized throughout the empire, it soon overcame its initial weaknesses.

A number of men rose to prominence and distinction in Yugoslav arts and sciences. In linguistics were Djura Daničić (1825–1882), Vatroslav Jagić (1838–1923), and Tomo Maretić (1854–1938). The latter wrote a scientific grammar of the "Croatian or Serbian" language in 1899, which helped to integrate the literary language of Serbs and Croats. In historiography eminence was achieved by Stojan Novaković (1842–1915), Ilarion Ruvarac (1832–1905), Franjo Rački (1828-1894), and Ivan Kukuljević (1816-1889). In the natural sciences the roster included the botanist Josif Pančić (1814–1888) and the mathematician Mihailo Petrović-Alas (1868–1943).

The advancement of culture generally was accompanied by the strengthening of cultural institutions. The Yugoslav Academy of Arts and Sciences was inaugurated in Zagreb in 1867, and in Serbia the Serbian Learned Society *(Srpsko učeno društvo)* was transformed by a law of 1886 into the Serbian Royal Academy. But until the very end of Austria-Hungary's existence, the Slovenes failed to acquire a university or an academy of sciences; in spite of this, science made considerable headway.

Theaters also were marked out for progress. The Serbian Theater was opened in 1861 in Novi Sad, where the first generations of actors were trained for the theaters in Belgrade and Zagreb. In Belgrade the National Theater opened its doors for the first time in 1869, and in Zagreb as early as 1861. By the century's end, a network of theaters had been set up in Croatia, Serbia, and Dalmatia. In Slovenia the political framework frustrated the development of this institution. Although the performing arts were flourishing as early as 1848, they were given firm foundations only with the opening of the New Province Theater in 1892. These were the principal cultural institutions, but many minor ones functioned alongside them.

A salient feature of this cultural growth was the advancement of cultural institutions in the more highly developed regions of the north and their intimate connection with national policies and ideology, as cultural institutions and the development of separate national entities paralleled each other in their evolution. Culture could hardly succeed, if indeed it ever tried to do so, in divorcing itself from its historic destiny to perform the role of an instrument of nation building, of promotion of separate national ideologies, or of the ideology of unification on an all-Yugoslav scale. Furthermore, cultural institutions, even when independent, like theaters and newspapers, were subjected to the ever-present supervision of the state. Some of them were also created and managed by the state.

A further striking characteristic of this cultural development was the more rapid headway of the arts in relation to the sciences, the latter associated mostly with schools, museums, and the two academies of science. Again, the social sciences recorded more rapid progress than the natural (notably linguistics, historiography, history of literature, and literary criticism). The young bourgeois society in formation required a culture that could best serve the interest of its emotional and social integration. This explains why literature experienced a far more thorough and tempestuous flowering than any other branch, with the number of literary critics outrunning the number of creative writers. Talented young men were wont to turn to literature, which enjoyed undeniable hegemony in culture. In the popular consciousness, culture *was* literature and conversely it was literature that penetrated that consciousness more than any of the other arts.

The sixties saw the appearance of the first purely literary magazines: the *Morning Star* (*Danica*, 1860–1872) and some others among the Serbs, the *Wreath* (*Vijenac*, 1869–1903) among the Croats, and the *Ljubljana Bell* (*Ljubljanski zvon*, 1881), among the Slovenes, although attempts along these lines had also been made earlier. The pattern of literary history is quite similar among all the Yugoslav peoples. The transition from romanticism to realism came about 1870. Also common to all of them is the fact that, at least until the appearance of realism, writers sought refuge for national ideology and policy in literature, as they wrestled ceaselessly with conservative circles, the state, hunger, and its fellow traveler tuberculosis, long the evil attendant of Yugoslav culture. But if this literature was a refuge for national ideologies, it was to an equal extent the reflection of their weaknesses: literature influenced only a select circle of the literate, chiefly residents of towns, and made its mark on a broader, nationwide basis only in the long run. Other themes found far fewer readers in a society obsessed by the national question.

The foundations for Yugoslav literature in the second half of the nineteenth century were laid by prominent writers of the first half. Among the Serbs, these were Vuk Karadžić, linguist and historian, and Petar Petrović Njegoš, poet and statesman. The latter's epic poem *Mountain Wreath* (*Gorski vijenac*) was published in twenty editions between 1847 and 1913, to become the most widely read literary work among the Serbs. It was *The Mountain Wreath* together with the myth of Kosovo that provided the Serbian national movement with its ethic in the following century. The greats among the Croats were linguist Ljudevit Gaj and the national poet Ivan Mažuranić, the latter the author of the epic poem *The Death of Smail-Aga Čengić (Smrt Smail-Age Čengijića,* 1846). Among the Slovenes it was the grammarian Jernej Kopitar, and national poet France Prešern with his book of sonnets *Sonnet Wreath (Sonetni venec).* This polarity of linguists and poets (only in the Slovene case was the poetry not epic in character) cannot be considered a coincidence. It was from these roots that Yugoslav literature was to develop later. The poet and satirist Jovan Jovanović Zmaj (1833–1904), destined to become the most eminent Serbian poet of the latter half of the nineteenth century, was a happy combination of lyricist, children's poet, and patriot. Djura Jakšić (1832–1878), also a many-sided personality, was poet, dramatist, and painter. Laza Kostić (1841–1910) gained prominence through his poems and national dramas. In the coastal area, prose writer Stjepan Mitrov Ljubiša (1824–1878) won distinction for his tales of Montenegrin life. Croatian romanticism found its most eminent exponent in the person of novelist August Šenoa (1838–1881), whose books gave generations of schoolchildren their basic insight into the world of literature. Also of significance were Mirko Bogović (1816–1893) and Luka Botić (1830–1860). Of the Slovenes, Fran Levstik (1831–1887) wrote both prose and poetry, as well as political essays, while he tried to purify the Slovene language of German influence. In his works Levstik posed the Slovene national question for the sophisticated reading public. In the most famous tale, *Martin Krpan of Vrh* (1858), he portrayed a Slovene peasant whose enormous strength made him the only person capable of saving the emperor in Vienna from deadly peril; as a reward, he was offered the role of court jester at the court in Vienna. Generations to come absorbed the moral of the story. Other writers of note were Simon Jenko (1835–1869), Janez Trdina (1830–1905), Simon Gregorčič (1841–1906), and Josip Stritar (1836–1923).

In contrast to the romanticists, who acted as nation builders in composing their lyrics, epic poetry, and national dramas in verse form, the new generation of realists began to look upon their surroundings after 1870 with more sobriety and introversion. The novel came to prevail, alongside short stories with a social bent and prose drama, which failed to make much of an impression. This was a sign not only of the new spirit in literature, but also of general maturity. With their poetry the romanticists had proved the worth of the language of their people, installing it among the other languages of the European community where it had previously been unknown. The realists went on from there to depict to the world the shortcomings of their society. The Croatian realists concentrated on themes of bourgeois and petty bourgeois life (possibly because most of them belonged to the Movement of Rights), whereas the Serbs focused more on the villages. Their critical attitude toward the society in which they lived derived not only from the fact that the foundations of the new movement in Serbia had been laid by socialists, and their ideas of democracy and a Balkan federation, but also from the political apathy typifying the regimes of the last members of the Obrenović dynasty.

Serbian realism sprang from the criticism of society inaugurated by Ljuben Karavelov and Svetozar Marković. Marković's articles *Singing and Thinking* (1868) and *Reality in Poetry* (1870) paved the way for the new generation of writers who were to follow up the ideas of their teacher about the democratization of society and liberation from within, to lay the foundations for the Balkan federation of nations and general social progress. It was at this time that the center of Serbian literature moved from Hungarian parts to Šumadija.

A few writers stand out among the many, and these few future generations will not forget: prose writers Jakov Ignjatović (1824–1889), Milovan Glišić (1847–1908), Laza Lazarević (1851–1890), Stevan Sremac (1855–1906), and Sima Matavulj (1852–1908), and the poet Vojislav Ilić (1862–1894). Outstanding among the Croats were novelists Evgenij Kumičić (1850–1904), Ante Kovačić (1854–1889), and the most prolific of them all, Ksaver Šandor Djalski (1854–1935). Also in this category are the poet Silvije Strahimir Kranjčević (1865–1908) and the short-story writer Vjenceslav Novak (1859–1905). From the older generation, the Slovene realists inherited a division into conservatives and liberals. Among them prominence was achieved by Janko Kersnik (1852–1897), Anton Aškerc (1856–1912), and Ivan Tavčar (1851–1923).

Toward the end of the century, when the wellspring of realism began to run dry, the new literature, the beginnings of which coincided with the dawn of the succeeding century, inherited from the old much that had suffered from underdevelopment. As it advanced, it first abandoned the influences of German literature, which had dominated the romanticists, and of Russian literature, to which the realists had looked. It was now French literature, the influence of which had run strong also during the period of realism, that came to the forefront. The critic and literary historian Jovan Skerlić, responsible for the "new wave" in Serbia, later explained that France was "the pathfinder for peoples to the bright truth and humanitarian ideals," whereas Russia was semi-Asiatic, Austria feudal and clerical, England plutocratic, and Germany a land with the mentality of a corporal. Under this literary banner, social progress generally began to move in the same direction.

In contrast to literature, the fine arts and music were not able to strike deep roots or to win the confidence of society. They focused on the towns and, toward the end of the nineteenth century, on the largest urban centers alone. Their development among the various Yugoslav nationalities was not as even as that of literature had been. Nonetheless, in the seventies a transition to a new phase, in motifs and techniques, is noticeable everywhere. The new century ushered in the era of modern art after attempts had been made since the middle of the nineteenth to wrest painting and music from their traditional dependence on the church and wealthy merchants, on religious compositions, portraiture, choral music, and rousing national songs and to invest them with more contemporary form and substance.

The most noteworthy development in music in the second half of the century was the appearance of the national opera, which at first surged forward more rapidly among the Slovenes and Croats than the Serbs. The establishment of musical societies and academies of music (the Zagreb Conservatory, the Opera of Croatia, the Ljubljana Conservatory—all in 1870) channeled this development toward European models. The enthusiasm for national motifs during the mid-century renaissance waned with the introduction of Bach's absolutism, only to revive after 1870. Two names dominate the scene among the Croats: Vatroslav Lisinski [the operas *Love and Malice (Ljubav i zloba*, 1846) and *Porin* (1897)], and Ivan Zajc. Among the Slovenes, those to gain distinction were Gustav Ipavec, Fran Gerbič, and Anton Foerster. Two names in Serbia provide the framework for the history of national music: Kornelije Stanković at the beginning of this period, and Steven Mokranjac toward the end. Mokranjac's fifteen compositions known as *Rukoveti* are considered the pinnacle of achievement in Serbian music.

Slowly painting and sculpture began to find their place in the course of European art. Traditionally painters received their training at home, in Temišvar, in Vienna, in Italian academies, and in Munich. But as the new century approached, a strong tendency to study in the European art center—Paris—became manifest. Vjekoslav Karas, a Croatian known as the "first Illyrian painter," was schooled in Italy. Succeeding generations of painters (Ferdo Kvikerez, Celestin Medović, Vlaho Bukovac) broadened horizons with their own culture and achievement. Croatian painting reached its zenith in the works of Josip Račić and Miroslav Kraljević. The construction of an art gallery in Zagreb with funds provided by Bishop Strossmayer gave important impetus to the development and guidance of painting.

A number of distinguished artists among the Slovenes (Miha Stroj, Matevž Langus, Janez Volf, and Marko Pernhart) won for their art a better place in the society of their nation than it had previously enjoyed.

Romantic painting among the Serbs is best represented by the works of Djura Jakšić, equally distinguished as painter and poet. By introducing national and secular motifs, Konstantin Danil was highly instrumental in ridding art of the classical tradition. On this basis, a style of painting dominated by compositions portraying scenes from the national history came to be developed (Uroš Predić and Paja Jovanović).

CHAPTER 28

Civil Liberties, Constitutional Systems, and Political Parties

Only a small stratum of the privileged took part in the affairs of state and official policymaking, their numbers kept down by the slack development of constitutional and electoral systems and also of political parties. In Serbia, where the common man had been drawn into the business of governing since Karadjordje's time, official policy relied in mounting degree on the relatively small number of people living in towns, and on the civil servants. In the lands under Hapsburg control, few could participate in political life: the landowners, the wealthier sections of the town population, intellectuals, and some of the richer peasants, although the peasantry as a whole was kept well in the background.

375

As the national movements advocated the new concept of the state, they were to become the medium through which the peasantry embarked upon political life, although it never came to partake in actual decision making. In countries under Turkish administration, there were, in principle, no policies that took public opinion into consideration at all, and the will of the people was expressed only in revolutionary movements.

Constitutional Changes in the Hapsburg Empire after 1861

In the Hapsburg empire the Constitution of 1861 introduced an inconsistent centralism and a central parliament whose 343 deputies were delegated originally by provincial representative bodies rather than elected directly. Of the Yugoslav lands, Dalmatia, Istria, Carniola, Carinthia, Gorizia, and Styria had such bodies. Croatia was by tradition linked with Hungary, the latter acquiring its own separate system only after the Croatian-Hungarian Compromise of 1868.

For the provincial representative bodies (called sabors in most South Slav lands), deputies were elected by a limited number of people, indirectly and orally, through electors and curiae—groups of voters selected in accordance with class and social criteria. The majority vote prevailed, but voting was oral rather than by ballot, the authorities were always at hand, and there was no question of any direct or secret vote. Different numbers of deputies were elected to the curiae: one-fourth from among the big landowners, one-fourth from the cities, and two-fifths from the wealthier peasants. Only a thin crust of the population was involved in this electoral system. In Carniola in 1861, it was only 8.4 percent of the people, and in Istria 8 percent. In practice the percentage was even smaller, as in such inert societies not all those enjoying the right to vote exercised it. The electoral system favored the urban centers, which, with the exception of Ljubljana and certain Dalmatian towns, were largely German and Italian.

The modified electoral system of 1848 was in force in Croatia. The electoral system of 1861, apart from seating appointed members from the ranks of the higher clergy, nobility, and civil servants, made provision for elections in the županijas, the free royal cities, the "free chartered market towns," and larger communes, and also among the Catholic and Orthodox clergy (seven Catholic and four Orthodox). Elections were public and indirect, as in other parts of the monarchy. Homeowners in the towns elected electors who in turn chose one deputy per district under the watchful eye of the authorities. Jews and Protestants could not be elected deputies. The system in Croatia was modified on a number of occasions. It was adapted to the compromise with the Hungarians in 1868, as the Croatian Assembly sent its deputies to a joint parliament. The electoral system was also changed through simplification of voting machinery and introduction of high poll taxes, but the number of people participating in elections was kept down. In Croatia it has been estimated as less than 2 percent of the population.

The electoral reforms of 1873 in the Austrian part of the empire, and of 1874 in the Hungarian, failed to produce any tangible improvement. The same applies to the reforms of 1882. More stress was laid on increasing provincial and national autonomy than on individual liberties. The consequence was a strengthening of the national oligarchies. In the electoral reform of 1896, the Viennese government endeavored, by instituting a fifth curia, to open the doors of parliament to the working class, but even after the electoral reforms of 1907 and 1910, it was difficult to democratize that system in both parts of the empire.

The Vojvodina Serbs, although lacking administrative autonomy and their own political representative body, had an irregular and inconstant representative body in their church synods, which discussed ecclesiastical and educational matters. Up to 1871 these sabors were elected on the basis of the old electoral provisions dating from 1779, according to which three estates (church, military, and civilian) sent twenty-five representatives each to the Assembly. From 1871 onwards, there were fifty temporal representatives to twenty-five ecclesiastical. The Hungarian government deprived this sabor of the right to discuss political affairs, limiting its competence to church and educational questions.

The Role of Law in the Empire

The restricted liberties in the Hapsburg empire (the Law on University Education of 1874, the Press Law of 1907) revealed the snail's pace of the process by which the modern citizen was taking shape. Such a system required solid legislation and a strong legal tradition to maintain it, and the empire truly was a state of law. The bureaucracy had developed the concept of the *Rechtsstaat*, in which law and the lawyer were needed to reconcile the new measures taken by the government with the living traditions upon which the system was based, and also to deal with the endless lawsuits in which the poor peasants engaged, entangled in their intricate agrarian relations. The state as absolute and supreme arbiter of individual affairs found fertile ground in the primitive agrarian community. The individual in that state enjoyed some protection, as the laws were generally applicable and did not depend on the will of the authorities. Resistance to despotism was manifested by intellectual and well-educated circles but mostly through patient waiting that dragged on for several successive generations in the absence of any democratic examples to draw upon in previous history. The net result was the creation of a mentality of obedience. The highly developed law resulted in the conspicuous tendency for political parties to be conducted by lawyers, and for all political ideology to emanate from them. These parties and ideology were therefore ridden with the spirit of legitimism and shallow high-flown rhetorics. Through the lawyers, the political parties were hitched by invisible threads to domestic and foreign banking circles. This type of law went hand in hand with despotism, with the congealing of undemocratic political practices into rigid legal norms. As the Croatian parties were led, apart from lawyers, also by writers and Catholic clergymen, they were all infected with the spirit of doctrine and dogma. By and large, they concerned themselves with determining national objectives based on historic rights and the past. The prevailing policy of the Hapsburg monarchy, as well as the existence of privileged groups called "political people" which influenced the state and government, was based entirely on the aristocratic persuasion that the people had to be ruled, even though this was done against the formal backdrop of parliamentary life. The vast majority of the people were not citizens who, having won political liberties, participated in the affairs of state, but rather political subjects to whom some freedom had been granted as a gift which, when the need arose, was taken away.

The inevitable upshot of this unpromising social state of affairs was that all political parties, without exception (including opposition parties and those termed people's movements by the historians, except for the socialists and branches of the socialist movement), adapted their programs, objectives, and organization to this social fabric.

The Development of the Parliamentary System in Serbia before 1903

Constitutional development in Serbia took a different turn. With no powerful upper classes or stable monarchy, Serbia slowly and laboriously developed its own peculiar brand of parliamentary system, adapted to the general upsurge of the bourgeoisie and the political retrogression of the peasantry, and making occasional concessions to the state bureaucracy which, as an institution, had emerged as a power above the people. The focus of state leadership was transferred more and more to the towns and the Serbian national bourgeoisie. The stratum which had run the state for four decades slowly withdrew, and the constitutional system was steadily changed for the better. Prince Mihajlo's Law on the National Assembly of 1861 gave the franchise to all those who paid taxes, but the decision to limit deputies to one per 2,000 people decreased the number of representatives to a quarter of the number elected by earlier custom. In contrast to previous practice, the Assembly was convened triennially. But the prince did not respect this rule; obsessed by the inevitability of war with Turkey, he instituted a personal regime independent of parliament. Even if the Assembly had been convened, the legal provision making a deputy liable to trial in court for remarks made in parliament would have reduced that body to a negligible force.

The death of Prince Mihajlo in 1868 was followed by public discussion of constitutional changes in Serbia, the lively debates registering not only demands for introduction of universal franchise, toward which the people had striven a full fifty years in the teeth of opposition from their arrogant rulers, but also seemingly exotic ideas about parliaments based on classes (with merchants, peasants, and civil servants sending deputies to the Assembly, much as in the Austrian curial system). There were also some champions of the type of bicameral system that would secure for the upper classes the right to rule the state.

The Constitution of December 1869 remedied the situation somewhat, but a third of the deputies were still appointed by the government, the remaining ones being elected. The executive branch acquired the right, in case of "danger to public security," to suspend civil and political liberties. The rigid centralized system of local administration was retained, and the government was not responsible to the Assembly. It was only in 1874 that a government fell for the first time in Serbian history after failing to win a solid majority in the Assembly. The 1869 Constitution also kept the tax census as a basis for franchise, thus limiting the electoral body by applying the criterion of class.

The Constitution of 1888 reduced the tax basis for voters. An abortive popular revolt of 1883 (the Revolt of Timok) resulted in the introduction of rather liberal provisions in the Constitution of 1888, which proclaimed that "all Serbs are equal before the law. Titles of nobility for Serbian citizens can neither be granted nor recognized. Personal liberty is guaranteed by this Constitution." By a coup d'état of 1893, the king revoked this Constitution and demanded the promulgation of a new one predicated on a higher tax as the basis for franchise, so that parliament might be dominated by the wealthier classes. The earlier Constitution of 1888 was a source of annoyance to the court because the Assembly had the right of full legislative initiative and discussion of the budget. The provision that ordinary deputies should be supplemented by "qualified deputies" with a university education was a concession to the high government bureaucracy, although it turned out to be ineffective in practice.

Some headway was made with the proclamation of the right of assembly, association and freedom of the press (1870), direct and secret elections, and communal self-administration (1875). Attempts to suspend these achievements proved unsuccessful. Proposals to institute a bicameral system in Serbia in 1901 failed, although perseveringly supported by the upper classes. After dynastic changes and popular movements in 1903, Serbia embarked upon an era of bourgeois liberalism. In 1904, 23 percent of the people in Serbia enjoyed the right to vote, the highest percentage in Europe, except Switzerland and France, from the latter of which the Serbian constitutional system took inspiration.

With the social advancement of the Serbian bourgeoisie, the peasants lost some of their earlier influence over the state. Two-thirds of the deputies to the Saint Andrew's Assembly of 1858 had been peasants; their number declined to one-third at the Assembly of 1874. Another section of the population that re-

FIGURE 35.   Paja Jovanović, "Cocks Fighting."

FIGURE 36.   View of Ohrid.

gressed together with the peasants were the village traders, who surrendered some of their influence to the urban merchants. Although this signified the retrogression of the ideology of an agrarian society, which slowly gave way to the political philosophy developing in the bourgeois towns, more than it did the actual backsliding of the peasantry, it was true that with the disappearance of the old ideas the peasant had fewer and fewer deputies to represent him in parliament.

Thus the unstable and deficient constitutional mechanism in Serbia determined the character, scope, ideology, and destiny of every political movement and every political party without exception. All of them felt the weight of the monarchy, police, and officer corps, and the veiled suspicions of the peasantry that freedom was not for them. Nonetheless, the system in Serbia offered the people incomparably more liberty there than in Austria and Turkey. Parties in Serbia were dominated by lawyers, professors, small proprietors, and clergymen. But even the monarchy had to react to the pressure of the people and the groups fighting for power, and to surrender to them from time to time. When it failed to do so, it was brought down. Between the time of Karadjordje and 1903, not a single Serbian ruler terminated his reign peacefully. They were banished, forced to abdicate, or even murdered.

Political Parties and Programs in the South Slav Lands

Under these constitutional systems, political parties acted as vehicles of the system. The essential difference between the political parties in Serbia and those in Austrian provinces of the Yugoslav lands was that the former accentuated civil liberties in an independent state and aspired to liberation of the Serbs in the neighboring lands of Austria and Turkey, whereas the latter directed their efforts largely to struggle for the independence of the nation as a whole, or for increased provincial autonomy. All these parties pursued certain paths that were typical of parties among all South Slavs: they tended to collect around a newspaper and a strong personality (or group) which then became the ideologue; their instability and interrupted continuity were provoked by the instability of the petty bourgeois party rank and file that made up the majority of their followers. The inconstancy of these groups manifested itself within parties in the form of factionalism and separatism. Among both Serbs and Croats, it was a popular saying that "two men make three parties."

Because of Croatia's geographic position, its parties in their foreign policy orientation were more inclined to pursue Central European than Balkan policies. The struggle of subjects for the status of citizens led in Serbia to the national state and in other Yugoslav lands to opposition to foreign states. In Montenegro and areas under Turkish rule, this dilemma was unknown to society. It beset only those who were beginning to doff their national costumes.

In Serbia organized political parties began with Serbian liberalism, which surfaced on the wreckage of the old police order of Prince Aleksandar Karadjordjević and Mihajlo Obrenović. Between 1859 and 1869 it was a loose-jointed movement striving for one idea; later, organized on firm political principles, it was led by Jovan Ristić and Jevrem Grujić, with Vladimir Jovanović as ideologue. Liberalism met the fate it did because of the conviction of its ideologues that in a monarchy which refused to renounce internal force, improvements could be achieved only peaceably. After 1893 the Serbian Liberals barely managed to exist, and after 1903 they stepped down from the political stage altogether.

In terms of social pattern, the Serbian Liberals were a combination of wealthy merchants, government employees, and rich peasants. The fact that the Serbian petty bourgeoisie was not attracted to them made them politically inconsistent. In annexes to their program (1881, 1888), when they had already begun to wane, the Liberals called for universal franchise, communal self-administration, free education, and a foreign policy predicated on confederation "among the eastern peoples who share the historical destiny and cultural interests" of the Serbian people.

When the Liberals were in the ascendancy as a political power, their principal rivals were the Conservatives, a group that had developed from the oligarchical Defenders of the Constitution under the leadership of Milutin Garašanin (1843–1898) and Jovan Marinović (1821–1893). With the police regime introduced by Prince Mihajlo, they disappeared from the political scene. But headed by the dynamic Aćim Čumić (1836–1901), they rose again between 1871 and 1873 in new guise, calling themselves the Young Conservatives. In 1881 they were renamed the Progressive party, but their broad program found few followers because its lofty and democratic promises were at odds with their movement's rigid tradition. The Progressives remained a party with a small number of adherents and little influence on society. As a matter of fact, their influence on official policy was greater than it was on society at large.

Even before the time of Svetozar Marković, the ideologue of Serbian socialism, there had been some socialist traditions in Serbia (Živojin Žujović), but it was Marković who laid solid foundations for this ideology. Educated in Russia and Switzerland under the influence of Europe's progressive thinkers, Marković gave philosophical formulation and impulse to modern Serbian democracy. His first political steps were taken within the United Serbian Youth, where all the rebels of the times found refuge. He was soon to object to its "having condemned itself to vegetate as a disorderly and useless literary society." It was his wish to galvanize the youth into a political party acting systematically and scientifically in line with socialist teachings.

In time Marković elaborated a systematic approach to the role of the Serbian people in modern history, most clearly set forth in his work *Serbia in the East* (1872). His thesis was that the Serbian people could liberate themselves only if the surrounding peoples still under Turkish and Austrian rule did likewise, although he did not envisage the Serbian state extending its administration to include them. Rather, they would all come together in freedom and equality. In order to perform its new role, Serbia would first have to emancipate itself internally. The initial step toward achieving this would be transformation of the old form of centralized state into a confederation of self-administered communes. Instead of replacing Turkish servitude by capitalism, Serbia should take advantage of its venerable social institutions, like the joint family and national assembly, to build a new society. The police force would be run on a communal basis, the courts would include panels of jurymen, and the standing army would be abolished. Formally speaking, his system was a republican one, but in a special way, for he had no particular respect for the republic as such, considering it an outmoded form of state. The historical objective of society was freedom based on the freedom of the individual. In this respect, Svetozar Marković was a rarity among Balkan politicians and ideologues, who were inclined to think of their own homogeneous nation as the final historical objective, and failed to look beyond.

Marković's ideas were first taken up by the young people and the small number of workers then in existence. But soon his writings found their way to even the remotest villages in Serbia. In 1871 and 1872, with his brother Jevrem and a group of like-minded men, he tried to start an uprising in Turkey, thus reversing the tendency of European socialists, after the failure of the Paris Commune in 1871, to renounce revolution as a political method.

Two political movements were to draw inspiration from Marković's thinking. His successors formed the Serbian Socialist movement. First, Mita Cenić (1851–1888) founded the General Workers' Society in Belgrade (1881), which adopted a program of struggle for a people's administration and Yugoslav federation. The tireless Vasa Pelagić, former Bosnian priest and convert to socialism, worked side by side with him. The early socialists had to shed many of the atavisms of the agrarian society, which both nourished and strangled them, and also the inevitable social demagoguery. In spite of all obstacles, they succeeded in creating a fine and powerful tradition on which later socialism was to develop. Red banners appeared in Kragujevac in 1876. When Dimitrije Tucović (1881–1914) founded the Social Democratic Party of Serbia (1903), it already had strong backing from the people.

This Serbian socialism was closely associated with socialism in the Austrian lands, for which the foundations were laid in the late sixties by foreign workers. The Society for Advancement of Workers was set up in Osijek in 1867. In 1871 a branch of the First International was also established in Osijek via Budapest, but the authorities refused to certify its rules and regulations. The Social Democratic Party of Croatia and Slavonia was founded in 1894, and in 1896 the Yugoslav Social Democratic party in Slovenia (within the frameworks of the Austrian Social Democratic Party), which was joined in 1903 by the Social Democratic Party of Dalmatia.

The Radical Party of Serbia was another organization that drew upon the ideas of Svetozar Marković, having developed from the peasant group of Adam Bogosavljević (1844–1880). As opponents of the regime, the Radicals expounded universal franchise, communal self-administration, and an up-to-date parliament. The ordinary Serbian soon directed his political activities to maintaining a steady barrage against the unpopular bureaucracy. The Radicals won the support of all those who "wore sheepskin coats and peasant moccasins." They were the first in Serbia to set up a radical party organization, which by 1883 had swelled to 60,000 enrolled members and just as many unregistered supporters. Without doubt, it was the most massive organized movement in the Balkan Peninsula of that time.

The leadership of the Radical party was in the hands of the petty bourgeoisie, and the party itself drew its adherents from small provincial towns. Its program of 1888, clear and pithy, was printed several times in thousands of copies. So popular did it become that some even styled it the political prayer book of the small town in Serbia. Its nine condensed chapters called for thorough reform of the Serbian state, including a parliament elected by direct and universal franchise of all adults, and self-administration in the districts. Other demands concerned elected courts and direct and progressive taxation. Education was to be "general, compulsory, and free," and a people's militia was proposed to replace the system of recruitment then in force.

In the course of the next two decades, the party lost its onetime vitality and turned more for support to the privileged classes in the larger towns; originally a petty bourgeois party, it became bourgeois, its nationalism adapted to the economic interests of the bourgeoisie. Questions of internal democracy in Serbia were subordinated to questions of the nation's position in the Balkan Peninsula. In 1901 the Independent Radical Faction, continuing to support the old program, broke off from it and in 1905 constituted itself as a separate party.

In the first phase of its development, until it degenerated into a party of the urban rich, the Radicals tried to invest their foreign policy platform with more flexibility than other Balkan nationalist movements, and in their program of 1881 they raised the question of creating a Balkan federation, beginning with Serbia, Bulgaria, and Montenegro.

Political parties in Croatia developed from the roots implanted during the time of the Illyrian movement. The National party in Croatia inherited the Illyrian traditions and shaped itself accordingly. It shed the name "Illyrian" and replaced it by "Croatian" for strategic reasons on the advice of Ivan Kukuljević in 1858, who stated that the new name would be necessary "until we Slavs in the South unify at long last and take a name that offends no one."

The National party in Dalmatia, and to some extent the National Free-

thinking party in Vojvodina, resembled the Croatian party politically and ideologically. In the early phase of development, all of them were more like national
fronts in their regions than real political parties. Ideas of self-administration
in the districts like those in Switzerland ("Eastern Switzerland") and of a Yugoslav federation were advocated by the National party in Vojvodina. It modified
its program in 1872 and in 1879 it disintegrated into a number of parties: national, liberal, and radical. The National party was a continuation of its predecessor, but with an altered program. It lasted until 1884 and during the period of its
duration was popularly known as the party of "notables." A group of Miletić's
friends went by the name of the Liberal party after they made an attempt to come
together again in 1885. Their program called for the independence of Hungary,
equality for all nationalities living in it, and equality for Serbs and Croats in
education, judiciary, and administration. Early in 1885 the foundations were
also laid for the Serbian Radical party in Hungary, Croatia, and Slavonia, and by
1887 its organization was completed. In 1895 the Liberals and Radicals effected
a rapprochement, brought together particularly by their joint support for the
program of the "Federation of the Three Nationalities of Hungary"—Serbian,
Slovak, and Romanian. Their platform stressed autonomous rule in the županijas,
universal franchise, and autonomy for schools and churches.

Prior to 1870 the National parties in Croatia and Dalmatia were a joint
movement of Croats and Serbs. In the eighties the Serbs in Croatia proper constituted 26 percent and in Dalmatia 17 percent of the entire population. Slowly
the Serbs and Croats in these parties parted ways. From then on, the Serbs tried
to form separate parties striving for recognition of nationality, and in doing so
usually leaned on the regime for support. The Serbian National Independent
party in Croatia began to function in 1887, defending the national individuality
of Serbs and equality between Serbs and Croats. They also asked that the name
and language of the Serbs be recognized in all official acts, that Serbian autonomous schools be opened, and that equality between the Orthodox and Catholic
churches be respected. In Dalmatia the Serbs detached themselves from the Croats
to form a separate party in 1879. There was also a separate movement of "Catholic Serbs" under the leadership of Baron Franco Gundulić of Dubrovnik. Its
ideologue was a Catholic priest, Ivo Stojanović, and the movement encompassed
a section of the educated Catholics in the Dalmatian towns.

The disintegration of the old national parties into separate groups illustrates the extent to which the onetime front movements had failed to clear up
certain unsettled accounts, and also points up the clash between various interest
groups who comprised the so-called "political people" within the frameworks
of the highly inappropriate constitutional mechanism. Factions broke away from
the National parties in Croatia and Dalmatia to form separate parties on the
grounds of political and not national considerations. In the sixties one of these
parties was the Autonomous National party *(Samostalna narodna stranka)*

headed by Ivan Mažuranić, which sought Croatian political reliance on Austria. In the eighties another such was the Independent National party *(Neodvisna narodna stranka)*; they were called the *Obzoraši*, from the name of the newspaper *Obzor (Horizon)*. In Dalmatia one wing broke off temporarily from the National party, calling itself the Land party *(Zemljačka stranka)* and pursuing a separatist policy.

The moving spirits of the National party in Croatia were the bishop of Djakovo, Josif Juraj Strossmayer, and the historian Franjo Rački. Strossmayer, former court chaplain in Vienna, assisted the National party financially after he became bishop of Djakovo, with a parish of 300,000 and income of a million forints annually. By financing a number of cultural institutions (the Yugoslav Academy of Arts and Sciences, the Art Gallery, and the university), he promoted a twofold objective: the nationalization of Croatian culture through the new institutions, and the pursuit of some of his South Slav convictions.

The platform and ideology of the National party in Croatia were determined not only by its Illyrian roots but also by historical events which proved stronger than it was. Its historical mission was truly Yugoslav, although in the beginning the focus was on Croatia. Moreover, until its illusions about the good intentions of the Viennese court were shattered in 1867, it thought along the lines of solving the complex of Yugoslav political problems (including Bosnia) within the confines of the monarchy and without Serbia. From then on, Serbia was regarded as the South Slav center, although at times belief faltered both in its strength and in the good faith of its Yugoslav intentions. For a time after 1868, the party supported the idea of Serbia's liberating Bosnia and Hercegovina, and thus laying the indispensable geographic and political foundation for Yugoslavia. Strossmayer believed that Serbia would thus be swerved from its narrow national objectives toward the general Yugoslav aim.

The Yugoslav ideals of the National parties in Croatia and Dalmatia retained a great deal of the premises of the old Illyrism, both formally and substantively. The Yugoslavs were considered one people, who had preserved their ancient ethnical names of Serbs, Croats, Slovenes, and Bulgarians as the "tribes" of a single nation. Miho Klaić (1829–1886), one of the leaders of the Dalmatian Populists, stated on one occasion in 1887: "As far as I am concerned, there are not two nationalities, the Serbian and Croatian. There are two tribes of one and the same nation." The basis for this Yugoslavdom was the common literary language and the need to develop it further. This unity served as the point of departure for all political plans and considerations. The languages of the Balkan Slavs had not yet been divided up, and the renaissance spirit from the time of Kopitar and Šafarik was still an invigorating force. According to these ideas, the Slovene and Bulgarian languages were variants of a single Yugoslav tongue, and the peoples concerned there were the tribal offshoots of a single nation. In 1861 the Croatian Assembly passed a decision by majority vote to call the language in

Croatia "Yugoslav." The deputies had had submitted to them four possible choices for the naming of the language ("national," "Croatian-Slavonic," "Croatian or Serbian," and "Yugoslav"). When the Assembly was dissolved soon afterward, that decision was revoked. Through the efforts of the imperial commissioner in Croatia, Ivan Mažunarić, the language came to be called Croatian.

But the Illyrian spirit of Yugoslav unity existed side by side with its invisible historical assumption—the struggle for prestige between the eastern and western sections of the South Slavs, which the hegemonic Germans and Hungarians did everything in their power to conceal. The National parties were bourgeois movements which failed to grow into large popular organizations although for a time they were the strongest political parties in Croatia and Dalmatia. Their ideology of Yugoslavhood was undermined by the realities of the defeats of 1868 and 1878, while the pressure of events relegated them to a realistic place in political life. The general tendency to assimilate what these parties called "tribes" into a nation invested their ideas of Yugoslavhood with an apostolic character that they were too fragile to promote. On the other hand, Croatian society itself was too weak to attain to leadership in the Balkan Peninsula through the medium of such ideas. Although these ideas achieved little that was practical or lasting, they were a vital and at times even a dominant force in the sphere of ideology and culture for many decades.

The chief rivals in the National parties were the Unionists (in Croatia) and the Autonomists (in Dalmatia). The former strove for a close alliance between Croatia and Hungary and the latter for Dalmatian autonomy in the Austrian section of the empire, with a separate Dalmatian assembly and administration conducted in Italian. The Autonomists represented the townspeople, largely landowners, civil servants, and a section of the intelligentsia. Their leader, Ante Bajamonti (1822–1891), a popular mayor of Split who made his town the principal stronghold of the Autonomists and kept it that way until 1882, devised the slogan "Whether Italians or Slavs, we are all Dalmatians." They themselves were also guilty of abusing the general Yugoslav character of the first phase of national awakening in Dalmatia and its powerful tradition. The common folk were truly conscious of being Slavs, especially those living south of the Neretva River. In Dubrovnik they formed a movement through which an attempt was made, during the crucial period 1878–1885, to preserve Serbo-Croat unity. The peasant masses of central Dalmatia, once they began to awaken politically, resurrected their old national names, which had long been suppressed, although in Dalmatia, as in all areas that spoke the same language but professed various religions, the role of national dividing line between Serbs and Croats was played not by the consciousness of belonging to one or the other nation but by religious affiliation.

In contrast to the National parties, the Croatian Party of Rights under the leadership of Dr. Ante Starčević and Eugen Kvaternik advocated Croatian independence from both Austria and Hungary, and emancipation of Croatian national ideas from powerful Serbian influence. Originally they drew support from the Unionist ban, Levin Rauch, who upheld them as allies against the National party.

The historical significance of the Rights movement lay in its providing the background for cultivation of an exclusive Croatian nationalism. It interrupted the continuity of the Yugoslav orientation in Croatian national ideology and endeavored to constitute a purely Croatian nation, divorced from its Yugoslav frameworks. Certainly the ground had been broken for this by the way the idea of Croatia had taken shape in 1848 and later, rather than by the efforts of the inconsistent exponents of Croatin nationalism.

When they said "Croatia," the Rights movement advocates meant "historical and natural" Croatia, as Kvaternik put it, extending from the Soča River in the west to an undeterminate boundary in the east. Sometimes this was the Drina River, sometimes the Timok and Bojana Rivers. In this area Slovenes, Serbs, and Muslim Bosnians would have to be assimilated by Croats. But these ideas remained in the sphere of ideology, as practically and politically the Rights advocates realized they had not enough strength to put their policies through. In contrast to other Croatian parties of the times, the Rights movement ideology possessed many elements characteristic of the great nationalist movements of the succeeding century: the geopolitical basis of the nation; the preservation of the old social order and the joint family; emphasis on the virtues of the peasants generally; avoidance of industrial civilization, railways, and the proletariat. They strove to sidestep a rift in the nation as the upshot of class struggle and preached class harmony for the general good of the nation as a whole. In his "Instructions" to party members in 1871, Starčević wrote: "The peasantry and the lowest class of townspeople on one side, and all the other classes on the other, are two inimical groups in Croatia. Neither of them can achieve anything by itself, but in harmony they are all-powerful. The party will weld those two large groups of people and all their parts together." The Rights movement made a particular point of insisting on the purity of the Croatian literary tongue. Starčević himself railed against the linguistic reforms of Vuk Karadžić. Although a staunchly Catholic movement, the Rights party objected that the Catholic clergy did not maintain sufficient purity of language. In 1871, defending his "theistic and Christian viewpoint," Kvaternik wrote that the liberation of Croatia would simultaneously signify the liberation of her religion. He attacked the Paris Commune for negating God, the nation, the state, and private property.

The Rights party waited patiently for an opportune moment in foreign affairs, hopefully expecting support from some big power to implement its ideas. In the beginning it turned to France (1860), then Germany (1871), for as Starčević put it, "Austrian and external Germanity will crush the Hungarians." They pinned some temporary hope on Russia in 1878, after being convinced of the obvious truth that Russia was not creating a great Orthodox Serbia in the Balkans, as the Rights party had been led to believe.

Starčević, under attack by his opponents for his narrow-minded views, nevertheless stuck to his ideas. The radically disposed section of Croatian society found him attractive for his tempestuous, solitary intransigence and fascinating personal appearance, enhanced by a magnificent leonine mane of gray hair. Even during his lifetime, he became a myth, partially because in that unintegrated and heterogeneous society, the leading national stratum in the towns felt the need for a messianic, chosen personality to reflect its national objectives and national spirit. Throughout the greater part of its existence, the Rights party remained anti-Serbian and anti-Slav, and even occasionally anti-Semitic. It was always to adhere to the feeling about the Serbs expressed by Kvaternik in 1864: "that Serbhood, it is a knife at the throat of my people."

The Rights movement as a political party was stronger on ideology than it was on organization. It did not have many followers or much political influence over society. In 1860 it was a small group of like-minded men around Starčević and Kvaternik. When Kvaternik attempted to create an uprising in Rakovica in 1871, without sufficient preparation, the Rights movement disappeared temporarily from the political scene. After 1878, feeding on the crisis of Croatian society during which everyone from the "palace to the hut" grumbled about high taxes, the Rights movement was resurrected as a political force, initially along the coast. Appraising Austria as "the greatest evil on which the sun shines," Starčević strove for democracy in the political system of Croatia, for an elected assembly and executive, and a ban responsible to the Assembly. The Rights movement then experienced a dramatic upsurge which was to make it for a time the strongest political party in the entire country. But in 1890 it began to decline.

Among the party masses of the Rights movement, certain ideas occasionally acquired overtones of revolution. Their radicalism was encouraged by Starčević's uncompromising attitude, as reflected in the phrase he coined himself: "despotism does not reform but collapses." Although the Rights movement did not succeed in winning over the Croatian rural districts, for a time it was closer to the peasants than any other group. It was largely a movement of the middle classes, drawing support from the petty bourgeois townspeople. Imbued with the petty bourgeois mentality, the Rights party gradually assumed conservative positions and began to break up into factions. The *Domovinaši*, or Homelanders (taking their name from the newspaper *Croatian Homeland*), headed by Franco Folnegović (1848–1903), made a pact in 1894 with the Independent National party and opted for participation in government, while Starčević himself formed the Pure Party of Rights in 1895. The followers of the Rights movement meandered ideologically and for a while even toyed with the ideas of a Balkan confederation.

In Dalmatia the Rights movement was late to develop, making headway only in the eighties. Its most prominent advocate was the editor of *Catholic Dalmatia*, Ivo Predan, whose clericalism was blunted by the appearance of younger leaders like Frano Supilo (1870–1917) of Dubrovnik and Ante Trumbić (1864–1938) of Split. The conflicts between the various currents in the Rights movement in Dalmatia terminated in 1894 with the founding of the united Dalmatian Party of Rights. The movement also echoed in Istria, the first stirrings traceable to the period after 1883, when a younger generation of politicians entered the Istrian Assembly. The Rights party made its way into Bosnia and Hercegovina in the eighties, but was unable to establish itself legally. Its ideas were first expressed by the *Voice of Hercegovina* in Mostar and a group of Hercegovinian Franciscan friars. The latter had clashed with the Catholicism of Archbishop Stadler (1843–1918) and were also up in arms against certain Serbian organizations over winning adherents among the Muslims for their nation. The Rights movement was capable of influencing the Croatian people in its entirety more effectively even than Illyrism or the National party that had preceded it.

Starčević's successor, Josip Frank (1844–1911), whose followers were called Frankists, rejected the oppositionist position of the Rights party in relation to the authorities, in his desire to make Croatia "a bridge over which Austria could cross into the Balkans."

The Slovenes made a belated acquaintance with the institution of political parties. It was only after 1867 that political societies came into being, although they were not yet to become political parties and candidates were not nominated for elections. The liberals and conservatives split radically at the close of the eighties, and both groups grew into separate political parties. Their first rift came in 1889 in Gorizia. Under the influence of the Second Catholic Congress (1889), the conservatives of Carniola established the Catholic Political Society in Ljubljana in 1890. In reply, the liberals formed the Slovene Society, also in 1890. Later, the Catholic society took the name of Catholic National party and the liberals first the National party and then the National Progressive party, drawing their support from the towns, wealthier peasants, teachers, and small-town intelligentsia. The Yugoslav Social Democratic party was founded in Slovenia in 1896.

Anton Mahnič (1850–1920) and the Ljubljana bishop Jakob Missia (1838–1902), who became the first Slovene cardinal in 1889, are names associated with modern Slovene clericalism. Attempts were made to implant Catholic principles in all spheres of political life and to promote them by intensifying social cooperation. Christian Socialism headed by Janez E. Krek (1865–1917), a well-educated priest supported by the peasants and a section of the workers, also was prominent in this trend. In the war "between the church and the factory smokestacks," as he was wont to call it, he gave precedence to the church. "One should begin on the ground, and then one will end up in heaven," he stated in 1901. Through

Janez Krek and his form of Christian Socialism, Slovene clericalism became widespread among the masses of Slovenia, developing particularly after 1890.

In 1897 all Catholic workers' societies merged in the Slovene Christian Social Workers' Alliance. In 1898 Slovene clericals established links with the Croatian Party of Rights. In Trsat (near Rijeka) that same year, their representative at the Party of Rights Congress stood up in favor of the annexation of "United Slovenia" to Croatia on the basis of Croatian state rights.

The appearance of clericalism on the South Slav political scene had, by default, certain positive consequences in the sense of presenting a challenge to democratic public opinion. It suggested to the youth the possibility of democratic cooperation among Yugoslavs as a political alternative to the gloom of the cathedral. The pope's slogan that all was restored in Christ *(Omnia restaurare in Christo)* was not followed; rather, political action was undertaken. The first great expression of organized clericalism was the All-Croatian Catholic Congress of 1900. On that occasion, an endeavor was made to fuse into a firm political amalgam the Croatian nationality and the Catholic religion, in the conviction that Christianity determined not only the historic boundaries of nationality but also its innermost substance.

The main consequence of development of political parties and their ideologies among the Yugoslavs after 1860 was their evolution into nationalist parties by the turn of the century. Parties were demonstrated as being the most efficient institutions for developing national consciousness and ideology; as a matter of fact they were so effective that the impression was that nationalism had come into existence only with parties. In the early twentieth century it was believed that there had been no nationalism before the eighties.

Political parties succeeded in shifting the historical accent from agrarian problems and the villages to the environment of the towns. The middle classes of townspeople and the petty bourgeoisie became the leaders of the nation in virtually all South Slav lands. The petty bourgeois outlook began to fashion the political mentality of all societies. After 1848 the tendency for the petty bourgeoisie to develop into a national oligarchy was the leitmotiv of social evolution among all South Slav nations outside Turkey and Montenegro. Social progress in its entirety was subordinated to this objective.

CHAPTER 29

The Failure
of Yugoslav-oriented Policies
and the
Predominance of Austria
in the Balkans,
1875-1903

UPRISING IN THE SOUTH SLAV LANDS, 1875–1878 / AUSTRIA AND RUSSIA CARVE OUT SPHERES OF INTEREST / THE CHARACTER OF GUERRILLA WARFARE BEFORE 1878 / THE CONSEQUENCES OF THE CONGRESS OF BERLIN / THE REGIME OF KHUEN-HÉDERVÁRY IN CROATIA / POLITICAL LIFE IN DALMATIA, ISTRIA, AND SLOVENIA / THE REGIME OF OCCUPATION IN BOSNIA AND HERCEGOVINA / MONTENEGRO AFTER 1878 / DEVELOPMENTS IN MACEDONIA / THE ILINDEN UPRISING

In 1875 a peasant uprising erupted in Hercegovina, whence it spread rapidly to parts of western and eastern Bosnia, the Sanjak, portions of Macedonia and Bulgaria, and even Albania, where it echoed strongly. A year later the war against Turkey was joined by Serbia, by Montenegro, and somewhat later by Russia, giving rise in the Balkan Peninsula and around it to the Great Eastern Crisis (1875–1878), one of the most important turning points in Yugoslav history.

The failure of this massive popular movement in the heart of the South Slav world acted to strengthen the position of Austria and generally promoted foreign influence on the Balkan Peninsula.

Uprising in the South Slav Lands, 1875–1878

The uprising started near Nevesinje in June 1875, after discontent had simmered for a number of years, finally to reach the boiling point. The Turks were forced to take refuge in the towns. In Hercegovina peasants belonging to both Christian religions rose in revolt. In August the conflagration engulfed the Bosnian Krajina, centering in Knežpolje and Kozara and followed by a revolt in the Sanjak in which the Vasojević tribe played a prominent part. When the villages in the vicinity of Višegrad and Nova Varoš took up arms, the overland route from Istanbul to Bosnia was temporarily cut off. A stream of refugees flowed over the boundaries, prompting an estimate at the Congress of Berlin in 1878 that over 200,000 people had crossed the Austrian border during the uprising.

The uprising of 1875–1878 was a great social turning point for the lower classes of the population in the Balkan Peninsula, for it was the first time they took part in such an undertaking after many centuries, with the exception of the Serbian uprisings of 1804–1815, of which this uprising was a spiritual and social continuation. It was also one of the major guerrilla wars in modern European history. It has been estimated that in the course of the uprising about 150,000 people disappeared from Bosnia and Hercegovina alone, more than in the Franco-Prussian and Austro-Prussian Wars together. The Orthodox and Muslims suffered the greatest casualties.

The uprising can be traced to the obsolete structure of society under Turkish rule and the fact that the oppressed national groups had matured to the point of being ready to create their own independent societies outside the bounds of the Turkish state mechanism. The Balkan part of Turkey was the last stronghold of feudalism in Europe. The historic cause of the uprising was undoubtedly the crisis of the agrarian system and the social aspirations of the small dependent peasants to break up the large landed estates and bring to fruition a different concept of private property in land and commerce. In both Bosnia and Macedonia the desire for a free peasant holding and small-scale proprietorship was the basic motive for social progress.

The profound social crisis affected all strata of society, including the Muslim nobility. For years the latter had tried to wrest the civil service from Turkey, to win command of the Turkish army, and to offer the people relief from high state taxes (especially the tithe, which was indirectly a burden for them as well).

The uprising resounded throughout the Yugoslav area, and it revived all the political motives that had temporarily lain dormant. Committees to assist the rebelling people and refugees were set up in all important towns; moreover, the insurrection was wider in its repercussions throughout the world than any event preceding it. The agrarian revolution was imbued with the character of a war for national liberation waged by the domestic bourgeoisie aided by all South Slav progressive opinion and parties. On the official Serbian side, the rivalries of the greedy princes of Serbia and Montenegro were temporarily stilled in June 1876 by the conclusion of an alliance of war against the Turks. The alliance was officially committed to "liberating the Christians while the immediate goal was to liberate the Serbian people in the European part of Turkey." The two principalities divided the territory in revolt between them.

During the insurrection several political groups were formed, the most significant of which was the Socialist, with the prominent socialist writer and agitator Vasa Pelagić as its leader. For a time, the Bosnian uprising was led by a Slovene, Miroslav Hubmajer (1851–1910), and the Hercegovinian by Mićo Ljubibratić (1839–1889), whom the Austrians captured and interned. In Macedonia the uprising broke out in Razlog on February 2, 1876; it was headed by a priest, an old member of Garašanin's secret organizations, Dimitrije Georgijević Berovski, who had mapped out a plan for the insurrection in Salonika and attempted to realize it himself. The uprising was brutally crushed although it was supported by the entire eastern part of Macedonia.

Austria had kept a watchful eye on developments since their very inception. For a time it declared a state of siege along the border in order to suppress in Croatia the hopes of the Croatian and Dalmatian National parties and their supporters that a territorial and political nucleus for the future Yugoslav community would result from the uprising. In the middle of 1876 the war was joined by Serbia and Montenegro, but defeat at the Djunis soon forced Serbia to sue first for truce and immediately afterward for peace with Turkey.

In the meantime the Bosnian insurgents had proclaimed the unification of Bosnia and Serbia in a united state. Command over them was assumed by a Serb, Mileta Despotović, who had emigrated to Russia, where he became a colonel of the Guard; later he was appointed regent of the Serbian prince in Bosnia. The uprising shed the features of a social revolution, for when he entered the war against Turkey, the Serbian prince announced that "our movement is purely national. It must close its ranks to all elements of social revolution and religious fanaticism." However, the attempt to win over Bosnian and Albanian Muslims by renouncing social revolution failed to achieve its objective.

The uprising resounded widely in Croatia, Dalmatia, and Vojvodina. Strossmayer and Rački were the most resolute representatives of the group that supported unification of Bosnia and Serbia. Their idea was that Bosnia should win at least some autonomy in Turkey to prevent occupation by Austria. To

Strossmayer, for whom "Croathood and Serbhood were only means, the final goal being national unity," this was only natural. Rački had developed a personal doctrine reflected in the conviction that Croatia historically was incapable of consolidating the Balkan Peninsula and that any attempt to do so would only whet Hungarian ambitions: "Here is another result," he declared in a letter of 1877, "of my historical studies: Croatia has never been capable of becoming a nucleus attractive enough for the creation of a larger state, but it has always been a rather firm lever for Hungary, which used it to prevent consolidation of the Balkan Peninsula. The Hungarians know this very well, and even today keep Croatia to this traditional path." A similar persuasion was voiced by the leader of the National party in Dalmatia, Miho Klaić, who saw the unification of Serbia, Montenegro, Bosnia, and Hercegovina as offering the possibility of "establishing *one* strong Yugoslav state, completely independent." However, some of the adherents of the National parties of Croatia and Dalmatia, influenced by highly integrated Serbian nationalism, did not share these views.

The uprising was also a great moment in the history of the Vojvodina Serbs. Miletić's National party based its entire program and activities on the expectation that the uprising would result in unification of the Serbs into a national state. When Serbia entered the war against Turkey, Miletić called upon the people of Vojvodina "not to lag behind the rest of Serbdom more than warranted by the duties of state." This was sufficient reason for the Hungarian government to order his arrest, and to search for a motive for having done so only later.

Turkey endeavored to pacify the insurrection by accelerating implementation of reforms. Promises were made of a new state order that, rather than allaying fears, struck terror into the people, as it was to commence with the more just dispensation of punishment. As far as the sultan was concerned, the reforms meant the consolidation of his own authority, which led the Muslims to rebel against him, too. Several rebellions in Istanbul, Salonika, and Bosnia threatened to undermine the whole effort. Fearing that the big powers might divide Turkey up between themselves, the sultan proclaimed a constitution in January 1877 and made provision for the convening of a parliament. The Constitution cunningly solved the question of nationalities by deciding that "all subjects of the Ottoman Empire are to be called Osmanlis, without exception, irrespective of their religion."

Austria and Russia Carve Out Spheres of Interest

The big powers profited from the uprising in the Balkans to divide it up into spheres of interest. Even before the outbreak of the insurrection, Austrian policy had succumbed to the pressure of military circles in Vienna, which called for Austria to occupy Bosnia and Hercegovina. Its basic design was to come to some manner of agreement with Russia, which it finally achieved in the conclusion of a secret convention signed in Budapest on January 1, 1877, in which Russia and Austria-Hungary agreed not to extend any assistance to the formation of a Yugoslav state, and to divide the Balkans up into spheres of interest. Austria thereby acquired Bosnia and Hercegovina, and Russia obtained Bulgaria; the extensive area between the two was to remain a buffer zone. Both powers attempted to increase their spheres at the expense of the indeterminate central zone. Russia favored the idea of a Greater Bulgaria including all Macedonia and parts of Albania and Serbia, in its quest to create a sound strategic basis for pursuing the struggle for a hinterland along the Straits and in the Mediterranean basin. Both consciously and unconsciously the trend was to sink the fate of Macedonia, Serbia, and Bosnia forever in the Straits. Austria was bent on increasing its sphere by infiltrating into the Sanjak, through which the road led to Salonika, its diplomacy anticipating the creation of a great Albanian state. Italy was also taking a mounting interest in Albania in the endeavor to make up in that area what it had failed to achieve in the northern Adriatic.

When Russia, assisted by Serbia and Montenegro, defeated Turkey in the second war fought by them, it created by the San Stefano Peace Treaty a great Bulgaria best suited to its own purposes. The big powers opposed this solution and adopted a more lasting decision at the Congress of Berlin (June 13–July 13, 1878): Bosnia and Hercegovina were temporarily to be administered by Austria-Hungary; Serbia acquired the Niš, Pirot, Toplica, and Vranje districts, and its state independence was recognized. Montenegro's territory was augmented and it was given an outlet to the sea, while Bulgaria was considerably reduced in size. Its southern portion, under the name of Eastern Rumelia, was granted autonomy within the Turkish Empire. Macedonia and Albania remained under the sultan's rule. Through their representative, Sava Dečanski, Macedonian emigrants in Serbia asked the Berlin Congress to grant Macedonia autonomy.

The Congress of Berlin represented a major defeat for the South Slavs. It was the greatest division of the Balkans ever made among the big powers, putting an end for the next twenty-five years to both secret and public movements for the creation of a Yugoslav state in the Balkans and to negotiations for Balkan cooperation and federation, and inaugurating an era of national egoisms which congealed on the consequences of the division of the Balkans into spheres of interest. The Balkans were apportioned out among the big powers, and Austria's share strengthened it appreciably. Having been defeated in Europe and accused of impotence in the face of various nationalist aspirations, Austria blossomed forth in the Balkans on the wreckage of South Slav movements for independence. The upshot was a deepening of the differences between the various societies, their social structures and the social mentality of the eastern and western Yugoslav peoples. National entities were broken up, the boundaries of nations petri-

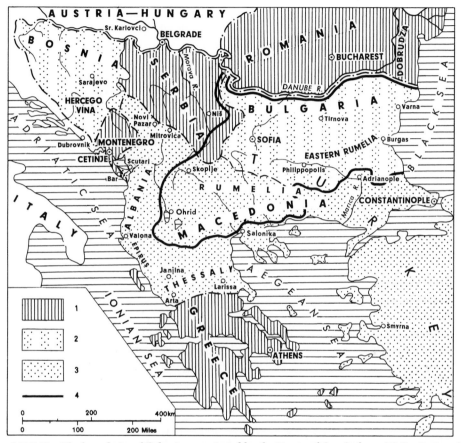

MAP 36.   The boundaries of Bulgaria as projected by the Treaty of San Stefano. (1) Territories of
independent states; (2) territories under the supreme authority of Turkey; (3) territories
of the Ottoman Empire; (4) boundaries foreseen for Bulgaria.

fied, and where they had not already been determined by religion, this role was
performed by the big powers. The Congress of Berlin disrupted the integral
Balkan market, turned Bosnia westward, and bound Serbia more closely to
Austria.

Soon afterward (1882) Serbia proclaimed itself a kingdom and acquired
an autocephalous church, but the defeat of its historical aspirations cost it the
high price of abandoning the ideology of the "Piedmont of the South Slavs." It
was no accident that the twenty-five-year period that followed was a time of
dissension and parting of ways between Serbs and Croats, naturally in terms
of their official policies. The former, in 1878, lost the opportunity to accomplish
something important in the Balkans, while the latter never got the chance.

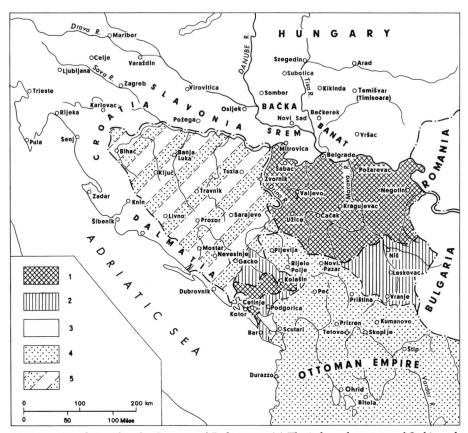

MAP 37.   Boundaries after the Congress of Berlin, 1878. (1) The independent states of Serbia and Montenegro; (2) additions to Serbia and Montenegro by the Treaty of Berlin; (3) territory of Austria-Hungary; (4) territory of the Ottoman Empire; (5) territory under Austro-Hungarian occupation.

The Character of Guerrilla Warfare before 1878

The Congress of Berlin marked the end of the last spontaneous guerrilla war of the nineteenth century, with the exception of the uprising in Hercegovina and Krivošije in 1882. From then on, internal wars were carefully prepared in advance, both ideologically and politically. The spontaneous peasant uprising, although firm in its internal strategic structure, never had rules that were valid for everyone. As long as the guerrilla war pursued the unwritten goal of a new social order, it demonstrated its incomparable superiority over classical warfare. In the Krivošije uprising of the peasants against Austria in 1869, it was officially estimated that the firing effectiveness of the insurgents in the battlefield as against that of the regular Austrian army had a ratio of 50:1. Such a force could be beaten only by time, by the doggedness of the opponent over a long period, and above all by internal dissolution provoked by the feeling of the people that the insurrection was not leading to the right goal.

The Consequences of the Congress of Berlin

In 1878 Serbia fell under Austrian influence to an extent which was tantamount to its becoming a protectorate. The trade agreements of 1881 and 1890 paved the way for a customs union, and a secret convention of June 28, 1881, gave Austria the right to supervise Serbia's foreign policy. It was Prince (and after 1882 King) Milan Obrenović who personally pursued this policy of reliance on Austria. Clashing with Serbian public opinion, he abdicated in 1889 in favor of King Aleksandar (1876–1903), a still a minor, although he did not renounce his ambition of keeping a finger in the pie of official Serbian policy. To a growing extent, Serbian foreign policy was directed toward the conquest of Macedonia, whereas internally, the Radical party was edging forward in influence. Through the Liberal and the Progressive parties, the government of King Milan suppressed the mounting authority of the Radicals under the leadership of Nikola Pašić (1845–1926) and Pera Todorović (1852–1907). Dissatisfied with the official policy, the public turned its back on the government. In the autumn of 1883 the Timok Revolt broke out in eastern Serbia. The king introduced martial law, his court-martial condemning almost 100 rebels to death, over 550 to imprisonment, and 5 to exile. The Central Committee of the Radical party was suspected of having fomented the uprising, and the court-martial sentenced its members to death, but they were amnestied by the king.

The king took advantage of temporary stabilization of the unpopular regime to suppress the Radicals, but after sustaining a serious defeat in the war with the Bulgarians in 1855, he was forced to make concessions to them. To general rejoicing, the Progressive party was deposed in 1887, and from that date forward the Radicals drew closer to the helm of state, first in conjunction with the Liberals and later on their own. As it achieved power, the party began to degenerate from what was once a party of the man in the street into a bourgeois group. Nonetheless, it made some attempt to implement parts of its radical program. Externally, it leaned toward Russia, whose prestige in Serbia had declined precipitously after 1878. Russian diplomacy persisted in attempts to restore its reputation by influencing the opposition and cultural groups and playing on Slavic feelings, while its legation in Belgrade was more an institute for sounding Serbian public opinion than a diplomatic mission. Nevertheless, only time and the pressure of new events succeeded in repairing its prestige.

Internally the Radicals strove to develop Serbia economically and culturally so as to wrench it from the claws of foreign economies. By the Law on Communes of 1889, they intended to realize their idea of communal self-administration. Domestic industries were given incentives and in May 1889, foreigners were deprived of their control over Serbian railways, which were transformed into a state enterprise. The Anglo-Austrian Bank was divested of its monopoly on salt, and in 1890 the Serbian government acquired the exclusive right to export, import, and process tobacco.

In conflict with the regency in 1892, the Radicals lost power. In April 1893 King Aleksandar effected a coup d'état, proclaiming himself of age although still a minor. He was intelligent, but crafty and unstable; the new ruler's autocratic behavior provoked violent reactions.

In the Hapsburg empire the old policy of the Viennese court was supplemented by fresh pressure from the Hungarian oligarchy on South Slav nationalities. The Law on Nationalities of 1868, which drew a distinction between the concepts of the "nation" and "nationality," exploited democratic ideas for purposes of perpetrating political tyranny and was soon transformed into a dead letter. In most cases Magyarization was carried out by legal means and in the guise of liberal laws, the aim being to fashion of political Hungary an ethnical Hungary with a single language. By pursuing this policy, the Hungarians did indeed succeed in upgrading themselves in their own state territory from a minority to an absolute majority in which 51.4 percent of the population was Hungarian in 1900, and in 1910 as much as 54.5 percent. Industry was predominantly in the hands of the Germans and Hungarians, as were most political posts. Differences in workers' wages made entire nations feel economically privileged. Workers' wages in light industry in Vienna amounted to 4.01 crowns whereas they were only 2.50 crowns in Zagreb at the same time. Most of the landholdings over 20 hectares in size (in Vojvodina 93.5 percent of the land) belonged to Hungarians. Slavonians constituted the larger part of the empire's emigrants. This Magyarization applied more to Vojvodina than it did to Croatia, where the policy of Magyarization was never systematically pursued.

In Croatia the Hungarians endeavored to reduce to a subterfuge even the unfavorable provisions of the Compromise of 1868. Croatia had no control over its own system of taxation and finances, whereas scant domestic capital did not suffice for the creation of a stable bourgeois society. As transportation was in Hungarian hands, no national market could develop. Between 1875 and 1900 the dualistic character of the monarchy consolidated, and Hungarian magnates thought along the lines of subordinating Croatia to their power even more. An attempt to hang signs in Hungarian on financial institutions in Zagreb in 1883 provoked demonstrations simultaneously with peasant unrest in the areas where conditions were most desperate. In reply to the disorders, a Slavonian landowner, Count Khuen-Héderváry (1849–1918), a capable, vigorous, and arrogant representative of the Hungarian nobility, was appointed ban of Croatia.

The Regime of Khuen-Hedérváry in Croatia

For twenty years (1883–1903) Khuen-Héderváry ran Croatia. In order to maintain the traditional forms inherited from earlier periods, he kept the Croatian Diet but worked from the inside to frustrate its functioning, setting Serbs and Croats against each other and goading Slavonian separatists. The existence of the Assembly provided him with the possibility of dressing up his absolutism in legal guise. His formula for running Croatia was a simple one, as intimated to a British politician, A. Nicholson, in 1889, for he considered that "a conviction was gradually permeating the Croat people that in a composite country like Hungary one race must govern, and that race must be the Magyar." But much more crucial than the question of why he pursued such a policy is how he managed to pursue it over a period of twenty years. The main reason is that he was operating in an unintegrated bourgeois society which had laid its foundations in 1848 but could not complete the process of formation on its own. It was a society in which all earlier political institutions had ceased to function as dynamic and decisive political factors.

Croatian national policy was the policy of the Croatian parties. Ideologically routed in 1878, the National party began to change from within and later (1880) took the name of the Independent National party. It continued to draw closer to the Party of Rights, whose star was rising rapidly just as that of the National party was setting. But the Rights movement also went into slow decline after 1887, to become a moderate opposition after 1900, thus eradicating the differences which had distinguished it from the Independent National party. The cleavage of the Rights movement into Frankists and Homelanders in 1895 caused it to ally itself with the Independent party, although for all these reasons it was not able to pull its weight even in this combination.

The growth of the youth movement introduced new elements into the situation beyond those ordinarily found in the programs of the various parties. Before 1901 the young people's influence was felt mainly along cultural and social lines, but from then on an emphasis on politics increased. The creation of the United Croatian and Serbian Youth in 1896 represented an attempt to bridge the gap in Croatian politics. From the very inception of the youth movement, one of the outstanding figures was the dynamic Stjepan Radić (1871–1928), who labored to find a new political formula including the neglected peasantry, especially after he inaugurated the newspaper *Dom (Home)* in 1899. The youth had little in common with growing clericalism or with the Rights movement's attack on Serbs (especially in its demonstrations, picketing, and pogroms of 1902), although they had not fully faced up to the inability of Croatian political parties to recognize the Serbs as a separate nation.

The Military Frontier was annexed to Croatia after it had been formally demilitarized and its population placed on a par with other subjects of the empire in 1873, although it actually came under the ban's administration only in 1881. Even then the actual annexation was not enforced until 1888.

Political Life in Dalmatia, Istria, and Slovenia

The government in Vienna was by no means deaf to the cries for unification with Croatia in Dalmatia. In 1889 it threatened to dissolve the Diet in Zadar if it dared to discuss the subject of unification, just as it occasionally banned the dissemination of opposition newspapers originating in Croatia. On the other hand, the principal political force in Dalmatia, the National party, stopped referring to unification after 1887, despite the fact that two years later it was to proclaim itself the National Croatian party. It took wing for a time after gaining the autonomous stronghold of Split in 1882, and winning the fight for recognition of the national language in 1883, when it was decided that the "Croatian or Serbian tongue" was to become the official language of the Diet. True, the government in Vienna pursued the same policy at this time in the other provinces under its control. The party's inclination to satisfy itself with trifling financial and political concessions from the Viennese government resulted in consolidation of the positions of the radical Party of Rights opposition.

The Croatian politicians in Istria made common cause with the Slovenes in western Istria. In 1884 they formed the Croat-Slovene Club in the Diet, with recognition of language equality in 1883 working in their favor. In reply to the inauguration of Italian national organizations (*Società politica istriana*, based on the platform of promoting the Italian national spirit, civilization, and culture, and the society *Pro Patria*, which, after being banned in 1890, transformed itself into the *Lega nazionale* for the opening of Italian schools), the Croats, with help from Zagreb, organized their own Slav League and the Society of Saints Cyril and Methodius for Istria. A rapprochement between Croats and Slovenes found political expression in the Political Society for Croats and Slovenes in Istria in 1902.

After 1878 Slovenes conducted their political activities under the aegis of intensifying dualism so that they, too, felt the pinch of the South Slav defeat of that year. Nationally oriented policies had even less reason for failing to respect the frameworks established by dualism and neglected to question them for quite some time, especially as it seemed that the Slovenes could progress as a nation within that system. In 1879 they sent thirteen deputies (rather than the earlier eight) to the central Parliament in Vienna. Reform and democratization of the Austrian system in succeeding decades enabled the Slovenes also to make some slow political progress. Slovene representatives in the Parliament of Vienna, together with the small number of their fellow countrymen from the other South Slav regions, supported the government of Eduard Taaffee, which claimed to be above parties. For the fourteen years that it was in power (1879–1893), they satisfied themselves with the political crumbs of minor concessions to their provinces and people. From 1882 onwards, the Slovene language advanced, as it began to be taught in elementary schools and was used in the courts and also partly in the administration. In other provinces, outside Carniola, the Slovenes as a people were exposed to a mounting menace. The Slovene national boundary crept southward, while the activities of German capital and German political parties indicated that the process would not be easy to stop. The Slovenes tried to respond in equal measure to their German opponents, although they were far too weak to defend themselves by taking the offensive. Through the endeavors of Ivan Vrhovnik (1854–1935), the Society of Saints Cyril and Methodius was formed in 1885, through which wider action was to be undertaken to found Slovene national schools. The cultural and scientific endeavors of the Slovene Matica organization helped promote Slovene national consciousness.

Political changes seemed to be launched at the beginning of each decade, as though history were trying by leaps and bounds to outrun the calendar. Blajvajz, the spiritual leader of the conservatives, died in 1881, as did Jurčič, the liberal leader. New faces appeared to enrich the political mosaic. Fran Šuklje (1847–1937), a deputy to the Parliament in Vienna, worthily represented the liberals, and Karel Klun the conservatives, although the spirit of opportunism on both sides smoothed the way for the strengthening of clericalism.

The Regime of Occupation in Bosnia and Hercegovina

The occupation of Bosnia and Hercegovina in 1878 was the initial phase in the new Austrian infiltration of the Balkans. By restoring the Three Emperors' League in 1881, Austria won the right to annex Bosnia and Hercegovina if possible, whereas Russia could round out its sphere of interest in Bulgaria by unifying Bulgaria with Eastern Rumelia. Through all these changes, Austria wished to increase its control over Serbia. It kept Serbia in a state of obedience by constantly posing the threat of a customs war or of stopping imports of Serbian livestock, and took exception to Serbia's program for railway construction (especially as it applied to the Adriatic railway after 1896). The Austrian "Bosnian Railways" project (Sarajevo-Uvac) of 1900 revealed its intention to obtain an outlet at Salonika.

Upon entering Bosnia in 1878, after subduing resolute popular resistance by the Muslims and partly by the Serbs, Austria was authorized by the big powers temporarily to occupy territories that legally remained under the sultan's sovereignty. By the Novi Pazar Convention with Turkey in 1879, the sultan's name continued to be glorified in occupied territory and Osmanli flags fluttered from the mosques. The old social system in Bosnia was retained, and soon the government was explaining to the people and especially to the serfs through the medium of its district chiefs that "the new authority had not entered Bosnia and Hercegovina in order to abolish the old laws but only to apply them equally to everyone." Austria made up for the shortcomings in earlier Turkish reforms by introducing an efficient gendarmerie and civil servants whose orderliness and extreme sense of obedience could distill some good even from a bad system. The new authorities had no wish to turn the Muslim nobles against themselves. Benjamin Kallay (1839–1903), who ruled Bosnia for twenty years, stated that he ascribed the "greatest importance to the retention of the Muhammadan beys and agas, a state-building element, who had a great deal of feeling for the country and the people." The occupation authorities did not trust the local Bosnian Croats and built their apparatus up by bringing in people from other parts of the monarchy. Neither did the authorities have much faith in the Franciscans, who finally had to reconcile themselves to a new state-financed hierarchy in the Catholic church introduced in Bosnia by agreement with the pope on June 8, 1881. The positions once enjoyed by the Franciscan clergy were lost forever. The new bishops paid by the state took special oaths of political loyalty to the Austrian emperor.

In addition to importing civil servants, the Austrian authorities started colonizing their own peasants in Bosnia. It has been estimated that by 1914 between 180,000 and 200,000 newcomers settled the area while 140,000 of the indigenous population had to move elsewhere. In the beginning, the settlers established their homesteads on free land, but later attempts were made to bring them together to form an ethnical wall along the Drina River and in the Bosnian Krajina so as to disrupt Serbian territorial continuity. As a result of this colonization process, the Catholics grew between 1879 and 1910 from 18.08 to 22.87 percent of the population while the Muslims decreased from 38.73 to 32.35 percent. In the meantime the Orthodox, owing to the stability of their natural increase, registered a negligible growth, despite resettlement, from 42.88 to 43.49 percent of the entire population of Bosnia. Of the Muslims who moved out, most were peasants who found it difficult to fit into the new system.

The Serbs acquired a new metropolitan, Sava Kosanović (1839–1903), who resigned in 1885 because of the pressure of Catholic propaganda. In 1882 the Bosnian Muslims were given a supreme religious body in the *ulema-mejlis* and a religious leader in the person of the *rheis-el-ulema*, signifying their separation from Turkey in affairs of faith. The new administration was a military one until 1882. Bosnia and Hercegovina were administered by a joint finance ministry from Vienna, headed by a general. Civilian administration was introduced in 1882, dominated by a civilian *adlatus* (aide-de-camp), who with a few officials composed the entire government. The region was divided up into six districts. The gendarmerie provided the system with its foundations; in 1906, to 200 gendarmerie stations (2,500 gendarmes) there were 239 elementary schools with 568 teachers.

In 1880 the country was incorporated into the Austrian customs zone. After the 1881 proclamation of military law and initiation of recruitment, an uprising broke out in eastern Hercegovina (1882). The Orthodox and Muslims (under the slogan "For the Honorable Cross and the Faith of Muhammad") created a joint command for the uprising (*Opština*), both separate and common military detachments, and a joint civilian administration (mejlis) consisting of six Orthodox and seven Muslims. After the collapse of the uprising, the administration of Bosnia was taken over by the dynamic Benjamin Kallay, who ruled it for two decades (1882–1903). He began to establish a new administrative, educational, and economic system. The attempt to solve the delicate national question by officially proclaiming a special "Bosnian nationality" failed in spite of a certain amount of domestic support for it in the beginning. The language was called "Bosnian" or the "land language," but in 1883 a concession was made to the local population through the introduction of the Karadžić-Daničić phonetic orthography.

The awakening of national consciousness also affected the domestic Muslim population, which both Serbs and Croats tried to win over. Muslim intellectual and political leaders themselves parted ways over this question. Some supported Croatian, others Serbian national ideas, as they opted for the nationality of their choice. This process did not strike deep roots among the ordinary Muslim people, Islamic in religion and culture, and under the influence of Turkish political tradition in the Balkans. Leading Muslims endeavored to form an authoritative national movement, and by 1891 the *Bosnian*, a newspaper edited by Mehmed Bey Kapetanović (1839–1902), was expounding the idea of a separate Bosnian nationality to which the Muslims belonged. But the movement's basis was not broad enough to assure its success. The Muslim political leaders, mostly from the ranks of the beys, negotiated with both Serbs and Croats. Under the circumstances, the regime gradually abandoned the idea of a "Bosnian nationality," especially since in the separation of the three people no natural basis for the idea was found.

Legal national movements purporting to achieve educational and political rights were instituted at the turn of the century. The Serbian townspeople struggled for educational autonomy between 1896 and 1905, and the Muslim between 1899 and 1909 (Džabić's Movement). This struggle for church and school communities was far broader in its implications than it might seem to be at first glance. As a form of political struggle, it was waged in Croatia, Dalmatia, Vojvodina, Bosnia and Hercegovina, and Macedonia. That it was a social and not a narrowly educational and religious question is evidenced by the opinion of the Serbian historian and statesman Stojan Novaković, in 1888, that "church and school communities perform the functions of the national state in every oppressed nation." They discharged those functions also in Bosnia and Hercegovina.

A secret agreement concluded between Muslims and Serbs in Slavonski

Brod in 1902 (or 1901) was an attempt with the help of Turkey to invest this movement with a political character. The two previously inimical groups were to unify, declare themselves an integral Serbian national movement, and jointly demand restoration of the sultan's power; autonomy for Bosnia in which the people would choose their own governors, a Muslim alternating with an Orthodox; the adoption of Cyrillic as the official alphabet; the banishment of all colonists; and the resumption of Franciscan administration of the Catholic church.

Gradually the occupiers developed a modern social mechanism in Bosnia. A bourgeois class came into being although politics, owing to the general lack of freedom, was reduced to skillful maneuvering within the triangle of the three confessions. This game was not a difficult one for the occupation authorities to play in a sealed, agrarian and extremely conservative society, staggering under the burden of the past. As time went by, the bourgeois class created small oligarchies which alternately bickered and negotiated, within their confessional triangle, over power under the aegis of Austria.

And so the new authority consolidated in Austria. A narrow-gage railway network was laid; this was not sufficiently linked with railways in Serbia or in Croatia, for its chief purpose was to control the routes to Salonika, Albania, and Istanbul. It was decided to lay a narrow-gage railway not for political reasons but on principle, as construction was to be covered by domestic financing. Sarajevo was on its way to becoming an important junction.

The Albanians also felt the consequences of the Congress of Berlin. Under its influence a meeting was held in Prizren on June 10, 1878, of Albanian representatives, most of them large landowners and tribal chieftains, who organized what was later known as the Albanian League (or more popularly the Prizren League). Initially, they called for the sovereignty of the sultan over Albanian lands and maintained contact with the Bosnian Muslims, to whom they were bound by a common enemy and past. On June 15, from Prizren they sent a memorandum to the big powers demanding state integrity for Albanian territory. In 1878 a turning point began in the history of northern Albania. The local revolts were transformed into a national movement and Albanian national renaissance which was supported particularly by the numerous Albanian emigrants abroad.

But soon the Prizren League began to split. From 1880 onwards, it broke up into two camps, one calling for reforms in Turkey and the other for Albanian national emancipation. In January 1881 the league clashed with the Turkish authorities (Prizren, Priština, Skoplje, Debar), but the Turkish army smashed the resistance and restored its hold over the province of Kosovo. The national awakening was paralleled by the process of social stratification among Albanians and the acquisition of fertile land in Macedonia and Kosovo. The herdsmen controlled the broad mountainous expanses surrounding the valleys, and later descended into the lowlands.

Montenegro after 1878

With the Congress of Berlin, Montenegro more than doubled its territory, acquiring an outlet to the sea, fertile land, and towns. The result was a change in the traditional direction of its state policies. From a small state upheld by the sword of every single able-bodied man and supported by European diplomacy, it began to develop a state mechanism on the model of other European states. The ruler remained an uncompromising absolutist but permitted the establishment of state institutions which had previously been nonexistent. The Assembly of Cetinje abolished the Senate and district offices in April 1879 and replaced them by a State Council, ministries, and High Court. The State Council was a legislative body in which the prince invited prominent personalities to take part, at his own will, in addition to the ministries. The state was divided into ten nahiyas, and these in turn into captainships. In July 1888 there came into force a General Property Code formulated by the legal historian Valtazar Bogišić (1834–1908). This administration remained in existence until 1903.

Development in Macedonia

The Congress of Berlin was followed by a number of uprisings along agrarian lines in Macedonia. The revolt around Kumanovo (the Kumanovo, Krivoreka, and Kratovo nahiyas) was crushed at the Battle of Čelopek in May 1879. The uprising in Kresna and at Pirin Mountain had to be quelled by 25,000 Turkish soldiers. The Brsjak Revolt of 1880, in western Macedonia, met the same fate.

Even after the Congress of Berlin, adjacent states scrambled for parts of Macedonian territory. Schools and churches were opened in considerable numbers by the Bulgarian, Greek, and Serbian governments, all of which set aside huge sums for this purpose in their budgets. By the turn of the century, 25 percent of the Bulgarian state budget was absorbed by activities in Macedonia. In 1885 the Bulgarians ran 306 schools in Macedonia; by 1890 that number had risen to 781, and the Greeks and Serbs had set up 200 schools each. All three were doing their utmost to establish as many church and school communities as possible, usually organized and supervised by their consuls.

For a time Serbia, in fear of Bulgarian domination over Macedonia, supported the idea of upholding Macedonian national separatism, and in 1888 Stojan Novaković wrote of a strong "tendency on the part of the Macedonians to be by themselves," adding that Serbia should win them over as allies "within certain wise limits including the promotion of the Macedonian dialect and Macedonian individuality." Serbia did not hold out long in the pursuit of this policy, which was not motivated by any honest intentions on the part of officialdom in any case, and soon reverted to its old activity through its teachers and consuls. The nature of this activity may be gauged from an assessment made by the Serbian scientist Sima N. Tomić in 1903, who said that Serbian agents in Macedonia "want to blot out the sun with their fists." Serbia grew ever more persistent in its overtures to Macedonia, especially as it was itself subjected to pressure from the west, from Austria. The Serbian statesman Milovan Milovanović (1863–1912) declared, "If Serbia does not obtain an outlet to the Aegean Sea, it will be forced to place itself in the hands of the Austrian dynasty."

The struggle to secularize Macedonian culture opened the problem of the literary language, as in the case of the Serbs and Croats a few decades earlier. Up to 1860 the Macedonians relied on the Serbs for support, and then switched to the Bulgarians for a time. This latter policy was dictated to an increasing extent by the church frameworks of the Exarchate and the interests of Russian diplomacy, which wielded a decisive influence over them as it did over all the Orthodox of the Balkan Peninsula. In their relations with Bulgarians, Macedonians struggled for their own literary language through newspapers and especially textbooks. Between 1857 and 1880 sixteen such textbooks were produced. Some of their authors strove to build the Macedonian language into a common Macedonian-Bulgarian language (on a fifty-fifty basis), whereas others worked to develop a separate Macedonian literary language. Those who advocated forming a combined language together with the Bulgarians took as their standpoint the conviction that "the study of Bulgarian grammar was one of the most difficult subjects for children in the Macedonian schools."

In evolving the Macedonian literary language, there were some who laid stress on separate Macedonian nationality. For instance, Gorgo Pulevski (1838–1894) wrote in his *Dictionary of Three Languages* that a nation consists of a people of the same origin, the same language, and the same customs. "Thus, the Macedonians are a nation, and their country is called Macedonia." The movement for a separate language was furthered also by a group of intellectuals connected with the newspaper (*The Vine, Loza,* 1891) and by several successive student strikes in Macedonian schools where instruction was given in foreign languages. This activity reached its culmination in 1903, when the learned Krste Misirkov (1875–1926) published a book in Russia, *For the Macedonian Cause.* Misirkov sensed the need for Macedonians, as a "separate and independent Slavic nationality," to codify their language, which stood somewhere between Serbian and Bulgarian in the Slavonic family of languages.

From 1880 onwards, attempts were made in Macedonia to set up revolutionary organizations, in Štip in 1885/86 and in Bitolj in 1891.

The Turkish authorities were kept busy watching these activities, which came to a peak in the nineties especially after the establishment, at a gathering in Salonika in 1893, of an organization called the Internal Macedonian and Odrin Revolutionary Organization (IMORO, later changed to IMRO). It had a central committee, after which its followers were called Centralists, and branches all over Macedonia (village, county, and district). Early in 1894 the organization acquired its first constitution. After the second congress, held in 1896, the IMORO also set up military detachments.

The organization strove for Macedonian autonomy over the entire territory which belonged to it, amounting to over 60,000 square kilometers according to a memorandum of 1904. With the slogan "Macedonia to the Macedonians," it was highly influenced by socialist ideas of a Balkan confederation. Owing to the mixture of peoples in Macedonia, it was not regarded as the state of one nation, but rather as a state and legal entity within the frameworks of a broader federation. IMORO proclamations referred to the fact that "our goal is far above any national or tribal differences." The organization soon desisted from its ambition of organizing activities around Edirne (Odrin, Adrianople) and confined itself to Macedonia alone. This change was evidenced in the name of the organization (IMRO).

In 1895 yet another organization for Macedonia and Adrianople was formed in Sofia under the leadership of Trajko Kitančev. It was headed by a supreme committee, from which its followers derived the name Supremists. The Centralists and Supremists were at odds on some matters, but there were certain similarities in their programs, whereas a lesser section of the IMRO, pressed by political considerations, thought of Macedonia itself as another Bulgarian state. But this section soon came to its senses and from 1896 onwards deliberately avoided the use of Bulgarian names in the organization. Goce Delčev (1872–1903), a village schoolteacher from the Štip area, and Djorče Petrov (1864–1921) were quick to rise to prominence in the movement.

The organization established a firmly knit network of committees and courts throughout Macedonia, which in some cases wrested the functions of state administration from Turkish hands. They even decided how much interest was to be paid on loans. In the villages workshops produced weapons and equipment.

Without doubt, IMRO was the most consistent and best-organized secret movement in the entire Balkan Peninsula, although its ideas of nationhood were extremely vulnerable on some points, owing to the enormous pressure put upon Macedonians by Turks and Greeks. It was slack in fostering the language as a means for integrating the nation and tended to dissipate its forces by pursuing inappropriate methods of struggle. Socialists endeavored, in the socialist custom of the times, to dodge the issue of national ndividuality rather than stressing it.

The Ilinden Uprising

The organization showed its mettle during the Ilinden Uprising of August 2, 1903, in the Veles-Debar area. [Ilinden is the Day of Saint Ilija (Elias).] The town of Kruševo was liberated, and there the first republic in the Balkans was proclaimed under the leadership of the socialist Nikola Karev (1877–1905). Turkey crushed the Ilinden Uprising by destroying the entire town. In any case, it took place against the background of intensive meddling by the big powers in Macedonia and Albania. In 1902 representatives of Austria-Hungary and Russia produced a draft of reforms which was submitted to the grand vizier. The Muslims in Macedonia and Kosovo took exception to it, particularly because of the suggestion that the Christians might also take part in the gendarmerie. A revolt broke out in Kosovo (at Vučitrn, Mitrovica, Priština) and there were disorders at Scutari. When the big powers again, on October 2, 1903 (at Mürzsteg), suggested that Turkey institute reforms, it formally agreed to do so. A new administrative setup based on ethnical considerations was proposed to Turkey. For fear of fresh Muslim unrest, the reforms failed to include the sanjaks of Novi Pazar, Debar, Prizren, and parts of the sanjaks of Ohrid and Peć with a large Albanian population. Thenceforward the Macedonian and Albanian national movements paralleled each other, their influence intermingling, although the Macedonian national renaissance, more resolute in its intention of destroying Turkey, paved the way for the Albanian, which it outlasted.

The year 1903 was a fateful one in Yugoslav history. In Serbia the population had grown sick and tired of the autocratic rule of King Aleksandar, who had perpetrated four coups d'état between 1893 and 1903, changed twelve cabinets, suspended and restored the constitution a number of times, revoked laws, and taken a generally high-handed attitude toward the dissatisfied political parties. His unpopular marriage with a lady of the court, Draga Mašin, only made matters worse in an atmosphere where public opinion was in any case inclined to slur over grave social problems by seeking their sources in the faulty behavior of the ruler. The general political retrogression was cut short by a group of conspiratorial officers who assassinated the king on May 29, 1903, an act they had been plotting since 1901.

In Croatia the youth and peasant movement brought down the regime of Khuen-Héderváry on the basis of the national question, finances, and the Hungarian flag. In Bosnia the administration of Benjamin Kallay came to an end, and it was felt everywhere that by 1903 the Yugoslav youth had brought on the dawn of a new era.

METROPOLITANS AND RULERS OF MONTENEGRO

Dynasty Petrović-Njegoš

Danilo I, Metropolitan (1697–1735)

Sava, Metropolitan (1735–1781)

Vasilije, Metropolitan and assistant to the Metropolitan Sava (1750–1766)

Arsenije (1781–1784)

Petar I (1784–1830)

Petar II, Metropolitan (1830–1851)

Danilo I, Prince (1851–1860)

Nikola I, Prince (1860–1910), King (1910–1918)

Part Four

UNIFICATION AND THE STRUGGLE FOR SOCIAL REVOLUTION

T he Yugoslav lands were among the last in Europe to undergo political and economic modernization. Some parts of Western Europe achieved national unification in the seventeenth and eighteenth centuries, and Germany and Italy followed in the second half of the nineteenth century; Yugoslavia did not come into existence as an independent state until 1918.

The Yugoslav realization of the right to self-determination was hampered by modern imperialism. Because of their geographic position and historical circumstances, the Yugoslav lands played a much greater role in contemporary international affairs than their size or economic strength would suggest. After the great rebellion of the Bosnian and Hercegovinian peasants in 1875–1878, which triggered a new international crisis, the Congress of Berlin was convened. It established a new balance of power. The shots of the Bosnian schoolboy Gavrilo Princip on June 28, 1914, at Sarajevo, not only ended the life of the heir apparent to the Hapsburg throne, Archduke Francis Ferdinand, but owing to the strained relations between the two blocs of the European powers, led to the outbreak of World War I. And again in World War II, the coup d'état in Belgrade of March 27, 1941, pushed Hitler to attack Yugoslavia and Greece and thus to delay his attack on the Soviet Union for several weeks. The conflict between the Soviet Union and Yugoslavia in 1948 pointed out the contradictions between socialist states and opened a new chapter in their relations.

The conflicts between great powers have always projected their shadow on the Balkans. Throughout history the line dividing competing spheres of influence has remained basically unchanged, despite the emergence of new great powers and new military technology. The Hapsburg emperor Joseph II concluded in 1781 with the Empress of All Russias, Catherine the Great, an agreement dividing up the South Slav lands and other Balkan areas along a line similar to that found in the secret agreements between Austrian and Russian statesmen in the nineteenth and twentieth centuries. In 1940 the Soviet foreign minister Vjacheslav Molotov and the German foreign minister Joachin von Ribbentrop quarreled over the establishment of spheres of influence in the Balkans, and even the British Prime Minister, Sir Winston Churchill and the Soviet leader Josip Stalin in 1944 agreed on spheres of interests in Eastern Europe and the Balkans. They could not agree on Yugoslavia and had to settle it on a fifty-fifty basis. The leaders of the new revolutionary Yugoslavia rejected all these secret agreements. As early as 1944 they had affirmed that the basis of postwar nonaligned policies of the third-world countries was the principle of equality of all states, large and small, in international relations, and their right to control their own destinies without becoming objects of negotiation among great powers.

In the struggle for independence and the right to self-determination, the Yugoslav lands, as in previous centuries, had to suffer mass violent death. In World War I their combined losses were over 1,900,000 out of a population of 11 million, and in World War II over 1,700,000 out of a population of 16 million. In this way the tragic element received a new reaffirmation in the social psychology of the Yugoslavs.

During World War II in Yugoslavia a resistance movement developed, and this had social aims also. The old Yugoslav regime had neglected the peasantry and workers and had imposed a centralized, unitaristic government, frustrating the national rights of other peoples in Yugoslavia. At the end of the war new social forces which were anticapitalistic in internal politics and anti-imperialistic in foreign policy came to power. The new Yugoslavia was organized on a federal basis with a constitution guaranteeing the rights of all Yugoslav peoples. Instead of capitalistic spontaneity, which caused social and economic inequality, the socialist principle was underlined, i.e., the need to introduce the element of reason and planning in all human relationships.

It was under these conditions in 1945, in a war-ravaged land, where a new conflict appeared likely with the recent Great Power allies, Great Britain and the United States, and where a potential conflict loomed with the Soviet Union, that Yugoslavia launched its struggle to build a new society on its own model: to become industrialized but at the same time to create a new social ethic.

CHAPTER 30

The Collapse
of Ottoman Rule

Yugoslav Lands on the Eve of World War I

Early in the twentieth century the balance of power struck at the Congress of Berlin in 1878 began to waver. Germany posed a threat to Britain's position as the world's leading power. The industrial revolution in Germany gave it
an economic potential equal to that of Great Britain. In order to pave the way
for expansion of their own capital, German monopolies triggered off a new
division of the world into spheres of influence. Between 1870 and 1912 Great
Britain had completed the conquest of 11.5 million square kilometers of new

colonies; its empire covered an area of 33.5 million square kilometers, that of the French 10 million, and that of the German only 3 million. At the turn of the century there were no more free colonies.

Intensification of Anglo-German Antagonisms and the Balkan Peninsula

The change in the balance of power gave rise to new coalitions. British-Russian conflicts, which had dominated the entire second half of the nineteenth century, were gradually relegated to the background as nascent Germany became prominent. The same was true of Anglo-French antagonisms. Two blocs of imperialist powers took shape: the Triple Entente (Great Britain, France, and Russia) and the Triple Alliance (Germany, Austria-Hungary, and Italy). Smaller states allied themselves with either of the two blocs.

The two coalitions acquired final form as World War I drew near: during the entire period, in spite of many common interests, members of the coalitions clashed over other, rival interests in various regions.

The Balkans figured significantly in the war plans of both sides. As the last hours struck for the Ottoman Empire, plans were made to fill in the vacuum it would leave. As the twentieth century broke, Germany succeeded in winning important positions in Istanbul. It took over the business of reorganizing the Turkish army and won the concession to build the Baghdad Railway.

Drang nach Osten and Drang nach Süden

In its strategic plans Germany had two variants: the naval and the continental. For the latter the geopolitical position of the Balkans was of overwhelming importance. The Balkans provided a bridge between Central Europe and the Middle East: the Ljubljana Gateway led to Trieste, the Danube ran toward the Black Sea, and the valleys of the Morava and Vardar Rivers toward Istanbul and Salonika.

With its population of 40 million, the Balkan Peninsula had also become an important market for the export of commodities and capital which neither bloc could afford to neglect. The rush was on: for raw materials, cheap manpower, government loans, arms purchases, construction of railways, consolidation of spheres of influence.

The deterioration of relations between the big powers affected 11 million South Slavs who lived under the domination of five states, eleven provincial administrations, and thirteen different legislative systems. The larger part of the South Slavs found themselves within the confines of Austria-Hungary; one-third lived in the independent states of Serbia and Montenegro. The Macedonians and some Serbs were under Ottoman rule, and the Venetian Slovenes were within the kingdom of Italy.

The importance of the Balkans loomed large for Austria-Hungary. After losses in the north and west in wars during the second half of the nineteenth century, Vienna directed its expansionist aims southward across the Morava and Vardar Valleys toward Salonika. Although Austria-Hungary found it necessary to rely ever more heavily on its powerful ally Germany, the two Germanic powers, especially at the beginning of the century, did not pursue an identical policy toward the Balkans. It was only immediately before the outbreak of World War I that Vienna, as the weaker partner, was forced to bow to Germany's foreign policy objectives.

The Quest to Fill In the Vacuum Left by the Ottoman Empire

The establishment of the two coalitions of great powers was reflected in the foreign policy of Serbia and Montenegro, and generally in the life of the South Slavs inside the Hapsburg monarchy. Until the turn of the century, the great powers, particularly Russia, tacitly agreed on Serbia's inclusion within the Austro-Hungarian sphere of influence. Imperial Russia curtailed its interest in the Balkans, especially in regard to the eastern part of the Peninsula. The first and foremost objective of Petrograd remained Istanbul and the Dardanelles. When Petar Karadjordjević (1844–1921) assumed the throne of Serbia in 1903, Serbia's posture in foreign affairs underwent a thorough change. The Party of the Old Radicals headed by Nikola Pašić (1845–1926), who had forged firm ties with Russia, took the guidance of state affairs into their own hands and kept it with minor interruptions. As France and Russia drew closer together, the Old Radicals party supported the adoption of an independent position vis-à-vis Austria-Hungary while maneuvering to the best of their ability between individual big powers so as to gain as much as they could for their state.

In view of its difficult position in the Far East, Russia was forced to exercise caution in its new policy in the Balkans. At a meeting in Mürzsteg on October 3, 1903, the Russian tsar Nicholas II and the ruler of Austria-Hungary, Francis Joseph, endeavored to conclude an agreement on division of the Balkans into spheres of interest. Provided with a motive by the untenable situation in Macedonia and Kosovo, they suggested to the other big powers that internal reforms be implemented in the three western, European vilayets (districts) of the Ottoman Empire. Seeking reform of the gendarmerie so as to protect the Slavic population from local Turkish authorities and Albanian feudatories, the great powers forced their own officers into positions of command over the gendarmerie. In this way Vienna acquired the right to control the entire eastern portion of the district of Kosovo.

The Russo-Japanese War of 1904 temporarily weakened Russia's influence in the Balkans, a circumstance fully exploited by Austria-Hungary. In order
to escape the consequences of the perilous situation, various Balkan countries
began a process of rapprochement. Montenegro and Serbia initiated talks of
alliance, while Serbia and Bulgaria concluded an agreement which made provision for a customs union between the two countries.

The Customs War

Austria-Hungary's response was quick and cutting. When Nikola Pašić
refused to revoke the alliance with Bulgaria, Vienna launched a customs war
against Serbia which lasted with interruptions for more than five years. The
economic blockade began with the closing of the borders to imports of Serbian
livestock and meat and to the transit of Serbian goods over Austro-Hungarian
territory. At this time, Austria-Hungary enjoyed a monopoly hold over Serbia's
foreign trade: 66 percent of its imports and 93 percent of its exports were in the
hands of Vienna and Budapest.

Arms purchases further threatened Serbia's relations with Austria-
Hungary. Vienna insisted that Serbia buy artillery at the Skoda factory in Pilsen
in which the Austrian court, and especially the heir to the throne, Francis Ferdinand, owned part interest. Tenders for the sale of arms were also submitted by
the French firm of Schneider-Creusot, the German Krupp firm, and some others.

In Serbia a group of older conspirators who had maintained contact with
the Austrian authorities while organizing their plot against King Aleksandar
Obrenović, demanded that the arms be bought from the Skoda Works. Nikola
Pašić opposed the demand in the interests of common sense, knowing full well
that heavy arms should never be purchased from a potential enemy who could
cut off the supply of spare parts and ammunition whenever it suited him. Furthermore, Petrograd advised giving the contract to the French.

Serbia rose to the challenge of the customs war. It sent its exports over
Turkish territory via Salonika and along the Danube to Brăila, found new
markets, and thus escaped what might have been the devastating effects of
economic blockade. Domestic manufacturing also developed and some meat
products were exported instead of livestock on the hoof.

The Penetration of French Capital into Serbia and the Weakening
of Austro-Hungarian Influence

But Serbia came to depend increasingly on foreign capital, the only
change being that Austrian influence was replaced by French and partially by

British. True, the Austrian foreign trade monopoly had ceased to exist, but subservience to French financial capital was total. From 1903 onwards, together with Austria-Hungary, France had the last word when Serbia concluded agreements for foreign loans. It augmented its influence through the medium of three state loans to Serbia, concluded in 1906 (a 4.5 percent loan for railway construction and army equipment), in 1909 (a 4.5 percent loan for railway construction and army equipment), and in 1912 (a 5 percent loan to meet the most pressing expenditures for war and urgent state requirements).

Serbia's economy suffered extensive damage from the low issue rates (for the loan of 1906, 86 percent; for the loan of 1909, 84.5 percent; and for the loan of 1912, 84.75 percent) so that the indebtedness of Serbia upon obtaining the loan was higher by that percentage than the resources it actually received. The expenses of subscription and issue were disproportionately high. Serbia was forced to convert earlier loans, that is, to incorporate them into the new ones. In order to obtain the loan of 1913, it was compelled to take over part of the state debt of the Ottoman Empire (the French *porteurs*, holders of loan shares, were the principal creditors of Istanbul).

The extent of the damage done to Serbia by these loans is best illustrated by the course of their repayment. Nominally, they amounted to 495 million francs in gold (95 million plus 150 million plus 250 million); by April 4, 1941, 630,711,913 gold francs had been paid against the interest alone, whereas the total balance to be paid for the three loans still stood at 327,072,000 gold francs.

France also penetrated into the sphere of communal, mortgage, and private capital. In 1910 an agreement for a loan with the Serbian National Bank was signed in Paris under the name of the "4.5 mortgage obligation of the Fund Administration" for 30 million gold francs; in 1911 another mortgage loan was concluded for 30 million gold francs, which was actually used for wartime requirements.

In 1904 the Mirabeau Bank began to extract copper in the Bor basin through the Compagnie Française des Mines de Bor. Clear profit from the Bor mines ranged up to 100 million francs annually, equivalent to the principal. Bor shares, issued in 1904 at 500 francs each, had risen to the value of 850 francs by 1913. Among Yugoslavs who acquired a small part of the shares was the industrialist Djordje Vajfert. Metropolitan (later Patriarch) Dimitrije held 200 shares. Another shareholder was King Petar (200 shares). His diary shows that he presented the shares in the form of dowry to his daughter Jelena when she married the Russian grand duke Constantine, brother of Tsar Nicholas II.

In 1910 the Franco-Serbian Bank was founded, with headquarters in Paris and a branch office in Belgrade, to handle the principal financial operations of French capital in Serbia. During the customs war with Austria-Hungary, French capital provided various Serbian banks with credit. This led to the founding of the Export Bank, in which the Party of the Young Radicals, headed by Milorad Drašković, had the main say.

French industry had primacy over Serbia's orders of arms. It also demanded a monopoly for railway construction, clashing with British, Belgian, and German capital.

As capital formation was not so high in Serbia that industrialization could be financed from domestic resources, French capitalists chose for their investments areas where returns were quick and profits high. In this respect, their wishes were met by Serbian industrialists, both the young and the old Radicals. Reports sent by the French envoy in Belgrade openly refer to the bribing of members of the National Assembly, cabinet, and army for the purpose of winning the best possible concessions and contracts. The highest circles in France were keenly interested in these matters. Raymond Poincaré, later president of the French Republic, was for a time the lawyer for the French arms factory of Schneider-Creusot.

A careful reading of French archives for the 1903–1914 period shows that even the old Radicals, who of all the political circles in Serbia were the most susceptible to bribes, endeavored from time to time to free themselves from the pressure of French monopoly. In 1906 French diplomatic representatives praised Pašić for his perseverance in winning an arms contract with the Serbian army for France rather than Austria although the French ambassador in Vienna informed Paris that Pašić was extremely adroit in exploiting the antagonism between Austria and Germany during the period when Serbia strove to extricate itself from the economic blockade imposed by Vienna.

When Serbia's dependence on French finance capital had become so great, the French envoy in Belgrade on November 31, 1910, complained that Serbia tried to play Austria off against Russia politically, and France against Germany economically. The French envoy to Belgrade had already, on June 16, 1910, called the attention of the Serbian government to the fact that France as Serbia's biggest creditor merited a privileged position in Serbia better than that of all other competitors.

German capital was particularly active in competing with French in Serbia for the construction of railways and in 1911 also for supplying the army with mountain artillery. The Serbian government had already expressed its readiness to purchase mortars from Krupp. This attitude did not change even after the Balkan Wars, and on December 28, 1913, the French envoy in Belgrade informed Paris that he had submitted the French government's demarche to the Serbian government protesting Germany's intensified economic activity. He explicitly stated that Pašić had granted German industry numerous concessions and that only on pain of French financial boycott had Serbia refrained from purchasing mountain artillery from Krupp. The French envoy quoted the Serbian finance minister, Lazar Paču (1853–1915), as having said to the German industrialist Karl Duremberg, "What can we do? The French have us by the throat and we cannot free ourselves of their grip. We cannot do any business with you now as that would only provoke fresh difficulties with the French."

In leading Austro-Hungarian circles, what was known as the war group slowly came to prevail. It was headed by Francis Ferdinand, the heir apparent, and Franz Conrad von Hötzendorf, the chief of staff. At certain periods one of their closest associates was Alois Lexa von Aerenthal, foreign minister from 1906 to 1912. Von Hötzendorf openly supported the view that Austria-Hungary had to secure for itself the Adriatic Sea, the Balkan Peninsula, the eastern part of the Mediterranean, and a part of North Africa. Toward the close of 1907, Aehrenthal told von Hötzendorf that Austria-Hungary should annex north-eastern Serbia with Belgrade, and allot other parts of Serbia to Bulgaria. An offer in this sense was made to the Bulgarian king Ferdinand.

Simultaneously the war group disseminated the idea of the triune re-organization of Austria-Hungary, with the South Slavs forming the third separate unit in the empire. Thus Vienna would draw within its fold even those South Slavs who lived beyond its boundaries, notably Serbia and Montenegro. Actually it was found later that Francis Ferdinand had never seriously accepted the idea of a triune empire—trialism. It served him merely as a means for intimidating Hungary and inducing friction among Croats and Serbs.

Late in 1907 Conrad von Hötzendorf and the German chief of staff, Helmuth von Moltke, harmonized their views, and 1908 saw Austria-Hungary launch a new effort to gain control of the road to Salonika. It succeeded in win-ning from the Turkish government a concession for the construction of a railway line from Uvac to Kosovska Mitrovica, from which point a railway already ran to Salonika.

On the other hand, this move led to a rapprochement between Russia and Italy. Although a member of the Triple Alliance, Italy feared the penetration of Austria-Hungary into the Balkans. Serbia continued to insist on the need for building a railway line to the Adriatic Sea to facilitate export of goods. The Serbian-Austrian customs war simply acted to accelerate these plans, acceptable to Russia and Italy, which saw the Adriatic railway as an instrument for suppress-ing Austrian influence in the Balkan Peninsula. Early in 1908 the Turkish govern-ment finally granted a concession for the construction of this line, planned to run from Negotin on the Danube River through southern Serbia and the Sanjak to northern Albania.

Annexation of Bosnia and Hercegovina

The course of events frustrated the implementation of these plans. Counter to the provisions of the Berlin Treaty, on October 7, 1908, Austria-Hungary announced the annexation of Bosnia and Hercegovina, while also mak-ing preparations for the invasion of Serbia. Serbia replied by mobilizing and a tense international situation ensued.

Initially the position of official circles in Russia was ambiguous. At a meeting in Buchlau on September 15 and 16, 1908, Aehrenthal revealed the intentions of his government to the Russian foreign minister, Izvolsky. The two statesmen tried to hammer out a new arrangement for dividing the Balkan Peninsula into spheres of interest. Izvolsky let it be known that he would agree to the annexation of Bosnia and Hercegovina if Austria-Hungary would assure Russia right of way through the Dardanelles.

But Russian public opinion reacted negatively to the news of the annexation and took Serbia's side. Although the government in Vienna had not informed the German government of its plans for annexation, the two Germanic empires nevertheless reached full agreement in the course of this international crisis.

Entente members were not of one mind. The German army had already progressed considerably in its reorganization, but the French and Russian armies were not yet fully prepared for war. When, on March 15, 1909, the Austro-Hungarian government published a mobilization decree and the German government delivered an ultimatum of sorts to Russia, the Entente powers advised Serbia to yield. On March 31, 1909, the Serbian government was constrained to state that "the new situation in Bosnia and Hercegovina does not encroach upon Serbia's rights."

During a closed session of parliament the Serbian foreign minister, Milovan Milovanović (1863–1912), developed the idea that the great powers did not recognize the right of peoples to self-determination. There was therefore no recourse but for Serbia, in the struggle against its powerful neighbors, to pose the matter as one concerning all Europe, that is, to show up Austria-Hungary as not only impinging upon the rights of a small nation but also jeopardizing the European balance of power. Basically this was the application of Garašanin's old guidelines to the new circumstances.

The annexation of Bosnia and Hercegovina brought to light the fact that the British government had altered its policy toward the struggle of the South Slavs. For over a hundred years any attempt by the South Slavs to liberate themselves from Ottoman power had been interpreted in official London circles as reflecting the growth of Russian influence in the Balkans. When the head of the opposition, Gladstone, endeavored between 1875 and 1878 to defend the rights of the insurgents in Bosnia and Hercegovina, Disraeli's government rejected his views. But in 1908 the British government saw the annexation of Bosnia and Hercegovina in an entirely new light, as the *Drang nach Osten*—the drive of the Germans eastward and the resulting threat to British positions in the Mediterranean and Middle East.

The Young Turk Revolution of 1908 failed to revitalize the Ottoman Empire. The suppressed peoples did not win liberty and Ottomanization was continued under new regimes. Revolts broke out in Yemen; the Greeks again took up arms on Crete, and disorders erupted in Albania. In 1911 Italy declared war on the Ottoman Empire and launched military operations in Libya and the Mediterranean.

Creation of the Balkan Federation

The Balkan states were already completing the modernization of their armies; Austro-Hungarian pressure after the annexation of Bosnia and Hercegovina simply served to accelerate their intention of settling accounts with the Ottoman Empire. Diplomatic negotiations proceeded slowly between the Balkan states; finally, in the spring of 1912 secret treaties were concluded. Russia and France gave their consent and later Italy also expressed its readiness to support the Balkan states.

First, a treaty was signed between Serbia and Bulgaria on March 13, 1912, for conducting an offensive against the Turkish army in the south while assuming a defensive stance toward Austria-Hungary in the north. Agreement was reached on the territorial dismemberment of Macedonia, and disputed zones were pinpointed. The Russian tsar Nicholas II was elected arbiter between the two kingdoms for division of the controversial areas. The treaty provided an outlet to the sea for Serbia via Albania. Treaties were also concluded between the other Balkan states, and a detailed plan of military operations was adopted.

In the summer of 1912 the Albanians raised an insurrection and entered Skoplje. The sultan recognized their authority in the Kosovo, Scutari, Bitolj, and Janjina districts, which aggravated the position of the Christian population to an even greater degree.

The End of Ottoman Power over the Balkan Peninsula and the First Balkan War

The first cannon was fired against the Ottoman Empire by the Montenegrin army on October 8, 1912. The Serbian forces smashed the Turkish army at Kumanovo on October 23 and 24 and at Bitolj on November 13 and 18. Serbian and Montenegrin troops merged in the Sanjak, and two detachments of the Serbian army advanced to the Adriatic Sea through northern Albania. After the initial victories, the Bulgarian army slowed down. The Turks put up stiff resistance at Edirne (Adrianople). Although it was not part of its obligation under the treaty, Serbia consented to send its Second Army under the command of Stepa Stepanović to help the Bulgarians at Edirne. It also dispatched 24,000 troops to support the Montenegrins along the front in Scutari.

The victory of the Balkan states, and especially Serbia, upset Austria-Hungary to such an extent that it demanded the undeferred withdrawal of the

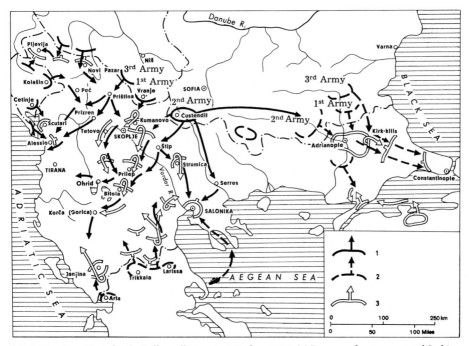

MAP 38.   Operations by the Balkan allies against Turkey, 1912. (1) Forces and movements of Serbian and Montenegrin armies; (2) forces and movements of Greek and Bulgarian armies; (3) forces and positions of Turkish army.

Serbian army from Albania. The demand was underwritten by the Conference of Ambassadors in London in December 1912, when the founding of independent Albania was announced. Vienna also insisted on the withdrawal of the Montenegrin army from Scutari and carried out a partial mobilization while the navies of the big powers threw up a blockade along the Montenegrin coast. Serbia and Montenegro were forced to yield.

The First Balkan War was terminated by the Treaty of London, signed on May 30, 1913. The Ottoman Empire was stripped of all its possessions in Europe with the exception of a narrow belt of land near Istanbul along the Enos-Midia line.

The Struggle of the Balkan Monarchies for Macedonia and the Second Balkan War

The Balkan states, especially Serbia and Bulgaria, clashed over Macedonia. Belgrade claimed that Bulgaria had not lived up to the treaty of 1912,

MAP 39.   Territory in dispute between Serbia and Bulgaria. (1) Boundaries according to the treaties
of 1913; (2) territories liberated from Turkey; (3) territories in dispute between Serbia and
Bulgaria.

having failed to send to the Vardar theater of war the number of troops it had
promised; also it had applied to Serbia for urgent assistance at Edirne which
had not been argued upon; Serbia had complied and dispatched its Second Army.
As Bulgaria had been sluggish in conducting war operations, the war had dragged
on an extra five months. Finally, Austria-Hungary had prevented Serbia from
acquiring an outlet to the sea via Albania. For all these reasons, Serbia asked
for revision of the treaty.

Viennese diplomacy sided with Bulgaria, a fact which prompted King
Ferdinand to decide not to wait for arbitration by Tsar Nicholas II, but rather

to send his army in the night of June 29–30, 1913, to take Serbian troops at Bregalnica and Greek troops in Aegean Macedonia by surprise. This step brought on the Second Balkan War. The other Balkan states, Romania and Montenegro, also rose against Bulgaria. Even Turkey ordered its troops to cross the new boundary. Bulgaria had to lay down its arms, and a treaty was signed in Bucharest on August 10, 1913, establishing new boundaries in the Balkan Peninsula.

The Yugoslav Lands and the Enmity of the Two Imperialist Blocs before World War I

Serbia's gain in strength in the two Balkan wars gave Austria-Hungary cause for concern. The militaristic group ceaselessly called for the launching of a preventive war against Serbia. In his memoirs von Hötzendorf admitted that between January 1, 1913, and June 1, 1914, he had asked the Viennese government twenty-four times to declare war on Serbia immediately. In the autumn of 1913 an Austrian invasion motivated by the Albanian uprising in Kosovo and the entry of Serbian troops into Albania was avoided by a hair's breadth. The Viennese government dispatched an ultimatum demanding that the Serbian government pull its troops out of Albania. Simultaneously Wilhelm II, the German kaiser, gave Vienna a free hand in dealing with Serbia. The Russian government again counseled Serbia to yield, and Serbian troops withdrew from Albania.

But Austro-Hungarian pressure was unremitting. A new motive was found in the question of the purchase of the Eastern Railways, in which Viennese capital had a vested interest. It was then that the highest circles in Vienna concluded that Serbia would finally have to be destroyed altogether. When Emperor Francis Joseph fell ill in May 1914, his putative successor Francis Ferdinand made preparations to assume the throne. In the instructions he had drafted on another occasion when the emperor's health had taken a turn for the worse, in 1911, he had refused to include Serbia in the list of his imperial and royal titles "as it is a sovereign state under international law." However, in the text prepared for his assumption of the throne in May 1914, he brushed these considerations aside and Serbia was inserted in the list as a crownland.

CHAPTER 31

Internal Relations in Serbia, Montenegro, and Macedonia, 1903-1914

The Serbian Peasantry and Peasant Democracy

The modernization of society in Serbia and its transition from agrarian to industrial economy proceeded rapidly during the first decade of this century only to be interrupted by the outbreak of World War I. Serbia was included in the network of world economic trends, and foreign capital made its way to the most profitable branches of enterprise. Railways were laid late in Serbia in comparison with other Yugoslav lands, beginning only in 1884; but by 1910 the length of line amounted to 1,664 kilometers. Domestic commercial capital concentrated on investing in industry. Industrial production increased ninefold between 1903 and 1910. After Bosnia and Hercegovina, Serbia at this time had the highest birthrate of all the Yugoslav lands. From 1,900,000 inhabitants in 1884, Serbia's population rose to 2,900,000 in 1910.

But despite its rapid advancement, Serbia remained an economically backward country. In 1910, 84 percent of its population made their living from agriculture. In contrast to other Yugoslav lands, there were no large holdings in Serbia, nor were there any remnants of feudalism in agrarian relation. In 1904 only 4 percent of the peasant holdings exceeded 20 hectares, whereas 542,000 agriculturists' families held, on an average, less than 3.7 hectares. The penetration of capitalism into the Serbian village engendered a certain amount of stratification marked by the basic tendency toward increase of small landholdings. A contributing factor was the institution of the *okučje*, the land minimum which could not be sold to pay off debts. But whereas in the nineteenth century the state could sell the *okučje* for taxes and other government levies, by a law of 1907 the peasant's holding was also protected from this danger. On the other hand, in Serbia the redundant population in the rural districts could not emigrate to the towns or other states; the people stayed in the villages, reducing the size of the already small holdings. The effects of social polarization began to be felt in the villages too.

The price gap between industrial commodities and agricultural products continued to widen to the detriment of the village, pushing up peasant indebtedness. The problem of property relations and their influence on agricultural production and distribution of income remained the key socioeconomic factor in the life of Serbia.

The peasantry also set its imprint on general political conditions in Serbia. Economic stratification in the villages led to changes in the Radical party. The older Radicals were now backed not only by merchants, but by the early industrialists and in the villages also by the wealthier section of peasants, whereas the young Radicals had behind them a section of the industrial bourgeoisie, and the small owners of town and country. Of the other two bourgeois parties, the Liberals split into two factions and the Progressive party reorganized.

The Party of the Old Radicals succeeded in attracting the majority of peasants to their program. In foreign policy they called for an outlet to the sea for Serbia through alien ethnical territory, taking advantage of the fact that Austria-Hungary had launched the customs war which struck at the entire population of Serbia. Seeking new ways of exporting livestock, especially pigs, as well as plums and grains, the Radical party won over to their side both exporters and the new manufacturers, in addition to the villagers whose products were the major part of Serbia's exports.

The idea of self-administration was still alive among the peasants; distrust of the towns was widespread, for the town was the personification of authority, taxes, and all the other evils that hounded the villages during the early period of capital formation. For demagogic reasons, the Old Radical party retained its slogan of self-administration and its principal political newspaper kept the name *Samouprava (Self-Administration)*, although the party did nothing practical at all to further this goal.

Social Democracy

The Serbian Social Democratic party was founded in 1903 with the objective of "relying on the working class, as everywhere in the world, and representing its political and economic interests, which are the interests of all the working people." The same year saw the founding of the Workers' Alliance of Serbia, as a general nationwide trade union organization. The number of workers in Serbia increased steadily to reach 55,000 in 1914. The number of trade union members grew to 8,000, and the party was influential not only in the principal towns but also in the villages, where it began to make headway.

The principal daily newspaper of the party was *Radničke Novine* (the *Workers' News*); a theoretical journal, *Borba (Struggle)*, was also published. The Anarcho-Syndicalists represented the left wing of the party but later withdrew from it. They had their own separate newspapers, *Hleb i Sloboda (Bread and Liberty)* and *Radnička Borba* (the *Workers' Struggle*). The most prominent of the Anarcho-Syndicalists were Nedeljko Divac, Sima Marković, and Krsta Cicvarić. The Anarcho-Communists were also active in Serbia at the time, publishing the *Commune* and a number of brochures by Michael Bakunyin and Peter Kropotkin.

When Petar Karadjordjević ascended the throne in 1903, a specific parliamentary system was introduced in Serbia which frequently went by the name of peasant democracy. Unlike former Serbian rulers, Petar I had no tyrannical leanings. Even before he was formally chosen king, he made the following statement on June 18, 1903, to a Munich newspaper:

> I have friends in all three parties and have always held genuinely liberal views. My father-in-law in Cetinje has jestingly called me an anarchist. . . . Above all, I am for honest freedom of the press. The country and people must be given unlimited possibilities to voice their wishes and complaints. Serbs are mature enough for the same kind of freedom of the press that modern states enjoy.

During the reign of Petar I, Serbia truly enjoyed freedom of the press. In Belgrade alone there were over fifteen dailies whose open criticism, often including epithets, was leveled against not only the government but the royal household. Various big powers took advantage of this to bribe individual newspapers, as attested by archives of France, Germany, and Austria-Hungary.

But this Serbian peasant democracy was a double-edged sword. On one hand full freedom reigned, and on the other political prisoners could be murdered with impunity by the Belgrade police (for example, the assassination of Milan and Maksim Novaković in 1907 whose perpetrators were not punished despite all the efforts of the opposition to bring them to justice). Although franchise was not universal in Serbia, a larger percentage of the population there exercised the right to vote than, say, in Hungary, Italy, Holland, England, Austria, and Germany. The peasants felt free in the state they thought of as their own, and well they might, for they had borne the brunt of grueling wars from 1912 to 1918. At the same time, flogging was used in the army until 1918. The gendarmerie terrorized workers on many occasions. During the strike in the sugar factory of Čukarica (financed by German capital) four workers were murdered on March 1 (Toma Dokić, Vasa Jovanović, Milutin Ilić, and Milan Matić). Strikes were ruthlessly crushed in the mines of Aleksinac and Majdanpek (Belgian capital) and Bor (French capital). Up to 1910 the workday was fourteen hours long. In certain mines and factories the *ailuk* system left over from Turkish times was still in force. Workers were hired for a certain period, but were not paid until that period was over; in the meantime they received coupons for food and other necessities from the factory store and canteen. Serbia acquired labor legislation in 1910, when the workday was set at ten hours. Children between fourteen and eighteen and women were exempted from night work. Workers won the right to conclude collective contracts. In defense of these rights, workers went on strike 175 times in 1911 alone.

Militarism

The army figured significantly in the country's life. This was partly the consequence of the fact that officers had deposed King Aleksandar Obrenović in 1903. Until the annexation crisis in 1908, there had been a tacit agreement between civilian and military authorities regarding the affairs over which each had charge; the army permitted no one to meddle in its affairs. At first King Petar himself found the former conspirators troublesome. They insisted on having their own way, tore up the king's decrees, and on one occasion confiscated an edition of the *Official Gazette* containing a decreee that was not to their liking. Some of them terrorized the workers, and even members of government.

After defeat in the annexation crisis, the conspirators concluded that they should also have a say in foreign policy. They called for more dynamic action against both the Ottoman and the Austro-Hungarian Empires. Militarism in Serbia was a specific type of phenomenon, its peculiarities arising from the country's economic underdevelopment, its weak bourgeoisie, and the preponderance of the peasantry, which was itself stratified. The working class was still in its infancy—an army of semipeasants: the "peasants' tails still peeped out from underneath the workers' blue overalls."

Against the background of belated social development, the bureaucracy and army played the role performed in advanced Western European countries by spontaneous economic growth. In this sense, Serbian militarism became a factor in the national liberation of the Serbian nation from the oppression of the Hapsburg and Ottoman Empires. But Serbian militarism was composed of a number of diverse elements. Some of them supported the tendencies of the big Serbian bourgeoisie, particularly in respect of its aspirations toward other South Slav peoples. In 1911 Dragutin Dimitrijević (1876–1917), known as Colonel Apis, founded the secret organization called *Ujedinjenje ili Smrt (Unification or Death)*, the seventh article of whose statute refers to Bosnia and Hercegovina, Montenegro, Old Serbia, Macedonia, Croatia, Slavonia and Srem, Vojvodina, and Dalmatia, as "Serbian provinces" whereas no mention is made of Slovenia, considered a Germanic land.

Military and Civilian Authorities Struggle for Power

After its victories in the Balkan Wars, the army's prestige soared. Colonel Apis stood at the head of the strongest group and in 1914 organized a putsch of sorts against the government of Nikola Pašić. The immediate cause was the so-called Decree on Priorities dealing with the question of who would have the last word in the administration of Macedonia and Kosovo—the army or civilian authorities.

The Serbian authorities' behavior in occupied territories left much to be desired. The Radical party sent their own people to those areas as civil servants whose principal purpose was to get rich quick by devious means. In Kosovo the situation was particularly grave after the revolt of the Albanians in the autumn of 1913.

The military commanders strove to set things in order in Macedonia, an important strategic position for the Serbian army. A clash resulted from an incident in the Russian consulate in Bitolj as to who would be the first—the military commander or the civilian district chief—to toast the Russian tsar Nicholas II. The newspaper dominated by Apis, *Pijemont* (Piedmont), launched a campaign against the government, calling Pašić a "dead corpse." King Petar I was on the point of asking for the resignation of the Pašić government when the Russian government extended its support to the Radicals. The fray was joined by the heir to the Serbian throne, Aleksandar, who was the exact opposite of his father. Reared in the page corps in Petrograd, he had all the makings of a tyrant.

Pašić remained in power, new parliamentary elections were scheduled, and King Petar I, a man of honor, took the consequences. On June 25, 1914, he issued a proclamation stating that illness prevented him from attending to his royal duties and abdicated in favor of his son.

The Absolutism of Knjaz Nikola in Montenegro

Montenegro was economically the most backward Yugoslav land. Lacking railways, it was not able to exploit its natural wealth (largely forests and mines). It was only in 1909 that a narrow-gage line was opened between Bar and Virpazar but with little economic effect, as it did not penetrate the country's interior.

In land relations, differentiation intensified, supported by Knjaz Nikola Petrović (1841–1921). At the turn of the century, one-tenth of Montenegrin families had no land at all, while certain chieftains, particularly those of the Petrović dynasty, had as much as 300 hectares of arable land. In districts rid of Ottoman power, along the Montenegrin coast and in Zeta, semifeudal relations lingered on, as they did on certain monastery and church lands.

Foreign capital (first British, and then Italian and Austrian) penetrated the subsistence economy of Montenegro. The Italians acquired a monopoly over tobacco and their Bar company began developing the harbor of Bar and a railway line to Lake Scutari. The Austrians were eager to exploit Montenegrin forests. In foreign trade Austria-Hungary enjoyed monopoly. Three-fourths of Montenegrin exports and one-half of its imports were accounted for by Austria-Hungary. The country's budget was never balanced. Two state loans were contracted for, one in 1909 in London and the other in 1913 from the Paris-Holland Bank and the Eastern Trading Company in Milan. On a number of occasions the Russian government saved Montenegro from bankruptcy. In the military convention concluded in 1910, Russia undertook the obligation to pay the annual sum of 1,500,000 perpers for the maintenance of the Montenegrin army. In 1912 alone, Russian resources covered half of Montenegro's budget (about 2 million perpers).

The Petrović dynasty, and especially Knjaz Nikola, enjoyed high prestige in Yugoslav lands, notably at the end of the nineteenth century, when Serbia cooperated closely with Austria-Hungary. Knjaz Nikola also established contacts with European courts. His daughter Jelena was the Italian queen, consort of Victor Emmanuel III. Two other daughters, Milica and Anastasija, were married to Russian grand dukes, Peter and Nicholas Nikolayevich. The fourth daughter, Milena, was the wife of Petar Karadjordjević. Nikola's oldest son, Danilo, married a German woman from the aristocratic house of Mecklenburg. Despite his vacillating between his powerful neighbors, Nikola was steadfast in his devotion to Russia. Tsar Nicholas II once called him "Russia's best friend."

Knjaz Nikola, an autocrat who depended for support on the chieftains and vojvodas, summoned the leaders of Montenegro in December 1905 to proclaim the Constitution, which did nothing basically to change the system of government as he continued to appoint officials. Voting at elections was public, and the Knjaz himself supervised and recalled civil servants. Two political parties took shape, the genuine National party, obedient to the knjaz, and the opposition National party, nicknamed the *klubaška* or "clubby" party.

Discontent at the knjaz's high-handed ways ran high. In November 1906 a strike broke out among the workers constructing the Bar-Virpazar railway line and in the printing shop in Cetinje. The latter strike made it impossible to publish the official newspaper *Glas Crnogorca* (the *Voice of the Montenegrin*). The youth were particularly active in their opposition to the knjaz. The Montenegrin students, like their counterparts in Bosnia and Croatia, formed a secret revolutionary society for which they obtained bombs from Serbia. When the bombs were discovered in Cetinje, Knjaz Nikola took advantage of the situation to bring the opposition leaders to court. Fifty-two persons were sentenced, six of them to death. The trial was popularly called the "bomb trial." It failed to discourage the opposition, and a plot was hatched against the knjaz in the Vasojević area. This too was disclosed, and in January 1909 forty persons were arraigned before the court in Kolašin, of whom seven were condemned to death.

The Problem of Unification of Serbia and Montenegro

The Montenegrin government accused Serbia of masterminding the conspiracies, and subsequently relations between the two Slav countries deteriorated rapidly. But Austro-Hungarian pressure and the annexation crisis compelled them to relegate their differences to the background. On the eve of World War I, negotiations for unification began, unification conceived as a personal union. The problem was under consideration until May 1914, and the negotiators ran into many obstacles: dynastic rivalries, mutual distrust, and pressure from Austria-Hungary and Italy. Vienna was of the opinion that unification of Serbia and Montenegro would mean war. In Montenegro the youth were particularly radical in their support of this cause whereas the tribal leadership of the old Montenegro was opposed.

In 1910 Montenegro was proclaimed a kingdom and Knjaz Nikola was made king. After the Balkan Wars the country's territory expanded and its population grew to 350,000.

The Čiftčija's Position in Macedonia Deteriorates

Up to 1912 Macedonians lived in three vilayets of the Ottoman Empire: Salonika, Skoplje, and Bitolj. Although railways had been laid in Macedonia relatively early in comparison with Serbia, general conditions were such that industrialization proceeded at snail's pace. Three-fourths of industry was concentrated in Salonika, with some in Bitolj and only 6 percent in Skoplje. Industrial workers numbered about 10,000.

The čiftlik was the prevailing form of agrarian relation. As the čiftčijas were not bound to the land, many of them fled to the towns, where 25 percent of the Macedonian population lived, or temporarily went into emigration—*pečalba*. There was an increase in the number of emigrants leaving for America and Canada. Large tracts of arable land were left uncultivated. Agriculture stagnated; as the new century dawned, over 90 percent of the Macedonian peasants still used the wooden plow.

The Macedonian peasant is thought to have been in the worst position of all the peasants in the Balkans. Compounding the other evils that pressed down on him was the general insecurity. In addition to the terror perpetrated by the Ottoman authorities and Albanian feudatories, the ruling classes of neighboring states—Greece, Bulgaria, and Serbia—sent detachments to Macedonia ravaging the local population. In Belgrade action along these lines was pursued by the Chief Committee of the Chetnik (guerrilla) organizations, behind which stood the Foreign Ministry as well as leading politicians in both the government and the opposition. In addition to Nikola Pašić, others involved in these matters were the young Radicals Ljuba Davidović and Ljuba Kovačević. The Serbian Orthodox church was also mixed up in Chetnik activities, like the Greek Phanariot vladikas, who sought to annex all Macedonia to Greece.

In the Internal Macedonian Revolutionary Organization—the IMRO—of Macedonia, members came to a parting of ways over strategy and tactics in the new situation. A left wing was formed, headed by J. Sandanski (1872–1915), which struggled against the pretensions of the bourgeoisies of Bulgaria, Serbia, and Greece to Macedonia. After the Young Turk revolution, a National Federative party came into being and was joined by certain Macedonian socialists. The first Social Democratic Conference of Balkan Lands in Belgrade, 1910, proclaimed the principle of creating a Balkan federation of equal nations. The decision received wholehearted support in Macedonia. It was also planned to found a separate Macedonian Social Democratic party, but the decision was not implemented because of the outbreak of the Balkan Wars.

No Change in the Situation after 1912

In declaring war on the Ottoman Empire, the Serbian government stressed that the feudal system of čiftlik would be abolished in Macedonia. Many Macedonian detachments helped the Balkan allies in their fight against the Ottoman troops. Nonetheless, Macedonia was divided up between Bulgaria, Greece, and Serbia. The latter expanded its area by some 40,000 square kilometers, acquiring an additional 1,660,000 inhabitants in Macedonia, Kosovo, and the Sanjak.

The Serbian government was not inclined to permit the liberal provisions of the Serbian constitution to be applied to Macedonia and Kosovo. Terror came to prevail; the Muslim section of the Macedonian population left en masse for Turkey. The Macedonian peasants failed to be relieved of the burden of the feudal system of čiftlik. This was achieved only in 1918.

Rebellion in Kosovo, 1913

Conditions in Kosovo were such that the Albanians rose in revolt in the autumn of 1913. Several divisions of the Serbian army had to be used to deal with the situation and they quelled the uprising savagely. In his book *Serbia and Albania*, Dimitrije Tucović condemned these war crimes in the following words:

> The bourgeois press called for merciless annihilation and the army acted upon this. Albanian villages, from which the men had fled on time, were reduced to ashes. At the same time, they were barbarian crematoria in which hundreds of women and children were burned alive. . . . It was once again confirmed that the popular revolt of the most primitive tribes is always more humane than the practices of standing armies used by modern states against such revolts. The Serbian propertied class has opened its annals of colonial murder and horror and may well take its place among the propertied classes of the English, Dutch, French, Germans, Italians, and Russians.

RULERS OF SERBIA AND YUGOSLAVIA

Dynasty Karađorđevic

Dorde Petrović "Karađorđe," "Vožd" leader (1804–1813)
Alexander I, Prince (1842–1858)
Petar I, King of Serbia (1903–1918), King of Yugoslavia (1918–1921)

Alexander I, King of Yugoslavia (1921–1934)
Petar II (1934–1945, with regency 1934–1941)

CHAPTER 32

The South Slavs under the Hapsburgs, 1903-1914

Intensified Germanization in Slav Lands

In the face of growing Germanization, especially in Styria and Carinthia, Slovene ethnical territory began to dissipate in the early twentieth century. The strategic significance of the Ljubljana Gateway and the port of Trieste impelled German capital to intensified efforts designed to make the area secure for its own purposes. Slovenes continued to live scattered about in Carniola, Styria, Carinthia, Primorska (Istria, Trieste, Gorizia), and in two Hungarian županijas, their dispersion preventing their unification and resistance to the pressure of the German glacier from the north. The sole exception was Carniola, where the accumulation of Slovene capital had given the Slovenes a breathing spell from this pressure.

The penetration of German capital into Slovene areas magnified the differences between Slovenia and the economically advanced parts of Austria; next to Galicia and Dalmatia, Slovenia stood lowest on the ladder of economic development in the Austrian portion of the Hapsburg empire. This was also reflected in the growth of population: from 1860 to 1910 the Slovene population rose by 21.6 percent and that of Austria by 51.7 percent (the rest of Europe by 59.3 percent). The slower growth of the Slovenes was due partially to Germanization and even more to massive emigration, particularly between 1890 and 1910. The rural districts could not provide enough work for everyone, and the fledgling industries were not capable of absorbing the superfluous manpower from the villages. Between 1900 and 1910 Carniola alone lost 33,965 people, or two-thirds of its natural increase. True, the Slovenes in Carniola kept their numbers up, but in Styria and Carinthia they declined rapidly. According to the newspaper *Slovenec* (the *Slovene*) of April 1, 1913, between 1900 and 1910 the number of Germans in Styria increased by 80,909 and Slovenes by only 152. In Carinthia the situation was even worse. Between 1880 and 1910 Germans increased by 62,702 while the number of Slovenes decreased by 21,040.

The state bureaucratic apparatus was a powerful instrument of Germanization, especially in schooling. On January 23, 1913, *Slovenec* published statistics to the effect that there were 559 high schools in Austria, of which 40 percent were German (for the 35.5 percent of the population that was German) and 23 percent were Czech (for 27 percent of the population that was Czech). Only the Slovenes and Ruthenians had no state high schools in their own languages.

Even in Carniola, teaching in the higher grades was in German; the Slovene professors had to lecture Slovene students in German. In most intermediary schools, except in Carniola, the majority of professors were German, especially for the more important subjects, like history, for instance, and the Slovene students were thus Germanized. The only Slovenian-language state gymnasium was in Gorizia.

The railways in Carniola carried signs in two languages, but by the time they reached Trbovlje, only German signs were in evidence. When Slovene youths were inducted for military service, they had to speak German, for according to Austrian law the *Dienstsprache* was German. In this respect the Slovenes did not enjoy the same privileges as the Hungarians, who could use their mother tongue in their Home Guard units.

The Austrian government did not permit the opening of a Slovene university. In the youth newspaper *Preporod (Renaissance)* of December 1, 1912, Janko Kos asked:

Do we have a single Slovene high school? Not a one. We have scientific books, we have capable men who could lecture on all subjects in the Slovene language, but the government does not permit this. Why should we not study history, language, and physics in Slovene in the higher grades?

Give us Slovene offices, Slovene schools, a Slovene university in Trieste, let us become economically independent, and we shall have no need of German.

In the same issue of this newspaper, in an article headed "Germanization," France Fabijančič wrote:

Great Germany wishes to become the most powerful state in the world, to which all nations must bow; it wants to spread in the Mediterranean, it wants Trieste. On the road to the achievement of these German desires stand the small Slovene people and that is why the Germans are united in the view that the Slovenes must be destroyed. We are constantly forced to read and listen to German politicians giving advice of various kinds to the effect that the Slovene people must be evacuated from areas that are of vital importance for Germany. Some say our land should be taken away and that we should be scattered around the earth, others advise forcible Germanization, and others again that we should simply be killed off.

Trieste as a Slovene Center

For centuries the ethnical line with the Italians remained unchanged. In the town of Trieste, owing to the influx of manpower from surrounding areas, the number of Slovenes increased steadily. (According to the census of 1910, 31 percent of the population of Trieste was Slovene and 62.3 percent Italian.) Austrian capital in Trieste developed industry; in 1912 the iron works in Škedanj produced 110,000 tons of iron. Trieste was an open port, one of the biggest in the Mediterranean. Italian capital in Trieste was powerful, but the Slovene commercial and banking bourgeoisie was also growing stronger. Their influence was felt in Croatian Primorje, Istria, and Dalmatia. Trieste figured as a significant Slovene cultural center. There Social Democracy had struck the deepest roots. At the turn of the century, Slovenes discussed at length the question of whether the first Slovene university should be located in Trieste or Ljubljana.

Of all the South Slavs, the Slovenes, as economically the most advanced, numbered the most workers. It has been estimated that the number of industrial workers in 1910 amounted to over 80,000. Among the workers the Yugoslav Social Democratic party founded in 1896 wielded the greatest influence. It was also influential, through Trieste, in Istria, Croatia, Primorje, and Dalmatia. The party conducted a persevering struggle to improve the position of the working class. In November 1905 the party helped demonstrators in Trieste (40,000 participants, Ljubljana (12,000), and other industrial areas of Slovenia where political demands for universal franchise were put forward. The success of these demonstrations was also promoted by the 1905 revolutionary events in Russia.

The liberal National Progressive party slid downhill swiftly, siding with the most conservative elements in the state on the question of electoral reforms in Austria. The party's leaders were influential among the bankers and industrialists of Slovenia, who controlled the Credit Bank, then spreading to Bosnia and Dalmatia and competing even with Hungarian capital.

In the elections for the State Assembly in 1907, the Liberals were badly defeated. The Slovene People's party (called the Catholic Progressive party before 1905) succeeded in advancing a more up-to-date program and won seventeen seats as against the Liberals' four; in 1911 the Liberals retrogressed even further. The younger people in the Liberal party, headed by Gregor Žerjav (1880–1929) and Albert Kramer (1882–1943), finally staged a revolt.

Up to 1918 the Slovene People's party had held a virtual monopoly over political life in Slovene lands; at elections it polled up to 65 percent of the vote. Two groups vied for power within the party. One, undemocratic and conservative, was characterized by militant clericalism and attacks on the idea of self-determination for peoples, claiming that national consciousness was only a form of Catholic conscience. The policy of clericalism revived medieval Catholic cosmopolitanism through the principle of legitimism. Every pretext was used to justify the domination of Catholic-feudal-capitalistic Austria over the Slav peoples. The spiritual leader of the movement was Bishop Anton Mahnič, and later the Slovene People's party leader, Ivan Šušteršič, who became the head of Carniola in 1912. Clericalism was also supported by Ljubljana's archbishop. Dr. Antun Bonaventura Jeglič.

The Slovene Peasantry and Dr. Janez Krek

The other group was led by Dr. Janez Krek (1865–1917). It was more democratic in its approach and expounded a Christian Socialist program, but still on the grounds of the Christian religion. At first Dr. Krek was under the sway of the Christian Socialists of Vienna, but as time passed, he delved deeper into the essence of social problems. He devoted his energies first to work among the Slovene peasants and placed himself at the head of their social revolt, setting up technical and agricultural cooperatives in the conviction that cooperatives were the principal cure for the ills of the village and a counterpoise to Germanization. By 1912 there were 600 such cooperatives in existence. Under his influence, a school for cooperatives was set up in Ljubljana, the first of its kind in Austria-Hungary, and the second in Europe. He then turned his attention to organizing workers in the spirit of Christian Socialist teaching. It was Dr. Krek who prevented the creation of a unified workers' party on a class basis.

Dr. Krek was one of the few Yugoslav politicians who had worked out a concept of modernization for Slovenia. In his attitude toward the other Yugoslav peoples, he demonstrated greater breadth than Šušteršič and the leaders of the Slovene People's party. For a time, he waxed enthusiastic over the idea of a triune Hapsburg monarchy, but not as clamorously as Šušteršič, who considered that the creation of a Yugoslav federal unit within the Hapsburg empire would offer wide opportunities for young Slovene capital in Carniola. Šušteršič, like the Liberals, developed the idea that the Slovenes should become the standard-bearers of industry and trade in other South Slav countries.

In 1912 the leading group in the Slovene People's party concluded an agreement with the Croatian Party of Rights, accepting their state-legal program in the spirit of legitimism and dedication of the Hapsburg court. The agreement recognized the individuality of the Croatian and Slovene peoples within the Hapsburg empire. Dr. Krek and other members of the Slovene People's party left wing felt that the Serbs in the Austro-Hungarian monarchy should also enjoy religious and political equality and national individuality, an idea vigorously rejected by the Croatian Party of Rights.

The extent of the rift between the leadership of the Slovene People's party and Dr. Krek is demonstrated in part by entries in the private diary of the Ljubljana archbishop, Dr. Jeglič, on the occasion of Krek's death in 1917. Jeglič complained that the late Krek had been praised by the public out of all proportion to his actual worth.

> True, the entire political movement here, and throughout the southern part of the monarchy, was begun by him. He did a great deal for the people, but what did he do for the church, for religious life? Those who praise him today say nothing about this. Admittedly in the Mohor Society he completed the translation of the Holy Bible, and sometimes preached. In this respect, his life was unusually sad. He did not even wish to take Holy Communion before his death. . . . This makes me mournful, and it seems to me strange that he is praised after death. . . . I think that God did right to call him from this world.

Dr. Janez Krek has gone down in history as a person who harked to the advice of wise Conservatives that a new program should be advanced to keep the old ship going. He advanced the idea of co-optation. But coming into contact with the masses, he spontaneously became a sort of rebel against institutions which impeded the struggle of the Slovene people for emancipation. Janez Krek influenced the Slovene modernists (writers and painters) and supported them in their freethinking ways.

Croatia Divided

The beginning of the twentieth century saw the desire for unification intensify among the Croats. In the Austrian and Hungarian parts of the Hapsburg empire, they were divided up into a number of separate units: Dalmatia and Istria formed part of the western section of the empire, and Croatia and Slavonia belonged to the eastern part.

This period also hastened the development of trade and industry. After the economic crisis of 1907, the First Croatian Bank, like the Serbian Bank, took over numerous smaller banks in the provinces. The influence of the Adriatic Bank, with headquarters in Trieste, intensified in Primorje and Dalmatia. But the influence of foreign capital, particularly Hungarian, increased apace. Domestic capital drew support from the Czech banks.

In agriculture, too, capitalist relations prevailed. Although industry developed and the number of industrial workers and craftsmen approached 90,000 in 1910, agriculture continued to hold first place as the principal branch of economic activity. In 1910, 78.5 percent of the population of Croatia and Slavonia made their living from farming, as against 84 percent in 1900. Some of the big landholdings were broken up, but peasants could not scrape together enough money to buy land. The banks benefited most, as did foreigners who had the means with which to purchase land. Before the Compromise of 1868, there were only 11,921 Hungarians in Croatia; by the beginning of the twentieth century that figure had risen to 105,948. Most of the big estates were owned by outsiders, and 520,000 farms possessed an average of only 2.8 hectares of arable land. In Dalmatia the small peasant holding predominated.

The Emigration of the Peasants to America

On the whole, the peasantry was being pauperized, indebtedness rose, and industry was not able to employ the superfluous village population. Between 1900 and 1914 roughly 230,000 inhabitants of Croatia went overseas, mostly to the United States of America.

In factories and workshops the workday was twelve to fourteen hours long, wages were low especially during times of depression, and prices were high. In the spring of 1905, large-scale strikes broke out in Zagreb, Osijek, and Mitrovica. In autumn of the same year, the railwaymen went on strike and there were demonstrations and clashes with the police in Zagreb. In the course of 1906, the number of strikes increased all over Croatia. In Rijeka workers stopped unloading ships.

Pursuit of the objective of financial independence from Hungary continued. A high percentage of the capital formation flowed from Croatia to Hungary, as the Assembly was unable to check on the implementation of the Financial Compromise, renewable every ten years.

The Position of Non-Magyar Peoples in Hungary

The position of the non-Magyar peoples in the Hungarian part of the empire was even worse than that of the non-Germanic peoples in the Austrian part. The Magyars, who made up only 45 percent of the population of Hungary, held 404 seats in the Parliament in Budapest, while the non-Magyar peoples occupied only 8.

The right to vote—publicly—was enjoyed by a mere 16.1 percent of the population of Hungary, that is, 27.6 percent of all males over the age of twenty-one. The disenfranchisement of virtually three-quarters of the male population was largely the result of rigid property classification based not on the amount of tax paid but on the assessed value of the land. Provisions such as these made it possible to place an arbitrary value on property, thus favoring the big landowners. Before 1906 only 1.8 percent of the people in Croatia could exercise the right to vote. In this respect Croatia was the most backward country in Europe next to Russia. In some electoral districts, like Karlobag, the local deputy was elected by only seventy-five persons, in Srb by seventy-four, and in Perušić by sixty-one. The electoral law of May 28, 1910, extended the franchise, but the workers and peasants remained deprived of their rights. The number of voters grew from somewhat under 50,000 to 200,000.

The Radić Brothers and the Croatian Peasant Movement

The unbearable conditions in Croatia were instrumental in winning greater participation by the peasants in the public life of Croatia. The Radić brothers, Antun (1868–1919) and Stjepan (1871–1928), founded the Croatian Plebeian Peasant party in 1904. As early as 1902 Antun Radić was asserting that it "is high time for the peasants to look after their own interests." The new party, imbued with a populist spirit, strove for democracy in public life and universal franchise. Antun Radić was a particularly sharp critic of the huge inequalities in Croatian society, pointing out the magnitude of the differences even in the civil service. While the ban drew an annual salary of 41,000 crowns, and the seven highest officials received between 15,600 and 21,000, the most junior civil servants were paid 1,200 to 2,300 crowns a year. On the national question, the Radić brothers opposed the Compromise, seeking rather a federated Slavic Austria with five units: the Alpine (German), Polish, Czech, Galician, and Croat-Slovene-Serb banovinas, the latter encompassing all South Slavs within the empire and with headquarters in Zagreb. Obviously the Radićs were attuned to the danger of oncoming German imperialism.

The new party opposed revolutionary changes in society and recommended evolution and the economic and cultural advancement of the people; it disagreed with the idea of class struggle and rather advanced the unity of all classes, while assuming an understanding attitude toward domestic capital.

The Radićs inveighed against exploitation by big capital, especially foreign, but regarded the peasantry as an integral body. They were blind to the fact that capitalism had penetrated the Croatian village, provoking a certain degree of polarization. While supporting agrarian reform with a maximum landholding of 300 hectares, they agreed to compensation for the owners of big landed estates.

All bourgeois parties condemned the new party. High clergy denounced the Radić brothers for allegedly pursuing antistate activities. It was true that the Radićs were anticlerical, but they considered Christianity part of the cultural heritage of the Croatian peasant. On the other hand, they frustrated the Clericalists in their attempt to form a large-scale party among the Croat masses in Bosnia and Hercegovina as they had in Slovenia.

The fact that so few people had the right to vote made it impossible for the new peasant party to demonstrate its strength; however, in 1910 Antun Radić was elected in Ludbreg, and for the first time in history the representative of a peasant party sat on the benches of the Croatian Assembly. Later, when universal franchise was introduced in Yugoslavia after 1918, the Radićs' party was catapulted into the position of the leading political force in Croatia.

The Social Democratic party of Croatia succeeded for a time in increasing its influence, thanks to the growth of the workers' movement. From purely economic demands for shortening the workday and raising wages, it went on to political demands for general political rights. During the regime of Khuen-Héderváry, the party was tolerated, but the trade unions were regularly banned under pressure from employers. It was only in 1907 that trade union activity became legal, only to be banned again. The workers then went underground, forming trade unions in secret which were actually combined party–trade union organizations. This arrangement endured, and later members of trade unions automatically also became members of the Social Democratic party.

The Third Congress of the Social Democratic party acclaimed the Russian Revolution of 1905, expressing the hope that "the victory of the Russian Revolution would be a sign of liberty for all the oppressed and disenfranchised in the world." In practice, the party leadership conducted an opportunistic policy of cooperating with the Croatian bourgeoisie. It had some influence over the villages, expecially in Srem, as was evidenced in the elections.

The Croatian-Serbian Coalition

The turn of the century saw a regrouping also in the right-wing sections of political life in Croatia. Ultraconservative Clericalists rallied to the newspaper *Hrvatstvo (Croathood)*, launching a struggle against the influence of the Social Democrats among the Croatian workers, preaching anti-Semitism, and denying the national individuality of Serbs in Croatia. These Clericalists had much in common with the pro-Hungarian National party and right-wing elements in the Croatian Party of Rights.

A rapprochement soon began between liberal Croatian bourgeois groups and Serbian political groupings. Undoubtedly this was partly a reaction to the danger of the *Drang nach Osten*, and also an endeavor by Croatian and Serbian capital to develop a joint platform in the struggle against the mounting inroads of foreign capital. It was then that the idea struck them of finding a common tongue with the Hungarian opposition in the face of the Germanic danger. This new course was particularly supported by Frano Supilo (1870–1917) and Ante Trumbić (1864–1938). On October 3, 1905, a group of politically conscious citizens from Croatia and Dalmatia met to sign the Rijeka Resolution. This historic document supported the Hungarian opposition in its idea of the formation of a personal union between Austria and Hungary, and stressed the need for defense from German imperialism. For the Croats, it asked for unification of all Croatian lands and full democratic liberties.

On October 19, 1905, Serbian politicians from Dalmatia and Croatia gathered in Zadar. They accepted the foundations of the Rijeka Resolution, especially unification of Dalmatia with Croatia and Slavonia, expressing the hope that the Croatian representatives would adopt the principle of equality between Croats and Serbs in Croatia and Dalmatia. The Dalmatian Italians also supported these two resolutions.

The Rijeka and Zadar Resolutions made it possible to form a Croatian-Serbian coalition, joined by the Croatian Progressive party, the Croatian Party of Rights, the Serbian National Radical party, and the Serbian National Independent party.

The rapprochement between Croats and Hungarians on the one hand, and Croats, Serbs, and Italians in Dalmatia and Istria on the other, and particularly joint action by Croats and Serbs, were blows to the tried and tested strategy of Vienna: Divide and Rule. But developments in Hungary favored the intentions of the Austrian government. When Ferenc Kossuth came to power in

Budapest, he could not bring himself to renounce Magyarization in Croatia, thus undermining the foundations of the Rijeka and Zadar Resolutions.

Absolutism in Croatia

Nevertheless, the Croatian-Serbian coalition stood firm in Croatia. At the elections in May 1906, it won a convincing election victory, obtaining forty-three of eighty-eight seats. A government under its influence came into power but fell in the summer of 1907. Vienna and Budapest decided to apply absolutist measures, which remained in force in Croatia until the end of World War I. The Croatian-Serbian coalition faltered, especially after Supilo left it. The fact that the new leadership frequently followed the moods of Serbian foreign policy acted to weaken the liberation struggle in Croatia.

Openly terroristic methods began to be applied in Croatia, particularly once Vienna accelerated expansion in the Balkan Peninsula in the direction of Serbia and Montenegro. During the annexation crisis, fifty-three leading Serbian politicians were arrested in Croatia, charged with conspiring to raise a revolution in Croatia with the help of the Serbian and Montenegrin armies. The charges were based on materials submitted by a paid Austrian agent, Djordje Nastić, a native of Bosnia. The indictment stressed the Clericalist-Frankist thesis that there were no Serbs in Croatia, meaning that their national individuality was not recognized. The objective of the trial was to create an atmosphere of pogrom in Croatia on the eve of the war being prepared against Serbia. In the meantime, the annexationist crisis subsided and the principal defendants, Adam and Valerijan Pribičević, were each sentenced to twelve years' imprisonment.

At the end of March 1909 the Viennese historian Heinrich Friedjung published a series of articles in which he tried to prove with the help of documents that the leadership of the Croatian-Serbian coalition had worked hand in glove with the Serbian government. The articles were part of a deliberate campaign for making war on Serbia; following their publication, all the leaders of the coalition were to be arrested for high treason. However, the coalition members brought suit against Friedjung, and a trial was held in Vienna in December 1909. The Czech leader Tomáš Masaryk and the Croat Frano Supilo were highly instrumental in helping establish the facts of the case during the Friedjung trial. It was proved in court that all the alleged documents had been forged in the Austro-Hungarian mission in Belgrade, and the exposé caused a scandal throughout Europe. According to reports from the French envoy in Belgrade, of December 8, 1910, the Viennese minister to Belgrade, Count Forgach, lodged a protest with the Serbian Foreign Ministry because people in the streets of Belgrade called him names ("jackass") and the Serbian press held him up to ridicule. The Ministry issued a statement to the effect that it could not interfere with the press. It has not been ascertained who forged the documents. According to one version, some Obrenović followers who wished to damage the reputation of the Karadjordjević dynasty were mixed up in the affair; according to another, the Serbian police had tricked the naïve Forgach by sending him *agents provocateurs*. The envoy swallowed their story whole in his anxiety to find justification for Austria-Hungary's planned aggression against Serbia.

Political conditions in Croatia continued to deteriorate. In January 1912 the Assembly was dissolved, and Slavko Cuvaj was appointed ban, signifying the establishment of outright absolutism in Croatia. The press was often confiscated, and demonstrations in which many workers participated broke out in Croatia. On March 12 a student strike spread not only throughout Croatia and Dalmatia but also to Bosnia and Hercegovina. The Hungarian government responded by setting up a commissariat in Croatia, headed again by Cuvaj. Now the youth stood in the front ranks of the fight against absolutism. On June 8, 1912, Luka Jukić, a student, attempted to assassinate Cuvaj. The outbreak of the Balkan War and the enthusiasm in Croatia at the news of the first victories by the Balkan states aggravated the situation in Croatia still further.

Francis Ferdinand's Speculations with the Trialism

In order to frustrate cooperation between Croats and Serbs, the Austrian aristocracy, together with the Viennese Christian Socialists, again revived the tactics of trialism, or formation of a third federal unit for the Hapsburg empire, headed by Croatia, which was to rally all the other South Slavs to itself. This program was adopted by a section of the Croatian bourgeoisie headed by Josip Frank and by the Clericalists.

In Vienna the policy of the trialism was supported especially by Francis Ferdinand and the circles around him, although the realization of the idea would actually have weakened his policy of centralization and Germanization of the empire. But to Francis Ferdinand, the trialism policy was only a tactical means, useful for fomenting dissension between Croats and Serbs, as the Frankists refused to acknowledge the individuality of the Serbian people in Croatia.

Francis Ferdinand's confessor and one of his principal political advisers was a Jesuit monk, Anton Puntigam; in a confidential letter sent to Friedrich Funder, editor of the *Reichspost*, on November 12, 1912, he wrote that the greatest danger threatening the cause of the monarchy was "rapprochement between Serbs and Croats in the South Slav provinces of Austria-Hungary." The letter went on to say:

> We all believe that it will most probably be impossible to prevent the creation of a large South Slav state. The danger is that the Austrian South Slavs, Croats and

Slovenes, might also join this state. Only two years ago, the Croats felt a strong antipathy toward the Serbs. Today that has changed: the suicidal policy in Croatia, the neglect of Dalmatia, the steady deterioration in the position of Catholics in Bosnia in favor of Orthodox and Muslims, and especially victories in the Balkan War, have influenced even those people who were previously not very enthusiastic. A large part of the Croats—virtually all Dalmatians—have turned their backs on Austria in internal affairs. And total secession may be expected when external relations favor this policy more. Catholicism is the only thing still holding back the Croats and especially the clergy, from joining the Serbs. . . .

Francis Ferdinand himself, in his confidential political instructions written in May 1914 for his prospective assumption of the throne, definitely rejected the idea of the trialism:

> Trialism should be regarded as a means for prevailing over the Hungarians. In my opinion, it is simply an appropriate instrument for intimidating the Hungarian chauvinists although it cannot bring the dynasty and Austria any genuine benefit.
> First of all, it should be noted that the South Slavs are more or less unreliable politically. This has been evident in Croatia and recently also in Bosnia. And who can guarantee that this new state unit within the empire—which would consist of Croatia, Bosnia and Hercegovina, and Dalmatia with Primorje, and to which Carniola would be added and perhaps a part of Styria—would always be on Austria's side. . . ? It is possible that present difficulties would simply be increased if three governments, three parliaments, and three delegations had to rule together, and the South Slav state unit were on the side of Hungary, where the Crown's interests cannot lie. . . .

Semicolonialism in Bosnia and Hercegovina

In the early twentieth century Bosnia and Hercegovina remained the sole colonial protectorate in Europe. After the death of Benjamin Kalaj, Count Stefan Burian was appointed the new joint finance minister for Austria-Hungary. Under his administration, Vienna and Budapest fought even more fiercely over who would supervise the affairs of Bosnia and Hercegovina. Meanwhile German capital was gradually acquiring key positions for exploitation of raw materials in Bosnia and Hercegovina.

During the early part of the twentieth century, 1,684 kilometers of railways were laid in Bosnia and Hercegovina, the lines planned in such a way as to meet primarily the requirements of Hungarian industry, of which the most important was wood processing. In 1913 this branch accounted for 25 percent of the total exports of Bosnia and Hercegovina. Coal, iron, salt, and manganese mines were opened and developed. In 1913 Vareš alone produced roughly 60,000 tons of pig and cast iron, and Zenica a little under 10,000 tons of steel.

Burian announced a new policy for Bosnia and Hercegovina, declaring that reforms had to come from the top so as to avoid their being instituted under pressure from below. Actually Burian's policy consisted of extending certain concessions to the Serbian bourgeoisie, which had begun to strengthen, and to the Muslim agas and beys. In 1905 a measure of autonomy was restored to the Serbian Orthodox church, and in 1909 the Muslim religious community succeeded in winning the same concessions. The Hapsburg regime generously backed action by the Catholic church, especially the Jesuits. Francis Ferdinand, together with General Potiorek, laid plans to construct fifty Catholic churches in Bosnia and Hercegovina.

The Constitution of 1910

In 1908 Austria-Hungary announced the annexation of Bosnia and Hercegovina, thus drawing those two lands into its boundaries also from the standpoint of international law. By the Imperial Patent of February 17, 1910, Emperor Francis Joseph decreed a constitution for the two provinces. The constitution made provisions for the establishment of a parliament—the Bosnian Sabor, or Assembly. However, the body had no authority. It had no right to elect, to supervise, or to control the work of the executive authorities (Article 31) headed by an appointed chief—a general; the government continued to be run by the joint Finance Ministry in Vienna. Moreover the Assembly did not have representatives of its own in the Delegations in Vienna. Only on certain second-rate matters of local significance did it have the right to submit an opinion.

The entire electoral system was undemocratic. Of the Assembly's ninety-two members, twenty-five were Virilists who became members on the basis of functions assigned them by the emperor. Catholics were in the majority. Seven of the Virilists were Catholics and only five Orthodox, although there were twice as many Orthodox as Catholics in Bosnia and Hercegovina. The president and vice president of the Assembly were also appointed by Vienna. A Muslim was named to the post of president of the Assembly, in spite of the fact that Orthodox Serbs were the largest national group in Bosnia and Hercegovina.

The remaining members of the Assembly were elected in line with the restricted franchise. Voters were divided up into curiae in accordance with their social and religious status. Large landowners had one representative per 80 voters, townspeople one per 2,300 voters, and peasants one per 10,000 voters. Young people had no right to vote, franchise being limited to adults over the age of twenty-four. Only those over thirty could be candidates.

Employment in the administration was also subject to discrimination. In 1904, of all the civil servants in Bosnia and Hercegovina, only 26.48 percent were natives of the province, most of them Catholics. Only 3 percent were Serbs, and 5 percent were Muslims.

The Serfs Buy Their Freedom

Agrarian relations also were aggravated as the regime in Vienna maintained the Ottoman feudal system. Burian refused to introduce compulsory emancipation of serfs; he announced the "gradual voluntary redemption of serfs" as the first step toward liberating the serfs from the grip of their feudal lords. Hungarian capital, having acquired privileges, founded the Privileged Agrarian Bank, which granted loans to serfs for the purchase of their liberty. But the interest rates were high and protests came from the villages. The landowners refused to sell serfs their land, from which they collected an annual rent of 12.4 percent. The joint minister of finances Leon Bilinski, perceiving that the gap was widening between the Serbian bourgeoisie, especially merchants and small bankers on the one hand and the masses of peasants on the other, decided to make this circumstance work to his political advantage. The number of local Serbian banks increased steadily until it reached twenty-six in 1914. These banks also granted loans to the peasants at high interest rates. The Serbian merchants themselves began to buy up land with serfs from the Muslim beys. According to statistics from 1910, 6.5 percent of all the feudal landowners in Bosnia and Hercegovina were Serbs. The first political organization of Serbian townspeople in Bosnia and Hercegovina, the Serbian National Organization, founded in 1907, split on the question of redemption of the serfs.

In the course of 1910, over 13,500 peasants and serfs were forced to leave the land for default in payment of taxes to the state and of the *trećina* or "third" (old feudal tax) owed to the landowners. Over 56,000 suits were brought against peasants and serfs. The first open conflict between peasants and the authorities occurred in August 1910 in the Bosnian March, when the so-called peasant strike was launched. Refusing to pay taxes and the third owed to the landowners, the rebellious peasants set fire to a number of buildings. Vienna issued orders to the military authorities to stop the peasant movement by any and all means. The Forty-ninth and Ninety-ninth Regiments from Sarajevo, as well as other units, were dispatched to the center of revolt. At Doboj the army opened fire on the serfs. Unrest spread to other parts of Bosnia, subsiding only in autumn of the same year. The serfs were subjected to reprisals, and in the district of Banja Luka alone over 200 peasants were brought to court.

On June 13, 1911, Emperor Francis Joseph issued an imperial charter proclaiming the principle of voluntary redemption of serfs. This introduced no essential change in the position of the serfs as it simply sanctioned the existing state of affairs. It was left up to the will of the landowners to grant the serfs their liberty upon receiving appropriate indemnity. The process of voluntary emancipation of the serfs dragged on. According to Karl Grünberg, a Viennese professor, the liquidation of serfdom in Bosnia and Hercegovina at that rate would have been completed in the year 2025. In his memoirs Bilinski later noted that the solution of the agrarian problem in Bosnia and Hercegovina "unfolded at snail's pace."

Social conditions in the towns were no better. Industrialization had produced a certain increase in the number of workers. At the turn of the century, there were about 50,000, but they were only a few percent of the population, the mass of which, or about 88 percent, still lived in the rural districts of Bosnia and Hercegovina. The workers had no rights whatsoever. The 1905 revolutionary events in Russia stimulated the workers to more militant activity. Early in May 1906 a general strike broke out in Sarajevo and spread rapidly to other areas. The workers demanded a nine-hour workday and regular payment of wages. The employees of the tobacco and brick factories in Sarajevo had been the first to come out on strike on April 30. On May 3 the police opened fire on a procession of workers, killing and wounding several. From Sarajevo the strike spread to factories in Mostar, Konjic, Ljubuško, Čapljina, Metković, Kakanj, Doboj, Vareš, Zenica, Travnik, Brod, Tuzla, and other towns. On May 14 three workers were killed in Zenica. Factory directors received instructions from Vienna not to comply with the workers' demands for higher wages. The army was sent to deal with the strikers, but in Vareš did not succeed in breaking up the demonstrations. Free peasants and serfs in the Sarajevo district joined the workers, asking that their demands be met. The same happened in Ljubuško. The strike was crushed only after severe action by the army.

Nonetheless in 1906 the authorities had to recognize the right of the workers to set up trade unions. Also, the Social Democratic party of Bosnia and Hercegovina was founded, the principal newspaper of which was *Glas Slobode* (the *Voice of Liberty*). Like most of the Social Democratic parties of the South Slavs, this one took as the basis of its activity the Erfurt Program of the German Social Democratic party.

Magyarization in Vojvodina and the Growth of the Agricultural Proletariat

Next to Slovenia, Vojvodina was economically the most highly developed Yugoslav land although characterized by slow capitalist industrialization. Between 1900 and 1910 the number of industrial workers rose from 22,150 to almost 30,000, with the sugar industry in the forefront, followed by flour mills. Some typical manufacturing activities in Vojvodina were hemp production, sawmills, brick kilns, and basketmaking.

Vojvodina's agriculture was among the most advanced in Austria-Hungary. Large landed estates (some of which ran to as much as 15,000 hectares) practiced capitalist methods of production; meanwhile the number of landless peasants grew steadily. Basically the agrarian proletariat consisted of emancipated serfs without land. As industrialization proceeded slowly, these serfs were unable to find employment in the towns. The resettlement of landless Hungarian peasants from northern Hungary in Vojvodina made matters in the rural districts even worse. The rich province of Bačka alone counted almost 60,000 landless.

The beginning of the century brought the acceleration of enforced Magyarization. In Bačka, for instance, between 1840 and 1918 the population grew 77 percent with the number of Hungarians increasing 310 percent, Germans 86 percent, Serbs and Bunjevci (Croats) 43 percent, and Romanians only 7 percent. According to the 1910 census, Vojvodina's population consisted of 38.6 percent Slavs, 31.7 percent Hungarians, 22.7 percent Germans, and 6 percent Romanians. But there were 560 Hungarian elementary schools, 157 Serbian, 120 German, and 41 Romanian.

In 1907 the Hungarian Parliament passed a law decreeing that teachers and students in all congregational schools had to study Hungarian and learn to speak it properly. In the summer of 1912 autonomy was abolished for Serbian church schools.

As World War I drew near, social hardships caused a growth in resistance in Vojvodina. Economic demands were raised alongside political. In the summer of 1906 a movement of the village poor and agricultural workers spread to twenty-three Hungarian županijas, including those in Vojvodina. At harvesttime work was stopped by the "harvesters' strikes." At the same time, the population insisted on the right to vote. In the autumn of 1907 a general political strike erupted in Hungary, conflicts with the police and army being recorded in Velika Kikinda, Subotica, Vršac, Veliki Bečkerek, and Pančevo.

The Hungarian Social Democratic party, founded in 1890, set up a special Serbian Agitation Committee for the Serbs in Vojvodina which organized the workers and published a number of newspapers, banned frequently by the authorities. The militant Krsta Iskruljev came to head the Serbian and Bunjevci Agitation Committee in 1909, but he was soon ousted by the opportunistic wing in the party. After leaving, he joined the Anarcho-Syndicalists.

CHAPTER 33

Modernism in Literature and Art

The Cultural Backwardness of the Yugoslav Lands

The complete induction of Yugoslav lands into the world economy resulted in changes in culture and education. The tempo of life picked up, and
economic contacts were established with virtually all large European states, wel-
coming new impulses in material and spiritual culture.

Technical culture remained predominantly German, not only in the
Yugoslav lands within the Hapsburg empire, but also in Serbia and Montenegro,
where German technology had also been instrumental in initiating modernization.

Cultural ties with Germany and Austria continued to be strong (French symbolism, for instance, penetrated to one section of western Yugoslavs through German and Austrian modernists) but the emphatic orientation of Serbia's economy to France was responsible for persuading young Serbs to study in Paris, where many of them came into direct contact with the latest development in French culture and thought.

The beginnings of a more pronounced industrialization and the greater flow of goods, accelerated urbanization, and the influx of population from country to town made it necessary to broaden the scope of general education. In this respect the Yugoslav lands were among the most backward in Europe. The only exception was Slovenia, where almost 90 percent of the population was literate even at the beginning of this century. But as one moved southward from the Sutla River, the number of illiterates increased to reach almost 90 percent in Bosnia and Hercegovina, and over 90 percent in Macedonia.

This was the era of imperialism, practiced by capitalist states large and small. In Germany and Austria-Hungary ruling circles deliberately pursued policies of denationalization and assimilation in the Slav lands, as Germanization and Magyarization paved the way for the penetration of their capital. We have seen in previous chapters the perseverance with which the Slovenes fought for their cultural individuality, for the right to use their mother tongue and to study in their own schools in Slovenia. The Serbs and the Bunjevci Croats in Vojvodina were in a similar position, threatened as they were by Magyarization.

However, some of the Yugoslav peoples, like the Macedonians, for instance, even after the collapse of Ottoman power which had ruled for five centuries, did not acquire the right to speak their own language or to be taught in their own schools. The Serbian authorities refused to permit this, considering Macedonians to be Serbs.

General material conditions, and the nature of society itself, did not allow of general education for all sections of the population. Education was a right that was unequally applied. Even as late as 1910, in Bosnia and Hercegovina only one-tenth of school-age children had the good fortune to attend school.

Some advancement was discernible in higher schools of learning, but certain Yugoslav peoples—the Slovenes, for example—were not able to establish a university of their own, for the Austrian government was loath to see the development of local Slovene cadres in science, education, and economy. The same was the case in certain other Yugoslav lands. Many young Yugoslavs who left their homeland to seek employment abroad found their way to the top of their chosen professions thanks to their talent and perseverance, as was the case in the United States with Nikola Tesla, Mihailo Pupin, and others.

In 1905 the Higher School of Learning in Belgrade became a university, and soon the level of teaching and the scientific achievements of professors and research workers reached that of other European centers. In the field of geography and sociology, there was Jovan Cvijić (1865–1927), in mathematics Mihailo Petrović (1868–1943), in astronomy Milutin Milanković (1879–1958). The University of Zagreb developed along similar lines in spite of the obstacles placed in its way by the Hungarian authorities. In Zagreb, too, the Yugoslav Academy of Sciences continued its fruitful activities. In its *Journal of National Life and Customs* Antun Radić published his meaningful "Bases for the Collection and Study of Materials about National Life." The geographer Andrija Mohorovičić (1857–1936) won a world reputation in his field. The philologist Vatroslav Jagić (1838–1923) taught at universities in Berlin and Petrograd, and in 1886 succeeded Miklošić as the head of the department of philology in Vienna. In Montenegro, Valtazar Bogišić (1834–1908) produced the draft of the Montenegrin Code of Property Laws.

The Significance of Books in Slovenia

Reading made rapid headway among the people. In this respect Slovenia held pride of place. For example, the Mohor Society, founded in 1852, published six books in the first year of its existence. Only 600 copies of each were printed at first, but by 1914, 88,500 copies of each were published—for a population of just over 1 million. Most of these books found their way to the villages of Slovenia, where they were read avidly. Against the background of the official policy of Germanization, books in the national tongue were an essential factor acting to strengthen national sentiments and were even helpful in maintaining the Slovenes as a nation. The fact that the leading Slovene poet of the romantic period, France Prešern, wrote in the Slovenian language gave the Slovene peasant a feeling of belonging to his nation. It is partly to this that the poet's prestige among the Slovenes may be attributed. In countries where the course of history ran differently, as in England, this was not the case. But the example of Slovenia may be compared with that of Scandinavia, more so with Bohemia and Slovakia, and perhaps even with Germany, where romanticism figured significantly in the national awakening of the masses. This tradition, dating from the romantic period in Slovenia, was consolidated further at the beginning of this century, when conditions for the existence of nations worsened to an even greater extent.

In Serbian areas the *Srpska Književna Zadruga* (the *Serbian Literary Cooperative*), founded in 1882 for the dissemination of fine literature, succeeded in offering selected works to a wide circle of readers. In Croatia the literary and scientific society, the *Matica Hrvatska*, published books and promoted cultural activity. It was particularly successful in its work of collecting folk songs and poems.

Literary journals played a role of growing importance in the spiritual life of individual nations. In Slovenia the outstanding magazines were *Dom in Svet* (the *Home and the World*) and *Ljubljanski Zvon* (the *Ljubljana Bell*); in Vojvodina *Venac (Marigold)* and the *Yearbook* of the Serbian Matica; in Croatia *Savremenik* (the *Contemporary*), which followed modernistic trends and published the best Croatian writers; in Bosnia and Hercegovina *Pregled (Survey)* and *Bosanska Vila* (the *Bosnian Fairy*). In Serbia the *Srpski Književni Glasnik* (the *Serbian Literary Herald*) was founded in 1901.

The Srpski Književni Glasnik and Jovan Skerlić

At the turn of the century, Jovan Skerlić, professor of literature at the University of Belgrade, became the editor of the *Glasnik*. Until his death in 1914, he wielded a decisive influence on the advancement of Serbian literature, in conjunction with Bogdan and Pavle Popović, in the spirit of modern French literature. Skerlić himself had the following to say about this:

> French influence is not confined simply to the translation of books and performance of French plays. Since the end of the nineties, it has been powerfully reflected also in original Serbian literature. This influence is facilitated by the great spiritual similarity between the French and Serbian mentalities and between the spirit of the French and Serbian languages. In large part, Serbian writers today draw inspiration from French literature; French influence is particularly strong in lyrics and in literary criticism, and to a certain extent in novels as well. The Serbian literary style is developing successfully on the great French model; punctuation, which had until recently been grammatical in accordance with the German, is now becoming logical in accordance with the French. Serbian literature today is advancing largely under the influence of French literature.

Bora Stanković (1876–1927) was the originator of the modern psychological approach to character portrayal in Serbian literature. As he delved into the centuries-old trauma and complexity of the soul of people living at the crossroads between East and West, Stanković, knowing nothing of the results of modern French literature in this sphere, achieved the same literary patterns as his European contemporaries in this art form.

Simo Matavulj (1852–1908) was eminently successful in depicting the mental anguish of Dinaric man as he clashed with oncoming civilization, his work reflecting palpably the influence of the Maupassant style in French literature. Ivo Ćipiko (1869–1923), also from the Adriatic coast, is an exceptional and singular example of the masterly application of Zola's naturalistic method to local characters and conditions.

The outstanding Serbian poets of the early twentieth century were Jovan Dučić, Aleksa Šantič, and Milan Rakić. The first two were Hercegovinians who founded the journal *Zora (Dawn)* in their native town of Mostar. Milan Rakić came from Belgrade.

The leading satirist of his time was Radoje Domanović. While castigating government bureaucracy, he also portrayed how the will could be bent under the pressure of authority's power. In Bosnia Petar Kočić, in his satire *Jazavac pred Sudom (The Porcupine on Trial)*, depicted the double-dealing morals of the Hapsburg authorities in Bosnia and their racist-ridden behavior toward the people.

Although inclined to modern trends in literature, Skerlić was impatient with trends toward pessimism. He had no understanding, nor could he have had, of the individualism and tragedy of Vladislav Petković-Dis or the futility of Sima Pandurović. The latter frequently published his works in the *Bosanska Vila*. Dimitrije Mitrinović, member of the Young Bosnians organization, had an ear more attuned to this type of poetry than Skerlić did.

The youthful Isidora Sekulić was another who did not pass the test of patriotism with Skerlić, the great and exalted national spokesman; her book *Fellow Travelers*, troubled and highly personal, was proclaimed by him to be unnecessary and even harmful during the great war effort of Serbia. Under the blows of the same whip, Milan Rakić, a poet of gentle atmosphere and eroticism, had to don sackcloth and ashes in his poem *At Gazi-Mestan* (the field of Kosovo, where the Serbian army was defeated in 1389):

> Today they tell us, children of this century,
> That we are unworthy of our history;
> That we have been caught up by the Western river
> And that our souls fear danger.
>
> My good land, they lie! Who loves you
> Today, he loves you, for he knows that you are the mother,
> While before our time, neither the fields nor the bare mountains
> Could give conscious love to anyone.

Modernism among the Croats and Slovenes

Modernism developed also in Croatia, where it lent fresh impulse to Croatian art as well as literature, breaking ground through the conflict between the older and the younger generation. The latter sought freedom of expression in all forms, destruction of narrow local frameworks, contact with the mainstream of world culture. Croatian modernists gained distinction in all fields, especially in poetry: Milan Begović (1876–1948), Vladimir Vidrić (1875–1909), Dragutin Domjanić (1875–1933). Ivo Vojnović (1857–1929) produced the most important plays in Croatian literature at the turn of the century.

FIGURE 37. Jovan Cvijić.

FIGURE 38. Ivan Meštrović,
"Mother and Child."

458

FIGURE 39.   Ivan Cankar.

FIGURE 40.   The writer Isidora Sekulić.

459

A. G. Matoš

Although not formally classified as belonging to the modernists, Antun Gustav Matoš (1873–1914) was the most distingushed representative of Croatian literature of his day, his influence extending beyond the boundaries of his own land. He was a connoisseur of French literature, his knowledge of it probably unsurpassed by any of his contemporaries. Matoš began his writing career with short stories and tales composed in the spirit of symbolic prose with roots in Croatian realism. But lyrics were his forte. He took no sides in the struggle between the younger and older generations in Croatia, although in terms of his conceptions he was actually the forerunner of the younger group. Emphasizing aesthetic criteria, he insisted that the poet owed allegiance to them alone; yet, at the same time, he demanded "engagement" from writers. For him, "the modern story is a study, actually an experiment, demonstrating some social idea." Matoš was highly influential with the younger generation of writers. A perennial rebel, he was simultaneously a conservative in his love of the past, and a visionary and wanderer who observed, measured, and compared everything he saw. Matoš also wrote all types of criticism and left behind him a number of unforgettable vignettes of Belgrade and Serbia, written with utter honesty. Some of them describe with telling insight the social psychology of Belgrade's atmosphere in the tumultuous days before 1912. Matoš's sharpness earned him many opponents, but the special method of polemics he introduced into criticism brought him numerous followers among writers and publicists.

Ivan Meštrović

Modernism also injected new conceptions into the arts. Academism was abandoned and new models were sought in French impressionism. Miroslav Kraljević (1885–1913) and Josip Račić (1885–1908) were the first painters to set out along the new road. They were followed by Vladimir Becić (1886–1954), Ljubo Babić (1890–   ), and others. Outstanding among sculptors was Ivan Meštrović (1883–1962), who looked to Rodin and the aesthetics of the Secession. His most important work dating from that period is the *Saint Vitus's Day Cycle*, its symbolism evoking the days of the Battle of Kosovo. After the victory of the Balkan States over the Ottoman Empire in the war of 1912, Meštrović created his *Allegory* group, representing emancipation from Ottoman tyranny. The monument was to have been placed on Terazije Square in Belgrade, but then World War I broke out. It was destroyed except for the figure of the Victor, placed in Kalemegdan Park in Yugoslavia's capital.

The modernists broke the bounds of narrow Balkan provincialism. Croatian painters and sculptors, together with their Serbian colleagues (Nadežda

Petrović, 1874–1915), and Slovene artists (Rikard Jakopič, 1869–1943; Matija Jama, 1872–1947; Ivan Grohar, 1867–1911) displayed their works at joint exhibitions in Ljubljana, Belgrade, and other Yugoslav towns.

In the realm of architecture, Viennese Secessionism reached out to influence Yugoslav areas as the twentieth century dawned. Ljubljana was forced to construct new buildings to replace those damaged by the earthquake of 1895; it did so in the Secessionist manner (the Kresija building, Hotel Union, the Bishopric High School in Šent Vid, and others). The Secession came to Belgrade via Russia and Hungary. In the very heart of town, the Moskva Hotel was erected in that style.

New trends were also discernible in acting, although the romantic style continued to hold its own. Petar Dobrinović ruled the Serbian stage. Dobrica Milutinović (1880–1956) rose to prominence among Serbian actors during the period of national resurgence (1903–1914), his temperamental style gaining him the enduring affection of the theater-going public. In Croatia the melodramatic pathos of the romantic style was abandoned, thanks to the efforts of Milica Mihičić and Mila Dimitrijević.

The Role of Intellectuals in Public Life

Modernism in literature was especially marked in its manifestation in Slovenia, where it arrived from Germany and Austria, retaining all its specific features: symbolism, decadence, individualism, and eroticism. The most famous representatives were Ivan Cankar, Dragotin Kette, Josip Murn Aleksandrov, and Oton Župančič.

Young poets found it hard to win the ear of the conservative public. In 1899, when Cankar published his lyrics under the name *Erotica*, the bishop of Ljubljana, Dr. Antun Bonaventura Jeglič, ordered the entire edition bought up and burned. Side by side with the poets appeared a new generation of Slovene literary historians and theorists (such as Ivan Prijatelj and France Kidrič).

To writers in the modern manner at the beginning of the century, whether Slovenes, Croats, or Serbs, Nikolai Chernyshevski's teaching was applicable: that the writer should be the "soldier of thought," that revolution in the spiritual life of individuals had to precede all social and political changes; that literature had to place itself in the service of progressive, national, and useful ideas.

Social conditions were such that the poet had to be a social reformer, no matter how pessimistic his poems might sound. Scientists followed the same rule. For example, while producing numerous important works in the field of geography and anthropogeography, Jovan Cvijić never forgot to point out the need for honest personal labor in the interests of the people, at a time when many a politician reeked of corruption. Cvijić knew the social psychology of his environment, and his words had a telling effect, especially on the younger generation. During the period of struggle by Balkan monarchies over Macedonia, Cvijić emphasized that the "Slav mass of that country is an independent entity neither Serbian nor Bulgarian."

New Conceptions of Yugoslavhood

In the early twentieth century, as the result of external pressure on one section of society in the Yugoslav lands, and especially on the youth, the idea emerged of the need for rapprochement and later even unification among certain peoples. The basis for this new concept of Yugoslavhood was the common ethnical origin and the danger of Germanic imperialism.

Various ideas were put forward as to how that unification should be effected. Bourgeois politicians of various Yugoslav lands, and especially the two largest—Serbia and Croatia—supported the assemblage of all Yugoslav lands around one center, the former around Belgrade and the latter around Zagreb. The fact that Serbia was an independent state and that its prestige had grown after the Balkan Wars bolstered these demands for unification. Illyrism also appeared in new form; voices could be heard denying the cultural individuality of various peoples and calling for the merger of all of them into one whole.

Dimitrije Tucović and Ivan Cankar

In contrast to such one-sided views, Socialists—in Belgrade Dimitrije Tucović and in Slovenia Ivan Cankar—submitted democratic proposals for the structure of the future state. The former, in the spirit of decisions taken by the Balkan Social Democratic Conference of 1910, saw a solution to the problem of Yugoslav unification in the form of a federation of Balkan republics on a footing of equality. In a lecture delivered on April 12, 1913, in Ljubljana, Cankar expressed his opposition to Neo-Illyrism and came out in support of a Yugoslav republic-federation with guarantees for preservation of the cultural specifics of each nation.

Simultaneously, overtones of chauvinism and support of the hegemony of one nation over others could be heard in the public life of all Yugoslav lands, stronger in some places, weaker in others. In Serbia this was noticeable in the posture of influential groups in the Radical and other bourgeois parties; in the top circles of the Orthodox church, where Nikolaj Velimirović endeavored to use the concept of messianism to justify ideas of the superiority of the Serbs over other peoples; and in the army and especially among the leadership of the secret organization *Unification or Death*, popularly called the "Black Hand." Among the Croats, the idea of hegemony by the Croatian people was assumed by the Frankists and the Clericalists, and in Slovenia by circles surrounding the Clericalist leader Šušteršić.

This intolerant trend was backed by the big powers, especially Vienna. The product of narrow-minded local views and utter lack of universality, these hegemonistic ideas were frequently supplemented by the personal complexes of those who expounded them. Lenin once pointed out that Stalin, "like all non-Russians, frequently overdid his Great-Russianism." Among the Croats, Dr. Frank's hatred of the Serbs was partially traceable to his non-Croat origins, for his father was a German Jew; Colonel Apis, in proclaiming Croatia and Dalmatia Serbian provinces, was goaded by his complex of being a Cincar rather than a Serb. Among the Macedonians, this was true of Vanče Mihajlov, who was also a Cincar.

Revolutionary Yugoslav Youth

The younger generation displayed its disapproval of such Balkan atavism and chauvinism. But they did not establish an integral, centralized organization; they were rather a part of the spontaneous revolutionary movement of the South Slav youth wherever they were: within the borders of Austria-Hungary, in Croatia, Dalmatia, Slovenia, Bosnia and Hercegovina, as well as in Serbia, Montenegro, and even among Yugoslav emigrants in America. These various groups were brought together by one objective: the revolutionary overthrow of the Hapsburg empire.

Youthful revolutionaries despised the Hapsburgs as the symbol of powerful state and military institutions which suppressed entire nations as well as classes, and also men as individuals. They opposed not only the Hapsburgs as the vehicle of foreign power but also the entire social system from which the Hapsburgs drew support, a system oppressive to young people. Consequently, where national and social conditions were the harshest, for instance, in Bosnia and Hercegovina, Dalmatia, and a part of Slovenia, the young people organized secret societies opposed to their own ruling classes as such. In Bosnia the rift between the two generations of Serbs ran deep; the Young Bosnians condemned their own compatriots who refused to fight to the end against the Hapsburgs but rather sought compromise in order to preserve their own special interests. In Croatia Vladimir Čerina and Janko Polić-Kamov held similar opinions.

The Young Bosnians, like similar secret societies in Dalmatia and Croatia, yearned for emancipation from parochial, patriarchal bonds everywhere: from stagnant society, from their conservative elders, from the conception that woman was the slave of man and his passions, from atavisms of all categories.

Vladimir Gaćinović, one of the ideologues of the Young Bosnians, cried on one occasion that "our fathers, our tyrants, have created this world on their model and are now forcing us to live in it."

These young people believed that society could be changed only by the action of morally strong and socially conscious individuals, who would set the example for the creation of a new and better type of person. Their ideas reflected the influence of Chernyshevski and other Russian Narodnjaks; in them there was something of Proudhon and also of Mazzini. But it was Svetozar Marković who carried particular weight with them. Markovic's socialist idealism was once formulated by Jovan Skerlić in the following manner: "In small countries especially, ideas are worth only as much as the people who support them."

They applied these ethnical principles in their own personal and public lives. Condemning the hypocrisy of leading sections of society in all spheres, they were horrified at the mutual intolerance of the Serbian, Croatian, and Muslim bourgeoisies, at the centuries of hatred, the carnage, and the refusal to recognize each other's rights. They saw a way out of the chaos in tolerance among nations and religions, and yearned to become a link helping man to bridge the gap of fratricidal massacre and bigotry generated by the history of conquest by foreign powers and the avarice of various ruling circles in each nation.

Groups of the Young Bosnia society established particularly close ties of cooperation with young Slovenes belonging to the *Preporod (Renaissance)* society. In its issue of January 1, 1913, the magazine *Preporod* published a poem sent from Bosnia, ending with the lines:

> Fear not, comrades; fear nothing; with you, brothers, are we from the Bosnian mountains, the land of the Neretva; with you in heart, soul and unerring arrow— gift of Perun—are we. Boldly forward to our common work—in the great struggle for Yugoslavia.

The Young Bosnians and other secret associations of the revolutionary youth were not concerned with ethics alone; they turned their attention also to other spheres of spiritual and intellectual life. As World War I drew near, one of the most active was the literary group which fought against academism and upheld modern trends in literature. For them, writing in free verse was a form of revolt against professors who tried to force them into the mold of classicism.

Sensing fully the extent of Europe's decay at the beginning of this century—and this intuitive awareness of the need for something new and fresh and audacious was far more developed among the young people—Dimitrije Mitrinović and Vladimir Čerina, two of the leading thinkers of South Slav revolutionary generations before 1914, proclaimed Ibsen's concept of permanent revolt as the principal law of life.

As for the older generation, the young revolutionaries respected Cankar (with whom they maintained contact from time to time), Frano Supilo (after his resignation from the Croatian-Serbian coalition), Jovan Skerlić as a literary historian and national spokesman (Gavrilo Princip laid a wreath at his grave a few weeks before his assassination of Archduke Francis Ferdinand in Sarajevo on June 28, 1914), Antun Gustav Matoš (for his preaching of the cult of energy), and Jovan Cvijić.

They took exception to the local Social Democratic parties, especially in Bosnia and Hercegovina. In the newspaper *(Zvono)*, on May 30, 1914, a member of the Young Bosnians, Danilo Ilić, took the Social Democratic party to task for being no different from bourgeois parties in terms of democracy, for its statutes were not

> regulative from the bottom up, in the federalist manner, but rather from the top down, in the centralized and hierarchical manner, like the Catholic church. The central party administration holds absolute power over members, who must obey it uncomplainingly, so that virtually all criticism by members is precluded. The party runs things according to its own will and the personal interests of a few top men; the people in this party, like those in others, do what the bosses order. If someone does not obey, he is expelled from the party, in the interests of party discipline. Consequently, this party, too, rests on undemocratic, conservative, and even autocratic foundations.

The Idea of Individual Acts of Terrorism as a Means of Achieving Liberation

Owing to the backwardness of their own society and the colonial conditions existing in Bosnia and Hercegovina, the Young Bosnians had become rebels so spontaneously that they were incapable of adapting to the modern ideologies of mass movements acting against oppressive systems.

Like similar societies in Croatia, Dalmatia, and Montenegro, they were therefore champions of the tactics of individual acts of terrorism. Between 1910 and 1914 they organized a number of assassination attempts on the lives of Hapsburg dignitaries: Emperor Francis Joseph in May 1910, during his visit to Bosnia; the head of Bosnia and Hercegovina, General Marijan Varešanin, at whom Bogdan Žerajić, a student from Hercegovina, fired five bullets on June 15, 1910, after which he committed suicide; on June 8, 1912, a Bosnian student, Luka Jukić, fired at the ban of Croatia, Slavko Cuvaj, killing a high-ranking official and a policeman and wounding two other policemen; a student of Zagreb, Ivan Planinščak, tried to kill Ban Cuvaj in Zagreb on October 31,1912; a Croatian youth, Stjepan Dojčić, who had emigrated to the United States of America, returned to his homeland to kill Cuvaj. In the meantime Baron Ivo Škerlec had become ban of Croatia; Dojčić attempted to kill him but succeeded only in wounding him in the hand on August 18, 1913. On May 15 another Zagreb student,

Jakov Šefer, made an attempt on the life of Archduke Salvador and Ban Škerlec as they were leaving the National Theater in Zagreb. He had already drawn his revolver when he was apprehended by a policeman.

The archives in Vienna contain numerous documents attesting that secret revolutionary societies among the South Slavs had laid plans for the assassination of many leading persons in the Hapsburg empire.

CHAPTER 34

The Assassination in Sarajevo and the Outbreak of World War I

The Motives of the Youthful Assassins

On Saint Vitus's Day, June 28, 1914, a group of students and workers belonging to the Young Bosnia society (Danilo Ilić, Nedeljko Čabrinović, Gavrilo Princip, Muhamed Mehmedbašić, Trifko Grabež, Vasa Čubrilović, Cvetko Popović), assisted by young like-minded Serbs, Muslims, and Croats, and also supported by others—some peasants (Mitar Kerović, Jakov Milović, Nedjo Kerović), intellectuals (the youthful teacher Veljko Čubrilović), and merchants (Miško Jovanović)—assassinated the heir to the Hapsburg throne, Archduke

467

FIGURE 41. Gavrilo Princip.

Francis Ferdinand, during his visit to Sarajevo following the completion of large-scale maneuvers in Bosnia by the Austro-Hungarian army.

It was Gavrilo Princip who shot and killed Francis Ferdinand "for the common good, as a tyrant," in protest against the colonial position in which Bosnia and Hercegovina were kept at a time of spreading struggle by the South Slavs for national liberation. The conspiracy was the work of the Young Bosnians, in cooperation with other revolutionary associations among the South Slavs.

It would be an exaggeration to claim that the Sarajevo assassination was the basic or immediate cause of the war of 1914–1918. Under other, more normal international circumstances, this event could not have triggered off such significant consequences. But the antagonisms between the big powers had generated such tension, and the reorganization and rearming of the German army had achieved such a level, that only a minor provocation was needed to touch off a conflagration.

The Warlike Group in Vienna Grasps Its Opportunity

The Sarajevo assassination was an unexpected gift from the god Mars to the warlike party in Vienna which had been searching since the annexation crisis of 1908–1909 for any kind of excuse to attack Serbia and pacify the South Slavs, and to expand Hapsburg power to the very gateway of Salonika. General Conrad von Hötzendorf, chief of staff of the Austro-Hungarian army, stated after June 28, 1914:

> This is not simply the crime of a fanatic; the assassination is Serbia's declaration of war on Austria-Hungary. . . . If we let this chance pass, the empire will be exposed to fresh explosions of Yugoslav, Czech, Russian, Romanian, and Italian aspirations. . . . Austria-Hungary must wage war for political reasons.

The Viennese government was poised to invade Serbia immediately, without warning of any kind. Germany backed the "hawks" of Vienna, as attested by documents from Austro-Hungarian archives and newly revealed materials from German archives. At a meeting of the Austro-Hungarian government on July 7, 1914, only the president of the Hungarian government, Stephan Tisza, advised caution, although General Potiorek considered "that Austria-Hungary has to go to war with Serbia if it wishes to remain in the Balkans." Consequently the Viennese government decided to attack Serbia while endeavoring to win over world public opinion by accusing the Serbian government of complicity in the assassination. The Austrian minister to Belgrade, Wladimir Giesl von Gieslingen, stated in Vienna that the "assassination has created a favorable moral atmosphere for us." All preparations for the aggression were made in secret so as to achieve surprise both against Serbia and among the big Allied Powers.

General Conrad von Hötzendorf even ostensibly went on his summer holiday.

A special envoy of the Foreign Ministry in Vienna, Friedrich von Wiesner, was dispatched to Sarajevo on July 10, 1914, to examine the materials from the interrogation and to bring back proof of the Serbian government's responsibility for the assassination. But as a conscientious public official, reared in the spirit of the Viennese administration's concept of Austria as a *Rechsstaat*, he telegraphed Vienna on July 13:

> There is nothing whatsoever to indicate the responsibility of the Serbian government for organizing or preparing the murder, or supplying weapons. There is also nothing to lead one to suspect anything of the kind. On the contrary, there is evidence seeming to indicate that nothing of the sort can be suspected. . . .

Why the Serbian Government Did Not Want War with Austria-Hungary

The Serbian government headed by Nikola Pašić obviously had no intention of provoking any kind of conflict with Austria-Hungary. After two grueling Balkan wars, and the great Albanian revolt in the autumn of 1913, the Serbian army was exhausted. Losses and casualties had been high, weapons were lacking (the army was about 120,000 rifles short). Beginning with 1912, the Serbian economy had fallen behind because of the wars.

The Serbian prime minister, Nikola Pašic, had tried to improve relations between the two countries. Serbian diplomacy also feared the outbreak of a new Balkan war. Greece and Turkey were on the brink of hostilities. The Serbian government had made considerable concessions to Vienna during negotiations to settle the problem of indebtedness for the Oriental Railway, and other economic concessions associated with railroads. Serbia had taken over the debt of 42 million francs owed by the Ottoman Empire to financiers of the Ottoman railways for a section of the line in Macedonia and Kosovo which was ceded to Serbia after 1912.

Moreover, internal conditions in Serbia were not peaceful. Although the antagonism between military and civilian authorities had been smoothed out formally, the conflict between the conspirators headed by Colonel Apis and Nikola Pašić's government continued unabated. On June 23 the National Assembly was dissolved, and new elections were scheduled for August 1.

The Inquiry in Sarajevo Establishes the Innocence of the Serbian Government

Seeking to avoid any incident with Vienna in connection with Francis Ferdinand's journey to Bosnia and Hercegovina, the Serbian government extended full assistance to the Austro-Hungarian authorities when a group of students from the teachers college in Pakrac fled to Serbia. These students had allegedly claimed that Francis Ferdinand would be killed and that a large number of terrorist acts would be undertaken throughout the Hapsburg empire. The Serbian authorities kept vigilant watch over all movements along the Serbian-Bosnian boundary. Through officials of the National Defense Ministry, the minister of internal affairs, Stojan Protić (1857–1923), was informed that certain persons armed with grenades and revolvers had crossed into Bosnia from Serbia. Protić informed Nikola Pašić, who discussed the case with some cabinet members. Protić received instructions to order civilian authorities along the border to conduct an inquiry; also, as minister of internal affairs, he issued an edict against the unlawful transportation of persons and weapons across the boundary. A similar edict was issued by the defense minister.

Nikola Pašić further instructed the defense minister to conduct an inquiry into the behavior of Colonel Apis, suspicion having been aroused as to the involvement of some of his subordinates in arms smuggling. Simultaneously, Nikola Pašić took steps through the Defense Ministry to stop the young men who had already crossed the border.

All those involved in the Sarajevo assassination were subjects of Austria-Hungary; they denied that they had had any connection whatsoever with Serbian officialdom or with the Serbian authorities. But directly before the assassination, three of the conspirators—Princip, Grabež, and Čabrinović—had lived in Belgrade, where they tried to purchase weapons. Without funds, they could not buy any and so they acquired them through some of their acquaintances, Bosnian Komitas, associated with Vojislav Tankosić, also from Bosnia, and otherwise Colonel Apis's right-hand man.

Colonel Apis's role in the organization of the assassination remains ambiguous. There is evidence that after the inquiry by the civilian authorities and interrogation of Apis himself, he tried to stop the assassins, but they rejected any meddling from the outside. Later in 1916, when Colonel Apis was arrested and accused of responsibility for the Sarajevo assassination, in order to save his life and that of his comrades, he magnified his role in the case.

The Ultimatum of July 23, 1914

Although the official representative of the Viennese Foreign Ministry, Wiesner, established that there was no evidence of responsibility on the part of the Serbian government for the assassination, the government in Vienna, desirous of squaring accounts with Serbia by force of arms, drew entirely different conclusions in a note and ultimatum to Serbia of July 23, 1914. Official Serbia was accused of inciting Serbs in Bosnia against the Hapsburg empire, and it was stated that the idea of the assassination had been hatched in Belgrade, that the assassins were supplied with weapons and ammunition by officers and government officials, members of the *Narodna Odbrana* [*National Defense*] organization, and that they had been transported across the border to Bosnia by officers of the Serbian Boundary Patrol.

The Viennese government further demanded that the Serbian government officially condemn all propaganda against the Austro-Hungarian Empire, that a statement to this effect be published on the front page of the *Official Gazette*, and that the king inform the Serbian army of this in his orders of the day. Furthermore, the Serbian government was asked to undertake an obligation involving the following ten points:

1. That it prohibit all publications inciting to hatred and scorn of the Empire and its general policies and against its territorial integrity.

2. That it immediately dissolve the *Narodna Odbrana* organization and undertake similar action against all other associations in Serbia conducting propaganda against the Austro-Hungarian Empire and take measures ensuring that the dissolved associations do not continue their activities under a different name or in a different form.

3. That it expel from the school system in Serbia all teachers and teaching aids that could be used in propaganda against Austria-Hungary.

4. That it discharge from military service and government administration all officers and officials who had erred by conducting propaganda against the Empire, whose names and misdeeds the Royal and Imperial Government in Vienna would later submit to the Royal Government of Serbia.

5. That it accept the collaboration of organs of the Royal and Imperial Government to quell the subversive movement directed against the territorial integrity of the Empire.

6. That it institute court proceedings against participants in the plot of June 28, who were apprehended on Serbian territory. Organs delegated by the Imperial and Royal Government would participate in the inquiry.

7. That it immediately arrest Major Vojislav Tankosić and the official Milan Ciganović, who had been compromised by the inquiry in Sarajevo.

8. That it take decisive measures to prevent unlawful trade in weapons and ammunition across the boundaries by Serbian authorities; that it discharge and severely punish officials of the Boundary Patrol in Šabac and Loznica who had helped the Sarajevo assassins by assisting them across the border.

9. That it supply the Imperial and Royal Government with an explanation for the unjustifiable addresses made by high-ranking Serbian officials in Serbia and abroad who, in spite of their official status, did not hesitate even after the assassination of June 28 to make hostile statements about the Austro-Hungarian Empire in interviews.

10. That it inform without delay the Imperial and Royal Government

of the implementation of measures it promised to undertake under the preceding paragraphs.

The Serbian public had not anticipated such sharp measures on the part of the Viennese government, whose deceptive tactics thereby achieved their goal. At that time Prime Minister Nikola Pašić was traveling through Serbia on an election campaign, and the chief of staff, General Putnik, had gone to a spa in Austria for treatment.

The Austro-Hungarian note and ultimatum were received by Pašić's deputy, Dr. Lazar Paču, on July 23 at 6 P.M. The entire Serbian government was in session, with the exception of Pašić and Stojan Protić, waiting to see the contents of the note. In delivering the note, the Austro-Hungarian envoy, Giesl, stated that he would leave Belgrade with the personnel of the Mission on July 25 at 6 P.M. unless the Serbian government submitted a satisfactory reply.

The Reply of the Serbian Government, July 25

The Serbian government discussed the note, the general opinion being that it should be rejected. According to the memoirs of the principal secretary of the Serbian Foreign Ministry, Dr. Slavko Grujić, after the Serbian ministers had read the note, the first to venture an opinion was the education minister, Ljuba Jovanović (1865–1927): "There is no recourse but to die."

The historic decision was adopted unanimously by the cabinet members. The same night Lazar Paču sent a circular cable to all Serbian diplomatic missions stating that Serbia would go to war if it were inevitable. It so happened that neither Russia nor France nor England had envoys in Belgrade at that time, but only junior diplomatic representatives. Paču called on the Russian chargé d'affaires Schtrandman to inform him that the Serbian government would appeal to the big powers friendly to Serbia for protection. If war was unavoidable, Serbia would fight. Regent Aleksandar also visited the Russian mission to declare that the Serbian government would not take a decision until Pašić returned.

At dawn the next day, July 24, Pašić arrived in Belgrade and paid a call on the Russian Mission at 5 A.M. He too favored rejecting the Austro-Hungarian ultimatum. The same morning, he met with the British chargé d'affaires and asked the British government to intercede with the government in Vienna to tone down its demands, which were "unacceptable to Serbia." Pašić also received the Montenegrin and Greek ministers. Regent Aleksandar dispatched an impassioned appeal to the Russian tsar and Italian king.

At a meeting of the government on July 24, Pašić asked that no decision be taken until Russia's opinion had been heard, and his suggestion was accepted. In the afternoon of the same day, the Russian government met. It decided to counsel Serbia to put up no resistance in case of Austro-Hungarian aggression but rather to withdraw Serbian troops gradually into the country's interior. At the same time, the Serbian government should declare that it entrusted its destiny to the big powers and request their mediation.

At the same session, the Russian government decided to mobilize four military districts bordering on Austria-Hungary.

In the course of July 24, the Serbian government ordered evacuation of Belgrade, remaining steadfast in its decision not to buckle down to Vienna. The draft of the Serbian government's reply was composed by Pašić and Stojan Protić, and the other ministers inserted additions. The French translation of the reply dragged on, the only typewriter with Roman letters in the Foreign Ministry broke down, and the last part of the Serbian answer had to be written out by hand. The translation was completed by 5:45 P.M., or fifteen minutes before the deadline set in the ultimatum. The question arose as to who would deliver the reply. As the other officials hesitated, according to Slavko Grujić, Pašić himself undertook the task:

> He put the big envelope containing our reply under his arm, left slowly and calmly, and descended the stairs from the top of which I was watching, thinking to myself, "There goes our destiny."

Pašić personally delivered the Serbian government's reply to Giesl. The Serbian government acceded to all the points in the ultimatum except the sixth, as that "would be a violation of the Constitution and Criminal Code." Tankosić was arrested the same evening that the reply was delivered, but Ciganović could not be traced. At the end of the reply, the Serbian government stated that it was ready to accept a peaceful agreement, and insofar as the Austro-Hungarian government was not satisfied with the reply, it was ready to submit controversial points for consideration to the International Court in The Hague or the big powers who had taken part in defining the declaration of the Serbian government of March 31, 1909.

Austria-Hungary Declares War on Serbia

Giesl immediately noticed that the Serbian government had not accepted all the points of the ultimatum. He informed Pašić that he was dissatisfied with the reply and would leave Belgrade forthwith. The same evening the Serbian government withdrew to Niš. On July 28 the Austro-Hungarian government declared war on Serbia, by telegram. The poet Sibe Miličić happened to be in a cafe in Niš, lunching at a table near that of Pašić when a gendarme presented Pašić with the telegram. Pašić stroked his long white beard, read the message, rose, and informed those present:

> "Austria has declared war on us. This is its end. God will grant us victory."

CHAPTER 35

The Collapse
of the
Austro-Hungarian Offensive
of 1914

POTIOREK'S DEFEAT AT CER, GUĆEVO, AND KOLUBARA / FRATRI-
CIDAL WAR AMONG THE SOUTH SLAVS / THE LONDON TREATY /
SERBIA'S WAR AIMS / THE NIŠ DECLARATION / THE CREATION OF
THE YUGOSLAV COMMITTEE

Potiorek's Defeat at Cer, Gućevo, and Kolubara

Austria-Hungary's aggression against Serbia terminated in total defeat during the first year of the war. Between August 12 and the middle of December 1914, the aggressors undertook three offensives, all of which ended in fiasco. In these battles, over 273,000 officers and men of the Austro-Hungarian army were immobilized, or almost one-fifth of its entire land army.

The Serbian Supreme Command headed by Crown Prince Aleksandar Karadjordjević, General Radomir Putnik as chief of staff, and Deputy General

Živojin Mišić had expected the principal strike to come from the north, for it was logical to anticipate that the enemy would strive to reach the Morava Valley and other Danube and Saba tributaries. But General Potiorek, commander of the Balkan front, between July 25, the day of partial Austrian mobilization, and August 12, concentrated his forces on the Drina River (Fifth and Sixth Armies, while the Second Army, as a reserve, took up position north of Mačva). The Austro-Hungarian army was thus faced with the task of conquering a number of mountain areas suitable for defense. It is not clear what persuaded the Supreme Command in Vienna and Potiorek to change the war plan. Potiorek himself, as governor of Bosnia and Hercegovina, feared deterioration of the political situation in the occupied provinces; the Sarajevo assassination and the discovery of a network of Young Bosnian organizations aroused his suspicion that an offensive by the Serbian army across the Drina River might provoke an insurrection, especially among Bosnian Serbs.

From General Potiorek's diary, kept from the very first day of the war and up to his replacement at the end of December 1914, it is obvious that his intelligence service possessed rather accurate information about the deployment of Serbian units, the Serbian army's short supply of armaments, and the scarcity of ammunition and clothing. This encouraged him to belittle his opponent. He thought of the attack on Serbia in terms of a punitive expedition, completely ignoring the factor of morale, and the readiness of the Serbian peasant to defend his land in spite of all material obstacles. At the same time, the Supreme Command in Vienna was in a hurry; Serbia had to be put out of commission in short order so that all Austro-Hungarian forces could be sent to the front in Galicia against Russia.

General Potiorek predicted that his Fifth Army would take Valjevo within six days, and that the Second Army would need simply to make a show of strength in the north. However, the Serbian army was ready for the enemy on August 12 when he crossed the Drina River at Loznica and Lešnica, and joined battle at Cer Mountain. Only twelve days after the launching of Potiorek's offensive, his last soldier had been expelled from Serbian territory. Roughly 25,000 men were immobilized. The Battle of Cer was the first allied victory in World War I.

The Russian and French Supreme Commands demanded that the Serbian army undertake the offensive without delay so as to relieve the pressure on the front in Galicia. Although the Serbian army had itself suffered great casualties in the Battle of Cer (over 16,000 men) and lacked ammunition, it crossed over into Srem while Montenegrin units penetrated deep into Bosnia all the way to Pale and Jahorina, and sections of the Serbian Užice Army reached Romania and Vlasenica.

In the meantime General Potiorek undertook his second offensive on September 8. The Serbian army withdrew from Srem. Potiorek advanced

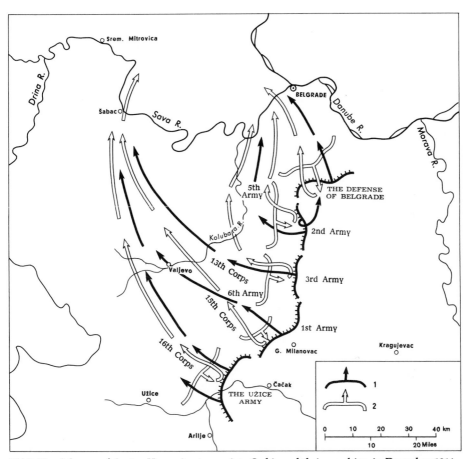

MAP 40.   Advance of Austro-Hungarian troops into Serbia and their expulsion in December 1914.
(1) Positions and movements of the Serbian army; (2) positions and movements of the
Austro-Hungarian troops.

methodically only to meet staunch resistance from the Serbian army at Mačkov
Kamen and Gučevo. Prince Djordje, commander of a battalion, was seriously
wounded at Mačkov Kamen. The second offensive bled both sides white. Almost
half of Potiorek's troops were thrown out of commission.

Potiorek took advantage of the lull to reinforce his units, whose number
rose to over 250,000 men. The Serbian army was in crisis particularly because of
the scarcity of ammunition. It had to abandon Valjevo and take up positions on
the right bank of the Kolubara. In order to shorten the front, Belgrade was
evacuated. Emperor Francis Joseph sent special congratulations to Potiorek for
his success in conquering Belgrade, and the Turkish sultan awarded him the high-

est Ottoman decorations. The total collapse of Serbia was expected at any moment.

The Serbian Supreme Command exploited the fact that Potiorek had spread his forces out too thinly in the north, and during a lull of several days gave its fatigued units a respite. Ammunition had finally arrived via Salonika; General Živojin Mišić, commander of the First Serbian Army, decided to counterattack. He took the mountain of Suvobar and broke through Potiorek's front. Pursuit of the Austro-Hungarian troops began, and on December 15 Belgrade was liberated again. Potiorek, previously the emperor's favorite, was retired, withdrawing to his brother's castle Brusnik, on the Sava River between Zagorje and Trbovlje. He had not even had enough time to receive the sultan's decoration.

The Serbian army also had sustained heavy casualties during Potiorek's three offensives. When the war began, it had had 250,000 men in the operational army. Of that number about 132,000 were no longer fit for active duty.

The Battle of Kolubara was the greatest victory of the Serbian army in World War I. The official British history of that war noted that although the Battle of the Marne was referred to as a miracle, it would be far more justifiable to speak of the miracle at the Kolubara River.

Fratricidal War among the South Slavs

In World War I the state and social structures of the belligerent countries by pressure and demagoguery goaded the masses under their rule into exterminating each other. A profound rift occurred in the international workers' movement. In spite of the resolutions adopted at congresses of the Second International of various Social Democratic parties to the effect that they would not permit the imperialists to conduct a war of extermination, the spirit of internationalism was relegated to the background from the very first day of hostilities. The three most powerful Social Democratic parties, those of Germany, France, and Austria, joined the bandwagon of the bourgeoisie.

Lenin's Bolshevik party was an exception among the Russian Social Democrats. The Serbian Social Democratic party also adhered to the principle of proletarian internationalism and voted in the National Assembly against war credits. Lenin acclaimed the position assumed by them, which caused them considerable political difficulties: the Serbian government banned various issues of *Radničke Novine* (the *Workers' News*) that castigated corruption in the army, especially concerning purchases of food and footwear for the troops. On the other hand, the Social Democrats realized that Serbia was waging a defensive war, as emphasized by Lenin himself in some of his wartime articles. The leader of the Serbian Social Democrats, Dimitrije Tucović, although condemning World War I as an imperialist war, did his duty as a Serbian officer and was killed in battle late in 1914.

The South Slavs could not avoid fratricidal warfare, especially in the early years of the war. The basic force of Potiorek's Balkan Army which attacked Serbia was the Fifteenth Corps (with headquarters in Sarajevo), the Sixteenth Corps (with headquarters in Dubrovnik), the Thirteenth Corps (with headquarters in Zagreb), and the Eighth Corps (with headquarters in Prague). In some of the divisions of these corps, 20 to 25 percent of the men were Serbs from Bosnia, Hercegovina, Croatia, and Dalmatia, and the number of Croats came to over 50 percent.

The bulk of these soldiers were peasants, backward and intimidated. This was not the first time in the history of the South Slavs that they had slaughtered each other for the sake of their masters. In the "Battle of Peoples" near Leipzig in 1813, the Hapsburgs sent South Slav soldiers from the northern districts of the Military Frontier to fight South Slavs from the southern part of the Military Frontier, which was under French rule. So South Slav blood was shed on both sides for the sake of the Hapsburgs and Napoleon.

As soon as the war broke out in 1914, the Austro-Hungarian authorities brought great pressure to bear on all South Slav lands, accusing of high treason all those who disagreed with the aggression against Serbia. The Vatican also approved the Austro-Hungarian assault on Serbia. Secretary of State del Val told Pálfy, the Austro-Hungarian representative to the Vatican, on July 29, 1914, that "he cherished the hope that the monarchy would finish the work it had begun and destroy Serbia."

Under the influence of the higher clergy, the Clericalists and Frankists in Slovenia, Croatia, Bosnia, and Hercegovina instigated fratricidal war against the Serbs. On July 27, 1914, the Ljubljana newspaper *Slovenec* (the *Slovene*) joyously announced that the state authorities had banned the publication of the Slovene Social Democratic papers *Zora (Dawn)* and *Rudar* (the *Miner*), and that the infamous Serbophile newspaper *Glas Juga (Voice of the South)* had also been silenced. Actually *Glas Juga* was the organ of the Slovene revolutionary, renaissance-oriented youth who maintained close ties with the Young Bosnians.

In the same issue of the Clericalist *Slovenec*, there appeared the slogan "Serbs on Willow Trees" (referring to the hanging of adversaries), in a poem dedicated to Franz Ferdinand under the title "Flash Attack":

A funeral dirge is heard in heaven
To avenge the blood of Ferdinand and Sophie.
You [Serbs] have been provoking us for a long time to massacre.

We have awakened after a long sleep.
With cannons we'll greet all Serbs,
And we shall make your cold home [gallows] the willow tree.[1]

---

[1] According to Franček Saje in the book *Belogardizam*, published in Ljubljana in 1951, p. 10, this poem was written by Marko Natlačen, who later became governor of Drava province (Slovenia). He led the legation of Slovenian bourgeoisie to Mussolini in 1941. The executive board of the Libera-

Vienna's military-minded circles gave their wholehearted support to the Clericalist *Slovene* and similar papers in Slovenia during World War I. In 1915, when the *Slovene* asked the Viennese government for a subsidy, General Conrad von Hötzendorf personally gave his recommendation, stressing that it was "the newspaper most loyal to the monarchy in Austria."

The court in Vienna and the Supreme Command were particularly desirous of widening the cleavage between Serbs and Croats. The Forty-second Croatian Home Guard Division, known as the Devil's Division, took part in the operations in Serbia in 1914. It was the only unit in the Austro-Hungarian army to which Emperor Francis Joseph sent a personal thank-you note for congratulations sent to him on his birthday. And Potiorek shuffled his troops about so as to permit the Twenty-sixth Infantry Regiment of Karlovac to be the first to enter Belgrade on December 2, 1914. Their entry was clamorously publicized, Emperor Francis Joseph himself issuing a proclamation of "gratitude to the Croats." In the battle at Mačkov Kamen in September 1914, fighting on one side was the Fourth Regiment of Užice and on the other a regiment from Lika including a large number of Serbs from that area whose forebears had for centuries been the most faithful soldiers of the Hapsburg emperors. Commander Purić of the Užice regiment led his men in fourteen charges, to which the men from Lika responded with lightninglike countercharges. In one of these Purić shouted to them, "Surrender, don't die so stupidly," and they replied, "Have you ever heard of Serbs surrendering?"

In a proclamation to the British people and Parliament of May 12, 1915, the Yugoslav Committee emphasized that the occupiers had forced a fratricidal civil war on the South Slavs, eight million of whom, living in the monarchy, had been "compelled to fight against their own brothers and liberators." The proclamation went on to state that a large number of people had been expelled from their homes, that many citizens had been condemned to death, and that jails were filled to overflowing with political prisoners.

The London Treaty

The imperialist character of World War I was reflected especially in the lack of respect for the right of peoples to self-determination. Secret agreements involving the destiny of territories belonging to small states and unliberated

---

tion Front sentenced Natlačen to death, a penalty executed by Slovenian partisans in summer 1942. In the *Slovenec* of July 27, 1914, no author was given for the poem "Flash Attack." But the *Slovenec* stated that on July 29, 1914, Dr. Marko Natlačen had given a warmongering speech on Star Square in Ljubljana.

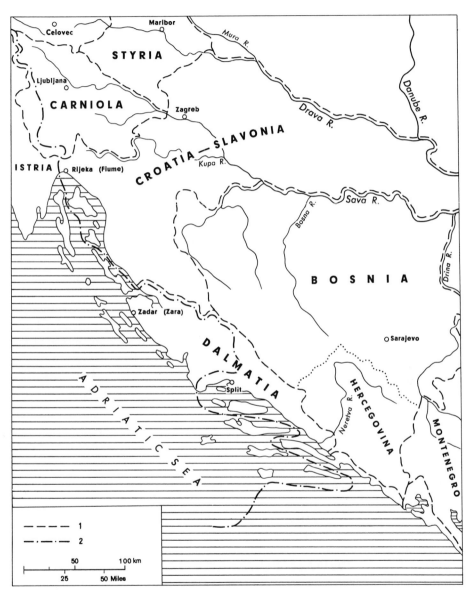

MAP 41.   Italy's boundaries by the London Pact of April 26, 1915. (1) Boundaries of 1914; (2) the line of the London Pact.

peoples were concluded behind their backs. The Yugoslav peoples in particular were victimized by such secret arrangements.

England, France, and Russia were anxious to win Italy to their side although it had been an ally of Germany and Austria-Hungary up to 1914. Rome asked the allies for southern Tirol, Trieste with Istria, a large part of Dalmatia, a portion of Albania, and even some districts in Asia Minor, thus initiating some painful bargaining. Russia was the most hesitant of all the allies. But when London informed Petrograd that the British government would comply with Russian demands for Constantinople, Russia's hesitancy vanished and the London Treaty was signed on April 26, 1915. The agreement provided that what was left of Albanian territory after Italy took what it wanted would be divided up among Greece, Montenegro, and Serbia.

Serbia's War Aims

The first year of the war also raised the question of future relations among the South Slav lands. All the big powers were firm in the view that the Austro-Hungarian monarchy should not be dismembered, which meant it would be impossible for the Yugoslavs to unite in one state. In Serbia the industrial and mercantile bourgeoisie felt that the state of Serbia should take advantage of the war to win new markets and to gain an outlet to the sea. Its program was to extend Serbia across the Sava and Drina Rivers to all lands where Serbs lived. The idea of unification of all South Slavs held no particular attraction for these circles, who placed their reliance above all on tsarist Russia. And ruling circles in Petrograd opposed the creation of a single South Slav state in which the Catholic Croats and Slovenes would also be influential.

The Niš Declaration

The Old Radical party, headed by Nikola Pašić, represented these views in Serbia, although Pašić, depending on the political exigencies of the moment, sometimes agreed to the program of unification of all Yugoslav peoples with Serbia as the pivot. The Independents, as well as most intellectuals, demonstrated greater understanding of the idea of a united Yugoslavia. On September 4, 1914, Nikola Pašić, in his capacity as foreign minister, sent a circular letter to all Serbia's diplomatic missions emphasizing that "a strong southwest-Slav state should be created out of Serbia, in which all Serbs, Croats, and Slovenes would be included." The Serbian government submitted its official public program relating to its war aims in a declaration in the National Assembly of December

7, 1914, in Niš. By and large, it repeated the ideas set forth in the circular letter of September 4, 1914.

The Creation of the Yugoslav Committee

The revolutionary youth in the Yugoslav lands under Hapsburg rule were the most persevering in the effort to create a community of Yugoslav peoples, although they had little influence over the masses once the war broke out because of the terror that reigned, and other circumstances. The leaders of the bourgeois parties of Croatia and Slovenia adhered more or less to the positions of the Hapsburgs. Exceptions were to be found among some of the politicians of Dalmatia: Frano Supilo, Ante Trumbić, and Ivan Meštrović, who were responsible for the idea of setting up a Yugoslav Committee in exile. They were joined by some Slovenes from Trieste and certain politicians from Bosnia who managed to emigrate.

The spiritual leader of the Yugoslav Committee was Frano Supilo. In talks with allied statesmen, he was the first to learn the details of the London Treaty. Supilo feared that Pašić might bargain with the big powers at the expense of the Croats and Slovenes. Although Supilo later resigned from the Yugoslav Committee for considerations of principle, the dilemma he raised remained until the end of the war: would the new state be an extension of Serbia or would the problem of the relation among the Yugoslav peoples in the future state be solved on a federal basis in line with the principle of equality?

CHAPTER 36

The Tragedy
of Serbia
in 1915

German Shock Divisions Arrive at the Serbian Front

No particular activity was recorded along Serbia's fronts in 1915 until
autumn, but the country suffered terribly from an epidemic of spotted typhus.
Between December 1914 and the summer of 1915, over half a million persons
contracted the disease, 100,000 of whom were soldiers. The contagion was
spread even more rapidly than it would otherwise have been because of the
fleeing population. From the Drina Valley area almost a quarter of a million
refugees fled in the face of the enemy army, from the Valjevo district almost

484

100,000, and from Belgrade almost 85,000. The country was insufficiently equipped to cope with the epidemic; food was scarce and the people went barefoot and
poorly clothed. At the time, Serbia had only 200 doctors. The raging infection
took a toll of roughly 150,000 lives.

In the spring of 1915 Italy entered the war on the side of the Allies. The
first skirmishes began late in May, followed by the great Italian offensive on the
Soča River toward the end of June. The Italian troops were stopped on the plateau
of Doberdob with casualties high on both sides. This was the first of eleven
offensives on the Soča front. It has been estimated that over 250,000 men were
rendered unfit for battle on both sides, Italian and Austro-Hungarian, among
whom there were many Slovenes. The people chanted:

> Oh Doberdob, Oh Doberdob,
> Graveyard of young Slovenes.

The Allies Attempt to Win Bulgaria to Their Side

In 1915 the situation at the front deteriorated for the Allies. The Italian
offensive had ground to a halt. The attempt by the Allies to capture the Dardanelles and establish contact with Russia by sea failed. German troops turned
first against Russia. With 90 divisions on the western front, the Germans hurled
140 divisions at the Russians. In May 1915 German troops broke through the
front at Gorlice, taking Poland, Lithuania, and even part of Byelorussia. Formally
neutral up until that time, Bulgaria now sided openly with the Central Powers,
while simultaneously negotiating with the Allies and asking that Serbia cede
all of Macedonia. The Allies were ready to meet some of the Bulgarian demands
and made a statement to this effect to the Bulgarian government without even
consulting the Serbian government. Serbia was simply informed that in return
for concessions in Macedonia, it would receive Bosnia and Hercegovina, northern
Albania, and southern Dalmatia after the war. But Pašić replied to the Russian
government that he preferred to retain Macedonia.

In 1915 the belligerents negotiated to stop the war, but to no avail. The
Central Powers also established contact with authoritative Serbian circles to
sound out the possibility of concluding a separate peace with Serbia. The negotiations were conducted through intermediaries with the knowledge of the
Serbian government and the Serbian Supreme Command. But as no decision was
forthcoming, the Central Powers determined to destroy the Serbian and Montenegrin armies in the autumn of 1915. First they came to agreement with Bulgaria
relevant to its participation in the war against Serbia and the Allies. Bulgaria
received territorial concessions from Turkey and the promise that it would be
given all of Macedonia and part of Serbia up to the Morava River after the

war. Serbia learned of the agreement between Bulgaria and the Central Powers, and consequently the Supreme Command considered it necessary to launch a preventive attack against Bulgaria for self-defense and to ward off the possibility of a stab in the back later. But the Serbian government disagreed and the Allied powers, even less enthusiastic about the idea, forbade the Serbian Supreme Command to concentrate divisions for defense along the Bulgarian boundary.

Mackensen's Offensive against Serbia

The Central Powers moved up the Eleventh German Army, commanded by General Mackensen, the 1914 victor against the Russians at Gorlice, to invade Serbia. The main line of attack ran from the north along the Morava River valley. At the same time, the Third Austro-Hungarian Army mounted an assault on Belgrade. Along fronts over 1,000 kilometers long, the Serbian army awaited the assault of 800,000 enemy troops.

Mackensen's offensive began on October 6, with his divisions crossing the Danube and moving along the Morava Valley. A fierce battle ensued for Belgrade, in the defense of which Russian sailors took part, alongside the troops manning long-range French and British guns. But faced by a far superior enemy, Belgrade fell. Major Dragutin Gavrilović, commander of the Second Battalion of the Tenth Regiment, issued orders to his troops beginning with the words: "The Supreme Command has erased our unit from its lists."

Bulgaria Strikes Serbia in the Back on October 13, 1915

In the night between October 13 and 14 the Bulgarian army struck the Serbian army in the back, and by October 16 Bulgarian units had cut communications in the valleys of the Morava and Vardar Rivers which were of strategic significance for Serbia, for they provided the sole link with the port of Salonika, where some Allied units had already landed. On October 22 Austro-Hungarian troops launched an offensive against Montenegro.

The Serbian Army Breaks Through Encirclement Three Times

The operational plan had been worked out by General von Seeckt, chief of Mackensen's staff. The plan anticipated the encirclement and destruction of the Serbian army. The superior enemy forces attempted to implement the plan three times, but failed. The Serbian army withdrew to Kosovo, tried to break through to Macedonia, but was repulsed by Bulgarian divisions entrenched in the canyon of Kačanik.

Allied Help Arrives Too Late

The Serbian government and Supreme Command then took stock of the situation. The 156th French Division under General Sarrail had already advanced from Salonika to Strumica, waiting for orders to move north to relieve the Serbian army, but the British government considered it was too late and that the Salonika front should be liquidated. Only after sharp intervention by the French Supreme Command did London desist from its intention.

The Calvary in Albania

The Serbian government and Supreme Command rejected the German demand for capitulation and decided that the Serbian army should withdraw through Albania, between the mountains of Šar and Prokletija, and also through Montenegro. Fleeing from the enemy in the north were also about 200,000 civilians, men, women, and children, moving together with the army. The huge mass of people on the march evoked memories of the great national migrations in Serbia's past. The people carried all their portable goods with them, including wagons, livestock, pets, mixing together in indescribable confusion with the supply trains, artillery, government treasury, archives. Borne aloft in front of the army were the relics of King Stefan Prvovenčani, taken from the monastery of Studenica, traveling on one of their twenty-odd trips during the five centuries of Serbian history. With their capes spread out, soldiers protected four great candles from being snuffed out by the wind until they reached their destination in the monastery of Ostrog in Montenegro. The military defeat, disease, bitter cold, hunger, and the long and hopeless withdrawal caused mass hysteria, leading some persons to commit suicide in this procession of death, among them the talented writer Milutin Uskoković.

Only one section of the people could accompany the army across the ravines; among them were about 30,000 young men and women. The retreat lasted over a month. Many soldiers and young people died along the way from starvation and exposure. It has been estimated that 15,000 of them lost their lives in the Albanian fastnesses.

One of the surviving youngsters, Rastko Petrović, later composed a poem, *Good Friend*, to the thousands of his companions who never made it through the snowdrifts of Albania.

The main force of the army, crippled and exhausted, arrived at a point between Scutari and Durazzo, but then had to withdraw all the way to Valona through marshland. At first the Italian military authorities refused to render any assistance to the Serbian army and refugees, fearing Serbian military superiority in Albania. They threatened to open fire on them at Valona while persistently refusing to give the Serbian troops transport ships. Even the ailing King Petar, carried on a stretcher by soldiers through Albania, was treated rudely. Only after intercession by the Russian tsar Nicholas II did the Italian authorities relent. The main burden of evacuating the Serbian army was undertaken by the French navy.

At the beginning of the offensive against Serbia, in October 1915, the Serbian army numbered 420,000 men. In Kosovo, late in November, that number had declined to about 300,000, and during the crossing of Albania and Montenegro in December and January to 220,000. From Valona the Serbian army was transported to Corfu and Vido, where the exhausted troops died by the thousands, to be buried in the depths of the Ionian Sea. A young Serbian poet, Milutin Bojić, author of several historical dramas and many solemn verses, suffered all the trials of the withdrawing army, which he accompanied. To them he dedicated his poem *Blue Grave:*

> Halt, imperial galleons! Fetter the powerful ships!
> Plow in silence, slowly,
> For I sing a dirge the heavens have never heard
> Over this water holy.

Later, the poet himself lost his life in the war. On Corfu the number of Serbian soldiers went down to somewhat less than 150,000.

Montenegro's Surrender

In the meantime, the Third Austro-Hungarian Army waged an offensive against the Montenegrin army, in straitened circumstances after the withdrawal of the Serbian troops. The Montenegrin army in the Sanjak, in the valleys of the Drina and Tara Rivers, resisted the far more powerful troops with whom it joined battle on January 5, 1916. Three days later the Austro-Hungarian troops began an offensive against Lovćen Mountain. Thus the Montenegrin army helped the Serbian army retreat toward the Adriatic Sea, where it was unable to follow the Serbs, however, especially as leading circles in Montenegro did not agree on how the war was to be prosecuted further. Among the Austrophiles was the heir to the throne himself, Danilo, married to a German princess. Some members of the cabinet and Assembly asked that a separate peace be concluded with Austria-Hungary. The king himself, Nikola, sent a telegram to Emperor

Francis Joseph, offering truce, while the Montenegrin government made a similar offer through Austro-Hungarian military commanders. This initiated negotiations in which Vienna called for the unconditional capitulation of Montenegro, and for the surrender of all Serbian troops then crossing Montenegrin territory.

The Montenegrin government was ready to agree to all the conditions of capitulation except the surrender of Serbian troops, and the negotiations were disrupted on this point. Cetinje fell on January 13; Lovćen was captured by Austro-Hungarian troops, who partly destroyed the chapel raised there by Vladika Rade Petar II Petrović Njegoš. King Nikola and Prime Minister Lazar Mijušković had already left Montenegro, while three ministers and the Supreme Command of the Montenegrin army remained behind in an endeavor to resume negotiations with the Austro-Hungarian military authorities. But no agreement could be reached. Montenegrin officials signed no convention, either for truce or capitulation. Montenegro was subjected to a regime of wartime occupation, remaining in a state of war with Austria-Hungary.

CHAPTER 37

The Third Year of the War

The Serbian Army at the Salonika Front

The men of the Serbian army rested on Corfu, where their health was more or less restored. In April 1916 they formed six infantry divisions and one cavalry, with about 130,000 officers and men. The troops were transported to the Salonika front, where they joined French, British, Russian, and Italian units. In September 1916 the Allied forces undertook an offensive. The Serbian army was assigned the task of breaking through the Bulgarian-German front, which it did at Gorničevo and Bitolj. The Drina Division captured Kajmakčalan. With interruptions, the offensive lasted three months, during which the Serbian and French troops captured Bitolj. The Salonika front stabilized, and war from these positions was waged until the autumn of 1918.

Yugoslav Volunteers

Some of the men in the Serbian army had volunteered in 1914. Most of them were youngsters, Serbs from outside of Serbia proper. Owing to the enormous casualties sustained by the Serbian army in 1915 and 1916, the question of reinforcements arose. A number of the Yugoslav emigrants from America volunteered. An even larger number were Austro-Hungarian soldiers of Yugoslav descent who had been captured at the Russian front or had surrendered voluntarily. In the spring of 1916 the first volunteer division was formed in Odessa, fighting side by side with the Russian army at the front in Dobrudža against the Bulgarian army. There it suffered heavy losses. A second volunteer division was soon formed. It has been estimated that almost 100,000 Serbs, Croats, and Slovenes from the Yugoslav lands under Austria-Hungary fought in the Serbian and Allied armies as volunteers against the Central Powers.

Regent Aleksandar Squares Accounts with Colonel Apis

Although the Serbian government and Assembly were in exile together with the army, there was no unanimity of views among them on many key issues. Serbia's military defeat in the late fall of 1916 revived the conflict between military and civilian authorities. Colonel Apis felt that the government was to blame for the retreat, as he and his companions had been of the opinion that a preventive incursion should have been made into Bulgaria. Regent Aleksandar hoped to bring both military and civilian authorities under his control and to institute a personal regime. For a time he hesitated between two alternatives: to square accounts with Nikola Pašić and the Party of the Old Radicals, or to unite with them to destroy Colonel Apis and his secret organization, who seemed to him the more dangerous of the two. Late in 1916 Colonel Apis and his principal associates were arrested and accused of having planned to assassinate Aleksandar and Pašić, plotting a coup d'état, and other crimes. It has since been established that Colonel Apis was not plotting to assassinate Aleksandar, but he was condemned to death and executed on June 26, 1917. Although many voices were raised abroad asking Aleksandar to pardon Colonel Apis, the regent was merciless. The Salonika trial and the methods used by the Serbian secret police threw an ugly shadow over the regime in Serbia and the tribulations suffered during World War I.

Persecution of the People in Occupied Serbia and Montenegro

The desire for peace appeared in the ranks of the Serbian army at the Salonika front. The men of the Second Serbian Army and the Forty-fifth Bulgarian Regiment left their trenches and came out into the open area between them, where they began to fraternize on December 28, 1916. Order at the front was restored only after artillery opened fire on the soldiers of the two fraternal nations, who asked only that the mutual slaughter be stopped.

The conditions of occupation in defeated Serbia and Montenegro made life extremely difficult. Serbia was divided up into the Austro-Hungarian and Bulgarian zones of occupation, separated by the Morava River. The Austro-Hungarian authorities banned the use of the Cyrillic alphabet and the Julian calendar. The poems of Branko Radičević and Jovan Jovanović Zmaj were placed on the blacklist. In the beginning each inhabitant was given a ration of 400 grams of bread daily, but this quantity was steadily reduced until the end of the war, when bran alone was dispensed. Over 50,000 people were displaced from Serbia by force. The Austrian authorities introduced compulsory labor. The population was single-minded in its resistance to the occupiers, except for a handful of the old conservative party Naprednjaks, who were on friendly terms with the alien authorities.

The Uprising of Toplica, 1917

Conditions in Montenegro were even worse and the economic situation was unbearable, as bread was far harder to come by in the rockbound land. In both Serbia and Montenegro spontaneous resistance developed through detachments of Komitas.

Early in January 1917 the Bulgarians introduced recruitment of the population in occupied areas, counter to international law. In Toplica an armed uprising broke out against the occupiers in February. The insurgents captured Kuršumlija, Prokuplje, and several other places, and took over 1,000 Bulgarian soldiers. The uprising was headed by Kosta Pećanac, Kosta Vojnović, and Rade Vlahović.

As the insurgents posed a threat to communications along the Morava River, jeopardizing the supply lines of Bulgarian and German troops at the Salonika front, the occupation authorities launched a big offensive with Austro-Hungarian and Bulgarian divisions and two German regiments. The insurgents, unprepared to wage frontal warfare against a regular army, were smashed. Commander Kosta Vojnović was wounded and committed suicide to avoid falling into enemy hands.

The occupiers and especially the Bulgarians took a barbaric revenge: whole villages were razed and the entire population slaughtered. The estimate is that Bulgarian troops massacred over 20,000 men, women, and children.

Genocide against the Serbian Population in Bosnia and Hercegovina

In Bosnia and Hercegovina persecution of the population, especially Serbs, was crueler than anywhere else in Austria-Hungary. One by one, the Young Bosnia organizations were discovered, in Sarajevo and also in other towns in Bosnia and Hercegovina. Secret youth organizations in Slovenia and Dalmatia who maintained contact with the Young Bosnians also were uncovered. In 1914 and 1915, not counting the trial in Sarajevo of the assassins of Francis Ferdinand, six groups of Young Bosnians, three groups of the *Preporod* movement, and several groups of Dalmatian youth were brought before the court. The Young Bosnians included not only Serbs but Croats and Muslims as well, a fact which the Austro-Hungarian authorities strove to conceal.

In Bosnia and Hercegovina, and in parts of Croatia, the crime of genocide was committed against persons of Serbian nationality. Elsewhere the Armenians were experiencing a similar fate.

Even before World War I, Austrian aristocratic and military circles close to Francis Ferdinand made plans to destroy the individuality of the Serbian people in Bosnia and Hercegovina. When the war broke out, material conditions were created that made it possible to implement those plans. In Bosnia and Hercegovina itself, the Viennese anti-Serbs could not muster massive support for committing genocide against the Serbs because the three religious communities there, despite disagreement, practiced a tacit, mutual tolerance. Consequently aggressive-minded Viennese government circles placed their reliance on the Croat conservative Frankists, who had for many years developed the thesis that the Serbs in Croatia and Bosnia and Hercegovina were not a separate people and had no individuality as a nationality. The principal "hawk" in Vienna, General Conrad von Hützendorf, met Dr. A. Horvat and J. Frank, the Frankist leaders, on July 16, 1914, to work out a plan of measures against the Serbs in Bosnia and Hercegovina and in Croatia.

In the crime of genocide, it is the intention, *animus injuriandi*, that is essential, that is, the intention of destroying the members of a nation, race, or religious group for the precise reason that they belong to their community. To this end, the warlike party in Vienna suspended the Constitution in Bosnia and Hercegovina, and partially also in Croatia, so as to have a free hand in taking discriminatory measures against the Serbian people with the aim of depriving them of their individuality. In Bosnia and Hercegovina the Cyrillic alphabet, although one of the recognized alphabets, was prohibited in official communication and in the schools. Also under ban were the display of Serbian flags, the celebration of Orthodox patron-saint days, and so on. Similar measures were undertaken in Croatia. By a decree of November 5, 1914, the government in Zagreb changed the name of the mother "Croatian or Serbian" tongue to "Croatian" only, and on January 3, 1915, it abolished by decree the use of Cyrillic in the administration.

Under the sway of the war party in Vienna, certain Frankist newspapers, or other newspapers under their influence, clearly made public the intention of destroying the Serbian people as such. The newspaper *Hrvatska (Croatia)* wrote on July 3, 1914: "The people announce a life and death struggle to the Serbs and their banishment from Bosnia and Hercegovina." On June 29, 1914, the same newspaper had written: "We must square accounts with them for once and for all and destroy them. . . . The Serbs are poisonous snakes from whom you are safe only after you have crushed their heads."

The intention of committing genocide was carried out by several criminal acts: direct physical extermination, forced evacuation, and banishment to concentration camps.

Austro-Hungarian courts-martial in Bosnia and Hercegovina, according to data from Vienna, condemned to death and executed 460 persons of Serbian nationality. However, the number of Serbs killed was far higher. On instructions from Vienna, General Potiorek established an auxiliary militia in Bosnia and Hercegovina—the so-called *Schutzkorps*, in which he mobilized the scum of town and country. These were given freedom to deal with the Serbian population with the tacit assistance of the Austro-Hungarian authorities and high-ranking Roman Catholic clergy. While committing their crimes, the *Schutzkorps* sang: an anti-Serbian song: "There is no three-fingered cross." At a session of the Austrian Parliament of January 22, 1918, Dr. Anton Korošec referred in an interpellation to these crimes in Bosnia and Hercegovina during the early war years, and mentioned instructions issued by the Supreme Military Command in Vienna regarding simplification of wartime judicial procedure. In the discussion that ensued, a representative of the Austrian government admitted that, apart from the death sentences meted out by military courts, "there had been many murders committed for religious reasons at the beginning of the war." By using this terminology, the government in Vienna tried to cover up the murders committed by the *Schutzkorps*. Their number has never been accurately ascertained. At one locality near the Drina, in Foča, the *Schutzkorps* hanged Josif Kočović (a presbyter), Vasilije Kandić (a clergyman), and three other Serbs. In Trebinje Serbs were killed directly by the Austro-Hungarian army. Thirty-seven Serbs were hanged, including the presbyter Stevan Pravica and the parson Vidak Parežanin. The Austro-Hungarian army also killed without benefit of trial, as was the case in the Foča area. On August 14, 1914, alone, 126 persons of Serbian nationality were put to death.

The extermination of the Serbian population was also effected by the forced evacuation of numerous villages along the Serbian and Montenegrin borders. The people were banished to other areas, where they perished of hunger and disease.

The most massive extermination took place in the concentration camps. In this respect war circles in Vienna conducted the first large-scale experiments in Europe which Adolf Hitler later applied on an even grander scale. There were several types of camps. The most infamous was the mustering camp in Doboj, through which passed 16,673 men and 16,996 women of Serbian nationality between December 27, 1915, and July 5, 1917, according to official data. Between 800 and 1,000 persons were assigned to a single barrack. The authorities doled out 100 grams of bread per person. When an epidemic of spotted and intestinal typhus broke out, an enormous number of internees died. Conditions were similar in other transit camps, especially in Žagar near Bihać and in the camp at Višegrad. The latter camp issued orders to the effect that each inmate had to fetch his food in person, meaning that meals could not be taken to those who were too sick to come themselves. Consequently a large number of persons suffering from typhus or weak from malnutrition died daily.

Permanent concentration camps existed in Arad, Nezsider, Talesdorf, Turony, Sopronnyek, and other places in Austria and Hungary. Tens of thousands of Bosnian Serbs died in these camps, including Risto Radulović-Rinda, one of the leading intellectuals of his day.

When the Serbian army advanced into Bosnia and Hercegovina in the autumn of 1914, some of the Komita detachments, in revenge, launched reprisals against the Muslim population, and so the fratricidal slaughter continued.

The Trial at Banja Luka

On April 22, 1916, in Banja Luka, sentence was passed on virtually half of the older generation of Bosnian intellectuals of Serbian descent. Brought before the court were one hundred and fifty-six persons including seven members of the Assembly, twenty-four professors and teachers, twenty-one priests, and eight students. Of these, sixteen were sentenced to death, and the others to long terms of imprisonment. The lives of the condemned were saved only by the pressure of world public opinion, and the desire of Emperor Charles, the successor to Emperor Francis Joseph, to make a liberal show in the Allied countries during the course of negotiations for a separate peace between Austria-Hungary and France.

CHAPTER 38

The Last Days
of Austria-Hungary

The Influence of the Russian Revolution on Yugoslav Lands

The Russian Revolution of 1917 had a profound influence on events in
Yugoslav lands. In March that year, when the tsarist regime was deposed, the
people in other countries were encouraged to hope for the end of other feudal
institutions, like the Hapsburg, Hohenzollern, and Ottoman empires. In the
Allied countries, too, the Russian Revolution gave the masses incentive. In
France widespread strikes broke out in which over 100,000 workers participated;
in Britain the number of strikers was almost a quarter of a million.

Ruling circles in all belligerent states took steps to pacify the masses in revolt and to maintain the existing social order. The Serbian government, particularly the Party of the Old Radicals, felt that the fall of tsarism in Russia had deprived them of an important pillar of support in their foreign policy. On the other hand, the Allied powers, France and England, and particularly Italy, had no intention of allowing the Austro-Hungarian monarchy to disintegrate, so that the outlook for unification of the Yugoslav peoples in a single state was bleak. In the spring of 1917 the United States of America entered the war, raising the chances of an Allied victory. However, in his fourteen-point program, President Wilson did not foresee the disruption of Austria-Hungary. He adhered to this position almost until the end of the war.

The Corfu Declaration

In summer of 1917 the Serbian government and representatives of the Yugoslav Committee agreed to meet on Corfu to examine the principles for creation of a future common state of the Yugoslav peoples. The historic meeting was devoted almost exclusively to discussion of the future relations between Serbs and Croats. Two theses were submitted: one unitaristic and the other federalistic. The first was expounded by Nikola Pašić, who thought that only a strong, unified state could withstand all external pressures; Dr. Ante Trumbić did not openly favor a federal system (the real protagonist of which was Frano Supilo, who had left the Yugoslav Committee in the meantime) but rather supported the view that the future state would have to be decentralized. At the same time, he accepted the idea of unitarism, especially under the Karadjordjević dynasty.

The interests of the remaining Yugoslav peoples were neglected at Corfu. Members of the Yugoslav Committee showed no understanding of the problem of unification of the Slovenes; even Supilo himself advocated in veiled form the old Party of Rights view that the Slovenes were "Alpine Croats." During the war he upheld the idea that all lands up to the Drina River should be administratively linked with the federal unit of Croatia. However, in this he was not consistent, just as he was not consistent in his insistence on the importance of Catholicism in Yugoslav culture. Further, he advocated the idea of a federation in which Bosnia and Hercegovina would be a separate unit. The question of Macedonia was not even posed at the Corfu meeting. The status of Montenegro was considered as a dynastic question of the precedence of the Karadjordjević line over the house of Petrović in the "unification of Montenegro and Serbia."

In the Corfu Declaration social problems were relegated to the background; participants took the view that the bourgeois order should be safeguarded. No decision was even taken to abolish the remnants of feudal agrarian relations. Trumbić opposed the abolition of serfdom and latifundia by government decree. His views were sharply countered by those of Dušan Vasilijević, representative of the Bosnian Serbs, but Trumbić won the day.

In Croatia and Slovenia the year 1917 brought a resurgence of political activity, which had almost died out altogether after the war broke out. In the Slovene People's party (Clericalists), the old guard, headed by Ivan Šušteršič, lost ground while party leadership was gradually taken over by younger people like Anton Korošec and Janez Krek. The Clerical party continued to reject the idea of revolutionary solution of the Yugoslav question. It supported the maintenance of Austria-Hungary and in this posture was upheld by the other political parties of Slovenia, both the People's Progressive party (Liberals) and the Social Democratic party. Only Ivan Cankar stood firm in the view that Austria-Hungary should be broken up and a Yugoslav republic established, with equality for all its peoples. Furthermore, he underscored the need for preserving the cultural individuality of each nation in the future federation.

The Slovene Clericalists maintained close ties with the right-wing Croatian parties. It was their view that Croatian state law should provide the basis for unification of Croats and Slovenes in an autonomous Yugoslav state unit, within the frameworks of Austria-Hungary, a variant of the old idea of a triune Hapsburg monarchy.

The Vienna Declaration of May

In the Parliament of Vienna on May 19, 1917, Anton Korošec proposed a resolution calling for unification of Croats and Slovenes under the Hapsburg crown and for parity with Hungary. The right-wing Clericalists, headed by Šušteršič, did not wish the May Resolution to mention the Serbs in Croatia, as it was considered that they had been outlawed on the day the war broke out, but they were outvoted because the club of Yugoslav deputies had already been formed in the Viennese Parliament including Croat, Slovene, and Serbian deputies. Somewhat later, Korošec became the president of the Slovene People's party.

The New Russian Authorities Publish the Secret London Agreement of 1915

The October Revolution of 1917 influenced the Yugoslav lands profoundly. The Congress of Soviets of Workers' and Soldiers' Deputies proclaimed the Decree of Peace on November 8, 1917, in which the governments and peoples of belligerent states were called upon to conclude a democratic peace immediately.

The Manifesto went on to say that the new peace had to be free of annexations and forcible acquisitions of alien territories and nationalities and that no contributions should be extorted, that is, no material or financial indemnity should be demanded from the defeated.

The new Soviet government simultaneously published all the secret agreements concluded between tsarist Russia and the Allied countries pertaining to spheres of interest. For the first time, the world and the Yugoslav public gained insight into the exact provisions of the London Treaty of 1915, in which many Slovene and Croatian areas were granted to Italy.

The Naval Mutiny in Boka Kotorska and Slovenia

Large numbers of Yugoslav prisoners of war who were set free in Russia joined the Russian revolutionary forces. Their number has been estimated at 35,000 to 40,000 in the ranks of the Red Army, within the framework of which a special Yugoslav Communist regiment was formed. In the Yugoslav lands themselves the revolutionary mood grew. On February 1, 1918, a mutiny on the flagship *Sankt Georg* of the Austro-Hungarian navy, part of which was then in Boka Kotorska, spread to other warships. Over 6,000 sailors on forty ships joined the mutineers. The red flag was raised in Boka, and implementation of Wilson's principles was demanded. The mutiny was crushed when the third division of warships belonging to the Austro-Hungarian fleet arrived from Pula. Over 800 sailors were arrested, some of whom were condemned to death: Franc Raš (of Czech nationality) and Anton Grubar, Jerko Šišgorić, and Mate Brničević (Croats), identified as the leaders of the mutiny.

Unrest broke out in Slovenia. During the early years of the war, the Austrian authorities had condemned 470 persons to death in Slovenia and interned a far larger number. In 1918 strikes broke out in mines and factories, and in the night of May 12–13,-1918, the Seventeenth Slovene Infantry Regiment in Judenburg mutinied. They were joined by Slovene soldiers in Murau and Radgona.

The Appearance of the Green Army in Croatia

The so-called Green Army was formed in Croatia and in Srem. Thousands of deserting soldiers fled to the forests, attacking big landowners and rich merchants. It has been estimated that near the war's end over 50,000 soldiers were roaming the Croatian forests with gun in hand.

The Green Army spread to Bosnia and Hercegovina. In April 1918 the assassin of Francis Ferdinand, Gavrilo Princip, died in prison in Terezina at the same time that his native Bosnia was lit by the fires of burning beys' mansions, signalizing the end of slavery that had endured for centuries. The shots fired by Princip in 1914 brought death not only to Archduke Francis Ferdinand but also four years later to the multinational Hapsburg monarchy and its archaic institutions, including the medieval system of serfdom in Bosnia and Hercegovina.

Mutinies also broke out in Hercegovina. In Mostar the Fifteenth Dalmatian Regiment rebelled, but its revolt was quelled with much bloodshed.

In Serbia the Seventy-first Slovak Regiment mutinied in Kragujevac on June 2, 1918. When the Slovaks reached the town, fierce fighting broke out with loyal Austro-Hungarian troops. The mutiny was crushed and fifty-nine of the seven hundred mutineers were brought before the court, forty-four of them sentenced to death and executed on Stanovljansko Polje, near Kragujevac.

The Allied Powers and Austria-Hungary

The October Revolution also had a bearing on the position of the big powers regarding the need to maintain the Austro-Hungarian monarchy. From the beginning of the war, France had felt that after the dissolution of the Hapsburg monarchy, the German element in Austria would join the great Germany, counter to France's interests. Furthermore, French capital had vested interests in Vienna. The Vatican's support of the Hapsburgs, as a Catholic dynasty, also found approval in French ruling circles. The social unrest that erupted in Austria-Hungary in 1918 convinced Paris that the old dynasty should be preserved as a dam against the new danger from the East.

The Hapsburg Monarchy Disintegrates from Internal National and Social Upheavals

In Great Britain Liberals as well as Conservatives considered Austria-Hungary a defense against both the German danger and the Russian. A group of intellectuals, including R. W. Seton-Watson and Henry Wickham Steed, who supported the unification of the South Slavs, were left in the minority. British nostalgia for Austria-Hungary was best expressed by Winston Churchill, who began his memoirs of World War II by asserting that the disintegration of Austria-Hungary was one of the greatest tragedies of the previous war.

Not much support was forthcoming from Italy for the plans to dismantle Austria-Hungary. Under the pretext that the new Yugoslav state could become a medium for the expansion of Russian influence in the Mediterranean, Rome thought to justify its own expansion in the Balkan Peninsula.

The Breakthrough of the Salonika Front

In September 1918 the Allied forces at the Salonika front undertook the offensive. Serbian and French troops broke through the front. On September 15 the Serbian Second Army drove a wedge 11 kilometers wide and 4 kilometers deep at Kozjak. At the same time, the French entered Pelagonia. Greek and British troops joined in the breakthrough. Seven days after the offensive was launched, Serbian units arrived in the Vardar Valley, and on September 29 French divisions entered Skoplje, refusing to allow the Serbian army to advance into Bulgaria. The same day Bulgaria sued for capitulation.

The German army fought as it retreated, but the First Serbian Army smashed German divisions at Niš and liberated the town on October 12. The advance northward continued, and Belgrade was finally liberated on November 1, 1918. Doing battle all the way, the Serbian army had come over 500 kilometers in forty-five days.

The Losses of the Yugoslav Peoples in World War I

So came the end of the war for the Yugoslav peoples, who had sustained huge human and material losses. According to a memorandum of the Yugoslav government to the Peace Conference of 1919, and also as estimated by several historians, the Yugoslav lands lost 1,900,000 lives, of which around 43 percent were Serbian. Serbia had mobilized 705,343 men in the war, or 20 percent of its entire population, and 40 percent of all males. The Serbian army also included 40,000 Serbs and Slavs from outside of Serbia proper, as well as 10,000 volunteers from America. All in all, Serbia had sent between 800,000 and 850,000 fighting men to war. Of this number, 369,815 were killed or died later from wounds sustained in the war—almost half of all the country's fighting men.

The civilian population also suffered serious losses. Over 600,000 people died from disease, starvation, and hardship in camps in Hungary, and in the Toplica uprising. Montenegro also was hard hit by the war as 20,000 of its 50,000 mobilized troops lost their lives. Altogether, Montenegro lost 63,000 people in the war, or one-fourth of its total population in 1910. Of the other Yugoslav lands, heavy losses were sustained by Bosnia and Hercegovina and Slovenia. It has been estimated that in proportion to the number of men mobilized, Slovenia suffered the highest losses of all Austrian lands.

These losses were especially great because it was mostly men of the younger generation that had been killed. For years after the war, the scarcity of males was noticeable in villages and towns. At the end of 1914, 1,300 students had been accepted in the Serbian army as corporals although they were still under age. Of that number, only 140 survived to see the end of the war.

CHAPTER 39

The New State in International Affairs

The Foundations of Foreign Policy

The dissolution of the Hapsburg empire was an irreversible historical process. That feudal contrivance, headed by the oldest European dynasty, fell to pieces in the autumn of 1918 under the impact of revolt by its subjects: Czechs, Poles, Romanians, Slovaks, Slovenes, Croats, and Serbs, all of them demanding their own national states. Furthermore, the cleavage between the Hungarians and the western part of the empire was total. Alarmed by the social ferment bordering

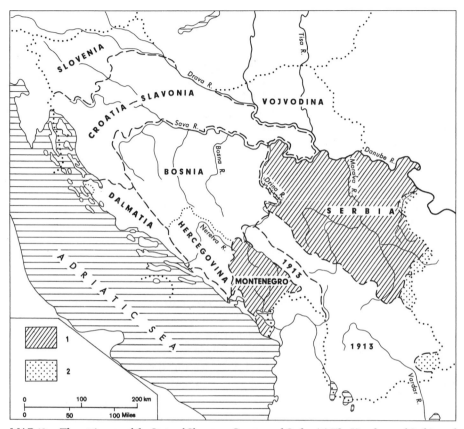

MAP 42. The setting up of the State of Slovenes, Croats, and Serbs. (1) The Kingdoms of Serbia and Montenegro before the additions of 1913; (2) additions at the expense of Bulgaria, 1919.

on revolution, the statesmen of the Allied powers strove in vain to preserve Austria-Hungary, once the bastion of conservatism in Central Europe.

At the end of 1918, however, they reconciled themselves to the course of events and adopted new tactics. As the Hapsburg empire could not be salvaged, reliance would have to be placed on the bourgeois forces among the Slavs of the Hapsburg empire, and on Serbia, in order to rescue the capitalist system in the heart of Europe.

The National Council of Slovenes, Croats, and Serbs, sitting in the Croatian Assembly on October 29, 1918, proclaimed itself the new supreme organ of the state administration of South Slavs in Austria-Hungary, thereby severing all ties with the Hapsburg monarchy. At the same time, the Council proclaimed the creation of a new state of the South Slavs, named the State of Slovenes, Croats, and Serbs.

The same sovereign body announced on November 24 the unification of the State of Slovenes, Croats, and Serbs with the Kingdoms of Serbia and Montenegro, into the integral state of Serbs, Croats, and Slovenes. Similar decisions were taken in Novi Sad in relation to Vojvodina and in Podgorica for Montenegro. On December 1, 1918, the formation of the Kingdom of the Serbs, Croats, and Slovenes was proclaimed in Belgrade.

The new state numbered somewhat over 11,900,000 inhabitants; its definitive boundaries were determined by the treaties of peace of 1919 and 1920, and later; its area came to 248,000 square kilometers. The following joined together to form the Kingdom of the Serbs, Croats, and Slovenes: the Kingdoms of Serbia and Montenegro; the greater part of the Austrian crownland of Carniola (Kranjska) and parts of the crownlands of Styria (Štajerska), Carinthia (Koruška), and Prekomurje; the crownland of Dalmatia (without Zadar and Lastovo); Croatia and Slavonia, which were semiautonomous territories of Hungary; Medjumurje; Vojvodina, a component part of Hungary; and Bosnia and Hercegovina, territories under the administration of the joint Austro-Hungarian Finance Ministry.

The first joint state of Serbs, Croats, and Slovenes was thus created on the wreckage of the Hapsburg empire. It was part of a Europe in which the balance of power among the big states had shifted. But the rule still applied that small states were simply objects and not subjects in international relations. In substantial measure, a change also took place in the foreign policy of the new joint state. Milovan Milovanović's dictum during the European crisis of 1908 over the annexation of Bosnia by Austria-Hungary was that the Serbian, and therefore also the Yugoslav, question could not be posed before Europe as such— that is, as a question of the right to self-determination, of the liberation of small nations from the Hapsburg and Ottoman Empires—but that it would rather have to be presented as a European problem, as the struggle against the *Drang nach Osten;* this foreign policy idea was no longer tenable. Germany and Austria-Hungary had been defeated, and among the victors, allies of Serbia, differences in view existed regarding postwar problems. France remained the principal protector of the new Yugoslav state; Britain assumed a reserved attitude in its search for an antithesis to French domination in Europe; Italy, considering the state of Serbs, Croats, and Slovenes as the main obstacle to its influence in the Balkans, did everything it could, even as early as the latter part of 1918, to disrupt it.

The Peace Treaties

At the peace conferences in 1919 and 1920, treaties of the nature of dictates were concluded with the defeated Central Powers: Germany, Austria,

Hungary, Bulgaria, and Turkey. The supreme council of these conferences consisting of representatives of the five big Allied powers—France, the United States, Great Britain, Italy, and Japan—decided everything alone, even matters relating to the other Allied powers that had taken part in World War I. Serbia and Belgium were classified as belonging to the second category of conference participants, as states with "special limited interests." The third category included all other Allied powers, who had the right to submit an opinion only on problems concerning themselves, but not on the foundations of the peace treaties.

In terms of the principles underlying them, the peace conferences of 1919 and 1920 were an extension of the Holy Alliance, symbol of defense of legitimism and the social order in Europe and in the world. The secret agreements concluded by the victors among themselves in the course of the war, relating to division of territories and to spheres of influence, provided the basis for establishment of new boundaries in Europe and the world, and consequently also the boundaries of the Kingdom of the Serbs, Croats, and Slovenes. As one of the five Great Powers, Italy was bent on implementing at all costs the clauses of the secret London Treaty of 1915. In order to undermine the new Yugoslav state, Italy advocated the drawing of a boundary line between Austria and Yugoslavia favoring the former to the greatest possible extent.

The Yugoslav government and its delegations to the peace conferences were not themselves in accord in their defense of the new state as a whole. Both Nikola Pašić and Ante Trumbić showed signs of particularism. The former felt that a bargain should be struck with Italy as soon as possible so that no great alarm would be raised over the annexation of Montenegro to the new Yugoslav state, whereas Trumbić focused attention on the interests of Dalmatia and the Croatian Littoral, neglecting the Slovene Littoral and Istria.

The Treaty of Rapallo

The definitive boundaries between Italy and Yugoslavia were established at Saint-Germain in 1919, in Rapallo in 1920, and in Rome in 1924. If compared with what the Great Powers had promised Italy in the London Treaty of 1915, it is evident that the government in Rome backed down on Dalmatia and the Croatian Littoral; on the other hand it grabbed all of Istria, Rijeka, the Slovene Littoral, and even a part of the Old Carniola. Over 600,000 Croats and Slovenes came under Italian rule. The Slovenes themselves fared the worst. The boundary between Yugoslavia and Italy left more Slovenes in Italy than the secret London Treaty of 1915 had provided for. This was the upshot of Rome's persistence in establishing what it called strategic boundaries with Yugoslavia, and of pressure brought by the Great Powers, France and Great Britain, on the Yugoslav govern-

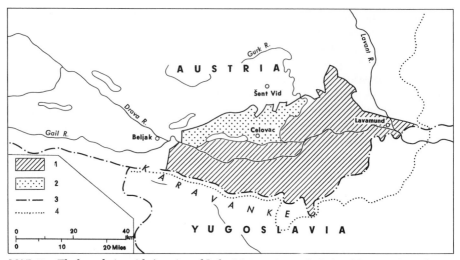

MAP 43.   The boundaries with Austria and Italy. (1) Zone A, in which the plebiscite of October 10,
1920, was held; (2) Zone B; (3) the boundary established in 1921; (4) frontier of province of
Carinthia in Austria before 1921.

ment to accept the dictate of the Rapallo Treaty. But the Slovene people were
split also because of Pašić's indifference, Trumbić's particularism, and the sub-
servient attitude of the Slovene Clericalists and Liberals toward the new regime
in Belgrade.

In Istria and the Slovene Littoral, the Italian authorities immediately
launched the forcible Italianization of Croats and Slovenes. All schools in the
Croatian and Slovene languages were banned and surnames were Italianized.
People were even made to change the names on gravestones. Leading persons
were placed under arrest. The Slovene National Hall in Trieste was set on fire.

The Plebiscite in Carinthia

The Slovene people fared no better at the peace conferences in regard to
their northern boundaries. A treaty with Austria was signed in Saint-Germain
on September 10, 1919, sanctioning the Germanization of Koruška (Carinthia).
Once the purest of all Slovene lands, this area's national structure had altered
rapidly, especially since the end of the nineteenth century. In Štajerska (Styria),
Germanization proceeded somewhat more slowly. Energetic action in 1918 and
1919 by Rudolf Meister, the Slovene general, was instrumental in preserving
Lower Štajerska with Maribor for Slovenia. The Treaty of Saint-Germain deter-

mined that a plebiscite should be held in Koruška in two zones, A and B. A smaller part of southern Koruška was annexed to Yugoslavia.

At the plebiscite held on October 10, 1920, the majority of the population voted to remain in Austria (22,025 votes against 15,279, or 59.04 percent for Austria and 40.96 percent for Yugoslavia). The reasons for this result are complex. First of all, the Commission for the Plebiscite was not altogether objective. One section of the Slovenes voted to remain in Austria. This was partly due to the influence of the Catholic church, and partly to the Slovene Social Democrats, some of whom declared that it would be better for the Slovene proletariat to remain in Austria, where the Socialists were the leading force, than in monarchist Yugoslavia, in which King Aleksandar persecuted the working class and had instituted a totalitarian regime.

The boundary with Hungary was established at the Grand Trianon in Versailles on June 4, 1920. One of the crucial questions was the boundary between Yugoslavia and Romania in the Banat. In a secret agreement of 1916, the Allied powers (France, Britain, Russia, and Italy) had promised Romania all of the Banat up to the Tisa and Danube Rivers in return for its entering the war on the Allied side. After lengthy negotiations, Yugoslavia and Romania divided up the Banat. A peace treaty with Bulgaria was signed in Neuilly on November 27, 1919, and with Turkey in Sèvres on August 10, 1920.

The question of Macedonia never came up at all in the peace treaties. Not a single bourgeois Yugoslav group considered the Macedonians a separate nation. The Treaty of Neuilly introduced certain corrections in the Yugoslav-Bulgarian boundary in Yugoslavia's favor: Strumica in Macedonia, Bosiljgrad in the north, Caribrod (Dimitrovgrad), and a few other areas.

Large masses of Greeks had moved to the Aegean part of Macedonia after the Turco-Greek War, when over a million of them had been expelled from Asia Minor.

Orientation to France

In essence, from 1918 onwards, Yugoslavia was simply a link in the chain of French domination in Europe. In this respect it had a twofold role to play. On the one hand, Austria and Hungary in Central Europe, and Bulgaria in the Balkans, had to be kept in a state of obedience so that there would be no revision of the boundaries established by the postwar peace treaties. To that end, under the patronage of France, Yugoslavia, Czechoslovakia, and Romania formed the alliance known as the Little Entente. The immediate motive for the creation of the alliance was the putsch in Hungary in March 1921, when Charles of Hapsburg made an attempt to restore his throne.

The Little Entente: *Cordon Sanitaire* against the Soviet Union

On the other hand, France, as the guardian of the bourgeois order in Europe, was the main force, together with Great Britain, engaged in interventions against the young Russian Soviet republic. The Little Entente served as a *cordon sanitaire* of sorts against the Bolshevik danger in Central Europe. The outbreak of revolution in Hungary presented new problems for the Little Entente countries. Romania and Czechoslovakia sent troops to crush the revolution in Hungary, but Yugoslavia did not, although influential circles in the Yugoslav government had already alerted several divisions to be commanded by General Petar Živković, the king's favorite.

The Labour party in Britain and the British Trade Unions, as well as the Socialist Party of France and the workers' trade unions in that country, issued a proclamation on July 20 and 21, 1919, calling upon the working class of Europe to organize a general strike in protest against the armed interventions in Russia and Hungary. The Socialist Workers' Party of Yugoslavia (communists) and the Central Workers' Trade Union Council responded to the appeal and on July 20 and 21 paralyzed economic activity in Yugoslavia. In Maribor and Varaždin spontaneous mutinies broke out in the army, forcing the government in Belgrade to reverse the decision to send Yugoslav troops to Hungary.

King Aleksandar was the champion of the anti-Communist course in Yugoslav foreign policy. This was partly the consequence of his education in the page corps of Petrograd and his ties with the Russian imperial family. When the interventionist forces were defeated in Russia, at the request of Aleksandar Yugoslavia became one of the principal refuges for the routed troops of General Vrangel. Special corps of pages were established in Yugoslavia to train refugee youths of Russian nationality as officers for future interventionist armies; schools were set up for the instruction of terrorists, who were infiltrated into Soviet territory.

Aleksandar and Pašić took a dim view of the new Bulgarian government, headed by the Bulgarian peasant leader, Aleksandar Stamboliski. Belgrade turned its back on all his attempts to reach an understanding between the two countries. In 1923 the Bulgarian court and Conservatives overthrew the Bulgarian peasant government by force, murdering its many followers.

Italy against the Territorial Integrity of Yugoslavia

Italy posed a constant threat to the territorial integrity of Yugoslavia. On December 3, 1918, General Pietro Badoglio, deputy chief of staff, submitted a memorandum to the Italian government regarding action to disrupt the new state of Serbs, Croats, and Slovenes.

In the introduction to this document (discovered in the captured Italian archives in World War II) Badoglio stressed that the idea of Yugoslavhood was supported only by intellectuals and a section of the well-educated bourgeoisie, whereas the peasants and workers were far more lukewarm in their attitude: "Imbued with Bolshevik principles, the proletariat will not support this petty bourgeois nationalistic program." Badoglio concluded in the introduction that the outlook was excellent for a potential internal conflict in Yugoslavia and that "all possible means" should be used to activate the forces so inclined. Badoglio went on to say that every possible method should be used to foment regional particularism. Rumors should be spread in Serbia to the effect that it would become the "unwitting instrument of Croatia, which was convinced of its intellectual superiority over·Serbia and would do everything it could to absorb the latter." For Croatia, Badoglio foresaw the following tactics: "The Croats are still dreaming of a Great Croatia, more than of Yugoslavia, and they should be supported to regard the Serbs with aversion, as hegemonists. But as the Croatian people are primitive and frequently barbaric, as well as fanatic and loyal to established authority, in using such tactics it is best to rely on the faithful." In Slovenia, Badoglio emphasized the role of the Roman Catholic church: "In view of their special language and different cultural tradition, separatist propaganda among the Slovenes has a good chance of succeeding."

Badoglio further stated that he needed 200 secret agents, divided up into four groups, for the unoccupied zone in Yugoslavia. He declared that he had already found the agents he needed for Serbia. For Slovenia, he said, "I am seeking to establish contact with the two principal newspapers in Ljubljana, *Slovenski Narod (Slovene People)* and *Slovenec* (the *Slovene*), and the three main newspapers in Croatia, *Horizont (Horizon)*, *Hrvatska Riječ (Croatian Word)*, and the *News*, to persuade them to come over to our side." Badoglio also calculated how much money he would need to pay his contacts in Yugoslavia: 2 million lira for the agents (10,000 lira for two months for each agent); 150,000 lira for each newspaper (he believed he would succeed in bribing three newspapers); and from 300,000 to 500,000 lira for clergymen. He also anticipated the sum of from 200,000 to 500,000 lira for adherents of former regimes. Badoglio added that as France was spending large sums of money to finance the program of Yugoslav unification, he too had to ask for such considerable amounts.

The Italian government approved Badoglio's proposal. Foreign Minister Sonnino informed him that the memorandum had been studied by Prime Minister Orlando and Chief of Staff Díaz, who had decided that implementation should begin immediately.

For many long years, Badoglio's memorandum served as the basis for Italy's foreign policy toward Yugoslavia, especially after Mussolini had ensconced himself in Rome.

Changes in the Balance of Power in Europe and the Weakening of French Influence

Rome and Belgrade struggled in particular over Albania. When the progressive Fan Noli came to power in Albania, the Yugoslav government financed a putsch by the feudalists who had rallied to Ahmed Zogu to bring down the Fan Noli government. They even sent help in the form of "volunteers," most of them Russian émigrés. But Ahmed Zogu chose to ally himself with the far stronger and richer Rome, leaving the Belgrade government without any influence over Albania. Later Ahmed Zogu proclaimed himself Zog I, king of Albania.

Italy and Great Britain also supported Bulgaria. Both Italian and British capital were making inroads upon the Balkan Peninsula. In order to maintain its dominance over this part of Europe, France pursued a policy of concluding new bilateral agreements with Czechoslovakia, Romania, and Yugoslavia. Although the Pašić-led Radicals claimed that a "family atmosphere" imbued relations between France and Yugoslavia, there was another point to view.

Toward the end of 1927, a treaty of friendship was signed with France providing for the extension of military assistance by either side in case of any kind of attack that might lead to change in the boundaries established in the peace treaties of 1919 and 1920. The Yugoslav government undertook the obligation to consult the French government in case of international crises, and to accept any advice that might be forthcoming from Paris.

The Balkan Pact

France and Britain took the initiative, in the early thirties, for the formation of a new regional alliance in the Balkans, known as the Balkan Pact, joined in February 1934 by Yugoslavia, Romania, Greece, and Turkey. The alliance was directed against German resurgence, gaining in momentum, and against the growing influence of the Soviet Union in international relations. After the revolution, interventions, and economic blockade, the Soviet Union had entered a period of accelerated industrialization. In 1934 the Soviet Union sought reliance on France and its system of alliances to defend itself from the burgeoning power of Germany. Although the Yugoslav government persisted in refusing to recognize the changes that had taken place in Russia, or the Soviet government, the Yugoslav delegate voted for admission of the Soviet Union to the League of Nations. King Aleksandar was in the course of strengthening his ties with France under the new circumstances created by Hitler's taking power when his assassination in Marseilles in 1934 put an end to these plans. Both Italy and Germany breathed a sigh of relief at the news of his death.

Germany's Influence Grows

In 1936 substantial changes occurred in Yugoslavia's foreign policy. The regent, Prince Pavle, was under the influence of right-wing British Conservatives who strove to strike a bargain with Hitler at the cost of destroying the entire French security system in Europe and also of diverting the main line of Hitler's drive eastward toward the Soviet Union. In doing so, this group of British Conservatives hoped to organize fresh interventions by the European bourgeoisie against the Soviet Union, with German militarism as the striking force. Prince Pavle wholeheartedly supported this policy.

This course in Yugoslav policy became more and more evident, first during the tenure of Bogoljub Jevtić and particularly after Milan Stojadinović became prime minister in 1936. Formally speaking, it was a neutralist position between the German and French blocs. Upon taking office, Stojadinović stated that in case of a conflict between Germany and France, Yugoslavia would remain neutral, and also that in view of Germany's renunciation of the Locarno Treaty, Yugoslavia would not take part in any sanctions against Germany, thus paving the way for German aggression.

The victory of the People's Front in France took Yugoslavia even further afield from the French security system. Ties with the Little Entente also weakened. Prince Pavle ordered the conclusion of treaties of friendship with Bulgaria (January 1937) and with Italy (March 1937).[1]

Czechoslovakia stood threatened by Germany. The last meeting of the Little Entente took place at Bled on August 28, 1938. As France and Britain had decided to leave Czechoslovakia to the mercy of Germany, Yugoslavia and Romania also refused to render it any assistance. The death knell had tolled for the Little Entente. Czechoslovakia was isolated. In Munich in 1938, pressurized by its onetime allies, it surrendered to Germany.

---

[1] Mussolini gave small concession to the Belgrade government, by ordering a slowdown in the *Ustaša* activities. [Pavelic called his men *Ustašas* (rebels) and used them in terroristic activities in Yugoslavia from their bases in Italy and Hungary.] But Pavelić applied new tactics in Croatia, by penetrating the different cultural and economic organizations. That was particularly the case of one of the most esteemed Croat cultural organizations, *the Matica Hrvatska*. Pavelić's two right-hand men, and later his two members of the government, Dr. Mladen Lorković and Mile Budak, worked their way into the inner sanctum of *the Mitica Hrvatska*. Lorković published as a *Matica* edition his book *Narod i zemlia Hrvata (The People and Land of the Croats)*, claiming that all the Slovenes, the whole of Bosnia and Hercegovina, and even Montenegro are parts of Croatia. When Pavelić came to power with the help of Hitler and Mussolini on April 10, 1941, the *Hrvatski Narod* (the *Croat people*), a daily, recorded on June 6, 1941, that the leadership of the Matica Hrvatska visited Pavelić. The president of the *Matica*, Filip Lukač, hailed Pavelić "as one of the greatest heroes of our era," and Pavelić in his answer stressed that in the old Yugoslavia "no one could do more and better against the Belgrade regime than what the *Matica Hrvatska* did."

Yugoslavia's Neutrality

Yugoslavia's policy of so-called neutrality also led to growing German influence over the Yugoslav economy. Germany became its principal partner in foreign trade, accounting for 48 percent of imports and 32 percent of exports, especially after the annexation of Austria to Germany in March 1938 and the occupation of Czechoslovakia in the spring of 1939. The influence of German capital over Yugoslavia also grew, finally outstripping that of British and French capital.

Certain more or less enduring factors had a bearing on the development of Yugoslavia's foreign policy: the country's strategic position, its place on the ladder of world economic development, its share of world trade, cultural achievements, and contacts along these lines with the outside world. But the foreign policy orientation also depended in large measure on the degree of readiness of the ruling social forces to subordinate their class and regional interests, or ideological preoccupations, to what common sense should have told them were the historical interest of the entire country.

CHAPTER 40

The Economy
of the
Kingdom of Yugoslavia

SLOW MODERNIZATION OF SOCIETY / YUGOSLAVIA'S NATURAL
RESOURCES / THE SEMICOLONIAL NATURE OF THE COUNTRY IN
COMPARISON WITH ECONOMICALLY ADVANCED STATES / THE
ROLE OF FOREIGN CAPITAL: STATE LOANS / THE ROLE OF FOREIGN
CAPITAL: INDUSTRY, MINING / CORRUPTION / IMPEDING THE COUN-
TRY'S ECONOMIC DEVELOPMENT / EXPLOITATION OF THE WORK-
ING CLASS / THE POSITION OF THE PEASANTRY / AGRARIAN RE-
FORM / TWO MILLION TINY HOLDINGS / THE INFLUENCE OF THE
GREAT DEPRESSION OF 1929 / THE UNEVEN ECONOMIC DEVELOP-
MENT OF VARIOUS PARTS OF YUGOSLAVIA

Slow Modernization of Society

In 1918 the Kingdom of Yugoslavia achieved independence, but only in
the formal sense of international law. Economically it continued to be a semicolonial land ruled by foreign capital.

The process of the modernization of society in Yugoslavia advanced
sluggishly between 1918 and 1941. Compared with the rest of Europe, the Yugoslav state could but be considered socially and economically backward. It paid
the price of its history: for too long it had been under the control of other, larger

states; it had been late in liquidating the feudal system particularly in the principal branch of the economy, agriculture; all this together caused it to develop belatedly as a capitalist economy. In the between-wars period, the gap between the economically advanced countries of Europe and Yugoslavia widened to the detriment of the latter. The tempo of industrialization in Yugoslavia during that twenty-odd-year period amounted to a little over 2 percent a year, whereas the world average was 3 percent. The surplus product of the Yugoslavs, whether in the form of profits or super-profits, flowed to the industrialized countries of the world.

Ruling circles had no coherent concept of the country's modernization, of industrialization, of urbanization as a social process involving the shift of population from country to town, with all its attendant manisfestations. Although individuals did put forward certain proposals from time to time, they were largely retrogressive. The archives of King Aleksandar contain a study by an unknown author, compiled in 1930, on the economic reorganization of Yugoslavia "on a cooperative basis, through the advancement of agriculture and cottage industries"; it was "opposed to the development of industry and foreign trade, and favored total agrarian isolationism." Not enough effort was expended to introduce the element of reason into the regulation of vital questions, nor did the will to do so exist, as capitalist models prevailed and the country was allowed to drift downstream. The blind forces of capitalist anarchy were permitted full play, and planning went by the board.

In size Yugoslavia was twelfth in Europe in 1918, in population tenth, but in natural resources needed for economic development it was among the first, especially as regards mineral wealth, sources of energy, arable land, and areas under forest.

Yugoslavia's Natural Resources

Contemporary science considers that twenty-six strategic raw materials should be used to gauge the mineral wealth of a country and its potential supply of raw materials for domestic industries. They are iron, manganese, chromium, wolfram, molybdenum, nickel, aluminum, copper, tin, lead, zinc, antimony, mercury, platinum, oil, coal, graphite, asbestos, bauxite, fluorite, sulfur, pyrite, phosphate, mica, and iodine. Of these twenty-five materials, seventeen were mined in Yugoslavia before 1941, four more were known to exist but were not exploited, and the other five were thought to be nonexistent in Yugoslavia (wolfram, nickel, tin, fluorite, and graphite), but deposits of tin and nickel were discovered after 1945.

In the opinion of experts, no other country has such a high number of strategic ores with the exception of the Soviet Union. In respect of reserves of metallic ores, iron deposits run below the general world average, but reserves of nonferrous metals per capita are higher than the world average, especially for lead, bauxite, and zinc. The same applies to reserves of nonmetals.

According to an estimate made in 1946, Yugoslavia ranked as follows in extraction of nonferrous metallic ores on the eve of World War II:

Bauxite—first in Europe, second in the world
Lead—first in Europe, fifth in the world
Chromium—first in Europe, sixth in the world
Antimony—first in Europe, fourth in the world
Mercury—second in Europe, second in the world
Copper—second in Europe, eighth in the world
Zinc—second in Europe, eighth in the world

Molybdenum, one of the most precious metals, is mined only in Yugoslavia and Norway inside Europe, and only in the United States and Canada outside. In 1939 Bor and Trepča were the biggest mines of their kind in Europe. Antimony output amounted to 10 percent of the world production of this metal, lead to 4 percent of world production, copper to 4 percent (1925) and 2 percent (1939), and zinc to 2 percent.

As regards natural sources of energy, Yugoslavia is far above the world average in waterpower. Per capita, its potential is over twice the world average in a mean hydrological year. But Yugoslavia is poorer in mineral fuels as sources of energy. Reserves of coal amount to only one-quarter of the world average; they are less than those of Britain, Germany, and Poland, but greater than France's and far greater than those of neighboring Austria and Italy. Reserves of gas and oil are extremely modest, but prospecting has not been completed. All in all, waterpower sources in Yugoslavia can easily make up for the unimpressive amount of oil found so far.

Yugoslavia was relatively well off in terms of arable land and forests. Of its total area, cropland, gardens, orchards, and vineyards accounted for 31 percent, pastureland for 26 percent, and forests for 36 percent, the remainder being unfertile. The country sustained great losses from the ruthless cutting of forests. In contrast to many other European countries, Yugoslavia produced a large number of agricultural products, and not simply two or three kinds of cereal crops; furthermore, it had considerable potentialities for growing a number of subtropical crops: cotton, olives, poppies, and also lemons and oranges.

The Semicolonial Nature of the Country in Comparison with Economically Advanced States

The widespread devastation of World War I was a great impediment to Yugoslavia's industrialization. In Serbia, Macedonia, Montenegro, eastern

Bosnia, and some parts of western Slovenia, a large percentage of the means of production, and in some places all of them, were destroyed during war operations. The same was true of means of communication.

Although the railways were the largest capitalist enterprise in the country in terms of investments and number of employed (in 1922, the country had 9,330 kilometers of railway lines), they staggered under the burden of the past, having been constructed by Austrian and Hungarian capitalists to suit their own economic interests. The railway lines radiated from Vienna and Budapest, leaving large parts of the new Yugoslav state poorly connected, or totally unlinked. The hinterland was not tied up with the seaports, and the railway lines were of different gages (in Bosnia and Hercegovina, all railway lines except for one in the north were narrow-gage). There were also no links by rail between Serbia and Bosnia.

Yugoslavia also fared poorly when the Austro-Hungarian merchant marine was divided up, receiving only 114,000 tons although its river shipping alone had amounted to 462,000 tons.

The country was badly in need of technically trained personnel. In 1918 the economy was in total disorganization. But difficulties in industrialization were also the result of the complete lack of a concept of industrialization on the part of the country's leaders. One of the essential reasons for this stagnation was the social conditions of production.

In the Kingdom of Yugoslavia, leading circles in society had very little independence in economic affairs, bound as they were to foreign capital. The latter in turn had little interest in the country's industrialization, maintaining it rather at the level of a producer of primary products and some semimanufactures, and as a source of cheap manpower. The country was not the master of its own economy, particularly as some groups of foreign capitalists demonstrated the tendency to transform Yugoslavia from a semicolonial into a purely colonial territory. As a result, leading groups in Yugoslavia could not have elaborated a plan for industrialization, even if they had wanted to do so. Their role was that of compradors, instruments of foreign capital for maintaining the Yugoslav economy in a position of subordination.

The Role of Foreign Capital: State Loans

Foreign capital acquired key positions in the Yugoslav economy not only through the medium of direct investments but by state loans as well. The country's position in this respect was extremely difficult as it had inherited the public debts of Serbia and Montenegro, and some of the debts of the Ottoman Empire in proportion to the territory allocated to Serbia and Montenegro. To this was added the burden of the war debts of Serbia and Montenegro.

Yugoslavia's war debt to France, contracted during the war years 1914–1918 in cash, military equipment, weapons, and maintenance of the Serbian army, was regulated by agreement between Yugoslavia and France on January 20, 1930. The agreement established the debt at 1.024 billion francs, which was to be paid over a period of thirty-seven years. Yugoslavia paid about 20 million francs of the debt but stopped in 1931, when Germany also ceased paying reparations; the same was done by other Allied states in their mutual repayments of wartime debts.

The war debt owed to Great Britain amounted to somewhat over 25 million pounds and to the United States of America around 63 million dollars. The debt derived partly from advances in cash placed by the American government at the disposal of the Serbian government on Corfu (26 million dollars) and partly for indebtedness involving the purchase of American military stores in France. All in all, up to 1931 installments in repayment of this debt amounted to 1,225,000 dollars.

Yugoslavia was also compelled to take over a part of Austria-Hungary's prewar debt, and the debts of public persons from former Austro-Hungarian territory that was allocated to Yugoslavia. The debt to the Joint Fund in Paris (for repayment of Austria-Hungary's public debts) amounted to 273,951,000 gold francs. Other debts were as follows: 4 million Austrian crowns to the Czech Savings Bank in Prague for a loan to the duchy of Carniola in 1907; 8 million French francs to the Steg, the Austro-Hungarian State Railways Company, as compensation for nationalization in Yugoslavia of a section of the local railways running through areas which went to the Yugoslav state in 1918; debts to other groups of local railway owners (twenty-four Hungarian companies) to the amount of 28,500,000 gold francs; and a debt to the privately owned Danube-Sava-Adriatic Southern Railways Company for that section of the line that linked Austria with Italy through Slovenia, to the amount of 261 million gold French francs. French banks were in possession of a large number of shares in the Southern Railways Company. The debt on April 5, 1941, amounted to 203 million gold francs, meaning that roughly 58 million gold francs of the principal had been paid plus over 12 million gold francs for interest.

As soon as World War I ended, the Yugoslav state asked for official loans abroad to finance industrialization. But the loans received for this purpose were usually spent otherwise. This was the case, for instance, with the so-called Blair loan contracted in the United States in 1922 for the nominal sum of 100 million dollars to finance the construction of a railway line from Belgrade to the Adriatic Sea and a harbor at Bar. The loan was guaranteed by the net profits of monopolies, customs, and railways, and was issued in two parts. In 1922, 8 percent, amounting to 15,250,000 American dollars, was issued. Of this sum, the government spent 15 million dollars for its own general requirements and only 250,000 dollars for the construction of the Belgrade-Bar railway. The issue rate was 86.5 percent. The second issue took place in 1927 to the amount of 30 million dollars at the rate of 86 percent.

By 1941, 26,797,625 dollars in interest alone had been paid on the Blair loan, and 15 million dollars in repayment of the principal.

On the basis of a convention of March 14, 1923, the Yugoslav government received from France a loan of 300 million francs for the purchase of military equipment. By 1941, 105 million francs had been paid for interest alone.

When the war ended, France and Yugoslavia came into dispute over the question of the gold clause in France's prewar loans to Serbia. Up to the middle of 1914, they had been paid in gold. After 1918, however, France canceled the gold clause for debtors who were French citizens, and the Yugoslav government took this as a basis for asking that the gold clause be canceled also for prewar Serbian debts, which it would pay in paper money, dinars and francs. A loud cry was raised in France over this. When the treaty of friendship was concluded between France and Yugoslavia in 1926, the French prime minister Aristide Briand told Vojislav Marinković, then Yugoslav foreign minister, that the convention would be signed only on condition that the Yugoslav government agree to go before the Court in The Hague and to pay French shareholders in gold for those sections of the loan to which the gold clause applied. This was a serious blow to Yugoslav finances and greatly to the benefit of the French *porteurs*. Since the beginning of the twentieth century, they had received more than double their money back through the low issue rates, high interest rates, and other means for the exploitation of small Balkan states.

In an endeavor to stabilize the dinar in 1931, Yugoslavia contracted a loan for 1.025 billion francs with a bank syndicate in Paris, headed by the Paris Union Bank. The issue rate was 87.60 percent, actually a net of 82 percent. By 1941, 240 million francs had been paid out in interest alone.

After the Great Depression of 1929, financial difficulties, shortage of foreign currency, and cessation of reparations payments by Germany made it necessary for Yugoslavia to declare a moratorium of sorts in 1932. It was no longer in a position to service its foreign debts. In order to establish repayment service installments, representatives of French shareholders inaugurated negotiations in Belgrade which terminated in the Convention of July 26, 1933. Three types of new bonds were issued: 5 percent French funding, 5 percent English funding, and 5 percent American funding. By 1941, for interest alone 131 million francs had been paid for the French funding, 1,500,000 dollars for the American, and 9,094 English pounds for the British.

It thus happened that next to Greece, Yugoslavia was the most highly indebted country in Europe between the wars. In 1925 the debt amounted to 25 billion dinars, in 1932 to 39 billion. This did not include short-term flying loans, or commune debts. By 1937 the external state debt amounted to 45 billion dinars, and the internal debt to 10 billion.

In the budget of prewar Yugoslavia, interest payments on all types of long-term loans accounted for 10 to 12 percent of all expenditures. According to a draft of the budget for 1941–1942, 1,370,300 dinars were set aside for debt repayment service.

The Role of Foreign Capital: Industry, Mining

Foreign capital also effected direct penetration of the Yugoslav economy in those branches in which it had the greatest interest and not for the purpose of promoting the country's productive forces. Foreign capital had almost complete control of Yugoslavia's mines of nonferrous metals, and employed over half the country's miners. Its aim was to keep Yugoslavia at the level of producing raw ores alone, rather than processed metals. In 1937 Yugoslavia produced 350,000 tons of bauxite, of which it processed only 300 tons. Aluminum production was hampered by an agreement among world monopolies. Yugoslavia was singled out as the source of raw materials for certain German concerns and was therefore prohibited from producing aluminum. The same was the case with zinc and lead ore. Only one-eighteenth of the lead and one-eleventh of the zinc were processed at home.

Foreign capital was divided as follows according to country of origin before the war:

	Percentage
1. Switzerland	19.5
2. Great Britain	16.4
3. Germany	15.5
4. France	13
5. United States	7
6. Italy	4.5
7. Belgium	3.8
8. Hungary	3.7
9. Sweden	2.8
10. Netherlands	2.1
11. All other	11.7

Foreign capital relied heavily on corruption, which was highly instrumental in helping it draw huge extra profits from the country. A typical case was the penetration of British capital into Yugoslav mining through three companies: the Selection Trust Company (lead mines at Trepča, Novo Brdo, Zletovo, Kopaonik), the Central Mining Investment Corporation and Alatini Mines (Mežice, and shares in Novo Brdo, Zletovo, and Kopaonik), and the Podrinski Antimony Mines.

Nikola Pašić had owned mining terrain in Kopaonik since 1906; he and his family also formally acquired other mining terrain in Kosovo after 1918. At an auction held in 1922, the Yugoslav government fictively sold Trepča to the National Bank and Novo Brdo to the First Croatian Savings Bank. Rade Pašić, son of Nikola Pašić, immediately repurchased Trepča and began negotiating with the London Selection Trust represented by an American, Chester Beatty, known for his interests in Rhodesian and Burmese mines. Soon the London Selection Trust was in possession of Trepča, where it began production in 1932, Trepča being the world's cheapest lead producer. Its output was always completely sold out for several years in advance. Between 1933 and 1937 Trepča paid tax-free dividends amounting to between 16 and 30 percent. After only five years of operation, Trepča shares rose to thirty times their value.

The court archives of the Karadjordjević dynasty contain documents revealing that a fund of 100,000 shares had been set up at Trepča and presented in the form of gifts to influential persons in Yugoslavia. King Aleksandar was offered 4,000 preferred shares.

Private French capital, too, was quick to gain a foothold in the Yugoslav economy. After 1918 the French took over the Trbovlje Coal Mines. The principal political intermediary in these transactions was Dr. Anton Korošec, who, according to documents, received a commission of over 2 million dinars.

Corruption

In techniques of corruption, foreign capital had recourse to a number of different methods. One of these was the intermediaries, fictive representatives or *štromani*, Yugoslav citizens; also, legal forms were satisfied pertaining to participation in the management boards of enterprises behind which stood foreign capital. Politicians did their part in legislation, passing financial laws in the parliament acknowledging and approving foreign concessions. Not a single political party in prewar Yugoslavia could claim that it was not involved in such practices, from the Radicals and Democrats to the Social Democrats and Republicans. When necessary, foreign capital also bribed the press. Even the newspaper *Politika* purchased paper at unusually low prices from Czechoslovakia, for which it returned appropriate favors. Groups were formed in the government administration who defended the interests of one or another foreign group. The same was true in the army, especially when the question arose of where to purchase arms, and which type. The corruption trickled down to the very bottom, to the level of chiefs and clerks in the districts where various enterprises were situated. The police also helped by crushing any attempt to strike or win better working conditions.

Between the two wars, Yugoslavia was essentially an agrarian appendage of the big industrial states. They extracted raw materials, impeded the development of manufacturing, and sold to Yugoslavia manufactured goods produced from its own raw materials at very high prices. In order to purchase one typewriter, Yugoslavia had to export 50,000 kilograms of iron ore, 3,000 kilograms of corn, or 334 kilograms of pork.

Key positions in the Yugoslav economy were in the hands of foreign capital. It accounted for 60.3 percent of electricity output, 55.5 percent brown coal production, 76.1 percent sugar, 100 percent copper and lead, 100 percent bauxite, 70 percent shipping, 98.2 percent cotton fiber, 100 percent matches, and so on.

Impeding the Country's Economic Development

All these factors acted together to keep the development of productive forces in industry and mining slow and uneven. On the average, growth amounted to between 2 and 2.2 percent annually. It was fastest between 1920 and 1923, when an annual growth of 5.2 percent was recorded. Between 1924 and 1928 that figure declined to 1.8 percent and virtually stagnated during the Great Depression beginning in 1929.

Mining registered a somewhat more rapid growth, as communications did. During the first ten years of its existence, the Kingdom of Yugoslavia constructed 922 kilometers of new railway lines, but in the next ten years only 300. By 1940 Yugoslavia had a total of 10,479 kilometers of railways.

The merchant marine grew to 232 ships with 418,000 tons, four times as much as the 1920 figure.

Yugoslavia's population also rose at a fairly rapid rate. According to the census of 1921, it had a population of 11,984,000, and in 1931 it had 13,934,036. The estimate for 1941 was 16 million. The birthrate fell steadily from 36.7 percent in 1921 to 25.9 percent in 1939. But this trend was paralleled by a decline in the death rate from 20.9 to 14.9 percent over a twenty-year period.

According to the 1921 census, 78.9 percent of the population made its living from farming; in 1931 this figure was 76.5 percent, and on the eve of the war it had declined very little, to 74.4 percent. Owing to the population explosion, the number of peasants rose steadily. Between 1931 and 1941 alone, 1,450,000 people were added to this section of the population.

The number of persons working in industry, crafts, and mining, together with their families, accounted for 9.9 percent of the population in 1921 and for 11 percent in 1931. Between 1918 and 1941 the number of new workers in industry amounted to a mere 8,900 annually. The result of this slow growth was that on the eve of World War II, of Yugoslavia's 16 million inhabitants only 380,000 were employed in industry, 240,000 in crafts, and 55,000 in mining.

Between 1918 and 1941 Yugoslavia's city growth rate was one of the lowest in Europe, reflecting the sluggish pace of industrialization. Urbanization as the social process of population shifting from the rural districts to towns was attended by other processes. For instance, a considerable number of industrial and especially mine workers continued to live in the villages while working in factories and mines and neglecting their duties on the land.

With the exception of Belgrade and Zagreb, towns grew slowly, Belgrade and its environs rose from 70,000 in 1900 to 102,000 in 1920, and to 300,000 in 1940. In the Kingdom of Yugoslavia, Belgrade, as the center of political power and state administration, numbered many government employees and their families. Also industry around Belgrade developed more rapidly than it did in other parts of the country.

In 1900 Zagreb counted about 60,000 inhabitants and in 1920 it had 101,000. During its twenty years in the Kingdom of Yugoslavia, it increased to 240,000. After 1920 Zagreb became the biggest industrial center in Yugoslavia and an important communications junction, besides having a large number of banks and mercantile establishments. In 1924 about 50 percent of all Yugoslavia's bank capital was concentrated in Zagreb.

Exploitation of the Working Class

From the very first day of its inception, the country was torn by fierce class conflicts reflecting its poor economic development. Factory and shop owners arbitrarily lengthened the workday, but owing to price spiraling, wages were considerably lower than they had been before the war. General strikes broke out in Trbovlje in December 1918, and later in Split; in February 1919, 30,000 workers went out on strike in Bosnia and Hercegovina. On September 12, 1918, the government was forced to issue a decree on the compulsory eight-hour work-day, but the workers' living standard continued to worsen in consequence of inflation and rising prices for food. In the spring of 1920 the strike movement reached its peak, with fifty strikes in Serbia and Vojvodina alone and twice as many in Yugoslavia as a whole. In 1920 a general railwaymen's strike broke out. On April 21 and 22, the central trade unions called a general workers' strike in support of the railwaymen, but the response was not sufficient to make it a success. In Trbovlje all miners left their pits. On April 24, 1920, the Clericalist government in Slovenia ordered the gendarmes to open fire on workers in Zaloška Street in Ljubljana; fourteen men were killed and seventeen wounded. The railway strike terminated in failure for the workers, who consequently harbored a great deal of bitterness toward ruling circles.

In the autumn of 1920 a miners' strike broke out involving 10,000 miners in Slovenia and 5,000 in Bosnia. The mines were placed under military administration. On December 17, miners from the Kreka Mines, in the village of Husinje, rebelled against these methods, with the result that seven miners were killed and around seven hundred were arrested.

Factory owners took advantage of the terror being perpetrated against the miners to prolong the workday. Real wages fell again, in places amounting to only 50 percent of the 1914 wages. The government promulgated three laws early in 1922 on labor inspection, on-the-job labor protection, and social insurance, somewhat improving the position of the workers. The laws also prohibited children under fourteen from working and banned nightwork for women and minors under eighteen.

The Position of the Peasantry

The peasantry, too, was exposed to a gradual but steady process of pauperization. In view of the fact that Yugoslavia was an explicitly agrarian country with a backward agriculture, the peasantry was the principal source of the surplus product which both domestic and foreign proprietors battled to appropriate. Over 60 percent of the national income was produced by the peasants.

In 1918 the peasantry in Yugoslavia encountered changed political and economic conditions. The internal market, like the foreign, had expanded; a new system of taxes and credit had been introduced.

In many parts of Yugoslavia, the peasants demanded abolition of the remnants of feudalism and division of the land. In Bosnia and Hercegovina, as in Macedonia, Kosovo, and parts of Montenegro, feudal relations still prevailed, whereas the tenant-farmer system of exploitation lingered on in Dalmatia, Istria, the Slovene Littoral, and other parts of Slovenia. In Croatia and Vojvodina large landed estates were prevalent, most of them owned by foreigners; peasant landholdings were so highly mortgaged that the peasant was only nominally the owner.

At war's end and during the first few years of peace, a veritable agrarian revolution threatened to erupt in these areas. Disorders were frequent, and unrest broke out for various reasons. The peasants hammered at the doors of mansions belonging to the landowners, who were given protection by the army.

Agrarian Reform

Ruling circles, fearing the same kind of social upheaval that had occurred in Russia, were forced to make certain social and economic concessions. One of these measures was the agrarian reform. It was extremely long in the implementation, beginning with the Preliminary Decrees that made the preparations for the agrarian reform of February 25, 1919, up to the Law on Liquidation of the Agrarian Reform of July 1931, although in places the reform had not been completed even by 1940. The first law abolished feudal relations throughout all Yugoslavia. Serfs were proclaimed free and big landowners were promised indemnity. The ninth article proclaimed the principle of expropriation of large holdings, but with compensation. An exception was made in the twelfth article in the sense that no indemnity would be paid to large owners of land in the hands of the Hapsburg dynasty and its members, and other hostile dynasties. The ninth article granted certain privileges to soldiers and volunteers in the liberation wars of 1912–1918.

Implementation of the reform dragged on. It was the motive for corruption, from junior officials in the field up to government ministers who endeavored to salvage some of the large holdings. The first law did not specify exactly what a large landholding was, and what the limits on estates were. In international agreements, the Italian government succeeded in assuring that its citizens in possession of large landed estates could retain them, the land involved covering some 13,000 hectares. Peace treaties with Austria and Hungary also granted certain privileges to some of the big landowners.

About half a million peasant families in Yugoslavia received land at the expense of 10,000 large landholders of various categories. The church managed to rescue a considerable part of its extensive holdings, over 95,000 hectares of land. Landowners were paid about a quarter of a billion dinars in indemnity.

The agrarian reform, having abolished feudalism, facilitated the penetration of capitalism into all the aspects of village life, but it also provoked a decline in yields. The maximum landholding was continually raised, first to 300 hectares and later even more.

Two Million Tiny Holdings

After the reform, an enormous number of tiny peasant farms came into existence, actually about 1,985,000. Holdings under 5 hectares accounted for 68 percent of all homesteads and 28 percent of farmland. Holdings between 5 and 20 hectares made up 29.5 percent of the total number of homesteads, these medium-sized farms accounting for almost half (49.3 percent) the farmland. Holdings over 20 hectares made up 2.9 percent of the total number of farms and 22.7 percent of farmland.

The twenties brought a certain improvement in the material position of the peasants, especially the middle and some of the poorer peasants, but this was canceled out by sporadic agrarian crises, falling prices for agrarian products and growing industrial prices, increased taxes, and greater peasant indebtedness. For a time, the peasant tried to help himself by setting up cooperatives, which were joined in particularly large numbers by the middle peasants. But these cooperatives began to slide downhill under pressure from government measures and in Croatia from the big Zagreb banks, which acted directly to disrupt them.

The rapid population increase continued to aggravate the agrarian situation. Agrarian overpopulation was accelerated. There were 118 inhabitants to 100 hectares of arable land; in Germany this number was smaller by half (59 inhabitants to 100 hectares). In view of the slow development of industry, the superfluous population could not find employment in the towns. Emigration was one way out, and about 250,000 persons left Yugoslavia, most of them peasant boys, between 1921 and 1931. After 1931 it became increasingly difficult to emigrate.

Agricultural production was primitive. As stated by Dr. Mihajlo Vučković, 1,000 peasant holdings in prewar Yugoslavia were in possession (and this in the twentieth century!) of 182 wooden plowshares and 439 iron plows; 379 homesteads had no plows at all.

The progressive pauperization of the rural districts was reflected in the per capita national income, which between 1931 and 1941 was lower in Yugoslavia, Albania, and Bulgaria than in any other European country. Yugoslavia was one of the biggest sugar beet producers in Europe but at the bottom of the ladder of European sugar consumption. Whereas England consumed 53 kilograms per capita annually, Yugoslavia consumed only 4 kilograms. Even that consumption was unevenly distributed. In unproductive areas like Bosnia and Hercegovina, Montenegro, Macedonia, Lika, Kordun, and Dalmatia, sugar was eaten only on holidays.

Health conditions in the villages were also extremely poor. According to statistics for 1938, 4,000 doctors were employed in towns accounting for 3.5 million inhabitants, whereas there were only 800 for the 11.5 million rural inhabitants. More persons, especially young ones, died of pulmonary tuberculosis than in any other European country. Malaria affected one-tenth of the Yugoslav population and in Macedonia even more. The government did very little to improve health conditions in the rural districts. The only exception was the National Health School administered by Dr. Andrija Štampar in Zagreb, who worked actively to organize preventive medicine throughout Yugoslavia, especially in the villages, on a cooperative basis.

The Influence of the Great Depression of 1929

The Great Depression of 1929 was especially disastrous for agrarian countries. When it struck Yugoslavia, certain enterprises trading with the rural districts failed and were replaced by privileged enterprises established by the government, thus strengthening state capital. Peasant debts increased to nearly 7 billion dinars. Private persons and private banks constituted 80 percent of the creditors. The state formed the Privileged Agrarian Bank, which extended cheap agricultural credit for farmers not on the basis of mortgages on their holdings but in the form of personal credit. This practice was soon abandoned, and the banks reverted to mortgages which favored the richer peasants. At the same time, the government raised taxes in the villages. In 1932 peasants were paying almost 4 billion dinars in taxes. Prices of agricultural products continued to show a downward trend, aggravating indebtedness and pauperization.

These tendencies generated new social movements in the rural districts. The peasant came to perceive that the measures undertaken by the new order established in 1918, and the promises made over the years, had not produced the desired result. On the eve of World War II the Yugoslav villagers were restive, and the same desire for change was felt that had been expressed so many times before in the history of struggle by the Balkan peasantry.

The Uneven Economic Development of Various Parts of Yugoslavia

The various parts of Yugoslavia developed unevenly. In 1918 the Serbian bourgeoisie had the advantage over the Croatian and Slovene, for it controlled the army and found it easy to establish a centralized, monarchistic order. Thus it acquired both political power and the possibility of economic domination. It dictated tax policies and decided personnel questions in the administration, army, and diplomacy.

Internal development in Yugoslavia was dependent on the legacy of earlier historical periods. The Yugoslav lands that had been part of Austria-Hungary, primarily Slovenia, Vojvodina, and Croatia, although economically backward in comparison with other sections of the Hapsburg empire, particularly Austria and Hungary, had had a better starting point and conditions more favorable for industrialization than those in Macedonia, Kosovo, the Sanjak, Bosnia and Hercegovina, and even Montenegro and Serbia. Macedonia, Montenegro, Hercegovina, and Serbia possessed only 15 percent of all factories in Yugoslavia in 1918. Up to that year, investment capital in industry per capita ran as follows:

	Dinars
Slovenia	192
Vojvodina	124
Croatia	113
Serbia	107
Bosnia and Hercegovina	73
Montenegro	13
Macedonia and Kosovo	3

As the capitalist system based exclusively on the profit motive prevailed in the Kingdom of Yugoslavia, and the blind laws of capitalist development were left free play, the gap between the economically advanced and economically underdeveloped regions of Yugoslavia continued to widen, to the detriment of the latter after 1918. In Slovenia, Vojvodina, and Croatia, a certain industrial tradition had already been established, labor productivity was higher, and financial and industrial capital was domestic in source to a greater extent. These areas were less dependent on foreign capital than the newly opened mines in Kosovo, for instance, and other underdeveloped areas.

In the opinion of one of the leading Yugoslav economists, Dr. Dimitrije Mišić, judging from the number of factories, the amount of capital, and the number of employees, most of the country's industry developed between 1918 and 1941 in the northern and northwestern parts of Yugoslavia, including Belgrade with Zemun and Pančevo, meaning in those areas where it was already advanced. The predominant part of industry was constructed in Croatia and Slavonia, followed by Serbia, Slovenia, and Vojvodina.

In relation to its population, Slovenia, followed by Croatia and Serbia, did more by way of industrial construction than other areas. The least industry was developed in Montenegro and Bosnia and Hercegovina. Macedonia was slightly better off, showing a high percentage of capital increase per capita in relation to 1918, when its level of industrial development, after liberation from Turkey, was very low indeed and when the amount of capital invested in industry per unit of population was only half that of Montenegro.

The amount of capital invested in Slovenia in new industries, on a per capita basis, was 2.5 times that of Serbia, 6 times that of Bosnia and Hercegovina, and 25 times that of Montenegro. This illustrates how the inherited disproportions in industrial development were not only maintained but even aggravated.

Dr. Mišić further considers that mining and smelting developed in a different direction. The dynamics of advance in this branch of economic activity showed the pace to be swiftest in Serbia, followed by Bosnia and Hercegovina. Slovenia remained at about its 1923 level in value of production, whereas Croatia's production developed more slowly than that of Serbia and Bosnia and Hercegovina. Following is the index for mining production and smelting in 1938 as against a base of 100 in 1925:

Serbia	412
Bosnia and Hercegovina	206
Croatia	163
Slovenia	102

Much greater divergence in degree of industrialization between various regions is noticeable when the value of industrial production is calculated on a per capita basis:

Slovenia	3,320	processing 3,140, mining 180
Croatia	1,560	1,540 + 20
Serbia	846	766 + 80
Bosnia and Hercegovina	683	562 + 121
Macedonia and Montenegro	156	149 + 7

The survey shows, concludes Dr. Mišić, that in per capita value of industrial production, Slovenia held pride of place (with 3,320 dinars), followed by Croatia, Serbia, and Bosnia and Hercegovina, with Macedonia and Montenegro in last place (with 156 dinars). In other words, Slovenia produced four times as much industrial goods per capita as Serbia, and twenty-two times as much as Macedonia and Montenegro.

At that time, the difference between the industries of Slovenia and Macedonia was greater than between those of Yugoslavia and the United States.

Most industrial production centered in the northern and northwestern parts of the country. The central and southern parts, including all of Bosnia and Hercegovina, Macedonia, Montenegro, and the part of Serbia belonging to the then Morava banovina and a section of the Drina banovina encompassing western districts in Serbia, accounted for only 15 percent of industrial production, as against its 39 percent of the country's total population.

In 1918 Bosnia and Hercegovina numbered 13 percent of the new state's population, somewhat more than Vojvodina and Slovenia together, but could count only 145 industrial enterprises, or one-sixth as many as Vojvodina and Slovenia.

In 1938, however, Bosnia and Hercegovina had about 15 percent of Yugoslavia's population but only 7 percent of its industrial enterprises. Slovenia and Vojvodina together also accounted for 15 percent of the Yugoslav population and 46 percent of industrial enterprises, 6.5 times as much as Bosnia and Hercegovina.

The central government did nothing to prevent exploitation of economically backward areas by industrial and finance capital. On the contrary, it supported this anarchic development which suited it politically. The centralistic regime appropriated part of the profits for itself while at the same time making compromises with capital in Slovenia, Croatia, Vojvodina, and Belgrade. The Cvetković-Maček Agreement of 1939 gave formal expression to this desire of the strongest bourgeois groups in Serbia and Croatia to divide the country up into spheres of interest at the expense of their own peoples and also of the other nationalities of Yugoslavia.

CHAPTER 41

Yugoslavia between Centralism and Federalism

Reasons for Submission by Croat and Slovene Bourgeois Circles to Serbian Centralism

Fear of social unrest was one of the principal reasons why leading bourgeois groups in Croatia, Slovenia, and Vojvodina agreed to the formation of a joint state of Serbs, Croats, and Slovenes on December 1, 1918, without having specified whether it would be a centralized or a federated state.

Toward the close of 1918 all Croatia, as well as Slovenia and Vojvodina, were caught up in spontaneous peasant unrest. The National Councils provided rallying points not only for all bourgeois groups but also for the big landowners, the high-ranking clergy (both Roman Catholic and Orthodox), and even many prominent civilian officials and army officers of the former Hapsburg dynasty. The peasant masses were promised immediate agrarian reform and the working class was promised an eight-hour day. Late in September, when it had become quite clear that Germany and Austria-Hungary were on the brink of defeat, the National Council of Slovenes, Croats, and Serbs was established as the supreme organ of state administration in the part of Austro-Hungarian territory inhabited by South Slavs. In the Croatian Assembly on October 29, 1918, this new body solemnly proclaimed the formation of the State of Slovenes, Croats, and Serbs, and severance of ties with the Hapsburg empire.

The Croatian Frankists were the only political party not admitted to either the National Council or the government of the new state. Since the annexation of Bosnia and Hercegovina, they had compromised themselves as a party on the payroll of the Military Office of Francis Ferdinand, heir to the throne. After the assassination of the Archduke in Sarajevo in 1914, and having received the go-ahead sign from Vienna, they had been largely responsible for organizing persecution of the Serbs, especially in Bosnia and Hercegovina, At the same time, they had waged a persistent and clamorous campaign in the Croatian Assembly against the leaders of the Croatian-Serbian coalition, calling them the "murderers of the Croatian heir to the throne," and it was at their instigation that Svetozar Pribićević had been arrested. During the war the Frankists had continued their activities along these lines, looking for any excuse to deepen the rift between Serbs and Croats. When Potiorek captured Belgrade in December 1914, they sent him congratulations. And in 1918, when the Hapsburg dynasty collapsed, the Frankist leaders made a statement confessing that their policies had suffered defeat and that they were therefore dissolving their party.

Bourgeois sections of the population of Croatia and Slovenia were alarmed not only by peasant restiveness and the deserters in the Green Army, but also by the advance of Italian troops from the west. The Italians refused to stop at the line of the truce or even at the boundary established by the secret London Treaty of 1915; they continued their thrust into Yugoslav territory. This fact was also responsible for the National Council's decision to ask for the urgent assistance of the Serbian army. Politicians from Dalmatia were particularly persevering in this respect, insisting that unification be proclaimed immediately in Belgrade. The Social Democratic parties of Croatia and Slovenia also joined the National Council and its government.

The Decision of the National Council of November 24 on Unification into One State

On November 24 the National Council passed a decision on the "unification of the State of Slovenes, Croats, and Serbs, over the entire Yugoslav territory of the former Austro-Hungarian Empire, with the Kingdoms of Serbia and Montenegro, into an integral state of Serbs, Croats, and Slovenes." The Social Democrats bowed to the will of the majority while voicing their reservations about a monarchy. The only one who voted against the hasty unification was Stjepan Radić, representative of the Croatian peasantry.

The Declaration of December 1, 1918

The delegation of the Council arrived in Belgrade on November 27, 1918, and was received by Regent Aleksandar on December 1 at 8 P.M. in the Krsmanović Building on Terazije Square. The regent was flanked by ministers Stojan Protić, Momčilo Ninčić, Ljuba Jovanović, and Commander Živojin Mišić. An address from the National Council was read out to the regent, stressing the danger presented by the Italians and the hope that Aleksandar would help establish the boundaries of the new state on ethnographical lines and in keeping with the "principle of national self-determination proclaimed by President Wilson of the United States of America and all the powers party to the agreement." Apparently, the Council delegation did not raise the question of the form of the future state, the manner in which the new constitution would be adopted, or other conditions posed by the National Council in its instructions before the delegation's departure for Belgrade.

Aleksandar replied that he accepted the announcement of the "historic decision of the National Council of November 24 proclaiming the unification into a state of the entire nation and the entire beloved, martyred but glorious homeland."

The ceremonies held on December 1 in Belgrade were not attended by Nikola Pašić although he had signed the agreement of November 9, 1918, in Geneva, which provided for an entirely different procedure of unification, and a different substance. Pašić had signed on behalf of the Serbian government, Anton Korošec on behalf of the National Council, and Dr. Ante Trumbić on behalf of the Yugoslav Council. The Geneva declaration had established: That a state of Serbs, Croats, and Slovenes would be formed as an indivisible state entity; further, that both the governments of the Kingdom of Serbia and of the National Council would continue to discharge functions in their internal legal and territorial jurisdiction and until the convening of the constituent assembly.

Actually, the Geneva agreement made provision for a dualistic state, as half of the new government which was to concern itself with joint affairs was to be selected by the Serbian government and the other half by the government of the National Council. One half of the members of the new government were to take their oath to the king of Serbia, and the other half to the National Council.

Historical sources have never ferreted out the entire political background of the Geneva agreement or presented an accurate picture of the game played by Nikola Pašić, who had both previously and afterwards staunchly supported the idea of a centralized government in Belgrade. He was disavowed in Belgrade as Korošec was in Zagreb. The question was raised in the National Council as to who had invested Korošec with the authority to conclude such an agreement.

Unification of Serbia and Montenegro

In Podgorica, Montenegro, the Great National Assembly was convened on November 25, 1918, to proclaim the deposition of the Petrović-Njegoš dynasty, the confiscation of all the property of the Montenegrin dynasty, and the unification of Montenegro with Serbia, Croatia, and Slovenia. Those responsible for convoking the assembly, and for the decisions it passed, included a considerable number of former members of the Montenegrin youth who had been persecuted by King Nikola for their democratic ideas and desire for unification of Serbia and Montenegro. In the new Yugoslav state many of them, headed by Marko Daković, were soon disillusioned with the system of rule, and some even withdrew from political life. Supporters of the Podgorica assembly were particularly sharp in their condemnation of Prince Mirko, son of King Nikola, for the capitulation of Montenegro in 1916, declaring that the time had come for Montenegrins to redeem themselves for this disgrace. Actually the Serbian government, and especially Regent Aleksandar, made haste to prevent any countermoves by King Nikola. Early in January 1919 an interallied commission arrived in Montenegro to "examine the mood of the people." However, they encountered a fait accompli. King Nikola's pleas for help were turned down even in Italy, on which he had pinned high hopes in view of the fact that his daughter Jelena was the Italian queen. When the agreement between Italy and Yugoslavia was signed in Rapallo in 1920, two secret clauses were inserted. According to one of them, Italy undertook the obligation not to assist "malcontents and renegades" in Yugoslavia. Opinions differ as to their identity. Momčilo Ninčić considered that Italy had promised not to help "Bulgarians and Croats" whereas Ante Trumbić stated in an address delivered in Split on December 5, 1920, upon his return from Rapallo, that the agreement with Italy had been signed because otherwise "elements calculating on the dissolution of our state would grow stronger, including the Montenegrin renegades."

The acts of unification of November 24 and December 1, 1918, made provision for the convening of a constituent assembly to pass the final decision about the new state system. Elections for the assembly were held on November 28, 1920. Among those participating were, first, the old political parties from prewar days (Radicals), the new united parties (Svetozar Pribićević and his political group joined the Democrats), and some new parties. Universal franchise for males was introduced. This was of particular significance for the peasant masses in Croatia, where the right to vote had been considerably limited. Although the Radical and Democratic parties won the most seats, ninety-three and ninety-two, respectively, it came as a surprise that the Croatian Republican Peasant party received fifty, and the Communist Party of Yugoslavia fifty-nine.

Stjepan Radić Supports the Idea of a Republic and Confederation

Dr. Antun Radić had died in February 1919, and the Croatian Republican Peasant party was then led by Stjepan Radić. He proclaimed it a republican party, and it was decided at a special assembly that the Croatian people would submit to the Peace Conference in Paris a memorandum asking for the right to self-determination and for the Croats to be permitted to express their free will in respect of joining an equal state community together with Serbia and Montenegro. Radić formulated the program as follows: "The Croats are a separate state and national individuality in the ethnographical community of the South Slavs." On March 25, 1919, Stjepan Radić was arrested; the widow of Dr. Antun Radić, in despair, committed suicide at the grave of her husband in Mirogoj. With a minor interruption, Stjepan Radić was kept in prison until the elections of November 28, 1920, from which the Croatian Republican Peasant party emerged as the largest political force in Croatia.

The Formation of the Communist Party of Yugoslavia; Elections for the Constituent Assembly

The Communist Party of Yugoslavia was founded at a congress held in Belgrade in April 1919, its original name being the Socialist Workers' Party of Yugoslavia. It supported a revolutionary platform and joined the Third International. At the general elections the Communists won a large number of votes. In Slavonski Brod and certain other industrial centers, they received an absolute majority at the polls, and in Zagreb a relative majority. The Communists also won the elections in Podgorica. At the Second Party Congress in Vukovar in June 1920, the party changed its name to the Communist Party of Yugoslavia. Dragiša Lapčević and Živko Topalović opposed the program of the Communist Party of Yugoslavia (CPY) but were left in the minority. Of the 305 members present, 242 delegates voted for the program. Sima Marković and Filip Filipović were elected secretaries of the Party. The CPY also won a convincing victory at the commune elections held in Serbia and Macedonia in the summer of 1920. In Belgrade Communist candidates, headed by Filip Filipović, came out first; this was also the case in Niš, Kragujevac, Užice, and almost all the large towns of Serbia. They were victorious also in Skoplje, Kumanovo, and Prilep. The minister of internal affairs, Milorad Drašković, assisted by the police, prevented Filip Filipović from taking power in the commune of Belgrade. At elections on November 28, 1920, the CPY became the third most powerful party in the country, polling almost 200,000 votes and winning fifty-nine seats. Over 40 percent of the voters in Montenegro and Macedonia cast their ballots for it.

The Proclamation of December 30, 1920

Fearing the strength of the CPY, the government in Belgrade issued a proclamation (*obznana*) on December 30, 1920, banning "Communist propaganda, stopping the work of Communist organizations, and confiscating all Communist newspapers." Using the proclamation as a basis, the government extended the persecution to include the strongest trade unions. A Law for Protection of the State was also passed.

The Saint Vitus's Day Constitution of 1921

The Communist deputies in the Constituent Assembly protested against these measures. They called for the new constitution to proclaim a soviet republic. Finally, on June 28, 1921, a new constitution was promulgated, later known as the Saint Vitus's Day Constitution. Voting for the constitution were 223 deputies, while 196 voted against it or were absent. The government won the day with the help of votes cast by Muslim landowners from Kosovo, the Sanjak, and Bosnia and Hercegovina who had been promised huge indemnity for land subject to the agrarian reform.

In protest against the terrorization of the working class, a house painter Spasoje Stejić, who had been a volunteer in the Serbian army during World War I, threw a bomb on June 29, 1921, at the carriage in which Regent Aleksandar was driving along Miloševa Street in Belgrade. The bomb exploded after the carriage had passed and the regent was well out of danger, but nine other people were wounded.

The police staged a provocation claiming that the leadership of the Central Committee of the CPY had organized the attempt at assassination. Filip Filipović, Vladimir Čopić, Nikola Kovačević, and Miloš Trebinjac, all members of the CPY executive, and deputies, were arrested. They were brought to trial in January 1922 and sentenced to two years in prison although all the statements made under duress claiming to prove their guilt had been withdrawn from court. Stejić was sentenced to death, but his sentence was later commuted to life imprisonment. In the summer of 1941, together with a group of communists, he escaped from the Ustashi prison in Sremski Mitrovica, joined the Partisans, and was killed in the Battle of the Sutjeska in June 1943.

Among the young Communists was a group who thought that assassination should be used as a method of fighting the regime. A carpenter, Alija Alijagić of Bijeline, acting on this persuasion, killed Milorad Drašković, the minister of internal affairs, in Delnice on July 21, 1921. Others in the plot were Rodoljub Čolaković, Dimitrije Lopandić, Nikola Petrović, and Stevo Ivanović. Alijagić was sentenced to death and executed on March 8, 1922, in the courtyard of the High Court in Zagreb; the other conspirators received long terms of imprisonment.

Self-government Founders

The Saint Vitus's Day Constitution established a centralized state and in essence did not recognize the existence of various nationalities in Yugoslavia although it did admit of a difference between what it termed the "various tribes." It confirmed the thesis put forward by Regent Aleksandar in his reply to the address of the National Council of December 1, 1918, relevant to the existence of a single nation in Yugoslavia.

In contrast to this thesis, the Croatian Republican Peasant party supported the view that Yugoslavia should be a confederate state of three nationalities: Serbian, Croatian, and Slovene. However, Stjepan Radić did not recognize the existence of the other nationalities in Yugoslavia, even Macedonian. Supporting the unitaristic system of state, however, in addition to the Radicals and Democrats, were the Serbian Agriculturists, although they sought also local self-government. It is interesting to note that the Communists had neglected the national question in Yugoslavia, considering it a bourgeois problem. It was only at the Third Congress of the CPY in 1926 that they finally took a stand against unitarism and for the right of the peoples of Yugoslavia to equality.

As a member of the Democratic party, Svetozar Pribićević supported

FIGURE 42. Stjepan Radić.

FIGURE 43. Nikola Pašić (on the right).

centralism. After leaving the Democrats, he formed the Independent Democratic party and concluded an agreement with Radić calling for division of the country into historical provinces, the first step toward federation; only later, after January 6, 1929, did he adopt the idea of a federated Yugoslavia. The most independent of the Radicals was Stojan Protić, who felt that the new state would soon be in crisis over centralism. But he remained isolated in his views. The Slovene Clericals bent with the wind, vacillating between one side and the other. This was also true of the followers of Mehmed Spaho in the Yugoslav Muslim Community.

The staunchest critic of centralism was Stjepan Radić, although he, too, occasionally faltered. His influence among the Croat peasants, and later the people in the towns, mounted from one election to another. The number of votes cast for him rose from 230,000 in 1920 to 473,000 in 1923 and 533,000 in 1925. Radić stuck to his concept of the state as a republic, and ceaselessly sent memorandums to international conferences insisting that the Croat people be allowed to exercise their right to self-determination. More than any other politician or political group, Radić sensed the profound influence of the October Revolution on Croatia: the land to the peasants, peace, the idea of a common humanity. Elements of ancient Bogomilism were noticeable in his public statements. He assailed the church as an institution susceptible to corruption and earthly sins, but defended the faith. His slogan was "Praise be to Jesus and Mary, down with the bishops." Having spent more time inside prison than at liberty, he took advantage of a breathing spell in 1923 to go abroad, visiting Vienna, London, and Moscow. In the U.S.S.R. he joined the Peasant International; upon his return home, he was placed under arrest and brought to trial. He and his followers were arraigned under the Law for Protection of the State.

Then came a turning point in Radić's career. Speaking on his behalf in the National Assembly in March 1925, his cousin Pavle Radić stated that the Croatian Republican Peasant party recognized the status established by the Saint Vitus's Day Constitution. Stjepan Radić publicly announced the resignation of the Croatian Republican Peasant party from the Peasant International. Radić and Rade Pašić, the corrupt son of Nikola Pašić, embraced publicly in Zagreb on a balcony overlooking a square where people had gathered for a meeting. King Aleksandar received Radić in audience, and in November 1925 he became minister of education in a coalition government with the Radicals.

There is some mystery surrounding the reason that led Radić to accept the "kiss of death" from the ruling regime. It may have been the result of the lowered morale, apathy, and feeling of futility that sometimes follows the enormous effort of revolt in a movement such as that of the peasants, where blind forces are frequently in play. But Radić soon pulled out of this lethargy. The Radicals were unwilling to share power with anyone. In the autumn of 1926 he withdrew into the opposition to create, with Svetozar Pribićević, the Peasant-Democratic coalition, where he remained until his death.

The Crumbling of Bourgeois Democracy

The central political figure in Yugoslavia was indisputably King Aleksandar. The Saint Vitus's Day Constitution had simply served to sanction his authority, already established in 1918. From the very beginning he had bent all his energies to liquidating the regime of liberal monarchy and introducing his own personal dictatorship, placing his reliance primarily on the army, which was utterly under his control after the execution of Colonel Apis in 1917. He was unswerving in his adherence to the Great Serbian program, in which he had the full support of the generals. Of the 165 generals in active service in 1926, all were Serbs except for two Croats and two Slovenes.

Reared in court circles in Petrograd, Aleksandar showed a patent weakness for fortune-telling, and he kept himself surrounded at court by various "clairvoyants."[1]

Through his many connections, the king systematically acted to undermine the prestige of the various political parties. He referred to them as a great evil and shifted to them the responsibility for the country's unsound condition, deposing one government after another in a deceptive attempt to demonstrate the instability of such a political system. Svetozar Pribićević later asserted that King Aleksandar himself provoked a crisis in twenty-one of the twenty-three governments that were in power between 1918 and 1929. Not a single government in prewar Yugoslavia lost power through elections. None of them ever fell from a no-confidence vote in Parliament; the cause was behind-the-scenes activity in court circles.

Autocratic by temperament, Aleksandar "did not know how to rule," frequently giving vent to his fury by screaming and shouting at his ministers and even at his wife Queen Mary, a cousin of the British Queen Victoria. It was he who was responsible for the death of Nikola Pašić. Receiving him in audience

---

[1] His papers reveal numerous details about this side of his life. Historians had been led to believe that century, a peasant named Tarabić had confided his visions to Zaharić. Tarabic's "auguries" during reasons, although the talks were tacitly desired by certain military circles headed by Colonel Apis; even the prime minister, Nikola Pasić, was not indifferent to German offers to conclude a separate peace treaty. However, a note has been found in Aleksandar's papers indicating that he had sought the advice of Presbyter Zaharije Zaharić of Kremna on this occasion. At the end of the nineteenth century, a peasant named Tarabić had confided his visions to Zaharić. Tarabić's "auguries" during confession, that the war "would be bloody and horrible and would bring about the downfall of Austria against the Obrenović dynasty, whose fall they claimed he had foretold. In the autumn of 1915, according to a letter in the court archives, Aleksandar sent an emissary to Presbyter Zaharić, who was then eighty-two years old, to ask what Tarabić had predicted about the duration of the war and the outlook for Serbia. Zaharić informed Aleksandar that forty years ago Tarabić had stated, during confession, that the war "would be bloody and horrible and would bring about the downfall of Austria and Turkey whereas Serbia would emerge from the war great and become an empire." The message from Presbyter Zaharić carries the date September 25 (12), 1915.

on December 9, 1925, he upbraided him so mercilessly that the elder statesman suffered a nervous breakdown and died the next day. In this manner the monarchy showed its ingratitude to the man who, for monarchy, betrayed his own political exemplars—Svetozar Marković, Mihailo Bakunjina, and Karl Marx—so that he could become a spokesman for the extreme right of Serbian society. That which the old statesman Pašić received as a reward, Stjepan Radić received as punishment.

The Murder of Stjepan Radić

On June 20, 1928, the Radical deputy, Puniša Račić, shot and mortally wounded Stjepan Radić during a session of Parliament, also killing two deputies of his party, Dr. Djuro Basariček and Pavle Radić. He also seriously wounded Dr. Ivan Pernar and Ivan Grandja. After a few weeks Stjepan Radić succumbed to his wounds.

King Aleksandar took advantage of this tragic occurrence to compromise the parliamentary system and introduce a monarchist dictatorship. The murderer, Puniša Račić, for years a close associate of General Petar Živković, claimed that he had committed the crime in a fit of rage, having been provoked by Ivan Pernar's allegations that he had "plundered the beys." The government endeavored to portray the crime as the personal revenge of an unstable personality, but the fact remains that Račić belonged to the intimate circle of the court camarilla. Many other facts also indicate that Račić committed the crime with malice aforethought. The question is: Did King Aleksandar himself know that plans were afoot for Radić's assassination? No reference to this has been found in court papers. The only documents available are the reports of the great župan of Zagreb about the course of Radić's health after the assassination attempt. Apparently the reports lay on Aleksandar's desk for a long time. On one of them he drew a number of graves with large crosses.

Puniša Račić was brought to trial in Belgrade and sentenced to twenty years' imprisonment in the summer of 1929.[1]

The Dictatorship of January 6

The unsettled national question, the peasant problem, and the dissatisfaction of the workers had caused a serious crisis for the regime in con-

---

[1] In October 1944, during the battle for Belgrade, fighting men of the Twenty-first Serbian Division found Puniša Račić in a village near Avala and passed sentence on him summarily. He was taken to the camp at Banjica and executed. Unfortunately, lacking a sense of history, they failed to question him about the role of King Aleksandar in the murder of Stjepan Radić.

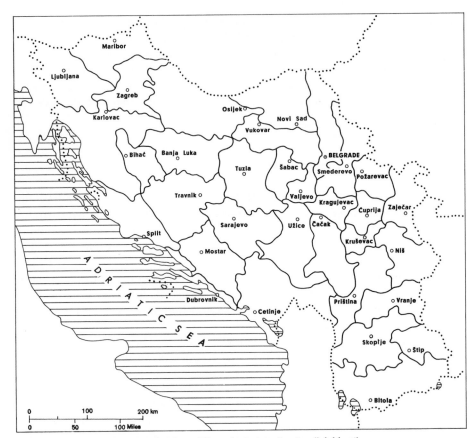

MAP 44.   The administrative division of Yugoslavia into "regions" (oblasti).

sequence of which King Aleksandar decided, on January 6, 1929, to effect a coup d'état eradicating all trace of bourgeois democracy and establishing the dictatorship of the king as the representative of the Serbian bourgeoisie.

In his proclamation for the occasion, the king stated that he "wished to remove the intermediaries between the people and the King," that is, the political parties, and further stated: "Parliamentarism, which remains My ideal as a political objective, in accordance with the traditions of My unforgettable Father, has been abused by blind political passions to such an extent that it has become an obstacle to any fruitful work in the state. For that reason I have decided to suspend the Constitution of the Kingdom of the Serbs, Croats, and Slovenes of 1921." The king appointed a new government, announcing that it was responsible to him alone. All political parties were abolished and the National Assembly was dissolved. Even commune administrations were dissolved. Thus

Aleksandar violated the most profound traditions of peasant democracy in the Serbian parts of Yugoslavia, where even in Turkish times the peasants had had the right to elect village representatives. Freedom of the press was restricted, and newspapers were brought under government control. Police clerks in the Belgrade Municipal Administration were given a list of words that were not allowed to be used in the press, and all articles in daily newspapers had to be sent to the Municipal Administration for approval. Later a Central Press Bureau was established to censor the press in a more intelligent but also more perfidious manner. Any political activity against the state was punishable under law by twenty years' imprisonment or death.

By his putsch of January 6 King Aleksandar removed the supreme state power completely from the control of the National Assembly and government and concentrated all authority in his own hands. He appointed General Petar Živković, commander of the Royal Guard, to the post of prime minister, replacing the incumbent Anton Korošec. When the latter tendered his resignation to the king, he asked; "When did I lose your confidence?" The king replied by offering him the post of minister of transportation in the government set up on January 6. Korošec accepted, making his Slovene People's party the sole party which supported the new dictatorship in its entirety. In this respect all the other parties were split. Radicals who joined the government included Nikola Uzunović, Boža Maksimović, and Milan Srškić. Some who refused to join were Miša Trifunović, Momčilo Ninčić, and Velja Vukičević. Democrats who became members of the government included Voja Marinković, Laza Radivojević, and Kosta Kumanudi, but the leader of the party, Ljuba Davidović, and Milan Grol were opposed to the dictatorship. None of the Serbian Agriculturists joined the government, nor did any of the followers of Mehmed Spaho, or the Slovene Liberals. It is true, however, that the king later inveigled various politicians, one by one, over to his side.

The president of the Croatian Peasant party, Dr. Vlatko Maček, who had assumed leadership of the party after Radić's death, vigorously opposed the dictatorship of January 6, in company with Svetozar Pribićević. Pribićević was arrested on the basis of the Law for Protection of the State, which he himself had helped to pass in 1921, and banished to Brus, from where he was permitted to emigrate, first to Prague and then to Paris. Dr. Maček was arrested in December 1929, accused of having provided terrorists with funds and weapons. Furthermore, the police claimed that in the Christmas issue of the newspaper *Dom (Home)* he had published an article, covering the entire front page, under the heading "Christmas, a Crown of Thorns, and the Bloody Croatian Emblem." However, after his trial in the spring of 1930, Maček was acquitted and released.

The Communist Party offered strong resistance to the dictatorship, which persecuted it relentlessly. The organizational secretary of the Central Committee of the CPY, Djura Djaković, and the secretary for Yugoslavia of the organization Red Help were arrested in April 1929. They were tortured savagely and slain at the Yugoslav-Austrian border. The list of murdered Communist leaders stretched out interminably: in the summer of 1929, the secretary of the Young Communist League (YCL), Mijo Oreški, and a member of the Bureau of the Central Committee of the YCL, Slavko Oreški, were killed in Samobor. In Belgrade Bracan Bracanović, member of the Politburo of the Central Committee of the CPY, was murdered along with Marko Mašanović. In Sarajevo Marijan Barun was killed, and in Zagreb the new secretary of the Central Committee of the YCL, Pera Popović-Aga. The murder of another high-ranking YCL leader, Josip Kolumbo, was soon followed by that of Josip Debeljak and Josip Adamić. Božo Vidas-Vuk, member of the Central Committee of the CPY, was killed in Zagreb.

Between January and September 1932, eighty-two groups of Communists, many of whom were sentenced to long terms of imprisonment, were arraigned before the State Court for Protection of the State.

The Frankists of Croatia also joined the opposition to the regime. Having lain low for the first few years following the war, they became politically active again after 1924. Following the institution of the dictatorship of January 6, their leader Ante Pavelić went first to Austria and then to Hungary and Italy, where he obtained both material and political assistance for his work to disrupt Yugoslavia. The IMRO organization, in the service of Bulgaria, also joined the action and found support in Italy and Hungary.

The 1931 Constitution

Soon the regime set up on January 6 was in a crisis caused by many factors, including the grave economic situation. King Aleksandar thereupon decided to promulgate a new constitution on September 3, 1931. It was a constitution in form alone. A bicameral system was also introduced with a Senate supplementing the National Assembly, but the government remained responsible to the king alone and not to the Assembly or Senate.

In point of fact the constitution legalized unitarism, both in international relations and in state organization. It was proclaimed that Yugoslavia consisted of a single nation. Even before the new constitution, the law dividing the country into administrative units changed its name on October 3, 1929, from the Kingdom of the Serbs, Croats, and Slovenes to the Kingdom of Yugoslavia. It was carved up into nine banovinas, or administrative regions: Drava, Sava, Drina, Vrbas, Primorje, Zeta, Dunav, Morava, and Vardar. In military units, all Serbian banners were replaced by new Yugoslav flags.

The government formed on January 6 also scheduled elections at which voting was public. But more voters abstained than at any other elections held in Yugoslavia between the two wars. Even the rectors of the country's three

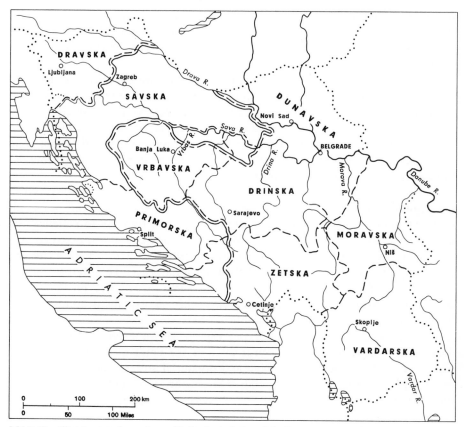

MAP 45.   Division into banovinas with the boundaries of the Banovina Hrvatska from 1939 to 1941.

universities in Belgrade, Zagreb, and Ljubljana refused to go to the polls in protest.

On both left and right, dissatisfaction with the January 6 regime was rife in Serbia as well as in other parts.[1]

The Punctation

On December 7, 1932, ten members of the executive board of the Peasant-Democratic coalition met in Zagreb: Vlatko Maček, Sava Kosanović, Hinko

[1] In Bosnia, even the old national fighters found the dictatorship unbearable. A priest, Simo Begović, Commissioner of National Defense and a native of the Romanija area, who had been condemned to death at the Banja Luka trial of 1916, led a group of peasants from Pale to protest in front of the ban's palace in Sarajevo against the abolition of their commune administration and the imposition of a representative by the authorities after the introduction of the dictatorship of January 6. The ban

Krizman, Josip Predavac, Juraj Šutej, Ante Trumbić, Većeslav Vilder, Mile Budak, Dušan Bošković, and Presbyter Dušan Kecmanović. They condemned the January 6 regime in a document called the *Punktacija* (the Punctation). It read:

1. Standing on the principle of democracy, we consider that national sovereignty is the backbone of any state organization and the people themselves the sole and exclusive source of all political sovereignty and all public power.

2. As the peasantry as a collective concept is the vehicle of all national culture, economic life, social construction (building), and moral values, and also includes the great majority of the people, the peasantry must be the foundation of the organization of our entire life.

3. We note that, because of its lack of ability, Serbian hegemony, which has imposed itself upon Croatia from the very beginning and on all our lands on this side of the Sava, Drina, and Danube, has had recourse to violence and immoral methods keeping all state power in its hands and acting destructively, destroying moral values, all our progressive institutions and achievements, the material property of the people, and their spiritual peace. This state of affairs reached its culmination under the absolutist regime inaugurated on January 6, 1929, which, strengthening that hegemony with all its fateful consequences, has moreover abolished civil and political liberties.

4. On the basis of this grievous experience we arrive at the inevitable conclusion that, returning to the year 1918 as the point of departure, it is an urgent necessity to launch a decisive and organized struggle against that hegemony with the objective of removing it from our lands and eliminating from them all the power and influence of that hegemony together with all its representatives.

5. On this assumption the only thing to do is to begin building a new system of the state community which, without going into a detailed elaboration of the foundations at this particular time, would in principle be founded on the idea that this community, precluding the prevalence of one or more of its members over the others, would represent an association of interests, based on the free will of its members so that each member in his own country, and all of them together working in cooperation on affairs of general interest to the community, which will be determined by agreement, can pursue individual and common interests, guarantee progress and the advancement of the moral and material life of the Serbian, Croatian, and Slovene people. The special interests of minorities speaking other languages will be fully guaranteed.

---

personally came out to meet the demonstrators and asked the priest to state their complaint. Begović asked the ban for 4,000 dinars, upon which the ban replied that he would give him 40,000 if he would only tell him what he needed the money for. Begović, with typical Dinaric violence and the inclination to slide from one extreme to another just for spite, answered: "I want to buy a ticket to Vienna to visit the grave of Francis Joseph, so I can tell him, 'Well, Francis, if I had only known what a mess Bosnia would be in after your death I would never have worked to depose you.'"

The opposition in Serbia and the opposition in Croatia tried to find a common platform against the January 6 regime, but no agreement could be reached. The former emphasized the restoration of the parliamentary system as it had existed prior to January 6 while the latter, especially after the Punctation, considered it most essential to establish the principles upon which a new state order would be based. In some of the Serbian opposition parties, such as the Agriculturists party, groups favoring a federal system were gaining in strength (Dragoljub Jovanović and others). Difficulties also ensued from the arrest of Maček, who was first sentenced to twenty years and later interned in Čajniče. Finally proceedings against him were instituted by the State Court for Protection of the State in Belgrade on the basis of the Punctation. Accused of masterminding the Punctation, he was sentenced on April 29, 1933, to three years' imprisonment without privileges and removed to the jail in Sremska Mitrovica to serve sentence.

The regime also brought pressure to bear on other politicians. Anton Korošec did not last long in the January 6 government, from which he withdrew; he, too, made statements voicing opposition and was soon arrested and interned on the island of Hvar.

King Aleksandar endeavored to win over to his side a section of the opposition politicians. In the spring of 1932 General Živković was withdrawn as prime minister and replaced by Voja Marinković, then by Milan Srškić and finally by Nikola Uzunović.

The Assassination of King Aleksandar

In October 1934, when King Aleksandar visited France, he was assassinated in Marseilles on October 9 by Vlada Makedonski, also known as Veličko Georgijev-Kerin. He died on the spot. The Yugoslav government later spread the word through the press that the king's last words had been "Guard Yugoslavia for me." The assassin was mobbed at the scene of the crime, and his accomplices were taken into custody: Zvonimir Pospišil, Mijo Kralj, and Milan Rajić. At their trial in Aix-en-Provence, they were sentenced to life imprisonment. Ante Pavelić, Eugen-Dido Kvaternik, and Colonel Perčević, as organizers of the assassination, were sentenced to death *in absentia* because they were in Italian prisons.[1]

History has not yet ascertained the roles of Hungarian and Italian

---

[1] Pavelić spent a full eighteen months in the prison in Turin, where he composed a novel, *The Lovely Blond*, giving many details of the preparations for and execution of the assassination. The French police established that the weapons had been smuggled to the assassins in France by a blond woman who pretended to be pregnant to deceive the police. Her identity was not discovered. In his novel Pavelić himself said that she left for America after the assassination. The first edition of Pavelić's novel appeared in 1941 and the second in Buenos Aires in 1954. Her identity was not disclosed in the second edition either.

officialdom in the assassination. The chief of the Historical Department in the Yugoslav Foreign Ministry, Vojislav Jovanović-Marambo, wrote that Mussolini had issued orders to Pavelić and Vanče Mihajlov to organize the assassination after the appearance of an article in the government newspaper *Vreme (The Time)* of Belgrade in which Stanislav Krakov referred denigratingly to the Italian defeat at Kobarid (Caporetto) in World War I. The Yugoslav prime minister himself, Bogoljub Jevtić, was inclined to believe this, but when the assassination was discussed in the League of Nations, the Yugoslav delegate did not dare say anything about Italy's responsibility. In his memoirs Milan Stojadinović absolves Mussolini of all responsibility. Some American historians, like Harry Howard, for instance, are inclined to blame Mussolini and Count Ciano.

In his book *Operation Teutonic Sword*, the Soviet historian Vladimir Konstantinovich Volkov stated that in his opinion the assassination had been organized by Hitler's followers for political reasons, that is, to obstruct Franco-Yugoslav rapprochement. Volkov cites some Nazi documents in the possession of the Democratic German Republic showing the assassination to have been organized by a certain Captain Hans Speidel, assistant military attaché in Paris, at instructions from Hitler and Göring. These documents from East Berlin were published in 1957, after the onetime Captain Speidel had become General Speidel and appointed commander of NATO land forces in Europe. These assertions were denied in West Germany, and the authenticity of the documents was disputed.

Government under Jevtić and Stojadinović

After the death of King Aleksandar, the crown prince came to the throne as Petar II. During the young king's minority, the regency was assumed by Prince Pavle, cousin of Aleksandar Karadjordjević. A new government was formed, headed by Bogoljub Jevtić and new assembly elections were scheduled for May 1935. The Peasant-Democratic coalition and the Serbian opposition joined forces to submit a single list of candidates headed by Vlatko Maček. Despite the advantage enjoyed by the government in elections through its control over the state administration, the united opposition won 1,076,345 votes as against the government's 1,746,000.

Jevtić's government fell, and a new one was formed by Milan Stojadinović, who also established a new political party called the Yugoslav Radical Union, which was joined by persons from the former opposition: Korošec of Slovenia and Spaho in the name of the Yugoslav Muslim Community. However, the Peasant-Democratic coalition would have nothing to do with the new government in spite of personal contacts between Maček and Stojadinović and the audience granted by Prince Pavle to Maček. Maček called for the promulgation of a new constitution, but Pavle felt that the Croatian problem should be solved in line with the existing constitution.

The Serbian parties in the United Opposition were mistrustful of Maček's talks with champions of the regime. Maček persisted in his view that the main objective was to achieve agreement on the state order. The Democrats agreed with this, but a section of the Radicals which had not entered the government was energetically opposed to Maček's demands. At long last a compromise solution was found, and all the heads of the opposition parties signed an agreement in Farkašić in October 1937. The priority of the state-legal question was recognized, procedure was mapped out for the transition to a parliamentary system, and a decision was taken that the new constitution could not be passed without the approval of a majority in Serbia, Croatia, and Slovenia. The agreement concluded in Farkašić was signed on behalf of the Croatian Peasant party by Maček, for the independent Democratic party by Adam Pribičević, for the Radicals by the elderly Aca Stanojević, for the Democrats by Davidović, and for the Agriculturists by Jovan Jovanović-Pižon. Maček visited Belgrade, where he was welcomed by a crowd of over 100,000 people cheering fraternity between the Serbs and Croats.

Regulation of Serbian-Croatian relations was postponed for a time by the need to attend to the question of a concordat with the Vatican. According to the census of 1931, 48.7 percent of the population in Yugoslavia was Orthodox, 37.5 percent Roman Catholic, and 11.2 percent Muslim.

The Serbian Orthodox church had set its relations with the state in order as soon as the war ended. Before 1918 there had been seven independent or affiliated Serbian church districts: the Belgrade archbishopric, the see of Karlovac, the see of Montenegro and the Littoral, the Serbian church in Dalmatia and Boka Kotorska, the Serbian church in Bosnia and Hercegovina, the Serbian church in Old Serbia and Macedonia, and the Serbian church in America.

The canonic unification of all churches was effected in June 1920. The Archihierarchic Synod of the Serbian Patriarchate decided that the archbishop of Belgrade and metropolitan of Serbia, Dimitrije, should be appointed Serbian patriarch, but the administration would not agree to this procedure as it wished to share in the selection of a patriarch. In October 1920 a decree was published prescribing the manner in which the patriarch would be chosen. Laymen were admitted to the synod. Furthermore, the supreme supervisory and administrative authority in all religious-political affairs of the patriarchate was to be the Ministry of Religion, as an organ of the Yugoslav government.

Relations between the Roman Catholic church and the state were to be regulated by a concordat, the draft of which had been completed during the lifetime of King Aleksandar. In July 1937 Prince Pavle and Prime Minister Stojadinović resolved to submit it to the National Assembly. The Serbian Orthodox church, considering that the draft of the concordat placed the Roman Catholic church in a privileged position, launched a fierce campaign against it. It was approved by the Assembly by 167 votes against 127. The synod of the Orthodox church excommunicated all deputies who had voted for the concordat, including Prime Minister Stojadinović. On the other hand, Stojadinović expelled from the government party, the Yugoslav Radical Union, all those deputies who had voted against it.

Demonstrations broke out in Belgrade. The gendarmerie attacked a religious procession and thrashed the vladikas (bishops) and priests. Great alarm was caused by the sudden illness of Varnava, patriarch of the Serbian church. After he died, an inquiry was conducted into the circumstances of his death and traces of poison were found. Rumors spread that Varnava had been poisoned deliberately. In his memoirs Stojadinović energetically refuted these accusations. However, the state archives contain a report from the administrator of Belgrade to Stojadinović regarding the discovery of traces of poison, to which Stojadinović had replied that it was not necessary to continue the inquiry.

Finally Stojadinović had to capitulate. The draft of the concordat was not submitted to the Senate, where Stojadinović feared he could not secure a majority. The excommunication of those who had voted for it was annulled in February 1938, and a new patriarch was chosen, Gavrilo Dožić, supported by the ministers who had the right to vote on these matters according to law. The concordat came to naught, and it thus happened that the Roman Catholic church remained the sole large religious organization in Yugoslavia which had not regulated its relations with the state.

In December 1938, when general elections were held in Yugoslavia, Stojadinović got 1,643,783 votes as against 1,364,500 for Maček. This was a grave defeat for Stojadinović (the ballot was open and there was pressure on the voters), and he was forced to resign in 1939. Acting in the name of Prince Pavle, Korošec was the principal agent in Stojadinović's replacement.

Attempts at Compromise between the Serbian and Croatian Bourgeoisies: the Cvetković-Maček Agreement

The international situation influenced Prince Pavle to try to find a compromise solution for Serbian-Croatian relations. Consequently he was ready to make certain concessions to Maček. The new prime minister, Dragiša Cvetković, met with Maček several times, and on April 27, 1939, an agreement was signed for the creation of the banovina of Croatia, to include the old Sava and Primorje banovinas and the town and district of Dubrovnik. Cvetković and Maček were not able to reach agreement on the division of Bosnia and Hercegovina, or Vojvodina including Srem, and these matters were left open. The central government was prepared to transfer competence to the banovina of Croatia, except for the affairs of the supreme state administration, national defense, and foreign affairs, which were to remain under the jurisdiction of the joint central government. It was also planned to set up a joint government charged with the task of reorganizing the state.

The regency rejected the agreement. Mehmed Spaho protested to Prince Pavle over the partition of Bosnia and Hercegovina by Belgrade and Zagreb. Maček took advantage of the interval to conduct negotiations with the Italian government, intended to bring pressure to bear on Belgrade. A section of the United Opposition was also vigorously opposed to this type of agreement, considering that it "violated the essential interests of the Serbian people." The outbreak of World War II was imminent, and on August 26, 1939, Cvetković and Maček finally signed the agreement. A government was formed with five of Maček's followers participating, in addition to one Independent Democrat. Members of the government from the opposition were Branko Cubrilović, an Agriculturist, and Laza Marković and Boža Maksimović, Radicals.

The agreement signified the division of Yugoslavia into spheres of interest between the Serbian and Croatian bourgeoisies. The banovina of Croatia came to include the former banovinas of Primorje and Sava and the districts of Dubrovnik, Ilok, Šid, Brčko, Gradačac, Travnik, and Fojnica. The final boundaries of the banovina of Croatia were to be defined when the state was reorganized, taking account of economic, geographic, and political considerations. Communes and villages not having a Croatian majority were to be withdrawn from the aforementioned districts attached to the banovina of Croatia.

The agreement, neglecting the totality of the national question of Yugoslavia, took no account of the right of other nationalities to equality. As in the turbulent days of the autumn of 1918, the Croatian and Serbian bourgeoisies found a common tongue in the face of the dangers that threatened them in 1939. The Cvetković-Maček government started bearing down on the masses of the people, who were demanding the solution of economic and social problems. In Croatia the reign of terror against the working class worsened. Class-oriented trade unions were banned in Croatia and throughout all of Yugoslavia, and many Communists and trade union functionaries were dispatched to concentration camps. In December 1939, during demonstrations in Belgrade, the gendarmerie opened fire, killing six and wounding over fifty people.

The Fifth Conference of the Communist Party of Yugoslavia

In the few years preceding World War II, the Communist Party of Yugoslavia succeeded in consolidating its ranks despite the grave blows it endured. In Moscow it stood threatened with dissolution. In his purges, Stalin had ordered the liquidation of over 800 of the Yugoslav Communists who lived and worked in the U.S.S.R., among them 120 functionaries headed by Secretary General Milan Gorkić.[1] Also partly responsible for these murders was the factional strife among the Yugoslavs themselves, who denounced each other to the Soviet police and accused each other of the most heinous crimes. Georgi Dimitrov was directly instrumental in saving the lives of the few Yugoslavs who survived Stalin's slaughters in Moscow. The new leadership headed by Josip Broz Tito moved back to Yugoslavia on Tito's own initiative. The Comintern appointed him the secretary-general of the CPY, and he chose Edvard Kardelj as his deputy. Time was no longer wasted in sending even the most minor leaflet to Moscow for approval. The Party also became financially independent, supporting itself from membership dues and contributions.

The Party was reinforced by an influx of young workers and students. In the villages, too, its influence grew apace. In November 1940 the CPY held an underground conference in Zagreb, attended by 105 delegates from all parts of the country. It was noted there that the number of Party members had grown by over 200 percent. The Party then numbered 9,000 members, and there were 30,000 members in the YCL. This, the fifth conference, was of historic significance, as it laid the groundwork for the CPY's strategy and tactics in the major events that were on the horizon.

A new Central Committee of the CPY with twenty-nine members and nine candidates was elected at the Fifth Nationwide conference. The Politburo members were Josip Broz Tito, as secretary-general of the Party, and Edvard Kardelj, Milovan Djilas, Aleksandar Ranković, Ivan Milutinović, Rade Končar, and Franc Leskošek.

---

[1] During the term of Nikita Krushchev the Soviet courts proclaimed the innocence of all the Yugoslav Communists who had been killed, including Milan Gorkić, annulling all accusations that they were foreign spies, traitors, etc.

CHAPTER 42

Trends
in Education
and Culture, 1918-1941

ONE OF THE HIGHEST ILLITERACY RATES IN EUROPE / ENORMOUS
CULTURAL DIFFERENCES BETWEEN VARIOUS PARTS OF THE COUN-
TRY / THE POSITION OF WOMEN AND LEGAL SYSTEMS / DIFFERENCES
IN LAW ENFORCEMENT / THE INFLUENCE OF FRENCH, GERMAN, RUS-
SIAN, AND ANGLO-AMERICAN CULTURE AND CIVILIZATION / LITER-
ATURE AND ART

One of the Highest Illiteracy Rates in Europe

Yugoslavia's general cultural and educational level, in both town and country, was below the world average. It lagged behind the rest of Europe, just like its economic development, upon which it depended. The census of 1921 showed that 51.5 percent of the total number of persons over the age of twelve were illiterate. In this respect Yugoslavia was far down toward the bottom of the ladder of European countries. In 1931, 44.6 percent of the population was illiterate.

The country showed the same uneven pattern of development in culture as it did in economy. For instance, according to the 1921 census the percentage of illiterates above the age of twelve was distributed as follows:

	Percentage
Slovenia	8.8
Vojvodina	23.3
Croatia	32.2
Dalmatia	49.5
Serbia	65.4
Bosnia and Hercegovina	80.5
Macedonia	83.8

Educational legislation also differed from one area to another. In 1882 Serbia's laws made provision for compulsory education up to the sixth grade; Slovenia's laws decreed eight years of schooling from 1869 onwards; in Croatia and Vojvodina it was six years. In regions under the Ottoman Empire, there had been no state system of schools at all. A law making eight years of school compulsory was passed in Yugoslavia in 1929, but it was not enforced, especially not in the economically backward districts.

Enormous Cultural Differences between Various Parts of the Country

Educational and cultural opportunities were not equal for all nationalities in prewar Yugoslavia, particularly the so-called national minorities, which were present in the following numbers according to the 1921 census:

	Number
Germans	505,790
Hungarians	467,658
Albanians	439,658
Romanians	231,657
Turks	150,000

National minorities composed 16 percent of the entire population. They were treated differently in respect of schooling in their mother tongue. The German and Hungarian minorities were protected by peace treaties according to the provisions of which the Yugoslav government was under the obligation to provide instruction in their native language. Elementary schools in German and

Hungarian existed from 1918 onwards, but high schools were opened far more slowly. The Romanian minority also acquired its own schools, although somewhat later. As Romania was a member of the Little Entente, its minority enjoyed a better position than some other minorities.

Minorities in the south had no rights whatsoever. We have seen that the Macedonians were not considered a separate nation. The official thesis was that they were Serbs, and Macedonia was even called "Southern Serbia." Instruction was given only in the Serbo-Croatian language. The same applied to the Albanians and Turks, who had no schools in their languages at all.

Under the system of schooling in Yugoslavia, the wealthy fared better than the poor, the towns better than the countryside. When the war ended, the country could count 5,600 elementary schools with 650,000 pupils. After twelve years, that number had gone up to 9,300 with 1,500,000 pupils. Nevertheless, each year 230,000 village boys and girls had to stay home because there were no schools for them to attend. The number of teachers also rose slowly. A beginner in the gendarmerie or police force was better paid than a teacher. The result was that the mass of peasants remained illiterate. Whatever education they received was self-taught; in the middle of the twentieth century, they were still forced to acquire their learning from the oral tradition of the country's folklore, which abounded with all manner of fallacious beliefs. It was widely believed in the rural districts that the towns did not want the peasant to learn to read and write because, illiterate, he was an easier object of exploitation.

The social pattern of the high schools and universities was quite different from that of the country's population. Sons of workers were rarely able to reach university level, but peasant boys were in a somewhat better position. Yugoslavia had two universities in 1918, one in Zagreb and one in Belgrade. A new university was established in Ljubljana, a law faculty in Subotica, and a faculty of philosophy in Skoplje. In twelve years the number of students rose from some 2,000 to almost 20,000, peasants making up about one-fifth of that number. In Ljubljana there were far fewer sons of peasant families attending college than in Zagreb and especially Belgrade. More than a third of all the students in Yugoslav universities took up law, the state being eager to produce cadres for its bureaucratic apparatus. Furthermore, at the University of Belgrade law was studied by the poorest students because attendance at classes was not compulsory. Students bought or borrowed "scripts" (notes on the term's work) and appeared in the early summer or fall to take their exams. A large number of boys from peasant families lived in the villages and came to Belgrade only for examinations. Most of the Belgrade students from peasant families hailed from unproductive areas: Montenegro, Bosnia and Hercegovina, the Užice area. Large numbers of them inclined to left-wing ideas and were the principal propagators of communism in the villages of those areas.

The Position of Women and Legal Systems

Cultural differences between men and women were marked in prewar Yugoslavia. The 1921 census showed that 59 percent of the men were literate, but only 38.8 percent of the women above twelve. Women in Yugoslavia did not enjoy the right to vote. They were discriminated against in employment, found it more difficult than men to advance in their professions, and were regularly paid lower wages and salaries. Even the legal system as it existed in Yugoslavia between 1918 and 1941 gave women a position inferior to that of men. Between the two wars there were six different legal areas:

1. The area of the Serbian Civil Code, that is, the territory of the former Kingdom of Serbia.

2. The area of the Montenegrin Property Code, that is, the territory of Montenegro.

3. The area of the Austrian Civil Code before the additions of 1914 and 1915. This included Croatia with Slavonia and part of Vojvodina (the territory of judicial districts of Žablje, Titel, Bela Crkva, Kovin, and Uljma and the entire area of the judicial district of Pančevo); further, the territory of the judicial districts of Kastav and of the islands of Rab, Pag, and Krk, as well as Čakovec and Prelog, and the entire territory of the former Military Frontier (Lika, Kordun, Varaždin, Brod, and southern Srem).

4. The area of the Austrian Civil Code with additions: Slovenia, Dalmatia, part of Istria, and Prekomurje.

5. The area of Hungarian law: Vojvodina minus the aforementioned districts.

6. The area of Bosnia and Hercegovina, where the Sheriat law applied to private property relations among Muslims, in addition to the Austrian Civil Code.

In prewar Yugoslavia, differences in public law were removed, but the opposite was the case in the domain of private law, where diversity increased. Even the proponents of centralism tolerated and fostered the retention of such differences in private law under the influence of custom. Private law governed the everyday existence of the people and provided a reliable reflection of the national life. Consequently it was the most difficult to modify. This process of the intensification of private law acted to undermine public law.

All six systems of private law placed the woman in a subordinate position, but in none of the six Yugoslav regions was woman in a worse position than in Serbia. Živojin Perić, a Serbian lawyer, once wrote, "Man is a kind of noble, and woman is a kind of slave." The Serbian Civil Code deviated considerably from its source, the Austrian Civil Code. Serbian chiefs and rulers acted in accordance with the national common law, which traced its roots to the medieval concept that woman was merely an object in the hands of man. Private law governing Serbs outside of Serbia proper recognized equality between male and female children in inheritance, but in Serbia proper, male children took precedence. In terms of private law, the ability of women to work was equated to that of children. Married women could conclude legal contracts in Serbia, but these could be annulled unless previously or subsequently approved by their husbands. In some cases under law, women were considered the equals of minors between seven and twenty-one, and in others of children under seven!

The position of women in Serbia was in some respects even worse than that of Muslim women. According to Sheriat law, a woman did not enjoy freedom of movement, and all her activities outside the home depended on approval by the husband. According to the Serbian Civil Code, women also had to execute all their husbands' orders. On the basis of Article 350 of the Penal Code, a husband could send a disobedient wife to jail for ten days. The Serbian Penal Code also drew a difference between unfaithful wives and husbands. A woman was considered to have committed adultery if she engaged in intercourse with another man, whereas a man was considered an adulterer only if he brought his mistress to live with him at home. The Muslim woman had the advantage over the Serbian woman in the sense that although inferior in private life she enjoyed equality of property rights. A Muslim man could divorce his wife simply by writing a letter to that effect, but Sheriat law made provision for separate property ownership. The woman managed, enjoyed, and could dispose of her property. She was not compelled to contribute to the family. True, husbands frequently found loopholes in these provisions of Sheriat law, but the woman did, nonetheless, enjoy a certain degree of economic independence, which was not the case in Serbia. In this respect Serbia was even more backward than Montenegro, where the joint family prevailed. The woman in Montenegro was inferior to the man, but the Montenegrin Property Code proclaimed total equality between men and women in business affairs as a general principle of the joint family.

This is only one side of the life of women in prewar Yugoslavia. Women were discriminated against under public law, and private law remained largely as it had been. The Yugoslav Criminal Code of 1930 placed men and women on a footing of equality in cases of adultery, and in certain others as well. Some changes for the better were also introduced in laws relating to debts and insolvency, and for procedure in lawsuits and settlements outside of court. The fact remains, however, that enormous differences in the life and rights of the two sexes lingered on until 1941. One of the principal reasons for such widespread participation of women in the National Liberation struggle of 1941–1945 was their desire to achieve the ideal of social equality with men.

Although women were somewhat better off in areas that had been administered by Austria-Hungary than in those where oriental influences had prevailed, even there the women did not enjoy all public rights. However, in terms of their ability to conduct business and their right to inherit, their social position was superior to that of women in Serbia, Macedonia, and Bosnia and Hercegovina.

Throughout the entire country differences between the sexes were considerable in regard to the right to contract marriage, manner of contracting marriage, and consequences thereof. In this sphere church law took precedence. The only exception was the area of Hungarian law, where civil marriages were permitted. But the churches also had different views on these matters; the Roman Catholic church did not permit divorce, but the Orthodox church did. The Orthodox were allowed to divorce as many as three times.

Great difficulties attended the contracting of marriage between persons of different faiths. Marriage between Muslims and Christians was valid under Sheriat, but not Christian, law. In this respect Muslim law prevailed and the state had to tolerate it. The consequence of these differences in marriage laws was that people switched religions in order to be able to divorce and remarry.

In Slovenia, Croatia, and other areas where the Catholic church predominated, many intellectuals desirous of dissolving the bonds of marriage joined the Orthodox church or even converted to Islam. Six professors at the University of Ljubljana resorted to this method. One of them, having joined the Orthodox church, later left it to become a Muslim, changing his name from Milan to Mehmed, so as to be able to obtain a divorce for the fourth time.

Differences in Law Enforcement

Appreciable differences in law enforcement also existed in Serbia, Montenegro, and other areas with a strong Turkish tradition on the one hand, and those beyond on the other. In the latter, the principles of the State of Law held sway. The emperor in Vienna had passed laws applying equally to everyone. Only he had the right to interpret the laws. If a certain law was not to his liking, he had a new one passed. No official had the right to interpret the laws in his own way. Officials appointed by the Imperial Office in Vienna had conducted the struggle against the feudatories with a sense of dedication to their duties and were highly ethical in their dealings. They were also paid well enough not to be tempted to steal. Consequently the Austrian government apparatus was among the most efficient in the world, on a par with the British.

In the other parts of Yugoslavia where Turkish traditions prevailed, every official interpreted the law as he saw fit. Subjects practiced all manner of machinations to evade law enforcement, to find loopholes. "God is on high, and the emperor far off," the people said, for they were dependent on the whims of poorly paid officials. As a result corruption was rife.

These contrasting tendencies in law enforcement were evident from the very inception of prewar Yugoslavia. In the Legislative Committee, Serbian lawyers explained matters this way to their colleagues from former Austro-Hungarian areas: "Where we come from, when a new law is passed, people first look for the loopholes, for ways of getting around it, but in your area the people obey the laws." It took the latter a long time to learn the ropes from Serbian politicians and their approach to law enforcement.

The Influence of French, German, Russian, and Anglo-American Culture and Civilization

In the between-wars period, Yugoslavia like the rest of the world was exposed to the growing development of technology, the multiplication of economic and cultural ties, and the possibility of learning quickly through communications media what was happening in other parts of the world.

A cultural mosaic, Yugoslavia grew less and less susceptible to the exclusive influence of either East or West, of one Great Power or the other. Slowly it entered the mainstream of world developments in all spheres of human activity.

French influence was at its zenith, especially in Serbia, in finances, politics, law, and culture (the surrealists Breton and Aragon held sway in Belgrade more than anywhere else outside of France). German expressionism dominated Croatia and Slovenia. German culture continued its presence in all branches of art; once Hitler came to power, however, the formerly fruitful contacts with Germany disintegrated rapidly.

In spite of the fact that Yugoslavia did not recognize the U.S.S.R., and that communications were poor, the influence of Russian culture was perhaps even stronger than it had been in many earlier periods. The poems of Esenin, Blok, and Mayakovski demonstrated to the younger generation of Yugoslavs that poets were the vanguard of revolution, that there could be no social change without rebellion, that rebels were the "salt" of revolution. Then came the January 6 dictatorship in Yugoslavia. The mere possession of, say, a copy of Gorki's book *Mother* or a work by any other Soviet writer was sufficient to lose a worker his job, to bring a high school student up before the principal, and even to provide a reason for arrest. On the other hand, the phenomenon of Stalinism lowered a curtain of silence over the Soviet Union.

But the influence of Russian culture continued to be felt. This was partly due to influx of a large number of Russian émigrés after the Russian Revolution. Among them were generals and police agents (some of the latter were extremely brutal professionals who taught the torture squads in Yugoslav prisons the methods used by the Imperial Intelligence Service, the Ohrana, in dealing with revolutionaries), but also scientists with a European reputation (Taranovski, Soloviev, Ostrogorski, Spektorski, Maklekov, Bilimovich, Saltikov, and others) who helped raise scientific research in Yugoslav universities to a higher level.

Legat and Knyazev laid the foundations for the Belgrade Ballet; other artists were active in opera, Zhedrinski in costume design. The same influence was evident, though to a lesser degree, in Slovenia and Croatia.

Anglo-American culture and civilization had been present even earlier, but between the two wars its influence expanded considerably, spreading to all areas. Through films, the new branch of art so available to the masses, English was heard throughout the land. The first cinema was opened in Belgrade in 1906, but the number of movie houses increased significantly only after the war. They became part of the local scene also in the small towns, and even villages, especially in Vojvodina.

During the early years of the war, on Terazije Square and in Krunska Street in Belgrade, signs written in Cyrillic characters could be found advertising *Hochglanzpeglerei* (collar pressing), *Schuster* (shoemaker), *Tischler* (cabinetmaker). At the same time, one of the first cinemas in Belgrade, the Elita Vitaskop, also displayed signs in Cyrillic with the names of the Belgrade public's new favorites: Бустер Кеатон (Buster Keaton); Мари Пицкфорд (Mary Pickford).

Films were produced in Belgrade even before World War I. A British film company recorded the coronation of King Petar I in 1904. The first film worker in Yugoslavia was Milton Manski, who started his activities in films in 1905. After the war, feature films began to be produced. In 1919 a film named after the medieval peasant rebel leader Matija Gubec was produced in Zagreb from a scenario by Marija Jurić-Zagorka. In Belgrade a well-known actor, Ilija Stanojević, popularly known as Uncle Ilija, directed the film *Karadjordje* in 1932. Two films were produced in Ljubljana: *In the Realm of the Golden-horned Ram* and *The Cliffs of Triglav*.

Yugoslav actresses Ita Rina and Štefica Vidačić performed in foreign films, and Slavko Vorkapić worked in Hollywood as a director.

The first Yugoslav radio station began broadcasting in Zagreb in 1926, followed by Radio Ljubljana and Radio Belgrade in 1928. But in number of radio sets, Yugoslavia again stood at the bottom of the ladder in Europe, as the accompanying table shows.

	Number of Persons per Radio
Denmark	3.7
Great Britain	4.2
Austria	6.8
Hungary	18
Bulgaria	34
Albania	37
Yugoslavia	65

The new mania, football (soccer), despite the voices raised against it by the older generation and even by preachers, brought thousands of fans to the football fields in what was once Belgrade's Aleksandrova Street. The Belgrade Sports Club and the Yugoslavia, Belgrade's two fiercest rivals, had their counterparts in Zagreb in the Gradjanski, HAŠKA, and Konkordija teams. The Haiduk team of Split broke the bounds of local separatism and exclusivity to win the hearts of fans all over Yugoslavia. Like other sports, football introduced hundreds of English words into the daily life and vocabulary of the ordinary Yugoslav without his even being aware of it.

In journalism innovations were introduced by the daily newspaper *Politika*, of Belgrade, not only in terms of technique but also in treatment of and approach to events. Correspondents trotted all over the country and the world to gather their reports. *Politika* acquired a reading public of 170,000 and could compare favorably with the best Central European papers. The principal newspapers were *Jutarnji List* (the *Morning Newspaper*) and *Novosit (News)* in Zagreb and *Slovenec* (the *Slovene*) and *Jutro (Morning)* in Ljubljana.

Literature and Art

In literature, the between-wars period saw the older and younger generations locked in the age-old struggle of conservatism versus vanguardism. The only one of the older writers who kept step with the times was Branislav Nušić. A Mediterranean by temperament, he distilled the best features from the small-town mentality of Serbia: a sharp eye for the double standard of morals and the conviction that satire was the strongest weapon in the hands of those who had no real power. Nušić was a profoundly committed writer, the "sorrowful Harlequin" of the period of early capital formation in Serbia; ostensibly he strove to make people laugh but actually felt deeply about the state of the world around him. He was left cold by all the attempts of leading Serbian circles to buy him out, to blunt the sharp point of his pen with flattering offers of official and even diplomatic posts. From the time he produced his first comedies, *The Deputy* (1883) and *Political Pull* (1889), he remained true to his ideas and his conscience; as evidenced in later plays—*Madame the Minister's Wife, The Mourning Family,* and *The Deceased*—and shortly before World War II in his articles for the left-wing magazine *Our Reality,* in which he spoke of the war in Spain with sympathy. What historians and sociologists failed to do, Nušić accomplished in his comedies: he laid bare the psychology of the primitive peasant arriving in town, forgetting his origins, joining the scramble for power, and achieving it through corruption, in accordance with the popular saying: "When God created the world, he made his own beard first." His world was one of petty usurers and money-lenders who "got rich quick" and rose to prominence as big-time merchants and bankers. Few were as successful as Nušić in tracing, with bitterness, the process by which power was achieved, unethically, through lies and cheating.

A group of Serbian surrealists (Marko Ristić, Dušan Matić, Aleksandar Vučo, Moni de Buli, Milan Dedinac, Koča Popović, Oskar Davičo, and others) charged the gates of conservatism in Serbian literature. Declaring that the time had come for a revision of all aesthetic values, these surrealists pursued the quest for new forms of linguistic expression, for which they were attacked by both left and right. But they left their mark for decades to come on Serbian literature. Around them gathered groups of young people who wanted to live their lives in their own way, to find their own answers to the questions troubling them, and to express themselves in their own language and style.

In Paris Rastko Petrović, rubbing elbows with the vanguard elite and particularly with the surrealists, absorbed the aspirations of modern thinking in his endeavor to produce a synthesis between the folk and rustic elements of the Balkans and modern modes of expression, in his search for the lost Slavic myth.

An important personality on the literary scene was Isidora Sekulić, travel writer, essayist, and philologist. The champion of the loftiest principles deriving from poetic and folk ethics, she found in Petar Petrović-Njegoš the personification of all her ideals. In her opposition to Balkan provincialism, she traveled far and wide, her essays demonstrating the possibility of pursuing the world's horizons. Well-educated, she managed to produce a synthesis of the national and international in her essays *From Native and Foreign Literature*, mapping out the roads which the culture of the South Slavs would follow in the future.

Belated critical realism stressing the social element found its clearest expression in *The Mown Field* by Branimir Cosić, one of the most prominent Serbian social novelists. Dying young, he never completed his opus.

Miloš Crnjanski, author of *Ithacan Lyrics* and *The Čarnojević Diary*, founder of Sumatraism, continued the gentle, melodic line of Serbian literature distinctive of the poet Branko Radičević. In *Migrations*, a historical novel, he described the unhappy fate of the wandering nation of Serbs (the Serbs who had been resettled in Hungary), landless, stateless, keeping body and soul together by waging war for others, and sustained spiritually by their Orthodox faith and belief in their great and powerful savior, the land of Serbia.

Ivo Andrić holds a special place in Yugoslav literature between the two wars. Seemingly uninfluenced by any other style or author, he was thoroughly steeped in the Bosnian environment to which he was born, and its ancient folkloric philosophy of life. A historian and ethnologist by profession, he not only knew the national legends and traditions from early youth, but reflected upon them as a mature man, tracing their roots down through the centuries. There is a great deal of truth in Isidora Sekulić's essay on Andrić, published in the *Srpski Knijiževni Glasnik*, about the influence of the East on him, the East that is such an indivisible part of everyday life in Bosnia, mirrored not only in Andrić's conception of woman, but also in the manner of his storytelling, the development of his characters. His work hardly lends itself to measurement by the rationalistic yardsticks of Europe, as his ear is attuned to the most delicate overtones of the national legend, the remains of Neo-Manichaeism in the soul of Bosnian man, the dislike of institutions, the feeling that the material world is fraught with evil and that death alone offers salvation. This Bogomil-like approach to history, the resistance to the material world, to any and all authority, even the most revolutionary, was expressed by Andrić in his early years in the *Tale from Japan*. In it, Andrić points up the difference between revolutionaries and rebels, between revolutionaries and poets, presenting the native, folkloric conception of permanent rebellion ever present in the life and death of the Bosnian serf.

The most highly individualistic writer among the Croats in the period between the two world wars was Miroslav Krleža. Although his antiwar tales are of the magnitude of works by German expressionists, his fame was slow to penetrate to the outside world, as is often the case with writers of small nations. No other writer between the wars did so much to prepare spirits for social change. This he achieved in his dramas *Golgotha, The Wolf, In Agony, The Glembaj Gentry*, and *Leda*, with his psychological insight into the bourgeois, semifeudal atmosphere of Croatia; and also in his essays and polemical writings, and his magazines *Flame* (1919), the *Literary Republic* (1924), *Today* (1934), and the *Seal* (1939).

Krleža belongs to the generation of postwar national revolutionaries who voiced their support for the young Soviet Republic in large numbers after 1917. Some of Krleža's intimate friends became leaders of the Communist Party of Yugoslavia. He himself traveled to the Soviet Union in 1926, after which he published his *Excursion to Russia*, standing firm in his defense of Soviet culture and the Soviet social system in defiance of the cry raised against him in prewar Yugoslavia by the official bureaucracy and state authorities.[1]

---

[1] In the twilight of socialism in the U.S.S.R. under Stalin, with its trials of old Bolsheviks and purges of Yugoslav revolutionaries residing in Russia, some of Krleža's friends lost their lives. As a poet and rebel, he found it impossible not to speak up and was among the first in Yugoslavia to give vent to his feelings, bringing fresh misfortunes down upon his head. Among the wealth of experiences of his lifetime is one involving an old comrade-in-arms, Pavle Bastajić, also a friend of Gavrilo Princip and a member of the Young Bosnia organization. In 1918 Bastajić and many other Young Bosnians, headed by Mustafa Golubić, had established contact with Soviet authorities through Russian Social Revolutionaries. As almost all of them believed in acts of individual terrorism as a means of struggle to liberate the working people, someone put them in touch with the GPU in the Soviet Union, and the Young Bosnians became professional terrorists, agents in that powerful apparatus. They served that apparatus not for money but for purely revolutionary ideals. For almost twenty years Pavle Bastajić operated in the Western European countries. When he learned the full truth, he began to wonder whether he had not been simply a blind tool in the hands of those who no longer had any revolutionary goals. Conscience-stricken, he refused to obey the strict disciplinary rules of the secret police and was consequently sentenced to death. Fleeing from paid murderers tracking him through various European capitals, he finally took refuge in his native Yugoslavia. One evening, Pavle Bastajić knocked at the door of his old friend, Miroslav Krleža, to tell him the whole bitter story.

In the *Pečat (Seal)*, Krleža launched a debate on many questions involving aesthetics and philosophy. It was thus that the found himself engaged in polemics with the CPY, which presented its replies to his arguments in the *Literary Notebooks*. There were a few people intimately associated with Krleža —Vasa Bogdanov, for instance—who, in the heat of polemics, "hating Nicholas, also came to hate Saint Nicholas," as the saying goes. They drew up a political platform, the main point of which seemed to be that nascent fascism made resistance futile. Lacking faith in the masses, they considered the Communist Party of Croatia too weak to play a decisive role in social developments. Consequently Bogdanov and those who shared his views, with Krleža's approval, advocated the idea that the Communist Party of Croatia should not nominate candidates for the elections in 1938, but should rather join Maček's Croatian Peasant party as a left wing. However, during the years immediately preceding World War II, Maček's Croatian Peasant party underwent a transformation that resulted in profound differentiation. Having become the Croatian National party, it was increasingly representative of Croatian businessmen and bankers rather than peasants. Accepting a left-wing position in a nationalist movement against which one had struggled one's whole life long seemed an utterly senseless thing to do.

Avgustin Tin Ujević was by all counts the most consistent of the rebel-poets of his period. As a youth, together with Vladimir Čerina and Janko Polić-Kamov, he had been the very soul of the national revolutionary movement in Croatia. Working closely with the Young Bosnians, he acted as their inspiration, and with them he found a common tongue. It was Ujević's belief that the individual should be freed of all the shackles binding him. It was not only the Hapsburg authority that had to be cast off, but atavisms of all kinds: the poet should abandon his servitude to classical models, high school students should not get poor marks for writing free verse, fathers should not force their views on their sons, women should stop being the slaves of men: in other words, liberation in all its aspects.

For him, deeds and words were one: he helped organize assassinations of Hapsburg dignitaries; came into contact with the head of the Black Hand organization in Belgrade, Colonel Apis; was pursued by all the police forces of the Balkans; in Paris he frequented Trotsky and Vladimir Gaćinović, while not neglecting the muse of poetry. He also labored to complete a "comparative grammar of the Croatian and French languages."

Furthermore, as a free poetic personality, he refused to be manipulated by anyone, either on the left or on the right, pursuing his own inspiration as he saw it. After World War I he continued his bohemian and nihilistic ways, occasionally calling himself a Communist. The author of neoclassical poems like *The Keening of the Commoner* and *The Medal*, which were taken up by the Belgrade surrealists, an essayist and translator from a dozen languages, Tin Ujević spun out his days between the café and the library, in permanent revolt against the ethics and aesthetics of petty bourgeois society, preaching disagreement with all systems, individualized revolt, a peculiar amalgam of Buddhism and psychoanalysis, and revolution of the spirit.

Others who gained prominence in Croatia were Ljubo Vizner, Gustav Krklec, Slavko Batušić, A. B. Simić, and the younger writers Novak Simić and Ivan Dončević, as well as Mihovil Pavlek Miškina with his village tales distinctive for their authentic ring.

In Slovenia one of the major literary figures was Oton Župančič. After publishing two books for children during World War I, *Ciciban and Thensome* and *One Hundred Riddles*, he wrote two books of lyrics in 1920. For some time thereafter he devoted his energies to translating Shakespeare and Galsworthy. In 1924 he published his drama *Veronika Desiniška*.

Another writer of the older generation was Franc Finžgar, who achieved fame with his historical novel *Under a Free Sun*.

Fran Milčinski (1867–1932) turned his attention to the problems of young people. His forte was his sense of humor and his pointed tales, based on Serbo-Croatian epics.

The most powerful Slovene writer of the period between the two wars was Prežihov Voranc (the pen name of Lovro Kuhar), who concerned himself with the psychology of the Slovene peasant in the war of 1914–1918 (the novel *Doberdob*), during the period of Austria's collapse and the struggle for Slovene Carinthia and Styria *(Holocaust)*. In his novel *Jamnica* he dealt with the life of the Slovene peasant in the new state. Prežihov Voranc was assisted in his literary development by the literary critic and writer Ferdo Kozak. In the *Contemporary Scene*, a magazine, he published a short story named *The Battle against the Devourer*, in the archaic Carinthian dialect of the Slovene language, portraying the tragedy of an impoverished peasant who could not eke a living from his land in spite of backbreaking efforts. In 1940 Voranc published *The Self-grown*, a collection of short stories and tales.

A name of distinction in the poetry of this period in Slovenia was that of Srećko Kovosel (1904–1926), who wrote in the modern manner. His exceptional talent for fresh discovery is particularly evident in the *Manifesto to a Free Spirit*.

France Bevk, a writer from the Slovene coast profoundly influenced by modernism, published *Poems*, his first collection of poetry, in Gorizia. His later tales and novels brought Trieste and Gorizia to life in Slovene literature.

Bratko Kreft won fame for his dramas *The Counts of Celje* and *The Great Insurrection* with their explicitly social motifs. He was also the editor of the progressive journal *Literature* between 1933 and 1939.

Also worthy of note are the poet Mile Klopčič for his works on a proletarian note, *Flaming Bonds*, *Book of Comrades*, and *Simple Songs;* the novelist Miško Kranjc for his work *Place in the Sun;* the poet Alojz Gradnik, and others.

The dignified poverty of the Macedonian laborer was sung by Kosta

Racin in his own native Macedonian tongue. He was unable to publish his collection *White Dawns* in Macedonia but succeeded, with the help of Communists, in doing so in Zagreb.

In architecture between the two wars, Josip Plečnik (1872–1957) laid the foundations for modern Slovene building, achieving fame throughout Europe for his creations. A disciple of Otto Wagner, founder of Viennese Secession in architecture, he won recognition even before World War I and was proposed as the successor to Wagner's chair in the Academy of Fine Arts in Vienna after the latter's death. However, Francis Ferdinand found him politically unsuitable for membership in the committee formed for the purpose of constructing Meštrović's Saint Vitus's Day Temple in Belgrade. (Other members of the committee were Jovan Cvijić, Bogdan Popović, Andra Stefanović, and Ivan Meštrović.) In 1920 he produced the blueprint for Meštrović's model of the Kosovo Temple.

Dissatisfied with the Secessionist style, Plečnik invested it with new functional elements. What he eventually evolved was not a national romantic style but rather a type of neoclassicism with overtones of national-ethnical elements using predominantly native materials. In Ljubljana Plečnik designed the Tromostovje, Congress Square, Žale, the University and the National Library, and many other complexes. President Masaryk of Czechoslovakia invited him to help with the reconstruction of Hradčany Castle (the Gateway of Paradise).

Plečnik and Milan Vidmar, a scientist of European fame in the field of electrotechnics, were the most eminent Slovenes of their time.

Croatian architecture, too, began to develop along new lines under the influence of Viktor Kovačić (1874–1924), also a pupil of Wagner. Soon, however, he set off in new directions in the quest for creative functionalism in architecture. Kovačić was an excellent pedagogue and passionately dedicated to the protection of historical monuments during a time when such pursuits were not supported by government officials.

A new generation of architects appeared on the scene, influenced to a growing extent by Corbusier. Outstanding among them were Drago Ibler and Zdenko Strižić.

In Serbia, too, the Secessionist style began to be abandoned. Momir Korunović tried to fashion a so-called Serbian style in architecture by using decorative elements from medieval buildings. His success in this attempt was not notable. He was responsible for the design of the Main Post Office in Belgrade and the Sokol Gymnasium in the Vračar section of the capital.

In Croatian painting, a group of three artists, Ljubo Babić, Vladimir Becić, and Jerolim Miše, sought to safeguard the principle of formal, individual qualities, in which they were opposed by the Earth *(Zemlja)* group with its explicit tendency toward association with social criticism, headed by Marijan Detoni, Krsto Hegedušić, and Oton Postružnik. The Earth group gave impulse to the development of naïve painters of the Hlebine School (Ivan Generalić, Franjo Mraz, and others). Milivoj Uzelac was in a category by himself. Having received a sound academic education, he left for Paris in his youth, where he was associated with the École de Paris and achieved an enviable reputation.

Ivan Meštrović continued to hold his own as the foremost sculptor. Some of his famous creations were the monuments to Grgur Ninski and Bishop Strossmayer, and the Tomb of the Unknown Soldier on Avala Hill near Belgrade, as well as the monument of gratitude to France in Kalemegdan Park in Belgrade. New trends appeared in Croatian sculpture, borne forward by Kršinić, Avgustinčić, Radauš, and Lozica.

Fresh influences in French painting had an observable effect on Serbian artists, especially Jovan Bijelić, Petar Dobrović, and Mile Milunović. Another group of "rational painters" included Sava Šumanović, Milan Konjović, and Zora Petrović. Ignjat Job appeared with his conception of cubism. A number of painters had made a name for themselves before the war broke out: Petar Lubarda, Mirko Kujačić, and others.

Prominent names in the nation's musical life were those of Josip Slavenski, Petar Konjović, Josip Hace, Jakov Gotovac, Antun Dobrović, Fran Lotka, and Stevan Hristić.

CHAPTER 43

The Subjugation and Dismemberment of Yugoslavia

TWENTY MONTHS OF YUGOSLAV NEUTRALITY / YUGOSLAVIA'S STRATEGIC IMPORTANCE IN THE WAR PLANS OF THE BELLIGERENTS IN WORLD WAR II / THE TRIPARTITE PACT OF GERMANY, ITALY, AND JAPAN / THE PUTSCH OF MARCH 27, 1941 / ATTACK BY GERMANY, ITALY, HUNGARY, AND BULGARIA ON APRIL 6 / CAPITULATION BY THE YUGOSLAV ARMED FORCES ON APRIL 17 / YUGOSLAVIA CEASES TO EXIST AS A STATE / THE OCCUPIERS' WAR CRIMES / THE DELIBERATE BOMBING OF THE CIVILIAN POPULATION / MISTREATMENT OF PRISONERS OF WAR / DISCRIMINATION AGAINST DIPLOMATIC AND CONSULAR OFFICERS / ECONOMIC PLUNDER / GENOCIDE / FORCIBLE RESETTLEMENT OF SLOVENES AND SERBS IN CROATIA AND BOSNIA AND HERCEGOVINA / LOOTING OF CULTURAL GOODS / MASSACRE OF SERBS, GYPSIES, AND JEWS IN THE INDEPENDENT STATE OF CROATIA AND IN BAĆKA

Twenty Months of Yugoslav Neutrality

Yugoslavia's neutrality in World War II lasted about twenty months. It was terminated by the attack of German, Italian, Hungarian, and Bulgarian forces on April 6, 1941, when Yugoslavia became the ninth victim of the Axis powers in Europe.

For a time it was in Germany's interest for Yugoslavia to remain neutral, as the German leader Adolf Hitler feared that Britain and France might open a front in the Balkan Peninsula. Germany gradually tightened its grip on the Yugoslav economy, for nonferrous metals from Yugoslavia were of paramount significance for the German war machine.

Yugoslavia's Strategic Importance in the War Plans of the Belligerents in World War II

Berlin also had to take account of Italian interests in the Balkans. Even before the outbreak of war in 1939, Hitler and Mussolini had agreed that the Mediterranean, and thereby also western Yugoslavia, were within Rome's sphere of interest. Early in 1940 Mussolini toyed with the idea of attacking Yugoslavia, but Hitler convinced him not to do so, pointing out that Britain was the principal enemy and that Yugoslavia could easily be "taken care of" later. In the autumn of 1940 the Balkan area gained in importance for both belligerent sides. British policy became increasingly active. Cooperation between Germany and the Soviet Union was nearing an end. Fresh negotiations between Ribbentrop and Molotov broke down for a number of reasons, including the question of the Balkans. Berlin would not agree that Bulgaria and the Dardanelles should become a Soviet sphere of interest and demanded the entire Balkan Peninsula for Germany. Hitler, already secretly preparing to assault the Soviet Union, was eager to have the Balkans as a peaceful hinterland.

The Tripartite Pact of Germany, Italy, and Japan

Mussolini's attack on Greece on October 28, 1940, of which he had not informed Hitler, complicated Germany's strategic plans. The Greek army halted the Italian aggression, and the first British divisions disembarked in the Balkans early in 1941. Hitler was forced to take vigorous action. Hungary and Romania joined the Tripartite Pact, which was followed by the entry of the German army into their territory with the approval of the local governments. On March 1 Bulgaria followed suit, after Hitler had promised King Boris Macedonia and parts of Serbia.

German diplomacy bent its efforts toward drawing Yugoslavia by peaceful means into the Axis sphere, but the pro-Western current still ran strong in ruling Yugoslav circles. The regent, Prince Pavle, adhered to the thinking of the British Conservatives, rallied around the former prime minister, Neville Chamberlain: that the principal opponent was the U.S.S.R., in consequence of which the European bourgeoisie should facilitate Hitler's eastward advance. This factor of class affiliation played an essential role when Pavle took the decision to join the Tripartite Pact. Visiting Hitler on March 1, he was told in confidence that

Germany would attack the U.S.S.R. Pavle was also upheld by a section of the Yugoslav General Staff, which was strongly under German influence. Support was also forthcoming from Maček, who maintained secret ties with both Rome and Berlin. Mussolini kept his stooge Ante Pavelić in Florence, and 600 of his Ustashi in a camp on the Lipari Islands, ready for any eventuality.

The mood in Serbia's opposition political parties, among the Democrats, Agriculturists, and Serbian Cultural Club, was anti-German and pro-Churchill. The same was the case among some of the generals and younger officers. In Slovenia the Clericalists and Liberals were against the Germans, knowing full well that Hitler was resolved to Germanize the Slovenes by sheer force. Also, the Soviet Union wielded some influence over a small group of Yugoslav Slavophile generals.

The Cvetković-Maček government used force to suppress all criticism of the Axis powers. Late in December 1940 a decision was taken to ban the activities of the United Workers' Trade Unions, and 2,000 Communists were thrown into concentration camps. Demonstrations were staged in Montenegro and Serbia against the methods to which the government resorted.

On March 25, 1941, the Yugoslav government signed papers signifying its accession to the Tripartite Pact. In a secret clause the Axis powers promised Yugoslavia Salonika at the end of the war, although they had previously promised it to Bulgaria.

Demonstrations broke out all over the country, especially in Serbia, Montenegro, Slovenia (Ljubljana), Bosnia and Hercegovina, Croatia (Split), and Macedonia (Skoplje). During the month of March the Communist Party of Yugoslavia issued a number of proclamations accusing the government of forfeiting the country's independence. Demands were raised for the conclusion of a mutual assistance pact with the Soviet Union and the formation of a popular government which would protect the interests of the masses. In Belgrade the CPY organized protest marches that began in the evening of March 26.

The Putsch of March 27, 1941

The general dissatisfaction with the government's pro-Axis policies and accession to the Tripartite Pact was also evident among part of the officer corps. Generals Dušan Simović and Bora Mirković executed a coup d'état with their help on March 27, at dawn. The heir to the throne, Petar II, was proclaimed king, the regency deposed, and the Cvetković-Maček government overthrown.

The exact identity of the initiators of the putsch has never been definitely established. Randolph Churchill claimed that the British intelligence service was behind the conspiracy, whereas certain American authors stress the role of General William J. Donovan, head of the American Office of Strategic Services

(OSS). The conspirators have denied these assertions. Certain facts would make it appear that Soviet intelligence agents (Mustafa Golubić) were preparing a conspiracy and even extended assistance to those involved in the plot (Božin Simić). Hitler publicly accused Britain and the Soviet Union of having overthrown the Cvetković-Maček government.

General Simović's government, in which virtually all bourgeois parties were represented, was not aware of Yugoslavia's predicament. Maček first attempted to strike a bargain with Berlin, but when he realized, on April 3, 1941, that Hitler had resolved to support Ante Pavelić, he agreed to enter the new government as vice president. Other persons inclined to capitulation also became members of the government. Upon the proposal of Milan Grol, the Democrats' leader, Momčilo Ninčić, otherwise a personal friend of Mussolini and president of the German Society in Belgrade, was appointed foreign minister. At his initiative, the cabinet took a decision to inform Germany and Italy that the new government recognized the signing of the Tripartite Pact, which Ninčić duly did, as attested by his circular telegram of April 3. When that government emigrated to Palestine after the German attack, this decision was not included in the official minutes of that session of the government (kept by the youngest member of the government, Sava Kosanović), which may therefore be considered a falsification.

How unrealistic their reading of the situation was, is evident from the fact that the new government decided to send its second vice president, Slobodan Jovanović, president of the Serbian Cultural Club, to Rome on April 6 to negotiate with the Italian government and persuade it to act as mediator in regulating Yugoslavia's relations with Germany. The prime minister himself, General Simović, also scheduled the wedding of his daughter for the morning of April 6 in Belgrade.

No appropriate military measures were undertaken. Instead of hurling all available forces at the Italian troops in Albania and thus creating a broad direct front with Greece, the government even failed to declare general mobilization.

But the Simović government did amnesty political prisoners and dissolve the military concentration camps, although this measure was not implemented in Croatia, where Maček's police detained all the Communists who had been arrested (they were later turned over to the Germans and Ustashi) and even made more arrests. On March 30 alone, over 200 left-wing citizens were taken into custody and also later surrendered to the Germans and Ustashi.

Attack by Germany, Italy, Hungary, and Bulgaria on April 6

When Hitler was informed of the events in Yugoslavia, his initial reaction was one of disbelief in the authenticity of the reports. Once convinced, he took swift and energetic action, calling his military and political advisers to a conference. Perceiving that the change in government in Yugoslavia could jeopardize preparations to attack Greece, and to invade the Soviet Union, he stated on the occasion that Serbs and Slovenes had never been friends of Germany. He then ordered that Yugoslavia should be destroyed as a state. A plan was drafted for the simultaneous invasion of Yugoslavia and Greece, with thirty-four German, forty-four Italian, and four Hungarian divisions being assigned to the operation. Romania and Bulgaria undertook to offer protection to the Axis powers attacking Yugoslavia in case of Soviet intervention. The new Yugoslav government had launched negotiations with the Soviet Union for the conclusion of a mutual assistance treaty, but agreement had been reached only on the treaty of friendship, which was signed early in the morning of April 6.

Falling in with Hitler's plans, Mussolini expressed satisfaction at the opportunity to square accounts with Yugoslavia, which he described as an "artificial contrivance of Versailles, godfathered by Wilson. Yugoslavia's recent behavior has no parallel in world history; it is an echo of Sarajevo 1914, provoked by the same incorrigible elements."

The Axis powers launched their operations in the night of April 5–6, when they took the Iron Gate section of the Danube by surprise to ensure freedom of navigation. At dawn on April 6, Belgrade was attacked by 450 German bombers with an escort of fighter planes, while Italian bombers struck at certain towns in Dalmatia. The German Twelfth Army, concentrated in Bulgaria, soon cut communications between Yugoslavia and Greece. By April 7 it had captured Skoplje. Yugoslav troops had begun to advance toward the Italians in Albania, but resistance faltered on all fronts. Zagreb fell on April 10, and Belgrade on April 12. Many of the senior commanders of the Yugoslav army were infected with the spirit of capitulation. In Croatia the Ustashi provoked a revolt in Bjelovar and other places, thus facilitating the German advance.

Capitulation by the Yugoslav Armed Forces on April 17

The government, together with King Petar, left by air for Greece on April 15, appointing Danilo Kalafatović chief of staff before departing. General Simović, the prime minister, authorized him to conclude an honorable cease-fire with the enemy. General Kalafatović designated Mihajlo Bodi, Colonel France Tomše, and Lieutenant Colonel Radmilo Trajanović plenipotentiaries of the Supreme Command. On April 16 they arrived in Belgrade, where the commander of the Second German Army, General von Weichs, handed them a document of unconditional surrender. The plenipotentiaries rejected the German conditions and returned to the Supreme Command in Sarajevo, which had meanwhile fallen into enemy hands. General Kalafatović was forced to appoint new plenipotentiaries: Aleksandar Cincar-Marković, who had been foreign minister in the Cvetković-Maček government, and General Radivoj Janković. On April 17 they signed an act of capitulation between Germany and the Yugoslav armed forces. From the standpoint of international law, the act was null, as it contained many purely political provisions. Such international agreements can be signed by governments alone, and not by individual military commanders.

On April 14 the Yugoslav Supreme Command took a decision to surrender its troops, positions, and communications and informed subordinate commanders that they should not offer resistance to the enemy in his advance. The commanders executed the order and surrender was thus effected, with the enemy occupying the country. German troops captured 337,864 men and NCOs and 6,298 officers.

Accordingly the Decree of April 17, 1941, could not deal with the question of war or peace between the two belligerent sides. The enemy had occupied the country and the state of war continued to exist, especially as the Yugoslav government announced in a declaration of May 4, 1941, that it was continuing the struggle against the occupiers.

Yugoslavia Ceases to Exist as a State

After the April War, the entire occupied territory of Yugoslavia was left to a twofold fate. The larger part was immediately annexed to adjacent states, contrary to the tenets of international law, and the remainder was placed under the enemy's military administration.

Germany annexed Gorenjska and Štajerska, and the remaining parts of Slovenia were annexed by Italy. On May 3, 1941, the formation of the Province of Ljubljana was proclaimed.

Hungary took Prekomurje, Medjumurje, Bačka, and Baranja.

Bulgaria occupied Macedonia up to Ohrid, a lesser part of Kosovo, and sections of eastern Serbia. On May 16 Bogdan Filov, the Bulgarian prime minister, spoke in the Bulgarian parliament and expressed gratitude to Mussolini and Hitler for the "creation of a great Bulgaria from the Lake of Ohrid to the Black Sea."

In Tirana on April 18 a group of Montenegrin émigrés, supporters of King Nikola, formed a Committee for the Creation of an Independent Montenegro. On May 7, however, civilian authority in Montenegro was assumed by a royal civilian commissioner of the Italian government and the committee of exiles was transformed into an advisory body. Preparations were made to proclaim Montenegro a kingdom under the protectorate of Italy on the basis of a personal union, under the aegis of the Italian queen Jelena, daughter of King Nikola, "the fairy of our mountains," as a proclamation of that period described

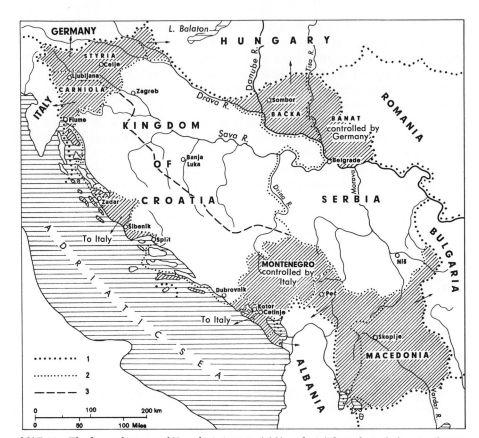

MAP 46.   The dismemberment of Yugoslavia in 1941. (1) Yugoslavia's boundaries before April 1941; (2) boundaries between divided territories; (3) the German-Italian demarcation line in the Independent State of Croatia.

her. Mihajlo Petrović, grandson of King Nikola, was offered the throne, but he rejected it. On May 18 the Italian king visited Cetinje. The outbreak of a popular uprising on July 13 frustrated the occupiers' plans.

Serbia was under the direct administration of a German military commander, its boundaries shrunk to where they had been before the Balkan Wars. The area of Trepča (because of the lead mines) and later also the Banat were attached to the military administration.

Kosovo and Metohija and part of western Macedonia (five districts) were annexed by Italy to Albania, over which it had established a protectorate.

The Axis powers created the so-called Independent State of Croatia, including Croatia, Slavonia, Srem, part of Dalmatia, and Bosnia and Hercegovina. The proclamation of the Independent State of Croatia was organized by Dr. Edmund Weesenmayer, a special emissary of Foreign Minister Ribbentrop, who had gone to Zagreb before April 6 to conduct talks with the leaders of the Croatian Peasant party and with the leader of the Ustashi in Zagreb, Slavko Kvaternik. At dawn on April 10, German troops crossed the northern Yugoslav border and the Fourteenth Tank Division entered Zagreb in the afternoon. Previously Maček had agreed to turn power over to the Ustashi. Kvaternik read a declaration over the Zagreb radio station announcing the establishment of the Independent State of Croatia, followed by a statement by Maček calling upon the Croatian people to submit to the new authority, and all members of the Croatian Peasant party to collaborate with it.

Pavelić himself was in Florence at the time and had no notion of what was happening in Zagreb. He heard Kvaternik's proclamation over the air. Mussolini ordered that Pavelić and his 600 Ustashi be transported to Zagreb immediately but first asked Pavelić for a guarantee that he would cede Dalmatia to Italy. With this objective, he sent Filippe Anfuso, foreign minister ad interim, to escort Pavelić on his trip to Zagreb. Thus Pavelić entered Zagreb only on April 15.

Although on May 15 Pavelić promulgated a law in Zagreb restoring the crown of King Zvonimir, which had "graced the Croatian kings and which again represented the sovereignty of the Independent State of Croatia," by a treaty of May 18 on "guarantees and cooperation between the kingdom of Croatia and the kingdom of Italy" he agreed that Croatia should become a protectorate of Italy. Simultaneously he conceded to Italy the Croatian Primorje, a large part of Gorski Kotar, Dalmatia from Zadar to Split, and all the islands except Hvar, Brač, and Pag. Pavelić requested the "Italian king and emperor to appoint a prince of Savoy to be Croatian king." The Italian king appointed his cousin, Archduke Aimone di Spoleto, Croatian king. The new king was given the title of Tomislav II; the coronation was to take place in Banja Luka, which Pavelić had selected for the capital of the Independent State of Croatia. In the May Treaty Pavelić promised that the Independent State of Croatia would not maintain a navy and that Italian troops would be permitted passage through neutral parts of Dalmatia.

In spite of the agreements between Hitler and Mussolini relating to spheres of interest, which specified that Croatian territory was to be exclusively an Italian domain, the Germans actually held power there. In this respect Hitler placed his reliance on the Austrian aristocracy and the old officer corps. On April 11, 1941, he appointed an Austrian, General Edmund Glaise von Horstenau, the ranking German general in Croatia.

The occupying states, disregarding the boundaries they had agreed would represent their borders in Yugoslav territory, concluded separate agreements on peaceful occupation which did not coincide with these specific state boundaries.

It thus happened that the demarcation line between Germany and Italy in April 1941 ran from Ljubljana to Samobor, south of Zagreb, thence to Glina, Bosanski Novi, Bugojno, Kalinovik, Priboj, Novi Pazar, Priština, Šar Mountain, Tetovo, and Ohrid.

Subsequent agreements altered this line, expanding the Italian zone by some 50 kilometers. The occupation line between German and Bulgarian troops also underwent modification. On January 15, 1942, Bulgarian troops took all of southeast of Serbia (the line running from Zaječar, Kragujevac, Raška, Kraljevo, Vučitrn). A year later, on January 7, 1943, the Bulgarian occupation zone was extended to western Serbia (the line running through Valjevo, Arandjelovac, Lapovo), and on July 31 the same year Bulgarian troops took possession of all of Serbia with the exception of Belgrade and one section of western Serbia (Mačva, Loznica, Valjevo).

In the Independent State of Croatia, Germany enjoyed sweeping rights reflecting introduction of the system of capitulation in Europe. In the nineteenth century the colonial powers had exercised such rights only in their colonies in Africa and Asia. Citizens of German nationality in the Independent State of Croatia were in certain cases exempted from the jurisdiction of the Independent State of Croatia and were held responsible only to local German courts. They were also not recruited into the army of the Independent State of Croatia but into special SS *(Schutzstaffel)* units under German command.

Axis diplomacy bent every effort to persuade the largest possible number of states to withdraw their recognition of Yugoslavia as a sovereign state and to supplant it with recognition of their arbitrary act of subjugation. In this respect some of the neutral states provisionally recognized the subjugation of Yugoslavia, either explicitly (the Soviet Union) or tacitly (the Vatican, Spain, Switzerland).

On May 9, 1941, the Soviet government issued a statement withdrawing recognition of the Yugoslav government in exile and closing the Yugoslav Mission in Moscow with the motivation that "the Yugoslav state as such no longer exists." The Soviet government acted in a similar manner toward some other states victimized by Hitler's aggression: Czechoslovakia, Belgium, Norway, and Greece. These acts ran counter to international law, which the Soviet government itself recognized a few weeks later when, after Germany's attack on the Soviet Union on June 22, 1941, it resumed diplomatic relations with the Yugoslav and other governments in exile.

The Occupiers' War Crimes

Germany, Italy, Hungary, and Bulgaria effected the *subjugation* of Yugoslavia, that is, its extinction as a subject of international law. However, at that time, as well as during the period when they kept Yugoslav territory under wartime occupation, they committed a number of other war crimes, or attempted to commit them.

The Deliberate Bombing of the Civilian Population

For instance, they deliberately bombed the civilian population. In preparing for the invasion of Yugoslavia, Hitler issued Directive No. 25 of March 27, 1941, ordering the destruction of Belgrade by steady day-night bombing. This military operation was given the operational name Punishment and was executed with particular efficiency and brutality despite the fact that the Yugoslav government had declared Belgrade an open city on April 3, 1941. During the raids a large part of the city was destroyed, and many historical monuments were razed; among those that went up in flames was the National Library with its many old manuscripts of inestimable value. Various estimates have been submitted regarding the loss of life, running from 2,000 to 5,000. A total of 4,891 persons are known to have been buried in Belgrade cemeteries as victims of the raid.

Mistreatment of Prisoners of War

Yugoslav prisoners of war were not allowed to exercise their right of applying to the protecting power. In special POW camps set up for them rules on nutrition and sanitation were not observed. POWs who escaped and were caught should by international regulations have been penalized by thirty days' imprisonment, but in certain cases the German authorities had them executed.

Hitler divided POWs into seven categories. The first category were nationals of Holland, Luxembourg, Belgium (Flemish), and Norway; the second were the British, the third French and Belgians (Walloons), the fourth Poles, the fifth Yugoslavs, the sixth Soviet POWs, and the seventh Italians captured after the Italian capitulation in 1943.

The lower the category, the greater the discrimination, thus violating to an even greater extent the Hague rules and the Geneva convention of 1929.

Yugoslav POWs were classified by Germany into seventeen groups: Serbs, Croats, Slovenes, Deutschervolk, Hungarians, Gypsies, Jews, Cincars, Montenegrins, Albanians, Sanjakians, Dalmatians, Croats of the Orthodox faith, Italians, Macedonians, Muslims, and Bunjevci. Upon submission of certain statements, all categories were permitted to return except Serbs from Serbia proper, Jews, and for a time Slovenes. Montenegrins were detained after the uprising of July 13, 1941, and Pavelić also endeavored to assure retention in POW camps of Serbs from Croatia.

Discrimination against Diplomatic and Consular Officers

Discrimination was also exercised against diplomatic and consular officers. When war breaks out between two states, diplomatic relations between them cease to exist; it is the international custom to permit the diplomatic representative of either state freely to leave the territory of the enemy state. The custom of conditional repatriation was introduced in World War II. In Yugoslavia's case, however, Germany broke this rule. It first interned Yugoslav diplomatic representatives in Germany and then sent them to Belgrade. There they were allegedly allowed to return home, but a large number of them were again placed under arrest and dispatched to concentration camps in Germany. Many Yugoslav diplomatic and consular officers lost their lives this way.

For its part, Yugoslavia permitted German diplomatic officers to leave its territory freely.

Economic Plunder

The plunder of the country's economy was another element in the occupation. One of the objectives of Germany's aggression against Yugoslavia had been to acquire Yugoslovia's raw materials and manpower for the German wartime economy. After the occupation, the Axis powers took all reserves of food and raw materials, dismantled a number of industrial enterprises (including the railway carriage factory in Kraljevo), and applied foreign currency and credit measures that stripped the occupied country clean, especially by printing a great number of so-called *Reischsmarkkassenscheine* (a special kind of marks). Property was confiscated, fines were levied, and collective punishment was meted out.

Big German trusts took over the basic sources of raw materials in Yugoslavia, especially nonferrous metals. The Hermann Göring Werke controlled the Bor Mine, from which Germany derived 21 percent of its wartime requirements of copper, as well as the Trepča mines, Danube shipping, and several other economic branches. Yugoslavia supplied 100 percent of Germany's requirements of chromium. Krupp directly controlled the chromium mines and Yugoslav ironworks (Jesenice, Zenica, and other smaller ones). The Germans also exploited Yugoslav bauxite, meeting 10 percent of their requirements with bauxite from mines in Hercegovina, while other deposits in Yugoslavia supplied another 20 percent.

Through the German minority in Vojvodina and Slavonia, the Germans also assured themselves supplies of Yugoslav grains.

Manpower from Yugoslavia was utilized in German factories. Roughly half a million Yugoslavs were working in Hitler's wartime enterprises at war's end.

Genocide

In line with his general war aims, Hitler intended to exterminate various Yugoslav nationalities so as to implement his conception of the Germanization of the territories where those nationalities lived. The idea of Germanization in the capitalist period had acquired specific forms as far back as 1848, particularly as applied to the Slovene people, and was implemented in that form until Hitler took power. Hitler invested the idea with elements of genocide, of the annihilation of nations as such, so that their territory could be used for repopulation by Germans. Hitler openly declared that it was not his objective for the Slovenes to know German laws and to speak German but for their territory to be inhabited by people of pure German blood.

The German authorities exploited the national, religious, and class antagonisms of prewar Yugoslavia to incite fratricidal war facilitating implementation of their Germanization plans. In this respect Hitler made ample use of the methods employed by the Austrian aristocracy, high-ranking Catholic clergy, and military circles who had for years relied in their policies on one or the other national and religious groups in the Balkans. General Conrad von Hötzendorf, leader of the "hawk" group in Vienna before World War I, described in his memoirs the occupation of Bosnia in 1878 and the uprising in Hercegovina in 1882, which he had helped to crush as a young officer, claiming that naked force alone could bring the people of the area to their senses. The war-minded party in Vienna calculated that its best ally in Bosnia was the mutual hatred of various nationalities and religions. Hitler simply continued these tactics. In this respect his objectives were eminently served by the right wing of the Croatian bourgeoisie headed by Ante Pavelić, who began exterminating the Serbs in the Independent State of Croatia. At a meeting held on June 7, 1941, Hitler advised Pavelić to solve the problem of the Serbs in the Independent State of Croatia in the same way that he, Hitler, was solving the question of the Poles along the Reich's eastern boundaries. According to official German documents, Pavelić explained to Hitler that "the Croats were cooperating so well with the German people because they were not of Slav origin at all. They were Goths in origin, and the idea of their being Slavs had been forced upon them." At the same meeting, Pavelić informed Hitler that the Serbian problem in Croatia had existed only over the past sixty years: "A part of the Croatian population was converted to the Serbian Orthodox religion and on that basis these people were mistakenly called Serbs, although they are essentially Croats."

Pavelić was a tool in the hands of German racists for implementing their plan of Germanization of Yugoslav lands in accordance with a new and total concept. In the harrowing days of 1941 there was a complete identity of views, ideology, and policies between German racists and the right-wing Croatian bourgeoisie racists headed by the Frankists and Ustashi. We have seen that the Frankists had always found support for their ideas in court circles in Vienna, among the Austrian aristocracy and high-ranking Catholic clergy, whose policies they had implemented in Croatia. These political ties were strengthened by ideological affinity. In the Vienna of the late nineteenth century, the ideology of racism developed, considering not only Jews but South Slavs as beings of a lower order. Karl Lueger, city mayor of Vienna and leader of the Christian Socialists, introduced a new element into the idea of racism: the physical extermination of other nations. His followers in the Viennese Parliament spoke publicly of Jews alone ("They should be baptized, but we must keep them under water longer than five minutes") although Francis Ferdinand and those around him were saying as early as 1906 and 1907 that the Serbs, the biggest national groups in Bosnia, should be eliminated the same way.

In *Mein Kampf*, Hitler tendered special homage to Lueger as a great German, and it is obvious that Hitler absorbed his ideas of racism as a young man in Austria. This is also an example of how extreme nationalism evolved into racism, how the idea of fascism developed on the basis of earlier nationalistic slogans.

Pavelić's idea of exterminating Serbs and Jews in the Independent State of Croatia was homegrown as well as imported from Germany under the influence of Hitler's ideology. In situations critical for the Yugoslav peoples, as, for instance, during the annexation crisis of 1908 and the outbreak of war in 1914, the Frankists at a sign from "hawk" circles in Vienna organized pogroms of the Serbian population. The Frankists in Bosnia and Hercegovina also played the main role in the organizing of the *Schutzkorps* in 1914. But these were only rehearsals for what was to happen on a much larger scale in 1941 to the Serbs both in Bosnia and Hercegovina and in Croatia. One of Francis Ferdinand's right-hand men in his Military Office during the period preceding World War I and in the course of the war, Nikola Mandić, vice president of the Bosnian Assembly, became prime minister of the Independent State of Croatia during Pavelić's time.

One of the essential elements in genocide is nonrecognition of the individuality of various nationalities and ethnical or religious groups. The Frankists refused to acknowledge the individuality of the Serbian people in Bosnia. Pavelić took this Frankist conception and carried it to its extreme limits. After Pavelić's talk with Hitler, Dido Kvaternik stated in June 1941 during the opening of the Croatian Assembly that "Serbs are not a nation but Wallachians and Kara-Wallachians." The Ustashi dug through all the archives of Croatia's political history to find the opinions of politicians who did not recognize the individuality of the Serbs in Croatia. As soon as Yugoslavia was occupied and the Independent State of Croatia created, the Ustashi published in Zagreb a special edition of the collected works of Ante Starčević, who, as early as the middle of the nineteenth century, did not recognize the individuality of the Serbs.

It thus happened in 1941 that there was complete identity of views between the two nationalisms rapidly evolving into racism. Pavelić adopted Hitler's method of denationalizing other nations, not only through assimilation by way of cultural genocide, as had been proposed by nationalistic politicians of earlier epochs, but through nationalization of territory and the thorough elimination of all members of nationalities condemned to extermination, that is, by pure genocide.

Hitler planned this fate not only for the Serbian nation but for others as well. Official German documents show that Hitler was also thinking of Germanizing the Croats after the end of the war. And Dalmatia was to be transformed into one large seaside resort for Germans. It is significant that even the right wing of Serbian bourgeoisie, headed by Draža Mihailović, also implemented Hitler's concepts of genocide (territorial annihilation) toward Muslims and Croats.

Forcible Resettlement of Slovenes and Serbs in Croatia and Bosnia and Hercegovina

The realization of Hitler's designs regarding the extermination of Yugoslav peoples depended in substantial part on the realistic possibilities open to him during the war. One of his projects was to create a German state called Eugenia on the Danube River, with Belgrade, renamed Festung in German, as the capital. In the late seventeenth and early eighteenth century, Prince Eugene of Savoy, the Hapsburg commander, had conquered those areas. Most of the population would be Germans from the Banat, and Serbs would either be resettled elsewhere or annihilated. The first concrete measures to establish Eugenia were undertaken (for instance, the resettlement of people living in certain sections of Belgrade), but the outbreak of the uprising in Serbia disrupted further implementation of these plans.

Even during the war, however, Hitler undertook certain large-scale measures to carry out his grandiose plan of Germanizing various Yugoslav peoples. Deportation was undertaken in various forms: economic emigration, recruitment of workers for labor in Germany, ordinary forced labor by sending prisoners and internees to factories in Germany, and the system of mass deportation of Slovenes and those Serbs who lived outside Serbia proper.

On April 18, 1941, the German authorities announced their guidelines for the deportation of outside elements living in the area of Lower Štajerska. According to these plans, 260,000 were Slovenes designated for deportation from this Slovene province: first, all Slovene intellectuals; second, all Slovenes who had moved to Styria after 1914; further, a belt 20 kilometers wide along the new border between Štajerska and the Italian Province of Ljubljana, and between Štajerska and the Independent State of Croatia, was to be cleared of Slovenes. The guidelines also provided for the expulsion of all peasants in Štajerska who showed obvious signs of having non-German blood.

The German authorities ordered all inhabitants of Štajerska to state, between May 17 and 25, 1941, to which of the above categories they belonged, and to list the languages they spoke: German, Slovene (Kranjski), or Wendish (the Štajerska dialect of the Slovene language).

At a conference in Zagreb of representatives of the German occupation authorities in Slovenia and Serbia, and representatives of the Independent State of Croatia, held on June 4, 1941, a decision was passed to resettle a part of the 260,000 Slovenes in the Independent State of Croatia, and the same number of Serbs from Srem and Bosnia in Serbia. A section of the Slovene population was also to be deported to Serbia. The deportations were planned in three waves. The first was designed to transport 5,000 Slovene intellectuals from Štajerska to Serbia, and 4,000 Slovene intellectuals from Gorenjska to Serbia. The second wave involved 25,000 Slovenes from Štajerska to Croatia and just as many Serbs from Croatia to Serbia. The third group were 65,000 Slovene peasants from Gorenjska to Croatia, and just as many Serbs from Croatia to Serbia.

The development of the uprising, and transportation difficulties, hampered implementation of the German plans. About 8,350 persons were deported from Štajerska and Gorenjska to Croatia, while 17,000 fled from the reign of terror. Somewhat less than 7,000 Slovene intellectuals were deported to Serbia. About 30,000 Serbs were sent to Serbia from Srem, Bosnia, and Zagreb; another 170,000 left on their own to escape the fate that would otherwise have awaited them. About 360 Roman Catholic priests were deported from Štajerska and Gorenjska and the Ustashi authorities expelled 334 Orthodox priests from Croatia to Serbia.

Serbs and Montenegrins were also resettled by force from Bačka, Kosovo, and Macedonia. On April 27, 1941, the Hungarian authorities ordered all Slavs, Gypsies, and Jews who had moved to Bačka after October 31, 1918, to leave their homes within three days. The first victims of the German occupiers were the Serbian colonists. All Serbs were expelled from Macedonia under similar circumstances, and many Serbs and Montenegrins were subject to the same measures in Kosovo and Metohija.

Looting of Cultural Goods

The German occupiers planned and organized the destruction of all historical monuments belonging to various Yugoslav nationalities to facilitate their plans of Germanization. Even before the invasion began on April 6, 1941, detailed plans had been worked out for executing this plundering policy. Archives and scientific and art collections were immediately confiscated and sent to German territory. The state archives (together with the court archives and the files of the Yugoslav Foreign Ministry) were sent to Vienna and Berlin.

In Štajerska and Gorenjska, Slovene schools were destroyed, Slovene signs torn down, place-names changed, and epitaphs on gravestones replaced. In Štajerska alone, 1,200,000 books in the Slovene language were burned during the first few months of the occupation.

The Fascist regime in Italy had pursued a policy of Italianizing the Slovenes along the coast since 1926. The Italians had their own plans for genocide in Slovenia. Although the same type of terror that prevailed in the Slovene provinces under German occupation was not applied in the Province of Ljubljana under the Italians in the early months of 1941, the Italian authorities introduced signs in two languages everywhere, and the principal newspaper of the Slovene People's party, *Slovenec* (the *Slovene*), began printing news in Italian as well as Slovene on May 14, 1941. According to some documents, Mussolini was considering deporting the Slovenes from the Province of Ljubljana at the end of the war.

In the Independent State of Croatia, Pavelić banned all books in the Cyrillic alphabet, proclaimed Croatian the sole language, and took measures to purify it of Slavic influence. According to the Rights theories that Slovenes were "Alpine Croats," Pavelić introduced discriminatory measures against the Slovenes. In Zagreb he changed Slovenian street names, as for example Ljubljanska and Cankareva Streets. He claimed that parts of Slovenia should be incorporated in the Independent State of Croatia. This was done according to plans of his main ideologue, the minister of external affairs of the ISC, Mladen Lorković, as elaborated in his book *The People and Land of the Croats*, published in Zagreb in 1939. In this book Lorković expanded "Croatian borders" to the Soča River on the west and to Beljak and Celovec on the north.

Because most of Slovenia was under German occupation in 1941, Berlin did not support Pavelić's claims for "his sphere of influence." Therefore the Ustashi had to stop their campaign for taking over Slovenian territories.

The Hungarian authorities in Prekomurje issued all orders in two languages, Hungarian and Slovene, although the Slovene used was not the literary language but the so-called Vendščina (Wendish), which had been spoken in Prekomurje 200 years earlier and which few people knew in 1941.

On May 3, 1941, the Bulgarian authorities in Macedonia issued orders making the Bulgarian language compulsory in all schools and offices in Macedonia.

Massacre of Serbs, Gypsies, and Jews in the Independent State of Croatia and in Bačka

Taking the Nürnberg laws as a model, Ante Pavelić passed a legal decree on April 30, 1941, on the protection of Aryan blood and the honor of the Croatian people, followed on June 4 by a decree on the protection of the national and Aryan culture of the Croatian people.

Andrija Artuković, minister of internal affairs, issued an order banning "Serbs, Jews, Gypsies, and dogs" from entering parks, restaurants, and public transportation services of Zagreb. The minister of education and religion, Dr. Mile Budak, stated in an address delivered in Gospić on July 22, 1941: "We shall kill some of the Serbs, we shall expel others, and the remainder will be forced to embrace the Roman Catholic faith. These last will in due course be absorbed by the Croatian part of the population."

The first massacres of Serbs began as early as late April 1941 and intensified during the summer. In Glina, Banija, 1,260 peasants and other citizens were locked up in the Orthodox church, murdered and incinerated.

It has still not been estimated how many Serbs were killed in Croatia. Some authors claim that the number of victims was 200,000; others put the figure at 600,000 at the least.

Among those murdered were the vladika (bishop) of Karlovac, Svetozar Sava Trlajić; the vladika of Banja Luka, Platon Jovanović, and Metropolitan Petar Zimonjić of Bosnia, together with 158 other clergymen.

The patriarch of the Serbian Orthodox church, Gavrilo Dožić, was arrested in the monastery of Ostrog in Montenegro at the end of April 1941. The Berlin newspaper *Das Reich* accused him of leading the putsch of March 27 and of visiting Prince Pavle on the eve of the signing of the Tripartite Pact to warn him for the last time not to sign it. Patriarch Dožić was brought to Zagreb on May 8, 1941, and from there he was sent into internment.

One section of the Catholic clergy in Croatia accepted the idea of forcible conversion from the Orthodox to the Catholic religion. It has been calculated that 200,000 Serbs in Croatia were forced to change their faith.

On January 21, 22, and 23, 1942, the Hungarian authorities organized the slaughter of Serbs and Jews in Novi Sad. According to official Hungarian data on these massacres, and on the massacre in Šajkaška, 3,309 persons were murdered, 1,000 of whom were cast into the Danube.

During the war the Germans and their satellites murdered 50,000 of the 70,000 Jews living in Yugoslavia, besides 60,000 Gypsies.

CHAPTER 44

The Attitude of Various Political Forces to the Occupation

Differentiation among Political Parties in Yugoslavia

The April War brought about differentiation among the legal political parties of Yugoslavia. The Royal government in exile announced that the war would continue to be prosecuted, but a dispute within it broke out between Croat and Serb nationalists. The latter claimed that the Croats were to blame for the quick collapse of the Yugoslav state and army, and the former asserted that the unsettled Croatian question in prewar Yugoslavia had been the reason for the low morale of Croat troops in the Yugoslav Royal Army.

A similar process unfolded within the leaderships of political parties in the country. They could not come to terms on a number of issues: what attitude to assume toward the occupation of the country, and what kind of state should emerge after the war.

Originally general confusion reigned within these parties, gradually transformed into doubt as to the justifiability of the policies being pursued by the leaders.

Mutual Accusations by Bourgeois Nationalistic Groups

World War II had just begun. It was not clear who would win, the Axis powers or Great Britain. Some groups immediately established contact with the occupiers, like the Montenegrin Federalists headed by Sekula Drljević; the Frankists and Ustashi in Croatia; Dimitrije Ljotić and his associates in Serbia. The Croatian Peasant party wavered. Irresolute by nature, Dr. Vlatko Maček thought it best "not to put all his eggs in one basket." He gave the right wing of his party the go-ahead sign to join Pavelić's regime, while some of his other close associates (Šubašić, Krnjević, Šutej) pinned their hopes on the British; these were members of the Royal government in exile. After calling upon the Croatian people to submit to the Ustashi government on April 10, 1941, Dr. Maček tried in May and June to wrench himself free from Pavelić's embrace; the Ustashi press attacked him for this, and especially for sending members of his party to London.

Similar tactics were applied by the Slovene People's party. A section of the leadership had gone to London with the government in exile, whereas the ban of the Drava banovina, Dr. Marko Natlačen, was the mainstay of the occupier's regime in Ljubljana and even headed a deputation of Slovenes to pay homage to Mussolini in Rome. A third group had severed ties with the official leadership of the Slovene People's party in 1940 and was biding its time to see how things would develop. A number of these maintained ties with progressives in Slovenia.

Colonel Draža Mihailović and His Chief Adviser Dragiša Vasić

Some Yugoslav army officers managed to hide out in towns and villages after the capitulation in April, refusing to surrender to the occupiers. Among them was a general staff colonel, Dragoljub-Draža Mihailović, assistant chief of staff of the Second Army. He was well known abroad, having attended higher general staff schools in Paris, where he became friends with Colonel Charles de Gaulle; later as Yugoslav military attaché in Prague and Sofia he widened his circles of acquaintance. It is assumed that some of these ties were intelligence contacts.

After the capitulation of the Second Yugoslav Army in Bosnia, Mihailović and a group of men remained in the vicinity of Doboj; on May 13, 1941, he left for the plateau of Ravna Gora with twenty-six officers and NCOs. He took no military action against the occupiers but gathered officers around him and established contacts with politicians. First Mihailović sought support from Dimitrije Ljotić, hoping that Ljotić would help him develop a political organization. Disagreement between the two men followed, and Mihailović was supported by Milan Aćimović, former minister of internal affairs in prewar Yugoslavia, who was appointed to head the German commissariat immediately after the occupation of Serbia.

There is still no accurate knowledge as to whether Draža Mihailović had been assigned this role earlier or, as one of the senior officers who were at liberty in 1941, undertook it of his own accord.

The first politician to arrive in Ravna Gora, where he became Mihailović's adviser, was Dragiša Vasić, one of the leaders of the Republican party. Not enough documents are available to present a well-rounded picture of his personality. A writer and lawyer, he defended Communists at many trials between 1921 and 1936. Before World War II he became secretary-general of the Serbian Cultural Club in Belgrade, the president of which was Professor Slobodan Jovanović. They represented the extreme right wing of the Serbian nationalists, which considered that, in his agreement of 1939 with Dr. Vlatko Maček, Dragiša Cvetković had "made great concessions to the Croats at the expense of the vital interests of the Serbian people." In this respect, Vasić found many points of contact with Mihailović, who from 1941 consistently implemented the policies of the Serbian Cultural Club.

Clarification of Vasić's role is further complicated by his ties with the Soviet intelligence service. For years he maintained contact with its center in Prague. This was considered the fourth line of Soviet military intelligence service for all three countries who were members of the Entente: Czechoslovakia, Yugoslavia, and Romania. This Vasić did out of Pan-Slav conviction, and not for reward. He specialized in work among the white Russian émigrés in Belgrade. Certain members of the CPY, who acted as couriers for the Soviet intelligence service, remember having taken Vasić's reports to Prague. When Mustafa Golubović arrived in Yugoslavia in 1941 to head the Soviet military intelligence service, he maintained close contact with Vasić, who hid a transmitter for him in Belgrade. Upon arriving at Ravna Gora, Vasić set up his own radio station and had a special code clerk at his disposal. History has not yet disclosed exactly with whom he maintained contact.

Dragiša Vasić and some of the Serbian bourgeois politicians still harbored illusions, dated from earlier periods, about Russia's policy in the Balkans: that it was the protector of the Orthodox, that is, of the Serbs, and would favor them rather than other religions and nationalities, in the spirit of Russian imperial diplomacy's advice to Nikola Pašić in 1914 and 1915 that Roman Catholics should not be included in the future state even if they were Slavs, meaning Croats and Slovenes.

In the summer of 1941, bourgeois parties were ridden by extreme nationalism, the total isolation of one people from another, and disbelief in the possibility of reconstructing a joint state.

Even before the attack on Yugoslavia in 1941, Berlin pursued a policy of exploiting all these antagonisms in Yugoslavia—political, national, and religious—so as to break down the country's cohesion and provoke the deepest possible internal conflicts. This it did even more relentlessly after the occupation by rendering direct assistance to the Ustashi in their genocide against the Serbs, although Serbian political groups were promised that they would get help against Pavelić, and in squaring accounts with Croatians and Muslims.

Prime Minister Simović's Warning

Bourgeois groups were divided in their attitude toward the occupiers. Supporters of Britain and France, once their initial demoralization following the collapse of the state in 1941 had subsided, came to believe that Yugoslavia's fate would be decided on the world's main battlefields. At home, they thought, it would be the better part of wisdom to leave the occupiers alone, lie low, and wait to see what would develop. The only thing that should be assured was the status quo of the social order. After the first German air raid on Belgrade on April 6, 1941, Yugoslavia's prime minister, General Dušan Simović, almost symbolically said to Bećarević, the chief of the political police: "Open your eyes so that the Communists and anarchists do not use this war for their own purposes."

The fear of social changes obsessed the Yugoslav bourgeoisie of all nationalities and subgroups from the first to the last day of the war. In many cases, interests of class prevailed over national and patriotic sentiments; as resistance to the occupiers developed, many bourgeois groups sided with the occupiers, at first timorously and later openly and completely, swayed by what they considered the interests of their class.

The Communist Party of Yugoslavia in the April War

When Germany and its satellites attacked Yugoslavia on April 6, 1941, the Communist Party of Yugoslavia assumed the position that no way should be left untried in strengthening the country's defenses to resist the occupiers. In Ljubljana, Zagreb, Split, and Podgorica Communists came out from underground and went to military command posts asking for arms for the workers so that they might fight the Germans.

During the first days of the war, ties were disrupted with the Central Committee of the CPY, which had its headquarters in Zagreb. For instance, the party organization in Sarajevo, where Ivo-Lola Ribar, member of the Central Committee's Politburo, was staying at the time, issued a proclamation stating that the "Communist Party has sent its best men to defend the homeland from the mad Hitler." In Split the Provincial Committee for Dalmatia published a leaflet on April 13 addressed to the "Croatian Working People and Patriotic Citizens" in which it condemned the aggression, Ante Pavelić, and Maček as well. In conclusion the leaflet stated: "Armed forces are resisting tenaciously and fighting against Pavelić's gangs in Croatia and German troops throughout the whole country, for the freedom and independence of all the peoples of Yugoslavia."

The Central Committee issued a proclamation on April 15, castigating the quisling regime of Pavelić and calling upon the people to offer continued resistance to the aggressors. The proclamation stressed that the Communists and working class of Yugoslavia stood in the front ranks of struggle against the attackers. Earlier, on April 10, the Central Committee of the CPY had taken the decision to form a military commission headed by Tito.

The Consultation of the Central Committee of the CPY in May 1941 and the Decision to Pursue an Armed Struggle Regardless of International Circumstances

Actually in the summer of 1941 the CPY had become an all-Yugoslav party operating in all parts of Yugoslavia. Early in May 1941 a session called the May Consultation was held in Zagreb, where consideration was first given to the behavior of Communists during the April War. Party organizations in Slovenia and Serbia were rebuked for creating separate detachments of Communists and sympathizers instead of sending Communists into regular army units where they could influence others. The Party organization in Bjelovar, Croatia, was admonished because fifteen of its members in one regiment sat passively by while "two or three Frankists organized a revolt against resisting the aggressors."

The May Consultation also raised the question of government under the occupation. It decided that an armed struggle should be prosecuted against the occupiers irrespective of international circumstances. The decisions passed at this consultation were published in the May–June 1941 issue of the *Proletarian*, organ of the Central Committee of the CPY. It was stated that there was no turning back, that the struggle would be waged for national and social liberation and for a better and happier future, and that the Yugoslav ruling class would be held responsible for its actions when the time came.

As soon as the Comintern received materials from the May Consultation, Moscow voiced its disapproval of the Central Committee's decision that national and social liberation would be the goal from the very first day of the uprising. The reply that arrived from Moscow after June 22, 1941, stated that "at this stage what you are concerned with is liberation from Fascist oppression and not socialist revolution."

The May Consultation pointed out how important it was to rely on the peasant masses in the uprising:

> Today, when the peasantry has completely lost faith in various bourgeois parties, when it has been sobered by the brutal reality and seeks only to find a way out of the situation, party organizations must pay the greatest attention to work in the villages. At the present stage of struggle, the most important thing is the alliance between workers and peasants.

The CPY's Organizational Preparations for the Uprising

During the war operations in April 1941, some Communists in the units of the regular Yugoslav army had been captured and sent to POW camps, but the entire Party organization as such remained intact, as did its technical sections, especially clandestine printing presses. Between the April War and June 1941, the number of Party members rose to 12,000 and the number of members of the Young Communist League to almost 50,000. The creation of military committees in the field was stepped up; many weapons that had been discarded by the troops on their way to POW camps were collected. A great deal was achieved along these lines, particularly in Dalmatia and Montenegro.

CHAPTER 45

The First Massive Uprising in Occupied Europe

The Spontaneous Uprising in June 1941 of Serbian Peasants in Hercegovina in Self-Defense

The first massive uprising in Hitler's "Fortress of Europe" broke out in Yugoslavia in the summer of 1941. From the initial spontaneous battles fought by the poorly armed peasants to save their very lives, the uprising spread throughout the lands of Yugoslavia as the rebellious masses developed their own government and National Liberation army. Within the frameworks of the integral mass

FIGURE 44. Hanged Partisan, Belgrade, 1941.

FIGURE 45. Ljubo-Čedo Čupic before his execution at Nikšić, May 5, 1942.

movement, which had far-reaching goals, the uprising in each of the lands of Yugoslavia demonstrated profoundly characteristic features, depending on the traditions and special economic and social conditions of each. The forms taken by the struggle also varied; in places the unarmed people, offering unanimous resistance, especially in certain towns, achieved duality of power in the full sense of the word with the occupiers; in others, self-defense unfolded through outright armed struggle. Too, the uprising progressed unevenly, sometimes smoldering, only to flare up again.

Peasants of Serbian nationality in Hercegovina and Bosnia, the homeland of guerrilla warfare, spontaneously rose in revolt to defend themselves from the extermination that threatened them at Ustashi hands, aided by Nazi Germany. From the beginning of June 1941, all of eastern Hercegovina rose to arms, although it was not alone; in May Serbian peasants in Lika and also those in the Bosnian March (Bosanska Krajina) resisted the Ustashi massacres. German documents show that on May 8 heavy artillery was used at Sanski Most against Serbian peasants of the Bosnian March and that several dozen were killed.

Extermination of Serbs in Hercegovina was pursued with appalling ferocity, to which the fanaticism of Catholic clergymen contributed not a little. All Serbs in the Neretva Valley who did not succeed in fleeing in time were killed. In Prebilovci near Čapljina, even all children who were caught were slain. The slaughter spread to eastern Hercegovina. In Korita, Gacko District, 180 persons were cast into pits. On June 1 thirteen Serbs were killed in Trebinje.

In the village of Drežnje, Nevesinje District, the Ustashi set out on June 3 to destroy all Serbs, but fifty of the more enterprising youths waited for them in ambush after digging up buried rifles hidden during the short war of April 6. Three Ustashi were killed, and another four were captured and shot. Like an avalanche, the insurrection roared through the districts of Nevesinje, Bileća, and Gacko. The entire area was liberated with the exception of the towns. Following the principles of the Montenegrin Popular army, the people elected detachment commanders (one detachment to a village); as soon as danger threatened, it sufficed for the commander to fire one shot to summon all able-bodied men not only from the village but from the entire district. The news of the uprising in Hercegovina sent spirits soaring in Montenegro, and a number of Montenegrin detachments came to the help of the Hercegovinians.

Imbued with atavistic ideas, the rebelling peasant masses called for "an eye for an eye, a tooth for a tooth." The strength of tradition, the extent to which the social psychology of the peasants of this area remained unchanged, had been attested by the Russian Narodnjak revolutionary, Sergei Mikhailovich Kravchinski, known under his pseudonym of Stepnyak. In 1875, hearing that the Hercegovinian serfs (Serbs and Croats) had risen in revolt against the Turkish feudatories, he rushed from Paris, where he was living in exile, to Hercegovina via Dubrovnik. But he soon went back disappointed, for he had cherished the illusion that he would find among the insurgents conscious fighters for social justice. "Religious fanaticism and the desire for plunder, those were the features that characterized them," Stepnyak concluded in his memoirs of the Hercegovinian uprising.

In 1941, at the instigation of former gendarmes and petty traders, the rebellious mass attacked the Muslim population, accusing them of responsibility for the massacre of Serbs. In the Bileća District the Ustashi had not succeeded in killing a single Serb (the Montenegrin boundary was nearby and they feared retaliation), but the Serbian insurgents, striking twice in that same district, killed over 600 Muslim men, women, and children.

The Communists Endeavor to Reeducate the Backward Peasant Masses

At that time, there were only 140 Communist Party members in all Hercegovina, most of them in the towns. There were few if any in the insurgent areas. They hastened to help the uprising and stop the fratricidal murder but were powerless in the face of the blind forces of hatred and revenge. Some of them, Muslims, were killed themselves. In the Bileća District Communists organized to protect 400 Muslims—women, children, and a few elderly men. Twelve chosen Communists escorted them to Stolac, but at Dabar they were intercepted by a group of former gendarmes, reinforced by insurgents from Dabar, who forced the patrol to withdraw and then killed all 400 Muslims.

Thus the Communists, in the midst of the uprising, began their struggle to reeducate the rebellious peasant masses, to make them socially and politically conscious, to invest them with humanistic principles, to emancipate them from the blind hatred that in the final analysis benefited only Nazi Germany and led to the self-destruction of the peoples of Yugoslavia.

Similar occurrences were registered in spontaneous uprisings in other parts of Bosnia, Lika, Kordun, and Banija. In the Bosnian March the town of Kulen Vakuf was razed. In the uprising of 1875 it had been the center of the Turkish forces and the Kulenović beys, who had terrorized the entire area.

Communist workers from Drvar helped the rebellious peasants dispel this grave psychological trauma, but the greatest achievement along these lines was recorded by the Partisans at Kozara Mountain. On the very first day of the uprising there, 10 percent of the units were Muslims and Croats, their number rising to 25 percent by war's end. The fact that the insurgents did not perpetrate reprisals against the innocent Muslim and Croat population made it easier to persuade the people to join the Partisans.

The U.S.S.R. Enters the War, Giving New Incentive to the Uprising

The Soviet Union's entry into the war on June 22, 1941, lent fresh impetus to the uprising in all parts of Yugoslavia. Those who had been undecided now realized that the anti-Hitler coalition had been reinforced and that Germany's chances of victory were waning. Progressive sections of the Yugoslav population had more reason to hope that the Western powers would not be able to dictate Yugoslavia's future policies, and it became realistic to expect that the influence of foreign capital in Yugoslavia would be suppressed.

The moral-political effect of the Soviet Union's entry was considerable. The old Slavic tradition lived on among the peasantry generally, and not only among the Serbs. It was manifest also among a part of the intelligentsia, Slovene, Serbian, and Croatian. As one Communist put it then, "Half the people are for Russia, and the other half for the Communists." There was a grain of truth in this.

The Decisions of the Central Committee of the Communist Party of Yugoslavia

As soon as the U.S.S.R. was attacked, the Central Committee of the CPY held a meeting on June 22 in Belgrade, where it decided to mobilize all party organizations and to appeal to the people of Yugoslavia to heighten their resistance to the occupiers. At a meeting of July 4 in Belgrade, it was resolved to send out a call for insurrection. Partisan warfare was chosen as the basic form for developing the uprising, which was to evolve from sabotage and diversionary activity into a nationwide insurrection. A directive was issued for the creation of shock groups headed by Communists; these were to leave the towns and spread around the countryside, among the people; Partisan detachments were to be formed. It was decided to send members of the Central Committee with special authorization to various parts of Yugoslavia where they were to invest every effort in transforming the uprising into an organized, armed struggle against the occupation forces. The General Headquarters of the Partisan Detachments, headed by Tito, was established and a Supreme Headquarters *Bulletin* began to be published. It was decided to introduce political commissars into all Partisan detachments.

Tito drafted instructions on the formation and tasks of the Partisan detachments of Yugoslavia, elaborating the fundamental premises of revolutionary war for the country, and the strategy and tactics of Partisan warfare.

Mass Uprising in Montenegro on July 13

After the Soviet Union's entry into the war, the first massive uprising in Yugoslavia broke out in Montenegro on July 13. Initiated by guerrilla detachments, overnight the uprising acquired a spontaneous and widespread character. Young and old took up arms. It has been estimated that the astonished Italians were attacked by over 30,000 armed Montenegrins. All of Montenegro was liberated with the exception of a few towns: Cetinje, Podgorica, Nikšić. In the Messina Division alone, over 5,000 soldiers were put out of commission.

There are a number of reasons why the uprising was such a success in Montenegro. In contrast to neighboring Hercegovina, Montenegro was not an object of genocide. On the contrary, the old Yugoslav gendarmerie stations in Montenegrin territory were empty and Montenegrin Communists had more freedom of movement than in the old Yugoslavia. The occupiers had also imported considerable quantities of food supplies into Montenegro in preparation for the proclamation of the "Independent Kingdom of Montenegro" and its unification with Italy.

Communists had a great deal more influence in Montenegro than in Hercegovina. Right after World War I, during elections for the constituent assembly, the CPY had polled about 40 percent of the Montenegrin vote, this being a form of protest by the Montenegrin masses against the conditions existing in their country after King Aleksandar had established his regime in 1918. In spite of many raids on Party organizations in Montenegro, the Party had preserved its network and cadres almost intact. There were many Communist students around the villages who were influential among the masses.

The fact that the U.S.S.R. had entered the war was also instrumental in assuring the success of the uprising there. It was widely believed that Russian paratroopers would descend in Montenegro at any moment. In many areas this conviction was so strong that peasants cut the grass in their fields to help the airborne troops land more easily.

The belief that the Red Army would make short shrift of the Nazi aggressors was strong, not among the people alone but also among many leaders of the CPY in and outside of Montenegro. In the summer of 1941 Veselin Masleša was brought before a commission of the Communist Party in Montenegro to answer for an article he had written for *Naša Borba (Our Struggle)*, organ of the Provincial Committee of the Communist Party of Montenegro, claiming that the war would last only six months. Immediately after the German aggression, the agitprop section of the Cental Committee of the Communist Party of Serbia had received directives from the Central Committee of the CPY to undertake measures for organizing the transfer of power in Belgrade.

Bosnia and Hercegovina

Optimism and belief in the early end of the war also ran strong in Hercegovina after June 22. A new wave of uprisings broke out in northern Hercegovina, during which a Communist peasant, Dukica Grahovac, and some other insurgents charged Nevesinje on June 24 with a red banner and cries of "Long live Russia." The Hercegovinians captured part of the town and forced the Ustashi to withdraw into their fortified garrison.

The further development of the July uprising in Montenegro revealed in full measure the social psychology of the peasantry in spontaneous insurrections. After its initial amazement, the government in Rome decided to send the Ninth Italian Army to quell the uprising. On July 18 six Italian divisions brought from Albania went into the offensive, all power having been placed in the hands of the commander of the Ninth Army. By August 10 the Italian troops had recaptured all liberated towns and stepped up their terrorization of the population, especially in villages near lines of communication. Some of the peasant masses wavered. The eruption of enthusiasm resulting from the first victories of the uprising gave way to lethargy. In some areas Communists who had led the uprising were hunted down. In Crmnica the district Party organization, under pressure from the peasants, confessed its "guilt" for "having driven the people into unnecessary slaughter" and then surrendered to the Italians. Fortunately this kind of behavior was rare; most of the Party organizations pursued the struggle and the insurgents continued to hold a large section of Montenegro with the exception of the towns and communications between them.

The dynamics of the uprising in Bosnia and Hercegovina also hinged upon the social psychology of the peasants. The struggle ebbed frequently, only to surge forward again when the Ustashi reign of terror drove the Serbian masses to fight in self-defense. The invaders, and especially the Italians, modified their policy only after the German and Italian authorities intervened in greater measure in Bosnia and Hercegovina—after they expanded their zones of occupation, having perceived that events were getting out of hand and that the uprising was seriously damaging their war potential. Their tactics were to offer certain minor concessions to the insurgents, most of them superficial and fleeting. But this new policy had some effect on the behavior of the peasant masses.

The uprising did not develop evenly in all parts of Bosnia and Hercegovina. In the Bosnian March the peasants rose en masse late in July, and in eastern Bosnia in late July and August. In August the insurgents succeeded in establishing control over the environs of Sarajevo.

During this period the uprising retained all the features of a spontaneous revolt. Serbian peasants fought to defend themselves from the threat of annihilation by the Ustashi. The confessional and national heterogeneity also had a bearing on the development of the insurrection. The Communist Party was still too weak to bridle peasant anarchy; to draw the line, organizationally and ideologically, at the chauvinistic groups among the insurgent Serbs upon whom the Chetniks under Draža Mihailović were wielding a growing influence with their slogan "Serbs above all." Thus Mihailović was pushing the Serbs to fight the Croats and Muslims—an attitude that served the Germans well. Consequently the Croatian and Muslim masses in Bosnia and Hercegovina were at first unwilling to join the uprising, except in rare cases such as that of Kozara Mountain, Mostar, and to some extent around Sarajevo, then the Husinje miners, Croats, who had joined the Partisans the very first day.

Many workers in Bosnia and Hercegovina (with one leg in the village and another in the city) were under the influence of bourgeois views and nationalistic and religious prejudices. In a report to Josip Broz Tito of August 15, 1941, Svetozar Vukmanović-Tempo immediately upon arriving in Sarajevo described the difficulties he encountered in Bosnia and Hercegovina. Referring to the Mostar area, he stressed that "the insurgents had plundered Muslim villages and thereby turned the entire Muslim population against themselves. . . . Furthermore, some Montenegrin Chetniks were looting and had transported food and other booty to Montenegro." Vukmanović explained in detail the difficulties that had cropped up in the Party organization of Zenica and gave at the same time his own simplified explanation of those very complex occurrences:

> We sent a comrade from the Municipal Committee of Sarajevo there to do a job (two power plants, a viaduct, and weapons stores—300 to 400 rifles and 4,000 kilograms of dynamite), and then to withdraw to the woods. The Zenica party organization disagreed with us for *political reasons*, claiming that we would have need of all these objects once socialism was established and also that if we did this the army would attack, reaction would set in, and the Zenica organization would be destroyed. It would be easy to blow up these objects as they are guarded by only a few workers. What is worse, the comrade from the Municipal Committee, who came back, agreed with them. I immediately sent another comrade, also a member of the Municipal Committee, to make matters very clear, to tell them that the tasks would have to be carried out and to convince them of the harm and senselessness of such a "political position." After three or four days he came back with another position: the Zenica organization did not agree with us politically for the following reasons: "The enterprises are not functioning at full capacity and are therefore not important enough to destroy. Furthermore, destruction of these enterprises would provoke revolt among the Muslim and Croat villages, and we do not want fratricidal war."

This is only one example of the type of difficulties besetting the CPY during the early days of the uprising in Bosnia and Hercegovina.

The Specific Features of the Insurrection in Croatia

Political conditions for launching an uprising were extremely complicated in Croatia. It flared up immediately in Dalmatia, the Croatian Littoral, and Gorski Kotar among the Croatian masses in areas under Italian occupation, but developed more slowly in other parts of Croatia. Disillusioned with the Belgrade government of prewar Yugoslavia, the Croatian peasant, influenced by the Catholic clergy, and particularly by Dr. Vlatko Maček (who had asked the Croatian people for loyalty to the Ustashi authorities), harbored certain illusions about the new regime during the first few weeks after the Independent State of Croatia was established.

On the other hand, the Serbian people in Croatia were immediately subjected to physical extermination. The reaction was the same as among the Serbian population in Bosnia and Hercegovina—spontaneous resistance. Communists operating in the field, especially those from Zagreb and other Croatian towns, quickly established contact with the insurgent masses. The Zagreb Party organization carried out a number of large-scale actions in the town: in broad daylight bombs were thrown at an Ustashi student detachment and the main telephone building in Zagreb was blown up. The arrival of the Sisak Partisan detachment, headed by Vlado Capo Janjić, a metalworker, in liberated territory in Banija, was historically important in the progress of the uprising. It undertook its first operations immediately after June 22, 1941. Made up exclusively of Croatian workers, it contributed considerably to the consolidation of fraternity and unity between Croats and Serbs.

The uprising in Croatia went its own way, particularly in the forms of struggle used against the occupiers. For instance, dual government was set up in the town of Split as early as 1941, and a number of National Liberation committees to which a large part of the population belonged were organized throughout the city. Large-scale actions were undertaken—a general strike, boycott of all Italian ceremonies, and attacks on functionaries in the occupation government. The same was the case in other towns, notably Šibenik, and on the islands.

The armed uprising in Dalmatia broke out somewhat later. On two occasions, young Partisan detachments, made up largely of workers from the towns, failed to break through to Lika and Bosnia, where territory had already been liberated. After heroic resistance, they were destroyed, but a third group succeeded in its thrust. Their arrival in Lika among the Serbian insurgents was also extremely helpful in promoting a feeling of brotherhood and unity.

As early as 1941, three partisan detachments were active in the vicinity of Rijeka.

The Liberation Movement in Slovenia

Compared with other European resistance movements, the National Liberation movement in Yugoslavia was an integral process. However, significant specific characteristics that came to mark the way the movement progressed among the various Yugoslav nationalities were due to different historical conditions. This was especially the case of the Slovenes.

Since 1848 German bourgeois circles had been pressing southward, denying the national individuality of the Slovene people and attempting to Germanize them in various ways.

Although Hitler's Germanization measures differed from those of earlier periods, their roots were the same. The immediate threat of genocide as posed by Hitler motivated the Slovene people to offer spontaneous resistance in self-defense and fostered broad unity throughout the entire nation.

As soon as he had taken possession of Gorenjska and Štajerska, Hitler turned his attention not only to Communists and other progressives but to the entire Slovene nation as such. For instance, of the 608 Roman Catholic parish priests of Slovene nationality living in those areas at the time of the occupation, by the end of 1941 Hitler had deported 487 to Serbia, the Province of Ljubljana, Croatia, or concentration camps.

In reaction to these conditions, the *Osvobodilna Fronta* (the Liberation Front) was formed, originally as a kind of coalition but changing its character as the war progressed. The CPY was the sole political party in the Front, whereas other groups who joined came from bourgeois political parties that had disintegrated; in some cases they were simply groups of like-minded, public-spirited citizens, or individuals who wanted to help.

The Liberation Front achieved unity among the working class, as an organization under the influence of Communists and also Christian Socialists (the working masses under the influence of the Social Democrats were only partially encompassed by the Front), and a common tongue was found with the majority of Slovene intellectuals.

One of the reasons for the Liberation Front's signal success was the strong support it was given by the peasants. Although the Slovene People's party, Clericals, had with the help of the hierarchy and over 200 branch organizations kept a virtual monopoly on political influence over the Slovene villages before the war, in 1941 the Community Party of Slovenia and the Liberation Front succeeded in attracting a large section of the peasant masses to their side, thus setting the scene for widespread support of Partisan units and Liberation Front organs in the field. There is a great deal of truth in the assertion that for the first time since the great peasant revolt led by Matija Gubec, the high-ranking Catholic clergy lost spiritual control over the countryside. This was without a doubt one of the major political achievements of the Liberation Front during the war.

In comparison with the way the uprising developed in other parts of Yugoslavia, resistance in Slovenia was characterized by even and balanced advancement, with each step in the struggle being prepared ahead through systematic activity by a whole network of auxiliary organizations, both political and military, throughout most of Slovenia.

Although Slovenia's position was strategically important (along the direct line of communications between Germany and Italy), and although most of it had been swallowed up by Hitler's Germany, Slovene Partisan units kept the enemy engaged throughout the entire war in this sensitive area, in spite of fierce enemy offensives.

Through 400 field committees of the Liberation Front, the Slovenes sustained a bitter struggle against the enemy in a variety of forms. Every household was active in one way or another. In Ljubljana the Liberation Front organized large-scale actions, calling upon the people to leave the streets and public places at specified hours. On two occasions in 1941, the entire city went dead, the first time on October 29, 1941, for the "twenty-third anniversary of the date when we Slovenes, together with the Croats and Serbs, were liberated from the Austro-Hungarian yoke" and the second on December 1, 1941, "the state holiday of Yugoslavia," for it was on that date in 1918 that the unification of Serbs, Croats, and Slovenes had been proclaimed.

The holiday was celebrated in other Slovene towns as well. In Novo Mesto all high school students went on strike; afterwards 125 of them were expelled from school.

In the autumn of 1941 the Italian authorities established a special military tribunal, *Tribunale Militare Speciale*, which passed sentence on 13,876 citizens of Ljubljana at 8,737 trials before the capitulation of Italy. From March 15 onwards, all Ljubljana was fenced in by barbed wire; arrests were made en masse, especially of the male population. In the spring of 1942 one-third of Ljubljana's population of 60,000 were in prison or internment.

As soon as the uprising started, the Central Committee of the Communist Party of Slovenia organized a special intelligence and counterintelligence service under the direct and exclusive control of the Central Committee; the Security Intelligence Service and the National Protection Organization undertook actions in the Ljubljana streets.

In Štajerska and Gorenjska conditions were far more difficult. The Germans had removed the intelligentsia by deporting them. They then began to resettle the peasants; further, they succeeded in breaking up and destroying the first Partisan detachments composed largely of workers. Apathy set in among a section of the population, particularly in the Zasavski basin, a working class center (Trbovlje, Zagorje, Hrastnik). Partisan units made a number of attempts to break through to Štajerska from Dolenjska, which was under Italian occupation, but failed to achieve their aim; during the entire duration of the uprising this area was the principal Partisan liberated territory and base although a predominantly peasant part of Slovenia.

Along the Slovene coast Liberation Front activities were a natural continuation of the resistance of the population during the full twenty years of Fascist occupation. Members of the Slovene organization *Tigar* joined the Liberation Front in large numbers and carried on the struggle to liberate the Slovene coast and annex it to united Slovenia and Yugoslavia.

In Prekomurje, under Hungarian occupation, the police immediately instituted a reign of terror, destroying Liberation Front resistance organizations and killing off the leading cadres.

The Conflict with the Bulgarian Workers' Party (Communists) over Macedonia

In Macedonia the population offered spontaneous resistance to the Bulgarian authorities from the very first day of Bulgarian occupation. Perpetrating cultural genocide, these authorities had forced the Bulgarian language upon the population in schools and administration. A decree was issued requiring every Macedonian to sign a declaration to the effect that he belonged to the Bulgarian nation. Just as the Great Serbian regime had forced Serbian names on the Macedonians, so did the Great Bulgarian regime change their names to Bulgarian. In certain high schools the students went on strike against these measures.

The Central Committee of the Bulgarian Workers' party (Communists) in Sofia had adopted the position of the Bulgarian bourgeoisie and the idea that Macedonia was a Bulgarian land with no national individuality of its own. In line with this, the Central Committee in Sofia asked the Provincial Committee for Macedonia of the CPY to break off ties with the Central Committee of the CPY and for all Party organizations in Macedonia to join the Bulgarian Workers' party. The Provincial Committee for Macedonia came to a parting of ways over this issue while the secretary of the Provincial Committee, Metodij Šatorov, sided with the Sofia Communists.

Šatorov refused to attend the May Consultation of the Central Committee of the CPY in Zagreb, and he rejected its decisions. In the meantime Bulgarian authorities had undertaken to deport all Serbs from Macedonia. Šatorov also ordered all Serbian Communists to leave Macedonia immediately. However, the Party organizations in Kumanovo, Bitolj, and Djevdjelija staged demonstrations and addressed protests to the Bulgarian authorities against the persecution of Serbs. The Skoplje organization collected contributions to help the afflicted families. In doing so, the Macedonian Communists demonstrated that they recognized the difference between the Great Serbian regime and the innocent Serbian families in Macedonia.

In the meantime the Central Committee of the CPY had sent Lazar Koliševski to Macedonia, Šatorov, his position supported by Sofia, remained adamant. The Central Committee of the CPY then applied to the Comintern for an opinion; the latter sided with the Central Committee of the CPY. Šatorov was suspended, and the Central Committee of the CPY sent an open letter to Macedonian Communists calling upon them to act vigorously in developing the uprising in Macedonia. Three Partisan detachments were formed in Macedonia and carried out their first armed attack against Bulgarian occupation troops on October 11, 1941.

The Development of the Uprising in Western Serbia

Conditions were ripe in Serbia for a spontaneous uprising by the masses, especially the peasants. The Communist Party perceived this in time to undertake systematic preparations. The signal for battle came from the YCL of Belgrade, which began taking action immediately after June 22, 1941, sabotaging in broad daylight German lorries, garages, communications, and newsstands selling German newspapers and attacking police agents and German soldiers.

These actions against the occupation authorities were also joined by persons who had no organizational connection with higher Party forums but wanted to fight. For instance, captured German documents show that in July 1941 a carpenter, Zoltan Vereb, tried to install a booby trap under the house at No. 10 Rumunska Street, Belgrade, where Göring's representative for Serbia, Neuhausen, lived. Vereb had been repairing the parquet in the house when he made this attempt; however, he was betrayed by some refugees from Bosnia, caught, and executed.

Partisan detachments were operating throughout Serbia. Ten detachments with 8,000 armed men were soon formed in western Serbia and Šumadija. Tradition played a meaningful role in the early days of the uprising. These were the areas of the First and Second Serbian Uprisings, and the great battles fought by the Serbian army in 1914 at the Cer, Drina, and Kolubara. In Vojvodina, too, a large number of smaller detachments were in operation. The insurrection spread in the Banat, and particularly in Srem. Assisted by Srem Partisans, thirty-two inmates of the penitentiary in Sremska Mitrovica made their escape on August 2, 1941. Among them were a number of Communists serving long sentences (Marijan Stilinović, Ivan Maček, Jovan-Žarko Veselinov, and others).

A large liberated area was soon created, extending from the suburbs of Belgrade to the towns of Užice and Kruševac. The first to be attacked were commune administration buildings and gendarmerie stations. Then the Partisans struck at the German troops. German troops stationed in the area suffered 6,000 casualties and 400 captured German soldiers. The growing Partisan attacks forced the Germans to withdraw from Užice, Čačak, Gornji Milanovac, and a few other places.

The uprising in Serbia had a galvanizing effect on the struggle of all the nationalities of Yugoslavia. This was not only because half of Serbia was liberated from the German occupiers and new organs of people's government were formed, but also because of the determined opposition of Partisans in

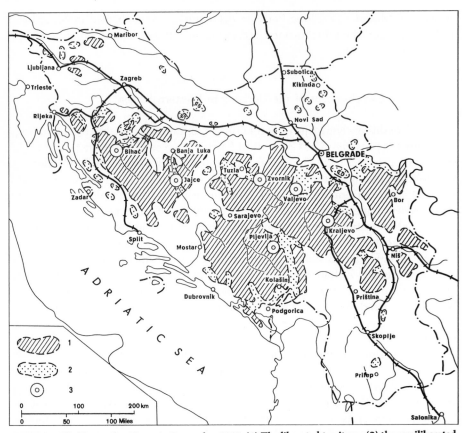

MAP 47.   The liberated territory in September 1941. (1) The liberated territory; (2) the semiliberated territory; (3) besieged enemy garrisons.

Serbia to the movement led by Draža Mihailović, grounded on the maintenance of centralism, nonrecognition of equality for the nationalities of Yugoslavia, and the old social system. The Serbian Partisans' achievements in the first year of the war demonstrated to the other nationalities of Yugoslavia that the future community of Yugoslav peoples would be based on acknowledgment of the individuality of each nation and on equitable relations.

In September the General Headquarters of the Partisan forces moved from Belgrade to liberated territory, first in Krupanj and then Užice. At Stolice near Krupanj, a consultation of commanders of Partisan detachments from all parts of Yugoslavia was held on September 26, 1941. The Supreme Headquarters was formed, and general headquarters for various territorial units. Measures were undertaken to strengthen the armed forces of the uprising and establish better contact between them. Plans for pursuing the struggle were worked out.

New Measures by Hitler to Crush the Insurgency

In the summer of 1941 the uprising covered one-third of the entire Yugoslav territory, provoking reactions not only in Berlin but among the leading Allied powers, especially Great Britain and the U.S.S.R. Forces within Yugoslavia also polarized. As the uprising had revolutionary objectives, committees of the new government were set up. Bourgeois circles began to waver; it was during this period that many of them decided that the capitalist order in Yugoslavia could be saved only by Nazi Germany's victory in the war.

The German Supreme Command realized the danger threatening from the uprising that jeopardized key communications along the Morava Valley and mining production in Serbia. It decided that the "dangerous development of the general situation in Serbia required that thorough measures" be undertaken. On September 16, 1941, Hitler ordered the Southeast Command "to crush the insurgent movement in the southeast by energetic measures." For reinforcement, he dispatched the 342d Infantry Division from France and a battalion of the 100th Tank Brigade. The 125th Infantry Regiment with two battalions of the 164th Infantry Division arrived from Greece; during the last phase of the offensive, the entire 113th Infantry Division was sent from the eastern front.

On the basis of experience acquired by German military experts in operations with Chiang Kai-shek's army against the Chinese partisans, German Headquarters in Serbia decided to quell the uprising not only by disrupting Partisan detachments but also by cutting them off from their rear. Consequently the German Supreme Command ordered special measures of reprisal against the people in the liberated areas, including the mass execution of the population in towns.

The Great Serbian Bourgeoisie Unites

Although suspicious, especially after March 27, 1941, of Serbian bourgeois groups and former generals who he thought would again support London at the first suitable opportunity, Hitler nevertheless agreed to collaborate with the leaders of the Great Serbian regime in Belgrade, in view of the situation in rebellious Serbia. Milan Aćimović and his government of commissars was replaced on August 29, 1941, by the government of "national salvation" headed by General Milan Nedić. Dimitrije Ljotić had initiated the unification of all groups of the Serbian ruling class and had been the principal mediator between them and the German authorities.

Joint mass psychological and propaganda measures were undertaken in occupied Serbia. Nedić mobilized 10,000 men who appeared in the field in the uniforms of the former Yugoslav army to show the people that "the old government was returning." The German authorities took the initiative for the signing of an appeal "against the Communists," actually an appeal against the uprising. On August 17 this shameful text was signed by hundreds of leading personalities in all walks of life in Serbia. Leading the list of signatories were Bishop Jovan of Niš, Bishop Nektarije of Zvornik and Tuzla, and Bishop Valerijan of Budimlje. Among those who refused to sign this call to treason were the author Isidora Sekulić, professors of Belgrade University Bogdan Popović and Nikola Vulić, the sculptor Sreten Stojanović, the writer Ivo Andrić, and Professor Miloš Djurić of the University of Belgrade, a Young Bosnian by persuasion. He happened to enter the auditorium of Kolarac University, where the appeal was being signed, and seeing what was afoot, he began sidling toward the exit. However, a composer and orchestra conductor spied him and publicly upbraided him, saying, "Don't run away. Miloš." The old professor replied in a loud voice in front of everyone, "It's easy for you, you play the bagpipe, but I teach ethics to my students."

The First Offensive

The offensive against liberated territory in western Serbia—known as the First Offensive—began on September 28, when the 342d German Division, newly arrived from France, forced the Sava River at Šabac. A stubborn battle followed, often frontal in character. The Partisans withdrew step by step, together with the fleeing people. After a month of continuous fighting, the 342d Division succeeded in reaching Valjevo, which the Partisans had kept surrounded for two months.

Draža Mihailović Attacks the Partisans

The development of the uprising provoked a reaction from the Yugoslav government in exile. Sensing that the armed people would want to establish their own form of government at the end of the war, King Petar and his government openly stated over Radio London, beginning at the end of October, that the time had not yet come to resist the occupiers. In the meantime Colonel Draža Mihailović at Ravna Gora had established wireless contact via British stations with the government in London, from which he received a message on October

28, 1941: "Except in case of dire necessity, do not provoke the enemy until the signal is given for joint effort."

Carried away by the popular uprising, some of Draža Mihailović's detachments in western Serbia participated against his will in operations against the Germans, frequently together with the Partisans. As Partisan Supreme HQ endeavored to establish contact with Draža Mihailović in order to coordinate joint operations, some local Partisan commanders visited him at Ravna Gora. Tito, the Partisans' commander, met Mihailović on September 19 in the village of Struganik, but the meeting was fruitless.

Desirous of preserving unity among the people, Supreme HQ continued to try to find a common language with Mihailović, sending new proposals for cooperation in the middle of October. On October 27, 1941, at another meeting in Mihailović's headquarters, an agreement was signed between the two commands concerning joint struggle against the occupiers, in which the Partisans agreed to give Mihailović rifles and ammunition from their stores.

In the meantime, a British intelligence officer, Duane Tyrrell Hudson, escorted by two Yugoslav army officers, had arrived over Partisan liberated territory at headquarters. Although he told Partisan Supreme HQ that he bore instructions from Britain to the effect that the Partisans and Chetniks should reconcile their differences, on November 2, 1941, while the main Partisan force was fighting the German divisions, Mihailović's Chetniks attacked Užice, the center of Partisan liberated territory. It was believed by some in the Supreme Headquarters that the British officer had persuaded Mihailović to launch a lightning attack designed to destroy Partisan forces in Serbia.

At the time, the British and Soviet governments exchanged views about the course of the uprising in Yugoslavia, especially after the government in exile in London had sent a request to the Soviet government to influence the Partisans to place themselves under the command of Draža Mihailović, as the leader of armed resistance in Yugoslavia.

During this period Partisan Supreme HQ had no regular radio connection with Moscow. A special radio station for contacting the Comintern, produced by Professor Pavle Savić in the Institute of Theoretical Physics in Belgrade, was destroyed during the bombing of the capital. Tito was therefore forced to send all his radiograms via courier to Zagreb, whence he also received replies. When Supreme HQ left for Užice, these contacts were rendered even more difficult by the fact that couriers had to make their way from liberated territory to towns controlled by the occupiers.

Contact with Moscow was therefore extremely slow. On November 11, 1941, the Free Yugoslavia radio station began broadcasting from Soviet territory; this was a great help to the liberation struggle in Yugoslavia.

Partisan units swiftly repulsed Chetnik attacks although the Chetniks in Milanovac had succeeded in capturing 350 Partisans in the first flush of battle.

Other Partisan units closed their encirclement around the headquarters of Draža Mihailović at Ravna Gora. Draža Mihailović and his men were not annihilated because Radio Moscow referred in a Serbo-Croatian language broadcast to Draža Mihailović as the leader of the resistance in Yugoslavia. Tito sent a protest about this to Moscow on November 25.

The Chetniks turned the 350 captured Partisans over to the Germans, and Mihailović himself met a representative of the 342d German Division at Divac on November 11. The Germans demanded the total capitulation of Draža Mihailović, their intelligence service having procured on October 27 the text of the agreement between Mihailović and Supreme HQ.

During this time German divisions were penetrating ever deeper into liberated territory, committing mass crimes against the population. In Kragujevac 7,000 citizens, including many youngsters, were shot on October 21 in retaliation for the uprising. Whole classes of students together with their teachers defied the German machine guns as they faced execution together. In her poem *Bloody Tale*, the poet Desanka Maksimović wrote:

> In the hilly Balkans
> In a peasant land
> A group of youths
> Died a martyred death
> On the day they made their stand.

In Kraljevo 6,000 persons were shot on October 18.

All these were measures of reprisal against the population and a warning not to assist the Partisans. The quisling units of Ljotić and Nedić advanced together with the Germans. All villages were searched and all progressives were executed or dispatched to concentration camps. It has been estimated that over 35,000 persons were put to death in western Serbia during the First Offensive.

The Heroism of the Užice Workers' Battalion at Kadinjača

Supported by tanks, German divisions entered the principal town on liberated territory, Užice, on November 29. The northern approach to the town was defended by the Užice Workers' Battalion. Having received no orders to withdraw, it fought on Kadinjača Mountain to the last man—240 workers from the Užice weapons factories and workshops in Užice. While withdrawing from Užice, Supreme HQ itself had been taken by surprise and many of its members had to fight to break through the German ranks. On Zlatibor Mountain, Germans executed about 150 wounded Partisans. Only the day before, Supreme HQ had ordered the release of all captured German soldiers.

The main force of the Partisans in western Serbia managed to withdraw

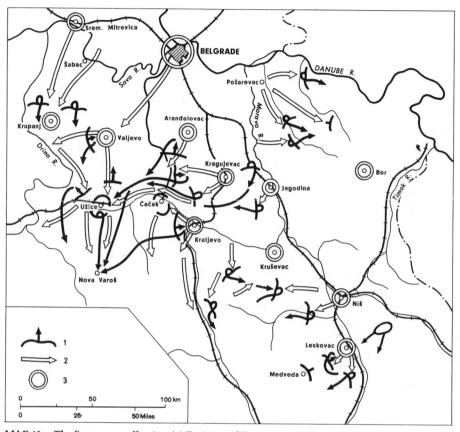

MAP 48.   The first enemy offensive. (1) Positions of Partisan units; (2) operations of the enemy; (3) the enemy garrisons.

to Bosnia and the Sanjak while about 3,000 men remained in western Serbia, where Germans and quislings began a hunt to track them down.

The First Offensive indicated that the Partisans were not yet experienced in frontal battles against technically superior enemy forces. They were not yet capable of attacking strongly fortified enemy strongholds in the cities. The attack on Plevlja, on December 1 and 2, 1941, was not successful and resulted in rather heavy losses: 203 Montenegrin Partisans were killed, and 269 wounded.

However, in the cities where people were strongly united, so-called "city guerrillas" were active. Attacks were undertaken against the occupiers' military installations, officers, and soldiers, and the leading quislings were liquidated. This often created a situation in which two authorities existed in individual cities. Ljubljana, Split, and Mostar were especially active in these struggles throughout the war, and Belgrade and Zagreb in 1941 and 1942.

The Ethics of the Revolution

Even in such a grueling war the Yugoslav revolution, despite all the horrors perpetrated against the population, began to acquire the elementary forms of a broad popular democracy. Within the Partisan units and in the rear as well, democratic-revolutionary trends were reflected in ethics of a new type, known as Partisan ethics, based on the tenet that there should be no difference between words and deeds. In most cases the fighting men chose their own commanders, and detachment conferences were genuine people's parliaments where leaders were freely criticized or tendered recognition. National liberation committees were established as the organs of a new revolutionary government with consistently democratic elements.

In this respect the revolution did not begin from scratch. As the peasants made up the overwhelming majority of the population, elements in their philosophical and emotional legacy were at work, issuing forth from the nation itself through its traditions of anti-imperialism in an area of major strategic significance. In 1941 the people's faith in the possibility of resisting the strongest enemy they had ever had was very much alive among the peasant masses. Interwoven with this faith was belief in their equality with other nations.

On the other hand, the negative aspects of the national mentality were also in play in 1941. Throughout centuries of struggle, always against far superior enemies, in towns where the occupiers' authority was strong, or among the peasant population living along the main arteries of communication, the factor of social mimicry was always present, as Jovan Cvijić had rightly observed in his main work, *The Balkan Peninsula*. In order to save their lives, not only individuals but whole groups of the native population were ready to come to terms with the aggressor. They took on his customs, clothing, language, and even religion. These elements in the social psychology of the masses were in evidence in 1941 as well; compounded by the main reasons mentioned earlier, like defense of class interests, they resulted in a situation giving wartime Yugoslavia (1941–1945) more quislings of various types than any other occupied country in Europe.

Application of the Principles of Equality among Peoples and the Role of Youth

What the Yugoslav revolution, one of the most democratic revolutions in twentieth-century Europe, accomplished in 1941 was the reflection of a clearly expressed desire for equality among nations, generations, and sexes.

The self-initiative of the masses was manifest on a nationwide scale among the various Yugoslav peoples. For the first time in the history of their land, Macedonian Partisans used their mother tongue and disseminated literature in the Macedonian language. And for the first time in the history of the Slovene people, they had their own army, part of the National Liberation Army of Yugoslavia. This was a factor acting mightily to mobilize the masses, especially the peasants.

In the history of Yugoslav lands, the youth had frequently played a very active role (the United Youth of the second half of the nineteenth century, the Young Bosnians and other revolutionary organizations of the youth at the beginning of the twentieth century), and this was also the case after the outbreak of the uprising in 1941. There is no doubt that a major role was played by the organization of young Communists, the Young Communist League, but it would not have succeeded so well in its operations had the youth not been imbued with a spontaneous desire to expel the occupiers and also to shape a new society in which young people would play a decisive role.

The collapse of the state in 1941, the gradual transformation of bourgeois political groups into pillars of support for the occupation authorities, or their degeneration into passivity, brought it home to the young people that the older generation was incapable of steering society toward a better future. The anticapitalist mood grew not only among the urban, working class, and student youth, but among young people in the villages. During the war the patriarchal structure of the peasant family showed a tendency to disintegrate, especially as reflected in the father's absolute power over his children. Young men began to feel freer; they joined the Partisans, often persuading their sisters, mothers, and other members of their families to follow suit. Among those interned in German camps were thousands of peasant families.

In the Partisan units, the young peasants came into contact with members of the YCL, who followed a new ethic and held new political ideas. In battle, in activities with their units, and in work in the field, the young people from the villages raised their ideological and cultural level with unprecedented speed.

Youngsters made up the main part of the Partisan army. Until 1943 they accounted for 75 percent of the total number of Partisans. According to official data, over 80,000 members of the YCL, meaning youngsters under the age of eighteen, lost their lives during the war. Of the 212 persons proclaimed national heroes by 1951, 90 percent were under twenty-three when they were killed, and over half, or 109 out of 212, were university and high school youth. From the Bijeljina high school alone (eastern Bosnia), 300 students laid down their lives on the battlefield.

A favorite Partisan song of 1941, "Hated Chains Are Being Forged for Us," speaks convincingly of the conscious sacrifices of the youth:

> To the end, fight we must
> Till the devil gets his due;
> Show the world that it can trust
> Youngsters under twenty-two.

At the First Youth Congress of Serbia, Josip Broz Tito described the young people's participation in the war:

> It will never be possible to say enough about the role the young people of Yugoslavia, and the youth of Serbia in the first place, played in this great struggle for the life and liberty of our peoples. In 1941, here on the streets of Belgrade, young boys and girls, virtually children, went to war in response to the call of the Communist Party. . . . When men go to war, when an army created by a state of adult men goes to war, they are doing their duty to their homeland, discharging the debt of every citizen and patriot. But when children of twelve, fifteen, and sixteen years of age go to fight voluntarily, without being mobilized, knowing that they are going to die, then that is more than discharging a debt to their homeland, that is superhuman heroism on the part of young people who sacrifice their own lives, although they have not yet even begun to live, so that future generations might be happy.

Participation by Women

In some parts of Yugoslavia in 1941, all youngsters over eighteen, of *both sexes*, had the right to vote in the elections for the national liberation committees, and for the Constituent Assembly in 1945 all young fighters regardless of age.

The egalitarian nature of the revolution was also expressed in the massive participation of women eager to win freedom through struggle. In some Partisan units, women accounted for as much as 15 percent of the fighting force. In organs of government in the field, women had the right to vote and to be elected. In some areas, as in the Bosnian March, for example, most of the committee members were women.

"I am proud of having followed in the footsteps of men; liberty will spring from my blood," cried a peasant woman, Krdžić by name, of the village of Andrijevica in Montenegro, when she was taken out to be shot for having given refuge to Partisans. These words express not only heroism under duress but a social and emotional attitude. The cry of the Montenegrin peasant woman, suppressed for centuries in her patriarchal and primitive environment, represents both the quintessence of an altruistic ethic and one of the basic elements in her nature—the desire for equality.

This human component of the revolution was mirrored also in the feeling on internationalism. When Ilya Ehrenburg wrote his article "Kill the Occupier, the Violator, Kill the German," Partisans responded with the slogan "Long live Telman, long live Stalin" in the liberated towns of western Serbia. (Ernst Thaelman was a German Communist leader in 1930, executed by Hitler during the war.) A German detachment called the Karl Liebknecht was formed in Slavonia. Germans captured during the liberation of western Serbia were not killed when the First Offensive began, but released in Jablanica near Zlatibor.

As in all revolutions, beginning with the English in the seventeenth century, revolutionary asceticism appeared in Yugoslavia in 1941. Also, as in all revolutions, it appeared spontaneously; the masses were destroying the old regime and wanted to live a life altogether different from that of the decadent ruling class. And the Communist Party stressed that there could be no double standard of morality, that the political activities of Party members could not be divorced from their personal lives, as only then could the confidence of the masses be won. A humane attitude and moral behavior were the components upon which the trust of the masses depended.

Nikola Vujović, a Communist peasant from the Nikšić area, expressed the responsibility of Communists in the following way: "We, Communists, must be the first to go hungry. All the fighting men look to us, do as we do. If we are the first to attack, we must be first in this, too."

The integrity of revolutionaries was best reflected in the fact that of the 12,000 prewar members of the Communist Party, 9,000 lost their lives in the war, in especially large numbers in 1941. It was this integrity that was responsible for the Communist Party's gaining the confidence of the people. By their behavior in 1941 and later, Communists demonstrated that the revolution was not being pursued for personal reasons but for the common good.

Casualties were particularly high among leading members of the Communist Party. Ten out of twenty-eight members of the Central Committee of the CPY were killed in the war.

The Instructions on the Duties of Partisans issued on October 11, 1941, by the Partisan Detachment for Kordun and Banija, stated: "Partisans, soldiers of the people, must not lie, steal or plunder. . . ." Other detachments had similar rules. Their implementation was assured in two ways: by the personal example of leaders and by disciplinary measures.

The staffs of Partisan detachments ate with their men in 1941. The first president of the Chief National Liberation Committee for Serbia was a Communist peasant, Dragojlo Dudić; he wrote about this in his diary before his death:

> Supper in the field at night. We had cooked food. I can't say what it was like because there was none left for me. In our detachment, leaders are last when it comes to the exercise of their rights, but first when it comes to duty, the reverse of the usual thing.

Alcohol was not drunk by Partisans in 1941. During the period of collaboration between Partisans and Chetniks in 1941, one of the big differences between them was that the Chetniks reeked of brandy.

According to an old peasant tradition, during wartime men did not sleep with women in deference to the mourning of the people; Partisans, even married couples, abstained totally from sexual intercourse.

In 1941 the high moral standards were the principal means for regulating relations within the Partisan units. The units were schools where young Partisans, especially those from peasant environments, were reeducated. In this human and moral transformation of people, an atmosphere of profound personal responsibility was created, making it extremely difficult to betray the ethical principles of the struggle.

In some units if, in spite of lengthy persuasion, a new Partisan violated these high standards, he was condemned to death. Dozens of cases were recorded of Partisans being executed for taking an apple or plum from a tree. The people often begged the authorities not to execute the culprit while the condemned man himself, standing in front of his own grave, asserted that he should be shot for sullying the Partisan banner.

At times this attitude was carried to extremes. Some of the older Communists thought that the Party should be a closed revolutionary group, as otherwise it ran the danger of dissolution under the pressure of peasant anarchy. The idea of messianism, of a chosen group to lead the people, was highly developed among such persons.

The fact that the Soviet Communist Party wielded a strong influence on the organization and working methods of the CPY was reflected in the uprising. In certain areas too much zeal was shown in stamping out what was known as factionalism. In the Župa area the Hercegovinian revolutionary, Čedo Kruševac, was shot as a Trotskyist although basically he merely wanted democracy in the Partisan detachments.

The Yugoslav uprising of 1941 is not simply a legend of the courage and endurance of the people crucified on the cross of a geopolitical junction, in which they came together of necessity, fought, and sacrificed their lives, hard in any case. The human component was extremely meaningful in the revolution. It succeeded only if and to the degree that it was capable of identifying itself with the national genius, expressed in the elementary self-initiative of the masses. The greatness of the Yugoslav revolution lay in its democracy, whereas the greatness of the Communists, the revolutionary leaders, lay only in the extent to which they grasped the fact that this national genius should not be stymied, that revolutionary self-initiative should not be obstructed, that the war should not be centralized to a measure greater than warranted by the given moral and spiritual frameworks.

The question arises as to the roots of this mass desire for social egalitarianism in the Yugoslav revolution. First of all, it was a spontaneous process, as in all other social revolutions of the nineteenth and twentieth centuries. In *The Peasant War in Germany* Engels showed how the masses, during times of the overthrow of tyrannical and oppressive systems, spontaneously create the ethical criteria of their revolution, criteria that are the exact opposite of those held by the ruling regime.

Principles of social equality are also injected subjectively. For instance, they were introduced into the Yugoslav revolution by the old Communists, especially former prisoners of the Mitrovica and Lepoglava penitentiaries who during their long years of confinement practiced the principles of egalitarianism inherited from other progressive movements.

Also not to be neglected is the fact that over a large part of insurgent territory, particularly in the region of Dinaric patriarchal culture, the national custom of working together was still alive as a vestige of cooperative life of the *zadruga*, the extended family. The *zadruga* had already disintegrated as an economic unit, but the institutions and customs of cooperative life, like the *moba*, *prelo*, *sijelo*, *pozajmica*, and *bačija*[1] were handed down from one generation to another in the life and work of the villages until 1941.

In the large hideaways on the mountain Kozara in 1942, as well as during the fourth offensive, internal organization was similar to that in people's uprisings in previous centuries.

In a way the National Liberation struggle revived certain forms of the national custom of pooling labor. The collective tradition with its long background merged with the Communist ideal. This was manifested in the youth work drives to cultivate lands abandoned during the war, and other forms of pooled, or associated, labor.

It should also be remembered that the tradition of the Dinaric warrior mentality still lived on in all its forms, particularly among the rebellious peasantry. In all tribal societies, warfare was a part of economic activity. This had been perceived with particular clarity by Vuk Karadžić, who described the so-called knightly economy of the Montenegrin and other tribes in the first half of the nineteenth century. On the barren heights life cannot be maintained without a leap over the fence into the barns of neighboring tribes to obtain food for one's immediate family and even distant relations. If one loses one's life in the process, there is always the halo of the martyr and hero as compensation. And if one comes back home alive with booty, again the heroic feat is celebrated and the family and clan has a full stomach. Elements of the knightly economy are found also in the concept of the Muslim holy war. If the warrior dies, he goes to *jenet* (paradise) where he is tended by *hurias* (maidens), and if he lives, then the "powers that be" endow him with spahilic or timar to enjoy.

All this was present, admittedly in specific form, in the minds of many of the rebelling peasants who rose to arms in 1941.

---

[1] *Moba* (bee), *prelo* (spinning bee), and *sijelo* (sitting) were bees for scouring wool, spinning wool, husking corn, pressing grapes, and other jobs well-suited for evening work. *Pozajmica* is a labor loan and *bačija* is a system of cooperative tending of livestock in summer pastures.

CHAPTER 46

The Uprising
in Crisis

The Formation of Proletarian Brigades

Early in 1942 the Partisans came to realize that final victory could not
be won by a series of lightninglike and massive uprisings such as those of the
summer of 1941. The view also came to prevail that the war would last much
longer than had ever been imagined when the Soviet Union entered the world-
wide conflict.

Yugoslav society continued to polarize. The upsurge of the liberation
struggle and the ever more appalling reign of terror perpetrated by the occupiers

created a dilemma for pro-Western bourgeois circles who had adhered to the view that they should bide their time to see how the war would develop on the world's main battlefields: should they make war on the occupier or fight with him against the liberation forces? The center soon melted away. Draža Mihailović's forces collaborated more and more openly with the occupiers against the Partisans.

In the outside world a conspiracy of silence surrounded the Partisan movement. Its only ties were with Moscow. In the meantime, the Great Powers were locked in a diplomatic struggle over the Yugoslav revolution. Powerful Western propaganda organizations ascribed all the Partisans' victories to Draža Mihailović. Moscow, too, changed its position gradually only after painful exchanges of views with the Partisan Supreme HQ. From the very beginning it had supported a war against the occupiers alone, an "anti-Fascist war" devoid of revolutionary elements. That is why it called for collaboration between the Partisans and the Chetniks. It was only from the middle of 1942 that Moscow began supplying the world with more accurate information about the state of affairs in Yugoslavia.

In the course of 1942 the National Liberation army acquired considerable battle experience and achieved a higher level of organization. The organs of the new government took on more permanent form, and political representative bodies of the National Liberation movement were created. As the army and government bodies became large-scale organizations, the original Partisan ethic of egalitarianism began to disappear.

The uprising continued to develop unevenly, not only because of enemy pressure but also and primarily because of wavering on the part of the peasant masses. Wartime conditions were nothing if not grueling. After the initial spontaneous explosion of revolt came a wave of decline, depression. Thus in 1942 the National Liberation movement responded to the waves of the vacillating peasant masses. After the initial successes of the insurgency in Montenegro, the uprising collapsed in the spring of 1942. The feeling of deflation also infected Hercegovina. A similar deflation took place in Slovenia although somewhat later, in the fall of 1942, and predominantly in the villages of the Bela Krajina area.

The Croatian peasantry in 1941 had lively recollections of the hard life it had led in prewar Yugoslavia; the peasants harbored illusions about betterment of their lot after the collapse of the former state, particularly as the leader of the Croatian Peasant party, Dr. Vlatko Maček, had asked the Croatian people to accept Pavelić's regime. However, their suspicions were aroused even more in 1942. Their attitude toward the Pavelić state and army grew passive. The Croatian Home Guard surrendered in large masses to the Partisans.

The lesson drawn by Supreme HQ from the wavering and scattering of the peasant masses during the fiercest enemy offensives was reflected in its forming the First Proletarian Brigade, under the command of Koča Popović, consisting of a firm proletarian nucleus of steeled, revolutionary workers, intellectuals, and peasants, in late December 1941. This unit was not bound to any particular territory but had the task of fighting where the going was hardest, where the peasant uprising showed signs of faltering, so as to set an example of true fighting spirit.

Early in 1942 Supreme HQ, together with the First Proletarian Brigade, arrived in eastern Bosnia, where the uprising was in crisis, for the Chetniks under Draža Mihailović had begun to operate in an organized fashion, to call upon the Serbian people to lay down their arms against the occupier, and to take revenge on Muslims and Croats for the crimes of the Ustashi against the Serbian people. At a consultation in Čevljanovići of insurgent leaders in Bosnia, a decision was taken for the First Proletarian Brigade, together with Bosnian Partisan units, to advance to the industrial area along the Bosna River and help mobilize the miners and workers for the Partisans. There were very few of them in Bosnia.

The Second Offensive

In the meantime the German Supreme Command had ordered in January 1942 the launching of the Second Offensive against the main Partisan operational group. The 342d German Division, accompanied by about 35,000 other German and Ustashi troops, crossed over into eastern Bosnia from Serbia.

By maneuvering in deep snow, Partisan units managed to evade the main enemy thrust. The First Proletarian Brigade conducted its long march over Igman Mountain, in a direction the enemy had not anticipated, passing very near the town of Sarajevo and advancing to liberated territory and the town of Kalinovik. The bitter cold left over 150 fighting men with severe cases of frostbite. German ski troops succeeded in taking by surprise only the Šumadija Battalion of the First Proletarian Brigade and sections of the Bosnian units at Pjenovac. The Partisans' automatic weapons stuck from the cold. Over a hundred men lost their lives, including the leader of the uprising in the Romanija area, Slaviša Vajner-Čiča. The commissar of the Šumadija Battalion, Draganče Pavlović, having been wounded in the thigh at the beginning of the attack, fired all his rounds of ammunition at the Germans, leaving only the last bullet for himself.

But the Partisan forces soon took the offensive. A broad liberated area was created in eastern Bosnia, the Sanjak, Hercegovina, and Montenegro. In the town of Foča on the Drina River, Supreme HQ and the Central Committee of the CPY remained over a hundred days. A people's government was established and the so-called Foča Decrees were issued, representing a step further in the development and consolidation of the new popular authority. They were applied,

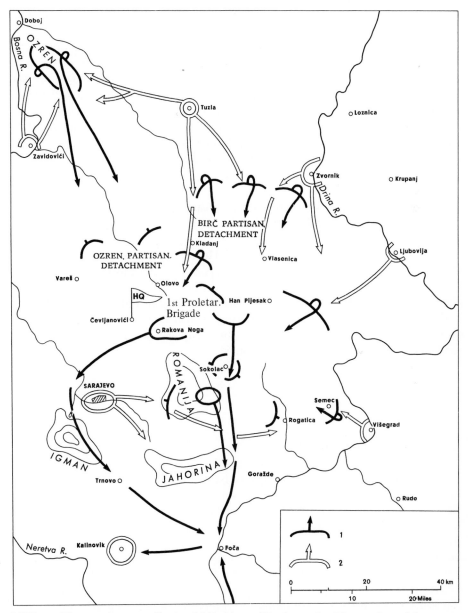

MAP 49.   The second enemy offensive. (1) Positions of Partisan units; (2) operations of the enemy.

however, not throughout the entire country but only in Bosnia, as being most suited to conditions there.

The German Supreme Command and the Italian Supreme Command launched in April 1942 the Third Offensive against the main body of Partisan operational troops. In this offensive Draža Mihailović's Chetniks fought against the Partisans together with the occupiers for the first time. Draža Mihailović himself, who had been promoted to the rank of general, minister of defense of the Royal army, and commander of all armed forces in Yugoslavia, had shifted to Montenegro. The Chetnik movement, having vegetated in Montenegro and Hercegovina up to the end of 1941, now surged forward.

The Problem of Vacillation by the Peasant Masses in the Uprising in Montenegro and Hercegovina

The peasants in Montenegro and Hercegovina were tired of the war; there was hardly any food to be had, and the poor peasants especially were forced to forage for it in the towns. The Italians and Chetniks skillfully turned the scarcity to their advantage. Many of the peasants who were not so badly off sided with the Partisans, who had concealed some wheat and were not so dependent on the towns. Peasants who hid "under the occupiers' skirts" in order to obtain food were the butt of malicious folk songs:

> For tin cans and corn bread
> They betrayed their very own.

Terror and Counterterror

The Italians and Chetniks instituted a reign of terror against all families and villages suspected of helping Partisans. This further weakened the will to fight. On the other hand, Chief Partisan HQ for Montenegro had taken the decision that any acts of mass terror against Partisan villages were to be answered by the same measures against villages where the Chetniks were influential. At the beginning of April 1942 fire was set to Ozrinići and all Chetnik families were banished to towns held by the Italians and Chetniks. Chief HQ for Montenegro informed Supreme HQ of these measures on April 11, 1942: "The people and the Partisans took these measures well but . . . there were unfortunately some Party members who wavered . . . we shall root out this wavering if necessary by sword and fire."

This severe policy had been pursued in Montenegro, except for the bigger

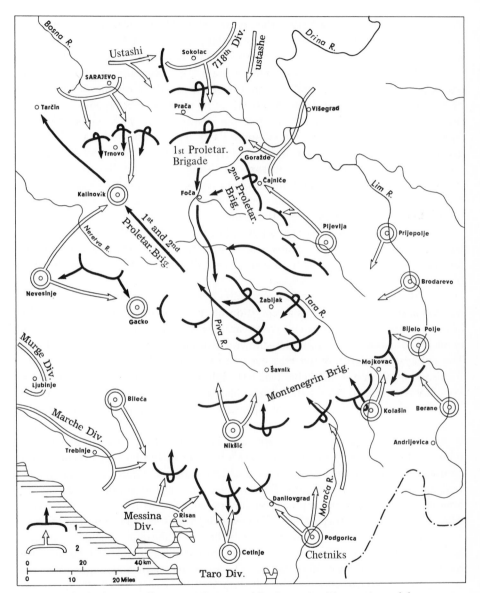

MAP 50.   The third enemy offensive. (1) Positions of Partisan units; (2) operations of the enemy.

part of Katunska Nahija under the influence of Veljko Mićunović, since the autumn of 1941. The Party organ *Naša Borba* printed in each issue lists of those killed for treason, ending with the words "To be continued."

In addition, dogmatism had appeared in Montenegro, Hercegovina, and some parts of Serbia. Stalin's concept of the stages of revolution was taken as a model, and the question was raised as to when the bourgeois-democratic revolution would evolve into a proletarian revolution in Yugoslavia. After the Partisan collapse in western Serbia, some Party leaders asserted that "the bourgeois-democratic stage is over and it is now necessary to go on to the stage of the proletarian revolution. All peasant Partisans should be disarmed and sent home." In some areas in Montenegro, as in Nedajno on the Piva River, a fairly well-off peasant was executed "as a future enemy, because he is a kulak," even though he had been helping the Partisans.

Attitudes such as these contributed to the decline of the uprising in Montenegro. This so-called sectarianism also infected eastern Hercegovina. During the war this province always followed in the footsteps of developments in Montenegro.

But the essential factor responsible for the temporary defeat in Montenegro and Hercegovina was a repetition of the same old story: the vacillation of the peasant masses in difficult war years. On May 21, 1942, Supreme HQ had to decide to withdraw Partisan detachments from Montenegro for the time being. The collapse in Hercegovina was even more sudden. Overnight only a single Partisan battalion out of twelve was left. Soldiers from the other battalions had gone home or joined the Chetniks. The insurgent leader in eastern Hercegovina, Miro Popara, a student and son of a peasant from Fatnica, in the Bileća District, was taken captive by his own Partisan peasants with whom he had fought side by side since the beginning of the uprising. They turned him over to the Italians, who executed him in Nevesinje. Popara's bearing in the face of execution was courageous. Among the peasant masses of Hercegovina, a cult developed around him, growing stronger with time. Their fashioning a legend out of Popara showed how conscience-stricken they were at having succumbed to the enemy's terroristic measures and betraying him. This was not the first case of its kind among the Hercegovinian peasants. In 1670 the bishop of Zahumlje, Vasilije Jovanović, had led the peasants of Popovo Polje in an insurrection against the Turks. After the entire area had been liberated, the Turks struck with a stronger force and set fire to one village after another. Bishop Vasilije was left virtually alone and barely escaped with his life from the very peasants he had led. He sought refuge in the wilderness of the Ostroške Grede, where he soon died. But the consciences of the Hercegovinian peasants gave them no peace; decades later a legend grew up about him, and Vasilije Jovanović was made a saint whom the peasants in Hercegovina worship above all others.

The Advance of Proletarian Brigades into the Bosnian March

In June 1942, after withdrawing from Foča, Supreme HQ formed the Fourth and Fifth Brigades of Montenegrin Partisans, the Third Brigade of Sanjak Partisans, and the Tenth of Hercegovinians. Then, together with the First and Second Brigades, it advanced into the Bosnian March, destroying the Mostar-Sarajevo railway in several places and capturing a number of towns along the way.

The Bosnian March was the stronghold of the uprising in Bosnia and Hercegovina. The Chetniks did not succeed in disrupting the movement there, and growing numbers of Muslims and Croats joined the Partisan units.

The Epic of Kozara

In May 1942 the units of that area liberated the town of Prijedor and the biggest iron ore mine in Yugoslavia, Ljubija. German troops, reinforced by Ustashi and Hungarian units, launched a big offensive against the liberated territory of Kozara Mountain, defended by the Second Krajina Detachment with 3,500 men. In July 1942 the enemy tightened his vise around the mountain; only half of the Partisans with 10,000 fleeing civilians were able to break through the encirclement. The Germans sent 70,000 people to concentration camps, of whom 25,000 died. Kozara was long barren of life.

The arrival of five brigades with Supreme HQ in the Bosnian March helped consolidate the uprising and establish firm ties with liberated territory in Croatia and Dalmatia.

One-fifth of Yugoslavia Liberated

The uprising continued to develop evenly in Slovenia; by early May 1942 a large area had been liberated in Dolenjska. In order to help those fighting in Štajerska, Chief HQ dispatched the Second Group of Detachments to northern Slovenia. It was their task first to advance across the Sava River, near Litija, into the Trbovlje mining basin, mobilize miners and workers for the Partisan detachments, and then spread the armed struggle throughout the entire territory of Štajerska. But the Second Group of Detachments failed. After withdrawing, it entered Reich territory a second time via Gorenjska, suffering heavy losses.

Joint operations by the Krajina and Croatian brigades liberated the town of Bihać and environs. At the time, Bihać was the largest town to fall into Partisan hands. This brought liberated territory up to over 50,000 square kilometers, one-fifth of Yugoslavia. A system of National Liberation committees was set up and elections were held. The Partisan army consolidated its organization, forming divisions and corps. These were tactical-operational units, highly mobile, conducting coordinated operations and attacking stronger enemy forces and even fortified towns and larger areas.

The Erosion of the Original Ethic

The type of discipline found in regular armies was introduced; this was considered necessary especially because the number of fighting men in the units was growing by leaps and bounds. Peasants, reeducated in the long fighting, brought to the Partisan army and new government organs not only their positive traditions but also their most negative features—avarice and nepotism. The new commanders sought growing privileges for themselves. The old government had been destroyed in the fighting, and on its foundations emerged a new revolutionary authority. But from the very first moment of its existence it was infected with the germ of the dilemma: would the soldier, the servant of the revolution, be transformed into the master of society? The Yugoslav revolution could not sidestep this process, which began to unfold on the basis of the most insignificant details. If the revolutionary is not on the alert, if he does not attend to these details immediately, they begin to corrode revolutionary ethics like a cancerous disease, innocuously and unnoticeably at first, only to erupt violently and jeopardize the existence of the revolutionary organism. And these "minor details" involved matters such as this: Would the revolutionary, because of his position, the power he wielded in the name of the revolution, have a greater right to the things around him, to food, to accommodation, to horses, than the other men around him fighting for the same objective?

Actually, the question that had to be solved was: Who decides on the way the surplus product is to be divided, what rights do those who produce the surplus product have in its distribution?

In the revolution the principal corrective was revolutionary public opinion, the self-initiative of the masses, the broadest possible democracy in the detachments and committees. The detachment conferences were an inviolable part of army life until the autumn of 1942, when the proletarian units were reinforced and their structure changed, altering the ratio of Party and YCL members, whose political and social consciousness lost some of its original firmness. These conferences continued to be held until the end of the war, but they were no longer the same; through them the commanders or Party organizations implemented measures they thought useful. Frequently it was impossible to criticize the staff, or such criticism was channeled in what was considered the proper direction.

Moscow's View of the Development of the Revolution in Yugoslavia

This modification in the original altruistic ethic of the Partisan units was caused also by transformations along these lines in the Soviet Union. For example, Soviet instructors had introduced into units of the Spanish Republican Army, and especially the International Brigades, great differences between staffs and soldiers, with privileges for the former, as well as strict discipline and abolition of the right of the troops to criticize their commanders. In the Red Army, during the revolution and in Lenin's time, a different spirit had prevailed, the principle of so-called egalitarianism, comradely relations; no difference existed between commanders and men in terms of food. Stalin changed all this, imposing his own ideas of discipline on the army on the basis of drill and subordination rather than ethics.

Yugoslavs who had fought in the Spanish war and arrived in Yugoslavia in 1941, via France and Germany, were extremely helpful in improving the military qualities of the fledgling Partisan detachments. But some of the Yugoslav commanders from the Spanish war brought Soviet concepts of discipline to Yugoslavia. On December 2, 1942, the staff of the Third Operational Zone had the following to say about the situation in the Third Partisan Detachment:

> The relation between the Partisans and commanders had been incorrect from the military point of view. There can be no egalitarianism in our army. The commanders must have complete authority. We do not hold anarchistic, petty bourgeois views about leaders. We recognize them, give them all the comfort possible, but demand full responsibility of them in directing the struggle.

This was totally at odds with the situation that had prevailed earlier in the Partisan detachments. Many authentic reports exist to show this. The secretary of the Party organization in the Bosnian March wrote to the instructor of the Central Committee of the CPY in Sarajevo on October 4, 1941:

> It is extremely disagreeable and throws a bad light on everything that life in HQ is not organized and regulated along lines of comradely mutual assistance. Food and clothing and other things are not divided up in a fair and comradely way. All of this provokes grumbling and dissatisfaction on the part of those who are neglected. . . . Owing to poor organization and unjust distribution, and the selfishness of certain responsible Partisans, even the wounded did not receive what they should. Consequently the complaints and protests of sick and wounded Partisan comrades are justified.

These "dangerous beginnings of bureaucracy" were often the subject of discussion in the Central Committee of the CPY of 1942. Similar manifestations were found all over Yugoslavia, even in Slovenia, where the influence of peasant anarchy was relatively insignificant; nonetheless the tendency existed, after the

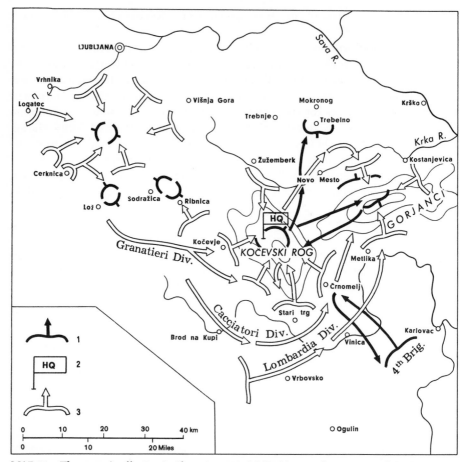

MAP 51. The enemy's offensive in Slovenia, 1942. (1) Positions and operations of Partisan units; (2) the General Headquarters of Slovenia; (3) positions and operations of the enemy.

initial successes of the uprising, to create a power above the revolution. In August 1942 Ivo-Lola Ribar received a letter from Edvard Kardelj saying:

> All the manifestations you refer to in connection with Hercegovina and Monte- negro have appeared among us in miniature as well. . . . There have even been individual cases of repugnant torture, rumors of which have spread among the people, casting a poor light on the character of the Partisan fighting man.

Kardelj said that after victories in fighting the Italians in May 1942, Partisan staffs began to behave in the following way:

> They have built themselves comfortable barracks in the woods, whole cities of them, installed electric lights, telephones, radios, typewriters, a large escort, and

women—often of suspect character. All of this has had a very harmful effect on the militant initiative of these staffs; they have become less mobile and frequently show signs of moral decadence.

At the close of the letter, Kardelj wrote that the Party had taken severe measures to deal with the situation:

> When I speak of "vojvode," don't think I am referring to outsiders. On the contrary, 80 percent of commanders, and all political commissars, are Party members. Furthermore, most of our commanders are workers by occupation. This and similar manifestations are therefore nothing that could not be removed with a minimum effort by our Party. All of it is caused by the dizzying effect of success. Some of the commanders and commissars simply say to themselves, "What can anyone do to us now that we have given the occupiers a sound thrashing?" Nonetheless, I feel that we shall remove these dangerous manifestations very quickly.

The strengthening of bureaucracy in individual parts of Yugoslavia began to weaken the powerful idea of equality of Yugoslav nations—a thought Tito had emphasized from the first. This erosion created the basis on which various expressions of nationalism and chauvinism could be revived. The Central Committee of the CPY was energetically and consistently opposed to such negative expressions. Because of this, the secretary of the Central Committee of the CP of Croatia, Andrija Hebrang, was removed from office, and in his place Vladimir Bakarić was nominated.

Global Policy or Misunderstanding of the Character of the Yugoslav Revolution?

In the course of 1942 the Soviet government gradually modified its attitude toward the development of the uprising in Yugoslavia. Although the Comintern let the Central Committee of the CPY know on several occasions that the Soviet government had to take account of global policy, that it could not undermine its good relations with Great Britain and the United States by accusing Draža Mihailović of treason or condemning the Yugoslav government in exile, the fact remains that the attitude of the Soviet government toward the young Yugoslav revolution depended upon Stalin's dogmatism and his suspicion of all revolutionary movements anywhere in the world. This was not therefore a matter of Moscow's lacking information about what was going on in Yugoslavia but rather of a specific policy, part of which was to "play on every card." In case Draža Milhailović won, this policy would secure Moscow certain positions in Yugoslavia.

It was only at the end of February 1942 that Supreme HQ reestablished direct radio communication with Moscow. Previously couriers had taken messages from liberated territory to Zagreb, where the Soviet intelligence service's radio station was situated.

All basic materials in abbreviated form about the advancement of the uprising were sent to Moscow from Foča, in eastern Bosnia, early in March 1942; on March 5 Moscow replied that "the impression is gained that circles close to the British and Yugoslav governments are to some extent justified in suspecting that the Partisan movement is acquiring a Communist character and is directed toward the sovietization of Yugoslavia." Moscow particularly resented the creation of proletarian brigades.

Tito and most of the members of the Central Committee of the CPY felt that the criticism was unjustified. In a radiogram sent on March 9, the Central Committee of the CPY dispatched a reply to Moscow to the effect that "erroneous conclusions have been drawn," that soviets were not being established in Yugoslavia but rather National Liberation committees, that detachments of the Volunteer Army were being formed parallel with the proletarian brigades.

Moscow proposed that Supreme HQ issue a proclamation to the enslaved peoples of Europe; this it agreed to do, but Moscow had a number of objections to the wording of the proclamation, among others, that the Central Committee of the CPY should not be mentioned as the organizer of Partisan detachments. On March 22, 1942, Moscow postponed publication of the proclamation on the plea that relations between the Soviet and Yugoslav governments would have to be clarified first.

In the meantime Supreme HQ asked the Soviet government to send planes with help for the Yugoslav Partisans, even if it were only token assistance. Moscow mentioned technical difficulties but intimated that help could be expected. Several weeks went by in the spring of 1942, but no help came. Obviously, the reason was the political reservations of the Soviet government.

Supreme HQ expressed its resentment at the fact that Soviet government information media were publicizing Draža Mihailović. Originally it was believed that Moscow's behavior was the result of scant information. On November 2, 1941, when the Partisans warded off Chetnik attacks, Tito stopped the encirclement of Draža Mihailović's headquarters upon hearing that, on that very day, Radio Moscow had referred to Mihailović as the leader of the resistance in Yugoslavia. Tito justified this action to his associates by invoking the need not to aggravate the Soviet Union's position in foreign policy, but he sent a radiogram to Moscow via Zagreb that the news about Mihailović was "a terrible stupidity."

Radio Moscow's attitude provoked disagreements in Yugoslavia. On December 20, 1941, the Provincial Committee of the Communist Party of Croatia for Dalmatia stopped dissemination of information about the treason of Draža Mihailović, issued by the Central Committee of the CPY, because Radio Moscow had "been broadcasting for several days the news that large-scale fighting against the occupiers was in progress under the leadership of Draža Mihailović."

Even the Free Yugoslavia radio station, which had begun operation in November 1941, broadcast the first reports about the conflict between the Partisans and Chetniks only in April 1942. But even for this the editors of the radio station's broadcasts, Yugoslav revolutionaries living in the U.S.S.R., headed by Veljko Vlahović, were reproached by the Soviet Foreign Ministry and asked to submit all their news reports for censorship.

The Central Committee of the CPY sent Moscow a protest asking why the Free Yugoslavia radio station had said nothing about Partisan leaders and Supreme HQ on the basis of data sent to Moscow earlier.

In the spring of 1942 many Communist parties pursued Moscow's line about the fighting in Yugoslavia. Through its organ *L'Humanité*, the Communist Party of France referred to Draža Mihailović as the leader of the resistance in Yugoslavia. In the summer of 1942 leaders of the Communist Party of the United States of America collected contributions for Mihailović, which were presented with ceremonies to King Petar during his visit to the United States.

Even as far back as 1941 Yugoslavs working in Moscow had been hearing Comintern opinions describing as pure adventurism the CPY's policy of developing a mass popular uprising. Soviet diplomacy adopted this view and, on a number of occasions in 1942 and 1943, Soviet diplomatic representatives told Royal Yugoslav government ministers in confidence that the "Yugoslav Partisans were Trotskyists and that Stalin did not trust them."

Opinions along these lines also reached Draža Mihailović from London, and from Moscow through Dragiša Vasić. In March 1942 Draža Mihailović's headquarters issued an official communiqué stating that although the Soviet government had on several occasions ordered the Partisans to place themselves under the command of Draža Mihailović, the leadership of the CPY was in the hands of Jews and refused to bow to Stalin's will

> as, ideologically, they are not with Stalin and therefore do not obey his instructions to place themselves under Mihailović's command. . . . As anarchists, and preaching the principle "kill everyone who is honest, God-fearing, and honorable" and anyone who gets in their way, they belong to Trotsky, whom Stalin had had killed by a hammer blow on the head in Mexico for such ideas.

Moscow modified its attitude toward Draža Mihailović as the ratio of forces in Yugoslavia changed. In the middle of 1942, when it became increasingly clear that the Partisan movement was developing successfully, the Soviet government took steps to criticize Draža Mihailović through the exiled Yugoslav government in London. At the same time, however, it offered to send a military mission to his headquarters and to extend assistance to him, although it had withheld assistance to the Partisans under the pretext of "technical difficulties."

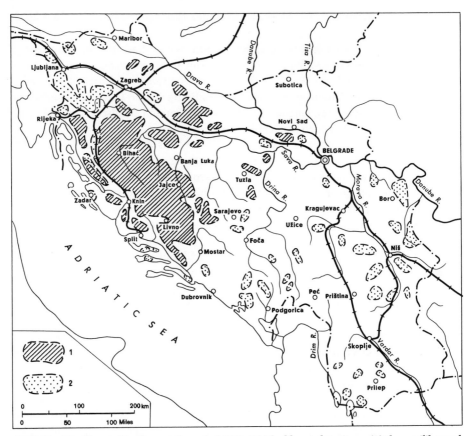

MAP 52.   The liberated territory at the end of 1942. (1) The liberated territory; (2) the semiliberated
territory.

Soviet Union Against Formation of the Provisional Government of the New Yugoslavia

In the autumn of 1942 the Central Committee of the CPY concluded that for the further successful development of the struggle in Yugoslavia, a popular government would have to be formed. It had held this view from the very first day of the uprising and Moscow had been informed of it on August 21, 1941, when it was told "that a kind of popular central government would probably be formed."

Once again, on November 12, the Central Committee of the CPY informed Moscow of preparations to establish a provisional popular government, but a quick reply came from Moscow: "At this stage, do not raise the question of abolishing the monarchy. Do not raise the slogan of a republic." The directive went on to say that the new committee should not oppose the Yugoslav government in London, as the question of the type of regime in Yugoslavia would be solved after the defeat of the Italian-German coalition and after the liberation of the country from the occupiers.

The Central Committee of the CPY therefore had to desist from its intention of establishing a political body invested with the rights of a new government at the constituent assembly of the Anti-Fascist Council for the National Liberation of Yugoslavia held in Bihać on November 26, 1942; this was attended by fifty-four of seventy-eight elected representatives of the people. On November 29, 1942, Tito sent a radiogram to Moscow stating his acceptance of the suggestion that a new government should not be formed and that the republic should not be proclaimed, but stated that the new Executive Committee of the AFCNLY would "nevertheless have to concern itself with all questions relevant to the state and the front, in which it would have the assistance of the National Liberation committees which have been set up in virtually all parts of liberated and unliberated territory. There are no organs of government in the country except these committees. . . ."

Even in 1942 it was obvious that Moscow and the Yugoslav Communists differed in their views on the development of the revolution in Yugoslavia. Essentially, Moscow did not want it to develop beyond the framework of an anti-Fascist war, whereas the successful advancement of the revolution required the clearest possible establishment of its final objectives, the nature of the future government, and particularly the relation between the nationalities of Yugoslavia: Would it be the old centralism, or a federation, monarchy, or republic?

CHAPTER 47

The Neretva and Sutjeska: Decisive Battles of the Revolution

Hitler's Decision to Destroy All Non-Axis Armed Forces in Yugoslavia

The upsurge of the liberation struggle in Yugoslavia toward the end of 1942 alarmed Hitler. In October he held a meeting in Vinnitsa in the Ukraine, the location of his Chief Headquarters, with the head of the Independent State of Croatia, Ante Pavelić, and the commander of the Twelfth German Army, General Alexander von Löhr.

Hitler was particularly concerned over the situation in the Independent State of Croatia. In a long monologue at Vinnitsa, he stressed that "the difficult conditions in the Croatian state could be repaired essentially if all armed forces were destroyed in that territory, and in the territory occupied by the Italians, unless those armed forces are regular Croatian or Italian units." Hitler further stated that the Independent State of Croatia had not discharged its role either as a supplier of raw materials for Germany or as a source of manpower for the German wartime economy and of troops for the eastern front.

Hitler was convinced that energetic military action could destroy the Partisan forces in the Independent State of Croatia, that the situation would then be corrected, and that German troops would be relieved for use on other fronts.

Developments along the eastern front and in North Africa confirmed the validity of Hitler's assessment of the Balkan theater of war. At Stalingrad the German armies were already encircled, and in Africa Rommel had begun to withdraw after the battle of El Alamein. Allied troop landings in North Africa led Hitler to conclude that the Balkan situation would have to be cleared up as soon as possible, as there was a danger of the Allies' launching an invasion on the Adriatic coast. If the Partisan forces were not destroyed, the German army would have them at its rear during an Allied attack on the Adriatic and its possibilities for maneuvering would be seriously curtailed.

The decision to open an offensive against Partisan forces in the western part of Yugoslavia was taken at a meeting in Hitler's Chief Headquarters, in eastern Prussia, on December 19 and 20, 1942. Invited to the meeting were the foreign ministers of Germany and Italy, von Ribbentrop and Ciano, and the chief of the Italian Supreme Command, Cavallero. Hitler said that "the Serbian conspirators must be destroyed" and that "the most ruthless methods would have to be used." At the end of November 1942 Hitler had issued orders regarding "procedures during battle with bandits" through which he wished to relieve his troops of any responsibility whatsoever during offensives in liberated areas behind his lines in the U.S.S.R. and Yugoslavia. In his orders Hitler authorized German soldiers to commit any crimes they wished, mercilessly and unrestrictedly, against the population of the liberated areas, regardless of the tenets of international law. At a meeting in Rastenburg, Keitel asserted that fire could be set to any village harboring Partisans.

Expecting the Allies to land in the Balkans, Hitler issued a special order, No. 47, relating to the command and defense of the southeast area. The Southeast Command was renamed the Supreme Command of Army Group E, and the chief of staff, General von Löhr, was made personally responsible to Hitler.

Differences with the Italians over Disarming Draža Mihailović's Chetniks

The Italians complied with Hitler's demand that they participate in this offensive although at the meeting of December 18 and 19, 1942, they had not approved of his insistence that the Chetniks be disarmed as well as the Partisans.

Hitler was certain that the Chetniks, in case of an Allied invasion, would turn their backs on the Axis powers. The Italians considered the Chetniks a pillar of support in the struggle against the Partisans and therefore not to be disarmed.

How exasperated Hitler was with the situation in Yugoslavia is evident from a letter he wrote to Mussolini on February 13, 1943:

> The range and extent of Tito's rebel organizations is a cause for anxiety and concern. We hardly have enough time to suppress the uprising if we wish to avoid the danger of an attack on our rear in case of an Anglo-American landing in the Balkan Peninsula. . . . If events develop as described above, during the Allied landing we shall have a situation in which the German divisions will be forced to deal with the Partisan bands rather than being available as effective defense troops for fighting the invasion armies.

Hitler also needed Bulgaria's help in the Fourth and Fifth Offensives. On January 5, 1943, he received the Bulgarian defense minister and told him that there was a weak spot in the fortress that defended Europe, and that was Partisan territory in Yugoslavia. He was therefore grateful to the Bulgarian government for agreeing to expand the Bulgarian occupation zone in Serbia so that the German Seventh SS Division, Prinz Eugen, might be able to take part in the offensive against the Partisans in eastern Bosnia. Hitler further said that the offensive would begin before spring and that the mop-up operation would soon be over.

Later, however, the German Command asked Sofia for even bigger favors. Two Bulgarian regiments, the Sixty-first and Sixty-second, took direct part in the battles of the Fifth Offensive, with the Bulgarian defense minister's consent, in early May 1943.

On December 29 General von Löhr issued a directive for the launching of the offensive. On January 3, 1943, he went to Rome to synchronize the course of operations with Italian commanders. Again, disagreement broke out over the question of disarming the Chetniks. Mussolini agreed with his commanders. It was decided to divide the offensive into three stages, called Weiss I and II and Schwarz. The first phase of the offensive, Weiss I, was worked out by General von Löhr and Commander Roatta at a meeting in Zagreb.

According to plan, Operation Weiss I was designed to encircle and destroy the Partisan army in Kordun, Banija, and the Bosnian March. The Seventh SS Division would advance from Karlovac and the 717th from Sanski Most and in two days' time should cut liberated territory in two and meet at Vrtoč. Operation Weiss II would destroy Partisan units that had succeeded in breaking out of the encirclement. Weiss I would be carried out with four German divisions, parts of three Italian divisions, about 10,000 Croatian Home Guards and Ustashi, and 2,000 Chetniks.

The German troops were under the command of General Lütters, who stated in his orders of the day:

The general war situation requires the pacification of the Croatia area. Expansion of the present focus northward could severely jeopardize the main railway line up to the point of disrupting supplies for the entire Balkans and Crete, and could therefore cause the collapse of the entire position of the Axis in the Balkans.

The offensive, scheduled to begin on January 15, was postponed until January 20 because the troops could not muster as planned, owing to atmospheric conditions.

Hitler wanted to be kept informed of all preparations and also asked General von Löhr to report twice a day on the course of the offensive.

At the end of November, Supreme HQ got wind of the possibility of an enemy offensive. Under its direct command the First Proletarian Division and the Third Division liberated large sections of central Bosnia and posed a serious threat to Banja Luka. The Second Proletarian Division smashed the Chetniks between Knin and Grahovo, liberated Livanjsko and Duvanjkso Polje, and joined forces with Dalmatian units.

The German offensive encountered fierce resistance. True, Bihać fell on January 29, but the Seventh SS Division and the 717th Division failed to meet as planned, two days after the launching of the offensive; they joined forces only after eighteen days. The enemy did not succeed in encircling the main operational force under the direct command of Supreme HQ.

On January 27 Supreme HQ decided on a counteroffensive in the direction of Montenegro and Serbia. A meeting of Supreme HQ was held in Drvar to work out the details for the advance of the Operational Group toward the Neretva River and Montenegro. On February 8 in Duvno, Tito informed the commanders of the First, Second, and Third Divisions of the plan for the counteroffensive.

The Problem of Rescuing Wounded Partisans

These operational plans depended on two factors. There were over 3,500 seriously wounded men in liberated territory. Supreme HQ faced the problem of saving their lives. In the first phase of the offensive, German units had surrounded the area of Grmeč in the hope of destroying the main Partisan force and the wounded Partisans. Consequently Supreme HQ could not leave the wounded anywhere in liberated territory. In Bosnia the Partisans had not yet acquired the same experience in coping with their wounded as the Slovenes, who had established well-camouflaged hospitals in inaccessible parts of Slovenia; in most cases the enemy never discovered them.

Care for wounded comrades was one of the basic premises of Partisan ethics. If a soldier fell wounded, several others would risk their lives to remove him from the battlefield, often being wounded themselves in following the Partisan principle that a wounded Partisan must not fall into enemy hands. This attitude toward the wounded was one of the sources of high Partisan morale.

Supreme HQ decided that the Main Operational Group should take the wounded with it. Although the winter was bitterly cold in western Bosnia, a long march of several hundred kilometers was undertaken through barren and mountainous territory without communications. The need to save the 3,500 wounded Partisans also decided the nature of the operation. The battle was fought to save them, among other things. The pace of the advance into the enemy rear and the execution of operations were subordinated to the necessity of transporting the wounded.

The operation would never have succeeded without the close ties between the Partisan army and the people in the liberated territory. During the Fourth and Fifth Offensives it was more than tangibly demonstrated that the unarmed people were the basic factor in the Partisan victory. It was they who kept the army supplied. It was they who provided reinforcements. The villages gave the wounded means of transportation and fed them. Frequently the people destroyed communications and hampered the enemy advance in various ways. In the Fourth and Fifth Offensives they performed tasks that various branches would have discharged in a regular army.

Consequently the German Command bore down hard on the civilian population to destroy the base on which the Partisan army rested. In the first phase of the Fourth Offensive, German units capturing Grmeč surrounded 15,000 older peasant men and women and children. On January 12 General Lütters had issued orders to the German army to hang or shoot anyone caught helping the Partisans. On January 18 General von Löhr stated that he "must establish peace, even if it be the peace of the grave." At Grmeč German troops carried out these orders, killing 3,370 persons. Losses from starvation and exposure were also high. It has been estimated that two-thirds of the population of Grmeč lost their lives.

The people moved along with the Partisan army, fleeing from the enemy. The estimate is that 40,000 women, children, and elderly men from Kordun, Banija, Lika, and the Bosnian March withdrew southward. The Partisan army and authorities did everything they could to accommodate the fleeing people and provide them with basic necessities. Enemy airplanes killed a large number.

The Partisan Counterattack and the Battle at the Neretva River

The Partisan counteroffensive began on February 9, taking the German and Italian Commands by surprise. The Third Division broke through Italian fortifications at Prozor and captured the town. Continuing the advance along the Rama Valley, it also liberated Ostrožac. The First Division arrived at Ivan Sedlo while the Second, together with the Dalmatian Partisans, liberated Imotski and Posušje, advancing to the valley of the Neretva and taking Jablanica and Drežnica.

At the time, Partisan units were hardly aware of the extent of the damage they had caused the occupiers. For instance, they cut off the bauxite mines situated between Imotski and Široki Brijeg, from which Hitler obtained 10 percent of the Reich's requirements of bauxite, tremendously important for the German war industry.

Partisan divisions advanced to the Neretva River along a front 80 kilometers wide, smashed the Italian Murge Division and captured vast quantities of war matériel and food.

The Italian Command, alarmed by the Partisan advance, asked the German Command to change the course of the Fourth Offensive and to start Operation Weiss II immediately, not in the direction of Livanjsko Polje but the Neretva Valley.

Hitler immediately dispatched General Warlimont, deputy chief of the operational staff of the German Land Army, together with Hermann Göring, to Rome to coordinate operations against the Partisans. The Germans were particularly disturbed by the "new situation created by the advance of Tito's forces in the direction of the bauxite area near Mostar." It was decided to start the Mostar Operation in the Neretva Valley and to continue the Weiss II Operation. But as fighting developed along the approaches to the Neretva, the Germans and Italians had to concentrate the main part of their forces to do battle with the Main Operational Group of the Partisans. On Šator Mountain, a section of the German force nevertheless succeeded in surrounding some units of the First Bosnian Corps, a large number of refugees, and wounded. The army and most of the people broke through, but the Germans managed to capture several hundred wounded, every one of whom they killed.

Were it not for the wounded (whose number was increasing steadily) being carried along toward the Neretva, the Partisan operational group would have had no difficulty in crossing that river. But the wounded had to be saved and the transport line moved slowly. In the meantime enemy forces had surrounded all Partisan units in the Neretva Valley and surrounding approaches, hampering the maneuverability of the Main Operational Group. Fighting began now to save not only the wounded but the Operational Group itself, almost 20,000 of the staunchest fighting men in the whole National Liberation army.

Did the Chetniks Fight Side by Side with the Germans and Italians with the Approval of the British Government?

Roughly 20,000 of Draža Mihailović's Chetniks participated in the Neretva operation along with the German, Italian, and Ustashi forces. This provoked a bitter reaction among the Partisan units, especially after documents.

were found on some captured Chetnik officers showing that the Royal Yugoslav government in London had given Draža Mihailović's units permission to participate in operations against the Partisans together with the Germans, Italians, and Ustashi. Their astonishment was even greater when Radio London, in its Serbo-Croatian-language broadcasts, transmitted orders regarding collaboration with the enemy—in code, of course, but the Partisans had already broken the code, revealed in captured documents.

After the capture of Draža Mihailović and his archives, it was concluded on the basis of documents that the Chetniks collaborated in this operation with the occupiers with the approval and knowledge of the Royal Yugoslav government and of certain responsible British circles as well. Draža Mihailović directed the entire operation through his deputy, Major Zarija Ostojić. The British liaison officer at Mihailović's headquarters, Colonel S. W. Bailey, moved with Ostojić's headquarters in the battlefield at the Neretva. Bailey advised that all forces should be used to "destroy communism." There is also evidence, available to the Partisans even during the fighting, that British planes dropped ammunition and light weapons to the Chetnik units.

The Chetniks, the Principal Threat to Development of the Revolution

At the same time, Supreme HQ had information that preparations were being made for an Allied landing on the Adriatic coast. This aroused suspicions that the Chetnik units had a special role to play, that is, their their purpose was, with the help of Allied weapons, to assure the retention of the old social order together with the monarchy in Yugoslavia. Also, the participation of Chetnik units in the Battle of the Neretva in the company of the occupiers awakened suspicions that a broad coalition had been formed in World War II—of Germans and Chetniks, and the latter's patrons in London—for the purpose of destroying the revolutionary nucleus personified by the Main Operational Group.

In March 1943 the conviction grew in Partisan ranks that the Chetniks would be the principal factor in the forthcoming landing of the Allies in Yugoslavia, bent on preserving the capitalist order, the centralistic system, and the monarchy. Supreme HQ therefore considered them the *principal threat* to the results achieved in the National Liberation struggle. Orders issued by Supreme HQ on March 30, 1943, state:

> As Draža Mihailović has mobilized all his forces in Montenegro, Hercegovina, Lika, and eastern Bosnia and concluded, in December, an agreement with the Italians, Germans, and Ustashi for a joint major offensive against us which began in January this year, we have resolved to use all our forces to smash and de~*~ · this treacherous band, which represents the greatest threat not only to th tional Liberation struggle but also to the future. . . .

Uglješa Danilović recorded in his diary on April 1, 1943, the details of a talk with Tito on that same day about the Chetnik danger:

> The Yugoslav government in London might attempt to take advantage of the situation to gather the fruits of our struggle, especially if the Allies make a landing in the Balkans.

A former officer in the Yugoslav army, Nedeljko Plećaš, claims in his memoirs (published in Chicago) that British intelligence had acquired German plans for the Fourth Offensive and that agreement had been given for Mihailović's Chetniks to participate. In British headquarters in the Middle East, the operation had been given the name *Accommodation;* officers Jovo Trbojević and Nedeljko Plećaš took a special course in Cairo connected with this undertaking and were parachuted to Mihailović's headquarters. Before they left for Yugoslavia, Trbojević and Plećaš were told by British officers of Allied plans to land in the Balkans and to put before the Soviet Union a fait accompli by "destroying Communist groups by spring." Plećaš claims Colonel Bailey brought Mihailović a message to the effect that the "Chetniks should liquidate the Partisans" and showed him a copy of German operational plans for the Fourth Offensive. According to Plećaš, Bailey informed Mihailović that the "destruction of the Partisans would be useful for both belligerent sides," meaning the British and the Germans.

At the beginning of March 1943, during the negotiations about the exchange of prisoners between the Partisan Supreme HQ and the Command of the German troops, the Partisan representatives did not hide their feelings toward the Chetniks and their protectors in London. There exist several German documents about these negotiations and the views of the Partisan representatives, which were later rejected by the highest German authorities.

Supreme HQ regularly informed the Soviet government through the Comintern of the Chetniks' collaboration with the Germans. In a radiogram of February 25, 1943, Supreme HQ told the Comintern that Mihailović was attacking the Partisans at the Neretva together with the Germans and Italians.

Again in March 1943, during the Battle of the Neretva, Supreme HQ asked the Soviet Union for help, albeit symbolic, but none came. In the meantime Supreme HQ had decided to take all possible measures to foil the plot between the Chetniks and those who helped them in London. Moscow did not approve the measures, and a rather sharp exchange of radiograms followed between Supreme HQ and the Comintern. The Comintern sent the following word:

> You must not for an instant doubt that, if there were the least possibility of giving you any material help in your wonderful, heroic struggle, we should long ago have done so.
> The Soviet people, together with its leaders, is entirely on your side, full

of enthusiasm and profound fraternal sympathy for the National Liberation army.

Josif Vissarionovich [Stalin] and myself have many times discussed ways and means of helping you. Unfortunately, hitherto we have not been able to on account of insurmountable technical difficulties (for planes). . . .

The moment it is possible, we shall do all we can.

Can you doubt this?

Try to understand the present situation and explain it all to your comrades-in-arms. Do not lose heart, but gather all your forces to bear the present exceptionally hard trials. You are doing a great thing which our Soviet land and all freedom-loving peoples will never forget.

With fraternal greetings to yourself, and best wishes to all the comrades in their heroic fight against the accursed enemy.

At the time, the contents of the radiogram were not known to the rank and file, who were extremely hopeful in spite of their own difficulties of being able to relieve the situation at the eastern front. The diary of Lt. Col. Vladimir Dedijer carries the following entry on March 9, 1943, the fateful day in the breakthrough at the Neretva:

We are approaching the turning point: will the Neretva be crossed or not? The enemy has sensed our maneuver. He is furious at our having outwitted him. He thought we were headed for Bugojno and now he wants to catch up with us. He is attacking fiercely along the whole northern front. . . . But the planes are the worst. They begin at daybreak and don't stop until nightfall. The bombers swoop almost to the ground, machine-gunning every stone, and have dropped a new load of the biggest bombs on Prozor. This has been the worst day.

The village of Duge with over 400 wounded has also been bombed. The village was damaged considerably but only one comrade was hurt. The Germans have paid particular attention to the Prozor-Jablanica road. All day long they have bombed Crna Ćuprija, the bridge across the Rama at Gračanica, but they have not put it out of commission. They bombed the curves in the road and whole cliffs of rock tumbled down, but still our drivers are transporting the wounded. The Dorniers 17 pursued the lorries, bombing and strafing, but not a single one was hit. Our courier, Mića, neatly puts it this way:

"Every bomb that falls on us is one less for Russia. Victory will come soon. And if we had surrendered to Hitler, there would be plenty of us at the eastern Front artd half a million in German factories. And they would have stripped us clean. . . . We would be eternal slaves. . . ."

The Partisans forced the Neretva in the night of March 6–7. A group of Dalmatians crawled on all fours along the wreckage of the bridge over the Jablanica, carrying hand grenades in their teeth to destroy the Chetnik blockhouse. Later three Dalmatian and three Serbian battalions widened the bridgehead. On March 8, the Second Proletarian Division kept the Germans back north of the Neretva.

And so the Neretva was crossed. It is true that all heavy weapons had to be jettisoned, but all the wounded were saved.

The German commander, General von Löhr, was forced to state:

> The Partisans succeeded in crossing the Neretva and in withdrawing down to the last man to the northern part of Montenegro. They broke through the section of the front held by the Italians and Chetniks. There is no booty or captured. Not a single wounded Partisan, not even a dead one has been found although, judging from our own bloody losses, the Partisans must have suffered even greater casualties.

As noted by Göring's representative in Serbia, H. Neubacher, Hitler had declared even before the breakthrough at the Neretva:

> Again they are reporting the encirclement of six of Tito's divisions. But I already know the outcome: in a few days there will be only three, then one, and when we finally close the circle, we'll find only a few Italians with frostbitten feet and some sick donkeys.

The Ordeal of the Wounded

While the Partisan units advanced rapidly toward Hercegovina and Montenegro, liberating Kalinovik and Nevesinje, the wounded remained in the upper reaches of the Neretva. Even while making for the Neretva, the long columns of refugees and wounded had no way of keeping clean, with the result that an epidemic of spotted typhus broke out, infecting over 1,000 fighting men. So it happened that the Central Hospital with 4,000 wounded and typhus cases found itself at Glavatičevo. Not only did it lack basic medicines and quarters for accommodating the sick and wounded, but the epidemic raged on, spreading to a large number of the medical personnel. Furthermore, there was no food, making the situation virtually hopeless. The army and people had never experienced a more severe ordeal since the calvary of Albania. The wounded and sick burrowed in the newly sown fields for barley and oat seeds to assuage their hunger.

The Main Operational Group developed offensive operations, drawing ever closer to the boundary of northern Albania and threatening German communications in the Vardar Valley via Kosovo. At the same time, the activities of Partisan forces in other parts of Yugoslavia also were gaining momentum. Croatian units restored territory lost in the Fourth Offensive and surrounded Gospić. They stepped up attacks on the Belgrade-Zagreb railway line while the Thirteenth Proletarian Brigade stormed the airport and Home Guard Glider school at Sveta Nedelja.

Slovene and Croatian brigades launched an offensive on the Zagreb-Ljubljana railway line, attracting the forces of four Italian divisions and of

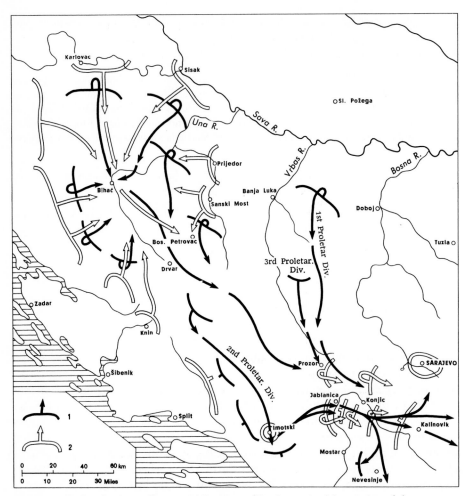

MAP 53.   The fourth enemy offensive. (1) Positions of Partisan units; (2) operation of the enemy.

one German regiment. At Jelenov Žleb a considerable enemy force was routed.

In Serbia (Toplica–Crna Trava), Macedonia, and Kosovo, the uprising spread. Delegates of the Central Committee of the CPY established close contact with the leadership of the Central Committee of the Communist Party of Albania, where the National Liberation struggle was growing rapidly.

Chetnik Massacre of Muslims and Croats

Even in 1941 Mihailović's Chetniks had had special "flying brigades" and "black threesomes" for the slaughter of supporters of the National Liberation struggle and Muslims. Together with the Yugoslav government, they succeeded in getting Radio London to send messages, before the Serbo-Croatian-language program began, stipulating who was to be branded with the letter Z, that is, singled out for liquidation.

In January 1943, in the district of Prijepolje, Mihailović's Chetniks set fire to more than thirty Muslim villages, killing over 1,500 people. In Foča and its environs they murdered several thousand Muslims. These crimes continued throughout the war. In the district of Ustikolina, they killed about 2,000 Muslims early in August 1943, and in the autumn of that year another 2,000 persons, mostly Croats, in the vicinity of Prozor.

Encirclement in Depth in Preparation for the Fifth Offensive

Battalions of the Fourth and Fifth Montenegrin Brigades advanced almost to the Albanian border. On May 14, at Bioče, they smashed strong Chetnik forces and wiped out the 383d Italian Regiment. Other battalions of those brigades, together with the Second Proletarian, had previously routed strong Italian units at Javorak, causing 1,000 casualties.

On March 30, 1943, Hitler himself decided to open the third phase of the operations, called Schwarz, against the insurgent forces in western Yugoslavia. The situation in North Africa worsened for the Axis, and there was a real possibility that the Allied forces would land along the Adriatic coast. Hitler was further worried by the direction in which the Partisan Main Operational Group was attacking. German commanders in the Balkans reported that these Partisan formations would move either along the Morava-Vardar Valley or into northern Albania.

Hitler was determined to disarm the Chetniks in western Yugoslavia in spite of the fact that the Italian Command held a different opinion. He realized that the Chetniks had been of little use against the Partisans in the Battle of the Neretva although their hostility toward the Partisans provided Rome with its main reason for seeking to rely on them. Hitler also felt that the Main Operational Group would finally be liquidated in the Schwarz operation, thereby depriving the Italians of their motive for using the Chetniks. The Chetniks would then be disarmed in order to make the Axis rear secure in case of an Allied landing along the coast.

In the Fifth Offensive the German Command massed its troops in secrecy. Until the last minute, even the Italian allies were not informed of German intentions. The Fifth Offensive came as a big surprise also for Partisan Supreme HQ. The order for the Fifth Offensive was issued by General Lütters on May 6, 1943. He had estimated that the encircled Partisan forces numbered some 15,000 men, a fairly accurate guess. The Main Operational Group consisted of over 16,000 soldiers, with somewhat over 4,000 men in the Central Hospital, wounded or sick with typhus.

The Appearance of Bulgarian Troops

Lütters concentrated a force of about 70,000 German soldiers (the First Mountain Division, the Seventh SS Division, Prinz Eugen, the 118th Pursuit Division, parts of the 369th and 104th Pursuit Divisions, and the Brandenburg Regiment). He also calculated on three Italian divisions, the Taurinense, Venezia, and Ferrara, and lesser parts of other Italian divisions. Pavelić placed about 11,-000 of his troops at Lütter's disposal, and the Bulgarian defense minister consented to the use of Bulgarian troops outside the Bulgarian occupation zone in Serbia and in Montenegro. This was the Sixty-first Bulgarian Regiment; another Bulgarian regiment was alerted to take part in the operations. All in all, Lütters had somewhat over 130,000 men in the Fifth Offensive. The air force was to be present in larger numbers than it had been in the Fourth Offensive.

The German Command predicted that the first stage of the operations (encirclement in depth) would take ten days and the second stage (destruction of Partisan forces in the basin) another ten days, and that another few weeks would be needed to comb the area thoroughly and carry out mop-up operations.

Supreme HQ, having no inkling of what was coming, held a meeting on May 8 in the village of Kruševo in the Piva River valley, to discuss the development of the Partisan offensive, a possible advance into Kosovo and to the boundary of Serbia. The first reports of German concentration were rejected as unfounded by the deputy chief of staff. It was only on May 15, when German aircraft, supporting shock troops, went into attack on all sides, that it was clear a major new offensive had begun.

Units of the Main Operational Group would easily have broken through the encirclement had the question of the sick and wounded not been raised again. Because Supreme HQ had to care for them, its ability to maneuver was impeded. Again a decisive battle had to be fought from the bottom of a caldron hemmed in by the enemy on all sides, initially to save the wounded, and later to save the Main Operational Group itself.

The Disarming of the Chetniks

In their first advance German units moving in the direction of Kolašin came upon Chetnik units under the command of Pavle Djurišić. The German commanders ordered the disarming of all Chetniks, and this was done. Almost 4,000 Chetniks were relieved of their weapons and were thenceforward considered POWs. These measures provoked protests from the Italian Command, and further disarming of Chetniks in the Fifth Offensive ceased. Some of the Chetnik formations with Italian divisions even took part in the fighting against the Partisans. Pavle Djurišić himself was later released, and excuses were made for his being taken as a POW. He immediately joined the German Command and fought to the end of the war along with the German troops against the Partisans.

German commanders issued special orders to kill not only Partisans but also the people in the surrounded area, and to foul the water. When the Fifth Offensive began, Supreme HQ instructed all military authorities in the rear, and operational units, to inform the people to take refuge in the inaccessible highlands of Durmitor, Sinjajevina, and other mountains in the vicinity.

After the first few battles in the valley of the Lim and Drina Rivers, Supreme HQ decided that an attempt to break through should be made northwards, in the direction of Bosnia. Orders were issued to stop the advance toward Serbia and to desist from attacking Mojkovac and Kolašin. The Partisans first tried breaking through to Foča, to which the First Proletarian Brigade had been transferred, but German troops offered stubborn resistance.

The movement of Partisan units was delayed also by the anticipated arrival of a British Military Mission in Supreme HQ. In April 1943 the British military authorities had sent a mission headed by Major William Jones to territory held by Croatian Partisans. Through this Mission the British Military Command in the Middle East informed Supreme HQ that it would send a mission directly to it, and agreement was given. The British Military Mission had been scheduled to arrive on May 22 in a liberated area near Žabljak, but its arrival was postponed to daybreak of May 28, entailing a loss of six precious days for Supreme HQ.

The British Mission was headed by Major William Stuart and Captain William Deakin, the latter a personal friend of the British prime minister, Winston Churchill, and his adviser on historical matters.

Before the British Mission arrived, Supreme HQ had sent a telegram to Chief Headquarters for Croatia, telling them to ask Allied military authorities via the British Mission to bomb immediately the starting bases of German and Italian troops in the Fifth Offensive in Pljevlja, Bijelo Polje, Berane, Andrijevica, Podgorica, Nikšić and Mostar, but the British Command turned a deaf ear to the request.

Late in May it became clear to Supreme HQ that a breakthrough northward could not be effected in the Foča sector. The valley of the Sutjeska was then selected as the best possible direction for penetration of German encirclement. Supreme HQ, realizing that the Vučevo Plateau between the canyons of the Drina, Sutjeska, and Piva was the key to the Sutjeska Valley, sent the Second Proletarian Brigade to take possession of that strategically important area. Serbian and Bosnian proletarian brigades arrived at the top of Vučevo only a few minutes before the Germans, whom they forced into the Sutjeska Valley. Simultaneously German troops were advancing on all other sectors of the front, closing the vise around the Main Operational Group and 4,000 wounded.

Tito kept Moscow informed in detail about the situation. His radiograms reflect the full gravity of the position in which the Main Operational Group found itself. There are in some of them elements of Vladika Danilo's monologue from Njegoš's *The Mountain Wreath*, the classical epic of Yugoslav literature.

Tito also informed Moscow of the arrival of the British Military Mission and asked for Soviet help as well. In a radiogram of May 23, 1943, Moscow asked for details: Were there airports on liberated territory? Was there fuel for airplanes? The Russians were thinking of sending planes, but in view of the distance from the Russian front, the planes would have to land in liberated territory in Yugoslavia before returning.

On May 24 Tito replied that a British Military Mission was expected and asked that a Soviet Military Mission also be sent:

> In this connection, we request the Supreme Command of the Red Army also to send a military representative as soon as that is possible. As regards the dispatch of your plane, it could easily land near Žabljak, but now the front is near there and we do not know how long we shall be here. We have no fuel for planes, but your representative could be parachuted. As soon as we find a suitable place, we shall inform you of possibilities for landing.

In the meantime German troops had taken the whole Sanjak, and all Partisan units had shifted to the left bank of the Tara River. The Germans modified their operational plan. They sensed that the Partisans had decided to break through at the Sutjeska and swiftly sent one division after another there. Supreme HQ divided all forces into two parts: the First and Second Divisions with ten brigades were to fight their way across the Sutjeska and into Bosnia, while the Third and Seventh Divisions with six brigades and the wounded would return, crossing the Tara River and making for the Sanjak. Supreme HQ would remain with the first group and the Executive Committee of the AFCNLY with the second. A message was sent to the Bosnian Corps to advance southward, strike the Germans in the rear, and thereby facilitate the breakthrough of the main force.

Orders were given to bury all heavy weapons so that the Partisan units could move faster, although their firing power was consequently reduced. Hunger again stalked the Partisan units. The battles were fought in uninhabited areas, and the few houses once in existence had been destroyed early in the war.

The Germans managed to gain control of the upper reaches of the Sutjeska but not the plateau of Gornja and Donja Bara defended by the Second Dalmatian Brigade. One of the most bitter battles of the Sutjeska was fought there between June 6 and 8. The command of the Second Battalion of this Dalmatian brigade sent a report on June 8: "The Germans are advancing with growing forces and increasing persistence; we have lost two-thirds of our men, but you can count on us just as though we were all here."

The Second Operational Group under the command of Milovan Djilas could not ford the Tara. Realizing this, it decided to take its wounded and join the first group, which controlled a narrow section of the Sutjeska between Suha

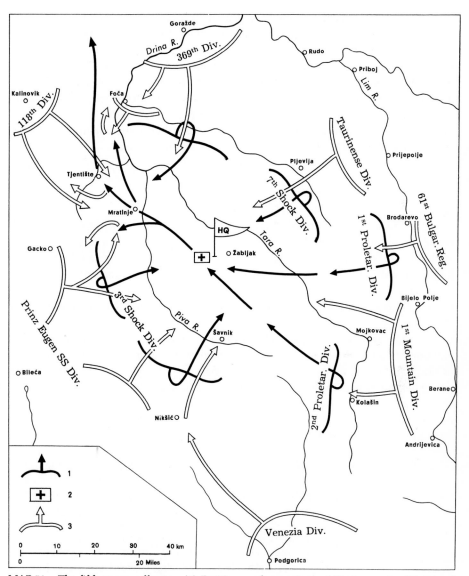

MAP 54.   The fifth enemy offensive. (1) Positions and operations of Partisan units; (2) Central
Hospital; (3) positions and operations of the enemy.

and Tjentište. Supreme HQ crossed the Sutjeska and on June 9 moved up the
slopes of Zelengora. German aircraft sustained a heavy barrage of the area, causing high casualties. The commander in chief, Tito, was among those wounded.
One of the heads of the British Mission, Stuart, was killed and the other, Deakin,
was wounded.

German aircraft bombed Supreme HQ almost daily. It was only at the end of the war after General von Löhr, commander of the Southeast Area for the Germans, had been captured, that we learned that German tracking stations had figured out the exact location of Supreme HQ during the Fifth Offensive, on the basis of the Supreme HQ wireless. The latter had to contact the Comintern station in Moscow every day, and the channels had to be left open for quite some time. Once the exact position of the Supreme HQ radio had been transmitted to the German air force, the area was bombed with uncanny precision, especially as the Partisans had no antiaircraft defensive at all.

The Breakthrough of the First Division

The First Proletarian Brigade took the initiative; without waiting to establish contact with the divisions behind it, it broke through the German front at Balinovac at daybreak on June 10. The entire First Proletarian Brigade, deployed in battle formation, stormed the German positions and took them. The same day, General von Löhr informed the German Supreme Command: "After heavy and unequal fighting the enemy succeeded in making a local breakthrough of the front held by the 369th Legionary Division."

The same day, some Italian POWs who acted as grooms for Supreme HQ horses fled to the enemy side. The groom responsible for the horse assigned to Vladimir Nazor, the poet, took the original diary of the venerable author with him when he joined the Germans. This was not a difficult thing to do, as the front line was frequently only a few hundred meters from Supreme HQ. The grooms told the German Command of the movements of Supreme HQ, and the news was passed on to Berlin:

> The strong enemy force in the Sutjeska-Piva area has been squeezed into a very small space. It has been established with certainty that Tito is with them. It is the last phase of the struggle; the time has come for the complete destruction of Tito's army.
>
> The importance of the order that not a single able-bodied man is to leave the encirclement alive and that women are to be searched to make sure they are not men in disguise, must again be drawn to the attention of the troops.
>
> Tito and his escort are allegedly wearing German uniforms. Military identity cards must be checked.

The First Proletarian Division, under the command of Koča Popović, took advantage of the tactical space and quickly widened it, arriving on June 12 at the Foča-Kalinovik road, which it crossed. The German vise was behind it.

The German Supreme Command issued new orders to close the vise; on June 12 General Lütters personally visited the Foča-Kalinovik road to raise morale. But the second wave of the Main Operational Group was already advancing toward this line of communication. On the eve of the breakthrough, Tito sent a radiogram to Moscow:

> Our position is still difficult. The enemy is again attempting to encircle us. Along the line of our advance in the direction of central and eastern Bosnia, the enemy has taken and fortified all heights, emplaced artillery and machine guns, and set up small garrisons, while his main force endeavors to close in on us. They are attacking constantly on all sides. The enemy is suffering heavy losses, as we are, particularly from aircraft. On June 9 and 10 our losses were especially serious. Also killed by aircraft on that day was British Captain Stuart, while Captain Deakin and I sustained light injuries. I was wounded in the arm by shrapnel. Captain Stuart was the head of the British Mission to our HQ. The British say they had no idea of the difficult battle we have been waging. They see that our units fight during the day and march at night. They do not sleep and they do not eat. Now they are eating up the horses without bread.
>
> Our situation is serious but we shall get out of it, even if with heavy losses. The enemy is making the greatest possible effort to destroy us, but he will not succeed.
>
> We ask for your support in these most difficult trials.

The principal breakthrough by the Second Division with Supreme HQ began on the night of June 12; on June 13 the main force crossed the Foča-Kalinovik road. That sector was defended by a German tank unit. The soldiers of the Second Proletarian Brigade who had refused to obey the order to bury their heavy weapons dragged an antitank gun with only three charges through the enemy encirclement. Concealing it in the thicket along the Foča-Kalinovik road, they let enemy tanks approach to a distance of 10 meters. Two charges put two tanks out of commission, and the others withdrew. In the meantime the Seventh Banija Division managed to catch up with the Second Division and cross the Foča-Kalinovik road.

The Tragedy of the Third Division and the Wounded at the Sutjeska on June 13

The German troops, having received reinforcements, closed the circle at the Sutjeska, Zelengora, and the Foča-Kalinovik road, making it impossible for the Third Division with the seriously wounded to get through. The First Dalmatian Brigade arrived at the Sutjeska on June 11, charged Tjentište, and seized it but could not hold the position until the arrival of the Third Division. Sections of it made their way northward one by one.

On June 12 the Third Division had its last radio contact with Supreme HQ; at daybreak of June 13 it began crossing the Sutjeska, the fighting men intermingled with refugees and wounded. German fire rained down on every square meter of the mountain torrent. They let the Partisans get near the other side and then opened fire. Exhausted and starving, the soldiers faltered. The order was given: "Communists up front," and the leaders, headed by Sava Kovačević, made the first charge. That day at the Sutjeska the Third Division lost half its men; after the death of Sava Kovačević, who was killed by machine-gun fire from an enemy blockhouse, chaos set in and the unit started breaking through in small groups.

Holding to the Partisans' rule of not permitting the enemy to take them alive, many of the seriously wounded committed suicide. The political commissar of the Third Sanjak Brigade, Božo Miletić, was wounded during the breakthrough. Seeing his thigh bone broken, he yelled to his comrades, "Go on, I won't let you die for me," and shot himself through the forehead. A few minutes later the wounded deputy brigade commander also killed himself so as not to be a burden to his comrades.

At the Piva and Sutjeska, the German and Italian troops killed over 1,300 wounded Partisans, as evident from German and Italian military documents impounded after the war. A similar fate was met by the medical personnel of the Main Partisan Operational Group. About two hundred nurses and thirty doctors lost their lives at the Sutjeska. This was half of the trained personnel of the Central Hospital.

Total Partisan losses at the Sutjeska amounted to over 6,000 men. More than 30 percent of the soldiers of the Main Operational Brigade lost their lives in the Battle of the Sutjeska.

It has never been estimated exactly how many fleeing refugees were killed. The German Seventh SS Division, Prinz Eugen, killed several groups of from 50 to 580 older men, women, and children in its sector. The Italian Ferrara Division also dealt savagely with the population. The Bulgarian Sixty-first Regiment executed twenty persons in the village of Palež near Žabljak. In the Durmitor district of Montenegro alone, 1,200 persons were killed, 5,000 buildings were burned down, and 60,000 head of livestock plundered.

Once out of the Sutjeska encirclement, the Main Operational Group hastened to break through toward Jahorina and Romanija, liberating Han Pijesak, Vlasenica, Drinjača, Srebrenica, Kladanj, and Zvornik. Fresh quantities of equipment were captured from the enemy.

The German Command was forced to admit that it had not achieved its objective at Sutjeska. General von Löhr later stated: "The original task of relieving German troops tied down in Yugoslavia for action on the eastern front was not achieved at all; on the contrary, at the end of the action, new German forces and commands had to be brought in."

The Battle of the Sutjeska reaffirmed the importance of the moral-political factor in the Partisan army; the operation also demonstrated that the fighting qualities of the men and their commanders, and their skill in warfare, were such as to enable them to outmaneuver military commanders as well-trained and an army as well-disciplined as the German.

CHAPTER 48

The Struggle
to Preserve
the Achievements
of the
Yugoslav Revolution

THE FIGHT FOR YUGOSLAVIA'S TERRITORIAL INTEGRITY / SECRET AGREEMENT ON DIVISION OF TERRITORY OR SPHERES OF INFLUENCE IN YUGOSLAVIA / CONSEQUENCES OF ITALY'S CAPITULATION / THE SECOND SESSION OF THE ANTI-FASCIST COUNCIL FOR THE NATION-AL LIBERATION OF YUGOSLAVIA: THE FORMATION OF THE PROVI-SIONAL REVOLUTIONARY GOVERNMENT / STALIN'S DISSATISFAC-TION WITH THE DECISIONS OF THE AFCNLY / TWO SERIOUS PARTISAN DEFEATS / CHURCHILL'S ENDEAVOR TO RESCUE THE MONARCHY / THE GERMAN AIRBORNE ATTACK ON DRVAR, MAY 25, 1944 / ŠUBAŠIĆ'S ARRIVAL ON VIS ISLAND / THE SECOND MEETING AND AGREEMENT WITH ŠUBAŠIĆ / THE TITO-STALIN MEETING / AGREEMENT BETWEEN STALIN AND CHURCHILL ON DIVISION OF YUGOSLAVIA INTO SPHERES OF INFLUENCE / THE BATTLE FOR BELGRADE; PARTICIPATION OF SOVIET TROOPS / YALTA AND YUGOSLAVIA / COALITION GOVERNMENT / FINAL BATTLES FOR THE LIBERATION OF YUGOSLAVIA / THE COLLAPSE OF DRAŽA MIHAILOVIĆ / THE TRÌESTE CRISIS / YUGOSLAVIA'S LOSSES IN THE WAR

The Fight for Yugoslavia's Territorial Integrity

The Battle of the Sutjeska was the turning point in the Yugoslav revolution, but final victory was still two years off. The heroic period of the Partisan struggle was not yet over, as demonstrated by the drive of the Fourteenth Slovene Division in Štajerska, the winter march of the Macedonian brigades, the slaughter of the First Šumadija Brigade near Prijepolje, wiped out to the last man. The German Supreme Command methodically conducted offensive after offensive, of which the sixth in the late autumn of 1943 was the most sweeping and the fiercest of the whole war. Many towns changed hands back and forth—for instance, Foča in eastern Bosnia forty-seven times. The population of liberated areas continued to be annihilated mercilessly. In Janja, western Bosnia, fire had been set to the villages so many times that finally the unfortunate peasants hit upon the idea of dismantling their cottages and hiding the beams in the forest as soon as German troops drew near, so they would have nothing to burn. When the enemy retired, the peasants set about the painstaking business of rebuilding their simple homes. As victory neared, the people in the areas of uprising grew ever more exhausted; hunger stalked the land; there were no longer any young people left to reinforce Partisan ranks, the usual case in long wars of liberation.

Secret Agreement on Division of Territory or Spheres of Influence in Yugoslavia

Fighting the occupier was not the only task of the Yugoslav revolution. Hitler's defeat was inevitable, and as it drew nearer, the differences in objectives between the three Allied powers grew more and more apparent. The great colonial empires—Great Britain, France, Holland, and Belgium—were living their last days. The United States and the Soviet Union came to the forefront as the two superpowers of the world. The diplomacies of the three Allied powers made plans for a new division of the world, concluding among themselves secret agreements for spheres of interest without the knowledge and to the detriment of the small and medium-sized states and nations.

For the Yugoslav revolution, the key question those days was whether the country would be an object or a subject in international relations, especially with regard to the following contingencies.

First, how was it possible to avoid Yugoslavia's becoming an object of agreements on division of spheres of interest among the Great Powers, in terms of either division of the country into spheres of *influence* or division of *territory?*

Second, how was it possible to preserve the *territorial integrity* of Yugoslavia, to prevent its dismemberment?

Third, how could the unification of the various Yugoslav nations be effected? For instance, parts of the ethnical territory of Slovenes, Macedonians, and Croats (Primorje with Trieste and Gorizia, Istria, Koruška, Aegean and Pirin Macedonia) had been wrested away from them during earlier periods.

Fourth, how would it be possible to prevent various Allied powers from invading Yugoslav territory toward the end of the war for the purpose of restoring the prewar social system and form of state? Up until the middle of 1944 the conviction prevailed among some British Conservatives that British troops should land in Yugoslavia to intervene, by force of arms, on behalf of the Yugoslav monarchy, as was done in Greece late in 1944.

In his guidelines of March 27, 1941, Hitler had announced his intention of destroying the Yugoslav state, and this idea had been adopted by his satellites in Yugoslavia: Ante Pavelić in Croatia, Marko Natlačen in Slovenia, Sekula Drljević in Montenegro, the leaders of the Albanian fascists (Ballisti) in Kosovo, and Dimitrije Ljotić in Serbia.

As soon as the April War was over, members of the extreme right wing of the Great Serbian bourgeoisie also pursued the notion of dismembering Yugoslavia, even if the Allies won, and of creating a Great Serbia. This program was upheld by Momčilo Ninčić and the Yugoslav ambassador to the United States, Konstantin Fotić. They were supported in their ideas by Slobodan Jovanović, for a time prime minister of the Royal government, and also by Draža Mihailović.

In a letter to Konstantin Fotić, Momčilo Ninčić wrote at the end of December 1941:

> I do not believe that Yugoslavia could be reconstructed again in the form in which it existed. We shall never have peace with the Croats. The Slovenes will be our friends only if we are strong. . . . We shall create a Great Serbia extending all the way to Ogulin. . . .

The right wing of the Great Serbian bourgeoisie found the greatest support in the United States of America for this idea of disrupting Yugoslavia after the war, especially during the last years of hostilities. Although Great Britain and the Soviet Union had at various phases of the war touched upon the question of division of Yugoslavia into spheres of interest, and also division of its territory, both of these great powers by and large favored agreements on spheres of interest, and influence, meaning that Yugoslavia's integrity would be maintained, but this was not the case with the United States. Particularly toward the end of the war, conservative American circles sought support among the most reactionary elements, in all nations, so as to secure supremacy for themselves under the cloak of struggle against communism (relying in China, for example, on Chiang Kai-shek and in Yugoslavia on Draža Mihailović).

Some American experts systematically submitted such views whenever the question of Yugoslavia's future came up at international conferences. Even

President Roosevelt repeated these positions on several occasions in 1942 and 1943. For instance, during a meeting with Anthony Eden, the British foreign secretary, on March 15, 1943, he declared that "the Serbs and Croats have nothing in common and it is foolish to force two such peoples who disagree to live together in one state." Roosevelt proposed that, after the war, only Serbia should be restored as an independent state, and that Croatia should be placed under the trusteeship of the United Nations as though it were an underdeveloped African territory!

Anthony Eden disagreed with Roosevelt's intention, submitting the view that a common state of Yugoslav peoples should be formed, under one dynasty, but along the lines of a confederation.

Later, at the conference between Roosevelt and Churchill in Quebec in August 1943, Churchill asked that troops be parachuted into Yugoslavia, but Roosevelt demanded that Germany be struck right in the heart by the shortest possible route—a landing in France. As for Yugoslavia, he thought that all forces, both Partisan and Chetnik, should be placed under the command of King Petar II, as the United States would not permit a change in social system to take place in any country in the world while the war was on.

Even after the Quebec meeting, however, strong groups in the United States supported the idea of separate Yugoslav states and the dismemberment of Yugoslavia as a single state. This was particularly true of the OSS (forerunner of the CIA), headed by General Donovan. The OSS leaned especially on Draža Mihailović and tried through him to accomplish contrarevolutionary intervention in Yugoslavia.

In this way it came about that the National Liberation movement in Yugoslavia was the basic force struggling for the integrity and indivisibility of Yugoslavia. The idea of fraternity and unity, fostered by the Central Committee of the CPY since the very beginning of the uprising in 1941, echoed favorably in Yugoslavia, especially among the peasants of all nationalities. These masses of peasants, who had occasionally fallen under the sway of bourgeois elements from the towns perpetrating mutual extermination, adopted the position of the Central Committee of the CPY after a number of brief crises, for the idea of a community of Yugoslav peoples was deeply rooted, especially among the peasantry.

Up to the beginning of the nineteenth century, and even later in some areas, few peasants had moved to the towns. In Serbia the small towns consisted of Turks, Cincars, Jews, Greeks, and Armenians, but in Croatia and Slovenia the Germanic element prevailed. It was only after the flow of peasants from rural districts to towns increased that the alien elements were Slavicized, although they continued to resist the ideas of unity held by the peasants. It thus happened that narrow nationalism and separatism had also struck deep roots in the towns of Serbia, Croatia, and Slovenia.

During the National Liberation war, when the peasantry took its political fate into its own hands, and while it provided the Partisan movement with the larger part of its members, the old idea of community revived; as a matter of fact, throughout history it had always been strongest when common danger threatened all the peoples of Yugoslavia.

Consequences of Italy's Capitulation

The capitulation of Italy in September 1943 lent fresh impulse to the liberation struggle. In Slovenia the Isonzo, Lombardia, Cacciatori degli Alpi Divisions and some other smaller units were disarmed. The White Guards (quislings in Slovenia) were smashed; 700 of the most obdurate were captured in Turjak. The majority were released but fled to Ljubljana and under German patronage became the mainstay of the German Home Guards. Most of them were recaptured by Partisan units in May 1945.

A spontaneous popular uprising broke out in the Slovene Littoral and Istria, in the course of which parts of three Italian divisions were disarmed; in the middle of September the National Liberation Committee for Istria proclaimed the unification of Istria with Croatia in a free Yugoslavia, while the plenary committee of the *Osvobodilna Fronta* proclaimed the unification of the Slovene Littoral to Slovenia and Yugoslavia.

The First Proletarian and Fourth Divisions advanced swiftly on Split, the principal Dalmatian town, toward which the German Supreme Command simultaneously sent three of its divisions. The people of Split themselves disarmed a part of the Italian forces. The town was free for a few days, only to fall into German hands again.

In Montenegro the Venezia Division joined the Partisans, and in Hercegovina the Taurinense Division followed suit. In Macedonia Partisans disarmed the Firenze Division.

A large number of Italian soldiers joined Partisan units. Special Garibaldi brigades were formed and distinguished themselves by their courage in fighting the Germans. Over 8,000 Italian Partisans lost their lives fighting in Yugoslavia.

Having captured large quantities of weapons, Partisan units were able to supply arms to all those who wanted to fight. The total number of fighting men in the National Liberation army grew to 250,000. Liberated territory, which had amounted to 50,000 square kilometers in the autumn of 1942, increased to 130,000 square kilometers within a year's time. Almost half the country's total population was now living in liberated areas.

The Second Session of the Anti-Fascist Council for the National Liberation of Yugoslavia: the Formation of the Provisional Revolutionary Government

Conditions were ripe for the formation of a people's government, for Yugoslavia to begin developing as a democratic, federal state, as a community of equal peoples. It was also considered necessary to strip the Royal government in exile of all the prerogatives of the legitimate government of Yugoslavia and forbid King Petar to return.

The Anti-Fascist Councils for Bosnia and Hercegovina, Croatia, Montenegro, and Slovenia, and Chief Headquarters in Macedonia and in Serbia, elected delegates to the Second Session of the Anti-Fascist Council for the National Liberation of Yugoslavia. Owing to war operations, some of the delegates were not able to reach Jajce, seat of the AFCNLY and of Supreme HQ. The following numbers of delegates set out for Jajce: seventy-eight from Croatia, fifty-three from Bosnia and Hercegovina, fifty-three from Serbia, eight from Vojvodina, forty-two from Macedonia, eleven from Montenegro, forty-two from Slovenia, and eleven from the Sanjak.

In a radiogram sent early in October, Supreme HQ informed Moscow that it did not recognize the government in exile and the king because of their collaboration with the occupiers, and that the people favored a democratic republican form of government for Yugoslavia in the future. The gist of these decisions was also transmitted to the Foreign Ministers' Conference of the three Allied powers held in Moscow at the end of October 1943.

The second session of the AFCNLY was held in the town of Jajce in western Bosnia on November 29, 1943, in the presence of 146 delegates from most parts of the country. Military operations prevented Macedonian delegates from attending the session. The session made the following decisions.

The AFCNLY was constituted as the supreme legislative and executive representative body of Yugoslavia and the supreme representative of the people and state of Yugoslavia as a whole. Yugoslavia was established as a federal community of equal peoples.

A new revolutionary government was set up—the National Committee of the Liberation of Yugoslavia, which thereby acquired all the features of a government, whereas the Royal government in exile was divested of all the prerogatives of the legitimate government of Yugoslavia. It was decided to examine all international treaties concluded by that government abroad to see whether they were in line with the interests of the people.

The AFCNLY confirmed the decision of the Slovene National Liberation Committee to annex the Slovene Littoral to Slovenia, and the decision of the Anti-Fascist Council for the National Liberation of Croatia to annex Istria, Rijeka, and Zadar to Croatia.

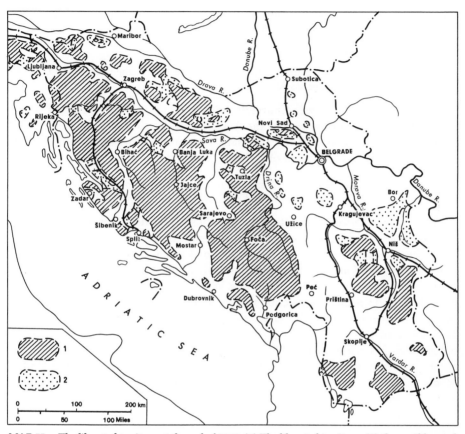

MAP 55.   The liberated territory at the end of 1943. (1) The liberated territory; (2) the semiliberated
territory.

Stalin's Dissatisfaction with the Decisions of the AFCNLY

Supreme HQ was resolved not to permit meddling from any quarter
whatsoever, to prevent a recurrence of what happened during the first session
of the AFCNLY when Moscow had not allowed the proclamation of the republic
and the formation of a revolutionary government. Consequently Moscow learned
of the decisions of the AFCNLY, especially those depriving the Royal government
in exile of legitimacy and placing a ban on King Petar's return, only after they
had been passed. Moscow's first reaction was strongly negative. The Free Yugoslavia radio station received orders not to broadcast the resolution forbidding
the king's return to Yugoslavia. Moreover, the Yugoslav representative in Moscow, Veljko Vlahović, was taken to task and all his broadcasts for Free Yugo-

slavia and Radio Moscow were subjected to censorship. Dmitrii Manuilski, nominally the chief of the Comintern, delivered Stalin's message to him:

> Hazyayin [among initiates in Moscow, Stalin was called Hazyayin—the host, the boss] is extremely angry. He considers this a stab in the back of the U.S.S.R. and the Teheran decisions.

The Stalin-Roosevelt-Churchill conference in Teheran was held at the same time as the second session of the AFCNLY. A decision was taken to open a second front in Europe, and the Partisans were also discussed. The first thing stated in the military decisions of Teheran was:

> It has been decided that the Partisans in Yugoslavia are to be helped to the greatest possible extent in supplies and matériel, and in commando operations.

Newspapers of the Western Allies published the decisions of the AFCNLY on December 4, but Free Yugoslavia broadcast them from Moscow only on December 15. Because political circles in London and Washington considered that the Yugoslav Partisans were blindly obedient to Moscow, the Jajce decisions were looked upon as a caprice of Stalin's. When Moscow saw that the Allies had published the decisions, the reaction was twofold. On the one hand, Moscow was persuaded to do the same, although its claim that the decisions had spoiled relations between the three Allied powers was shown to be exaggerated. On the other hand, Stalin's mistrust of Tito's leadership in Yugoslavia deepened. The Soviet government had had to wait sixteen years for recognition by the United States, which recognized the government of the new Yugoslavia immediately, albeit informally.

Germany kept a close watch on developments concerning Yugoslavia. The conviction grew that the landing of Allied troops in the Balkans was simply a matter of time. Late in October 1943 a decision was taken to launch a big offensive directed against Partisan forces in Yugoslavia, Albania, and Greece. This was the so-called Sixth Offensive, which lasted until the middle of January 1944.

Two Serious Partisan Defeats

This time, too, Partisan forces emerged victorious although they suffered two particularly serious defeats. After Italy's capitulation, over 18,000 interned Yugoslavs had succeeded in making their way home via the Partisan base in Bari. After a short training course, most of them joined Partisan brigades as reinforcements or formed their own overseas brigades, five in all. In their first clashes with the Germans, these men were killed off fast. In the first place, they were overly zealous, desirous of distinguishing themselves in battle and proving that they were not to blame for having been interned or imprisoned. This made them dis-

FIGURE 46. Partisans of the Slovene National Liberation Army approaching the railway line Graz–Zidani Most–Ljubljana–Trieste to destroy one of the most vital strategic communication links of Hitler's Third Reich (summer 1944).

FIGURE 47. A Slovene farmer giving a drink to a wounded soldier after the attack of the Slovene Partisans on German rail communications (summer 1944).

regard many of the basic rules of warfare. Furthermore, they had been physically weakened by the terrible conditions of internment in Italy. Long Partisan marches and poor food increased their exhaustion.

In the battles for the island of Korčula on December 22, 1943, two of the Partisan brigades of the Twenty-sixth Division counted among their number many of these "overseas" fighting men. Vigorous action by German troops soon routed them and several hundred were killed or captured. German troops took possession of all liberated Dalmatian islands with the exception of Vis.

The second tragedy concerned the men of the First Šumadija Brigade in Prijepolje. All of them were guerrillas who had stayed in the area to fight superior enemy forces after the withdrawal of the Partisans from western Serbia in the winter of 1941. Toward the end of 1943 they formed a separate brigade and joined the main Partisan force in the Sanjak. In this unit of seasoned Partisans, the egalitarian ethics of the early Partisan days in Serbia in 1941 still held good. They were temporarily garrisoned in the town of Prijepolje on the Lim River. One night the Germans entered the town, surrounding the building in which most of the men of Šumadija were quartered. The Partisans refused to surrender and died to the last man.

It was only after the war that the whole story of this tragedy was learned from German documents. The German counterintelligence service had deciphered a message sent from one Partisan unit to another. (They never succeeded in breaking the code used between Moscow and Supreme HQ.) They therefore knew exactly where the Šumadija soldiers were quartered. With the help of some of their intelligence agents in the town of Prijepolje, they took the Partisans unawares.

Churchill's Endeavor to Rescue the Monarchy

After the second session of the AFCNLY there was a complicated struggle over recognition of the new revolutionary government of Yugoslavia. Not a single Great Power—neither the U.S.S.R., Great Britain, nor the United States—wanted to recognize it *de jure* although the conference in Teheran had granted the National Liberation army the status of an Allied cobelligerent.

British Prime Minister Churchill hastened to secure the monarchy's position in Yugoslavia even at the price of sacrificing Draža Mihailović himself, whose military force, the Chetniks, had been defeated. At the same time, Great Britain and the U.S.S.R. negotiated to divide all Eastern Europe and the Balkan Peninsula, including Yugoslavia, into spheres of influence. At that time, that is, toward the end of 1943, the conviction was growing in Britain that Yugoslavia should be divided into *spheres of influence*, and not territorially, although the British representative attached to Draža Mihailović, Colonel Bailey, held the view that Yugoslavia should be divided into two spheres, the eastern (largely Serbia) to belong exclusively to Draža Mihailović, and the western (Croatia and Bosnia) to be Partisan. And in some circles in the Soviet Union, the belief persisted that the Chetniks had Serbia firmly in hand, and that the Partisan movement was largely Croatian. This opinion was publicly expressed by General N. Korneyev, the first chief of the Soviet Military Mission to Supreme HQ, when he visited wounded Partisan officers in Cairo on his way to Drvar in January 1944. He asked them point-blank whether there were any Partisans among the Serbs, despite the fact that at this time almost half of all Partisans in Yugoslavia were of Serbian nationality (according to Supreme HQ data, 44 percent of all Partisans were Serbs).

Churchill informed Stalin of his idea of a compromise solution for Yugoslavia. On December 21, 1943, the Soviet ambassador to London told Anthony Eden, the British foreign secretary, that the Soviet government agreed with the view of the British government that it was in the interests of the struggle of the Yugoslav peoples against the German occupiers to find a basis for cooperation between the two sides in Yugoslavia and that the Soviet government was ready to do everything within its power to effect a compromise between them.

Churchill immediately sent his son Randolph to liberated territory in Yugoslavia with the task of saving the monarchy and the old social order, even if Draža Mihailović had to be sacrificed. The young Churchill brought Tito a personal letter from his father. In the meantime the Soviet Military Mission had also arrived at Supreme HQ, supporting the idea of a compromise, although more cautiously. Otherwise, that Mission was primarily interested in knowing whether the Partisans had political police and advised them to establish such a force immediately; they also believed that all egalitarianism in the Partisan army should be suppressed and that the Yugoslav political system should follow the Soviet example.

The National Committee of the Liberation of Yugoslavia found itself in an intricate situation. News had been received that the government in exile had worked out a plan for mustering an army of 100,000 men (to include Poles under the command of General Anders) which, with the help of Allied troops, was to land in the Zadar area and thence advance to the interior and take charge of all means of communication. That army was to serve as a guarantee that the Partisans would be forced to accept the compromise proposed by the British government. These plans were upset by the mutiny in the Yugoslav Royal army in the Middle East. A considerable number of officers, especially airmen, announced that they were joining the National Liberation army. Finally the Partisan leadership decided that a compromise would have to be struck, although only temporarily. They modeled their approach on Lenin's flexibility in World War I, during the Brest Litovsk period.

The National Committee dispatched a Military Mission to London and another to Moscow to negotiate help for the Partisans and to discuss other questions.

The German Airborne Attack on Drvar, May 25, 1944

In the meantime German paratroopers had descended on Drvar on May 25, 1944, with the objective of capturing Supreme HQ and the Allied Military Mission; a strong land force was also dispatched to Drvar to destroy Supreme HQ and the units defending it. The attack did not succeed, and Supreme HQ was transported by Soviet plane from Kupreško Polje to Bari and from there by British warship to the liberated island of Vis in the Adriatic Sea.

Pursuing his idea of a compromise, Churchill persuaded King Petar to entrust the former ban of Croatia, Ivan Šubašić, with the task of concluding an agreement with the leaders of the National Liberation movement.

Šubašić's Arrival on Vis Island

Escorted by Ralph Stevenson, British minister to the Yugoslav government in London, Ivan Šubašić arrived on Vis Island on June 14, 1944, for two days of negotiations with the National Committee. Agreement was finally reached on the forming of the new Yugoslav government. Anyone who had been compromised by collaboration with the occupiers was excluded. It would be the responsibility of this government to assist the National Liberation struggle. Šubašić's new government also undertook the obligation to issue a public declaration recognizing the National Liberation struggle under Tito's command, condemning all traitors, and calling upon the people to unite in the fight for victory. For its part, the National Committee would publish a declaration of cooperation with the Šubašić government and would not take the initiative for any definitive regulation of the state system as long as the war lasted.

In August 1944, when Winston Churchill toured Allied fronts in Italy, he invited Tito to visit him. Tito had previously met with General Wilson, General Alexander, and other Allied commanders, their discussions including the question of assistance to the Partisan army. The Allies had opened their hospitals in Italy to 11,000 wounded Partisans; this was a great help to the National Liberation forces.

Churchill and Tito met three times in the course of August 12 and 13. The most important meeting was the first on August 12 between 12 noon and 1:15. On the Yugoslav side, there was only the translator, Olga Ninčić-Humo, who did not have time to take official minutes. The English version of this meeting was composed by the diplomat Pierson Dixon. At the other meetings between Tito and Churchill more Yugoslavs were present. They later composed the minutes of those meetings as well as notes of what they had been told about the first meeting.

On that first historic meeting between Churchill and Tito the following questions were discussed:

FIGURE 48. More than 27,000 refugees from the liberated territory of Dalmatia, after the Sixth German Offensive in autumn 1943, were evacuated to a camp near El Shatt in Egypt.

FIGURE 49. Josip Broz Tito (right) with Edvard Kardelj and Vladimir Bakarić in Tito's headquarters in a cave on the island of Vis (July 1944).

1. Coordination of military operations against the Germans in northeast Italy.

2. Churchill's position on Draža Mihailović and the monarchy, with proposed compromise between Partisans and individual Chetnik commanders in case Mihailović were to leave Yugoslavia. Tito rejected that position, recalling the decisions of the second session of the AFCNLY.

3. Churchill's interest in the future social system of the new Yugoslavia and Tito's explanation.

4. The relationship of Yugoslavia with neighboring countries in postwar Europe.

5. Churchill's concern for transfer of wounded Partisans from the Yugoslav mountains to Allied hospitals in Italy.

6. The information that would be given to Stalin and Roosevelt about these talks.

7. Future meetings between Churchill and Tito, after the experts had studied some questions of a military technical nature.

8. Agreement on a meeting between Marshal Tito and representatives of the king's government—Šubašić, Kosanović, and Cankar.

The Second Meeting and Agreement with Šubašić

In August Šubašić came to Vis Island for a second meeting. On behalf of the Royal government, he promised that assistance would be sent to the Partisans and people, that King Petar would publicly renounce Draža Mihailović, and that all reactionaries would be removed from the Royal diplomatic corps, such as Fotić and a number of others. Šubašić asked that a new joint government be formed immediately, made up of representatives of the Royal government and National Committee.

The Tito-Stalin Meeting

Churchill himself also sent messages along these lines. In the meantime Tito went to Moscow, where he met Stalin. In their talks, Stalin insisted on an agreement with King Petar and, in essence, annulment of the decisions passed by the second session of the AFCNLY, all of which Tito refused. At one point Stalin said, "Reinstate King Petar, and then later knife him in the back." Stalin made inquiries as to what the Partisans would do if the British landed in Yugoslavia without the approval of Supreme HQ. Tito replied that the Partisan units would throw them into the sea.

At this same meeting Tito asked Stalin to assign a tank division for joint operations by Soviet and Partisan units in Yugoslavia against the Germans; Stalin replied that a tank corps would be dispatched. Agreement was reached on the extent to which the country would be liberated by joint operations, on the points to which the Soviet troops, and also those to which the Partisan troops, would advance, and on how long Soviet troops would remain in Yugoslav territory. A separate agreement on these matters was signed on September 23, 1944, between the National Committee and the Soviet Supreme Command, referring to the conditions for entry of Soviet troops into Yugoslav territory.

While Tito was in Moscow, a delegation from the new Bulgaria came to Krayovo (headed by Dobri Terpeshev). Tito signed an agreement with them, terminating the state of war between the two countries "in order to help them redeem themselves and to permit them to fight together with us."

Agreement between Stalin and Churchill on Division of Yugoslavia into Spheres of Influence

British-Soviet negotiations continued for definitive division of Eastern Europe and the Balkan Peninsula into spheres of influence. Churchill finally had to desist from the idea of a landing in Yugoslavia. Harold Macmillan, a member of the British government in the summer of 1944, and the principal political adviser in the Allied Forces command in the Mediterranean, as well as prime minister for a time after the war, wrote, in his wartime memoirs published in 1967, that if British General Alexander had been permitted to make a landing in Yugoslavia, history would have taken a different turn. Yugoslavia would never have been proclaimed a republic and Draža Mihailović would not have been executed.

At the Stalin-Churchill meeting in Moscow, agreement was reached on the division of Yugoslavia into spheres of influence on the fifty-fifty principle. The United States government later agreed to this arrangement. Stalin and Churchill together asked the National Committee to set up the joint Yugoslav government as soon as possible.

During this time bourgeois groups in Yugoslavia bent all their efforts to changing the situation in their favor. Dr. Vlatko Maček tried to create a common front with Ante Pavelić. For the purpose of staging a fictive coup d'état in the Independent State of Croatia, Maček's deputy, August Košutić, contacted two of Pavelić's ministers: Dr. Mladen Lorković, minister of external and internal affairs and also ambassador of the Independent State of Croatia to Berlin, and Ante Vokić, minister of the Armed Forces. The Ustashi army would be dissolved and the Home Guards would form a common front with Draža Mihailović's Chetniks in western Yugoslavia, take possession of part of the Adriatic coast, and invite the Allies to land. Pavelić would be permitted to go to Switzerland, and Dr. Maček would assume the post of president of the Croatian republic. Pavelić,

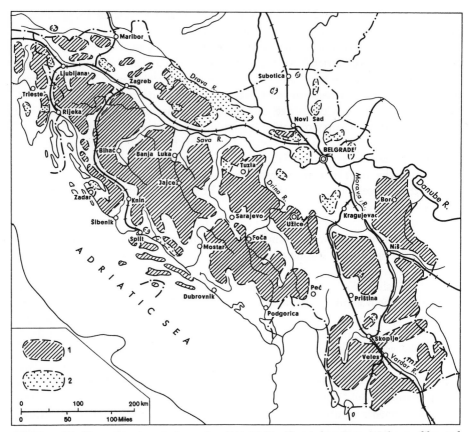

MAP 56. The liberated territory in September 1944. (1) The liberated territory; (2) the semiliberated territory.

loath to give up power, began to waver. In the meantime the Gestapo discovered these plans and ordered Pavelić to arrest the conspirators, which he did. Draža Mihailović established contact with Maček to find a joint platform at the eleventh hour. On September 17, 1944, an agreement was signed according to which Yugoslavia's future system would be discussed after the war. The Croatian Peasant party undertook the obligation not to conclude any kind of agreement with the Partisans, and its leadership stated that it was following with sympathy the work of the Central National Committee of the Kingdom of Yugoslavia under Draža Mihailović.

The high-ranking Catholic clergy in Croatia, headed by Archbishop Alojz Stepinac, also endeavored to mediate between Maček and Pavelić. Stepinac himself tried to persuade Pavelić to resign in favor of Maček, to proclaim Croatia a democratic republic, and to call upon the Allies, as soon as this was done, to land in Yugoslavia.

All these plans to dismember Yugoslavia and restore the power of the bourgeoisie were frustrated primarily by the development of the struggle in *all* parts of Yugoslavia. In the summer of 1944 the National Liberation army numbered thirty-nine divisions, as well as a large number of independent detachments, with a total of 390,000 fighting men. In Macedonia a number of brigades and the Forty-first Macedonian Division were formed. The Anti-Fascist Council for the National Liberation of Macedonia, as the supreme organ of the Macedonian nation, was established in the monastery of Prohor Pčinjski. In southern Serbia, Toplica, Crna Trava, another four divisions, the Twenty-second, Twenty-fourth, Forty-sixth, and Forty-seventh, were formed under the command of the Thirteenth Corps. Macedonian and Serbian liberated territory was merged. To the west, in Istria, the Forty-first Division was formed, and in eastern Bosnia the Twelfth Corps.

Supreme HQ again called upon all Yugoslavs in various quisling units to join the Partisans. At the same time, the Second Proletarian Division, and the Fifth and Seventeenth Divisions from eastern Montenegro, were ordered to advance into Serbia and join the Serbian Thirteenth Corps. The German Command tried to stop the advance, but to no avail. At Kopaonik a Partisan operational group smashed 8,000 Chetniks, liberated Brus and Aleksandrovac, and merged with the Serbian divisions.

The First Proletarian Division moved into Serbia and the Twelfth Corps crossed the Drina River at Višegrad. The insurrection welled up again in Serbia, just as it had in 1941. The First Proletarian Division alone was reinforced by 8,000 new men. On September 15, 1944, Supreme HQ formed the First Army Group in Serbia, including the First Proletarian Corps (the First Proletarian Division, and the Fifth, Sixth, Seventeenth, and Twenty-first Divisions), and the Danube Corps (Sixteenth, Thirty-sixth, and Eleventh Divisions).

The forces were assigned the task of acting as a shock group in liberated Serbia, together with the Thirteenth and Fourteenth Serbian Corps, which had seven divisions. They broke the resistance of the German troops and liberated a large part of Serbia.

The Battle for Belgrade; Participation of Soviet Troops

According to the agreement reached between Stalin and Tito, on September 29 the troops of the Third Ukrainian Front, the Sixty-eighth and Seventy-fifth Corps, crossed the Danube and captured Negotin, where they met up with units of the Fourteenth Serbian Corps. Joint forces of Soviet, Yugoslav, and Bulgarian

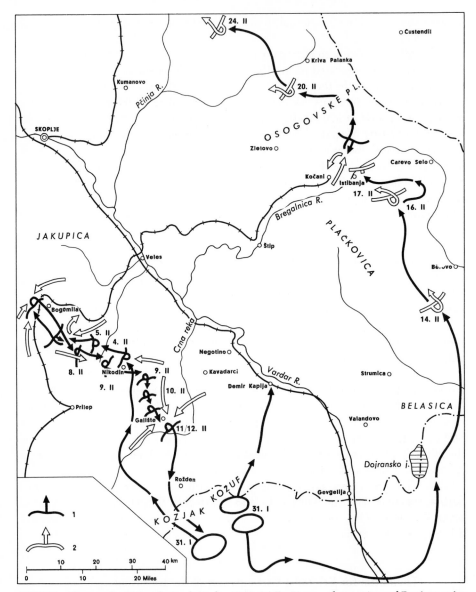

MAP 57.   The march of Macedonian brigades, 1944. (1) Positions and operations of Partisan units;
(2) positions and operations of the enemy.

troops liberated the eastern parts of Serbia, and on October 14 the battle for Belgrade began, with the First Yugoslav Army Group and the reinforced Soviet Fourth Mechanized Corps participating. After six days of fierce fighting, Belgrade was finally liberated. A group of over 2,000 armed citizens assisted the attacking Yugoslav and Soviet troops behind the German lines.

Tito and Šubašić resumed their talks in Belgrade for the formation of a joint government in the spirit of the Churchill-Stalin recommendations. On November 2, 1944, they took a decision on the composition of an integral Yugoslav government. The decision of the AFCNLY to forbid King Petar to return was to remain valid until the people had a chance after the war to decide the kind of government they wanted. In the intervening period the Royal government would be represented by a regency appointed by the king on the proposal of Šubašić and with the agreement of Tito.

Yalta and Yugoslavia

At the Yalta Conference in February 1945, Churchill, Stalin, and Roosevelt met again. They decided that the Tito-Šubašić agreement should be implemented immediately, and that deputies of the National Assembly elected in 1938 under Milan Stojadinović, who had not collaborated with the occupiers, should join the AFCNLY. All laws passed by the AFCNLY would have to be confirmed by the constituent assembly.

The Yalta decisions dealt a hard blow to the Yugoslav revolution. The National Committee had not been informed in advance by a single one of the Great Powers as to what was coming.

Coalition Government

The Provisional People's Government of Democratic Federal Yugoslavia was formed on March 7, 1945. The National Committee and the Royal government withdrew, and the king appointed a regency. The Great Powers recognized the Provisional Yugoslav government—Great Britain on April 20, the United States on April 28, and the U.S.S.R. on April 29.

Final Battles for the Liberation of Yugoslavia

Final operations for the liberation of Yugoslavia began in April. Over 250,000 new men were mobilized in Serbia to reinforce the front in Srem. Units of the First and Third Armies broke through the German front in Srem and

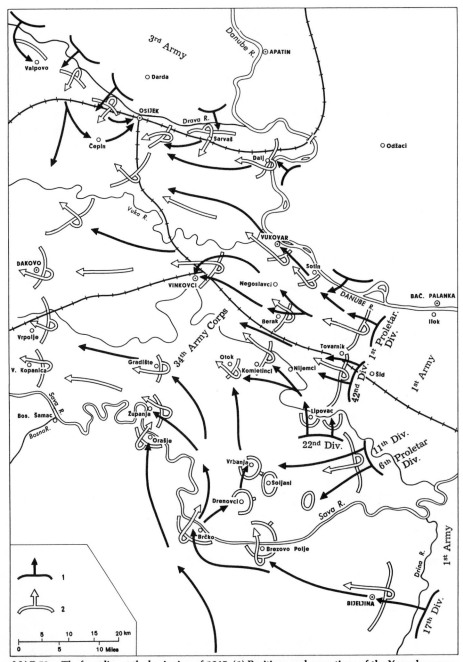

MAP 58.   The front line at the beginning of 1945. (1) Positions and operations of the Yugoslav army;
(2) positions and operations of German and quisling forces.

advanced toward Zagreb. Units of the Second, Third, and Fifth Corps liberated Sarajevo. Units of the Fourth Army and the Ninth Corps liberated Istria and entered Trieste, where they fought the German garrison a full three days. The entire town was liberated with the exception of one casern. In the meantime the Second New Zealand Division of the British Eighth Army reached Trieste and met up with the Yugoslav units. Had the command of the Ninth Corps blown up the bridges over the Soča River, this New Zealand division could not have entered Trieste, which was already liberated.

Although German military power had capitulated on all fronts by May 9, German units in Yugoslavia received orders to continue fighting. Together with the Ustashi, Home Guards, and Chetniks, they offered resistance until May 15, when they were finally annihilated and General von Löhr, the chief German commander for Yugoslavia, surrendered with his staff.

The Collapse of Draža Mihailović

On May 3 the Slovene quisling General Rupnik proclaimed the Independent Slovene State, which lasted only two days. Draža Mihailović with 12,000 men, mostly gendarmes, NCOs, and officers, exploiting the engagement of Partisan forces in fighting the Germans, made an attempt in April 1945 to enter Serbia from central Bosnia. Partisan militia prevented his crossing the Bosna River and he had to make a detour. Crossing Igman Mountain and Zelengora, he arrived at the Sutjeska, where the second battle of the Sutjeska took place in May 1945. Forward units of Mihailović's troops got as far as the village of Plužine at the Piva, where they were stopped in the canyon of this mountain torrent by a unit of the National Defense Corps. Peasants from the village of Mratinja acted as scouts for Mihailović, but when they saw that the Chetnik commanders were amply supplied with British pounds in gold, they attacked them from the rear in the Piva canyon. Mihailović ordered a quick retreat toward the Sutjeska, where troops of the National Defense Corps, supported by aircraft, smashed his units. The people of Mratinja stoned the captured Chetnik commanders to death and took all the gold found on them. Mihailović with a small group of men advanced toward Višegrad. Along the way, his commanders deserted, surrendering one by one.

The Trieste Crisis

Early in May 1945, a crisis arose in relations between the Western Allies and Yugoslavia. After an ultimatum of the British and the Americans, the Yugoslav forces had to retreat from those parts of Carniola which they had earlier liberated. Churchill also wished to solve the question of Istria, the Slovene Littoral, and Trieste by force. He demanded that Yugoslav troops withdraw from these territories. On May 12 President Truman agreed with Churchill's position. Threatening military demonstrations by British and American troops followed. Finally, on June 9, 1945, a compromise was reached according to which the territory of the Slovene Littoral and Istria was divided into two zones, A and B. The former was occupied by Allied troops, and included Trieste, Gorizia, the Slovene Littoral, and the northwestern part of Istria; in the south Yugoslav troops entered Pula, the remainder of Istria, and part of the Slovene Littoral.

Because of this, the Slovenian people did not accomplish total unification, although the old border was significantly corrected. It was even more difficult for the Macedonian people. In Vardar Macedonia they finally achieved their rights, but the Macedonians in Aegean and Pirin Macedonia were not so lucky.

Yugoslavia's Losses in the War

Thus ended World War II during which Yugoslav lands were once again in their history the scene of violent death on a massive scale. Over 1,700,000 Yugoslavs had lost their lives. Most of these casualties were young people between the ages of sixteen and twenty-one, for in contrast to earlier wars, it was the youth that bore the brunt of the Yugoslav revolution of 1941–1945.

In Germany during the war there were 240,000 prisoners of war, hundreds of thousands of workers in military industry, as well as 36,000 in concentration camps. In Italy, to the end of 1943, there were 143,000 internees as well as 46,000 captured officers and soldiers.

CHAPTER 49

Partisan Culture

Democratizing Culture

As the revolution progressed, the desire for education and culture increased. One of the harsh realities of the prewar period was inequality of educational opportunity, victimizing rural districts more than urban. In the midst of the
devastations, mass killings, and ravages of war, the thirst for knowledge and belief in education developed spontaneously. First the Partisan units and later the
National Liberation authorities labored to raise the educational and cultural level
of the people. Ideally, each and every Partisan was not only a soldier but an ex-

ponent of the objectives of the struggle. He popularized it in the first place by his own personal behavior in the countryside or in the newly liberated towns; one moment looking down the barrel of the enemy's rifles, the next he was eloquently explaining why he fought to the people gathered in the liberated villages. It was the ideal of all Partisan units to have not only a machine gun but also a typewriter or Multigraph machine for mimeographing news, songs, anecdotes, or brief accounts of objectives.

As the war proceeded, the conception grew that the aim of the National Liberation struggle was not only to expel the invaders and create better living conditions, but also to produce a new type of human being, new human relations.

The new social structure that emerged in the course of the National Liberation war required that new principles of education and schooling be established. Power passed from the hands of the one class where it had rested to the hands of all sections of the population, most of whom did not possess the knowledge needed to discharge the functions they had to take over.

Consequently, even during the first few months of fighting, the National Liberation movement was confronted with the reality of the country's situation in terms of education as it applied both to schoolchildren and to adults. In view of the fact that half of the population of the Kingdom of Yugoslavia had been illiterate, older people, too, wanted to learn reading and writing.

The System of Schooling in Liberated Areas

At first these problems were solved, or attempts were made to solve them, by the Partisan units themselves, which provided special literacy courses for illiterate fighting men. During the brief intervals between battles, courses for adult illiterates were improvised in the villages. Youth organizations, and especially the Young Communist League, were particularly active, especially after the area of liberated territory had expanded. In the Bosnian March, for instance, children begged passersby not for money or candy but for paper and pencils. National Liberation committees established special departments for schooling. It was their task to open the old schools as soon as feasible, if they were still whole. Where there had been no schools (and this was most frequently the case), they had to find suitable quarters where the children could gather. When nothing at all was available, classes were held in barns or under trees.

Even more difficult was the problem of finding teachers. Many of them had been killed or interned in POW camps, or had joined Partisan units. But Partisan initiative came into play and the duties of teachers were taken over by convalescents or older women from the towns whose age did not permit them to sign up with fighting units. When enemy offensives began, whole villages fled to the mountains and schoolwork was discontinued.

But as the war went on, liberated territory grew; the longer the Partisans succeeded in retaining it, the longer the schools were maintained. Greater attention could then be paid to the entire problem of schooling and the new objectives of education.

In this respect, particular success was recorded by the National Liberation committees on liberated territory in Croatia (Gorski Kotar, Lika, Banija, and other areas), in western Bosnia, and the Bosnian March. Toward the end of 1943, for instance, over a hundred elementary schools with 2,800 pupils were functioning in liberated territory in Lika; ninety-four schools with 2,900 pupils in liberated territory in Slavonia; forty schools with 3,300 pupils in Gorski Kotar. It is interesting to note that before 1941 there were only twenty-three schools in Gorski Kotar; under wartime conditions, difficult as they were, the Partisans succeeded in opening twice as many. Most of the teachers in these schools were not fully qualified for their occupation, and so special courses had to be arranged for them. In 1944 about 90 percent of school-age children attended these improvised schools in Gorski Kotar.

In the spring of 1944, elementary schools were opened in liberated territory in the Zagreb and Kupa River areas. At the end of the school year 1943–1944, liberated territory in Croatia could boast of 1,051 elementary schools with 53,895 pupils and 965 teachers; by the beginning of 1945 there were 1,343 elementary schools and 83,983 pupils. A highly developed system of schooling existed also in Srem, despite the fact that there was no stable liberated territory.

When the Partisans captured the first printing press, they published not only Partisan newspapers like *Slovenski Poročevalec* (the *Slovene Messenger*), *Borba (Struggle)*, *Naprijed (Forward)*, and *Glasnik* (the *Herald*) and periodicals like the Supreme Headquarters *Bulletin*, *Proleter* (the *Proletarian*, organ of the Central Committee of the CPY), and *Naša Žena (Today's Woman)*, but also alphabet books and other textbooks needed for the Partisan elementary schools. In 1944, according to data provided by the Croat leader Ivo Frol, the Partisan press in Italy printed 80,000 copies of an alphabet book that was sold out immediately, making a second edition necessary. An alphabet book was published also in the Bosnian March, where the county National Liberation committee produced a uniform teaching program in 1944 for all grammar schools in liberated territory. The schools were sadly lacking in teaching aids and teachers frequently had to use doors for blackboards.

Another high school was opened in Banija and yet others in Glina, Delnice, and other liberated towns. As far back as 1942, a number of junior high schools were functioning in Dalmatia. Toward the end of 1943, over 27,000 women, elderly men, and children were transported by ship from Dalmatia to the camp of El Shatt in Egypt, near the Suez Canal, out of the reach of vengeful German and Chetnik forces. Four intermediate schools were opened there with 1,194 pupils and 48 teachers.

A ramified system of schooling also existed in Slovenia. A Department of Schools was attached to the Slovene National Liberation Council. In 1943, 432 schools with 29,150 pupils were functioning in liberated territory, and in 1944 there were 531 schools with 34,479 pupils. However, immediately before final liberation, there were only 28,774 for, as the Germans retreated through the Balkan Peninsula, many teachers left for the army and some of the schools had to be closed.

By decision of the Executive Committee of the Liberation Front of Slovenia, dated January 11, 1944, an Institute of Sciences was formed in liberated territory to concern itself with the historical and ethnical problems of Slovenia while making preparations for the peace conference. Dr. Fran Zwitter, a prominent historian, was among the scientists working in this Institute.

In Croatia and Bosnia adult education centers provided courses of lectures on a higher level.

Thirst for Knowledge

It should be noted that appreciable differences in cultural life in Partisan-liberated areas existed not only between various Yugoslav lands but also within the frameworks of a single region. In the occupied towns a different approach was needed. There, supporters of the liberation movement were better educated and politically more conscious, asking only for news, information, and more sophisticated articles. In the villages a broad process of the awakening of the masses was in progress, and it was there that the Partisans did most of their educational work.

Each nationality had its own specific tasks and specific methods of cultural activity during the occupation. In Slovenia culture had for centuries served as a stand-in for statehood and politics and so retained a certain continuity. On the one hand, a rudimentary archaism had been maintained in the remote mountain villages to which Germanization had never penetrated and where the old Slovene language had been perpetuated; although Germanization in the Middle Ages had divested the Slovene people of many specific and enriching aspects of their way of life, including their old folk songs, the peasants jealously though passively guarded this essential element of their cultural identity. On the other hand, the lyrics of poets like Prešern and many others had been instrumental in preserving the national language.

Slovene Brigades Named after Poets

In 1941, when the Slovenes faced the danger of total extermination as a nation, their instinct of self-preservation asserted itself in all spheres, including culture. This was perceived particularly by the leader of the Slovene Partisans Boris Kidrič, who strove to see that this cultural element was introduced into the revolution in an organized fashion. Prešern's anniversary was proclaimed a national holiday, and the first Partisan brigades bore the names of Prešern, Levstik, and Cankar. Gatherings of Party, military, and social organizations were sure to have verses by Slovene poets tacked to the walls, one of the most popular being that by Cankar:

> The people will write their destiny alone
> Without tuxedoes, or the beads of priests.

In the Partisans' contacts with people in the villages there was far more poetry than politics. As the men of the Second Group of Detachments fought their way through Štajerska to Koruška, they often stopped, frozen and hungry, at the doorways of Slovene homesteads to sing the old Slovene songs. This was enough for the people to receive them kindly and give them shelter.

Along the Slovene coast during the long years of Italian occupation, Slovenes had not been permitted to speak their mother tongue. The development of the National Liberation movement meant the establishment of elementary schools in the Slovene language, the printing of leaflets and even books by secret Partisan printing presses. During the war an edition of Prešern's poems was published which even in peacetime would be considered a masterpiece of the printer's craft.

Restoration of the Mother Tongue in Istria

The same process unfolded in Istria, where the Croatian people under Italian fascism had had no possibility of speaking their mother tongue in government offices, courts, and schools. Although there were no qualified teachers, or books, the people themselves opened schools. A report of the Educational Department of the Regional National Liberation Committee for Istria of February 17, 1944, stated:

> Peasants in some of the villages of Buzet County have started courses in the Croatian (literary) language. The people do not wait for us but help themselves as best as they can. . . . Probably there are similar courses in other parts of Istria, but we have no details about them.

Actually these were schools and not courses. Tone Crnobori, historian of Croatian education in Istria during the National Liberation struggle, wrote:

> The people considered the resumption of Croatian schools as the most convincing sign of their national liberation; their national servitude had begun with the closing down of Croatian schools after the Italian occupation of Istria in 1918. It is therefore no wonder that at village gatherings the people seek ways to restore

schooling and that the National Liberation committees in the villages open schools on their own initiative.

In March 1944 a special course for teachers was given in the village of Klarići near Buzet; it was followed by a second and a third. But the last one was suddenly interrupted when German troops attacked the school where classes were held.

According to incomplete data, 150 schools and courses for adults were functioning in Istria between the end of 1943 and liberation in 1945. This figure does not include courses given in Istrian Partisan brigades or those organized by youth and other organizations.

In 1944 a primer was published for Croatians and Italians, 15,000 copies for each in their own tongue.

The First Schools and Books in Macedonia

In Macedonia the Macedonian language was systematically spread by the Partisan units, especially after September 1943, when territory in western Macedonia was liberated. The first Macedonian elementary schools were opened in this area. A special department for education was established in General Headquarters for Macedonia to work out an educational program for elementary schools and publish the first primer in Macedonian. Schools had no teaching aids whatever. Here and there a small blackboard was available, but in many schools, for lack of supplies, the pupils had to learn everything by heart. At the end of 1944 the first books printed in liberated territory in Macedonia, in the Macedonian language, came out stamped "in free Macedonia."

One of the most important tasks of the National Liberation committees, as they set about establishing the new government, was to institute schools for children and adult education courses. It was fully demonstrated then that "hunger for liberty is hunger for knowledge." The illiteracy of large masses of the population was considered a burden on the nation left by history. Sima Milošević, professor at the University of Belgrade and a member of the National Committee of the AFCNLY of 1942, said once in speaking to peasants gathered in Drinići, in the Bosnian March, "It is now the duty of our generation to complete the work begun many centuries ago by Saint Sava." Professor Milošević was killed by the Chetniks as he lay wounded after the Battle of the Sutjeska.

Folk songs were still a living tradition throughout a large section of liberated territory, especially in Bosnia, Hercegovina, Lika, Kordun, Banija, Montenegro, western Serbia. New songs welled up from the people in the familiar ten-beat line, singing of new motifs and new heroes, but still in the spirit of the patriarchal heroic folk poems.

Oral folk poetry was functional, having always represented the principal means of communication between people in these mountainous areas. Each Partisan unit had its own group of performers who established contact with the people in liberated villages through the medium of folk songs and poems, or short plays. These ensembles steadily improved in quality, especially after being reinforced by the influx of professionals from the towns. As far back as the autumn of 1941 a group of actors from the Croatian National Theater of Zagreb made preparations to join the Partisans; they finally managed to do so in the spring of 1942. This first group included Ivka Rutić, Joža Rutić, Vjeko Afrić, Salko Repak, Žorž Skrigin, and Milan Vujnović. In retaliation the Ustashi murdered a number of Zagreb actors: Janko Rakuša, Ivica Štrk, Nikola Vodopivec, Veljko Ilić, and Eugen Lesel.

In the autumn of 1942 the Croat actor Vjeko Afrić recited the poem *The Peasant Knapsack* in Bosanski Petrovac to a large mass of people, who greeted him with thunderous applause. The same year, the Theater of National Liberation, numbering twenty-six members, was founded in the liberated town of Bihać. In addition to actors from Zagreb, Ljubiša Jovanović, Braco Borozan, J. Medjedović, Mira Sanjina, and others joined this theater.

Oskar Danon, musician and conductor from Sarajevo, joined the Theater of National Liberation after he was seriously wounded as commissar of a detachment in Bosnia.

During the early days of the uprising, Partisan units first began to sing Yugoslav revolutionary songs, then Russian and Spanish. In Bosnia, Croatia, and especially Slovenia, poets who joined the Partisans composed new poems and songs. This was the beginning of the cult of Partisan poetry. True, these poems sometimes seemed rather didactic, but that is what the people in the villages wanted. Poets had to compose to suit the taste of the people, fostering their hope for personal and national freedom. The most popular song written in Slovenia was the famous *Hej Brigade* by Matej Bor (Vladimir Plavšić).

A large number of writers, poets, painters, scientistŝ, and doctors fought with the Partisans, especially in Slovenia. Such a large-scale organization as the Liberation Front of Slovenia naturally numbered masses of intellectuals, a great many of whom had joined the Partisans. Among scientists in Serbia who joined the Partisans was the theoretical physicist Pavle Savić. Of the painters there were Marijan Detoni from Croatia; Vojo Dimitrijević and Ismet Mujezinović from Bosnia; Božidar Jakac from Slovenia; Bora Baruh, Djordje Andrejević-Kun, and Pivo Karamatijević from Serbia; and many others. Between battles, several young fighters developed artistic abilities and later became known artists: Aleksandar Tomašević, Edo Murtić, Ive Šubić, Boško Karanović, Stojan Čelić, Jovan Kratohvil, Ivan Seljak-Čopič, and others.

When the Croatian bard and laureate Vladimir Nazor arrived in liberated territory in January 1943 with the young poet Ivan Goran Kovačić, it was decided to convene a congress of artists and scientists to discuss the question of the place and role of culture, art, and science in the new state. The launching of the Fourth Offensive by the enemy nipped this idea in the bud, however, and the congress was not held until the summer of 1944 in Topusko, Banija. At that time there were in liberated territory ten theatrical ensembles and three Partisan printing presses. The congress concerned itself more with the immediate task of reconstructing the country than with the problem of culture in the revolution or its place in the future system. The Slovene intellectuals held a similar congress in January 1944 at Semič.

Literature as Social Action and Moral Dilemma

Literature, prose and poetry, as part of social action, as depiction of a historically dramatic period, as the didactic and utilitarian expression of revolutionary aspirations, played a special role during the war. Many poets and writers who had participated in the revolution turned their attention to a different kind of literature after the war in an endeavor to express the new ethical, aesthetic, moral, and philosophical values that had emerged from the revolution.

One of the writers who displayed a special talent for delving into the social psychology of the peasant in the revolution was Branko Ćopić. He began his career by writing war poetry, and his poem *Song of the Dead Proletarians* is inscribed in the annals of Partisan poetry as a classic. In this poem Ćopić describes a few dozen proletarian fighters from the Bosnian March, surrounded near a hospital in the mountains, making their last charge against a far superior enemy and dying a heroic death in the unequal battle. The poem is illustrative of the mood of the peasant-fighters at the height of the war:

> In our land the wheat is sprouting, sown by our hands.
> The harvest awaits us and the song of girls,
> An evening song, melancholy, low.
> And we have fallen, comrade,
> The wheat has fallen, young green, the early spring harvest.
> Misty sorrow, with the whisper of rain, circles over the
> dead song.
> . . . .
> New youth will come, bringing new days,
> And carry on our unsung song
> forged in living fire.
> Oh, those songs were begun by us, through them we speak
> from afar,
> In them the sister will recognize her brother, the girl her
> beloved,
> And the sorrowful mother her son.

And the day of glory will come, and victory will be ours.
The savage beasts will disappear.
And the detachments of Liberty will march
With the dead proletarians.

Ćopić's novel *Prolom (Cloudburst)*, published in 1952, could serve as a textbook on the social psychology of the Bosnian March peasants during the spontaneous uprising of 1941. Despite wavering and atavisms, the feeling of common humanity prevails and good triumphs over evil.

The literary opus of Branko Ćopić, and that of most Yugoslav writers, reveals a function of literature which does not typify this generation of writers alone. Just as Antun Matoš in Croatia and Radoje Domanović and Branislav Nušić in Serbia, to name only a few, were ahead of the history and sociology of their times in elucidating the basic moral and philosophical values of their society, so did this generation of writers discharge a similar function. They preceded the political scientists, sociologists, and historians in delving into the aesthetic and ethical problems posed by the revolution, launching discussion of heroes and antiheroes in the revolution, the evolution of both former and latter under different postwar conditions. In short, they raised the crucial question of the revolution: In the final analysis, had the objective of developing new human relations, a new human being, been achieved?

In this respect, too, Ćopić was one of the pioneers. His well-known humorous bent was patently present in the *Heretical Tale* (1952), which laid the foundation stone for postwar Yugoslav satire and represented a continuation of the best tradition of Domanović and Nušić. Like other stories and novels of this type, this tale is a bold portrayal of the bureaucratization of the revolution. In his novel *Deaf Gunpowder*, he deftly avoided the cliché of the revolutionary as a man singularly free of dilemmas.

The portraits of the ordinary heroes of the revolution, the rank-and-file fighting men, in the *True Legends* of Jovan Popović, are slightly naïve, somewhat in the manner of the life stories of early Christian martyrs. This book was no doubt intended as the manual of a new mythology, a collection of life stories of latter-day "saints" for believers and disciples.

An exceptionally talented poet was Radovan Zogović, champion of socialist realism, utilitarianism, and didactic literature. Zogović is a strict man first toward himself and then toward others, and he defends his aesthetic principles with exemplary consistency even under the most difficult circumstances— in the revolution, and whether in or out of power. He developed his aesthetics or anti-aesthetics on the basis of the work of Russian postrevolutionary poets, especially Majakovski.

Mihailo Lalić, a participant in the revolution, also passed through a number of phases in his development. After his first short stories, in his novels

The Mountain of Lament and *Pursuit* he worked out the ethical problems of the revolution in a particularly creative way. Lalić's works show the dilemma of the peasant in the revolution, the peasant who is not a hero, who is rent by doubts and fears but resolved to endure to the last breath. Lalić worked his way to the forefront of Yugoslav literature.

Carrying over to his later works the turbulent and metaphoric language typical of his surrealistic days, Oskar Davičo portrays in his novel *Poem* the dilemmas of young participants in the liberation movement. The hero is torn between dry revolutionary asceticism and the youthful instincts of his nature. The climax seems paradoxical: having learned the pleasure of love, the young hero sacrifices his life to the cause, seeming almost to be punished for his blind dogmatism.

In his novel *Far Is the Sun*, Dobrica Ćosić was the first Serbian author to break the chain of writing that seemed more like wartime reporting, of the depiction of Partisans as men but rarely beset by dilemmas. He reveals the tragic fate of man in wartime, admitting that even a hero can be executed in the revolution, and by his own cofighters at that.

In his novel *Divisions*, Ćosić unravels the social psychology of the Serbian peasant in wartime. And in his last novel, *Time of Death*, especially in the second volume, he creates some of the most beautiful prose in contemporary Serbian literature.

What Ćosić accomplished in the literature of Serbia, was done in Slovenia by one of its greatest writers, Edvard Kocbek. As a participant in the revolution who had shouldered responsibility for its course, in his novel *Fear and Courage* (1951) he posed the problem of the thirst for blood in revolution and counterrevolution, of man in war, of mutual extermination, as questions which even progressive revolutions cannot dodge. In essence this is the same question that Prešern had raised in his great work *The Cross at the Savica*.

The most popular Slovene Partisan poet was Matej Bor (Vladimir Pavšić). As an integral personality, he was one of the first after the war to signalize the danger that altruistic Partisan ethics might get lost along the way, an issue dealt with in his dramas *Difficult Hours*, *The Blažonovs*, and *The Wheels of Darkness*.

The greatest lyrical poet among the Slovene Partisans was Karel Destovnik-Kajuh, who was killed in a battle in 1944, at the age of 23.

In his trilogy *Deceptions*, Tone Svetina does not present the Partisan epic with a black-and-white palette but rather realistically reveals the quandaries of both sides, avoiding the platitude of heroes and antiheroes, neatly classified.

The tragic inspiration of the revolution motivated two Croatian poets, Vladimir Nazor in *To an Orthodox Mother* and Ivan Goran Kovačić in *The Pit*, as well as Skender Kulenović in *Stojanka, Mother of Kneževolje*, to elaborate upon the theme of extermination of the Serbian people in 1941 and to condemn the horrors of Ustashi crimes. Ivan Goran Kovačić wrote *The Pit* in the forests of Bosnia. After the Fifth Offensive he was captured and killed by the Chetniks in the village of Vrbnica near the Sutjeska River. *The Pit* was translated into twelve languages, including Vietnamese. The painter Pablo Picasso, inspired by the poetic vision of Kovačić and his tragic end, took *The Pit* as the motif for one of his canvases.

This literature of the troubled conscience won an adherent in Antonije Isaković, whose wartime tales pose the problems of ethical principles, sacrifice for ideals, the psychology of guerrillas, abuse of power, the blind subservience to ideas from which all dogmatism is born. Isaković takes a Hemingway-like view of the revolution in his creation of expressive portraits.

Jure Kaštelan, author of *The Cock on the Roof* and the famous cycle of *The Typhus Cases*, stands out among Croatian writers who participated in the revolution and wrote about it. In the latter book typhus and the hallucinations it produces symbolize all the forces of the old world, of counterrevolution, and of evil.

A poet of the middle generation, Vasko Popa adapts, in his cycle of poems *The Eyes of Sutjeska*, the lapidary language of the folk to modern subject matter, showing the rootedness of every revolution in its region and clime, in the language and national character of the people participating.

Meša Selimović is one of the best known Yugoslav writers. His life's work is to reveal the sociopsychological layers and phenomena that were influential in creating the Yugoslav's consciousness in historic continuity. Even in the Yugoslav revolution those traces of the past were visible. In his works Selimović shows that the revolution opened the issue of man's liberation of himself from his past and from the oppression which bound him.

The theme of the revolution was elaborated upon also by Čedomir Minderović, Tanasije Mladenović, Risto Tošović, Mladen Oljača, Radonja Vešović, and others in Serbia; by Vjekoslav Kaleb, Petar Šegedin, and Slobodan Novak in Croatia; Miško Kranjec in Slovenia; Slavko Janevski and Živko Čingo in Macedonia. Their range runs from apologetics and feature stories, through one-sided descriptions of the war, to critical attitudes, sometimes with biblical and apocalyptic overtones.

Poets of the youngest generation, Branko Miljković and Blažo Šćepanović, both of whose lives ended in tragedy, were the coauthors of a book symbolically named *Death against Death*; they spoke in reverberating tones of the revolution, their work devoid of pathos, expressive rather of the humanity and tragedy of war.

Writer-revolutionaries have already presented a complex and suggestive portrayal of what happened between 1941 and 1945. But the war and revolution remained one of the principal preoccupations of intellectuals in Yugoslavia in later decades as well: in research and the collecting of historical materials, in the evocations of memoirs, in the creation of integral visions in literature and the arts.

Work on the historical reconstruction of the revolution was long devoted to the collection, preservation, and publication of materials and documents. Numerous institutions have been formed for this purpose, and government authorities have also done their share. The most enduring results along these lines have been achieved by the Military-Historical Institute.

As time goes by memoirs accumulate, but their value remains limited by narrow horizons and the fear people have of seeing themselves in historical perspective. Self-censorship is frequently present, although there is no need for it and it is not imposed from the outside.

Efforts in historiography have a wealth of documents to draw upon, not only domestically but from foreign archives, especially German and Italian. The achievements of the new methodological approach are visible, and study has been advanced by the far more favorable climate for scientific research that now exists. Numerous research workers have dedicated themselves to this field of endeavor and many works have been published. However, the scientific vision of the events of 1941 to 1945 is broken into numerous regional and local frameworks and is still not free of the mannerisms of apologetics.

Literature and art have found the least obstruction to the creation of a well-rounded picture of revolutionary events. Innovations are being introduced, particularly by writers of the younger generation who did not participate in these events and have therefore been able to dissociate themselves in terms of time and emotion, as they are not the writers and actors of their own dramas. Under the influence of trends in modern world literature, and their own critical mood, they developed the antiwar complex present more or less in all parts of the world. After two world wars and killing on a huge scale unprecedented in the history of mankind, and in the era of preparation for a third world war which threatens even biological life on this planet, these writers are subjecting all ideologies and all structures to reexamination.

An outstanding author of this younger generation is Miodrag Bulatović, a writer of great talent, who deals with internecine war in a biblical manner, bringing antiheroes out on the stage and endeavoring to demystify artificial revolutionism, Balkan mythomania, imaginary and overstressed sexual potency. Like Bulatović, many younger authors are obsessed with the problem of men who suffer for the heroism of others.

Among the younger poets, Matija Bećković is especially esteemed for his razor-sharp verse and cultural profundity.

The picture of the revolution presented by films has become increasingly complex and true to life, frequently following the aesthetic and artistic example set by world art in its treatment of war and revolution. The first films about the war (*Slavica, This Nation Will Live, Immortal Youth*) depicted the revolution in rather simple declarative form and with pathos. Later, and especially after 1948, films began to present the war and occupation in a far more complex manner (*The Sky through the Branches; Don't Turn Around, Son; Five Minutes of Heaven*) and from the highly individual and personalized standpoint of the author (*The Three, Noon, Ambush, The Mountain of Lament*). For his work in the fields of aesthetics and history of film, Vladimir Petrić is widely known.

In the 1900s, the Zagreb School of Animation [headed by Dušan Vukotić from Bileća] became significant in the world of cinema, producing a number of original cartoons which revealed their own philosophic attitude and a specific style essentially different from the classical, Disney-like concept of animation.

These sociological, philosophical, ethical, and aesthetic problems of the revolution have lost none of their timeliness and remain open and waiting for new answers.

CHAPTER 50

The Historical Significance of the Yugoslav Revolution

During the occupation of 1941–1945, a resistance movement developed
in Yugoslav lands which, by virtue of its massive scale and the heroism of its
participants, represents one of the high points in the world history of struggle
against tyranny. Yet the fact remains that at the same time no other occupied
country in Europe produced so many quislings, and such stubborn ones, as Yugoslavia.

A Part of the Resistance Movement of Europe

The Yugoslav resistance movement was linked with the struggle of other occupied nations in Europe and with the war waged by the three principal powers of the Allied coalition against Nazi Germany and its satellites. In those trying and troubled years, a common anti-Fascist ideology was forged, and similar methods of struggle were employed. But the European movements cannot be considered identical in spite of their resemblance.

A Specific Type of War under Specific Conditions

Within the frameworks of the general war against Nazi Germany and Fascist Italy, Bulgaria, and Hungary, each occupied country waged a *specific type of war under specific conditions*. Consequently each resistance movement bore its own special features, to a greater or lesser degree.

There are a number of reasons for this. In the first place, the occupied countries were not on the same level of social development. In some the process of national self-determination had been completed (France, the Netherlands, Norway, Denmark, etc.); these were nationally stable states where the transition from agrarian to industrial society had already taken place. Elsewhere, in eastern and southeastern Europe, certain nations were only beginning the process of achieving self-determination and modernizing the means of production, relationships, institutions, and superstructures. Although some of these states had acquired formal independence at the end of World War I, the process of self-determination there unfolded under a set of historical circumstances different from that in the western European states. These parts of Europe had undergone the process of modernization in the period of imperialism. In them the struggle for national liberation was predicated on a parallel demand for changes in the social structure in keeping with the principles of social equality. The masses strove to rid themselves of the presence and pressure of foreign capital and of the primitive and sometimes even semifeudal capitalist class which, for the benefit of foreign capital, impeded the development of productive forces in these countries.

Consequently the degree of social and national cohesion was not the same in all occupied states, particularly not in the states where a number of nationalities lived together. In such states the suppression of various nationalities before the war, and after it broke out, weakened their power to defend themselves from the aggressors.

It is not a coincidence that the fiercest forms of resistance to the occupiers during World War II in Europe were found in the least economically developed countries, those with the most profound social antagonisms and unsettled national questions, naturally on condition that subjective factors existed and were skillful enough to organize the spontaneous resistance of the masses and raise it to a higher level. Albania, Greece, and Yugoslavia are good examples of this thesis.

Intensity of resistance in World War II did not depend only on the class affiliation of the fighting men. True, in some industrial countries, where the working class had a revolutionary tradition, as in France and northern Italy, it was the backbone of the resistance.

The Role of Social Classes

But the question comes up of the role of the working class in Germany and Austria in the struggle against Hitler. Why was that working class not more active; why, until the end of the war in 1945, was there not a single rebellion by German workers, dressed up in the military uniforms of Hitler's army?

This is a complex question, with deep historical roots; in answering it, one of the factors that must be taken into account is the social psychology of Germans. Reasons for this psychology include the fact that their state had been split up for centuries, from the end of the Thirty Years' War to 1871, and also the German teaching that the state and its power are above all classes and all individuals. Also influential was the tragic rift in the European working class in 1914, when the great majority of workers' organizations, previously highly class-conscious, followed the lead of their belligerent bourgeoisies. From the very beginning of his fight for power, Hitler struck out against workers' parties and trade unions, killing their leaders or committing them to concentration camps. The masses of workers were thus bereft of leadership and fell prey to Nazi ideology.

The problem of the behavior of the German working class in World War II is linked generally with the problem of the attitude of the working class of Western Europe and the United States of America toward the colonial wars waged by their bourgeoisies after World War II. What did the French working class do to stop the French army in its war against the liberation movements in Indochina and Algeria, or what have American workers done during the war in Vietnam?

The masses of workers did not immediately rise in revolt in all economically underdeveloped countries of Europe either. The only exception in this respect is Greece. First of all, the workers were only a small section of the population. Most of these workers were actually still peasants who lived in their villages and went from there to their jobs in factories or mines. Their class consciousness was on a very low level, and they themselves were frequently under the influence of the atavisms and backwardness of leading circles in their region.

Most of the participants in the resistance movements of these countries hailed from rural districts. Most often they reflected the social psychology of rebelling peasant masses. Spontaneous uprisings were quick to reach their peak, and afterwards the people who had revolted became lethargic. As a rule, during the long years of occupation, the peasant masses faltered during times of acute crisis when the nucleus of resistance was composed of steeled workers and intellectuals who transmitted, by persevering efforts, their higher level of consciousness to the peasants, many of whom developed similar characteristics.

Different Conditions of German Occupation

Spontaneous resistance by the masses also depended on the particular conditions of occupation. The war objectives of Hitler's Germany were not everywhere the same. Hitler did not have the same fate in store for all suppressed states and peoples. He left some of the states a kind of satellite status; others were subjugated outright and removed from the scene as subjects of international law (this was, for instance, the case with Yugoslavia). Hitler acted on the racist ideology of German imperialism. Some peoples, like the Nordic, were able to preserve their cultural identity, while others were to be assimilated, according to German plans, after the most vital forces among them had been physically annihilated. For these reasons Hitler imposed different terms of occupation on different peoples. Although some Slavic nations (Russians, Poles, Slovenes, Serbs, and others) were immediately subjected to mass extermination, for tactical considerations Hitler postponed a similar fate for the other Slavic peoples until the end of the war. Further, the Nordic peoples were not exposed to genocide. During reprisals in Norway and Denmark Hitler ordered two or three Scandinavians killed for each German, but in Poland and occupied parts of the Soviet Union the figure went up to a thousand persons for one German, and in Yugoslavia from fifty to a hundred.

These differing criteria applied by Nazi Germany were no doubt instrumental in fanning greater resistance in states and among peoples where the reign of terror was worse, and where the lives not only of individuals but entire nations hung in the balance.

It also bears remembering that the military-strategic importance of various countries for Germany in World War II influenced Hitler's attitude. For instance, Poland was the chief operational bridge for movements by the German army along the eastern front, large military forces were steadily concentrated there, acting as a powerful deterrent to the possibilities that the Polish people would develop resistance to the Nazis.

On the Relation between Spontaneity and Ideology

There was spontaneous resistance to the German occupation in all countries, to a greater or lesser extent. But its development and transformation into fiercer, more effective forms of struggle depended largely on conscious, subjective social factors, on their ideology and organizational abilities.

Spontaneity and ideology complement each other and make it possible to develop resistance movements rapidly; history has shown that one without the other does not produce results. Even the most spontaneous movements in the war were soon extinguished unless ideological factors were present to guide them, to explain to the masses where they were headed and what the concrete objectives of struggle were. On the other hand, ideology itself cannot be effective unless the feeling of revolt is spontaneous, unless the masses refuse to stand for the present state of affairs and rise against it.

On the Subjective Factor in Resistance Movements

In European resistance movements, subjective factors were not everywhere the same, nor did they behave the same way in all countries. In some— for instance, in Norway, Denmark, Holland—bourgeois circles played a role of considerable importance in organizing resistance. Their ideology was civilian or secular in character. Within the Protestant church in Scandinavia, the desire for resistance arose from philosophical disagreement with the Nazi ideology. Despite the fact that the Roman Catholic church is a centralized organization in which the idea of monolithic unity is a norm of everyday life, various sections of it in a number of countries assumed divergent attitudes toward Hitler's regime during World War II. In Germany Catholic church dignitaries defended Hitler's aggression as a justified, holy war. But in Holland, Belgium, and even France, part of the hierarchy and a large section of the clergy were staunchly opposed to the German occupiers.

The Communist Parties did not behave the same way during World War II, nor did they represent a monolithic bloc. Although they more or less received directives from Moscow, there were essential differences between them, as evidenced, for instance, in the attitude of individual Communist Parties in Europe toward the question of war, toward Nazi Germany and the defense of their own countries during the period between the signing of the Ribbentrop-Molotov Pact in late August 1939 and Germany's attack on the Soviet Union.

Successful guidance of the masses undoubtedly also depended on the objective conditions in individual countries. Nonetheless, consideration must be given to the extent to which various Communist Parties were capable of assessing the situation and choosing appropriate strategy and tactics. The closer their ties with the people, the less chance there was of their adopting dogmas emanating from "the center," in spite of the strict discipline on which the Comintern insisted. If they had rid themselves of a schematic approach, they would have been able to take a more creative attitude to the problems arising from the given situation.

After the occupation of France in 1940, the French Communist Party tried to become legal and requested the German authorities for permission to publish its daily *L'Humanité*, whereas the Norwegian Communist Party publicly defended the German occupation. The secretary of the Central Committee of the Communist Party of Norway, Firboten, called for condemnation of the occupation, but the majority of Central Committee members disagreed. On April 20, 22, 23, 24, 26, and 27 and May 1 as well as on several occasions up to August 13, 1940, the Party daily *Arbeiderer* defended the occupation of Norway, claiming that Hitler had been forced to take this step to prevent Britain and France from making a war base out of Norway; further, the Norwegian Communist newspaper appealed to the working class to continue work in the factories.

Belonging to another group of Communist Parties who condemned the Nazi regime even before their countries were invaded by Hitler, and also immediately after occupation, were the Communist Party of Belgium, the Communist Party of Holland, and particularly the Communist Party of Yugoslavia. They were more closely attuned to the masses and were also influenced by the thinking of Palmiro Togliatti, who had said at the Seventh Congress of the Comintern in 1935 that the foreign policy of parties in power need not be a dogma for the foreign policy of parties in other countries that are struggling to win power. This line was pursued steadily by the Communist Party of China from 1927 onwards; it refused to subordinate the interests of the Chinese revolution to various foreign policy moves of the Soviet Union. Of the European Communist Parties fighting for power, the most independent in this respect was the Communist Party of Yugoslavia.

Although the Communist Party of Yugoslavia acknowledged the Ribbentrop-Molotov Pact of 1939, it did not cease criticizing the Nazi regime, or the danger posed by Germany to the independence and integrity of Yugoslavia. When Hitler attacked the Soviet Union on June 22, 1941, the Foreign Ministry in Berlin published a note containing the reasons for the German aggression. A section of the note was devoted to an explanation of the "hostile activities of the Comintern in Europe." Special mention was made of the Communist Party of Yugoslavia as proof of the faithlessness of Moscow despite the fact that an independent position was assumed by the CPY in consequence of activities by the new leadership of the Party in Yugoslavia, and not instructions from Moscow.

Ribbentrop stated that the CPY issued leaflets "calling for protest against the Cvetković regime's compacting with the imperialist governments in Berlin and Rome" and further cited a leaflet published by the CPY on the occasion of the

Ribbentrop-Molotov Pact of August 23, 1939, in which "the Yugoslav government is attacked for pursuing a policy of rapprochement with Rome and Berlin, and for wishing to hitch itself to the imperialist wagon of Germany and Italy." Ribbentrop further declared that a Communist leaflet disseminated in November 1940 in Zagreb attacked the leader of the Croatian Peasant party, Vlatko Maček, "for wanting to sell the country to the Fascist imperialist in Berlin and Rome." The German note also mentions a proclamation issued by the Communist Party of Slovenia on November 7, 1940, protesting against the "fraternizing of Cvetković's regime with the imperialist governments in Berlin and Rome."

The U.S.S.R., Great Britain, the United States, and Resistance Movements

The development of various resistance movements also depended in substantial part on the attitude of the three leading nations in the Allied coalition against Hitler: the Soviet Union, the United States of America, and Great Britain. They coordinated their military activity during the war and had the same objective—the unconditional capitulation of Germany—but they were three nations with different ideologies and postwar aims. All three Allied powers assumed their own positions toward individual resistance movements and extended them a certain amount of political and also military assistance.

Ruling circles in Great Britain strove to prevent the rebellious masses in occupied Europe from influencing the ratio of social forces, that is, to preserve the predominance of European conservative classes at the end of the war. Consequently London pursued a specific policy toward the resistance movements, advising them not to be too hasty or extreme in their choice of forms of struggle, in the endeavor to prevent the masses from arming themselves and posing the question of their own objectives in the postwar order of Europe. This line was followed especially in Eastern Europe and in the Balkans, Poland, Yugoslavia, Albania, and Greece.

At first Washington did not interfere much in the struggle of the European resistance movements, but as the war unfolded, its influence grew. Reactionary circles in the United States began to give direct assistance to conservative sections of society not only in France but in Yugoslavia as well during the latter half of the war, proclaiming openly anti-Communistic goals.

The Soviet government opposed these aims of the Western powers, less at the beginning of the war, when its own military situation was extremely difficult, and more as the war progressed. However, the tendency of so-called Realpolitik was present in the foreign policy of the U.S.S.R. during the war. Attempts were made, on the one hand, to subordinate certain resistance movements, especially in Eastern Europe and the Balkans, to direct control by Moscow;

on the other, bargains were struck by the Soviet Union with Great Britain and the United States for the division of Europe, and not only Europe, into spheres of interest.

Numerous historical facts confirm that Moscow tried to persuade various Western European Communist Parties, and through them even the resistance movement in various countries, not to take their struggle to extremes which would call forth the disapproval of ruling Western circles in whose sphere of influence France or Italy belonged, for instance. Toward the end of the war, workers in Italy, especially in the north, spontaneously took over all the factories in Milan, Turin, and other industrial centers. This action was approved by all four leading groups in the Italian resistance movement (Accione, Catholics, Socialists, and Communists), but Palmiro Togliatti, obviously not on his own initiative, reprimanded the Party organization of northern Italy for "sectarian behavior." The workers had to withdraw from the factories under the influence of Communists carrying the red banner with hammer and sickle! Togliatti's attitude also had inherent in it elements of the conviction that socialism in Italy would not have to be implemented by force although he was aware that Italy belonged to the Western sphere of influence and not the Soviet.

The case of Greece during its liberation from the Germans was even more tragic. At secret negotiations with Great Britain, it was written off by the Soviet Union as a Western sphere of interest. In December 1944, after the Germans had retreated, the liberation movement had almost complete control over Greece. But Winston Churchill ordered an invasion by tank units to restore the monarchy and the old social order in Greece. Stalin did not move a finger to prevent this aggression.

Perhaps the Greek leadership is to blame for not having seen through Stalin's position, for not having fought more actively to prevent the country from becoming an object of bargaining among the Great Powers.

In this respect, the behavior of the leadership of the Yugoslav resistance movement is instructive for, in spite of negotiations among the Great Powers to divide Yugoslavia into spheres of interest, it found means to assure the country a better fate than that of Greece, for instance.

The Specific Features of the Yugoslav Resistance Movement

Specific objective and subjective conditions in Yugoslavia invested the Yugoslav resistance movement with specific features, the most salient of which are mentioned here.

The resistance movement in Yugoslavia grew from a struggle for national liberation into a revolutionary struggle for the social transformation of the state. Profound historical processes unfolded during the war, and new social forces came to the direction of the state. The basic means of production were wrested from the hands of capitalist owners, and at war's end 82 percent of industry and banking was in the new state's hands. The peasantry's prewar debts were canceled; a thorough agrarian reform was implemented on the principle of expropriation without compensation to former owners. About half a million peasants from insurgent areas descended from the mountains to settle fertile land in the valleys of northern Yugoslavia. By these and other measures, wealth and income were more fairly distributed, especially to the benefit of the unproductive areas which had been the focus of struggle for all four years. The ratio of forces between the city, as the center of power and capitalism, and the rural districts, the object of exploitation, changed in favor of the latter.

The National Liberation movement was explicitly anticapitalistic within the country, and anti-imperialistic toward the outside world. Nazi Germany and its satellites wished not only to deprive Yugoslavia of its national liberty but to fasten a yoke around its neck economically. In the struggle against German imperialism the Yugoslav peoples won not only national independence in the narrow sense but also freedom from the presence of other imperialist states in Yugoslavia, and especially from the meddling of their capital in the country's economic and political life. Toward the end, material foundations had been laid for the more rapid industrialization of the country. Owing to the influence of foreign capital and the role played by the domestic bourgeoisie, this had not been possible in prewar Yugoslavia.

During the four years of war, Yugoslavia created a new type of army, and hammered out a new strategy and tactics. There were no specific fronts between the occupiers and the Partisan forces. Rather, the whole country was the front with encirclement on both sides; the Partisans were cut off from the main Allied fronts, and the enemy garrisons were surrounded by the Partisan forces. There was no rear in the classical sense of the term, either for the Partisans or for the enemy. Geographic and hydrographic factors were not the primary ones in determining Partisan strategy and tactics. The militant spirit of offensive was the decisive element in the defense. The enemy was not permitted to fight the Partisan forces along classical lines, as he was always taken by surprise by Partisan initiative.

So superiority over the enemy was achieved, not in the technical or numerical strength of units, but in the morale of the fighting men, their political consciousness, and tactical resourcefulness. An essential element in this respect was the tie between the fighting men and the masses, for the fact remains that the unarmed people, fully realizing the aims of the war they waged, were the principal factor in victory.

The end of the war found Yugoslavia with a government that differed totally in terms of the social forces on which it relied from the government that had been in existence at the beginning of the war.

The National Liberation government in Yugoslavia also created new foundations for solution of the national question, i.e., the relation among the various nations composing the country. The ground was prepared for a new federalism based on Partisan self-initiative, on respect for the cultural specifics and free development of all the nations in the equal Yugoslav community. The idea of brotherhood and unity was reflected in the social system at the end of the war.

Women were proclaimed equal with men in all spheres of life. Legislation also recognized the right of young people to a much greater influence over public affairs than had been the case before the war.

Parallels between the Yugoslav, Russian, and Chinese Revolutions

The Yugoslav revolution, the armed part of which was implemented under conditions imposed by World War II, was a specific type of manifestation in the forms it took. In terms of substance—the overthrow of the exploiting class and the taking of power by the exploited masses—it did not differ radically from the Russian revolution of 1917 or the Chinese revolution of 1926–1949, but in the forms through which it was implemented, the Yugoslav revolution was a new phenomenon.

Whereas the Russian revolution had been carried out under the slogan of *abandoning the front* in an imperialistic war, the revolution in Yugoslavia, and in China, unfolded under the conditions of a liberation war in which the masses rose—against the occupiers and those who assisted them—in an all-national and revolutionary war of all the people.

Owing to these specific conditions, it may be concluded that the base of the revolutions in Yugoslavia and in China was broader than it had been in Russia in 1917. All three, Russia, China, and Yugoslavia, were largely agrarian countries with a high percentage of peasants in the population on the eve of war, but at different levels of solution of the agrarian question. In Russia the poor peasants joined the revolution en masse, for the agrarian question had not been solved. The rich and middle peasants in Russia, however, were mainly on the side of the counterrevolution. In Yugoslavia the agrarian question had been solved in part between 1918 and 1941. During that period the agrarian reform did away with most of the remnants of feudalism and expropriated the big landed estates, although it is true that compensation was paid. In 1931 Yugoslavia counted 1,985,000 farms under 5 hectares. The peasant felt the pressure of capitalism; the price gap struck him hard, as growing indebtedness did. He had many points of contact with the working class in the struggle for democratic rights for national equality. Consequently, in the revolution of 1941–1945, the Partisans received mass support from the middle and even from the richer peasants, against the background of the particular type of rural social stratification that existed in Yugoslavia. Frequently the poor peasant was not on the side of the revolution. He was too backward, too dependent on the city for his daily bread; consequently bourgeois circles could manipulate him as they wished, and through them the occupier also could wield an influence over him. The phenomenon of the Vendée has been known since the French Revolution: owing to their backwardness, the poorest sections of the population in the villages become the victims of the most conservative forces in society. In Yugoslavia the peasant who was fairly well off was less dependent on the towns than the poor peasant; he was better educated and more autonomous in making decisions. All these were reasons why the villages, and especially the middle peasants, were the foundation of the Partisan movement. The villages fed them, hid them, reinforced their ranks.

In Yugoslavia the peasant masses participated with the proletariat in much larger measure not only in destroying the remnants of feudalism after 1918 but also in the revolution with its purely anticapitalistic slogans (the slogan of the creation of a new and free Yugoslavia) which was reflected concretely from the very first day of the uprising in the formation of new organs of government to replace the old, undemocratic, antinational, and antipeople's authorities.

The strategy and tactics of partisan warfare were developed in Yugoslavia in line with the nature of the base of the revolution. This revolution was carried out not only in a number of large centers with a dense concentration of the proletariat, as had been the case in the Russian revolution; the struggle was pursued outside the towns, among the peasantry. Until the end of the war, not a single large town was in Partisan hands except for a few days on occasions. They were all liberated at the end of the war.

A similar and yet somewhat different process took place in the Chinese revolution. After ridding itself of Comintern tutelage, which tried to persuade Chinese revolutionary forces to copy blindly the strategy and tactics of the Russian revolution, the Chinese revolution from 1927 onwards focused attention on the villages rather than on the towns. It was only in 1948 and 1949 that the victorious revolutionary forces entered the big towns of China.

In view of the fact that the Yugoslav revolution unfolded under different international conditions from those that prevailed during the Russian revolution of 1917, and that German imperialism between 1939 and 1945 resorted to total war, genocide, and the annihilation of entire nationalities as such, the base of the revolution in Yugoslavia was broader than it had been in Russia. For instance, Yugoslavia's intellectuals were in good part, and in some areas in the majority, on the side of the insurgent people from the very first day; this was not the case in Russia.

Further, a section of the lower clergy sided with the revolutionary forces, for the occupier, in waging total war, also persecuted various churches. Consequently a section of the clergy also felt itself jeopardized, and some of the priests participated in the war on the side of the revolutionary forces. (The first proletarian brigades even had something like chaplains, regularly ordained priests who held services, not in the brigades themselves but in the areas through which the brigades passed, for those peasants who wanted to hear services but had no priests of their own, as the occupiers had either killed or banished them.) In the Russian revolution, owing to the specific development of historical conditions in Russia, the church and the majority of clergymen fought actively against the revolution.

The Yugoslav revolution was a *phenomenon peculiar to Yugoslavia.* It proved the rule that no two social revolutions in the twentieth century followed the same pattern. In terms of sequence, it was Russia's experience that a bourgeois-democratic revolution had to be carried out first, and then a proletarian. In Yugoslavia the sequence had its own order and pursued its own logics. In Russia the revolution culminated in the creation of the Soviet government of workers and peasants in October 1917, whereas the first phase of the revolution, the overthrow of tsarism, had taken place in February 1917. Yugoslavia had its new organs of powers, with their own judiciary and executive branches, from the very first day of the revolution; the new government was democratically elected by secret vote directly by the people wherever wartime conditions permitted, and there was no continuity between it and the organs that had disappeared with the old state. Therefore one of the essential premises of a proletarian revolution was created at the very beginning of the revolution, whereas one of the primary tasks of a bourgeois-democratic revolution, like the abolition of monarchy, was effected only at the end of the revolution in Yugoslavia with the proclamation of the republic on November 29, 1945.

The Russian revolution had been more doctrinaire, for Russian revolutionaries, like the French revolutionaries of 1789, spent almost half a century discussing what forms the revolution would take. The Yugoslav revolution was less doctrinaire and more pragmatic. Owing to the danger of total annihilation of the nation, the revolution was implemented under the slogan of brotherhood and unity despite the tendency toward class divisions in various periods of the revolution when bourgeois circles placed class interests above patriotism. This was a rational, and the only possible, answer in the given situation to Kropotkin's concept of *mutual aid* in major elemental and social crises, although there was no direct ideological influence.

Owing to the specifics of the Yugoslav revolution, there developed a concept of the kind of relations that should be maintained with other states that did not have a capitalist social order. The idea of internationalism ran strong during the entire Yugoslav revolution, but so did the conviction that the revolution was being carried out for the sake of the working masses of Yugoslavia, and not for the sake of one state or another. This process of awakening unfolded slowly. In the beginning of the revolution the conviction prevailed that Yugo-slavia would become one of the republics of the U.S.S.R. But when the first difficulties cropped up with Moscow over the character of the revolution, over the attitude toward Draža Mihailović and the Great Serbian bourgeoisie, over the right to develop the revolution autonomously, over the question of secret treaties for spheres of interest, the new revolutionary government of Yugoslavia was bolstered in its conviction that an independent revolutionary Yugoslavia would emerge from the war, independent of friend and foe alike. In this respect the decisions passed by the Second Session of the Anti-Fascist Council for the National Liberation of Yugoslavia were decisive, as they laid the foundations for the new Yugoslav state. Thus the logics of the Yugoslav revolution led to the conflict with the U.S.S.R., for the two states had entirely different conceptions of the nature of relations between socialist states and of the forms to be employed in the building of a socialist society.

The New Phase of Modernization in Yugoslavia and the Circumstances under Which It Began

At war's end, new people came to the head of state in Yugoslavia. The large majority of them were of peasant origin. Of the prewar Communists who had led the revolution, most of them politically conscious workers and intellec-tuals, three-fourths had laid down their lives for their people. The masses of the peasants in Yugoslavia, who composed nearly 80 percent of the population, joined the liberation movement and took active part in the revolution, in some areas in large numbers, in others to a lesser degree, in some for a longer period, in others briefly, and with more or less hesitation. But basically they were on the side of the revolution, under the leadership of, and in alliance with, the Com-munists until the final liberation of the country. From them emerged the military and state leaders of the new Yugoslavia. In 1941 the Yugoslav working class was numerically small. The most class-conscious among them, the Communists, were the first to go into battle in 1941, and most of them gave their lives to the struggle. Actually, owing to Yugoslavia's economic backwardness, there were few real proletarians. In most cases they were still half peasants, bound to the soil, either directly or by tradition. Even the most highly conscious proletarians, like the miners of Husinje who took up rifles in 1941 to fight the occupiers, felt a nos-talgia for the land. Their favorite song, which they sang as they went into battle, was:

> With plow the peasant tills the soil;
> Without the plow, no use to toil.

The chief working-class centers in Yugoslavia began to send large numbers of men to the Partisans only toward the end of 1942. But the fact remains that in the Yugoslav revolution the peasant masses were governed by the ideology of the revolutionary section of the working class. In this respect the idea expressed by the Vietnamese revolutionary leader, General Giap, that contemporary liberation war in economically underdeveloped countries is a war waged by peasants governed by the ideology of the working class, is applicable to Yugoslavia.

In the Yugoslav revolution, as in any other, the problem of reciprocal influence should not be neglected. The revolutionary working-class ideology elevated the consciousness of the backward peasantry, showed them what the objectives of the struggle were, opened up the prospect of common struggle against imperialism throughout the world. But the social psychology of the peasantry also brought influence to bear on the situation during the four-year war; its imprint was borne by the men who rose from the rank and file of peasants to take over responsible posts in the army and later in the government. In Bosnia and Hercegovina, Montenegro, Croatia, Serbia, and somewhat less in Slovenia, 90 percent of the cadres in the Partisan army and sociopolitical organizations at the end of the war were of peasant or semipeasant origin. It was inevitable that they should also leave *their* imprint on the institutions in which they worked and in many cases headed; they developed their own working methods and gradually came to influence the revolutionary ideology which had carried them to victory. There appeared in the conception of the warrior in peacetime and in wartime the old Dinaric tradition that when there is peace, the warrior should enjoy the fruits of his wartime exploits; in his conception of power, he identifies himself with the general social good.

It was under these conditions in 1945, in a war-ravaged land that had sustained enormous losses in manpower and material goods, where a new conflict loomed with the Great Powers—the recent allies, Great Britain and the United States—where danger threatened from a potential conflict with the U.S.S.R., and with cadres such as those described above, that Yugoslavia launched its struggle to build socialist relationships to construct a modern society.

Chronology of Events, 1945-1973

November 29, 1945

The Constituent Assembly proclaimed that Democratic Federal Yugoslavia would be a people's republic under the name of the Federal People's Republic of Yugoslavia. It would be a unified state with a republican form of government, a community of equal peoples who had freely expressed their will to remain united within Yugoslavia. This decision abolished the monarchy in the name of the peoples of Yugoslavia, and Petar II Karadjordjević, together with the entire Karadjordjević dynasty, was deprived of all rights.

January 21, 1946

The Constituent Assembly promulgated the Constitution of the Federal People's Republic of Yugoslavia, whose two basic principles were the unity of authority and democratic centralism. The FPR Yugoslavia was to be composed of the People's Republics of Serbia, Croatia, Slovenia, Bosnia and Hercegovina, Macedonia, and Montenegro. The Serbian republic was to encompass within its borders also the autonomous provinces of Vojvodina and of Kosovo and Metohija.

The first Yugoslav Republican Constitution was modeled on the 1936 Constitution of the U.S.S.R., and many rights which each republic obtained during the Partisans' struggle were yielded to the central government. Also the principles of the administrative leadership of the economy were adopted. Bureaucratic-statistic routines replaced in many fields the revolutionary self-government of Partisan times.

March 18, 1946

Tito visited Poland, where a treaty of friendship and mutual assistance was signed.

April 19, 1946

The new Yugoslav regime was recognized by the United States. A pro-Yugoslav lobby composed of Americans of Yugoslav descent was working hard in Washington. Most prominent among them was Nick Bez, fishing magnate of the Pacific Northwest, who came to America at the turn of the century as an illiterate fisherman from Dalmatia. Before recognition, the Yugoslav government had to give assurances "that it was ready to observe existing treaties and agreements between the United States of America and the Royal Yugoslav government." This statement later became the basis for requests by the United States and other Western governments for compensation for their enterprises in Yugoslavia, which were nationalized in 1945, as well as for the settlement of all debts of the old Yugoslav regime. Faced with the economic blockade organized by the Soviet Union in 1948, Tito's government compensated all Western powers for their lost investments in Yugoslavia.

The United States resumed full diplomatic relations with Yugoslavia, at the end of April 1946, with a statement that "this step does not imply American approval of Yugoslav internal policies, but was the result of Tito's acceptance of the international obligations of the old royal regime in Yugoslavia."

May 10, 1946

In Belgrade, Czechoslovakia and Yugoslavia signed a treaty of friendship, mutual assistance, and cooperation.

July 11, 1946

A twenty-year treaty of friendship and mutual assistance was signed in Tirana between Yugoslavia and Albania.

July 15, 1946

After a trial begun on June 10, the Supreme Military Court in Belgrade found General Draža Mihailović and twenty-three other persons guilty of collaboration with the enemy, among other charges. The death sentence was imposed on Mihailović, who in early March had been betrayed by his illegal Belgrade organization and, particularly, by Major Nikola Kalabić, the commander in chief of the King's Mountain Guards, who took part in his capture in a village at the border of Serbia and Bosnia. At the trial Mihailović pleaded not guilty. At the same trial, two former presidents of the Yugoslav Royal governments, Slobodan Jovanović and Milan Purić, were sentenced, *in absentia*, to sixteen years of hard labor. Mihailović was executed at the end of July, by a firing squad commanded by Slobodan Penezić-Krcun, the minister of interior of the Serbian People's Republic.

August 19, 1946

The Yugoslav Air Force shot down two transport planes of the European Air Service of the U.S. Army over Yugoslav territory in Slovenia. The American Secretary of State, Dean Acheson, described these attacks as "outrageous" and presented two notes to the Yugoslav government, setting an ultimatum of forty-eight hours for freeing the crew and passengers of one of the planes. The Hearst press demanded editorially that President Truman drop an atomic bomb on Yugoslavia as a reprisal. The Yugoslav government answered that Yugoslav sovereignty had been infringed by the American military aircraft; in fact, between July 18 and August 8 a total of 171 unauthorized American aircraft had flown over Yugoslavia, among them 88 bombers, 39 fighters, and 44 transport planes. The Yugoslav government accepted the American ultimatum, and Marshal Tito deplored the loss of American lives and gave assurances that no foreign plane would be shot at under any circumstances.

At the Paris Peace Conference, Soviet Foreign Minister Molotov, in a private talk with Yugoslav Foreign Minister Edvard Kardelj, deplored the whole incident, stressing the fact that the United States possessed atomic weapons.

October 11, 1946

The People's Court in Zagreb sentenced Alojzije Stepinac, the archbishop of Zagreb and Roman Catholic primate of Yugoslavia, to sixteen years of hard labor. The Court found him guilty of collaboration with the Nazis and their *ustasha* quislings during the war and of sanctioning the compulsory conversion of 200,000 East Orthodox Serbs to the Roman Catholic church. Archbishop Stepinac pleaded not guilty.

November 29, 1946

Voluntary youth brigades from all parts of Yugoslavia, assisted by a great many boys and girls from abroad, completed the Brčko-Banovići railway line in Bosnia after six months' work, linking an important coal mining district with the main industrial centers of Yugoslavia.

December 1, 1946

About 80 percent of Yugoslav industry had been nationalized, as well as all mines, transport, banking, and wholesale trade. In agriculture the Law on Agrarian Reform of August 23, 1945, was implemented. By this the last remnants of the feudal system were destroyed and capitalist relations in the village were limited by the principle that "the land belongs to those who will till it." All estates over 45 hectares or those with 25 to 34 hectares of arable land were expropriated; 1,566,030 hectares of land were taken over from 60,000 owners. At the same time new forms of land socialization were initiated: in 1946 there were 454 peasant working cooperatives with 75,184 members and almost 120,000 hectares of land, while state farms organized production on 288,000 hectares. Yet less than 10 percent of the land was socialized. In 1945 there still existed 2,650,000 private farms, of which 92 percent had less than 10 hectares of land.

February 10, 1947
A peace treaty with Italy, Bulgaria, and Hungary was signed in Paris. A new frontier was established between Yugoslavia and Italy. The Zadar (Zara) enclave, the former Italian islands off the Dalmatian coast, the greater part of the Soča (Isonzo) Valley, and the greater part of the Istrian Peninsula were returned to Yugoslavia. The Free Territory of Trieste was established. Yugoslavia did not accept the Trieste ruling of the Conference. Italy also had to pay to Yugoslavia reparations of 125 million dollars.

April 28, 1947
The National Assembly passed the First Five-Year Plan for the Industrialization of Yugoslavia. It called for a fourfold increase in steel and iron production and an increase in the production of oil from 1,000 barrels to 450,000 barrels and a 274 percent increase in mining. The Assembly stressed the need for rapid improvement of the backward Yugoslav economy and a strengthening of the socialist sector of the economy.

September 9, 1947
At a closed meeting in Poland of the representatives of the Communist Parties of the Soviet Union, Yugoslavia, Czechoslovakia, Poland, Romania, Bulgaria, Italy, and France, the Information Bureau, or the Cominform, was formed. During the meeting the Yugoslav delegates Kardelj and Djilas strongly criticized the French and the Italian Communist Parties "for opportunistic attitudes both during the war and afterwards." It was decided that the seat of the Cominform should be in Belgrade. The newspaper *For Stable Peace and People's Democracy* became the organ of the Cominform with the Soviet official Pavel Judin as the editor.

November 27, 1947
Tito visited Bulgaria and signed at Varna a twenty-year treaty of friendship, cooperation, and mutual assistance. The treaty had been prepared at the Bled conference, August 2, with Georgi Dimitrov. The possibility of a customs union was discussed as well. Tito also announced that Yugoslavia would donate 25 million dollars to Bulgaria, which Bulgaria should have paid to Yugoslavia

as reparations for damages done by the Bulgarian army during the occupation of Yugoslavia in World War II.

December 19, 1947

Warmly received by masses of people in Romania, Tito signed a treaty of friendship and mutual aid with Romania. A similar treaty had been signed with Hungary on December 8.

January 14, 1948

The Yugoslav government demanded the unconditional release by the United States government of some 60 million dollars of Yugoslav funds which had been sent to the United States just before the Nazi invasion, on April 6, 1941. The American government rejected the Yugoslav request, stressing "if Yugoslavia was willing to provide the United States government and its nationals with adequate and effective compensation for losses and expenditures to which they are justly entitled, it will be possible to achieve at an early date a satisfactory general settlement."

February 10, 1948

At a meeting in Moscow, Stalin gave an ultimatum to a delegation of the Central Committee of the Yugoslav Communist Party (Edvard Kardelj, Milovan Djilas, and Vladimir Bakarić) that a federation between Yugoslavia and Bulgaria should be realized at once. This represented the beginning of the open breach between Moscow and Belgrade. Negotiations for Soviet economic aid and the purchase of war materials were begun. The Yugoslavs had to sign pledges for obligatory consultation with the Soviet Union in the field of foreign affairs.

March 1, 1948

At a meeting of the Central Committee of the Yugoslav Communist Party in Belgrade, Kardelj reported on Stalin's ultimatum and the Central Committee rejected it. One member, Sreten Zujović, then informed Anatolij Lavrentijev, the Soviet ambassador in Belgrade, about the meeting.

March 15, 1948

The census showed that the population of Yugoslavia was almost 16 million. Serbia had 6,523,224, Croatia 3,749,039, Slovenia, 1,388,085, Bosnia and Hercegovina 2,561,961, Macedonia 1,152,054, and Montenegro 376,573. Belgrade had 388,246, Zagreb 290,417, Ljubljana 120,944, Sarajevo 78,173, Skoplje 91,557, and Titograd (formerly Podgorica) 12,226.

March 18, 1948

The Soviet government decided to withdraw all Soviet military advisers in Yugoslavia. Tito wrote a letter of protest to Molotov.

March 20, 1948

The American, British, and French governments proposed that the whole Free Territory of Trieste should be placed under the sovereignty of Italy. Up to that time Zone A of the Territory was under Anglo-American military government and Zone B was under Yugoslav military government. The Yugoslav government protested against the Tripartite declaration on Trieste and proposed direct negotiations with Italy on the matter.

March 27, 1948

Moscow sent a letter to the Central Committee of the Yugoslav Communist Party accusing its leadership of anti-Soviet attitudes and ideological deviations.

April 12–13, 1948

After two days' deliberation, the Central Committee of the CPY rejected Moscow's accusations. Tito warned members of the Committee that ideological issues were not the cause of the conflict but rather "Russia's refusal to treat Yugoslavia as an independent state." It was decided that all members of the Party should be acquainted with Moscow's letters.

May 4, 1948

Stalin and Molotov answered the Yugoslav letter of April 13 with repeated charges of ideological deviations and anti-Soviet actions; they also claimed that the Yugoslav Partisans achieved no greater results than the resistance in neighboring countries. The Central Committee of Yugoslavia rejected all the charges and presented a list of violations of relations between the two countries, by the Soviet espionage service, for example.

May 22, 1948

The Economic Committee of the United Nations Economic and Social Council ruled that the American-Yugoslav dispute on the return of 56 million dollars of the Yugoslav gold held in the United States was outside the Council's jurisdiction. In its complaint the Yugoslav government stressed that the United States government's failure to return its gold reserves, deposited in the United States for safekeeping during the war, was damaging the Yugoslav economy and its recovery program.

June 28, 1948

At a meeting of the Cominform in Bucharest, attended by the representatives of the Soviet Union, Bulgaria, Poland, Czechoslovakia, Romania, France, and Italy, the Yugoslav Communist Party was expelled from the Cominform because of "pursuing a policy of nationalism and Trotskyism," "deviation from Marxism and Leninism," "hostile attitude toward the Soviet Union," and failing to take any action against the rich peasants.

June 29, 1948

The Central Committee of the CPY decided to publish the full text of the Cominform resolution together with the Yugoslav reply, which refuted the charges and described them as lies and slanders.

July 28, 1948

The Cominform resolution was read at the Fifth Congress of the CPY, held between July 21 and 28, and was unanimously rejected. The press of the Soviet Union and satellite countries now began open attacks on the Yugoslav leadership. The Cominform Headquarters were transferred from Belgrade to Bucharest. Albania broke off economic relations with Yugoslavia. Provocateurs were infiltrated into Yugoslavia to incite dissatisfaction among the different nationalities. The Soviet Union started to apply an economic blockade against Yugoslavia.

August 15, 1948

The Conference on Freedom of Danubian Navigation was opened in Belgrade on July 29. Yugoslavia together with the Soviet Union and other Eastern European countries presented a solid block against the British, French, and American delegations.

May 11, 1949

In Tirana, Koci Dzodze, the organizational secretary of the Communist Party of Albania, was sentenced to death as a Yugoslav spy.

June 10, 1949

The Chinese leader Liu Shao-chi published an article in *Pravda*, giving full support to Stalin's accusations against Yugoslavia.

July 25, 1949

The official leadership of the Greek Communist Party, headed by Nicolas Zahariades, under instructions from Moscow had been attacking the Yugoslav government as "traitors," although the Yugoslav government was extending substantial help to the Greek guerrillas. Because Zahariades persisted in his attacks against Yugoslavia, the Yugoslav government decided to close its border with Greece.

August 18, 1949

Protesting the arrest of Soviet citizens in Yugoslavia (i.e., Russian émigrés who had fled to Yugoslavia after the 1917 revolution in Russia), who had been charged with espionage for the Soviet Union, Molotov delivered an ultimatum to Yugoslavia that all of them should be released at once, "otherwise other more effective means will be employed" against Yugoslavia. Tito ordered Yugoslav troops to the northern borders of the country, and Partisan detachments throughout Yugoslavia were alerted.

September 16, 1949

The former Hungarian minister of the interior, Laszlo Rajk and several other persons were brought to trial, where they stated that the Yugoslav leaders were agents of foreign intelligence services and that they were trying to organize a counterrevolution in Hungary.

September 28, 1949

The Soviet government broke off the treaty of friendship and mutual aid with Yugoslavia concluded on April 11, 1945, branding the Yugoslav government as "a foe and enemy of the Soviet Union." The Polish, Hungarian, Bulgarian, Romanian, and Czechoslovak governments took similar steps.

October 5, 1949

The Yugoslav government recognized the new government of the People's Republic of China, even though the Chinese Communist Party sided with Moscow against Yugoslavia.

October 20, 1949

Soviet troops were concentrating on the Hungarian and Romanian borders with Yugoslavia; over the past months Yugoslav borders had been violated by armed incursions from all the satellite countries. Under these conditions Yugoslavia took steps to be elected to the Security Council of the United Nations.

November 29, 1949

The Cominform published its second resolution on Yugoslavia, stating that the leadership of the CPY is "in the hands of assassins and imperialist spies" and called all the Communist and workers' parties in the world to join in the struggle against Tito and his men.

December 23, 1949

The government and the Trade Union issued *Instructions for the Establishment and Procedure of Workers' Councils in State Economic Enterprises.* Copies were sent to all the main trade union councils in the various republics and to the pilot enterprises selected for the establishment of workers' councils. At first they were to have a consultative role. The first pilot workers' council was elected in the cement factory near Split, Dalmatia.

January 8, 1950

The governments of the United States and Yugoslavia signed an agreement for the sale of surplus United States farm commodities.

February 22, 1950

Despite pressure from some Western governments, Yugoslavia recognized the government of the People's Republic of Vietnam.

June 27, 1950

The People's Assembly enacted the Basic Law on the Management of State Economic Enterprises and Higher Economic Associations by the Working Collectives. The law established the principles for the election and removal of delegates to the workers' councils of enterprises by the working collectives.

September 28, 1950

A heavy new concentration of troops on the Hungarian border with Yugoslavia was reported.

August 23, 1951

In a speech in Bucharest Soviet Marshal Kliment Voroshilov called upon the Yugoslav population to mutiny against the Yugoslav government.

September 10, 1951

The East German Communist leader Walter Ulbricht mentioned at a press conference the possibility of an armed invasion against Yugoslavia and a local war in the Balkans.

November 14, 1951

Having information that the Soviet Union with its satellites was preparing an armed invasion of Yugoslavia, Tito made a formal request for military equipment from the Western powers. A formal military assistance agreement was signed between the governments of the United States and Yugoslavia. Tanks, jet fighters, and other weapons soon arrived. Also several hundred Yugoslav officers were sent to the United States for training.

November 27, 1951

Because of the sharp increase in the number of border incidents initiated by Soviet satellites in 1951, the Yugoslav government decided to complain of the aggressive behavior of the Soviet Union and its satellites to the General Assembly of the United Nations. The Yugoslav complaint was accepted by fifty votes against five (the Soviet Union, Poland, Czechoslovakia, Ukraine, and Byelorussia), while Iran and Afghanistan abstained.

November 7, 1952

The Sixth Congress of the Communist Party of Yugoslavia was held in Zagreb between November 2 and 7. The name of the Party was changed to the League of Communists of Yugoslavia. Various measures were adopted for the increase of workers' control and for liberalization in the country in general.

November 20, 1952

The Czechoslovak Communist leaders Rudolf Slanski, Vladimir Klementis, and several others, went on trial in Prague as foreign spies.

December 24, 1952

Yugoslavia broke off diplomatic relations with the Vatican.

January 13, 1953

The Federal People's Assembly adopted various amendments to the 1946 Constitution on the structure of government and on the relations between the organs of state authority and the organs of state administration. A federal Executive Council, headed by the president of the republic and four vice presidents, was formed. Also a Council of Nationalities and a Council of Producers were introduced. Marshal Tito was elected president of Yugoslavia.

February 28, 1953

Yugoslavia, Greece, and Turkey signed a treaty of friendship and cooperation, on the basis of which regular consultation between the three states was envisaged.

March 28, 1953

Tito visited Great Britain between March 23 and 28.

March 29, 1953

By a decree of the government, members of peasant working cooperatives were permitted to withdraw from these farms and return to individual farming; in addition the cooperatives themselves could be disbanded by a majority vote of their members. The peasants also were permitted to create other forms of cooperative organizations. By another decree the maximum of 45 hectares that had been fixed in 1945 was reduced to 10 hectares. This measure affected 66,000 peasants, and 276,000 hectares were expropriated and added to the state farms.

August 15, 1953

An Egyptian military mission visited Yugoslavia.

January 10, 1954

After Stalin's death on March 6, 1953, the attacks against Yugoslavia in the Soviet press were toned down, the number of border incidents began to decrease, and ambassadors were again exchanged between Yugoslavia and the U.S.S.R. and its satellites.

January 20, 1954

Milovan Djilas, the president of the Federal Assembly and one of the secretaries of the Central Committee of the League of Communists of Yugoslavia, was dismissed from the Central Committee because of his articles in the Party paper *Borba* and other journals demanding "a faster process of democratization of the Party and the country." The Central Committee stated in its decision that Djilas's articles were basically opposed to the policy adopted at the Sixth Congress of the Party and that by causing confusion among the members of the Party, he "damaged the organizational unity of the Party."

August 9, 1954

The Balkan Pact, a formal military alliance between Yugoslavia, Greece, and Turkey, was signed.

October 1, 1954

After six years of trade war against Yugoslavia, the Soviet Union ended it officially by signing a trade agreement with Yugoslavia in Belgrade.

October 6, 1954

The settlement of the Trieste issue was at last achieved by direct negotiation between the Yugoslav and Italian governments. Italy got the city of Trieste and part of Zone A, and Yugoslavia obtained Zone B, part of Zone A, and the right to use Trieste as a free port.

December 26, 1954

Tito made his first state visit to India, meeting Pandit Jawaharlal Nehru.

January 10, 1955

Although the Yugoslav government had recognized the People's Republic of China as far back as October 5, 1949, diplomatic relations between the two countries were not established until January 10, 1955.

January 25, 1955
   Tito visited India and Burma from December 16 to January 25. In his speech to the Indian Parliament, Tito gave his views on the policies of nonalignment and on the inequalities between economically developed and underdeveloped countries.

March 2, 1955
   Passing through the Suez Canal, Tito met President Nasser of Egypt.

June 2, 1955
   After a visit of an official Soviet Party and government delegation to Yugoslavia, headed by the Party leader Khrushchev and Prime Minister Bulganin, a joint declaration, signed by Tito and Bulganin, was issued, in which it was said among other things:

> In examining the questions which were the object of the negotiations . . . the Governments proceeded from the following principles:
> 1. The indivisibility of peace, upon which collective security can alone be based.
> 2. Respect for sovereignty, independence, and territorial integrity, and for equality between States in their mutual relations and in their relations with other States.
> 3. Recognition and development of peaceful coexistence between nations, irrespective of ideological differences and differences of social systems, which implies the cooperation of all States in international relations in general, and in economic and cultural relations in particular.
> 4. Mutual respect and noninterference in internal affairs for whatever reason— whether of an economic, political, or ideological nature—since questions of internal organization, of differences of social systems, and of different forms of socialist development are exclusively a matter for the peoples of the different countries.
> 5. Development of mutual and international economic cooperation, and the removal of all those factors in economic relations which hamper trade and retard the development of productive forces, both in the world and within the bounds of national economies.
> 6. Assistance through the appropriate United Nations agencies, and also in other forms that are in conformity with the principles of the United Nations, both to the national economies and to economically underdeveloped areas, in the interests of the peoples of those areas and in the interests of developing the world economy.
> 7. Discontinuation of all forms of propaganda and misinformation, as well as of other actions which spread mistrust or which in any way impede the creation of

an atmosphere for constructive international cooperation and peaceful coexistence among the nations.

8. Condemnation of all aggression and of all attempts to establish political and economic domination over other countries.

9. Recognition of the fact that the policy of military blocs increases international tension, undermines confidence among the nations, and increases the danger of war.

July 7, 1955

Nehru spent seven days in Yugoslavia.

January 6, 1956

From December 28, 1955, to January 6, 1956, Tito paid his first state visit to Egypt.

February 25, 1956

In his secret report to the Twentieth Congress of the Communist Party of the Soviet Union, Nikita Khrushchev described the conflict between the Soviet Union and Yugoslavia in 1948, stating that Stalin had expected a quick victory and had said on the eve of the conflict: "I will shake my little finger and there will be no more Tito."

April 15, 1956

It was announced in Moscow that the Cominform, the international organ of several Communist Parties, headed by the Soviet Communist Party, which had expelled Yugoslavia from its ranks in 1948, was dissolved.

June 1–20, 1956

Tito arrived in the Soviet Union, and after three weeks of discussions and sight-seeing he signed a joint Soviet-Yugoslav declaration in which the principles of the earlier 1955 Belgrade declaration were underlined:

> Yugoslavia and the Soviet Union both adhere to the ideas of Marx, Engels, and Lenin, but this does not mean that the two states have identical views on all subjects. All the Communist Parties should be independent and equal and not dominated from one center. There are many roads to socialism, and Communists in each country should be free to adapt their policies to the local situations and are not obliged to follow any model.

At private receptions several Soviet leaders confessed that they were forced by Stalin to take anti-Yugoslav attitudes during the crisis of 1948–1953.

July 19, 1956

Nehru, Tito, and Nasser met at the island of Brioni in Yugoslavia and issued a declaration denouncing the division of the world into antagonistic blocs.

November 11, 1956

In a speech at Pula, Tito denounced the first Soviet military intervention in Hungary, on October 24, as unnecessary, but claimed that the second Soviet military intervention was necessary, because of the alternative of massacres of Communists, of civil war, of the infiltration of Western agents, and of the reappearance of supporters of the former Admiral Horthy regime in Hungary. Yugoslavia also opposed putting the case of Soviet aggression against Hungary to the Security Council of the United Nations.

November 22, 1956

The Yugoslav government had given the right of asylum to the former prime minister of Hungary, Imre Nagy, and his colleagues in the Yugoslav embassy in Budapest. After the Kadar government guaranteed that nothing would happen to them, Nagy and his men left the Yugoslav embassy, but they were immediately arrested by Soviet security agents.

December 12, 1956

Milovan Djilas, the former president of the Federal Assembly, was sentenced to three years in prison during a trial held *in camera*. He was tried because of an interview he gave to the Agence France-Presse, criticizing Yugoslavia's abstention at the United Nations on the question of military intervention of the Soviet Union in Hungary, and he stated in particular that "Yugoslavia was threatened by the same imperialism which menaced the independence of Hungary."

October 15, 1957

Yugoslavia recognized the German Democratic Republic and established diplomatic relations with it. Following the Halstein Doctrine, the government of the West German Federal Republic (Bonn) broke off diplomatic relations with Belgrade.

November 10, 1957

A delegation of the League of Communists of Yugoslavia, headed by Edvard Kardelj and Aleksander Ranković, attended the fortieth anniversary celebration of the October 1917 revolution in Moscow. The Yugoslavs signed the peace declaration, but refused to add their signatures to the declaration of twelve Communist Parties, because it seemed to them that it did not take into consideration the principle of the equality of Communist Parties or recognize the right of every country to its own form of socialism.

April 26, 1958

The Seventh Congress of the League of Communists of Yugoslavia was held in Ljubljana between April 22 and 26. A new program was adopted which stressed the idea "that mankind is indomitably moving into the era of socialism along a variety of different roads." The draft of the program was sent to all the leading Communist Parties; the Soviet Union criticized it strongly, branding it as "petty bourgeois nationalism." The original draft was amended at the Congress, and all references to the policies of spheres of influence as practiced by the Great Powers during World War II at the Teheran, Yalta, and Potsdam conferences were omitted. Despite this compromise the Soviets did not send an official delegation to the Congress.

June 15, 1958

The Chinese ambassador left Belgrade, and the Yugoslav ambassador left Peking. The Chinese press opened an attack on "Yugoslav revisionism," as expressed in the Program of the Seventh Congress of the League of Communists of Yugoslavia.

June 28, 1958

The Soviet Union proposed to Yugoslavia that changes should be made in the economic agreements concluded in 1956 between the two countries. A postponement of utilization by Yugoslavia of the Soviet and East German long-term loans totaling 285 million dollars was introduced. The Soviet, Chinese, Albanian, and Polish press increased the attacks against Yugoslavia.

December 1960

In his book *Socialism and War*, Edvard Kardelj discussed the Chinese criticism of the policy of coexistence. He also presented his own views on social contradictions in a socialist state and criticized strongly "the Chinese inclinations toward social egalitarianism."

August 1, 1961

At the 1961 census Yugoslavia had 18,549,000 people: Serbia had 7,642,000, Croatia 4,160,000, Bosnia and Hercegovina 3,277,000, Slovenia 1,592,000, Macedonia 1,406,000, and Montenegro 472,000.

September 6, 1961

The heads of twenty-five nonaligned states met in Belgrade at a conference convened jointly by Tito, Nehru, and Nasser. The conference adopted a twenty-seven-point declaration, denouncing colonialism, demanding the immediate ending of all armed action and repressive measures directed against dependent peoples, and paying tribute to the struggle of the Algerian people, as well as that of the people of Angola. The conference condemned South Africa's *apartheid*.

November 1, 1961

The Yugoslav writer Ivo Andrić was awarded the Nobel Prize in literature.

January 15, 1962

During the Second Five-Year Plan (1957–1961) the average growth rate in Yugoslavia was 13 percent, the highest in the postwar period. Agricultural production expanded by 10.5 percent per year, industrial output by 14.1 percent, and building by 16.2 percent.

May 14, 1962

Milovan Djilas, the former president of the Federal Assembly, was sentenced to a total of eight years and eight months' imprisonment. Because of his book *The New Class*, published in 1957 while he had been serving his first sentence of three years, that sentence had been extended to seven years altogether, but after serving 3½ years Djilas had been released at the beginning of 1961. He was rearrested on April 7, 1962, because of the publication of his book *Conversations with Stalin*. The prosecution based its case on Article 320 of the Yugoslav Constitution, which provides up to ten years of punishment for revealing state secrets. This trial also was held *in camera*. Djilas pleaded not guilty and protested because the trial was secret.

April 7, 1963

The new Constitution of the socialist Federal People's Republic of Yugoslavia was adopted. The new state was defined as a sociopolitical community of the nation, nationalities, and working people of Yugoslavia, a multinational community, and a socialist community. The relation between the federation and the republics was to be, in fact, a relation between two essentially equal and mutually dependent and interlinked sociopolitical communities, which would reflect and constitute the social community of Yugoslavia as a whole.

The Constitution also stressed the importance of further development of workers' management. By its provisions this constitutional system should ensure "the stability of the socioeconomic position and social security of working men, i.e., man as an autonomous subject with equal rights in economic relations, in work and in creative activity."

In Article 254, the Constitution stated that no one has the right to enter in the name of the federation into capitulation with an enemy and recognize the occupation of the country.

April 15, 1965

Yugoslavia joined the East European Council of Mutual Economic Assistance as a qualified observer.

July 1965

During the months of June and July Tito visited the Soviet Union, Algeria, Egypt, Norway, Czechoslovakia, and East Germany.

July 25, 1965

The Yugoslav Federal Assembly introduced a far-reaching economic reform program, allowing a much greater degree of market freedom and increased decentralization.

December 1, 1965

The number of state farms increased from 279 in 1950 to 356 in 1965, and their total area from 424,000 to 1,100,000 hectares. The peasant cooperatives decreased in number from 9,060 in 1950 to 2,424 in 1965, but their total area increased almost tenfold, from 95,000 to 903,000 hectares.

July 1, 1966

At a meeting of the Central Committee of the League of Communists of Yugoslavia, the vice president of Yugoslavia, Alexander Ranković, was expelled from the Party's Executive Committee and Central Committee, on the grounds that he was responsible for the abuses in the work of the UDBA, the Yugoslav civil secret police. The Central Committee also decided that the UDBA should be reorganized and that a special commission should be set up to investigate the abuses.

January 15, 1967

According to official statistical data, the following changes in the population's economic structure took place in Yugoslavia over the last four decades: In 1921, 81 percent of the total population belonged to the agricultural community; in 1931, 76 percent; in 1948, 67 percent; in 1953, 61 percent; and in 1967, 47 percent.

June 15, 1967

Per capita national income, calculated at current prices in dinars, was as follows:

Yugoslavia	4,649	Macedonia	3,132
Slovenia	8,100	Bosnia and Hercegovina	3,039
Croatia	5,577	Montenegro	2,927
Serbia	4,572	Kosovo	1,610

June 12, 1968

After ten days of demonstrations, occupation of several university buildings, and sit-in strikes, the students of Belgrade University ended their action, which was triggered off on June 2 by the intervention of and the use of violence by the local police against the students. The most violent assault took place on June 3, when the police stopped a students' march through the streets of Belgrade by using tear gas and even firearms. More than sixty students were injured. After that the students occupied the main university administrative buildings. Among their demands, they insisted on improved housing conditions at universities, better food in university cafeterias, and more jobs for students after graduation because many of them had to emigrate from Yugoslavia in order to find work, often under appalling conditions. The students also denounced the brutality of the police and asked that all officials who were responsible for brutalities should be dismissed. The students also put up several political demands criticizing social inequality in Yugoslavia, as being against the basic principles of true communism. Support for the strike was almost 100 percent and many faculty members joined it. Students from Sarajevo, Skoplje, Zagreb, and Ljubljana sent their messages of solidarity. On June 4 the rebelling students renamed their university the Red University of Karl Marx. The authorities were divided on how to deal with the students' action. Some advised harsh measures and repression. In a speech on June 12 President Tito pledged to deal honestly with students' grievances.

August 21, 1968

President Tito strongly denounced the invasion of Czechoslovakia by the Soviet Union and other East European countries, stressing that this act "has violated the sovereignty of a socialist country and dealt a grave blow to socialist and progressive forces all around the world."

August 24, 1968

Tito met the head of the Communist Party of Romania, Nicolae Ceausescu.

February 2, 1969

Tito visited President Ceausescu of Romania in Timişoara, and both presidents denounced the Soviet's "limited sovereignty" doctrine.

February 11, 1969

The Federal Assembly of Yugoslavia passed a law creating Partisan units of territorial defense in all parts of the country. The first such units had grown up spontaneously in the days of the invasion of Czechoslovakia, when it seemed possible that the same states might attempt a military invasion of Yugoslavia. According to the new law all males up to sixty-five years of age, and every woman between nineteen and forty, would be assigned to military, paramilitary, or civil defense Partisan units.

March 16, 1969

The Ninth Congress of the League of Communists of Yugoslavia was held between March 11 and 16; it was boycotted by the Soviet Union and all Eastern European Communist Parties except that of Romania. The Yugoslav criticism of the invasion of Czechoslovakia was repeated at the Congress. A fifteen-man Executive Bureau was elected as the collective leadership of the League. Tito was elected president of the Bureau.

June 4, 1969

The workers in the biggest Yugoslav port, Rijeka, went on strike on June 3, protesting 25 percent wage cuts and the reduction of some benefits. Some violence was recorded. Most of the workers' demands were met.

December 20, 1969

Yugoslavia initiated a radical change in its foreign investment policy. The foreign partner should in the future be guaranteed that eventual changes in law would not affect his financial interests. Also the foreign cocontractor is entitled to the transfer of the invested property or may withdraw it partially even during the time of the contract. Thus the Yugoslav laws provide full security in the field of business cooperation. Among foreign investors Italy, Czechoslovakia, and the German Democratic Republic were most prominent, while the United States of America was among the least.

April 17, 1970

As a sign of the improvement in relations between the People's Republic of China and Yugoslavia, new ambassadors were named in Peking and Belgrade.

August 15, 1970

According to official figures, the national per capita income in Yugoslavia rose from 375 dollars in 1955 to 750 dollars in 1970. Slovenia had the highest income of all republics—1,000 dollars; the autonomous province of Kosovo the lowest—200 dollars. Despite a partial price and wage freeze, the cost of living rose about 14 percent in 1969. Yugoslavia had a trade deficit of 1.2 billion dollars with a gross national product of only 14 billion. It had been partly covered by two invisible assets. Tourism brings to Yugoslavia about 400 million dollars per year, while 800,000 Yugoslav workers employed abroad send home over 400 million dollars each year.

August 17, 1970

After a period of eighteen years full diplomatic relations were established between the Vatican and Yugoslavia.

September 14, 1970

At the third Summit Conference of nonaligned countries held in Lusaka, Zambia, and attended by the heads of fifty-four states, including Tito, a Declaration on Nonalignment and Economic Progress was adopted, as well as a number of other resolutions, among which one demanded "the immediate, complete, and unconditional withdrawal of all foreign forces from Vietnam" and expressed the hope that the Paris peace talks might lead to the war's rapid conclusion.

September 21, 1970

Although he did not specify when the transfer of power would take place, President Tito made public a succession plan by which a collective leadership would be formed to succeed him. This new body would have representatives from every republic and each autonomous region as well as all major political and social organizations in Yugoslavia.

March 25, 1971

Tito began an official visit to Italy at the invitation of Italian President Giuseppe Saragat. Tito described the friendship between the two nations as an example of how different systems can establish fruitful economic and political relations. Tito also met Pope Paul VI in the Vatican.

March 31, 1971

Provisional results of a census gave the population of Yugoslavia as 20,504,516. The approximate population figures for the six republics were as follows: Serbia, 8,437,000; Croatia, 4,423,000; Bosnia and Hercegovina, 3,743,000; Slovenia, 1,725,000; Macedonia, 1,647,000; Montenegro, 530,000.

April 8, 1971

The Croat fascist organization *Ustashi*, through its members in Sweden, murdered the Yugoslav ambassador in Stockholm, Vladimir Rolovic.

April 16, 1971

Due to the Yugoslav free market economy and decentralization, tendencies toward chauvinism and separatism were growing among the top local Communist leadership in all six Yugoslav republics, especially Croatia and Serbia. In a public speech Tito warned that nationalistic differences among leaders in different republics were so great that he might have to resort to purges to preserve the unity and integrity of Yugoslavia. There was sharp antagonism between the leadership of Croatia and Serbia over which would dominate the economy of Yugoslavia.

June 8, 1971

The Yugoslav Foreign Minister Mirko Tepavac visited Peking and opened a new era in the relations between China and Yugoslavia.

September 15, 1971

Tito attended the Persian monarchy celebrations.

September 26, 1971

The Soviet Party leader Leonid Brezhnev visited Yugoslavia and held a series of talks with Tito on international and other problems. In the official document a new Belgrade declaration was signed reaffirming Yugoslavia's political independence and right to develop its political system.

September 29, 1971

Tito visited the United States and met President Richard Nixon. On his way home he stopped in Canada and London.

November 23, 1971

University students struck in Zagreb. According to the official version, they were under the influence of the separatist leadership of the League of the Communists of Croatia and had links with emigration groups abroad. On the other hand, students claimed that they were striking because of the exploitation of Croatia by the federal government and to protest their own unbearable conditions in Zagreb University dormitories and other dissatisfactions.

December 3, 1971

At a meeting at Karadjordjevo, Tito harshly rebuked the Communist leaders of Croatia for not preventing the student strike in Zagreb, accused them of tolerating unconstitutional activities endangering the unity of Yugoslavia, and demanded "sharp measures against counterrevolutionary groups behind the strikes." Savka Dabčević-Kučar, president of the Croat Communists, and Mika Tripalo, member of the Executive Committee of the Presidency of the League of Communists of Yugoslavia, resigned. The official Yugoslav agency *Tanyug* reported that "400 students and other elements" in Zagreb started demonstrations in support of the Croatian communist leaders who resigned. Disturbances continued for several days, and according to an official statement, "170 students and other violators of the peace" were arrested.

December 23, 1971

At the anniversary of the formation of the First Proletarian Brigade, Tito said he would not hesitate to use the army to crush dissidents who threaten the unity of Yugoslavia. Political crisis and recent events in Croatia might have plunged Yugoslavia into civil war, but hostilities were averted "thanks to the unity of the Yugoslav Communist League."

January 28, 1972

The Ustasha terrorist organization in Sweden claimed credit for the crash of a Yugoslav airliner in Czechoslovakia that killed twenty-seven persons. A bomb in the express train Vienna-Zagreb-Belgrade killed six persons.

May 17, 1972

The hydroelectric dam at Džerdap on the Danube, one of the biggest in the world, was opened. It was a joint Yugoslav-Romanian project.

June 5, 1972

Tito opened a long visit to the Soviet Union, the first in seven years. He was awarded the Lenin Order and the Sabre of Stalingrad.

July 3, 1972

After many trials of intellectuals accused of separatism in Croatia, four student leaders, charged with conspiracy, were brought to trial.

July 4, 1972

A group of Ustasha terrorists crossed into Yugoslavia from Austria with modern arms and went to Eastern Bosnia to organize an uprising among the Croat population. In an encounter with the local militia, the Ustashas killed one officer and four men, but later most of the terrorists were either killed or captured. The newspaper *Borba* criticized the West for aiding the terrorist organization.

September 17, 1972

The *Filosofija*, the organ of the Serbian Philosophical Society, was banned in Belgrade for protesting the arrest of M. Djurić, professor at Belgrade University, and his sentencing to two years in jail. Tito spoke harshly of "some philosophers," warning that "they should be pensioned or find new employment, because they were poisoning the minds of their students." Later professors Mihailo Marković, Ljuba Tadić, Zagorka Pešić-Golubović, S. Stojanović, and four others were publicly criticized, and requests were made that they be purged. The group rejected the accusations, stating that they were Marxists, opposed to Stalinist dogmatism.

September 30, 1972

Tito and S. Dolanc, the secretary of the Executive Committee of the League of Communists of Yugoslavia, issued an open letter with the purpose of "revitalizing the Party," asserting that priority action was essential to reinstate the Party's authority and achieve unity of ideas and action. They asked for a purge of all deviationists as well as of rich managers and grafters in the economy.

October 25, 1972

Top Serbian Communist leaders Marko Nikezić and Latinka Perović resigned as Tito pushed his campaign to rebuild a disciplined and obedient Party. They were accused of being "liberals." *Tanyug* hinted that thirty to forty members of the Central Committee of the League of Communists of Serbia sided with Nikezić. Secret meetings of the Central Committee lasted several days, and no defense of Nikezić and others was published.

October 27, 1972

Mirko Tepavac, the Yugoslav foreign minister, resigned.

October 29, 1972

Koča Popović, one of the most esteemed Partisan leaders and former vice-president of Yugoslavia, resigned.

January 18, 1973

The New York Times reported from Belgrade that Overseas Private Investment Corporation (OPIC—an arm of the United States government chartered to guarantee that private American companies investing in developing nations are not adversely affected by internal politics and confiscatory actions) had signed an agreement with the Yugoslav government to "assist and encourage capitalist investment in joint ventures." B. Mills, the president of OPIC, who was present at the ceremony, said that over twenty-four United States firms had applied to the OPIC envisaging investments in Yugoslavia.

February 23, 1973

Dušan Makavejev, director of the film *Mysteries of Organism*, was expelled from the League of the Communists. Several other film directors were purged, among them Saša Petrovic, one of the leading Yugoslav film makers.

April 6, 1973

A new, modern National Library of Serbia was opened in Belgrade on the anniversary of the destruction by the Germans of the old Library on April 6, 1941, when many valuable historical manuscripts were destroyed.

July 3, 1973

New draft legislation was introduced to regulate mass migration by Yugoslav workers to the West; about 1 million workers, or 10 percent of the country's adult population, were employed in Germany, Austria, Switzerland, France, Sweden, Holland, and other European countries.

September 15, 1973

In Algeria, Tito attended and took an active part in an assembly of heads of states and governments of the nonaligned countries.

September 24, 1973

Soviet Premier Alexei Kosygin visited Yugoslavia for a week to strengthen long-range economic cooperation and discuss use of the U.S.S.R.'s 500-million-dollar credit, granted in 1971 for thirty-eight development projects. In his speech in Sarajevo Kosygin praised Tito's efforts to strengthen discipline and ideology and implied that Yugoslavia could benefit from the Soviet example of central planning management. The Yugoslav authorities seemed embarrassed by Kosygin's statement, and in the final document of his visit, it was stated that the "U.S.S.R. accepts the Yugoslav system of self-management of enterprises" and "dynamic development of economic relations."

October 6, 1973

As reported in *The New York Times*, U.S. Treasury Secretary George P. Shultz and Commerce Secretary Frederick B. Dent had talks in Belgrade on the expansion of economic relations between the two countries. Shultz underlined the rapid growth of U.S.-Yugoslav economic relations in the last four years. He noted that the Export-Import Bank had extended to Yugoslavia 335 million dollars and had made preliminary commitments for more than 630 million dollars.

October 20, 1973

The Belgrade Communist organization increased the pressure for ousting Prof. Mihailo Marković and seven other professors from Belgrade University.

November 12, 1973

Tito went to Kiev to meet the Soviet Communist Party leader Leonid Brezhnev. In the official communiqué it was said that they discussed the Middle East and relations between Yugoslavia and the Soviet Union.

November 20, 1973

A new constitution for the Yugoslav Federation, as well as for each of the republics and autonomous regions, was adopted.

November 29, 1973

The thirtieth anniversary of the formation of the Yugoslav Federation was celebrated in Jajce, Bosnia, and was attended by Tito, Kardelj, and other Yugoslav leaders. In his speech Tito indicated that he might step down as president if his mental and physical abilities fell below the level required for the position. He defended the nonaligned position of Yugoslavia and its political system. Mijalko Todorović, president of the Yugoslav Federal Parliament, in the name of the participants, read a petition urging Tito to remain as Yugoslavia's lifelong president. In the petition Tito was praised as "a hero in war and peace, a leader who overcame nationality hatred and became a tireless fighter for peace and independence."

INDEX

Germany, in World War II (*Cont.*):
  war crimes, 575
  working class, 686–687
  Yugoslav annexation, 571, 651
  Yugoslav bourgeoisie, 603–604
  Yugoslav diplomats, 576
  Yugoslavia and: cultural influence, 557
    economics, 512
    foreign investment, 519
    foreign policy, 511
    internal political antagonisms, 586
    World War II, 566–567, 569–570
Getaldić, Marin, 161
Gieslingen, Wladimir Giesl von, 469
Glagolitic, 35, 102
Golden Bull of 1222 (Croatia), 75
Golubić, Mustafa, 569, 585
Gorazd (Caranthian prince), 29
Göring, Hermann, 635
  assassination of King Aleksandar and, 546
Gorki, Maxim, 557
Gorkić, Milan, 550
Gothic art, 106–108
Goths, 14–17
Gotovac, Jakov, 565
Government (*see specific countries*)
Grabež, Trifko, 467, 471
Gradec, 78
Gradnik, Alojz, 563
Grahovac, Dukica, 594
Grand vizier (Ottoman), 173, 221
Grandja, Ivan, 539
Grdan, Voivode, 196
Great Britain, 326
  Anglo-German antagonism in Balkans, 417
  Bulgaria and, 510
  Czechoslovakia and (Munich, 1938), 511
  London Treaty (1915), 482
  Mihailović's collaboration and, 636, 637
  political parties of: Conservative party, 511, 650
    Labour party, 508
  radios in, 558
  South Slav policies of (1908), change in, 423
  sugar consumption in, 525
  trade unions of, 508
  in World War II: Balkans, 567
    meeting with Partisans, 643, 644
    prisoners of war, 575
    resistance movements, 690
    Serbian resistance, 605
    Yugoslav invasion, 651, 662, 663
  Yugoslavia and: cultural influences, 558
    diplomatic recognition, 667
    foreign investment, 519
    formation of government, 660, 662
    monarchy, 658–660
    spheres of influence, 658, 663–665
    territorial integrity, 652
    war debts, 517
Greater Caranthania, 48, 54
Greece, 435
  Balkan Pact and, 510
  Germany and, 570

Greece (*Cont.*):
  Hungary and, 570
  Italy and, 567, 570
  Macedonia and emergent nationalism of, 290, 348
  Montenegrin alliance (1867), 351
  Serbian alliance (1867), 352
  working class in, 686
  in World War II, 574
    Churchill, 691
    Germany, 570
    Italy, 567, 570
    resistance movements, 691
    Stalin, 691
  Yugoslavia and, 705, 708
Greek colonies, 8
  Roman conquest of, 9, 13–14
Greek literature, 99–102
Greek Orthodox church, 62, 332
  Austria and, 330
  of Bosnia, 404
  Bulgaria-Macedonian national movements and, 349
  Bulgarian influence (870 A.D.) of, 39
  Croatian conflicts of, 42
  Cyril and Methodius and spread of, 35–37
  deportation of priests of (1941), 580
  frescoes of, 109–112
  medieval social integration and, 80–81
  Ohrid autocephalous bishopric, 45
  Ottoman conquests and patriarchal culture, 184–188
    resistance to, 198–199
  Peć patriarchate and Ohrid archbishopric, abolition of, 222–223
  sacred and secular literature and, 104–106
  Serbo-Croatian clericalism, 354–356
  1375 reconciliation with Serbian church of, 115
  (*See also* Serbian church)
Green Army (Croatian), 499–500
Gregoras, Nicephorus, 87
Gregory VII (Pope), 49
Grol, Milan, 541, 569
Grosus (Serbian coinage), 71
Grujović, Boža, 268
Grujuć, Slavko, 473–474
Gubec, Matija, 558, 598
Gubernium (Austrian provincial government), 230, 253–254
Gučevo, battle of (1914), 477
Guerilla warfare, 276
  1875–1878 peasant uprisings and, 393, 398–399
  Guerrilla Activities and Guerrilla Warfare (Ivanović), 323
  individual terrorism and, 465–466
  Macedonian, 435
  (*See also* Resistance movements in World War II)
Guilds, 149, 253
  forerunners of, 81
  Macedonian, 290
Gundulić, Dživo, 245
Gypsies, 178
  in World War II: deportations, 580
    massacre of, 581–582

Paču, Lazar, 421, 473
Pagania, 46
Painting, 374
  of Croatia, 564–565
  fresco, 109–112, 185
  modernism, 460–461
  Renaissance, 168
  in Serbia, 565
  (*See also* Art)
Pajsije (patriarch of Peć), 198
Paleolithic settlements, 6–7
Pandurović, Sima, 457
Pannonia, 9, 17, 30
  arrival of Magyars, 38–39
  Croatian spread into, 41–42
Pannonian basin, 5
Papacy, Croatian conflict and, 48-50
  (*See also* Roman Catholic church)
Papal states, 49
Parliamentary organizations (*see* Elections and
  electoral bodies; *and listings under specific
  countries*)
Partisans (*see* Resistance movements in World
  War II)
Pashalics (Ottoman sub-divisions), 173
  abolition of Serbian, 265
Pašić, Nikola, 399, 418–419, 421, 432, 435, 491
  Bulgarian government and, 508
  Corfu Declaration and, 497
  death of, 538-539
  December First Declaration (1918), 531-532
  mining and, 520
  Niš Declaration and, 482–483
  Radić and, 537
  Soviet Union and, 585
  World War I and, outbreak of, 470-471, 473-474
  World War I peace conferences and, 505-506
Pašić, Rade, 520, 537
Passarowitz Treaty (1718), 217
Patarenes, 92
Patriarchal Ottoman culture, 184-188
Patriciate in Dalmatian towns, 77-79
Paulucci's Convention (1807), 270
Pavelić, Ante, 542, 545, 546, 568, 569, 573, 651
  Communists and, 587
  genocide by, 581–582
    of Jews, 578
    of Serbs, 577–579
  Lütter and, 642
  Maček and, 663, 664
  Slovenes discriminated against by, 581
Pavle (Prince of Yugoslavia), 511, 546-549
  in World War II, Hitler and, 567-568
Pavle Bakić (Serbian Despot), 143-144
Pavle Subić (Ban of Croatia), 89
Pavlinović, Don Mihovil, 354
Pavlović, Draganče, 616
Pavlovići family (Bosnian), 119
Peace conferences of 1919 and 1920, 504-506
Peasantry:
  Austrian urbarial regulations and, 235-236
  Bosnian, 289, 367, 450-451, 523
  Croatian, 284-285, 358, 443-445, 523, 530
  Dalmatian, 363, 523

Peasantry (*Cont.*):
  deportation of (1941), 580
  1875–1878 uprisings of, 393-395
  feudal, 67–68, 74
  in Hercegovina, 552
  Hungarian Revolution (1848) and, 312-313
  in Macedonia, 523
  "Open Command" (1853) and, 329
  raya (Ottoman), 173-176, 191, 262-263
  Serbian free peasantry, 279-284, 361-362
  significance of Serbian Revolution of, 276
  Slovene, 287, 440-441, 523, 530
  uprisings of, 149-151
  Venetian communal systems and, 151-152
  in Vojvodina, 523, 530
  of Yugoslavia, 523-526, 693, 694, 696, 697
    community, 653
    education, 553
  (*See also* Serfs)
Peć, patriarchate of, 185, 217–218
  abolition of, 222-223
Pejčinović, Kiril, 309
Pelagić, Vasa, 346, 383, 394
Perić, Zivojin, 554
Perišić, Toma Vučić, 358
Pernar, Ivan, 539
Perović, Latinka, 719
Persia, 28
Petar (Emperor of Bulgaria), 43
Petar I (King of Yugoslavia), 558
Petar I (Montenegrin bishop), 291-292
Petar II (King of Yugoslavia), 546, 568, 570
  Stalin's support of, 662
Petar Gojniković (Serbian prince), 39–40
Petar Karadjordjević (King of Serbia), 418, 430-431,
  698
  abdication of (1914), 432-433
Petranović, Božidar, 304
Petrić, Vladimir, 683
Petrov, Djorče, 409
Petrovaradin, 217
Petrović, Karadjordje, 265–266, 268–269, 271,
  273-276
Petrović, Mihailo, 455, 572
Petrović, Nikola, 535
Petrović, Rastko, 487, 560
Petrović, Vladika Vasilije, 225
Petrović, Zora, 565
Petrović family (Montenegrin family), 224, 291
Petrović-Njegoš, Petar, 224
Petrović-Njegoš dynasty, 532
Petrović-Pečija, Petar, 327, 332
Phanariots, 222, 435
Pharos, 8
Phocas (Byzantine Emperor), 21
Picasso, Pablo, 681
Piedmont, 326
Pivljanin, Bajo Nikolić, 197–198
Plavšić, Vladimir, 677, 680
Plećaš, Nedeljko, 637
Plečnik, Josip, 564
Plowshare, 66
Poetry, 188, 372, 677-681
  drama and, 160-161

2/10 /--